CORNELL STUDIES IN CIVIL LIBERTY

ROBERT E. CUSHMAN, *Advisory Editor*

The House Committee on

Un-American Activities

The House Committee on

Un-American Activities

1945-1950

ROBERT K. CARR

*Joel Parker Professor of Law
and Political Science, Dartmouth College*

Cornell University Press

ITHACA, NEW YORK, 1952

Editor's Preface

THIS volume is one of a series made possible by a grant from the Rockefeller Foundation to Cornell University. Beginning in 1948 a group of scholars working individually under my direction have studied the impact upon our civil liberties of current governmental programs designed to ensure internal security and to expose and control disloyal or subversive conduct. The research has covered the work of federal and state "un-American activities" committees and the operation of federal, state, and local loyalty and security programs. The first report, published in 1950, was *Security, Loyalty, and Science,* by Professor Walter Gellhorn of the Columbia University School of Law. This dealt with the problems of government-imposed secrecy in scientific investigation and the loyalty and security clearance procedures applicable to government scientists. This was followed in 1951 by *The Tenney Committee,* by Edward L. Barrett, Jr., Professor of Law at Berkeley; *Un-American Activities in the State of Washington,* by Vern Countryman, Associate Professor of Law at Yale; and *Loyalty and Legislative Action,* by Lawrence H. Chamberlain, Dean of Columbia College. These volumes present the records of legislative loyalty investigations in the states of California, Washington, and New York. In 1952 appeared *The States and Subversion,* edited by Walter Gellhorn. This contained chapters on six states together with a general analysis of the problems posed by state efforts to deal with the problem of loyalty. Professor Carr's present volume is to be followed by one on the President's loyalty program and the summary dismissal statutes, by Miss Eleanor Bontecou, formerly an attorney in the Department of Justice. In a short final book I shall summarize my own conclusions with respect to the problems covered by the entire study.

v

The House Committee on Un-American Activities has been the subject of bitter controversy almost from the time of its establishment in 1938. It has been accused of using unfair procedures and of ruthlessly abridging civil liberties; it has been stoutly defended as the necessary, valiant, and successful protector of our internal security. In 1945 it was made a standing committee of the House, and Robert K. Carr, Joel Parker Professor of Law and Political Science at Dartmouth, begins his study of it at that point. His accurate and objective review of the committee's policies, procedures, and accomplishments; his judicious appraisal of its worth and its shortcomings; his wise comments upon the important problems generated by the committee's purposes and methods—all these are valued examples of the services which a scholar may hope to render in a democratic state. He places at the disposal of thoughtful citizens the facts and the reasoned judgments on which an informed and prudent public opinion must rest.

The volumes in this series state the views, conclusions, and recommendations of the individual authors. There have, of course, been consultation and discussion among the group engaged in the entire study. Valuable aid and criticism have been received from a number of distinguished persons outside this group. Each volume, however, remains the work, and states the opinions, of the person who wrote it.

ROBERT E. CUSHMAN

Cornell University
Ithaca, New York

Author's Preface

The Un-American Activities Committee of the House of Representatives was created in 1938 as a temporary investigating committee. Taking its name from its chairman, Representative Martin Dies of Texas, it remained in existence until the end of 1944. Its record during this six-year period has been carefully analyzed in an admirable volume by Father August R. Ogden, entitled *The Dies Committee* (2d ed.; Washington: The Catholic University of America Press, 1945).

In January, 1945, the committee was made a standing committee of the House of Representatives. This volume deals with the first six years in the life of this permanent agency and traces its record through three Congresses, the Seventy-ninth, the Eightieth, and the Eighty-first. It should be noted that, whereas the temporary committee was dominated throughout its six-year life by its chairman, Mr. Dies, the permanent committee had three different chairmen in its first six years, and that its character changed materially in each of the three Congresses covered in this study. Thus it is not entirely accurate to talk of *the* Un-American Activities Committee as though its record in such years as 1946, 1948, and 1950 was made by one and the same body. If, in the pages that follow, I have myself seemed to refer to the committee as a continuing, homogeneous body, the reader should bear in mind the difficulties of such generalizations.

Many people gave invaluable help in the preparation of this volume. Cornell Research in Civil Liberties, through a grant from the Rockefeller Foundation, made it possible for me to undertake the study. Robert E. Cushman, director of the Cornell study, gave me unfailing encouragement and assistance. Members of the Un-

American Activities Committee and of its staff, witnesses before the committee, and others were generous and co-operative in granting interviews and in permitting me to examine certain records pertaining to the work of the committee. In the main, however, this study is based upon the official record of the committee's work as revealed in its printed hearings and reports and upon the reporting of the committee's activities in the *New York Times,* the *New York Herald Tribune,* and the *Washington Post.*

At one stage or another of its preparation, the manuscript was read by Robert E. Cushman, Walter Gellhorn, Eleanor Bontecou, Erwin Griswold, and Vern Countryman. All made criticisms and suggestions of great value. But it should be emphasized that in a work dealing with so controversial a subject as the Un-American Activities Committee, the author alone must accept final responsibility for what he has written.

I must also express a very great obligation to Ann Dishman, who labored long and faithfully over a three-year period to keep notes, newspaper clippings, and correspondence in convenient working order and to produce a typescript that took shape with more than the usual difficulty out of a complex of quoted materials, longhand drafts of text, and last-minute revisions and additions.

The author of a book about the Un-American Activities Committee should state his general beliefs concerning the threat offered to our national security by communism and the danger to individual freedom inherent in a program to control subversive or "un-American" activity. Accordingly, I offer the following general observations as indicative of the attitude of mind with which I have approached the task of writing this book.

Loyalty to a national state and concern for its security have a high moral and practical value. As national states go, the United States is one of man's greatest achievements. It has brought liberty and welfare to millions of people. We should give it our high loyalty, and we should fight to maintain its security.

We live in an age of revolution. The great issue of our times is whether the individual is to remain free and the state remain an instrument to serve him, or whether the individual is to become a mere unit in society and the state become a totalitarian manifestation of some principle of group solidarity. Against the revolutionary forces which are loose in the modern world, it is inevitable that established orders, such as our own, shall seek to defend themselves. There cannot, in the very nature of things, be any legal right of revolution.

The great revolutionary force of modern times is totalitarianism, and its twin agents are fascism and communism. At the moment fascism lies weak and defeated. On the international scene it has no powerful home state to serve as a base for its operations. Within our own land the native fascists have been put to rout. But this is not to say that the fascist threat to our free society is forever dead. There is a strong, latent fascist force in America that awaits only a favorable combination of circumstances to assert its ugly power. In the long run, the internal danger of a fascist revolution in the United States may well prove to be more serious than the danger of a Communist revolution.

At the moment communism is strong and aggressive. On the international scene it does have a powerful home state, the Soviet Union, from which to carry on its conspiratorial campaign to gain dominion over the world. The conspirators have made much headway in the last decade. No intelligent man can doubt that international communism is a revolutionary force of great strength and cleverness and that it has placed the Western way of life in mortal danger. But we must recognize that danger for what it is. To the United States the danger is in very large measure a military one. To meet this danger we must bend every effort to achieve the speedy completion of our rearmament program. We must also strive through diplomacy and generous economic support to weld together the free nations of the world in an effective alliance against the danger of Communist attack.

In addition to this military threat there is also a danger that communism will win men's minds. That the people of Asia, Africa, and even western Europe and South America may yet be persuaded to accept communism voluntarily as the most desirable way of life in the modern world is a very real possibility. Here our best hope is to win the non-Communist nations of the world as our allies and their peoples as our friends by showing them that Western democracy is in theory and *in practice* superior to communism.

At home our native Communist movement is small and weak. The possibility that this movement can attract any number of Americans through the mere advocacy of its doctrines is nonexistent. No major radical political group in American history has ever been less successful in winning converts. Accordingly, the threat to the American way of life resulting from the mere advocacy of communism can safely be met by continued reliance upon the free market place of thought and expression. With respect to this point is there any reason to doubt the continuing validity today of Jefferson's words: "If there be any among us who wish to dissolve this union, or to change its republican form, let them stand undisturbed as monuments of the safety with which error of opinion may be tolerated where reason is left free to combat it"?

At the same time, it must be recognized that a small, highly disciplined group of American Communists, co-operating closely with the international Communist conspiracy, can do grave damage to this country. But the damage they can do is not the subversion of the American people; it is the damage that criminals can do—criminals who infiltrate our private social institutions and our public agencies for the purpose of committing such offenses against the law as espionage and sabotage. The way to prevent such damage is not to silence men's tongues or to undermine confidence in our private organizations or the government. The way to meet the danger is the traditional one of providing an adequate body of law defining forbidden criminal conduct and of building up an adequate police force or counterintelligence system to ferret out the law-breakers.

In the end, the problem that confronts the United States is to find a satisfactory balance between the demands of national security and the interests of individual freedom. Finding a satisfactory solution to this problem, while difficult, is not an impossible task. The reconciliation of authority and liberty may be a never-ending process, but it is always possible. Indeed, the only liberty that can have real meaning to modern man is liberty in an organized society in which law and order are maintained and the security of the group is safeguarded. Liberty, then, is dependent upon authority for its very existence. Thus, efforts to safeguard national security cannot be condemned out of hand because of the danger that such efforts, if badly conceived or unwisely administered, may jeopardize civil liberties. At the same time, a free people must be ever on guard lest this rationalization be used to justify unnecessary encroachments by government upon the individual's freedom. John Frank has recently written, "Mankind has never learned the art of suppressing by littles. The violence of the spirit of suppression too quickly reaches beyond the truly wicked to mere non-conformists."

Edmund Burke, the great English statesman, has supplied us

with a sound working principle for the proper balancing of liberty and authority:

Liberty, too, must be limited in order to be possessed. The degree of restraint it is impossible in any case to settle precisely. But it ought to be the constant aim of every wise public counsel to find out by cautious experiments, and rational, cool endeavors, with how little, not how much, of this restraint the community can subsist.

ROBERT K. CARR

February, 1952
Hanover, New Hampshire

Contents

I: Congress and Subversive Activity

No CONGRESSIONAL investigating committee in history has provoked more controversy or criticism than has the Un-American Activities Committee of the House of Representatives. No such committee has been more bitterly attacked or more vigorously defended. To some Americans it has constituted one of the gravest threats to civil liberty our nation has ever known; in less than a decade it has managed to create and impose a loyalty standard upon the nation that has dangerously narrowed our traditional freedoms of thought, expression, and association. To other Americans the committee has been our chief bulwark against subversion; almost singlehandedly it has saved the nation against enslavement by the Communists.

In part the controversy that has raged about the committee has been of its own making. Created in 1938 by resolution of the House of Representatives as a temporary investigating committee, given a renewal of authority from time to time, and ultimately, in 1945, added to the list of the House's permanent committees, it has for more than a dozen years so conducted itself as to attract a maximum of attention, praise, and denunciation. Throughout the years one spectacular hearing has been succeeded by another; sensational report has been followed by still more sensational report. Again and again the committee has asserted that America is in great danger, its institutions threatened with corruption by subversives. From the committee have come reports of labor unions captured by Communists in their midst, government agencies overrun by spies, the secrets of American science betrayed at one moment by eminent scholars and at another by mysterious agents X, Y, or Z, and a motion

1

picture industry shot through with Communist directors, actors, and script writers. Often the committee has taken credit for sensational developments on the American scene. Without its labors Alger Hiss would not be in jail. William Remington would not have been prosecuted in federal court on the charge of perjury. President Truman would not in 1947 have established the loyalty program in the federal service, under which hundreds of civil servants have been dismissed from their jobs and thousands more have resigned. The most far-reaching law against subversion in American history would not today be found upon the federal statute books. Moreover, these assertions and claims to credit have been voiced in language as colorful and vigorous as any ever employed by a Congressional agency. Small wonder then that the Un-American Activities Committee has become perhaps the best known investigating committee in the history of Congress. Nor is it strange that its advocates have been so staunch and aggressive, its detractors so bitter and angry.

And yet the controversy that has raged about the Un-American Activities Committee reflects more than the committee's own sensational conduct and findings. Even if its hearings had always been calmly conducted, the behavior of its members thoroughly circumspect, and the language of its reports completely dispassionate, it is likely that its career would have been a stormy one, its friends and enemies numerous and vociferous. Two factors beyond the particular sensations with which this committee has been concerned help to explain why it was destined to become so well known and so controversial. One is the nature of the investigating power of Congress, a power whose exercise has occasioned much dispute and acrimony for more than a century and a half, regardless of the use to which it has been put. The other is the subject matter of this particular investigation. Subversive activity *is* an explosive subject to investigate, as Senator Millard Tydings and a Senate foreign relations subcommittee were to discover in 1950, when after a decade of industry by the Un-American Activities Committee it might have been supposed that the subject had lost some of its sensational quality. For all its efforts to do the job assigned to it in a fair and honest way, the Tydings subcommittee itself became a sensation, the center of violent controversy, its chairman marked for political destruction because he had dared to question the accuracy of charges that the State Department was overrun with Communists. It is not too much to say that the subject the Tydings subcommittee was ordered to investigate allowed no other culmination to the undertaking than a sensational one. The use of the investigating power of Congress to search for evidence of subversive activity is bound to produce an explosive result.

The Investigating Power of Congress

The first Congressional investigation took place just three years after Congress was established, when in 1792 the House of Representatives appointed a committee to look into the disaster that befell the St. Clair expedition against the Indians. Since then the use of the investigating power by Congress has been virtually continuous and there has been no long period without some spectacular inquiry.[1]

Controversy over the use of the investigating power of Congress is also an ancient tradition. As early as 1860 the use of the power to inquire into John Brown's raid on Harpers Ferry provoked a famous debate in the Senate. The power of inquiry was vigorously defended and bitterly attacked. The vehemence of the attack is indicated by the remarks of Charles Sumner:

> I know it is said this power is necessary *in aid of legislation*. I deny the necessity. *Convenient*, at times, it may be; but *necessary never*. . . . Such a power as this—which, without sanction of law, and merely at the will of a partisan majority, may be employed to ransack the most distant States, and to drag citizens before the Senate all the way from Wisconsin or from South Carolina—may be convenient, and, to certain persons, may seem to be necessary. An alleged necessity has, throughout all time, been the apology for wrong.
>
> "So spoke the Fiend, and with *necessity*,
> The tyrant's plea excused his devilish deeds." [2]

On the other hand, the power of inquiry was staunchly defended by Senator Fessenden in the following words:

[1] There are three excellent general studies of the investigating power of Congress. These are E. J. Eberling, *Congressional Investigations* (New York: Columbia University Press, 1928); M. E. Dimock, *Congressional Investigating Committees* (Baltimore: Johns Hopkins Press, 1929); and M. N. McGeary, *The Developments of Congressional Investigative Power* (New York: Columbia University Press, 1940). The Eberling and Dimock volumes cover the period from the St. Clair inquiry through the famous investigations of the 1920's. The McGeary volume is largely confined to the investigations of the 1930's. The spring, 1951, issue of the *Univ. of Chicago Law Review* is entirely devoted to the subject of Congressional investigations and contains a number of useful articles.

[2] *Congressional Globe*, 36th Cong., 1st Sess., Pt. 4, p. 3007.

Sir, with regard to myself, all I have to inquire into is: is this a legitimate and proper object, committed to me under the Constitution; and then, as to the mode of accomplishing it, I am ready to use judiciously, calmly, moderately, all the power which I believe is necessary and inherent, in order to do that which I am appointed to do; and, I take it, I violate no rights, either of the people generally or of the individual, by that course.[3]

The well-known inquiries of the 1920's into the scandals of the Harding administration also provoked much controversy. The Teapot Dome and Justice Department investigations have been much praised both for the manner of their conduct and the importance of their findings. But even these inquiries had their critics as is indicated by the vigorous language of such an eminent legal scholar as Dean John H. Wigmore:

The Senatorial debauch of investigations—poking into political garbage cans and dragging the sewers of political intrigue—filled the winter of 1923–24 with a stench which has not yet passed away. . . . As a prosecutor the Senate presented a spectacle which cannot even be dignified by a comparison with the prosecutive scoldings of Coke and Scroggs and Jeffreys, but fell rather in popular estimate to the level of professional searchers of municipal dunghills.[4]

The range of criticism of Congressional investigations has been extremely wide. Many inquiries have been attacked because of their subject matter, the argument being made that, because of either the limitations of its constitutional power or the impropriety of the situation, Congress should not investigate the particular subject under scrutiny. Other inquiries have been criticized because of the procedural methods employed. When Congressional inquisitors have seemed overly vigorous or thorough in their methods, they have been accused of conducting a "witch hunt." When they have gone about their work in calm and unspectacular fashion, their efforts have been belittled as amounting to a "whitewash." There has been little consistency in these criticisms. During the 1920's and 1930's Congressional investigations were generally progressive in their orientation. Liberals were pleased and praised the work of the investigating committees that looked into the Harding scandals, Wall Street stock exchange and banking practices, lobbying, and civil liberties. Conservatives denounced these investigations and, in particular, attacked their procedural shortcomings. For example, the

[3] *Ibid.*, Pt. 2, p. 1102.

[4] John H. Wigmore, "Legislative Power to Compel Testimonial Disclosure," 19 *Ill. Law Review* (1925), 452–453.

Senate lobbying investigation under Senator Black's chairmanship in 1935 was vigorously condemned on the ground that it showed insufficient concern for the rights of its witnesses. But in the 1940's as the orientation of investigation shifted somewhat from liberal to conservative, progressives took up the cry that witnesses were being unfairly treated, and conservatives rushed to the defense of the committees.

Much of the praise and blame that has been heaped upon the heads of Congressional investigators has unquestionably been stimulated by the specific methods or findings of particular inquiries. But in part, at least, the controversy reflects general uncertainty as to the nature and purpose of the investigating power itself. The power of investigation is not mentioned in the Constitution, and its development has been largely informal and pragmatic in character. Congress itself has never attempted by resolution or statute to define the purposes, powers, or procedures of its investigating committees. As will be indicated in a later chapter, the courts have attempted to remedy this defect. But judicial rulings in this area are spotty in character and fall far short of providing a coherent statement of the law of Congressional investigations. Accordingly, it has remained for students of Congress to supply systematic analyses of the investigating power. But these analyses have been unofficial in character and have been somewhat misleading in suggesting the presence of more rhyme and reason in the record made by Congress in the use of its investigating power than is warranted by the facts.

Not the least difficulty about the subject has been a fundamental problem of definition. What is a "Congressional investigation"? In its strictest sense the term has been used to refer to a special study of a particular problem made as a result of the adoption of a formal resolution by the House or the Senate, or the two houses acting jointly. In a looser sense, however, the term has sometimes been applied to the regular, routine hearings on a wide variety of subjects which are being made by the standing committees of Congress at their own initiative all the time. The former differ from the latter in several ways. A resolution authorizing a special investigation usually defines the purpose and subject matter of the inquiry with some precision and fixes a time limit for the undertaking. The body making such an investigation is customarily given the power of subpoena and a special appropriation to cover its costs. Some of the most famous investigations have been made by special committees, but not infrequently they have been turned over to standing committees or subcommittees thereof. In the latter instance, the dividing line between normal committee activity and the special investigation is not always entirely clear. In any case the use by Congress of the investigating power over a period of more than a century and a half has been subject to so many organizational and procedural variations that the subject is not an easy one to analyze or describe.

In spite of these difficulties, it is generally agreed that the investigating power of Congress may validly be used for three purposes. First, the investigation is a means of supplying Congress with accurate and detailed information essential to the intelligent exercise of its express constitutional powers—in particular, the enactment of laws. A good illustration of this motivation at work is seen in the Wall Street investigation in 1933, when Congress sought and obtained information about banking and stock exchange practices that led to the enactment of a series of statutes, notably those establishing the Securities and Exchange Commission. Second, the investigation is used to supervise or check the work of administrative agencies which have been charged by Congress with law enforcement duties. The House Committee to Investigate Acts of Executive Agencies beyond the Scope of Their Authority, created in 1943, by its very title illustrates this motive for investigation. Third, the investigation is used to influence public opinion by giving circulation to certain facts or ideas. The La Follette civil liberties investigation, conducted by a subcommittee of the Senate Education and Labor Committee in the 1930's, illustrates this motive at work. While it resulted in little or no legislation, this investigation had much to do with the American people's increased consciousness of civil liberties problems during the last decade and a half.

Only the first of these three purposes has formally been approved by the Supreme Court as a proper reason for the making of a Congressional investigation.[5] But it is generally agreed that the other two purposes are entirely legitimate ones. Since Congress is responsible for the creation and continued existence of virtually all administrative agencies of the national government and also makes, amends, and repeals the laws that these agencies enforce, it is clearly acting within its constitutional authority when it investigates the adequacy of the administrative mechanism for the enforcement of laws or the degree to which Congressional purposes have been followed in the carrying out of the law. Congressional efforts to influence public opinion are perhaps less easily defended. The Constitution suggests

[5] *McGrain v. Daugherty*, 273 U.S. 135 (1927).

no easy rationalization for such activity. But accepted democratic ideology holds that a national legislature, such as the Congress of the United States, must not only show a high sensitivity to the wishes of the people, but also supply the public with information essential to the emergence of intelligent opinion. As far back as 1885 Woodrow Wilson called attention to "the instruction and guidance in political affairs which the people might receive from a body which kept all national concerns suffused in a broad daylight of discussion." And he concluded, "The informing function of Congress should be preferred even to its legislative function." [6] Later students of American government do not quarrel with this assertion.

In addition to the three more or less formal purposes for which Congress has used its investigating power, three other motives, somewhat more informal and questionable in character, have also influenced the particular uses to which the investigating power has been put. These have been a desire for personal publicity and political advancement by Congressmen identified with investigations, a desire to advance the cause of one political party or to embarrass the cause of another through sensational investigation findings, and a desire to expose to public scrutiny allegedly unlawful or improper conduct by specific individuals, both public servants and private citizens.

It is harder to estimate the propriety of these latter motives than to pass judgment upon the three more formal purposes of the Congressional investigation. For one thing, two or more of these purposes and motives are often present in particular investigations and in varying degrees. For the chairman of an investigating committee charged with supplying Congress with factual information essential to wise policy-making to entertain modest hopes of personal political gain if he does the job well is hardly a motive to be deplored. On the other hand, if a Congressman schemes to gain authority to conduct a sensational investigation so that he may improve his personal political fortunes and then overlooks no opportunity during the course of such an inquiry to gain favorable notoriety, it is probable that the caliber of the inquiry itself will suffer accordingly. Much the same can be said of partisan motivation in the use of the investigating power. It is part of the theory of party government that rival political parties should seek to expose each other's shortcomings and to profit by so doing. Thus, a vigorous effort by the

[6] *Congressional Government* (Boston: Houghton Mifflin Co., 1885), pp. 297, 303.

minority party members of an investigating committee to demonstrate the shortcomings in the record of an administrative agency that has been dominated by the majority party is not inappropriate. But if an investigating committee is torn by partisan conflict and its members seek only to "point with pride" or to "view with alarm," the committee's search for impartial information will in all likelihood not be conspicuously successful. Similarly, both a good and a bad word can be spoken of an investigation which is aimed against specific individuals. If the latter are public servants and the purpose is to force them to mend their ways or even to drive them from office through exposure of their unsatisfactory records such a purpose cannot be criticized. The departure of members of the Harding Cabinet from office as the result of the Teapot Dome and Justice Department investigations has always been viewed as one of the finest achievements which can be set down to the credit of the investigating power. But where the purpose of an inquiry is to threaten a man's good name and means of livelihood through turning a legislative inquiry into a "trial" the situation may well be a deplorable one.

That the investigating power of Congress readily lends itself to abuse has been demonstrated all too frequently. Nevertheless, all students of the legislative process agree about the valuable uses to which the power has been put again and again in American history and insist that the continued vitality of Congress depends upon the preservation of the power. When he retired in 1944 as chairman of one of the most successful investigating committees in Congressional history, Senator Harry S. Truman said on the floor of the Senate:

It is important that Congress not only continue but enlarge its work of investigation. In my opinion, the power of investigation is one of the most important powers of Congress. The manner in which that power is exercised will largely determine the position and prestige of the Congress in the future. An informed Congress is a wise Congress; an uninformed Congress surely will forfeit a large portion of the respect and confidence of the people. [7]

Congress and Subversive Activity

Subversive activity, or more properly, the threat of subversive activity, has given Congress sporadic concern almost from the begin-

[7] 90 *Cong. Rec.* 6747 (Aug. 7, 1944). (All citations of the *Congressional Record* refer to the permanent, bound volumes unless otherwise specified.)

ning of our history. However, apart from the enactment of laws defining such specific offenses as treason, espionage, sabotage, and conspiracy, this concern has largely been limited to the present century. The one great example of an earlier interest occurred in 1798 when Congress, confronted with the threat of a war with France, and badly frightened by the seeming spread of the doctrines of the French Revolution, passed the Alien and Sedition Laws. These laws were worded in shockingly broad language. The Alien Act gave the President sweeping power to deport aliens considered dangerous to the peace and safety of the United States. The Sedition Act made it a criminal offense to publish false, scandalous, or defamatory writings with an intent to discredit the government, the President, or the Congress, or to excite the hatred of the people against them, to stir up sedition, to excite resistance against the law, or to aid hostile foreign designs against the United States. Persons convicted under this act could be fined up to two thousand dollars and imprisoned up to two years.[8] In the year or two following its adoption the Sedition Act was vigorously enforced by the Federalist administration for narrow partisan reasons. In the words of Arthur Schlesinger, Jr., "A New Jersey editor . . . was fined $100 for hoping in print that the wad of a cannon fired in a presidential salute might hit President Adams on the seat of the pants. A Vermont Jeffersonian, who accused the President of 'unbounded thirst for ridiculous pomp, foolish adulation, and a selfish avarice,' received a thousand dollar fine and four months in jail." [9] It is generally agreed that this early peacetime attempt to develop the crime of sedition contributed to the defeat of Adams and the Federalists in the election of 1800. When Jefferson became President in 1801 he pardoned all persons imprisoned under the Sedition Act, and Congress ultimately ordered all fines repaid.[10] The act itself was allowed to expire on March 3, 1801.

More than a century elapsed before Congress again attempted to curb subversion by placing statutory restrictions upon freedom of speech and press. Then in 1917 and 1918, with the entrance of the United States into World War I, Congress in the so-called Espionage and Sedition Acts defined as crimes such activities as willfully mak-

---

[8] Acts of June 25 and July 14, 1798, 1 *Stat.* 570, 596.

[9] *The Vital Center* (Boston: Houghton Mifflin Co., 1949), p. 193.

[10] Zechariah Chafee, Jr., *Free Speech in the United States* (Cambridge: Harvard University Press, 1941), p. 27.

ing or conveying false statements with intent to interfere with the success of the American war effort or to promote the success of its enemies, willfully obstructing the recruitment of military personnel or attempting to cause the disloyalty of such personnel, saying or doing anything with intent to obstruct the sale of government bonds, uttering or writing any disloyal, profane, scurrilous, or abusive language to cause contempt, scorn, contumely, or disrepute in regard to the form of government of the United States, the flag, or the uniform of the Army or Navy, or urging the curtailment of production of anything necessary to the prosecution of the war.[11] According to Zechariah Chafee over nineteen hundred prosecutions and other judicial proceedings took place under these acts before the end of the war. In one case a woman was convicted for saying in conversation, "I wish Wilson was in hell, and if I had the power I would put him there." [12]

Some twenty years after the close of World War I the deepening international crisis led Congress once more to turn its attention to the threat of subversive activity. In 1940 it passed the first peacetime sedition law since the infamous Sedition Act of 1798. This was the Alien Registration (or Smith) Act, one of whose provisions made it unlawful for any person knowingly to teach or advocate the overthrow of government by force or violence, or to help organize or to become a member of any organization so teaching or advocating the overthrow of government.[13] The act has thus far been invoked in only two or three cases, most notably in 1950 in the successful prosecution of eleven top leaders of the Communist Party of the United States. At the time of writing there are reports that some 12,000 persons are to be prosecuted under this statute.

And finally in 1950 Congress passed over a presidential veto the Internal Security (or McCarran) Act. This is an omnibus piece of legislation aimed at outlawing or curbing a wide variety of activities by Communists or other "totalitarians." Its best-known, and perhaps most controversial, section requires the registration with the govern-

[11] Acts of June 15, 1917, and May 16, 1918, 40 *Stat.* 217, 553. The Espionage Act of 1917 also dealt with such matters as actual espionage and protection of military secrets.

[12] *Free Speech in the United States*, p. 3. "Sedition," 13 *Encyclopaedia of the Social Sciences*, 638. The 1918 law was repealed in 1921. The 1917 law, which is confined to wartime offenses, is still in effect. The conviction of the woman occurred under the Act of Feb. 14, 1917, 39 *Stat.* 919, which defines certain threats against the President as crimes.

[13] 54 *Stat.* 670.

ment of all Communist and Communist front organizations as well as the individual members of the former.[14]

If the legislation of 1798 be ignored, Congress was almost as prompt in using its investigating power to strike at the threat of subversive activity as it was its lawmaking power. On February 2 and 3, 1919, less than three months after the armistice ending World War I, two rallies were held in Washington theaters in support of the Soviet forces, then fighting to establish their control of Russia against, among other opponents, Allied forces which included American soldiers. These meetings were reported in sensational fashion in Washington newspapers. Among other things it was stated that the establishment of a "Bolshevik" regime in the United States had been advocated. The Senate was disturbed by these reports and promptly took two steps to investigate the character of these meetings.[15] It adopted a resolution stating as fact that speakers at these meetings had "advocated the cause of the present Bolsheviki government of Russia, which is now at war with the United States" and had "advocated the use . . . of force and violence . . . for the subversion of the Government of the United States," and directing the Attorney General to report to the Senate what steps he had taken to investigate the meetings and "to enforce the laws of the United States in the premises." [16] It also adopted a resolution directing a subcommittee of the Senate Judiciary Committee, which under the chairmanship of Senator Lee S. Overman of North Carolina had been investigating "the brewing industry and German propaganda," to broaden its inquiry so as to cover "any efforts being made to propagate in this country the principles of any party exercising or claiming to exercise authority in Russia, whether such efforts originate in this country or are incited or financed from abroad, and further, to inquire into any effort to incite the overthrow of the Government of this country, or all government, by force, or by the destruction of life or property or the general cessation of industry." [17]

The Attorney General quickly reported to the Senate that he had had the two meetings under investigation even before being ordered

[14] Public Law No. 831, 81st Cong., 2d Sess. (Sept. 23, 1950).

[15] This account of the 1919 episode and of subsequent investigations of subversive activity by Congress up to January, 1945, when the House of Representatives created a standing Committee on Un-American Activities, draws heavily upon an excellent study by Father August R. Ogden, *The Dies Committee* (2d ed.; Washington: The Catholic University Press, 1945).

[16] 57 *Cong. Rec.* 2654, 2730 (Feb. 4 and 5, 1919).   [17] *Ibid.* (Feb. 4, 1919).

to do so by the Senate. He implied that no speakers had advocated the subversion of the government of the United States by force and violence, as had been asserted in the Senate resolution, and stated that he would appreciate it if the Senate would transmit to him the evidence upon which the statement had been based.[18]

The Overman subcommittee quickly held seventeen public hearings on "Bolshevik propaganda" and also heard certain unnamed witnesses in executive sessions. The hearings seem to have been centered on the nature of the Bolshevik regime in Russia rather than on the dissemination of Communist propaganda in the United States. In June, 1919, the subcommittee submitted its report, which according to August R. Ogden, consisted largely of "a description of the workings of the Russian Government." Ogden also says: "In order to make the picture more graphic, the report showed what the application of Soviet doctrine would mean in this country." [19] Thus did a Congressional committee whose original interest had been the brewing industry undertake the first investigation of Communist propaganda and subversive activity in the United States.

This post-World War I flurry of excitement about Bolshevik propaganda quickly died down, and, apart from sporadic proposals by individual Congressmen, no further efforts were made to use the investigating power of Congress to check subversive activity during the 1920's. But in May, 1930, the House of Representatives suddenly adopted by an overwhelming vote a resolution calling for an investigation of communism. This action was the result of sensational charges made before the House Committee on Immigration and Naturalization by Grover Whalen, then police commissioner of New York, that the Amtorg Trading Corporation was disseminating Communist propaganda in this country. The resolution provided for the creation of a special committee

[18] *Ibid.*, 3247 (Feb. 13, 1919). Later in 1919 the Senate directed the Attorney General to supply it with information regarding the activities of the Department of Justice in suppressing subversive activities. The Attorney General reported that the almost total absence of peacetime laws against subversion rendered such activities difficult, but he stated that he had ordered the Department of Justice to co-operate with the Department of Labor in deportation cases. *The Dies Committee*, p. 18.

[19] *The Dies Committee*, p. 17. The hearings were published under the title, *Bolshevik Propaganda; Hearings before a Subcommittee of the Committee on the Judiciary*, Feb. 11 to March 10, 65th Cong., 3d Sess., 1919. The report was published under the title, *Brewing and Liquor Interests and German and Bolshevik Propaganda; Report of the Subcommittee of the Committee on the Judiciary*, Sen. Doc. No. 61, 66th Cong., 1st Sess., 1919.

to investigate communist propaganda in the United States and particularly in our educational institutions; the activities and membership of the Communist Party of the United States; and all affiliated organizations and groups thereof; the ramification of the Communist International in the United States; the Amtorg Trading Corporation; the Daily Worker, and all entities, groups, or individuals who are alleged to advise, teach, or advocate the overthrow by force or violence of the Government of the United States, or attempt to undermine our republican form of government by inciting riots, sabotage, or revolutionary disorders.[20]

Representative Hamilton Fish was named chairman of the committee, and hearings were held between June and December, 1930. Ogden states that the committee "followed no set plan," and he calls attention to "a curious feature of the hearings"—"the fact that a large part of the testimony consisted of comparatively brief statements accompanied by lengthy and ponderous documents." [21] The committee's report was a fantastic document, for, as Ogden says, there was little or no connection between the committee's findings and its recommendations. The committee found that the charge against the Amtorg Corporation was not supported by the evidence and also that the Communist movement in the United States was pitifully weak. But its recommendations were numerous and drastic. In Ogden's words they were "aimed to suppress the Communist Party in the United States, root, lock, stock and barrel." Representative John E. Nelson of Maine filed a long minority report which even today remains a remarkably wise and sane estimate of the Communist danger and of the ability of the United States to meet this danger without encroachment upon fundamental civil liberties.

No action was taken on any of the Fish committee's legislative recommendations, although a bill providing for the deportation of alien Communists, which Representative Martin Dies of Texas sponsored in several succeeding Congresses, passed the House in 1932. However, in 1934, after Hitler's rise to power in Germany, the House of Representatives, again by an overwhelming vote, adopted a resolution, sponsored by Representative Samuel Dickstein of New York, calling for the creation of a special committee:

for the purpose of conducting an investigation of (1) the extent, character, and objects of Nazi propaganda activities in the United States, (2) the diffusion within the United States of subversive propaganda that is instigated from foreign countries and attacks the principle of the form of

[20] 72 Cong. Rec. 9390 (May 22, 1930).
[21] The Dies Committee, p. 24.

government as guaranteed by our Constitution, and (3) all other questions in relation thereto that would aid Congress in any necessary remedial legislation.[22]

John McCormack of Massachusetts, the present majority floor leader of the House, was named chairman of the committee and Dickstein was one of its members. Witnesses were carefully examined in twenty-four preliminary executive hearings, and seven public hearings were then held. Ogden calls this "a very wise procedure" and also states that "throughout the hearings McCormack sought to keep the proceedings on a high plane." [23] The committee's report, which was filed in February, 1935, contained separate sections dealing with Nazi, Fascist, and Communist organizations in the United States.[24] In general the committee found that fascism and communism were making little headway in the United States, and it contented itself with making a series of modest recommendations, one of which was ultimately enacted into law. This was the so-called McCormack Act, passed in 1938, which provided for the compulsory registration of agents of foreign governments disseminating propaganda in the United States.[25]

Following the report of the McCormack committee certain members of Congress continued to agitate for further investigation of subversive activity. The indefatigable Dickstein, who regarded fascism as offering the greatest threat to the United States, was now joined by Martin Dies, whose major interest from the start seems to have been communism, in urging the House to establish a new investigating committee. A Dickstein resolution calling for such a committee was defeated in the House in April, 1937, by a vote of 184 to 38. But shortly thereafter, Dies introduced another resolution, and, when this was called up in May, 1938, it was passed by a voice vote. The Dies resolution was patterned very closely after the McCormack committee resolution. It called for the creation of a special committee of seven members to investigate:

(1) the extent, character, and objects of un-American propaganda activities in the United States, (2) the diffusion within the United States of subversive and un-American propaganda that is instigated from foreign countries or of a domestic origin and attacks the principle of the form of government as guaranteed by our Constitution, and (3) all other ques-

---

[22] 78 *Cong. Rec.* 4934 (March 20, 1934).   [23] *The Dies Committee,* p. 34.
[24] The report was entitled, *Investigation of Nazi and Other Propaganda,* House Rept. No. 153, 74th Cong., 1st Sess., 1935.
[25] 52 *Stat.* 631.

tions in relation thereto that would aid Congress in any necessary remedial legislation.

This language has served unchanged to the present day as the directive upon which the work of the Un-American Activities Committee has been based.

The debate in the House on the Dies resolution was sharp and prolonged. It makes extremely interesting reading today in the light of the subsequent history of the Un-American Activities Committee.[26] Although communism was mentioned frequently throughout the debate, fascism—and more particularly Naziism—was clearly regarded as offering the greater danger to the United States, and the substantial majority given to the resolution unquestionably reflected this fear of fascism. Even such an implacable enemy of communism as J. Parnell Thomas emphasized the danger of Nazi propaganda and called attention to a Nazi camp that had been established in his district in New Jersey.[27] It is also clear from the debate that the excellent record made by the McCormack committee influenced many representatives to vote to establish a new investigating committee. Particularly striking in the debate were the calm, dispassionate words of Martin Dies, promising that if he had anything to do with the new investigation it would be conducted with scrupulous respect "for the undisputed right of every citizen in the United States to express his honest convictions and enjoy freedom of speech." Dies said also:

Let me say . . . that I believe all depends on the way the committee is handled. I can conceive that a committee constituted or composed of men whose object is to gain publicity, or whose object it is to arouse hatred against some race or creed, or to do things of that sort, might do more harm than good. On the other hand, investigations have a useful purpose. . . . I am not in a position to say whether we can legislate effectively in reference to this matter, but I do know that exposure in a democracy of subversive activities is the most effective weapon that we have in our possession. Always we must keep in mind that in any legislative attempt to prevent un-American activities, we might jeopardize fundamental rights far more important than the objective we seek, but when these activities are exposed, when the light of day is brought to bear upon them, we can trust public sentiment in this country to do the rest.[28]

[26] 83 *Cong. Rec.* 7567–7586 (May 26, 1938).   [27] *Ibid.*, p. 7577.
[28] *Ibid.*, pp. 7569, 7570. Equally interesting is the introductory statement made by Dies at the first hearing of the committee in August, 1938:
"The Chair wishes to reiterate what he has stated many times—namely that

Support for the resolution was also unquestionably won by Dies's statement that the investigation would last but seven months and by his acceptance of an amendment directing the committee to report to the House by January 3, 1939, or earlier.[29] Actually the House was establishing an investigating committee which more than thirteen years later was still going strong.

Although the final vote against the resolution was small, several

---

his committee is determined to conduct its investigation upon a dignified plane and to adopt and maintain throughout the course of the hearings a judicial attitude. The committee has no preconceived views of what the truth is respecting the subject matter of this inquiry. Its sole purpose is to discover the truth and to report it as it is, with such recommendations, if any, as to legislation on these subjects as the situation may require and as the duty of Congress to the American people may demand.

"We shall be fair and impartial at all times and treat every witness with fairness and courtesy. We shall expect every witness to treat us in the same way. This committee will not permit any 'character assassination' or any 'smearing' of innocent people. We wish to caution witnesses that reckless charges must not be made against any individual or organization. . . .

"The Chair wishes to emphasize that the committee is more concerned with facts than with opinions, and with specific proof than with generalities. Opinions, conclusions, and generalities have no probative force in any court of justice and they cannot be made the basis of any findings on the part of this committee. It is the Chair's opinion that the usefulness or value of any investigation is measured by the fairness and impartiality of the committee conducting the investigation. Neither the public nor Congress will have any confidence in the findings of a committee which adopts a partisan or preconceived attitude. Statements and charges unsupported by facts have no evidentiary value and only tend to confuse the issue. It is easy to 'smear' someone's name or reputation by unsupported charges or an unjustified attack, but it is difficult to repair the damage that has been done. As I previously stated, this committee is determined to be fair and just to everyone, and when an individual or organization is involved in any charge or attack made in the course of the hearings, that individual or organization will be accorded an opportunity to refute such charge or attack.

"In investigating un-American activities, it must be borne in mind that because we do not agree with opinions or philosophies of others does not necessarily make such opinions or philosophies un-American. The most common practice engaged in by some people is to brand their opponents with names when they are unable to refute their arguments with facts and logic. Therefore, we find a few people of conservative thought who are inclined to brand every liberal viewpoint as communistic. Likewise, we find some so-called liberals who stigmatize every conservative idea as fascistic. The utmost care, therefore, must be observed to distinguish clearly between what is obviously un-American and what is no more or less than an honest difference of opinion with respect to some economic, political, or social question." *Investigation of Un-American Propaganda Activities in the United States; Hearings before the Special Committee on Un-American Activities,* 75th Cong., 3d Sess., Aug. 12, 1938, I, 2–3.

[29] *83 Cong. Rec.* 7569, 7586.

Representatives spoke out against the proposal in vigorous fashion. Representative Gerald J. Boileau of Wisconsin called attention to the danger implicit in the exceedingly sloppy and vague wording of the resolution and offered an amendment which would have defined "subversive and un-American propaganda activities" in much more limited and meaningful fashion. His amendment called for an investigation of "the extent and character of propaganda activities in the United States which have as their objective the overthrow of the Government of the United States by force and violence." [30] But the Boileau amendment was not even voted on. Representative Dies had been recognized for one hour when his own resolution was called up, and under the rules of the House he controlled the floor and was entitled to move the previous question on his resolution when the hour was up, which he did. The House could have paved the way for a debate and vote on the Boileau amendment by rejecting Dies's previous question motion, but the latter was adopted by a vote of 191 to 41. Boileau tried to force the members of the House to go on record in taking this vote, but the necessary support of one-fifth of the members for a yea and nay vote was not forthcoming.[31] It is not too strong to say, then, that the manner in which the un-American activities investigation was originally approved by the House of Representatives did not reflect credit upon that body.

The so-called Dies committee thus came into being in May, 1938, and lasted until the close of 1944 when it expired with the 78th Congress. During this seven-year period it was given renewal of authority five times by the House of Representatives, always by overwhelming votes.[32] In January, 1945, at a time when it was thought that the Dies committee at long last was to become a thing of the past, the House of Representatives suddenly approved a proposal that the investigation of un-American activities be made a permanent one, and the present standing committee was created.

It is impossible here to say more than a word concerning the seven-year period of activity of the Dies committee. The story is told in considerable detail in Father August R. Ogden's excellent volume,

[30] *Ibid.*, p. 7579.   [31] *Ibid.*, p. 7586.

[32] These actions were as follows: (1) 1939 (344 to 34); (2) 1940 (344 to 21); (3) 1941 (354 to 6); (4) 1942 (331 to 46); and (5) 1943 (302 to 94).

In each instance the committee was renewed for a one-year period, save in 1943 when the renewal was two years.

According to Ogden the Dies committee was given the following appropriations by the House: 1938, $25,000; 1939, $100,000; 1940, $75,000 + $35,000; 1941, $150,000; 1942, $110,000; 1943, $75,000 + $7,500; 1944, $75,000; total, $652,500.

The Dies Committee. In the closing months of 1938 the committee was exceedingly active. Among the subjects of its early hearings were: the German-American Bund; communism in the CIO; J. B. Matthews; communism in Brooklyn College; the Federal Theatre; the Federal Writers' Project; Nazi activities; communism in the Farmer-Labor Party of Minnesota; sit-down strikes; anti-Semitism; and the American Civil Liberties Union. In addition to those held in the District of Columbia the committee also conducted hearings in New York, Michigan, California, and Ohio. After 1938 the number of public hearings conducted by the committee declined each year until August, 1941, when such hearings virtually ceased and the committee became thereafter a one-man show carried on by Dies. After commenting on the two or three public hearings held early in 1941, Ogden writes:

Any effort to trace the public action of the Committee henceforth becomes increasingly difficult. There is little evidence of activity of the Committee as such and all attention must perforce be given to the Chairman speaking in the name of the Committee or utilizing the information obtained from its files.[33]

The analysis of the Dies committee's record provided in the Ogden volume, while calm and dispassionate, is a generally critical one. Only in 1939 did the committee, in Ogden's opinion, make a good record. Much of the credit for this brief period of responsible activity is attributed by Ogden to the committee's counsel, Rhea Whitley.[34] But thereafter the influence of such staff members as J. B. Matthews and Robert J. Stripling increased, and the Dies committee fell into the practices which made its name so infamous in the annals of Congressional investigating committees.

[33] *The Dies Committee,* p. 245.   [34] *Ibid.,* p. 117.

II: The Committee in the Seventy-ninth Congress: 1945-1946

THE CREATION of a standing Committee on Un-American Activities early in January, 1945, was one of the most remarkable procedural coups in modern Congressional history. It was engineered almost singlehandedly by Representative John Rankin. The indefatigable Mississippian has always been an able and shrewd student of parliamentary procedure, a fact frequently overlooked by his detractors and opponents. Again and again in his career as a member of the lower house of Congress he has used this ability effectively in advancing causes meeting with his favor, and, in particular, in harassing his enemies and thwarting proposals which he has opposed. But the clever and successful way in which he caught the House of Representatives by surprise and forced it, probably against its will, to authorize a permanent Un-American Activities Committee is likely to remain the crowning achievement of his career as a parliamentarian.

That there was any possibility that the House might be asked to set up such a committee on the first day of the first session of the 79th Congress must have been furthest from the thoughts of the members, for there is no evidence that Rankin had taken any of his colleagues into his confidence as he laid his plans. The old Dies committee had seemingly been dying a slow death for some time. After the United States entered the war in 1941 it had become increasingly inactive, and during 1944 it held but a few, brief hearings. Finally, the decision of its unique chairman, Martin Dies, not to seek re-election to the House from his Texas district in the 1944 election looked like the deathblow to the committee so long identified with his name. For some time the committee had functioned as a one-man show, and without its flamboyant and tenacious chairman it seemed likely that it would expire for want of interest, support, and a willingness on the part of individual Representatives to offer their services in keeping the show going.

But all such calculations overlooked the mind and purpose of John Rankin. Hardly had the House of Representatives convened on January 3 for the brief, formal session characteristic of the first day of a new Congress when his opportunity came. The usual resolution was offered by Representative Sabath, chairman of the Rules Committee in the previous Congress, that the rules of the House in the 78th Congress remain in effect for the new Congress. Immediately, Rankin was on his feet with an amendment to this resolution to the effect that the Un-American Activities Committee be added to the list of the standing committees of the House. The cleverness of Rankin's move lay in the fact that the Sabath resolution had to be voted upon at once and could not be referred to the Rules Committee for deliberation and a recommendation, since technically no committees existed until the resolution itself was adopted.[1] Normally, major changes in the rules of the House of Representatives or the creation of new committees are proposed in resolutions offered after a new session gets under way, in which case they must necessarily be referred to the Rules Committee for what often proves to be prolonged consideration and ultimate pigeonholing. But the wily Rankin saw that the customary reluctance of the House to support any attempt to railroad through a change in the rules on the first day might well be overcome by the fear of House members, often indicated in the preceding years, that any kind of vote against the un-American activities investigation would be politically unwise.

Apart from Rankin's general desire to see the committee kept alive, and even made permanent, it appears that his immediate motivation was a concern about the preservation of the voluminous records and files accumulated by the Dies committee during the eight years of its existence. Rightly or wrongly, Rankin was convinced that there was a move afoot to destroy these records. In the debate on his amendment to the Sabath resolution he asserted that only the maintenance

[1] Even following the adoption of the rules it is usually a matter of days before a new House approves committee personnel and the committees are actually ready to function.

of a police guard over the records had theretofore prevented their destruction.[2]

In view of the very large majorities by which the House had always supported the Un-American Activities Committee, it is surprising that the Rankin amendment encountered the opposition that it did and that it passed by so narrow a margin. The debate on the amendment, while brief, was sharp. Representative Cochran, who as chairman of the Committee on Accounts had in the past taken an increasingly unfriendly view of the Dies committee's numerous requests for additional funds, opposed the amendment and argued that the intelligence officers of the State Department and the armed services could continue using the records of the Dies committee with the approval of the clerk of the House. In his opinion this would satisfy the need for a continuing check upon subversive activities in the United States.[3] Speaker Rayburn also pointed out that under the rules of the House the records of a defunct committee were placed in the hands of the House clerk for safekeeping and presumably would be sent by him to the Library of Congress.[4]

The first vote on the Rankin amendment was by division and went against the proposal, 134 to 146. Rankin immediately asked for a record vote, and his request received the necessary support of one-fifth of the membership of the House. When the roll was called the amendment was carried by a vote of 207 to 186, with 40 members not voting. A breakdown of this vote shows that supporting the Rankin proposal were 137 Republicans and 70 Democrats. Voting against the

[2] 91 *Cong. Rec.* 11 (Jan. 3, 1945). Members of the committee's staff also stressed this threat of destruction of the records in interviews with the writer. The publication in the closing weeks of 1944 of the controversial "Appendix Nine" seems also to have been motivated by a fear that the Dies committee records were about to be destroyed. The six volumes of this Appendix are nothing less than a very generous sampling of all the material in the committee's files. For a discussion of Appendix Nine, see pp. 338–339.

[3] Cochran pointed out that the Dies committee had spent in all about $675,000 and had established offices in six cities outside Washington. And yet, he said, "in recent years the Dies Committee has been a one-man committee. Outside of one investigation, meetings were seldom held during the past two years." Cochran also charged that one member of the Dies committee had even been unable to obtain the names, salaries, and duties of members of the committee's staff. Representatives Rankin and Thomas immediately challenged the accuracy of this last charge. 91 *Cong. Rec.* 11.

[4] 91 *Cong. Rec.* 14. The Speaker referred to House Rules 37 and 38 and to 2 USC § 147.

amendment were 150 Democrats, 34 Republicans, 1 Progressive, and 1 American Laborite.[5] Sixty-three of the Democrats voting for the Rankin resolution were Southerners. Thus it was a coalition of Republicans and Southern Democrats which was responsible for the creation of a permanent Un-American Activities Committee.

The Rankin resolution of 1945 provided for the creation of a committee of nine members with the following powers and duties:

The Committee on Un-American Activities, as a whole or by subcommittee, is authorized to make from time to time investigations of (1) the extent, character, and objects of un-American propaganda activities in the United States, (2) the diffusion within the United States of subversive and un-American propaganda that is instigated from foreign countries or of a domestic origin and attacks the principle of the form of government as guaranteed by our Constitution, and (3) all other questions in relation thereto that would aid Congress in any necessary remedial legislation.

The Committee on Un-American Activities shall report to the House (or to the Clerk of the House if the House is not in session) the results of any such investigation, together with such recommendations as it deems advisable.

For the purpose of any such investigation, the Committee on Un-American Activities, or any subcommittee thereof, is authorized to sit and act at such times and places within the United States, whether or not the House is sitting, has recessed, or has adjourned, to hold such hearings, to require the attendance of such witnesses and the production of such books, papers, and documents, and to take such testimony, as it deems necessary. Subpenas may be issued under the signature of the chairman of the committee or any subcommittee, or by any member designated by any such chairman, and may be served by any person designated by any such chairman or member.

The language of this resolution was derived almost without change from the original resolution creating the Dies committee in 1938, and it was carried over without any change into the Legislative Reorganization Act of 1946, which gave the committee further recognition as a standing committee of the House of Representatives.

On January 4, the House adopted a resolution submitted by Rankin directing that all of the files and records of the Dies committee be turned over to the new committee.[6] And on March 7 the House voted 315 to 54 to give the committee an appropriation of $50,000 (in addition to its regular clerk allowance) for use during an indeterminate period.[7]

[5] 91 *Cong. Rec.* 15. *N.Y. Times,* Jan. 4, 1945.
[6] 91 *Cong. Rec.* 35.   [7] 91 *Cong. Rec.* 1857.

The organization of the new committee, which took place shortly, was marked by a rather complete turnover in personnel. Six of the nine seats were filled with Democrats, none of whom carried over from the Dies committee. The Republicans had three seats, two of which were assigned to members of the 1944 Dies committee: Representatives J. Parnell Thomas of New Jersey and Karl E. Mundt of South Dakota. The House rule limiting Representatives to one committee chairmanship made it impossible for Rankin to claim the chairmanship of the new committee since he was already chairman of the Committee on World War Veterans' Legislation. Accordingly, the Democrats assigned the post to Edward J. Hart of New Jersey. Halfway through 1945 Hart gave up both the chairmanship and his seat on the committee, and John Wood of Georgia was appointed to both posts. An even division was arranged between Southern and non-Southern Democrats. Joining Hart were J. W. Robinson of Utah and John R. Murdock of Arizona. Joining Rankin were J. Hardin Peterson of Florida and Herbert C. Bonner of North Carolina. The third Republican member was Gerald W. Landis of Indiana. Ernie Adamson was named counsel and headed the committee's staff.

The record made by the Un-American Activities Committee for 1945 and 1946 suggests that, from his own point of view, Representative Rankin in his coup of January third won the battle but lost the war. Throughout the 79th Congress the committee plodded along, concerning itself with essentially minor and unimportant matters. It remained for the Republican-controlled 80th Congress to bring the committee to life and to exploit some of the potentialities that Rankin undoubtedly had in mind in making it a standing committee.

The 1945 Hearings

In 1945 the Un-American Activities Committee published no reports and conducted two brief sets of hearings. The first, in June, was a three-day hearing concerning radio publicity sponsored by the Office of Price Administration; the second, later in the year, was a six-day hearing dealing with the Communist Party of the United States.[8]

[8] The 1945 hearings were published in two volumes by the Government Printing Office under the following titles: *Investigation of Un-American Propaganda Activities in the United States (Office of Price Administration)*, June 20, 21, 27, 1945; and *Investigation of Un-American Propaganda Activities in the United States (Communist Party)*, Sept. 26, 27, Oct. 17–19, Nov. 8, 1945. The first is

The OPA hearings were about as futile an undertaking as the committee ever attempted. The opening of the hearings on June 20 coincided with bringing to the floor of the House of Representatives a bill providing for the renewal of the basic OPA legislation—the Price Control Act and the Stabilization Act, both originally passed in 1942. There is a strong suggestion that Adamson and Thomas were not without political motives in their part in the proceedings. The hearing opened with the following statement by the counsel: "Mr. Chairman and members of the committee, at this hearing I wish to raise before the committee some evidence in connection with numerous complaints we have received against the script radio broadcast of the New York region of the OPA. We are informed that these scripts are prepared by a man named Tex Weiner." [9] More specifically the charge was that a series of thirteen weekly fifteen-minute radio programs entitled "Soldiers with Coupons," which were prepared by a group of writers in the OPA and broadcast over station WOR in Newark, New Jersey, under the sponsorship of Standard Brands, Inc., contained subversive propaganda. Chester Bowles, OPA administrator, was the first witness and almost at once some members of the committee undertook to query Bowles about the OPA generally. Chairman Hart protested against this: "May I suggest that questions be kept in line with the purpose of this hearing? This is not an interrogation into the general conduct of the OPA nor the patriotism of volunteers that are helping the Government. We have a specific problem before us, and let us confine ourselves to that question." [10] Later, when Adamson by his questioning of witnesses suggested that it was improper for a private business concern like Standard Brands, Inc., to finance a government informational program, Hart again protested: "Let me say this: This inquiry does not include the propriety of business organizations sustaining programs in the hands of the Government, so let us not go into that. It has no part in this hearing. This hearing is devoted to a single subject: Whether or not the broadcasts were of a subversive nature, and I wish we could get down to the heart of the subject and let us find out whether they were or not." [11]

It was not until the third day of the hearings that Hart's plea that

abbreviated hereafter to *OPA Hearings;* the second is abbreviated to *Communist Party Hearings.*

For a full list of the hearings, reports, and other publications of the committee for the years 1945–1950, see Appendix, Table I.

[9] *OPA Hearings,* p. 2.   [10] *Ibid.,* p. 13.   [11] *Ibid.,* p. 66.

the committee get on with the search for subversive propaganda was heeded. On page 76 of the 88-page volume of published hearings, the first reference to alleged subversive activity is encountered. The witness at this point, George V. McDavitt, one of the committee's own investigators, testified that Tex Weiner, under whose direction the scripts were prepared, was once heard to voice "communistic ideas" and was also known to be irreligious. McDavitt began his testimony by alleging that Weiner had falsified his education and employment record at the time he secured his position with OPA. When Representative Robinson interrupted and asked what this had to do with subversive activity McDavitt endeavored to document his charges concerning Weiner's communistic and irreligious ideas. He reported that in one of the "Soldiers with Coupons" scripts the proprietor of a rooming house was made to place in each room a statement showing the price of the room: "The script ran something like this: 'Where will we hang this?' The reply in the script 'Put it in the Bible. Nobody looks in there.'"

Representative Robinson, seemingly unconvinced by this evidence, asked, "Is there anything un-American in that?" [12]

Other passages from the script quoted by McDavitt were: "As often is the case, tenants do not have high priced lawyers to advise them, but they do have the OPA, which is their bulwark against violations." "The overwhelming majority of landlords are patriotically cooperating with OPA, and the few that try to evade the law make it harder for the landlords who play square with his [sic] tenants." "Sure thing, Joe, OPA was set up for little guys like you and me." [13]

McDavitt then read part of an OPA official's criticism of a Weiner script: "This is one of the best ways to build up for a damn big run I've yet seen. It does not make the point that there are reasons for the shortage. It does not make the point that there is enough to go around if we restrain buying. It does not make any plea for restraint or conservation. It does intimate that OPA has let prices go clear up to heaven. I'd vote to tell them nuts on the whole thing."

Representative Robinson, still unconvinced, met this last bit of testimony with the query, "Apparently he didn't think much of the script, but where is the subversive part . . . ?" [14] The printed record of the hearing follows in part:

Mr. McDavitt: I will show you the objective of the communistic propaganda and how it fits into such broadcasts as this.

[12] *Ibid.,* p. 78.   [13] *Ibid.,* pp. 80–82.   [14] *Ibid.,* pp. 84–85.

Mr. Robinson: I am not interested in that. I am interested in these scripts. . . .

.   .   .   .   .

Mr. McDavitt: I might say this, that the people who today are disseminating the propaganda of a communistic nature no longer can be identified as the propagandists of 10 or 15 years ago. They are approaching the subject today on a highly cultural basis. . . .

The subversive activities of this particular script lie in the fact that it tends to generally indict the landlord, generally indict industry, as a violator of law, and in that way it makes the person on the street antagonistic towards these various individuals, such as capitalists, industry, and such as a man who owns a piece of property.

.   .   .   .   .

Mr. Rankin: . . . I am wondering if it is your contention that this is a propaganda line of the old Communist Party.

Mr. Adamson: Absolutely.

Mr. Rankin: And it was the Communist Party that was originally dedicated to overthrow this Government?

Mr. Adamson: There is no mistake about that.

Mr. Rankin: The overthrow of what they call the capitalistic economic system. That is the system of the ownership of private property. Is that what you contend that this all is?

Mr. McDavitt: Yes, sir.

Mr. Rankin: This is all driving to that end?

Mr. McDavitt: That is right.[15]

At the end of the third day of hearings the committee agreed to meet again and to listen to recordings of the Weiner broadcasts. There is no indication that it ever did so meet. Moreover, the only reference ever made to these OPA hearings in reports of the committee was a single paragraph in an annual report published more than a year later in June, 1946. The paragraph is as follows:

In addition to the comments concerning the radio commentators . . . the committee has conducted investigations concerning certain radio programs conducted by Government agencies. One of these programs was conducted by the Office of Price Administration and was the subject of several complaints received by the committee. It was alleged that the program was fostering the spreading of racial hatred and religious prejudice. The author of the program and two officials of the Office of Price Administration soon after the investigation was instituted by the

[15] *Ibid.,* pp. 85, 87.

committee resigned their positions and subsequently the committee dropped the matter of the investigation.[16]

Throughout the years since its creation in 1945 the major interest of the Un-American Activities Committee has been the Communist Party and the alleged subversive activity in which party members and fellow travelers have engaged. This, in itself, has been a reasonable and proper interest. With the defeat of the fascist powers which was imminent at the time the committee was created, the world-wide Communist movement became the great rival force to the Western capitalist and democratic way of life. Accordingly, if there was to be an un-American activities committee in the postwar period its major attention must inevitably have been given to communism.

A careful reading of the hearings on the Communist Party held in the fall of 1945 makes it clear that a fair amount of work had gone into their preparation and that the committee was following an investigatory pattern of sorts. The two chief witnesses were Earl Browder—who had been deposed as leader of the Communist movement in the United States just two months earlier in July, 1945, when the short-lived Communist Political Association was abolished and the Communist Party was re-established—and William Z. Foster, Browder's successor. The questioning of these two men indicated that the committee was seeking information on two crucial issues: (1) the extent to which the American Communist Party was subject to control by foreign agencies, and (2) the extent to which the party was an advocate of revolution by force and violence. More specifically the hearings were seemingly designed to throw light upon the curious action of the American Communists in first dissolving their party in 1944 and replacing it with the Communist Political Association, and then in 1945 in re-establishing the party and replacing Browder with Foster. There was good reason to believe that these changes had been ordered by the international Communist hierarchy and accepted by American Communists without question. In particular, it seemed probable that the signal for the 1945 action had been given by Jacques Duclos, a prominent member of the French Communist Party, in an article originally published in France and reprinted in May, 1945, in this country, in the *Daily Worker*.[17]

But if this was the pattern which the 1945 hearings of the Un-

[16] *Report of the Committee on Un-American Activities,* June 7, 1946, p. 11.

[17] See *The Communist Party of the United States as an Agent of a Foreign Power,* House Rept. No. 209, April 1, 1947, p. 31. Abbreviated hereafter to *1947 Communist Party Rept.*

American Activities Committee was supposed to follow, the actual conduct of the investigation fell short of the indicated purpose. The questioning of Browder and Foster suggests that if the committee intended to make a systematic investigation of the American Communist movement, insufficient attention had been given to details. Moreover, Browder and Foster were wily, clever witnesses. Adamson, Wood, Thomas, and Rankin, who did much of the questioning, again and again proved themselves incapable of subjecting the two witnesses to the kind of consistent and relentless questioning necessary to achieve the purposes of the inquiry. Their questions were so rambling and unsophisticated that Browder and Foster were never pinned down to a discussion of the all-important points concerning their party's relations with foreign agencies or their views with respect to the use of force and violence. Perhaps even wiser questioning could not have forced the two men to have testified openly concerning the strategy and policies of American communism. But an intelligent, sophisticated approach to the matters under inquiry would have made it harder for the witnesses to avoid giving such information.

Several examples of the questioning may be noted. When Browder was on the stand he was pressed hard to tell his side of the story concerning his recent deposal from office. The questioning turned to the Duclos affair:

Mr. Thomas: Who is Mr. Duclos?

Mr. Browder: Mr. Duclos, author of the article which has just been handed me, is the leader of the Communist Party in France.

Mr. Rankin: Do you agree with him, with his statement?

Mr. Browder: I would refer you to the fact that my opinions have been a matter of public record, and I have nothing to add to the record.

Mr. Rankin: I don't care anything about them being a matter of public record; I am asking you now if you agree with that statement by Duclos?

Mr. Browder: That is impossible to answer.

The Chairman [Wood]: Why is it impossible, Mr. Witness? You are familiar with the article, aren't you?

Mr. Browder: I am familiar with the article.

The Chairman: Do you agree with every observation made in it?

Mr. Browder: With every observation made in it? I don't think that in all my life I ever read an article in which I agreed with all observations, except my own articles of course. [Laughter.]

The Chairman: I was not asking you about your past experiences; I want to know if you agree with the statement of principles embodied in that article.

Mr. Browder: I do not know what statement of principle you mean.

The Chairman: Any of them.

Mr. Browder: It is subject to many interpretations, and a "yes" or "no" answer will not clarify but will only create further confusion.

Mr. Adamson: You mean by that, Mr. Browder, that you doubt the ability of the members of the committee to understand your explanation?

Mr. Browder: No; I do not.

Mr. Adamson: Well, why do you assume that it will create such a confusion in their minds?

Mr. Browder: Because the question is not defined whatever, and a "yes" or "no" answer to such a question, no matter what the question refers to, always creates more confusion than clarity.

Mr. Adamson: Suppose you answer it to the best of your ability. It is not necessary that you give categorical answers here. You are the witness, of course. Suppose you make an effort.

Mr. Browder: I really am unable to summon the tremendous energy required for such an effort as that at this time.[18]

The ease with which the witnesses were able to turn the proceedings in a farcical direction is suggested by the following exchanges:

Mr. Foster: Everybody who has Fascist leanings is dangerous.

Mr. Landis: If we had a few more men like MacArthur in this country we would be better off. I will say that.

Mr. Rankin: Amen.

Mr. Foster: Well, everybody is entitled to his own opinion, as the old lady said when she kissed the cow.

(This dialogue occurred after Adamson had brought Laski's name into the questioning.)

Mr. Rankin: Who is Mr. Laski?

Mr. Adamson: Mr. Laski is, I believe, one of the leaders in England of the Communist movement.

Mr. Foster: That is an example of how little you know about the Communist movement. Mr. Laski has nothing whatever to do with the Communist movement in England.

. . . . .

I hope Mr. Laski is not supposed to be un-American too. Is he?

Mr. Adamson: I don't know very much about Mr. Laski, Mr. Foster. You know more about him than I do.

Mr. Rankin: Is he an American? [19]

On the other hand, the investigation was not without its effective moments. Now and then committee members were able to press or

[18] *Communist Party Hearings,* p. 26.   [19] *Ibid.,* pp. 119, 162.

taunt the witnesses into meaningful and revealing statements concerning the nature of communism. A good example is seen in the following exchange between Representative Mundt and Foster:

Mr. Mundt: I was intrigued by an answer that Mr. Foster gave the chairman in response to a question—I believe you said that the people of Russia enjoy greater political liberties than the people of the United States, speaking of the working classes?

Mr. Foster: That is right.

Mr. Mundt: Would you say that the right to organize and operate in an opposition party is an inherent part of political liberty?

Mr. Foster: No. It is under capitalism, but not under socialism.

Mr. Mundt: You think you can have political liberty without having the freedom to dissent?

Mr. Foster: Parties represent classes, generally, and there are no opposing classes in the Soviet Union, so there is no basis for more than one party.

Mr. Mundt: You do not think there is?

Mr. Foster: I know there is just one party in the Soviet Union. I don't have to affirm or deny that. Everybody knows it.

Mr. Mundt: Would you say that the right to publish an opposition newspaper was inherent as part of political liberty?

Mr. Foster: If there is an opposition it should have a right to publish newspapers, and the fact of the matter is that for many years there were such newspapers published.

Mr. Mundt: Can you name an opposition newspaper in Moscow today?

Mr. Foster: There are none. Well, I don't know of any, because there is no opposition. The people are united. It is a difficult thing for you to realize that.

Mr. Mundt: 190,000,000 people over there are all of one opinion?

Mr. Foster: It may seem very humorous that the Russian people are united, but I think if they had not been united, you would probably have a gauleiter in New York and probably in Washington.

· · · · ·

Mr. Mundt: What was the great educational process employed by which in the course of say, 20 years, 190,000,000 people all came to think simultaneously about the same thing in every way?

Mr. Foster: Well, that is a long story.

Mr. Mundt: But it would be very informative. That is a great educational achievement.

Mr. Foster: I would like to know what all this talk about the Soviet Union has got to do with un-American activities here. I don't think this committee should permit such talk.[20]

[20] *Ibid.,* pp. 119–120.

In the end, however, these 1945 hearings on the Communist Party cannot be viewed other than as a false start. The committee was still two years away from any activity that might be characterized as a systematic effort to obtain an intelligent understanding of the Communist movement in the United States.

The 1946 Hearings

If the Un-American Activities Committee got off to a lame start in the first year of its existence, its record for 1946 was hardly more impressive. There were, in all, only three days of hearings. Gerald L. K. Smith, an alleged leader of the native fascist movement in the United States, was the sole witness on the first of these days at the end of January. On April 4, the committee placed upon the witness stand a number of recalcitrant officers of an organization known as the Joint Anti-Fascist Refugee Committee who had refused to comply with the committee's subpoena that they turn over to it the agency's files and records. And late in November the committee heard the ex-Communist, Louis F. Budenz, testify. The committee was only slightly more active than it had been in 1945 in submitting reports on its work to the House of Representatives and the American people. Three reports were published: one, a brief five-page study, *Sources of Financial Aid for Subversive and Un-American Propaganda,* and the other two, the committee's "annual" reports for 1945 and 1946.[21] The content and quality of these and subsequent reports by the committee will be examined in Chapter IX.

In a 1948 speech reviewing the ten-year record of the Dies-Wood-Thomas committee, Representative Thomas stated that in 1946 Gerald L. K. Smith was "questioned at length . . . regarding his anti-racial propaganda."[22] Actually, a reading of the printed hearing makes it plain that the questioning of Gerald L. K. Smith was most unsatisfactory. The committee had let it be understood that Smith would be subjected to a searching investigation, but the hearing was a relatively brief one and on the whole Smith was treated as though he were a "friendly" witness.[23] Rankin, Thomas, and Adamson fed

[21] For the list of the 1946 published hearings and reports of the committee, see Appendix, Table I.

[22] 94 *Cong. Rec.* A3473 (May 26, 1948).

[23] The committee issued a blanket invitation to all members of the House of Representatives to participate in the questioning of Smith. At the opening of the hearing Representative Ellis Patterson appeared and asked permission to read a series of nine questions directed to the committee concerning the procedure

the witness questions which allowed him to range widely and discuss at length his views concerning Communist activity in the labor movement, in religion, and in the motion picture industry.[24] Smith was allowed to name a number of well-known persons and to make irresponsible charges against them concerning alleged subversive activity. As the testimony turned in this direction, any thought of spreading on the record the story of Smith's own activity slipped from sight. In the final analysis the hearing was essentially worthless as a means of throwing light upon the alleged existence and activity of a native fascist movement in the United States.

The Joint Anti-Fascist Refugee Committee, as its name suggests, was a private organization which had as its ostensible purpose the

---

that would be followed if he and four other Representatives (Celler, De Lacy, Marcantonio, and Savage) accepted the invitation. The written statement of the questions was received, but Patterson was not allowed to read them, and his group did not participate in the hearing. Representatives Rankin and Thomas bitterly attacked the five Congressmen for their questions. *Gerald L. K. Smith Hearings*, pp. 1–4.

[24] "*Mr. Rankin:* The charge has been made that a certain element, largely under control of the moving-picture industry in Hollywood, is using it to spread communism and to destroy the morals, I will say, of America; and I should like for you, if you know anything about it, to discuss that; because this committee has been called on to investigate it, and from the side-line interferences we are receiving from that immediate community, especially from Members of Congress and left-wingers generally, it has indicated to me that there is one subject that this committee is going to have to go into.

"*Mr. Thomas:* We have already made a preliminary investigation, but we haven't done anything about it.

"*Mr. Rankin:* I understand that. I just wanted to know if the witness has any information on that subject, and if that had anything to do with these interferences and with these disturbance [*sic*] out there.

"*Mr. Smith:* When I first went to California, the naive and uninitiated just assumed that the smear stories that went out ahead of me were true. Then, when these people began to demonstrate and speak to five, ten, fifteen thousand people, and responsible citizens recognized in the leaders of these demonstrations the most notorious Communists in the State, they found that they enjoyed the financial cooperation of some of the most influential and highly paid personalities in Hollywood. Would you like me to give you four or five instances?

"*Mr. Rankin:* Yes.

"*Mr. Smith:* I am not going to speculate. I am going to give you illustrations that have come within the circumference of my own personal experience.

"The man who led the campaign before the school board to deny me the right of free speech, in cooperation with this Mobilization for Democracy, which Senator Tenney says is definitely controlled by the Communist Party—the man who led the campaign was Mr. Eddie Cantor.

"Before I spoke, the Communist element organized a high school strike. They went out with a loudspeaker appealed to the children of the Roosevelt High

rescuing of victims of fascism in Germany, Italy, and Spain. The House committee became interested in the agency in the course of a study of "the various means and methods employed by subversive organizations in collecting and disbursing funds." Chairman Wood told the House of Representatives that the committee had received 8,000 requests that it investigate the Refugee Committee.[25] In February, the committee subpoenaed Dr. Edward K. Barsky, chairman of the Refugee Committee, to appear before it and to bring with him the organization's books and records relating to receipts and disbursements of money, and correspondence with persons in foreign countries. Barsky appeared but informed the committee that

---

School to jump over the fence, desert the school, and picket the school board. They came down and picketed the school board, deserted the school, and I point out, gentlemen, that before I spoke in that schoolhouse I appeared before the school board of Los Angeles and my enemies had twice before brought in everything they could think of against me, and when all the facts were in—and it was a very expensive hearing both times—the school board unanimously agreed to permit me to use the high school auditorium.

"Some 500 of these children were suspended. Then the superintendent called them in and said to their parents that if they would sign a statement agreeing to try to prevent the repetition of such things they would remove the suspension; 92 refused. They were expelled.

"Shortly after that the Youth for Democracy, which is the successor of the Young Communist League, held a banquet at the Ambassador Hotel.

"*Mr. Adamson:* Is that the American Youth?

"*Mr. Smith:* The American Youth for Democracy, successor to the Young Communist League. The most conspicuous personality used in advertising this meeting was the much-publicized crooner, Frank Sinatra. Then Sinatra entered into a campaign to exonerate these children who had been the leaders in this organization for truancy.

"At this same meeting the much-publicized movie star, Ingrid Bergman, appeared and spoke. At this banquet were the most outstanding Communists of the State.

"The semiofficial night-life publication of Hollywood, called Hollywood Nite-Life, the current issue, January 18, carries a front-page editorial entitled 'The Unholy Three—Smith, Tenney, Rankin.' I would like to give you that.

"*Mr. Rankin:* Is that Tenney, of the State senate of California?

"*Mr. Smith:* Yes.

"*Mr. Thomas:* You wouldn't say Frank Sinatra was a Communist, would you?

"*Mr. Smith:* He may not be that intelligently, but he certainly is being used by the Communist Party, because when you take a man that is publicized as he is, and then direct the spotlight that leads right to a Young Communist banquet, you overtake millions of young people unprepared for that sort of persuasion and lead them to believe that communism is respectable.

"*Mr. Thomas:* Would you say he was sort of a Mrs. Roosevelt in pants? [Laughter.]" *Ibid.*, pp. 45–46.

[25] 92 *Cong. Rec.* 2745 (March 28, 1946).

he had laid the matter before his executive board and that the board had instructed him not to produce the records. Late in March the Un-American Activities Committee asked the House of Representatives to cite Barsky and fifteen members of the executive board for contempt. In the course of the debate it appeared that Barsky alone had been subpoenaed to produce the records and that the case against the members of the executive board depended solely on Barsky's word. When it appeared that the House might well refuse to approve the contempt citation, Representative Wood offered an amendment striking from the resolution all of the names save that of Barsky. So amended, the resolution was then passed by the House by a vote of 339 to 4.[26]

The hearing of the House committee on April 4 undertook to remedy this difficulty. This time sixteen members of the executive board and the executive secretary of the agency were subpoenaed and directed to bring with them the books and records. All of the subpoenaed witnesses appeared, but none brought the desired documents. The hearing was an executive one, but the testimony was ultimately made public. Almost all of the questioning related to the failure of the Refugee Committee's officers in their individual and collective capacities to produce the records which the House committee was seeking. Virtually no effort was made at this hearing to question the witnesses concerning the character of the organization or of its activities. In the end, the House committee had little choice but to renew the contempt charges against all of the witnesses, for the testimony made it clear that they had deliberately flouted the committee's subpoenas and had willfully refused to produce the records. Indeed, it was a bit like the game of "button, button, who has the button." Barsky had originally contended that he could not produce the records since the executive board had refused to grant him permission to do so. It was now the contention of each member of the executive board that they did not have custody of the records, since, legally, they were in the care of the executive secretary, Miss Helen Bryan. But Miss Bryan testified that she had not brought the records because the executive board had instructed her to take steps, within her legal rights, to protect the records against the House committee! She then submitted a prepared statement listing, on the advice of counsel, five reasons why she would not produce the records.

The Joint Anti-Fascist Refugee Committee hearing was thus the

[26] *Ibid.*, 2744–2749.

first in which the permanent Un-American Activities Committee encountered the problem of recalcitrant witnesses. The hearing's importance lies almost entirely on the side of procedure. All of the
witnesses were eventually prosecuted and convicted in the courts
for contempt of Congress. The Court of Appeals of the District of
Columbia sustained the conviction of the witnesses, and the Supreme
Court denied certiorari.[27]

In the November hearing, at which Louis Budenz was the lone
witness, the committee once more sought substantive evidence concerning the nature of the Communist movement. Budenz, by his
own testimony, had been a member of the Communist Party for
ten years, during six of which he was a member of the party's national committee. In 1945, at a time when he was managing editor of
the *Daily Worker*, he broke with the Communist Party in highly
dramatic fashion. Simultaneously with his break from the party,
Budenz returned to the Catholic Church. Subsequently, he became
an assistant professor of economics at Notre Dame University, and
at the time of his appearance before the House committee he held
a similar position at Fordham University.

It is difficult to evaluate the Budenz testimony before the House
committee. Budenz has become one of the leading, if not the chief,
ex-Communist upon whom dependence has been placed in the last
few years for factual information concerning the nature of the international Communist movement and the organization and policies
of the Communist Party of the United States. He was one of the chief
witnesses for the government in the successful prosecution of the
eleven Communist leaders in 1949 for violation of the Smith Act.
Budenz is an articulate, highly literate person, and there is little
doubt that much of the information he has supplied concerning
communism is both accurate and significant in the highest degree.
But any careful evaluation of the testimony Budenz has freely supplied again and again in recent years is beyond the scope of this
book.

Budenz' testimony before the House committee was rambling
and disorganized but exceedingly informative. He was allowed to
talk at great length, and the committee and its staff made almost no

[27] *Barsky, et al. v. United States,* 167 F. 2d 241 (App. D.C. 1948). Certiorari
denied, 334 U.S. 843 (1948). See also: *United States v. Bryan,* 339 U.S. 323
(1950). Same case below: 174 F. 2d 525 (App. D.C. 1949). *United States v.
Fleischman,* 339 U.S. 349 (1950). Same case below: 174 F. 2d 519 (App. D.C.
1949). The legal and constitutional aspects of these cases are examined in detail
in Chapter XI.

effort to guide him. Budenz stated that his appearance before the committee was the result of a radio speech he had made a month earlier in which he had asserted that the Communist International continued to exist "in fact, if not in form," that it continued to give instructions to local Communist parties throughout the world, and that there was in the United States "a specific individual," named Hans Berger, also known as Gerhart Eisler, who was the equivalent of a representative of the Comintern. Budenz' testimony before the committee was in good part an elaboration of his charge that ties existed between the American Communist Party and the international Communist movement. In particular, he discussed the "conspiratorial apparatus" which he said lay back of the regular party organization and was largely made up of shadowy foreigners. Budenz stressed the frequency with which forged passports, sudden disappearances, and even assassinations occurred in the careers of these people.[28]

[28] The character of Budenz' testimony before the House committee is illustrated by the following excerpt:
"*Mr. Landis:* How do you account for the fact that the intellectuals in America can follow this party line?
"*Mr. Budenz:* Because it gives them a kind of certainty. They see certain weaknesses in our present system, with all of its merit, and that is, for instance, the constant return of the business cycle and other things of that character. They start out with the idea of remedying that condition, and they get enmeshed into the whole system of this conspirational and lying character.
"Secondly, I would like to say at this point that the intellectuals, and particularly the so-called liberals, are of course meat for the Communists. The Communists, as I have said in quotation marks, called them 'soft-headed and soft-hearted liberals,' and to some extent that is a correct designation. They rush out to defend the Communist line, without any responsibilities on their part. It is a very comfortable position to be in, by the way. You do not have any of the responsibilities of the Communist leadership, and on the other hand you have the satisfaction of acting very progressively, as they call it, because the Communists keep harping on progressive as they do opponents Fascist [*sic*]. The liberals are the first line of defense for the Communists. When I say liberals, I want to be thoroughly understood. I mean by liberals those who ally themselves with the Communist cause. There are also liberals who are opposed to Communists. These pro-Communist people, among whom the intellectuals are very much represented, first start out with good will toward the world with the idea of reforming it, and then before you know it you find that they represent a certain viewpoint; they are parroting every current Communist phrase and let me tell you from my own experience, Congressmen, it is the hardest thing in the world to admit that you are wrong. I know that from my own hesitancy for 2 years to admit that I was wrong and to hope that things would turn out different from what they were in fact. Therefore, the intellectually proud liberals are enmeshed in this thing." *Budenz Hearings*, pp. 46–47.

III: *The Committee in the Eightieth Congress: 1947*

THE REPUBLICAN victory in the 1946 Congressional election resulted in a major change in the organization and policies of the Un-American Activities Committee. Once more there were important changes in personnel. Representative Wood surrendered the chairmanship to J. Parnell Thomas of New Jersey, who, alone among the committee's members, had served on it continuously since the establishment of the Dies committee in 1938. Democratic representation was reduced from six to four. Representatives Wood, Rankin, Peterson, and Bonner remained on the committee as Democrats. Bonner resigned from the committee at the end of 1947, and his place was taken during the second session of the 80th Congress by F. Edward Hébert, Democrat, of Louisiana. Republican representation was increased from three to five. Representative Mundt was the only other Republican carry-over, three new members of the majority party being appointed to the committee. These new members were John McDowell of Pennsylvania, Richard M. Nixon of California, and Richard B. Vail of Illinois. Ernie Adamson departed from the staff, his place being taken by Robert E. Stripling, who was given the title of chief investigator.

Much more important than the changes in personnel was the new life which Chairman Thomas and the Republican members breathed into the committee. Before the end of January the committee held an organization meeting and authorized Thomas to announce an eight-point program. This program was as follows:

1. To expose and ferret out the Communists and Communist sympathizers in the Federal Government.
2. To spotlight the spectacle of having outright Communists controlling

and dominating some of the most vital unions in American labor.

3. To institute a countereducational program against the subversive propaganda which has been hurled at the American people.

4. Investigation of those groups and movements which are trying to dissipate our atomic bomb knowledge for the benefit of a foreign power.

5. Investigation of Communist influences in Hollywood.

6. Investigation of Communist influences in education.

7. Organization of the research staff so as to furnish reference service to Members of Congress and to keep them currently informed on all subjects relating to subversive and un-American activities in the United States.

8. Continued accumulation of files and records to be placed at the disposal of the investigative units of the Government and armed services.[1]

Whatever one may think of the caliber of the committee's work under Chairman Thomas, it was at least to make good during the two-year life of the 80th Congress by covering the ground announced in this program. The only point that perhaps was lost from sight as the committee moved from one sensation to another during the two-year period was Number 6. But while "communism in education" was never to become the subject of public hearings or published reports, there is evidence that the committee's staff has been continuously engaged in assembling data on alleged subversive persons in American universities, colleges, and schools.

During 1947 the Thomas committee conducted seven sets of hearings which occupied twenty-seven days, and published four reports.[2] The hearings ranged widely but all had as their central purpose the search for subversive activity by Communists. By 1947 postwar relations between the United States and the Soviet Union had deteriorated to a point where the danger from communism became the all-consuming interest of the House committee. As it turned out, the feeble questioning of Gerald L. K. Smith in 1946 was the last attempt of the committee to investigate the threat of subversive activity on the right. Four of the 1947 hearings concerned prominent personalities in the Communist movement: Gerhart Eisler, Leon Josephson, Eugene Dennis, and Hanns Eisler. The other three dealt with legislative proposals to curb the Communist Party, communism

[1] N.Y. Times, Jan. 23, 1947. The text of the eight-point program is taken from the Report of the Committee on Un-American Activities to the United States House of Representatives, Eightieth Congress, Dec. 31, 1948, pp. 2, 3. Such annual reports are hereafter abbreviated to Annual Rept. with date.

[2] For the list of 1947 published hearings and reports of the committee, see Appendix, Table I.

in labor unions, and communism in the motion picture industry. One of the reports concerned the Communist Party as an agent of a foreign power, and the other three dealt with private organizations accused of being Communist fronts: American Youth for Democracy, the Southern Conference for Human Welfare, and the Civil Rights Congress.

The Eisler-Josephson Hearings

The first public hearing was held on February 6, and the subject under investigation was Gerhart Eisler, alleged representative of the Communist International in the United States. This was a follow-up on the Budenz hearing of the preceding November at which Budenz had charged that Eisler had been for many years the real boss of the Communist Party of the United States.

Eisler proved to be an arrogant, unco-operative witness. He refused even to be sworn, insisting that he must first be allowed to make a prepared statement. The committee wasted little time arguing with Eisler, and almost before he knew it he was ordered from the stand and cited for contempt. Here, as elsewhere, the committee may be criticized for failing to pamper an unco-operative witness in the hope that he might be persuaded ultimately to answer some, if not all, of the committee's questions and thereby supply evidence pertinent to the subject under investigation. However, the defiant attitude with which Eisler took the stand indicated that the committee would get nothing out of him.[3] Moreover, upon Eisler's de-

[3] The proceedings are reported in the printed hearings as follows:
"*The Chairman [Thomas]:* Now, Mr. Stripling, call your first witness.
"*Mr. Stripling:* Mr. Gerhart Eisler, take the stand.
"*Mr. Eisler:* I am not going to take the stand.
"*Mr. Stripling:* Do you have counsel with you?
"*Mr. Eisler:* Yes.
"*Mr. Stripling:* I suggest that the witness be permitted counsel.
"*The Chairman:* Mr. Eisler, will you raise your right hand?
"*Mr. Eisler:* No. Before I take the oath—
"*Mr. Stripling:* Mr. Chairman—
"*Mr. Eisler:* I have the floor now.

.   .   .   .   .

"*The Chairman:* Now, Mr. Eisler, you will be sworn in. Raise your right hand.
"*Mr. Eisler:* No.
"*The Chairman:* Mr. Eisler, in the first place, you want to remember that you are a guest of this Nation.
"*Mr. Eisler:* I am not treated as a guest.

parture from the stand the committee's procedure made it clear
that it felt that it could obtain sufficient evidence from other witnesses
to prove the charges against Eisler without persuading him to
incriminate himself by his own words.

The other witnesses heard on February 6 were William O. Nowell,
an ex-Communist, Louis Budenz, and Ruth Fischer, sister of Eisler.
All three testified in considerable detail concerning Eisler's important role in the international Communist movement. The most dramatic moment in the hearing occurred when Miss Fischer said of
her brother, "I consider Eisler the perfect terrorist type. . . ." [4]

A reading of the printed record shows that this hearing had been
much more carefully prepared than were any of the 1945–1946 hearings. Stripling was to prove himself a much more competent head
of the staff than Adamson, for it was at once apparent that a good
deal of careful staff work had gone into the undertaking. Moreover,
the questioning of the witnesses proceeded along much more systematic lines than it had under Adamson's direction. Thomas allowed

---

"The Chairman: This committee—

"Mr. Eisler: I am a political prisoner in the United States.

"The Chairman: Just a minute. Will you please be sworn in?

"Mr. Eisler: You will not swear me in before you hear a few remarks.

"The Chairman: You refuse to be sworn in? Do you refuse to be sworn in,
Mr. Eisler?

. . . . .

"Mr. Eisler: I am ready to answer all questions, to tell my side.

"The Chairman: That is not the question. Do you refuse to be sworn in? All
right.

"Mr. Eisler: I am ready to answer all questions.

"The Chairman: Mr. Stripling, call the next witness.

. . . . .

"Mr. Mundt: Mr. Chairman, suppose you ask him again whether he refuses
to be sworn.

. . . . .

"The Chairman: Mr. Eisler, do you refuse, again, to be sworn?

"Mr. Eisler: I have never refused to be sworn in. I came here as a political
prisoner. I want to make a few remarks, only 3 minutes, before I be sworn in,
and answer your questions, and make my statement. It is 3 minutes.

"The Chairman: I said that I would permit you to make your statement when
the committee was through asking questions. After the committee is through asking questions, and your remarks are pertinent to the investigation, why, it will be
agreeable to the committee. But first you have to be sworn.

"Mr. Eisler: That is where you are mistaken. I have to do nothing. A political
prisoner has to do nothing." *Gerhart Eisler Hearings,* pp. 1–3.

[4] *Ibid.,* p. 31.

Stripling to direct the original questioning of each witness along obviously planned lines and then gave each member of the committee a chance to ask random questions. The obstreperous Rankin was sat upon by the chairman and was not allowed to disrupt the proceedings as he had done again and again in the preceding two years.

The Leon Josephson hearings were in reality a part of the Eisler proceedings. The committee had evidence that Josephson had helped procure a fraudulent passport for use by Eisler and that Josephson was an important Communist "functionary" in his own right. Josephson, like Eisler, refused to be sworn, and contempt charges were ultimately brought against him in the courts. Following Josephson's refusal to be sworn the committee employed a technique used later in the year with great effectiveness in the Hollywood hearings. It placed on the stand one of its own investigators, Louis Russell, and by skillful questioning allowed him to put into the record much of the detailed information which had been accumulated by the staff in a Josephson dossier.[5] A minor figure in the hearing was one Samuel Liptzen in whose name the passport used by Eisler had been made out. The committee attempted to find out whether Liptzen had been a party to this duplicity. Liptzen was originally subpoenaed to appear before the full committee in Washington on February 6. He failed to appear and instead sent a wire that the "illness of one very dear to me" required his presence elsewhere. Ultimately, he appeared before a subcommittee in New York and, while admitting membership in the Communist Party, denied knowing either Eisler or Josephson.[6]

The Dennis Hearing

The story of the Eugene Dennis hearing on April 9 is quickly told. Dennis, at the time general secretary of the Communist Party of the United States, had been subpoenaed to appear before the committee on this day. When the hearing was called to order Dennis was not present. Instead, his attorney appeared and submitted a statement challenging the legality of the committee. The statement was received by the committee but was not made part of the record. Stripling suggested that the failure of Eisler, Josephson, Liptzen, and Dennis either to appear or to be sworn suggested the existence of a conspiracy to commit contempt, and he urged the committee to consider a request to the Department of Justice that it prosecute

[5] *Leon Josephson Hearings*, pp. 32–50.   [6] *Ibid.*, pp. 5 ff.

Dennis for conspiracy to violate federal law. Louis Russell once more took the stand and testified concerning Dennis' activities, licit and illicit, through the years.[7] At the end of the brief session, Representative Nixon's motion that the committee recommend to the House of Representatives that Dennis be cited for contempt, and to the Department of Justice that it investigate the conspiracy charge, was adopted unanimously.

The Hanns Eisler Hearings

The ostensible purposes of the three-day Hanns Eisler hearings in September were, in the words of Investigator Stripling, to show (1) that the International Music Bureau, "which Mr. Eisler conceived," was "a section of the Communist International" and "a major program of the Soviet Union in their effort to bring about a world revolution and establish a proletarian dictatorship," and, (2) that "Mr. Eisler was permitted to go in and out of this country time and time again when the immigration laws of this country say a Communist shall not be permitted in this country." [8] An underlying purpose was to badger the State Department and attack the New Deal. The committee, by subpoenaing the records of the State Department in the Eisler case, had obtained a letter written by Eleanor Roosevelt to Sumner Welles in 1939 intervening in Eisler's behalf, and also further evidence that Eisler's status had been the concern of top officials in the department.

Unlike his brother, Hanns Eisler appeared before the committee readily and permitted himself to be sworn without protest. Moreover, his manner was one of sweet innocence. But it was soon apparent that the committee was dealing with a wily, resourceful witness. This was shown when Eisler described a little poem he had "put together," which read (in translation),

> Terrible it is to shed blood
>   Hard it is to learn to kill
> Bad it is to see people die before their time
>   But we must learn to kill
> We must see people die before their time
>   We must shed blood
> So that no more blood will be shed,

[7] *Eugene Dennis Hearings*, pp. 3–10.   [8] *Hanns Eisler Hearings*, pp. 26, 43.

as "a little philosophic poem directed against gangsters" and one that expressed "correct anti-Fascist sentiment." [9] The sardonic humor of the situation degenerated into farce when Representative Rankin asserted, "I suppose that I am as familiar with American poetry and with English poetry generally as any member of either House. And anybody that tries to tell me that this filth is poetry certainly reads himself out of the class of any American poet that has ever been recognized by the American people." That Mr. Eisler had made no claim to being an "American poet" was irrelevant to the scholar from Mississippi.

The facts in the Hanns Eisler case, much simplified, are these: He first entered this country in February, 1935, as a temporary visitor on a three-month permit. He was readmitted later in 1935 and again in 1938 on temporary permits. After this last entry he managed to remain in this country for over a year until April, 1939, when he went to Mexico. He then re-entered the country in September, 1939, on a two-month permit, although he seems to have remained here until September, 1940. Finally, in October, 1940, he was admitted as a nonquota immigrant for permanent residence in the United States. The story of these comings and goings is a confused one, and it is apparent that Eisler enjoyed favorable treatment by the immigration authorities. He managed to spend a very considerable part of the more than five years between February, 1935, and October, 1940, in the United States on temporary-visitor visas, and he finally gained admission on a permanent basis. But the efforts of the House committee to prove that there was any real wrongdoing on the part of the Immigration Bureau or the State Department were never quite successful. Since the allegations of wrongdoing depended entirely upon Eisler's status as a Communist, it is significant that as late as 1947 the Un-American Activities Committee itself was not able to demonstrate that Eisler had been a continuing member of the Communist Party through the years. Eisler himself admitted that he had applied for Communist Party membership in Germany in 1926, but he claimed he had immediately allowed the membership to lapse. There was considerable evidence that Eisler was a staunch fellow traveler and Communist sympathizer all during the 1930's, but that there was any clear-cut violation of the immigration laws of this country in Eisler's comings and goings was never established.

Mrs. Roosevelt's letter to Welles was written in January, 1939,

[9] *Ibid.*, pp. 60–61.

when Eisler was trying to get a nonquota visa from the United States consul general in Havana. The House committee's thesis was that Eisler was trying to get assurance before he left the United States to go to Cuba that his application would be acted upon favorably there. He certainly was never given any such assurance, and in April, 1939, he transferred the application to Mexico City and departed for Mexico. Mrs. Roosevelt's letter read:

Dear Sumner: All these papers were brought to me yesterday by a friend of Mr. Eisler. The man who brought them is a perfectly honest person and very much disturbed. He thinks the State Department has really told the Cuban consul that they do not wish to admit the Eislers, and he is perfectly sure that the Eislers are not Communists and have no political affiliations of any kind. He is sure that they believe our form of government is "heaven" and would be entirely agreeable without reservation to take an oath of allegiance.

I believe that it is said that the Labor Department did not examine the case carefully enough. Why not do it all over again and bring it out in the open and let the Eislers defend themselves?

Cordially,
ELEANOR ROOSEVELT [10]

Welles replied with a perfectly proper letter which he concluded by saying:

Mr. Eisler may be assured that the Department only desires that the question of his qualification and that of his wife to receive visas shall be determined in the usual manner by the consular officer who is responsible under the law for deciding this question. Mr. and Mrs. Eisler may also be assured that the consul general will accord them every possible consideration. . . .[11]

Both Sumner Welles, who was Under Secretary of State during the period of Eisler's efforts to enter the country permanently, and George S. Messersmith, who was an Assistant Secretary of State at this same time, were summoned as witnesses. The line of questioning, which was mainly controlled by Stripling, made plain the committee's strong bias in the case. Members of the committee quite obviously thought that they had caught Mrs. Roosevelt and high State Department officials in improper political activity, and they seemed dominated by the desire to prove this point. Here, as elsewhere, the committee seemed either completely disinterested in the

[10] *Ibid.,* p. 64.   [11] *Ibid.,* p. 66.

climate of opinion that may have existed at the time of the events being investigated or totally unable to realize that men may have honest and commendable motives for conduct which, as a matter of hindsight, later appears to have been incorrect. Welles was asked by Stripling, "You have heard the testimony and the evidence which was presented here today. Are you of the opinion that Mr. Eisler was inadmissible at the time he applied for a nonquota visa in Habana, Cuba, in 1939?" Welles's long answer to this question is worth quoting in full:

Mr. Chairman, I would like to make a statement of one or two sentences in reply to that question, with your permission.

It is very easy, Mr. Chairman, for officials of this Government, or ex-officials of this Government, to be accused of negligence or dereliction on account of hindsight. It is perfectly obvious that if some of the facts that have now been brought out by this committee had been in my possession at that time, the action which I took would probably have been more far reaching and more careful, but I also want to make this point, Mr. Chairman: At the time of which we are speaking the atrocities that had been committed in Germany had already been going on for some years. I think there is no responsible official of the Department who is not anxious to have the United States live up, within all proper limits of security, to its great record and its great traditions as a home for refugees from political persecution and from racial and religious persecution. And I think for that reason, Mr. Chairman, that insofar as we felt it possible within the limits of the law and of security of the country, that in cases of that kind we always gave the most sympathetic consideration.

It is for that reason that I wanted to answer to Mr. Stripling's question that, of course, a great deal of this information now available to me and to my associates was not available. We didn't have the means of having it available. And the Department as early as the early winter of 1941 took measures to strengthen up the security regulations with regard to the issuance of visas. An interdepartmental committee was constituted; a higher board was set up within the Department of State. Of course, cases of this kind make it very clear indeed that those measures of precaution and security should have been taken earlier.[12]

Messersmith was bullied by Stripling and members of the committee because it appeared that in 1938 and 1939 he had a certain sympathy for the idea that refugees from Nazi Germany should be allowed to enter and remain in this country if at all possible. The following exchange between Stripling and Messersmith bears this out:

[12] *Ibid.*, p. 71.

Mr. Stripling: . . . There is a handwritten notation at the foot of the letter which I will show you, Mr. Messersmith. I don't know whether you have any objection to it being read or not. I don't think you do. [Exhibits document.]

Mr. Messersmith: My eyes are very poor and I can't read that. I am sure I have no objection to your reading it.

Mr. Stripling: It says:

"And with my particular appreciation—you have done so much for my friends in trouble! Most cordially—"

Do you know—

Mr. Messersmith: That is Marie Davenport, his wife.

Mr. Stripling: You are acquainted with Mr. [Russell] Davenport and his wife?

Mr. Messersmith: Well, I think I knew Mrs. Davenport, Mr. Chairman, better than I did Mr. Davenport. Mr. Davenport at that time was the editor of Fortune, and the only connection that I had ever had with him was that he was planning to write an article on the State Department, about functions and that sort of thing, for Fortune, which was after it was published. But Mrs. Davenport I had met from time to time in New York socially.

What reference Mrs. Davenport there makes is only that I was one of those persons at the time who, having lived in Germany for 4 years and having seen when the Nazis came in first the members of the Communist Party in Germany and all labor leaders, and anyone connected with labor, with any labor organization, Communist or otherwise, put into concentration camps and literally hundreds of them disappear during the first days of February 1933, and then seeing men like Dr. ——.

The Chairman [Thomas]: I think you have answered the question. I think you completed your answer to the question.

Mr. Messersmith: What I am getting at is this, Mr. Chairman: I did what I could within the law to help persons who were in difficulty when I was in Europe and when I was over here, and I am very glad that I did it.

Mr. Wood: You mean irrespective of their political affiliations?

Mr. Messersmith: I think that question is a very improper one. It is an improper remark. It is an improper remark for you—and I say this with all respect—to make to me, who has had a long, and I believe honorable, career in the service of our Government, and who would not have been entrusted with the post which he was if I had not been a person who always loyally did my duty.[13]

Over a year after the Hanns Eisler hearings, the committee in its annual report dated December 31, 1948, asserted, "The evidence before the committee disclosed that Hanns Eisler's admission to

[13] *Ibid.*, p. 133.

this country in violation of our immigration laws was advanced by
certain individuals in the highest circles of the Government." [14]
This statement is utterly unfounded. The report further notes that
"at the end of February, 1948, the immigration authorities agreed
to halt deportation proceedings and Mr. and Mrs. Hanns Eisler were
permitted to depart by plane for Czechoslovakia." The critical comment is added, "The fact that he had sworn falsely as to his Communist record was ignored." [15]

Had the Un-American Activities Committee been willing to limit
its purpose in the Hanns Eisler affair to a demonstration to the American people of the pattern of international communism and of the
way in which the International Music Bureau and Eisler fitted into
that pattern, it might justly have claimed to have performed an
important service. But in choosing rather to emphasize the charge
of wrongdoing on the part of important New Deal officials, a charge
never really substantiated, the committee allowed the political motive to outweigh all others.

Communism in Labor Unions

The 1947 hearings regarding communism in labor unions occupied
four days, February 27, and July 23, 24, and 25. They dealt with
Communist penetration of three specific unions: the United Automobile Workers; the Food, Tobacco and Agricultural Workers; and
the United Electrical, Radio and Machine Workers—all at the time
affiliated with the CIO. For the most part the witnesses were of the
"friendly" variety, union men who had opposed the Communists in
their organizations. On the first day the committee heard three men
who had been members of Local 248 of the UAW. At the time of the
hearing members of this local had been out on strike for a period
of ten months against the Allis-Chalmers Manufacturing Company
in Wisconsin. An earlier strike in the same plant in 1941 had lasted
seventy-six days. All three witnesses testified that Local 248 was
Communist-dominated and that the two strikes were Communist-
inspired. Among the charges made by the witnesses were these:
(1) some fifty Communists were able to dominate a union of 8,700
members by clever parliamentary tactics, by the dishonest count
of ballots in union elections, and by outright methods of intimidation
and violence; (2) Communist leaders of the union had deliberately
held down wages during the war so as to keep rank-and-file mem-

[14] *Annual Rept.*, Dec. 31, 1948, p. 8.   [15] *Ibid.*

bers dependent upon them for help and guidance; (3) Communists in the union used their positions to distribute Communist literature, to solicit subscriptions to the *Daily Worker* and other Communist publications, and to encourage union contributions to such Communist front organizations as the American League for Peace and Democracy; (4) the ten-month-old strike was being prolonged by Communist leaders in an effort to support R. J. Thomas in his struggle with Walter Reuther for domination of the National UAW, since under UAW rules a local's voting power at a national convention depended upon its membership at the time a strike began—the assertion being that Local 248 had lost so many members during the long strike that when the strike was settled its national representation would be greatly reduced.

On July 23 the committee heard six witnesses testify concerning the strike of members of Local 22 of the Food, Tobacco and Agricultural Workers against the Reynolds Tobacco Company in Winston-Salem, North Carolina. All six were officers (or ex-officers) of the local. Three were friendly witnesses, and three were "unfriendly" —the latter refusing to answer all questions concerning their Communist affiliations on the ground of self-incrimination. The three friendly witnesses told essentially the same story of Communist penetration and control of their local as had the Allis-Chalmers witnesses. On July 24 and 25 the committee's attention was turned to the United Electrical Workers union, with particular emphasis upon the situation in Local 203 at the General Electric Company's plant in Bridgeport, Connecticut. Two witnesses, one the president of the local and the other its business agent, testified concerning a successful campaign which had been made to destroy Communist influence in their local. As a result of the campaign a Communist member of the executive board had been unseated, and twenty-six Communists had been expelled from the local union. These efforts had brought the local into conflict with the national union, in which Communist influence was strong, and an unsuccessful attempt had been made to revoke the local's charter.

On the whole these hearings were fairly and carefully conducted. The friendly witnesses were for the most part intelligent, honest, and persuasive. The questioning of them, particularly by Representative Nixon, was frequently able and resulted in convincing, systematic evidence concerning the pattern of Communist penetration of labor unions. At times the hearings were marred by the antilabor sentiments of such committee members as Thomas and

McDowell,[16] and the witnesses were allowed great freedom in making unverified charges against named members of their unions.[17]

The pattern of Communist activity in labor unions which emerged from the hearings is worth noting. In addition to the evidence already referred to, the following points were emphasized by the witnesses: (1) Communists in the union movement are numerically small but they are usually found in important positions; (2) these Communists are dedicated men of iron discipline, and they are indefatigable workers;[18] (3) Communists are able to capture and dominate a national union like UEW because the election of delegates to a national convention is often a cut-and-dried affair easily manipulated by a few Communists in locals; (4) Communists use their knowledge of parliamentary procedure to put across party-line resolutions at local meetings and national conventions, and generally to use labor unions for Communist "good works"; (5) an ultimate purpose is to recruit union workers as members of the Communist Party, and some progress, however slight, has been made.

It may be asked whether the Un-American Activities Committee was, as late as 1947, bringing to light any really new or striking evidence concerning communism in the American labor movement. Certainly the Communist background of the Allis-Chalmers strike was by this time known to many people. On the other hand, the committee did give publicity to the specific facts concerning the situation in three unions. Two years more were to pass before the national CIO would get around to expelling the two of these three

[16] *Hearings regarding Communism in Labor Unions in the United States*, 1947, pp. 47, 53.

[17] On the final day of the hearings one witness, James J. Conroy, asked the committee to take steps to verify his charges: "I would like to request that the committee give to all persons I have named as Communists an opportunity to defend themselves against my charges. I certainly don't want to be a party to the same type of procedure that they used and are using against people who are opposed to them. I think these people I have named should have a chance to come here and defend themselves against my charges." Chairman Thomas replied, "That is a very fair request on your part. The Chair will say the committee will take that under consideration." *Ibid.*, p. 210.

[18] For example:

"*Mr. Stripling:* What is your explanation as to how the Communists, people you have identified as Communists, all occupied high positions in the union, how can such a small group capture these positions, how do you explain that?

"*Mr. Conroy:* The explanation I can give is that, first of all, they have a program; secondly, they have iron discipline; and, thirdly, and most of important of all, they work like beavers." *Ibid.*, p. 200.

unions—the electrical and tobacco workers' unions—which were unquestionably Communist-dominated. Moreover, in 1947 the pattern of Communist penetration of such social institutions as labor unions was only beginning to be understood by the American people generally. This knowledge was to become widespread in the next year or two as the evidence piled up concerning the tactics of Communists in fighting the cold war. The further gains of international communism in the satellite countries, the confessions of numerous ex-Communists, and the role played by the Communists in the 1948 presidential election in this country all helped to educate the American people concerning the nature of the Communist threat. But in 1947 the facts about communism were not so well known, and even today the 1947 hearings make good reading for anyone who seeks the details of Communist strategy and tactics.

Hearings on Bills to Curb the Communist Movement

The 1947 hearings on H.R. 1884 and H.R. 2122 marked the first time that the Un-American Activities Committee gave its attention to proposed legislation in the field of subversive activity. The two bills which provided the excuse for these hearings had been introduced by Representative Rankin and Representative Sheppard of California. Both were brief bills which in effect outlawed the Communist Party.[19] Neither bill was a careful or serious piece of legisla-

[19] *Investigation of Un-American Propaganda Activities in the United States: Hearings on H.R. 1884 and H.R. 2122: Bills to Curb or Outlaw the Communist Party of the United States*. Abbreviated hereafter to *Hearings on H.R. 1884 and H.R. 2122*. For volume citations for separate witnesses, see Appendix, Table I.

H.R. 1884, the Rankin bill, would have made it unlawful: (a) for any person to seek election to a state or federal office (1) as the candidate of the Communist Party, or (2) if a member of the Communist Party even though not running as such; (b) "to advocate, or express or convey the impression of sympathy with or approval of, communism or Communist ideology" in the course of instruction or teaching in a public or private school or college; (c) to send through the mails any publication "which advocates . . . expresses, or conveys the impression of sympathy with or approval of, communism or Communist ideology."

H.R. 2122, the Sheppard bill, would have made it unlawful "for any individual to be a member of the Communist Party, or any organization known to him to be" (a) one which has as its purpose or aim "the establishment, control, conduct, seizure, or overthrow of Government in the United States . . . by the use of force or violence . . ."; (b) one "engaging in political activity in the United States which is affiliated directly or indirectly with, or the policies of which in relation to such political activity are determined by or are subject to the direction or control of, a foreign government or a political party in a foreign country, or which receives financial assistance or support of any kind from a foreign government or from a political party in a foreign country."

tion warranting a series of public hearings by a Congressional committee. In particular, the Rankin bill was an outrageous proposal. Among other things, it would have rendered a teacher liable to a fine of $10,000 and a prison term of ten years for him merely to *convey the impression of sympathy with . . . Communist ideology.*"

Seven days were devoted to hearings on these two bills, and the parade of witnesses included such well-known persons as William C. Bullitt, William Green, J. Edgar Hoover, and Eric Johnston. It is not surprising that each of these persons declared himself in opposition to the two bills, as did many other persons who testified. The committee had to go to such organizations as the Daughters of the American Revolution, the American Legion, and the Veterans of Foreign Wars to find anyone willing to speak in support of the bills. James F. O'Neil, vice-chairman of the Legion's Commission on Americanism, boasted to the committee that the legion had eliminated "the Rugg textbooks" from the schools of San Francisco.

The committee also listened at some length to George Earle, former governor of Pennsylvania and United States minister to Austria, who, while venturing no opinion on the two bills, talked at length about an atomic bomb attack upon our shores. When Chairman Thomas interrupted this testimony to observe, "Well, Governor, I can't quite understand what this has to do with these particular bills that we have," [20] he might have extended his remark to cover much of the testimony presented at these hearings.

William Green, president of the American Federation of Labor, suggested, as have many witnesses during the lifetime of the committee, that the best long-run attack upon communism is made through efforts to perfect our own democracy. He said,

> The fires of communism and every other totalitarian ideology are fed by poverty, privation, injustice, and strife. Human misery is the combustible fuel of subversive activity. The enactment of progressive legislation, designed to serve broad public welfare and responsive to the needs of the great mass of the people, is a vital safeguard against Communist inroads. Since the American people won the victory over the Fascist rule, their Congress has remained unresponsive to the pressing needs of America's own postwar reconstruction. The urgent, often desperate, need of the people for housing, for greater social security and improved health services, for minimum wage protection and other standards essential to maintain a high level of employment, production, and prosperity in the years to come have [sic] not been enacted.
> These are the antidotes against communism.[21]

[20] *H.R. 1884 and H.R. 2122 Hearings*, p. 329.   [21] *Ibid.*, p. 58.

The questioning of Green by committee members was in general intelligent. There was real give-and-take between witness and committee, and one gets the impression from these pages of the hearing that, here at least, some members of the committee were learning by listening.

It is significant that Victor Kravchenko, a former economic attaché of the Soviet Purchasing Commission in Washington, who renounced his allegiance to the Soviet Union in 1944, made much the same point as did William Green concerning the best way to fight communism. He said,

It is quite evident that it is impossible to defeat communism as an ideology, only through police and financial means. Especially this is true in free countries where people enjoy the freedoms of personal liberty, and ideas, the press, and of speech. It is possible to defeat it by serious political enlightenment of the people, and by the solution of the economic, social, and political contradictions of society in which lie the sources which nourish the Communist movement.[22]

Kravchenko's testimony took a more sensational turn when he asserted that "every responsible economic, political, and military representative [of the Soviet Union] in the United States may be regarded as a possible economic, political, or military spy." [23]

The most bizarre moment in the committee's hearings on the Rankin and Sheppard bills came on July 21 when Walter S. Steele was heard. Steele had been one of the first witnesses to appear before the Dies committee in 1938, and his testimony now, nearly ten years later, was very similar to the story he had told on the earlier occasion. Steele identified himself as "chairman" of the National Security Committee of the American Coalition of Patriotic, Civic, and Fraternal Societies, and also as managing editor of the *National Republic* magazine. Steele had apparently been running a private un-American activities committee for years and had built up files of his own on allegedly subversive individuals and organizations that rivaled those of the committee. He boasted that his files had been used extensively by the FBI, Military Intelligence (G2 and ONI), the State and Treasury Departments, and the Civil Service Commission, and that during World War II he had spent "approximately 50 per cent of my time serving the Government" without pay.[24] The American Coalition was identified by Steele as an association of eighty-four organizations, the character of which is indicated by the following

[22] *Testimony of Victor A. Kravchenko*, p. 25.   [23] *Ibid.*, p. 16.
[24] *Testimony of Walter S. Steele*, p. 5.

names taken from Steele's list at random: American War Mothers; Associated Farmers of California, Inc.; Colonial Order of the Acorn (New York Chapter); Dames of the Loyal Legion of the United States; Eugenics Society of Northern California; General Society of the War of 1812; Ladies of the Grand Army of the Republic; National Council of the Patriotic Women of America, Inc.; Order of the Colonial Lords of Manors in America; Order of Three Crusades, 1092–1192, Inc.; Southern Vigilant Intelligence Association, Inc.; Tax Evils Committee of Council Bluffs, Iowa; and The Wheel of Progress.[25]

It is possible that Steele's testimony was the most irresponsible ever presented to the Un-American Activities Committee. Almost without interruption by members of the committee he was allowed to testify at great length concerning the allegedly subversive activities of literally hundreds of organizations and thousands of individuals whom he was permitted to name. Unquestionably, much of his material was authentic and described the activities of undeniable Communist fronts and fellow travelers. But Steele obviously had little power of discrimination, and the innocent were listed with the guilty. For example, Steele testified concerning some 122 publications or publishing houses which he insisted were Communist-dominated, and he was permitted to name hundreds of persons identified with these as editors and writers. Two excerpts from this part of the testimony will give an impression of the kind of detailed material Steele was allowed to place in the record.

Public Affairs Committee, Inc., with offices at 122 East Thirty-eighth Street, New York, N.Y., entered the pamphleteering field several years ago. It issues higher quality pamphlets on subjects related to those adopted for propagation by the Communist Party. Maxwell S. Stewart, former editor of Moscow News, and with other front connections, is editor of the pamphlet service. Violet Edwards is education and promotion director. Frederick V. Field, of New Masses—Communist organ—is a member of the board.

Ruth Benedict, a member of the East and West Association, and Gene Weltfish, a leader in the Congress of the American Women, have written pamphlets for the Public Affairs Committee. One of them, Races of Mankind, was barred by the War Department after Congress protested against its use in orientation classes of the Army, declaring that its aim was to create racial antagonism.

I list herewith a few of the pamphlets issued by the committee: Why Women Work, Labor on New Fronts, Farm Policies of New Deal, How

[25] See ibid., pp. 3–4, for the complete list.

We Spend, How Can We Teach about Sex, Security or the Dole, Machines and Tomorrow's World, Who Can Afford Health, Safeguarding Our Civil Liberties, Read Your Labels, Radio Is Yours, For a Stronger Congress, What To Do about Immigration, and Will Negroes Get Jobs.

· · · · ·

Associated Magazine Contributors, Inc., possibly an outgrowth of the Mainstream Conference, has recently made its appearance. It maintains offices at 68 West Forty-fifth Street, New York, N.Y. It is described as a cooperative enterprise, and will publish, among other things, a pocket-sized magazine. The following are officers: John Hersey, president; Jerome Ellison, vice president; William A. Lydgate, secretary; and Maxwell S. Stewart, treasurer. Directors include Christopher La Farge, Robert St. John, John D. Ratcliff, and Mortimer S. Edelstein. Initial contributors, in addition to the above, are John Steinbeck, Stuart Cloete, Pearl Buck, Margaret Culkin Banning, Clifford [sic] Fadiman, Robert Butterfield, Ernest K. Lindley, Raymond Gram Swing, Austin Briggs, Rene Robert Bouche, Richard Sargent, Dwight Shepler, Sam Berman, Alan Dunn, Jack Markow, Gardner Rea, Robert Disraeli, Andrew Kertsz, Herman Landshoff, and Gjon Mill.[26]

The Steele testimony provides a shocking commentary on the character and activity of many of the "patriots'" organizations with which this country seemingly abounds. His unconscious revelation of the existence of a widespread vigilante movement in the United States is most disturbing. But the most shocking aspect of this hearing was the uncritical way in which the staff and members of the Un-American Activities Committee accepted everything that Steele said. Stripling went out of his way to indicate sweeping approval of the Steele data:

Mr. Stripling: Mr. Chairman, for the benefit of the record, we had Mr. Steele submit a list of those publications which we in turn submitted to our research department. The research department checked them with our files and without a single exception all of them are either official organs of what the committee considers to be a Communist front organization or an outright Communist publication.[27]

And at the close of the hearing, Thomas said, "Mr. Steele, in behalf of the committee, the Chair wants to express its appreciation for your coming here today and making the very complete statement that you have. In my 8 years with the committee I have never seen a more complete and more documented statement on this subject

26 *Ibid.*, pp. 40–41.   27 *Ibid.*, p. 46.

than you have presented here today. You are to be congratulated. For all of us, I just want to thank you very much." [28]

The Hollywood Hearings

During the last two weeks of October, 1947, the Un-American Activities Committee staged the most flamboyant and widely publicized hearings of its history. Not even the Hiss-Chambers hearings of the following year quite matched the sensations of the nine days in which the Great and Not-So-Great of Hollywood testified, or refused to testify, as, in the words of Max Lerner, the committee tried "to track down the footprints of Karl Marx in movieland." [29] By and large, the Hollywood hearings reveal the committee at its worst. In no other committee undertaking were the motivating forces of politics and the personal prejudices of the committee members more apparent; in no other hearing were the over-all strategy and specific procedures more subject to criticism; no other major investigation of the committee ever ended so anti-climactically or produced so little tangible evidence in support of a thesis which the committee set out to prove.

The committee's interest in Hollywood dated back to the early days of the Dies committee. In 1940, when the committee was being run as a one-man show by its increasingly reckless and irresponsible chairman, the motion picture industry was investigated in a series of closed hearings. In the words of Ogden, this "Hollywood affair . . . was a credit neither to the Committee nor the manner in which it was conducted." [30] Again in 1945, soon after the committee was made permanent, the lure of Hollywood once more exerted a pull upon it. In the period between the resignation of Representative Hart as chairman and the appointment of John Wood as his successor, the indefatigable Rankin served as the committee's "acting chairman." Rankin seized upon this opportunity to force a renewal of

[28] *Ibid.*, p. 173.

[29] *PM, Oct. 22, 1947.* The hearings were published under the title, *Hearings regarding the Communist Infiltration of the Motion Picture Industry.* Abbreviated hereafter to *Mot. Pict. Ind. Hearings.*

[30] Ogden, *The Dies Committee*, p. 213. Ogden adds that the investigation "had been hanging fire almost from the beginning of the operations of the Committee," and he concludes that "in reality it was a sensational one-man show with only a part of the evidence being released to the public. Either a public airing of the entire affair, or a closed inquiry from which no information would have been allowed to leak, would have been far superior to the course actually followed."

committee interest in Hollywood. With an incredible lack of initial impartiality in starting such an undertaking, Rankin announced that he had received reports that "one of the most dangerous plots ever instigated for the overthrow of this government has its headquarters in Hollywood." And he added, "The information we get is that this is the greatest hotbed of subversive activities in the United States. We're on the trail of the tarantula now, and we're going to follow through. The best people in California are helping us." [31] On Rankin's motion the committee voted to undertake an investigation of the film industry. A few days later on the floor of the House, Rankin announced, "we are out to expose those elements that are insidiously trying to spread subversive propaganda, poison the minds of your children, distort the history of our country, and discredit Christianity." And he spoke of "the loathsome, filthy, insinuating, un-American undercurrents that are running through various pictures." Later in the year Rankin informed the House that he had received a letter from a Scotland Yard detective calling attention to "the fact" that "during the war . . . there were coded German messages going through the moving pictures that were shown all over England, and some of them were made in Hollywood." [32]

Chairman Wood made it clear upon his appointment that he did not share Rankin's zeal for hunting subversives in Hollywood. He announced, "The Committee is not going to do any witch hunting." And he added, "We are not going to waste time on small birds. We are going to save ourselves for the big game, if there is any around." [33] Toward the close of the year Wood and Ernie Adamson conducted a one-day closed hearing in Los Angeles, and Adamson told the press that they had found evidence of a "definite communistic plan" to gain control of the movie industry. As the Wood committee lapsed into inactivity in 1946 the Hollywood investigation slipped from sight.

The "eight-point program" announced early in 1947 indicated that the Thomas committee planned to renew the Hollywood investigation. In May, a subcommittee consisting of Thomas, McDowell, and Wood, accompanied by two staff members, Robert Stripling and Louis Russell, went to Hollywood and heard a dozen witnesses in closed sessions. These witnesses were all "friendly" and included such prominent Hollywood figures as Robert Taylor, Adolph Menjou, and Jack Warner. This testimony has never been released, but the

[31] N.Y. Herald Tribune, July 1, 1945.
[32] 91 Cong. Rec. 7372, 7386, 10033 (July 9, Oct. 24, 1945).
[33] Washington Post, July 14, 1945.

subcommittee returned to Washington convinced that Hollywood was a hotbed of communism. In June, Thomas read into the *Congressional Record* the report of the subcommittee to the full committee. This report contained a series of sensational findings. "Scores of screen writers who are Communists have infiltrated into the various studios and it has been through this medium that most of the Communist propaganda has been injected into the movies." Communists "have employed subtle techniques in pictures in glorifying the Communist system and degrading our own system of Government and Institutions." Lest this charge might fail to impress movie-goers unaware that they had been witnessing dangerous propaganda, Thomas stated that the subcommittee had been "furnished with a complete list of all the pictures which have been produced in Hollywood in the past eight years which contain Communist propaganda." It was further reported that studio heads "until recently" had taken no steps to discharge Communists. On the other hand, "a number" of loyal actors and directors had refused to participate in the making of pictures containing Communist lines, written by Communists, or in which Communist actors were to play. To make clear the devious lengths to which Communists in Hollywood had gone to effect their evil purposes, it was stated that Communists had prevented "certain good American pictures, which sought to glorify America and the American system, from being produced." In the light of these findings the subcommittee recommended to the full committee that it hold public hearings in Washington at the earliest possible date and that it subpoena "Communist actors, writers, directors, and producers and confront them in public session with the testimony and evidence against them." [34]

Thomas and other committee members made no effort to conceal the initial bias they brought to the Hollywood hearings in Washington or the political motivation that lay back of the undertaking. Again and again, Rankin and Thomas made it clear in their public utterances that they had made up their minds that the corruption of American motion pictures by the insertion of subversive propaganda by Communists occupying strategic posts in the movie industry had been carried to extreme lengths. Such a careful newspaperman as Cabell Phillips of the *New York Times* wrote in the course of the Washington hearings, "The Hollywood investigation now going on is one toward which the committee has been pointing for several months. . . . What is being heard verbatim from the stand here

[34] 93 *Cong. Rec.* A2687 (June 6, 1947).

today is, apparently, a careful synthesis designed for maximum impact on the public consciousness. Its substance is that Communists have elected the film industry as the principal vehicle for poisoning the American mind." [35] During the preliminary hearings in California Thomas announced to the press that Robert Taylor had told the subcommittee that government officials had prevented him from entering the Navy during the war until he made a pro-Russian film, *Song of Russia*. And at the close of the hearings Thomas announced that they had produced "recorded testimony that the White House exerted its influence on certain people to have pro-Russian motion pictures filmed during the regime of the late President Roosevelt." [36] And in the subcommittee report read into the *Congressional Record* he stated flatly that "some of the most flagrant communist propaganda films were produced as a result of White House pressure." [37]

The October hearings in Washington proved to be a two-act performance. Each act had its sensations; each had its own plot development and even its separate cast of characters. The second-act curtain was, however, exceedingly poor theater, and, while the play clearly needed a third act and seemingly one had been written and rehearsed, no such act was performed.

Through press releases and an introductory statement made by Chairman Thomas on the first day of the hearings, the committee indicated that the evidence to be produced at the hearings would prove three things: (1) that Communists had infiltrated the motion picture industry and that important jobs were held by card-carrying party members; in particular, it would be shown that many prominent script writers were Communists, and that the Screen Writers Guild had been dominated by Communists; (2) that Communists had succeeded in introducing actual subversive propaganda into motion pictures; and (3) that the White House had brought improper pressure to bear upon the industry to produce pro-Soviet films.

The committee's plan of procedure was an ingenious one. During the first week it would hear a series of "friendly" witnesses, many of whom had testified earlier at the closed hearings in California. These would include people from all phases of the motion picture

[35] *N.Y. Times*, Oct. 26, 1947.   [36] *Ibid.*, May 15, 1947.
[37] See note 34. In this report Thomas also charged that the National Labor Relations Board had "given great aid to the Communists in their efforts to infiltrate and control the motion-picture industry."

industry—producers, directors, writers, actors, and technicians—who would make clear, by relating their firsthand experiences, the extent of the Communist influence in Hollywood. Thereafter, a series of "unfriendly" witnesses would be placed on the stand and confronted with point-blank questions concerning their alleged participation in subversive activity. The culminating question was to be, "Are you now or have you ever been a member of the Communist Party of the United States?"

The parade of "friendly" witnesses was one that was bound to catch the public attention. It included such top-ranking producers as Jack L. Warner, Louis B. Mayer, and Walt Disney; such directors as Sam Wood and Leo McCarey; such writers as Rupert Hughes and Morrie Ryskind; and, above all, such famed actors as Robert Taylor, Gary Cooper, and Adolph Menjou. Included also were two women whose past activities in warring against the Soviet Union and communism placed them virtually in the class of professionals: Ayn Rand, the novelist, and Lela E. Rogers, mother of the actress, Ginger Rogers. The testimony of these witnesses during the first week was exceedingly varied and ranged all the way from intelligent, penetrating analysis of the Communist influence in Hollywood, to the strange, the bitter, and the stupid.[38]

[38] It is not entirely fair to single out passages from the testimony of various witnesses, for a completely accurate impression of the hearings can be obtained only by reading everything that was said. Nonetheless, the caliber of the testimony of a witness can at least be suggested by excerpts. For example, when Stripling asked Lela Rogers upon what she based her statement that Clifford Odets was a Communist, she replied: "I have here a column of Mr. O. O. McIntyre, datelined January 8, 1936, in which Mr. McIntyre says Mr. Clifford Odets, play writer, is a member of the Communist Party. I never saw that denied." *Mot. Pict. Ind. Hearings,* p. 231.

It is true that when prodded by Stripling Mrs. Rogers supplemented this reference to the ten-year-old writings of a newspaper columnist with information derived from the findings of the Tenney Subversive Activities Committee of the California legislature.

The ease with which Mrs. Rogers found subversive propaganda in a literary classic is indicated by the following:

"*Mr. Stripling:* Mrs. Rogers, . . . as your daughter's manager, so to speak, have you and your daughter ever objected to or turned down scripts because you felt that there were lines in there for her to speak which you felt were un-American or Communist propaganda?

"*Mrs. Rogers:* Many times.

"*Mr. Stripling:* You have turned down many scripts for these reasons?

"*Mrs. Rogers:* Yes, sir. We turned down Sister Carrie, by Theodore Dreiser, because it was just as open propaganda as None But The Lonely Heart." *Ibid.,* p. 233.

From the beginning it was evident that the investigation would show that Communists or fellow travelers held jobs in the motion picture industry. But whether the committee could prove its oft-repeated assertion that these Communists had introduced actual Communist propaganda into films was much more uncertain. Much of the questioning of the witnesses during the first week was directed toward this end, and an analysis of the testimony on this point will give a reasonably accurate impression of the general character of the Hollywood investigation. While the Un-American Activities Committee repeatedly insisted that it had a list of films which contained Communist propaganda—and the inference was that the list was a long one—no such list was made public at the time of the hearings or at any other time.[39] Nonetheless, as the first week of hearings proceeded, four pictures were mentioned by name, and a good deal of time was spent trying to show that these films did

---

Adolph Menjou indicated his distaste for Communists by saying, "I would move to the State of Texas if [communism] ever came here because I think the Texans would kill them on sight." *Ibid.*, p. 107.

When asked for his opinion concerning proposals that the Communist Party be banned by law, Robert Taylor replied, "If I had my way about it [communists] would all be sent back to Russia or some other unpleasant place [loud applause] and never allowed back in this country." *Ibid.*, p. 170.

On the other hand, the actor, Ronald Reagan, answered much the same question in these words, "Fundamentally I would say in opposing those people that the best thing to do is to make democracy work. In the Screen Actors Guild we made it work by insuring everyone a vote and by keeping everyone informed. I believe that, as Thomas Jefferson put it, if all the American people know all of the facts they will never make a mistake.

"Whether the party should be outlawed I agree . . . is a matter for the Government to decide. As a citizen I would hesitate, or not like, to see any political party outlawed on the basis of its political ideology. We have spent 170 years in this country on the basis that democracy is strong enough to stand up and fight against the inroads of any ideology. However, if it is proven that an organization is an agent of a power, a foreign power, or in any way not a legitimate political party, and I think the Government is capable of proving that, if the proof is there, then that is another matter." *Ibid.*, p. 217.

[39] That the committee toyed, momentarily at least, with attempting to prove an alternative theory concerning the evil done by Communists in the motion picture industry is suggested by the following statement made by H. A. Smith, a special investigator with the committee, during the questioning of James K. McGuinness: "Mr. McGuinness, my investigation reflects that it isn't necessary for these Communist writers to actually put any material into pictures, but that it is possible for them to receive large salaries each week and from that salary donate to the Communist Party and actually further and operate their activities throughout the United States. . . ." *Ibid.*, p. 147.

contain pro-Communist or pro-Soviet scenes which had been consciously and deliberately inserted by Communists or their sympathizers. These films were *Mission to Moscow*, a 1943 Warner Brothers film based upon the autobiographical book of the same name by Joseph E. Davies, American ambassador to the Soviet Union from 1936 to 1938; *Song of Russia*, a 1943 Metro-Goldwyn-Mayer film, starring Robert Taylor and featuring the music of Tschaikowsky, which told the story of an American orchestra leader who visited the Soviet Union and fell in love with a Russian pianist; *North Star*, a 1943 Sam Goldwyn production, based upon an original story by the playwright, Lillian Hellman, which told of the impact of the German invasion of Russia in 1941 upon a small village in the Ukraine; and *None but the Lonely Heart*, a 1944 RKO production, based upon a novel by Richard Llewellyn, directed by Clifford Odets, and starring Cary Grant and Ethel Barrymore, which was concerned with life among the poor in London.

The producer Jack L. Warner bore the brunt of the committee's attack upon *Mission to Moscow*. Warner readily qualified as a "friendly" witness and proved his co-operative spirit in his opening statement. He said, "Ideological termites have burrowed into many American industries, organizations, and societies. Wherever they may be, I say let us dig them out and get rid of them. My brothers and I will be happy to subscribe generously to a pest-removal fund. We are willing to establish such a fund to ship to Russia the people who don't like our American system of government and prefer the communistic system to ours." [40] But he made it clear at once that his company was not prepared to admit that it had erred in filming the Davies book. "If making *Mission to Moscow* in 1942 was a subversive activity, then the American Liberty ships which carried food and guns to Russian allies and the American naval vessels which convoyed them were likewise engaged in subversive activities. The picture was made only to help a desperate war effort and not for posterity." [41] But he was not to be let off so easily. Robert Stripling, the committee's chief investigator, questioned him as follows:

[40] *Ibid.*, p. 10.

[41] *Ibid.* The *Time* review of *Mission to Moscow* said in part: "The movie is a blunt, high-spot review of world power politics between 1936 and Pearl Harbor. For the most part a faithful translation of Joe Davies' book, the picture departs from its text only to leave out Ambassador Davies' occasional reservations about the Soviet Union. Without doubts or reservations of any kind, the film devotes itself unabashedly to endearing the Russians to U.S. audiences." May 10, 1943, p. 23.

Mr. Stripling: Well, is it your opinion now, Mr. Warner, that *Mission to Moscow* was a factually correct picture, and you made it as such?

Mr. Warner: I can't remember.

Mr. Stripling: Would you consider it a propaganda picture?

Mr. Warner: A propaganda picture—

Mr. Stripling: Yes.

Mr. Warner: In what sense?

Mr. Stripling: In the sense that it portrayed Russia and communism in an entirely different light from what it actually was.

Mr. Warner: I am on record about 40 times or more that I have never been in Russia. I don't know what Russia was like in 1937 or 1944 or 1947, so how can I tell you if it was right or wrong?

Mr. Stripling: Don't you think you are on dangerous ground to produce as a factually correct picture one which portrayed Russia—

Mr. Warner: No; we were not on dangerous ground in 1942, when we produced it. There was a war on. The world was at stake.

Mr. Stripling: In other words—

Mr. Warner: We made the film to aid in the war effort, which I believe I have already stated.

Mr. Stripling: Whether it was true or not?

Mr. Warner: As far as I am concerned, I considered it true to the extent as written in Mr. Davies' book.

Mr. Stripling: Well, do you suppose that your picture influenced the people who saw it in this country, the millions of people who saw it in this country?

Mr. Warner: In my opinion, I can't see how it would influence anyone. We were in the war and when you are in a fight you don't ask who the fellow is who is helping you.

Mr. Stripling: Well, due to the present conditions in the international situation, don't you think it was rather dangerous to write about such a disillusionment as was sought in that picture?

Mr. Warner: I can't understand why you ask me that question, as to the present conditions. How did I, you, or anyone else know in 1942 what the conditions were going to be in 1947? I stated in my testimony our reason for making the picture, which was to aid the war effort—anticipating what would happen.

Mr. Stripling: I don't see that that is aiding the war effort, Mr. Warner —with the cooperation of Mr. Davies or with the approval of the Government—to make a picture which is a fraud in fact.[42]

In the end the evidence obtained by the committee revealed no more than was already known: that the Davies book—and the film which was a reasonably accurate reproduction of the book—was a controversial one which had always had its critics who complained

[42] *Mot. Pict. Ind. Hearings,* pp. 38–39.

that Ambassador Davies had seen the Soviet Union through rose-colored glasses. But no one had ever questioned Davies' loyalty to democracy and capitalism or his distaste for communism. Nor was it ever shown that the making of a film based upon a highly successful book, at a time when there was a tremendous interest in Russia, was anything other than a normal Hollywood effort to turn a successful penny or—to give Warner credit for honesty in his statement of motives—to aid the war effort.

Louis B. Mayer, head of the powerful MGM studio, bore the brunt of the attack upon *Song of Russia*. To support its claim that the film contained Communist propaganda the committee also queried Ayn Rand, who had been asked to make a detailed analysis of the picture.

In his preliminary statement Mayer defended his film as follows:

> Mention has been made of the picture, Song of Russia, as being friendly to Russia at the time it was made. Of course it was. It was made to be friendly. . . . It was in April of 1942 that the story for Song of Russia came to our attention. It seemed a good medium of entertainment and at the same time offered an opportunity for a pat on the back for our then ally, Russia. It also offered an opportunity to use the music of Tschaikowsky. We mentioned this to the Government coordinators and they agreed with us that it would be a good idea to make the picture. . . . The final script of Song of Russia was little more than a pleasant musical romance— the story of a boy and girl that, except for the music of Tschaikowsky, might just as well have taken place in Switzerland or England or any other country on the earth.[43]

Questioning of Mayer by a committee investigator, H. A. Smith, on the subject of *Song of Russia* ran in part as follows:

Mr. Smith: Do you recall scenes in there at the night club where everybody was drinking?

Mr. Mayer: They do in Moscow.

Mr. Smith: Do you feel that that represents Russia as it is today?

Mr. Mayer: I didn't make it as it is today, I made it when they were our ally in 1943.

Mr. Smith: Do you feel it represents Russia in 1943 as conditions were in Russia?

Mr. Mayer: That is what I understood, that they go to night clubs there in Moscow. If only the rest of the Russians had a chance to do the same thing, it would be fine, but they don't. The picture was laid in Moscow.[44]

[43] *Ibid.*, p. 71. The *Time* review of *Song of Russia* said in part: "Many U.S. soldiers find this naive propaganda one long howl of laughter. Many civilians may find bits of it acceptable. . . . The music . . . is a boundary-melting pleasure to hear." Feb. 7, 1944, p. 56.

[44] *Mot. Pict. Ind. Hearings*, p. 76.

The testimony of Ayn Rand has to be read in its entirety for a proper appreciation of its bizarre quality. Identified by Stripling as "a qualified reviewer," Miss Rand was called to the stand for the clear purpose of refuting Mayer's contention that *Song of Russia* was just a boy-meets-girl musical film with no serious political implications. The witness prefaced her statement with these words, "Nobody has stated just what they mean by propaganda. Now, I use the term to mean that Communist propaganda is anything which gives a good impression of communism as a way of life. Anything that sells people the idea that life in Russia is good and that people are free and happy would be Communist propaganda. Am I not correct? I mean, would that be a fair statement to make—that that would be Communist propaganda?" [45]

Miss Rand then proceeded to give a 4,000-word detailed scene-by-scene analysis of *Song of Russia* that could only have been the product of a mind obsessed with a fear and hatred of all things radical. Even such conservative members of the committee as John Wood and John McDowell were obviously a bit skeptical about her vehement attack upon the film. Wood queried her, "Do you think, then, that it was to our advantage or to our disadvantage to keep Russia in this war, at the time this picture was made?" Miss Rand replied imperiously, "That has absolutely nothing to do with what we are discussing."

McDowell's exchange with the witness ran as follows:

Mr. McDowell: You paint a very dismal picture of Russia. You made a great point about the number of children who were unhappy. Doesn't anybody smile in Russia any more?

Miss Rand: Well, if you ask me literally, pretty much no.

Mr. McDowell: They don't smile?

Miss Rand: Not quite that way; no. If they do, it is privately and accidentally. Certainly, it is not social. They don't smile in approval of their system.

Mr. McDowell: Well, all they do is talk about food?

Miss Rand: That is right.

Mr. McDowell: That is a great change from the Russians I have always known, and I have know [sic] a lot of them. Don't they do things at all like Americans? Don't they walk across town to visit their mother-in-law or somebody? [46]

[45] *Ibid.*, p. 83.

[46] *Ibid.*, p. 90. It may be noted that Miss Rand had not been in Russia since 1926.

The attack upon *North Star* was more tangential since none of the witnesses before the committee had had any connection with the making of the film. It was, however, referred to in the testimony of James K. McGuinness, an MGM script supervisor, who made the following statement concerning the allegedly Communist content of certain movies:

> During the period of the war, when I would prefer to call them pro-Soviets more so than pro-Communist, there were three pictures made which have been discussed before this Committee: Mission to Moscow which, in my opinion, distorted history; North Star, and Song of Russia, which represented Russia as a never-never land, flowing with milk and honey. I never regarded them too seriously since they were made during the war. In fact, I looked on them as a form of intellectual lend-lease. . . .[47]

[47] *Ibid.*, p. 138. The *Time* review of *North Star* said in part: "It is the first major attempt by a major U.S. producer (Sam Goldwyn) to present Russia's war with the Nazis in the way that Winston Churchill saw it when the war began—not primarily as a struggle for Communism, but as a heroic defense by the Russian people of their homes. Only by implication is *North Star* revolutionary propaganda." Nov. 8, 1943, p. 54.

It was McGuinness who supplied some slight documentation of the assertion in the subcommittee report on the California hearings that Communists had tried to sabotage "certain good American pictures, which sought to glorify America and the American system. . . ." The film which he claimed had met with Communist opposition was *Tennessee Johnson,* which was based upon the life of Andrew Johnson. According to McGuinness the picture displeased Communists because it depicted Thaddeus Stevens as a villain, whereas Communists were using Stevens as something of a folk hero in appealing to Negroes. An amusing exchange between McGuinness and McDowell illustrates the ridiculous confusion which sometimes results when the attempt is made to read a Communist-line pattern into controversies which separate people who have nothing to do with communism:

"Mr. McDowell: Just to keep the record straight, Thaddeus Stephens [*sic*] was a great American patriot and citizen. Pennsylvania is very proud of Thaddeus Stephens and the role he played in American history.

"The Chairman: What were you going to say, Mr. McGuinness?

"Mr. McGuinness: I don't want to get into a political debate." *Mot. Pict. Ind. Hearings,* p. 139.

Dorothy Thompson in her column (Dec. 3, 1947) supplied a comment on the efforts to prove that *North Star* contained deliberate Communist propaganda that might also have been applied to *Song of Russia.* She wrote, that *North Star* "was bad, not because it glorified the Russian war effort but because it was false and silly. So are hundreds of other Hollywood pictures." No one seems to have pointed out at the time Ayn Rand saw signs of Communist taint in *Song of Russia* in the fact that its hero and heroine posed against backgrounds that were much too opulent and attractive for Russia that exactly the same fault is to be found in almost every film depicting middle-class life in America.

The committee's efforts to prove that American films do in fact contain Communist propaganda approached the ridiculous in the case of the picture, *None but the Lonely Heart*. Lela E. Rogers, one of the committee's "friendly" witnesses, was called upon to develop the case against this film. While the witness made it clear by her testimony that she was a dedicated and implacable opponent of communism she seemed to lose heart as she developed her argument against the picture:

I can't quote the lines of the play exactly but I can give you the sense of them. There is one place in which—it is unfair, may I say, to take a scene from its context and try to make it sound like Communist propaganda, because a Communist is very careful, very clever, and very devious in the way he sets the film. If I were to give you a line from that play straight out you would say "What is wrong with that line?" unless you knew that the Communist is trying in every way to tear down our free-enterprise system, to make the people lose faith in it, so that they will want to get something else—and the Communists have it waiting for them.

I will tell you of one line. The mother in the story runs a second-hand store. The son says to her, "You are not going to"—in essence, I am not quoting this exactly because I can't remember it exactly—he said to her, "You are not going to get me to work here and squeeze pennies out of little people poorer than I am."

Now, laid upon the background of—that is the free-enterprise system —trade, and we don't necessarily squeeze pennies from people poorer than we are. Many people are poorer and many people are richer.

As I say, you find yourself in an awful hole the moment you start to remove one of the scenes from its context.[48]

Efforts such as these to demonstrate the presence of Communist propaganda in motion pictures can only be characterized as stupid and vulgar.[49] If the Un-American Activities Committee had in its

[48] *Mot. Pict. Ind. Hearings*, p. 234. The *Time* review of *None but the Lonely Heart* said in part: "It is one of the pictures of the year, a feather in the cap of all concerned in its making. In the U.S., major productions have rarely dared to tackle so wholeheartedly so harshly human a subject. . . . On the whole, Writer-Director Odets has kept his sociology . . . subdued. . . ." Nov. 20, 1944, p. 92.

[49] Other efforts to obtain from witnesses information pertaining to Communist content in motion pictures may be noted:

(1) John C. Moffitt, motion picture critic of the magazine, *Esquire*, balked when asked to name pictures in which the Communist influence was apparent, although he offered to supply the committee with a list in executive session. He testified as follows:

"*Mr. Stripling*: Would you give the committee those instances?

"*Mr. Moffitt*: Yes, sir, I could, but I beg you not to ask me to. I think that the

files any solid evidence which would support the charge which its members and staff repeatedly made, such evidence was never made public.[50]

At the same time that it tried to indict the motion picture industry for permitting Communist propaganda to creep into films, the committee and its investigators badgered a number of witnesses about Hollywood's failure to make pictures containing anti-Communist propaganda.[51] The film director, Leo McCarey, indicated his opposition to pictures of the latter type: "Pictures should be entertainment. I think that because of the number of people in all lands who see our pictures. I believe it only tends toward causing more enmity if we are partisan and take any sides in our pictures." Chairman

---

most infamous aspect of [John Howard] Lawson's technique is that of involving innocent people. I think that many a time an actor plays that 5 minutes without knowing the significance of what he is doing. [Moffitt is referring to his own allegation that he once heard Lawson say that it was the duty of every Communist writer in Hollywood to work 5 minutes of subtle Communist propaganda into each script.] I think on many occasions—I think on practically every occasion that I know of the producer, both the associate producer and the studio heads, was in complete ignorance of what was done. I think very often the director may not know.

"Now this is done occasionally in pictures involving budgets of one and a half or two million dollars. That gets into the picture, and if I name that picture I will be working a hardship on innocent people. I would very much prefer, with your permission, to name those pictures in executive session." *Mot. Pict. Ind. Hearings,* p. 121.

However, Moffitt made it clear that he thought the Communist line could be seen in films depicting bankers who opposed GI loans to war veterans (the reference was quite obviously to the film, *The Best Years of Our Lives*), or pictures which criticized Congress.

(2) Leo McCarey, a prominent director, testified that Communists had succeeded in injecting propaganda into specific films, but Stripling, who was questioning him, did not ask him to name the pictures he had in mind. *Ibid.,* p. 227.

(3) Adolph Menjou, actor, when asked by Stripling whether he had "observed any Communist propaganda in pictures," replied: "I have seen no Communist propaganda in pictures—if you mean 'vote for Stalin,' or that type of communistic propaganda. . . . I have seen in certain pictures things I didn't think should have been in them." *Ibid.,* p. 92.

[50] While no list of propaganda films was ever released, the committee was reluctant to let go of the idea that it had such a list or could obtain one. Two weeks after the Hollywood hearings were adjourned, the *N.Y. Times* (Nov. 14, 1947), stated, "Chairman Thomas told reporters . . . that the committee was hiring 'expert analysts' to study films and scripts to find Communist propaganda, if any."

[51] See *Mot. Pict. Ind. Hearings,* pp. 144, 170.

Thomas saw the point and asked, "We would be doing the same thing Soviet Russia is doing?" [52]

The attempt to show that "the White House" had improperly tried to persuade Hollywood to make pro-Soviet films was no better supported in the testimony of witnesses than was the charge concerning the Communist content of films. Two efforts were made to support the contention. One concerned the film, *Mission to Moscow*, and the claim was that the firm of Warner Brothers was persuaded to make the picture as the result of "White House" or "government" pressure. In the preliminary hearings in California Stripling and Thomas did their best to get Jack Warner to admit this was so.[53] The most that Warner had admitted in California was that Joseph Davies had approached Warner Brothers with a proposal that it make a film based on his book. But in his Washington appearance Warner stated that even this was incorrect and that he now wished to state that the first approach had been made by the company to Davies.[54] Later in the testimony, when Stripling casually implied that the government had had a part in the making of the picture, Warner objected immediately:

Mr. Warner: I want to correct you, very vehemently. There was no cooperation of the Government.

Mr. Stripling: You stated there was.

Mr. Warner: I never stated the Government cooperated in the making of it. If I did, I stand corrected. And I know I didn't.

Mr. Stripling [presumably referring to the California testimony]: Do you want me to read that part, Mr. Chairman?

The Chairman: No; I think we have gone into this Mission to Moscow at some length.[55]

The second effort to catch the Roosevelt administration playing the Soviet Union's game in Hollywood was the contention that Robert Taylor had been forced to delay his desired enlistment in the Navy to play what was for him a distasteful role in the pro-Soviet film, *Song of Russia*. Here, too, there is evidence that Taylor went along with the allegation in his appearance before the subcommittee

[52] *Ibid.*, p. 227.

[53] In his Washington appearance in October, Warner was a somewhat unpredictable witness. When he failed to answer certain questions to Stripling's satisfaction, the latter proceeded to read into the record testimony taken by the subcommittee in California at which time Warner had been a more articulate witness.

[54] *Mot. Pict. Ind. Hearings*, pp. 33–35.   [55] *Ibid.*, p. 39.

in California, only to back down somewhat in his Washington testimony. In effect, the committee through its investigator, Robert Stripling, tried to show that Lowell Mellett, chief of the Bureau of Motion Pictures of the Office of War Information, compelled Taylor to delay his Navy duty so that he might star in a pro-Soviet film. In his Washington appearance Taylor reiterated his belief that *Song of Russia* "did contain Communist propaganda," but he repudiated the notion that there had been any compulsion to get him to act in the film: "If I ever gave the impression in anything that appeared previously that I was forced into making Song of Russia, I would like to say in my own defense, lest I look a little silly by saying I was ever forced to do the picture, I was not forced because nobody can force you to make any picture." [56]

The second week of the Hollywood hearings in Washington was largely devoted to the task of documenting the committee's assertion that Communists and fellow travelers had succeeded in infiltrating the motion picture industry as actors, writers, and directors. The committee's technique was to subpoena persons suspected of being Communists and confront them on the witness stand with the point-blank question: Are you now or have you ever been a member of the Communist Party of the United States? It is clear that the committee felt that it had convincing proof of the Communist Party membership or sympathies of a large number of persons. At one point Thomas publicly announced that the committee had in its files evidence showing the party membership or affiliation of seventy-nine "prominent people." [57] The publicity which preceded the Washington hearings indicated that nineteen such persons had been subpoenaed and would be placed on the witness stand. In the end eleven were actually called to testify. One of these witnesses, Berthold Brecht, a German playwright and poet, who had sold stories to Hollywood, flatly denied that he was a Communist. The other ten

[56] *Ibid.*, p. 167; see also pp. 80–81. At the time of the preliminary hearings in California, Thomas announced in one of his characteristic statements to the press that Taylor had told the subcommittee at a closed hearing that he had been prevented from entering the Navy by "government officials" until he made a pro-Russian film, *Song of Russia* (*N.Y. Times*, May 15, 1947). Lowell Mellett requested the committee to let him appear as a witness and to testify concerning the allegation that he had anything to do with compelling Taylor to act in the film. When the committee suddenly adjourned the Hollywood hearings without having met his request, Mellett stated publicly, "The committee deliberately avoided letting me give them the truth." *Washington Post*, Oct. 31, 1947.

[57] *Mot. Pict. Ind. Hearings*, p. 522.

persons, known as the "unfriendly witnesses," were truculent and unco-operative and refused to answer the question concerning membership in the Communist Party.[58]

The first of the unfriendly witnesses was John Howard Lawson, a well-known screen writer. His experience as a witness may be examined in some detail, for, with minor variations, the pattern in his case was repeated in the case of each of the other nine witnesses.

Upon being sworn in, Lawson produced a written statement and asked permission to read it. Chairman Thomas glanced momentarily at this statement and immediately announced that the first line convinced him that the statement was improper and should not be read. It was apparent from the start that the witness was prepared to match the chairman's truculence. When asked whether he had been a member and officer of the Screen Writers' Guild, Lawson replied that, while it was a matter of public record that he had been both a member and an officer, he would refuse to give a direct answer to the question on the ground that the question was beyond the authority of the committee to ask and an invasion of his personal right of association. The showdown between the committee and Lawson came when the witness was queried concerning membership in the Communist Party. The questions and answers ran as follows:

Mr. Stripling: Mr. Lawson, are you now, or have you ever been a member of the Communist Party of the United States?

Mr. Lawson: In framing my answer to that question I must emphasize the points that I have raised before. The question of communism is in no way related to this inquiry, which is an attempt to get control of the screen and to invade the basic rights of American citizens in all fields.

Mr. McDowell: Now, I must object—

Mr. Stripling: Mr. Chairman—

[The chairman (Thomas) pounding gavel.]

Mr. Lawson: The question here relates not only to the question of my membership in any political organization, but this committee is attempting to establish the right—

[The chairman pounding gavel.]

Mr. Lawson [continuing]: Which has been historically denied to any committee of this sort, to invade the rights and privileges and immunity

[58] It may be argued from a close reading of the testimony that most if not all of the unfriendly witnesses never actually *refused* to answer the question, but only *failed* to answer it. This is a technicality at best, and there is no doubt that these witnesses had determined not to answer the question. Moreover, in the subsequent trial of Lawson and Trumbo for contempt, the verdict of guilty implied a finding of fact by the jury that they had refused to answer the question.

of American citizens, whether they be Protestants, Methodist, Jewish or Catholic, whether they be Republicans or Democrats or anything else.

The Chairman [pounding gavel]: Mr. Lawson, just quiet down again. Mr. Lawson, the most pertinent question that we can ask is whether or not you have ever been a member of the Communist Party. Now, do you care to answer that question?

Mr. Lawson: You are using the old technique, which was used in Hitler Germany in order to create a scare here—

The Chairman [pounding gavel]: Oh—

Mr. Lawson: In order to create an entirely false atmosphere in which this hearing is conducted—

[The chairman pounding gavel.]

Mr. Lawson: In order that you can then smear the motion-picture industry, and you can proceed to the press, to any form of communication in this country.

The Chairman: You have learned—

Mr. Lawson: The Bill of Rights was established precisely to prevent the operation of any committee which could invade the basic rights of Americans.

Now if you want to know—

Mr. Stripling: Mr. Chairman, the witness is not answering the question.

Mr. Lawson: If you want to know—

[The chairman pounding gavel.]

Mr. Lawson: About the perjury that has been committed here and the perjury that is planned.

The Chairman: Mr. Lawson—

Mr. Lawson: You permit me and my attorneys to bring in here the witnesses that testified last week and you permit us to cross-examine these witnesses, and we will show up the whole tissue of lie—

The Chairman [pounding gavel]: We are going to get the answer to that question if we have to stay here for a week.

Are you a member of the Communist Party, or have you ever been a member of the Communist Party?

Mr. Lawson: It is unfortunate and tragic that I have to teach this committee the basic principles of American—

The Chairman [pounding gavel]: That is not the question. That is not the question. The question is: Have you ever been a member of the Communist Party?

Mr. Lawson: I am framing my answer in the only way in which any American citizen can frame his answer to a question which absolutely invades his rights.

The Chairman: Then you refuse to answer that question; is that correct?

Mr. Lawson: I have told you that I will offer my beliefs, affiliations, and everything else to the American public, and they will know where I stand.

The Chairman [pounding gavel]: Excuse the witness—

Mr. Lawson: As they do from what I have written.

The Chairman [pounding gavel]: Stand away from the stand—

Mr. Lawson: I have written Americanism for many years, and I shall continue to fight for the Bill of Rights, which you are trying to destroy.

The Chairman: Officers, take this man away from the stand—

[Applause and boos.] [59]

With Lawson's removal from the stand the committee made immediate use of a technique which had clearly been planned for just such an eventuality as had developed, and which was used following the refusal of each of the remaining nine unfriendly witnesses to testify. It called to the witness stand one of its investigators, Louis Russell, and had him read into the record the detailed dossier which the committee had assembled on Lawson. The most sensational revelation made by Russell was that during his investigation of Lawson there had come into his possession a Communist Party "registration card" for the year 1944 made out in the name of John Howard Lawson and bearing the number "47275." The remaining information about Lawson occupies more than seven pages of fine print in the published record of the hearing.[60] The material is divided into thirty-five numbered paragraphs which purport to show Lawson's affiliations with Communist front organizations and his varied activities in the Communist movement. It ranges all the way from such clear-cut statements of fact as that Lawson was once a "correspondent" of the *Daily Worker* and a regular contributor to the *New Masses,* and in one way or another affiliated with such Communist front organizations as the International Labor Defense, the American League Against War and Fascism, the American Peace Mobilization, and American Youth for Democracy, to such inadequately developed assertions as that Lawson "has shown an active interest in the Soviet Union," that he has "hailed" "the rise of the revolutionary theatre," and that he "advanced" the Communist Party line in the screen play which he wrote for the movie, *Blockade.* But in spite of the idiosyncrasies common to all Un-American Activities Committee dossiers which find their way into the public record, it must be admitted that a careful reading of these pages forces one to the conclusion that the committee does prove its allegation that Lawson was an enthusiastic, persistent worker in causes and organizations following the Communist line, even if the authenticity of the Communist Party registration card be doubted.

The unfriendly witnesses who followed Lawson to the stand were

[59] *Mot. Pict. Ind. Hearings,* pp. 293–295.   [60] *Ibid.,* pp. 296–304.

Dalton Trumbo, Albert Maltz, Alvah Bessie, Samuel Ornitz, Herbert Biberman, Edward Dmytryk, Adrian Scott, Ring Lardner, Jr., and Lester Cole. All of these men were screen writers, with the exception of Dmytryk, who was a director, and Scott, who was a producer. In every instance the witness failed to answer the question concerning Communist Party membership, and in every instance Louis Russell stated that he had in his possession a card indicating such membership.[61] Following each appearance of Russell, Chairman Thomas announced that the subcommittee conducting the hearings was unanimously recommending to the full committee that the witness be cited for contempt.

The sudden ending of the Hollywood hearings on Thursday of the second week has never been satisfactorily explained. As has been indicated, other witnesses had been subpoenaed and there were several additional persons identified with the motion picture industry who were presumably prepared to refuse to testify and thereby to place themselves in the unfriendly witness category. The committee had, however, advertised for several days the news that it had "mystery" witnesses who would take the stand and give "sensational"

[61] The authenticity of these cards seems never to have been *directly* challenged by any of the witnesses. In an interview with Bert Andrews (*N.Y. Herald Tribune*, Jan. 7, 1948), Ring Lardner, Jr., did challenge the cards obliquely. He speaks of the committee's "shy reluctance to let any witness, lawyer or newspaper man get a glimpse of its 'evidence' "; he says he is "wounded" by the suggestion that he would conceal his identity by using the pseudonym, "Ring L.," which appeared on his alleged registration card, and he points out that the cards read into the record were allegedly issued late in 1944 and used the terminology, "Communist Party" in spite of the fact that at this time the "Party" had been dissolved and replaced by the "Communist Political Association." Lardner observes, "Whether that change of name represented a technicality or an actuality is beside the point. Obviously the Communists themselves must have taken it seriously enough to alter their official documents."

In a tract by Dalton Trumbo entitled *The Time of the Toad: A Study of Inquisition in America,* reference is also made to the fact that the cards were registration cards and not membership cards. As such Trumbo argues they were "the alleged office record of an alleged card" (p. 19).

It may be noted that in two instances Russell's testimony concerning the cards in his possession varied from the pattern as indicated. In the case of Edward Dymtryk, Russell states that he was issued "Communist Party book No. 84961, for the year 1944," and he adds, "when the party was reportedly dissolved in the summer of 1944 and the Communist Political Association organized in its stead, he was issued 1944 Communist Political Association membership card No. 46859, and for 1945 the Communist Political Association card No. 47238" (*Mot. Pict. Ind. Hearings*, p. 462). In the case of Adrian Scott, Russell also identifies the cards issued to him as "Communist Political Association" cards. *Ibid.*, p. 468.

testimony.[62] On Thursday afternoon such a witness was produced, but he turned out to be only Louis Russell, the committee's well-known investigator. Russell's testimony broke completely with the subject of communism in the motion picture industry and dealt instead with alleged wartime atomic espionage in the Radiation Laboratory of the University of California at Berkeley. This was a subject that was to interest the committee periodically through the following years, but it had so little to do with what had been concerning the committee during the preceding days that the abrupt transition was confusing to press and public alike. The confusion was only heightened when Chairman Thomas, upon completion of Russell's testimony, suddenly adjourned the hearings with the statement: "While we have heard 39 witnesses, there are many more to be heard. The Chair stated earlier in the hearing he would present the records of 79 prominent people associated with the motion-picture industry who were members of the Communist Party or who had records of Communist affiliations. We have had before us 11 of these individuals. There are 68 to go. . . . I want to emphasize that the committee is not adjourning sine die, but will resume hearings as soon as possible. . . ." [63]

Members of the committee's staff have told the writer that the hearings were adjourned because the committee had evidence that Communist sympathizers were planning a demonstration in Washington against the investigation. Having proved to its satisfaction that prominent writers, directors, and producers in Hollywood were Communists, the committee decided to frustrate this move by bringing the hearings to a close for the moment.[64] An alternative explana-

[62] For example, the *Washington Post* (Oct. 23, 1947), in reporting on the third day of hearings stated that Thomas "announced after a closed session yesterday that the committee will present two mystery witnesses Monday whose testimony will link the Communist Party with espionage. Thomas said the evidence would be 'sensational.' . . ."

[63] *Mot. Pict. Ind. Hearings*, p. 522. "As soon as possible" turned out to be March, 1951, when the Hollywood hearings were resumed in the 82d Congress. One of the "ten," Edward Dmytryk, reappeared before the committee during these new hearings and freely testified that he had been a member of the Communist Party from the spring of 1944 to the fall of 1945. *Communist Infiltration of Hollywood Motion Picture Industry—Part 2* (82d Cong., 1st Sess.; April 17, 23–25; May 16–18, 1951), pp. 408–440.

[64] In a radio broadcast in the middle of November, Thomas once more asserted that the hearings so far were "only a beginning" and that they would be resumed "in a few weeks." He added, "We are exposing communism in Hollywood. We will continue to expose communism in Hollywood. . . . They would like to

tion is that the subcommittee members had wearied of the undertaking and were disappointed by newspaper reaction to the hearings. In spite of the fact that no Congressional hearing of modern times had received broader coverage in the press, the proceedings as reported in the news columns took on more than a faintly ridiculous character, and editorial comment, particularly in respected journals, was distinctly unfavorable. For example, in the middle of the first week of hearings the *New York Herald Tribune* commented, "Some attempt was made to show that Communism was being permitted to creep into films, but in each case the attempt dissolved into the ludicrous. . . . Not Hollywood but Congress is being investigated here. . . ." [65] And following the sudden shift of attention on the last day of hearings to atomic espionage the same paper observed, "This may be taken—perhaps ungraciously—as Mr. Thomas's confession that the Hollywood investigation has been producing a good deal of nonsense and very little else." [66]

Certainly the committee had failed to demonstrate that Hollywood was a hotbed of Communist activity. The only one of its oftrepeated assertions concerning communism in the motion picture industry that it was able to prove was that Communists or nearCommunists held important jobs in the industry, particularly as writers. It may be argued that this was a proper fact for a Congressional committee to publicize and that this alone justified the undertaking. In the light of the factual information available in 1947 concerning the nature of the Communist International movement, certainly the presence of Communists in a business having such important propaganda potentialities as the motion picture industry was something that the American people were entitled to know about.

In any case, the committee may fairly be criticized for inadequate questioning of the unfriendly witnesses in the Hollywood hearings. Presented with an opportunity to subject a group of witnesses, whose records made it clear that they were either Communist Party members or, at the very least, fellow travelers, to searching questioning concerning their interests and activities, the committee allowed the hearings to bog down over the issue of the witnesses' refusal to answer the single question concerning actual membership in the party. The committee apparently felt that in asking this question and

think that this is the end of this hearing and this investigation. Their activities are going to be exposed and they are going to be exposed for what they are. . . ." 93 *Cong. Rec.* A4277 (Nov. 20, 1947).
    [65] Oct. 22, 1947.   [66] Nov. 1, 1947.

in publicizing the refusal of the witnesses to answer it, it was acquainting the American people with the most important fact about alleged subversive activity in Hollywood. The committee seemed perfectly prepared to quarrel with its witnesses over this one issue and to match their bravura and self-righteousness with its own pompous indignation. Indeed, when the witness Ornitz was testifying, Thomas got so angry that he ordered him to leave the stand before Stripling had a chance to ask him the all-important question. Stripling, however, persisted, managed to ask the question, and got the expected refusal to answer into the record.[67]

By insisting that their refusal to answer was a matter of principle and that it was designed to· protect the right of association and privacy of political affiliation, the witnesses were able to confuse the issue, and, indeed, to pose as heroes before a part of the public. Little or no public attention was paid to the detailed information concerning each witness which was read into the record by Louis Russell. While much of this information was merely curious or even meaningless, a good deal of it, if true, was highly revealing concerning the strategy and tactics of the Communist movement in the United States. Persistent, intelligent questioning of the witnesses concerning their past activities, many of which were matters of public record, would have thrown a great deal of light on what it means to be a Communist. The witnesses might have refused to answer these questions too, but in so doing they would have condemned themselves far more than they did in refusing to answer the question about party membership. For example, in the material read into the record concerning Albert Maltz was a most interesting account of two articles written by him for the Communist magazine, the *New Masses*. In the first of these articles Maltz deplored the tendency to judge literary works by their ideological orthodoxy and called for more Communist toleration of writers of the non-Communist left, such as James T. Farrell, Richard Wright, and Lillian Smith.[68] This article met with the extreme displeasure of the Communist hierarchy, and Maltz was subjected to a barrage of relentless, dialectical criticism, under which he quickly gave way. In a second article he recanted and confessed the erroneous lines

[67] *Mot. Pict. Ind. Hearings,* p. 403.

[68] Maltz wrote: "Writers must be judged by their work, and *not* by the committees they join. It is the job of the editorial section of a magazine to praise or attack citizens' committees. It is the job of the literary critics to appraise the literary works only." *New Masses,* Feb. 12, 1946, pp. 19, 20.

of thought into which he had fallen in the first article.[69] This rather pitiful exhibition of the intellectual slavery into which communism forces its followers might well have been explored by the committee and the facts concerning it widely publicized. The committee might properly have argued that the American people were entitled to know the facts about the intellectual bondage shown by a leading writer of motion picture scripts to a political movement whose record on the international scene since the close of World War II had established it as a dangerous enemy of the democratic way of life.[70]

In the end, the most striking indication of the inadequacy of the Hollywood investigation was the failure of the Un-American Activities Committee to submit a formal report of its findings. Apart from statements concerning the contempt proceedings against the unfriendly witnesses the only reference made by the committee to the investigation was a single sentence in its "annual" report published more than a year later, where it is stated: "While the committee could not within the limits of its time and resources examine every single phase of Communist activity in the industry, the outlines and the pattern of such activity was clearly disclosed." [71]

In the light of the sensational build-up given to the 1947 hearings, the seriousness of the charges levied against the motion picture industry, and the spectacular manner in which the hearings were

[69] See the attacks by Howard Fast and Joseph North in the *New Masses* (Feb. 26, 1946, pp. 6, 8), Alvah Bessie (March 12, 1946, p. 8), John Howard Lawson (March 19, 1946, p. 18). In his second article (*New Masses*, April 9, 1946, p. 8), Maltz writes: "I consider now that my article—by what I have come to agree was a one-sided, non-dialectical treatment of *complex* issues—could not, as I had hoped, contribute to the development of left-wing criticism and creative writing. I believe also that my critics were entirely correct in insisting that certain fundamental ideas in my article would, if pursued to their conclusion, result in the dissolution of the left-wing cultural movement." And of one of the writers he praised in his first article he now writes: "Farrell's history and work are the best example I know of the manner in which a poisoned ideology and an increasingly sick soul can sap the talent and wreck the living fibre of a man's work." In this article Maltz even chastises those who had defended him during the controversy over the first article.

[70] As a matter of fact this episode of the Maltz *New Masses* articles and similar items in the professional careers of the unfriendly witnesses were explored during the first week of hearings when the friendly witnesses were testifying. But the testimony was secondhand, and it was difficult to separate the authentic from the doubtful in the testimony of the friendly witnesses, some of whom were disgruntled, prejudiced persons.

[71] *Annual Rept.*, Dec. 31, 1948, p. 9.

finally held, the committee had an obligation to Congress and to the American people to prepare a systematic report on the under-taking—however difficult a task that might have been! Its failure to do this reveals the erratic and careless policy—or lack of policy—which the committee was following as of 1947.

Some four years later the Hollywood investigation was resumed by the committee in the 82d Congress. These later hearings lie out-side the time period covered by this study. At the time of writing the hearings were still continuing, and no committee report had yet been filed. The new hearings supplied abundant additional evidence of the presence—present or past—of Communists or ex-Communists in the motion picture industry. However, once more there was little or no evidence that Communist propaganda had actually been in-troduced into specific motion pictures. As revealed in the testimony of "friendly" witnesses the committee's purpose in holding these new hearings seemed to be to show rather that highly paid Com-munist employees in the industry made significant financial con-tributions to the party, that support of Communist causes by Holly-wood stars was sought by the party as a means of "glamorizing" its program, that Communists had infiltrated Hollywood unions looking toward their ultimate control, and so forth. But once more any strong evidence that the Communists in Hollywood had been guilty of truly subversive (or un-American) activity was not forthcoming. This is not to say that the degree of success enjoyed by the Com-munists in their efforts to infiltrate the motion picture industry was not a significant thing for the committee to attempt to reveal. But the committee's primary assignment is, after all, a search for un-American *activity*, and it may be wondered whether the committee's Hollywood investigations have not from start to finish fallen rather wide of this mark.

This third year in the life of the permanent committee also saw the establishment of an elaborate program of publications. Up to this time the committee had issued only three reports of any con-sequence—its "annual" reports of June, 1946, and January, 1947, and the very brief report dealing with "sources of financial aid" en-joyed by "subversive" groups. In April, the Thomas committee pub-lished the first of two rather elaborate reports dealing with the Communist Party of the United States. This 1947 report was a fifty-six-page document examining the party "as an agent of a foreign power." It was followed in 1948 with a 160-page analysis of the party "as an advocate of overthrow of government by force and violence." The other three 1947 reports all dealt with specific private organizations which were charged with being Communist-dominated. One of these reports examined the American Youth for Democracy, one the Southern Conference for Human Welfare, and one the Civil Rights Congress. These were to be followed in subsequent years by similar reports on other organizations.

IV: The Committee in the Eightieth Congress: 1948

IN ITS second and last year the Thomas committee was even more active than it had been in its first year. There were only three sets of public hearings in 1948, but they occupied thirty-five days as against the twenty-seven days of hearings in 1947. Moreover, one set of the 1948 hearings dealt with the subject of Communist espionage in the United States. These hearings were to prove more consequential than any others conducted by the committee since Representative Dies started his investigations in 1938. The espionage hearings opened on July 31 when Elizabeth Bentley exploded a bombshell by charging that numerous employees of the federal government, whom she named, had been members of spy circles which had turned confidential government data over to Soviet agents during the war. Thereafter, twenty-six days in all were spent pursuing the details of the espionage story, until on December 14 the committee reluctantly let go of the Pumpkin Papers sensation and allowed the Department of Justice and the federal courts to take over.

The other hearings of 1948 were devoted to testimony concerning proposed legislation for the control of the Communist Party, a continuation of 1947 hearings on the same subject, and to the investigation of alleged efforts of Communist agents to ferret out the secrets of the atom bomb. During the year the committee also released eight reports. One was an "annual" report published at the end of the year (actually this report covered the two-year period of the 80th Congress), two dealt with legislative proposals to curb the Communist Party (one of these was a subcommittee report), one was the famous report of the "Subcommittee on National Security" dealing with Dr. Edward U. Condon, one was a report on the Communist Party "as an advocate of overthrow of government by force and violence," two reported on Communist espionage in the United States government, and one on Soviet espionage in connection with the atom bomb.[1]

Hearings on Legislation to Curb the Communist Party

The hearings on proposed legislation occupied seven days in February and were conducted by a subcommittee under the chairmanship of Representative Nixon. The other members of the subcommittee were Vail, McDowell, Peterson, and Hébert. Rankin attended certain of these hearings, to the rather obvious disgust of the members of the subcommittee. The Rankin and Sheppard bills of the previous year had gone into the discard, and taking their place as the object of the subcommittee's attention were two new bills—H.R. 4422, introduced by Representative Mundt, and H.R. 4581, introduced by Representative McDonough. By April the famous Mundt-Nixon bill had taken shape out of these hearings and was introduced as H.R. 5852.

These 1948 hearings on legislation were a decided improvement over the rather aimless hearings of the previous year on the absurd Rankin and Sheppard bills. Under Nixon's leadership the hearings were well conducted, and with one exception the atmosphere throughout was reasonably calm and judicial. The exception occurred at the hearing on February 11. That morning Representative Nixon fell on the ice and was injured. McDowell was the only member of the subcommittee present, but the irrepressible Rankin showed up. McDowell as acting chairman gave Rankin a free hand, and the latter turned the hearing into a shambles. In particular he disrupted the testimony of Adolf Berle, Jr., in a shameful manner.

On the whole, the printed record of these hearings contains many intelligent and penetrating comments on legislation to curb the Communist Party. For the most part the witnesses were invited and included such well-known persons as Donald Richberg, Louis Waldman, Arthur Garfield Hays, Morris Ernst, Admiral W. H. Standley, Adolf A. Berle, Jr., Tom Clark, James Burnham, and Ferenc Nagy. In addition, the committee received written statements from James Truslow Adams, Eugene Lyons, Thomas Reed Powell,

[1] For the list of 1948 publications of the committee, see Appendix, Table I.

and John Foster Dulles. So far as the eminence of its witnesses was concerned, the subcommittee may perhaps even be pardoned for its exuberant statement in its report to the full committee that the witnesses constituted "perhaps the most outstanding panel of legal talent ever to appear before a congressional committee." [2]

Like their predecessors the year before, the two bills before the subcommittee were brief, and, while vastly more intelligent than the earlier bills, they still represented rudimentary attempts to suggest a statutory policy for the nation to follow in dealing with the Communist threat. Less attention was given to the McDonough bill than the Mundt bill, and the former received almost no support from the witnesses. Representative McDonough's proposal was entitled "A Bill to define communism and to make the practice of communism a treasonable act in the United States." Beginning with three "whereases" concerning the nature of communism,[3] it proceeded to define communism "to be not a political policy, but . . . an international conspiracy" having for its purpose the overthrow of democratic government by force and violence,[4] and it concluded with the statement "that any person . . . actively practicing communism should be exposed and treated as a treasonable enemy of the United States and dealt with accordingly."

The Mundt bill was a much more imaginative, and at the same time practicable, proposal. It definitely foreshadowed the Mundt-Nixon bill which later became the committee's definitive proposal for a statutory attack upon Communist subversive activity. Representative Mundt's proposal was entitled "A Bill to provide that all members of the Communist Party and organizations controlled

[2] *Report of the Subcommittee on Legislation of the Committee on Un-American Activities on Proposed Legislation to Control Subversive Communist Activities in the United States,* April 10, 1948, p. 3. Abbreviated hereafter to *Rept. of the Subcommittee on Legislation.*

[3] Communism is declared "inimical to the people of the United States"; many people are said to "have been influenced to believe in and sympathize with communism" because its real purposes "are clouded and misunderstood"; and there is said to be "a pressing need for a clear and easily understandable definition of communism in order to protect the people of the United States from its insidious influence."

[4] The full statement here is "That communism be defined and declared to be not a political policy, but is [sic] an international conspiracy and an atheistic and an antireligious ideology which advocates and practices deceit, confusion, subversion, revolution, and the subordination of man to the state, and which has for its purposes and intentions the overthrow of any democratic or other form of government by force and violence, if necessary. . . ."

by it must register as agents of a foreign principal and that all printed matter distributed by such members and organizations shall be clearly labeled as being in compliance with the terms of this legislation. . . ." As this title suggests, the main purposes of the bill were to require the Communist Party and all Communist front organizations to register with the Department of Justice and supply the names and addresses of all officers and members, and to require that any publication or propaganda of said party or organizations sent through the mails be labeled, "Published in compliance with the laws of the United States governing the activities of agents of foreign principals." The officers of such organizations were made responsible for compliance with the terms of the bill, and minimum penalties of a fine of $1,000 and a prison term of one year were provided for noncompliance.

The tenor of these hearings on legislation was set at the beginning of the first day when Nixon announced that the subcommittee was seeking answers to three basic questions:

First of all, we should like to know whether or not the Communist Party or the American Communists constitute at the present time a real danger to our national security.

Second, are our present laws adequate to cope with that danger, and, if not, what new laws are necessary to meet it.

Third, is there any possibility or any substantial risk that by the adoption of any of the proposed legislation we will impair any fundamental constitutional rights? [5]

Whether all of the members of the subcommittee approached these hearings with the open mind and concern for civil rights of which Nixon speaks may be doubted, but it was at least refreshing to learn that the Un-American Activities Committee could open a series of hearings without a characteristic introductory statement in which the chairman made it plain that the committee already knew the answers.

In general, the registration and disclosure principle of the Mundt bill found considerable favor with the witnesses, and the arguments advanced in favor of this principle by such men as Waldman, Berle, and Ernst are impressive. Contrariwise, there was relatively little support for any step toward outlawing the Communist Party, although such a witness as James Burnham did advocate this policy.

[5] *Hearings on Proposed Legislation to Curb or Control the Communist Party of the United States,* Feb., 1948, p. 3.

Representative Mundt, who appeared as a witness in support of his own bill, made clear his position in this respect:

I have been one of those who has not looked with favor upon proposals to outlaw the Communist Party or to declare its activities illegal, because I fear such action on the part of Congress would only tend to drive further underground the functions of forces which are already largely concealed from public view. What I want to do is to drive the Communist function- aries out of the ground, into the open, where patriotic Americans of every walk of life can come to learn their identity and understand their objec- tives. . . .

My bill will publicly identify the Communists of this country for the foreign agents that they actually are, and enable both public and private employers to be on guard against them. . . . H.R. 4422 will bring the whole mechanism of communism into the open. Once that is done, I have complete confidence in the capacity and determination of patriotic Amer- icans everywhere to curtail the effectiveness of communism and to defeat its traitorous plots and plans to destroy our American way of life.[6]

Almost alone among the witnesses Arthur Garfield Hays counseled the committee against the enactment of any legislation directed against the Communist threat:

In my judgment no laws should be passed. It is about time our legisla- tors realized that the American people are to be trusted and need no laws to save them from bad propaganda or bad thinking. After 150 years of history, our people have shown that they are entitled to be trusted.

. . . . .

How far have the Communists gotten in the United States in the last 25 years? They have gotten nowhere. What is all the excitement and danger about, Congressmen?[7]

In asking his rhetorical question Mr. Hays was unconsciously raising one of the most troublesome of the issues that must be faced in evaluating the Communist threat and of considering how far it is wise to go in meeting this threat. If the threat is merely that com- munism as an ideology may prove attractive to large numbers of American people, then Hays is correct in stating that there is no evidence that this is taking place. Moreover, he is correct in suggest- ing that we do violence to the American tradition of freedom of speech when we seek to curb the mere advocacy of a radical ideology. But members of the subcommittee were quick to disagree with Hays that the Communist danger is confined to the intellectual world of

[6] *Ibid.*, pp. 11, 12.   [7] *Ibid.*, pp. 212, 214.

ideas. For example, Mr. Hébert said: "Your expression, 'They got nowhere,' and my opinion are two different opinions. When I see what happened in different countries and in this one with Communist-influenced strikes that kept planes on the ground when they were instantly needed in other parts of the world, I think they have gotten somewhere." [8]

This response by Representative Hébert led to an interesting exchange of remarks concerning the issue of fact as to the extent of Communist success in the world of acts as opposed to the world of ideas.

Mr. Hays: If they have been responsible for them. Nothing outrages us more than the general idea that the Communists deserve all the credit in the United States. They don't deserve that credit. It is that kind of credit that builds up the Communist Party. . . . I think all this publicity builds up the Communist Party more than the Communists themselves can do in 10 years. They have gotten millions of dollars worth of publicity.

I think we ought to regard them as the ridiculous, insignificant, futile crowd that they are.

Whenever there is any difficulty in the labor unions the Communists are blamed. You would think that a couple of Communists could lead millions of Americans around by the nose. That is an insult to Americans. Every time there is a disorder in the United States the Communists must be blamed for it, and I don't think they deserve the credit for all of it. . . .

. . . . .

Mr. Hébert: However, when a disease is spreading either on the body politic or on the body human, it behooves us as intelligent human beings to do something to retard it. We ought to treasure our way of life. If you want to live in the way you were brought up in freedom and believe in free speech, you must know that freedom can destroy freedom.

. . . . .

Mr. Hays: I know Foster. I know Bob Minor. I knew Earl Browder. I knew all these men. To me they are confused, futile men with wild ideas, who have been able to get nowhere in all these years. Why we treat them as important people developing a big political movement is beyond my comprehension. If we just ignore them and laugh at them, as I often do, and kid them along, and treat them as they deserve to be treated, we would get rid of Communists a lot sooner in this country.[9]

[8] *Ibid.*, p. 214.   [9] *Ibid.*, pp. 214, 215, 231.

The Communist Espionage Hearings

In examining the investigation of Communist espionage which
began with sensational charges by an "ex-spy queen" and ended with
seemingly irrefutable proof of espionage drawn from a hollowed-
out pumpkin, one is confronted at the outset with the factor of timing. The hearings began on the last day of July, just three months
before a presidential election was to be held, and in the midst of
a special session of Congress called by President Truman in the
course of his speech accepting the nomination for the presidency
at the Democratic National Convention in Philadelphia in July. That
this was not an auspicious moment for the calm, judicial sifting by
a Congressional committee of controversial charges concerning espionage in the public service and that political motivation played an
exceedingly strong part in the undertaking cannot be denied.

Similarly, it is apparent that the Un-American Activities Committee was persuaded into action to protect its jurisdiction as watch-
dog against subversive threats to the American way of life. From the
earliest days other Congressional committees had looked with en-
vious eyes upon the game-laden woods in which the Un-American
Activities Committee had been hunting, and always the latter committee had jealously guarded its valuable preserves. This time the
poaching threat was exceedingly serious. Over on the other side of
the Capitol, the well-regarded Senate Investigating Committee,[10]
pursuing its way through the unexciting labyrinths of American
export policy, had stumbled upon the aforementioned ex-spy queen,
one Elizabeth T. Bentley, who told a lurid story of the alleged cooperation she had received as a Communist agent from an employee
in the Department of Commerce, William W. Remington, who had
headed an important interdepartmental committee having juris-

[10] The so-called Senate Investigating Committee was a standing subcommittee
of the Senate Committee on Expenditures in the Executive Departments. In the
Legislative Reorganization Act of 1946 the Senate accepted the spirit if not
the letter of the recommendation of the La Follette-Monroney Committee on the
Organization of Congress that special investigating committees be dispensed
with. This subcommittee was created as an agency to which all investigations
would be entrusted which did not fall within the jurisdiction of the other standing committees of the Senate. In the 80th Congress the subcommittee was under
the chairmanship of Senator Ferguson of Michigan, and there was a tendency to
think of the Ferguson committee as the successor to the Truman committee,
which had enjoyed an excellent reputation because of its investigations into
defense production during World War II.

diction over the licensing of exports during the war. Miss Bentley appeared before the Senate committee on July 30, and while it is highly unlikely that the committee had any notion of pressing forward on a broad front in a search for subversive activity, there is little doubt that its rendezvous with Miss Bentley had the effect of encouraging the House committee into action.

An even more serious threat to the House committee's exclusive possession of the area in which it had been working existed in New York City. There a federal grand jury, for more than a year, had been looking into the whole matter of subversive activity and, in particular, into the Communist threat to American institutions. On July 20, 1948, it had indicted twelve top officers of the Communist Party of the United States, charging them with violation of the Alien Registration Act of 1940, known also as the Smith Act. Even more important, there were numerous, well-founded leaks to the effect that it had been hearing various witnesses concerning the presence of Communists in the federal government. There is little doubt that, as *Time* magazine put it, "the House Un-American Activities Committee caught the scent and acted." [11] Thus, one is faced at the beginning with the issue of conflict between the Congressional power of investigation and the jurisdiction of the courts. As far back as 1881, Congress and the courts had tangled over the issue of which should probe the reasons for the failure of Jay Cooke and Company and the resultant loss of federal funds. The Supreme Court ruled in *Kilbourn v. Thompson* (103 U.S. 168) that since the matter under investigation had already resulted in litigation the courts should have priority over Congress. This ruling has always had its critics, who have argued that the investigating power of Congress can never be subordinated to judicial power and that there is no constitutional reason why Congress should not concurrently investigate a matter that is being adjudicated in the courts, if the public interest so dictates.

Whether the public interest dictated that the House committee encroach upon the area already under examination by the grand jury is debatable. Once its inquiries began the House committee at several points came into conflict with the judicial proceedings, and there is evidence that the grand jury's work was rendered more

[11] *Time*, Feb. 13, 1950. Stripling writes that a newspaperman, Ed Nellor, told him about Chambers' appearance before the grand jury. Robert E. Stripling, *The Red Plot Against America* (Drexel Hill: Bell Publishing Co., 1949), pp. 95–96.

difficult by the tactics of the House committee. On the other hand, the House committee could claim then and later that years of activity and investigation in this area by the FBI and other federal administrative and judicial officers had resulted in little or no action and that the time had come for a Congressional committee to conduct a public inquiry into the many rumors and charges concerning espionage, communism in the public service, and so forth. Moreover, at the end of 1948, the Un-American Activities Committee was able to point to tangible, unmistakable, and irrefutable evidence that espionage agents had penetrated to the heart of the federal government—evidence that almost certainly would not have been brought to light had the committee not undertaken its own investigation in the middle of the summer.

The story of the espionage hearings of the committee is an intricate one whose details are often exceedingly hard to follow.[12] It is not possible to piece together a wholly coherent or complete story on the basis of the printed hearings and reports of the Un-American Activities Committee alone. It was characteristic of the leading witnesses that they told their stories in piecemeal fashion, that their memories were frequently faulty, and that they often contradicted themselves. Many leads suggested in the testimony were never run down. In the end, one of the chief witnesses, Alger Hiss, was twice to stand trial on the charge that he perjured himself in his testimony before the grand jury. The evidence brought to light at the two Hiss trials frequently conflicts with the evidence presented to the House committee and at many points adds considerable detail to the testimony given during the committee hearings in August, 1948.

In its main outlines the story unfolded at the 1948 hearings was as follows. Two "friendly" witnesses, Elizabeth Bentley and Whittaker Chambers, by their own word ex-Communists, described their roles as "couriers" in the days when they served the Communist Party.

[12] The first phase of the espionage hearings ran from July 31 to Sept. 9, 1948, and is reported in *Hearings regarding Communist Espionage in the United States Government.* The second phase ran from Dec. 7 to 14, 1948, and is reported in *Hearings regarding Communist Espionage in the United States Government—Part Two.* The pagination for the two volumes is continuous. Abbreviated hereafter to *Communist Espionage Hearings.*

The two espionage reports are *Interim Report on Hearings regarding Communist Espionage in the United States Government,* Aug. 28, 1948 (abbreviated hereafter to *Interim Rept.*) and *Soviet Espionage within the United States Government: Second Report,* Dec. 31, 1948 (abbreviated hereafter to *Soviet Espionage, Second Rept.*).

Their stories were very similar. As underground "functionaries" of the party each had been brought in contact by various means with a number of persons in the federal service in Washington who were either themselves members of the Communist Party or Communist sympathizers. Miss Bentley testified that over a period of time these persons supplied her with confidential and restricted information and material which she turned over to party officials. Chambers' relations with his Washington contacts were at first described in quite hazy terms, and it was only over a period of time that he made clear his role as a courier. In general, the activity of the two couriers seems not to have overlapped, and for the most part they were in touch with different groups of federal employees. In all, the two witnesses named more than fifty persons who were alleged to have co-operated with them as members of Communist cells or as "free lancers," although it was characteristic of both witnesses to be inexact about the number of contacts they had had. They tended to add names each time their stories were repeated and to intimate that there were many more such contacts in wartime Washington than those whom they had specifically named.

Apart from these two friendly witnesses, the more than fifty witnesses who appeared before the Un-American Activities Committee during the espionage investigation fell generally into two categories. The largest of these consisted of persons named by Bentley and Chambers as contacts. Some of these—notably, Alger Hiss and Harry White—appeared at their own request and testified at great length in denying the charges against them.[13] Others—notably, Nathan Silvermaster, Victor Perlo, John Abt, and Nathan Witt—appeared only after being subpoenaed and then refused to testify on grounds of self-incrimination.[14] The second category consisted of witnesses called by the committee in an effort to corroborate the testimony

[13] Others who testified willingly and denied the charges against them were Duncan C. Lee, Robert T. Miller, Lauchlin Currie, Bella and Sonia Gold, Frank Coe, and Donald Hiss. In her autobiography, Out of Bondage (New York: Devin-Adair Co., 1951), Elizabeth Bentley repeats her charges against certain of these persons.

[14] Those other witnesses who refused to answer questions on the ground of self-incrimination were Alexander Koral, William L. Ullman, Henry H. Collins, Charles Kramer, Abraham Silverman, William Rosen, Alexander Stevens (J. Peters), and Mrs. Addie Rosen. Lee Pressman did not actually refuse to testify on grounds of self-incrimination. But he was an uncommunicative witness and stressed other reasons, such as the protection offered by the First Amendment, in refusing to answer questions. Communist Espionage Hearings, pp. 1023 ff.

of Chambers and Bentley and included such persons as Adolf Berle, Sumner Welles, Francis Sayre, and Isaac Don Levine.

As usual the committee did not hesitate to indicate an initial bias. On the first day of the hearings several members of the committee made it clear that they were already convinced that many government employees had committed acts of espionage. Chairman Thomas stated that preliminary research by the committee's staff confirmed "the fact that there is a tremendous need for such an investigation *and exposure and a conviction in many cases in this country.*" And he added that the committee "recommends that a special grand jury be convened in Washington, D.C., in order to give special attention to the matter of espionage in the Government, and to bring the matter to an early conclusion." [15] That such a recommendation might more properly have been made at the conclusion of the hearings than at the very beginning of the first day of hearings seems not to have occurred to Mr. Thomas. Representative Rankin hastened to back up the chairman and asserted that it was "about time" President Truman and Governor Dewey "got behind this committee and helped to clean this proposition up and drive these rats from the Federal, the State, and the municipal pay rolls." [16]

Apart from these statements the committee wasted no time with preliminaries. The first witness called was Elizabeth Bentley, who quickly plunged into the details of her sensational story. Miss Bentley, a student of foreign languages, had graduated from Vassar College in 1930 and thereafter studied in Italy and also obtained a Master's degree at Columbia in 1935. At about this time she also taught at a girls' preparatory school. One does not have to do much reading between the lines of the testimony of the witness to obtain a picture of a woman who, during the 1930's, strongly desired to lead the life of an intellectual but who never succeeded in becoming more than a sadly confused idealist who was used by persons shrewder and cleverer than herself. [17]

[15] *Ibid.,* p. 501. Italics added.   [16] *Ibid.,* p. 502.

[17] For example, Miss Bentley answered Representative Mundt's question as to how she became a Communist as follows: "I am afraid that is an awfully difficult question to answer. Thinking back on it, it is rather hard to remember my state of mind at that particular moment. As I said, I was quite infuriated with what I had learned about fascism in Italy, and the only people who would listen to me were the people in the American League Against War and Fascism, and, as I said, I gradually got into that, and gradually there I met Communists, both in Columbia and downtown, and gradually my ideas began to change. I suppose, in a way, I was a very confused liberal, and, unfortunately, we confused

About 1935, Miss Bentley was drawn into a Communist group in New York City, and in 1938 she met and apparently fell in love with Jacob Golos, a functionary in the Communist Party. Thereafter, she became a close associate of Golos in his professional work as president of World Tourists, Inc., a travel agency. According to her testimony, after Germany attacked the Soviet Union in 1941, she became, under Golos' influence and direction, a courier between Communist headquarters in New York and two groups or cells of Communists in the federal service in Washington. She identified one of these cells as the "Silvermaster group" because it had been under the leadership of Nathan Gregory Silvermaster, an economist who held during the war years several important jobs in such federal agencies as the Farm Security Administration, the Board of Economic Warfare, and the Office of Surplus Property. The other cell was identified as the "Perlo group," led by Victor Perlo, also an economist, who was employed in the Office of Price Administration and later the War Production Board. Miss Bentley freely named a score or more of persons who, she said, were either members of or closely associated with one or the other of these groups. Among the persons so named were such prominent individuals as Harry D. White, Assistant Secretary of the Treasury, and Lauchlin Currie of the White House secretariat.

According to Miss Bentley the two cells were tightly organized groups which saw to it that their members were placed in desirable spots in the government service where they would have access to classified information. Miss Bentley's role is suggested by the following testimony:

Mr. Stripling: Now that we have completed the naming of the personnel which comprised each group, I wish you would describe to the committee the mechanical operation of the group, just how they operated, what you did, what the group did.

Take the Silvermaster group first.

Miss Bentley: It was my policy to come down almost regularly every 2 weeks. I would go to the Silvermaster home, very often have dinner with them, spend the evening, and collect from them the information which they had previously collected from the members of the group.

. . . . .

liberals have a tendency to look for guidance some place and a tendency to admire efficient people who know where they are going and seem to be doing a good job in the right direction." *Communist Espionage Hearings,* pp. 539–540.

Her naïveté is indicated by her insistence that no courses in government were taught at Columbia during the period she studied there. *Ibid.,* p. 549.

Mr. Stripling: What type of information was actually turned over to you, and which you transferred to Mr. Golos?

Miss Bentley: Military information, particularly from the Air Corps, on production of airplanes, their destinations to the various theaters of war and to various countries, new types of planes being put out, information as to when D-day would be, all sorts of inside military information.

. . . . .

Mr. Stripling: Could you elaborate on the military information which you secured from the Silvermaster group?

Miss Bentley: Well, the military information came largely from George Silverman and Ludwig Ullmann, and, as I said, it was information of the most varied things you could think of. We had complete data as to almost all of the aircraft production in the country, as to types, how many were being produced, where they were allocated, and so on. We had all sorts of inside information on policies of the Air Corps. As I said, we knew D-day long before D-day happened, and we were right. Practically all the inside policies that were going on inside the Air Corps. We got quite a bit of information about the General Hilldring's activities.[18]

Miss Bentley also revealed that she had established contacts with government employees who were not members of the two groups and with whom she kept in touch on an individual basis. One of these was William W. Remington, whose relations with Miss Bentley were being investigated by the Ferguson committee in the Senate at this same time. Another was Duncan C. Lee, an army officer who was assigned to the Office of Strategic Services during the war.

Miss Bentley seems to have been active as a courier from 1941 until 1944 or 1945. Toward the end of that period Jacob Golos died, and the witness testified that she began her break with the party about July, 1944, when she stopped paying dues. The break took about a year to complete, and, finally, in August, 1945, Miss Bentley went to the New Haven office of the Federal Bureau of Investigation with her story.[19]

[18] *Ibid.,* pp. 521, 522, 525.
[19] *"Mr. Mundt:* When did you quit the party, and why?
"Miss Bentley: I actually stopped paying dues to the party in July of 1944, but it took me about a year to more or less get it out of my system and get to the point where I could get in the frame of mind of going to the authorities about it. As to why: Having worked with Mr. Golos, whom I took to be a great idealist, a man who was working for what I considered to be the betterment of the world, I had been terrifically shielded from the realities behind this thing, and when he died I was thrown in direct contact with Russians who had just come over from Russia—at least as I understand it.

Four days after Miss Bentley's appearance, the Un-American Activities Committee heard its second witness, Whittaker Chambers, a senior editor of *Time* magazine.[20] It is significant that the committee heard Chambers before attempting to run down the many leads supplied by Elizabeth Bentley in her testimony. Thereafter, the committee did hear as witnesses persons named by both Bentley and Chambers, but the Chambers story, as it unfolded, proved to be so much more sensational than Miss Bentley's that the committee

"They thought that I was much more sophisticated than I was.
"They thought that I knew what was going on, and unfortunately they landed on me with both feet, made no bones of the fact that they had contempt for American Communists with their vague idealism, no bones of the fact that they were using the American Communist Party as a recruitment for espionage, and, in general, they were about the cheapest type of person I have ever seen—the gangster type." *Communist Espionage Hearings*, p. 540.

[20] How the committee got wind of Chambers and whether it knew in advance the direction that his testimony would take (including the naming of Alger Hiss as a Communist) are questions that have been given contradictory answers by committee members and agents.

Stripling has written that Chambers was subpoenaed as "a forlorn shot in the dark" in an effort to find someone who could corroborate Elizabeth Bentley's story. *The Red Plot*, p. 94.

Nixon told the House of Representatives at the time of Hiss's conviction that the committee came upon Chambers and his sensational story pretty much by chance:

"On August 3, just a week after Miss Bentley appeared before the committee, the committee called before it a witness we thought might be able to corroborate some of the Bentley testimony, because up to this time all we had was Miss Bentley's testimony about the espionage ring that she said she worked with. No other member of the ring had broken, and consequently it was only her word against the word of some who denied the charges and others who refused to answer questions on the basis of self-incrimination. . . .

"Consequently we subpoenaed him to appear before the committee for the purpose of seeing whether he could corroborate Miss Bentley's testimony in any respect.

"This was the first time any member of our committee had had the opportunity to see Mr. Chambers. . . ." 96 *Cong. Rec.* 1000 (January 26, 1950).

On the other hand both Stripling and Nixon admit that the committee knew that Chambers had made charges as early as 1939 concerning the presence of Communist agents in the federal service and that Chambers had been interviewed before he appeared as a witness. Nixon told the House: "The committee went to Mr. Chambers. We had learned that he had made charges many years ago, in 1939, to the officials of this Government concerning Communist activities among Federal employees in the period between 1934 and 1937." *Ibid.*

On January 26, 1950, the day on which Nixon made his speech to the House of Representatives, John Rankin read a letter to the House that he had just received from the committee's senior investigator, Louis Russell, in which it is

came increasingly to devote its attention to his charges. In the end, a number of the persons named by Bentley were never heard as witnesses, and parts of her story were left dangling in mid-air.

In its main outlines the Chambers story was not unlike that of his feminine counterpart. Having become a member of the Communist Party about 1924, Chambers came to Washington in 1932 or shortly thereafter to serve as courier for a Washington "apparatus" of underground Communists in the government service. Chambers testified that he began to break with the Communist Party in 1937 and that the break was complete by the time of the Berlin-Moscow pact in 1939. Indeed, he made his first attempt to communicate his story to government authorities two days after the signing of the pact. It is with respect to details such as the date of his break with communism that Chambers was vague in his first appearances before the committee. Some of this information was made clear only at the time of the Hiss trials. At first, Chambers insisted he had broken with the party in 1937. Later, however, in producing documents which he admitted receiving from espionage agents in the federal service early in 1938, he revised his testimony on this point and finally settled on April, 1938, as the date of his emancipation from communism. In December, Chambers told reporters covering the grand jury proceedings in New York, "Originally I thought I left the Communist Party about the end of 1937. But in developing the narrative before the Committee it became clear that I left in 1938. I think it was about the second week of April, 1938." [21] To make this matter a little more confusing, the Un-American Activities Committee in its second and final report on the Communist espionage hearings, released on December 31, 1948, stated, "Forty-eight hours after publication of the Russo-German pact of August 23, 1939, one Whittaker Chambers, a Communist agent, decided to abandon communism." [22]

If the Bentley and Chambers stories were not dissimilar in their

---

stated categorically that Chambers had been interviewed in April, 1948, by two committee investigators and that Chambers had specifically identified Witt, Abt, Pressman, Alger and Donald Hiss, Perlo, Collins, Kramer, and Ware "as having been members of a Communist apparatus in Washington, D.C., for the express purpose of infiltrating the Government." Ibid., p. 974. This hardly jibes with Stripling's assertion in The Red Plot that the investigators returned from the session with Chambers "empty-handed" (p. 96).

Chambers, himself, implies in Witness (New York: Random House, 1952) that he had had no previous contact with the committee when he appeared before it to testify on Aug. 3 (pp. 529 ff.).

[21] Washington Post, Dec. 9, 1948.   [22] Soviet Espionage, Second Rept., p. 1.

main outlines, there was a striking contrast between the two witnesses. In contrast to the confusion and naïveté that characterized Elizabeth Bentley's career as a Communist, Chambers' testimony made it clear that he had acted with assurance and sophistication in becoming a Communist and in playing his role as a party functionary. Moreover, he was never unaware of the dramatic aspects of his actions and thoughts, and it is not unfair to say that he took pleasure in stressing "the grandeur and misery" of his story. In his public appearances before the committee, he revealed an emotional as well as an intellectual side. The following long excerpt from the introductory statement which Chambers made on his first appearance before the committee throws a good deal of light on the character of the witness:

Almost exactly 9 years ago—that is, 2 days after Hitler and Stalin signed their pact—I went to Washington and reported to the authorities what I knew about the infiltration of the United States Government by Communists. . . . I regarded my action in going to the Government as a simple act of war, like the shooting of an armed enemy in combat.

At that moment in history, I was one of the few men on this side of the battle who could perform this service.

I had joined the Communist Party in 1924. No one recruited me. I had become convinced that the society in which we live, western civilization, had reached a crisis, of which the first World War was the military expression, and that it was doomed to collapse or revert to barbarism. I did not understand the causes of the crisis or know what to do about it. But I felt that, as an intelligent man, I must do something. In the writings of Karl Marx I thought that I had found the explanation of the historical and economic causes. In the writings of Lenin I thought I had found the answer to the question, What to do?

In 1937 I repudiated Marx' doctrines and Lenin's tactics. Experience and the record had convinced me that communism is a form of totalitarianism, that its triumph means slavery to men wherever they fall under its sway, and spiritual night to the human mind and soul. I resolved to break with the Communist Party at whatever risk to my life or other tragedy to myself or my family. Yet, so strong is the hold which the insidious evil of communism secures on its disciples, that I could still say to someone at the time: "I know that I am leaving the winning side for the losing side, but it is better to die on the losing side than to live under communism."

For a year I lived in hiding, sleeping by day and watching through the night with gun or revolver within easy reach. That was what underground communism could do to one man in the peaceful United States in the year 1938. . . .

For a number of years I had myself served in the underground, chiefly in Washington, D.C. The heart of my report to the United States Government consisted of a description of the apparatus to which I was attached. It was an underground organization of the United States Communist Party developed, to the best of my knowledge, by Harold Ware, one of the sons of the Communist leader known as "Mother Bloor." I knew it at its top level, a group of seven or so men, from among whom in later years certain members of Miss Bentley's organization were apparently recruited. The head of the underground group at the time I knew it was Nathan Witt, an attorney for the National Labor Relations Board. Later, John Abt became the leader. Lee Pressman was also a member of this group, as was Alger Hiss, who, as a member of the State Department, later organized the conferences at Dumbarton Oaks, San Francisco, and the United States side of the Yalta Conference.

The purpose of this group at that time was not primarily espionage. Its original purpose was the Communist infiltration of the American Government. But espionage was certainly one of its eventual objectives. . . .

It is 10 years since I broke away from the Communist Party. During that decade I have sought to live an industrious and God-fearing life. At the same time I have fought communism constantly by act and written word. I am proud to appear before this committee. The publicity inseparable from such testimony has darkened, and will no doubt continue to darken, my efforts to integrate myself in the community of free men.[23]

It is important to note that in his first statement before the committee, Chambers, while admitting that "espionage was certainly one of [the group's] eventual objectives," did not stress this angle but suggested rather that the purpose of the group at the time was to infiltrate the government service and place loyal Communists in strategic posts. He said: "I should perhaps make the point that these people were specifically not wanted to act as sources of information. These people were an elite group, an outstanding group, which it was believed would rise to positions—as, indeed, some of them did— notably Mr. White and Mr. Hiss—in the Government, and their position in the Government would be of very much more service to the Communist Party—" [24]

Ultimately the committee heard many of the persons named by

[23] *Communist Espionage Hearings*, pp. 564–566. Chambers' tendency toward delusions of grandeur was further illustrated at the close of the first Hiss trial when an Associated Press dispatch reported him as saying, "I am a man who grudgingly and reluctantly, step by step, has been destroying himself so that this Nation and the faith it lives by may continue to exist." *Washington Post*, July 10, 1949.

[24] *Communist Espionage Hearings*, p. 577.

Chambers. Had Harry White not died shortly after he appeared as a witness, it is possible that the conflict between his vigorous assertion of innocence and Chambers' charge that he was a conscious collaborator with a Communist "apparatus" might have commanded the committee's close and persistent attention, for with Lauchlin Currie he had occupied the most important government post of any of the persons Chambers named. As it was, Chambers' accusation that Alger Hiss had been a member of the Communist Party and an active and loyal member of the Washington cell came to hold the committee's main attention. The Hiss-Chambers "case" was quickly to become a *cause célèbre* and the House committee, as well as the country, was to show far more interest in the personalities of the case and the solution to the mystery than it was in the broader problem which underlay the details of the story. This tendency to personalize has marred much of the work of the committee and has, indeed, been a shortcoming of the entire approach of the government and public alike to the problem of controlling subversive activity in the postwar period.

It is difficult to avoid the suspicion that Chambers intended the case to take a strongly personal turn and that he hoped and expected that the committee would devote most of its energies to investigating his charges against Hiss. It is true that he mentioned many other persons, several of whom were just as well known as Alger Hiss, and two of whom were even better known. But in the end he managed in this first appearance to emphasize his charges against Hiss. This is apparent in the following testimony:

Mr. Stripling: When you left the Communist Party in 1937 did you approach any of these seven to break with you?

Mr. Chambers: No. The only one of those people whom I approached was Alger Hiss. I went to the Hiss home one evening at what I considered considerable risk to myself and found Mrs. Hiss at home. Mrs. Hiss is also a member of the Communist Party.

Mr. Mundt: Mrs. Alger Hiss?

Mr. Chambers: Mrs. Alger Hiss. Mrs. Donald Hiss, I believe, is not.

Mrs. Hiss attempted while I was there to make a call, which I can only presume was to other Communists, but I quickly went to the telephone and she hung up, and Mr. Hiss came in shortly afterward, and we talked and I tried to break him away from the party.

As a matter of fact, he cried when we separated; when I left him, but he absolutely refused to break.

Mr. McDowell: He cried?

Mr. Chambers: Yes, he did. I was very fond of Mr. Hiss.

Mr. Mundt: He must have given you some reason why he did not want to sever the relationship.

Mr. Chambers: His reasons were simply the party line.[25]

In a later appearance before the committee, Chambers, under Nixon's encouragement, returned to the matter of his relationship with Hiss:

Mr. Nixon: Why did you go to him? Did you go to all the others that were in this group?

Mr. Chambers: No; I went to two or three others.

Mr. Nixon: Why did you go to see Mr. Hiss?

Mr. Chambers: I was very fond of Mr. Hiss.

Mr. Nixon: You were very fond of Mr. Hiss?

Mr. Chambers: Indeed I was; perhaps my closest friend.

Mr. Nixon: Mr. Hiss was your closest friend?

Mr. Chambers: Mr. Hiss was certainly the closest friend I ever had in the Communist Party.

Mr. Nixon: Mr. Chambers, can you search your memory now to see what motive you can have for accusing Mr. Hiss of being a Communist at the present time?

Mr. Chambers: What motive I can have?

Mr. Nixon: Yes. I mean, do you—is there any grudge that you have against Mr. Hiss over anything that he has done to you?

Mr. Chambers: The story has spread that in testifying against Mr. Hiss I am working out some old grudge, or motives of revenge or hatred. I do not hate Mr. Hiss. We were close friends, but we are caught in a tragedy of history. Mr. Hiss represents the concealed enemy against which we are all fighting, and I am fighting.

I have testified against him with remorse and pity, but in a moment of history in which this Nation now stands, so help me God, I could not do otherwise.[26]

The explanation of this initial emphasis which Chambers gave to the name of Alger Hiss may be found in the later accusation by Chambers that Hiss was indeed procuring restricted documents for him from the State Department. On the other hand, it was seemingly Chambers' intention at this stage never to reveal the real evidence of espionage, and it is unlikely that he then intended to put the committee on the trail that was to lead ultimately to the production of the pumpkin documents. He did not even mention the names of four

[25] *Ibid.,* p. 572. Chambers testified that he also approached Harry White when he left the party and asked White to join him, but there was not the same effort on Chambers' part to personalize White's case. *Ibid.,* p. 574.

[26] *Ibid.,* pp. 1190–1191.

other persons whom he was later to charge with having supplied him with government documents—such as Henry Julian Wadleigh. One feels that Chambers was as much interested in this first appearance in putting the spotlight upon Alger Hiss as he was in bringing to light general information concerning espionage in the federal government.

At this point one encounters the theory that Alger Hiss was singled out for exposure as a Communist agent by Whittaker Chambers and/or the Un-American Activities Committee because as a symbol of the New Deal he could be used to discredit the Democratic administration and to influence the result of the 1948 election. There is no doubt that, as the case developed, Hiss came to have such a symbol-value both for liberals and conservatives.[27] Moreover, the House committee had too often frankly revealed its political motivation, and its chairman, J. Parnell Thomas, had too often engaged in raucous attacks upon the New Deal for the theory to be laughed aside. Certainly, members of the committee and its staff later did their best to emphasize Hiss's importance as a member of the Roosevelt administration. In a speech in the House of Representatives after Hiss's conviction for perjury, Nixon observed, "You know his phenomenal record in Government service." And he went on to imply that Hiss had played a role of incredibly great significance:

Five years ago, at the time of the Dumbarton Oaks Conference in 1944, when Alger Hiss served as director of our secretariate [sic], the number of people in the world in the Soviet orbit was 180,000,000 approximately the population of the Soviet Union. Arrayed on the anti-totalitarian side there were in the world at that time, in 1944, 1,625,000,000 people. Today there are 800,000,000 in the world under the domination of Soviet totalitarianism. On our side we have 540,000,000 people. There are 600,000,000 residents of United Nations countries which are classified as neutral, such as India, Pakistan, and Sweden. In other words, in 1944, before Dumbarton Oaks, Teheran, Yalta, and Potsdam, the odds were 9 to 1 in our favor. Today, since those conferences, the odds are 6 to 3 against us.[28]

[27] See Alistair Cooke, A Generation on Trial (New York: Alfred A. Knopf, 1950), pp. 8–10. Cooke concludes that "the House Committee . . . succeeded, before he ever came to trial, in making a large and very mixed public identify Hiss with what was characteristic of the New Deal." See also the interesting article by James Reston (N.Y. Times, June 9, 1949), discussing the role of Hiss as a New Deal symbol. In Witness, Chambers makes it plain that from 1939 on he regarded the New Deal as a revolutionary movement that differed from communism only in degree rather than in kind. See pp. 471–472.

[28] 96 Cong. Rec. 1007.

Stripling later spoke of "Alger Hiss, who sat with Roosevelt at Yalta when Poland and the rest of Eastern Europe were abandoned by the West, and the Far East was laid open to Communist aggression. . . ." [29]

Actually, during the heyday of the New Deal, Hiss was a minor government employee at best. It was only in the middle 1940's that he became at all prominent—as executive secretary of the Dumbarton Oaks Conference, as secretary general of the United Nations Charter Conference in San Francisco, as a subordinate figure in the United States delegation to the Yalta Conference, and, at the time of his retirement in 1946 from the government service, as director of the Office of Special Political Affairs in the Department of State. Even then, his positions were always just below those of first rank, and he was never a leading architect of American foreign policy or a top adviser of Roosevelt or Truman. [30] At the time when Chambers said Hiss had been engaging in espionage he was an assistant to Assistant Secretary of State Francis B. Sayre.

On the same day that Whittaker Chambers told his sensational story to the Un-American Activities Committee Alger Hiss wired the committee as follows:

My attention has been called by representatives of the press to statements made about me before your committee this morning by one Whittaker Chambers. I do not know Mr. Chambers and insofar as I am aware have never laid eyes on him. There is no basis for the statements made about me to your committee. I would appreciate it if you would make this telegram a part of your committee's record, and I would further appreciate the opportunity to appear before your committee to make these statements formally and under oath. I shall be in Washington on Thursday and hope that that will be a convenient time from the committee's point of view for me to appear. [31]

[29] *The Red Plot*, p. 15.

[30] James Reston has written (*N.Y. Times*, June 9, 1949): "Mr. Hiss . . . will undoubtedly continue to be portrayed as the man who sat at Franklin Roosevelt's right hand at Yalta, a great power in the direction of the nation's policy. This, of course, was not true. He did not make policy at Yalta. He was one of many technicians who did small jobs when he was told."

[31] *Communist Espionage Hearings*, pp. 585–586. It has been pointed out that, assuming Hiss's guilt, he acted at several points along the way as though he were subject to a psychic compulsion to destroy himself: (1) he sought an appearance before the Un-American Activities Committee; (2) he sued Whittaker Chambers for libel; (3) he ordered his attorneys to turn the documents produced by Chambers at the Baltimore pretrial deposition over to the Department of Justice; (4) he found the missing Woodstock typewriter and introduced it as evidence

Two days later he appeared before the committee as a voluntary witness. There was nothing equivocal about. Hiss's introductory statement. He said,

I am not and never have been a member of the Communist Party. I do not and never have adhered to the tenets of the Communist Party. I am not and never have been a member of any Communist-front organization. I have never followed the Communist Party line, directly or indirectly. To the best of my knowledge, none of my friends is a Communist. . . .

To the best of my knowledge, I never heard of Whittaker Chambers until in 1947, when two representatives of the Federal Bureau of Investigation asked me if I knew him and various other people, some of whom I knew and some of whom I did not know. I said I did not know Chambers. So far as I know, I have never laid eyes on him, and I should like to have the opportunity to do so.

. . . . .

Except as I have indicated, the statements made about me by Mr. Chambers are complete fabrications. I think my record in the Government service speaks for itself.[32]

Hiss did acknowledge varying acquaintances with several of the other persons whom Chambers had identified as members of the Washington apparatus, but he persisted in his statement that he did not know Whittaker Chambers. In answer to Stripling's question, "You say you have never seen Mr. Chambers?" Hiss replied, "The name means absolutely nothing to me, Mr. Stripling." [33] And then occurred the first of the committee's efforts to see whether Hiss could identify Chambers from a photograph:

Mr. Stripling: I have here, Mr. Chairman, a picture which was made last Monday by the Associated Press. I understand from people who knew Mr. Chambers during 1934 and '35 that he is much heavier today than he was at that time, but I show you this picture, Mr. Hiss, and ask you if you have ever known an individual who resembles this picture.

Mr. Hiss: I would much rather see the individual. I have looked at all the pictures I was able to get hold of in, I think it was, yesterday's paper which had the pictures. If this is a picture of Mr. Chambers, he is not particularly unusual looking. He looks like a lot of people. I might even mistake him for the chairman of this committee [Mundt]. [Laughter.]

Mr. Mundt: I hope you are wrong in that.

at his trials. Of course, it can be said he took each of these steps to strengthen his appearance as an innocent man. But the effect of each step was to bring him closer to final result—conviction in a federal court for the crime of perjury.
    [32] *Ibid.,* p. 643.   [33] *Ibid.,* p. 647.

Mr. Hiss: I didn't mean to be facetious but very seriously I would not want to take oath that I have never seen that man. I would like to see him and then I think I would be better able to tell whether I had ever seen him. Is he here today?

Mr. Mundt: Not to my knowledge.

Mr. Hiss: I hoped he would be.[34]

One gains a firm impression that at this first hearing the lawyer in Alger Hiss was very strong. He watched constantly for inaccuracies, correcting Mundt when the latter referred to seven members of the alleged apparatus and then named eight; he was careful not to state flatly that he had never known the man who called himself Whittaker Chambers, and he repeatedly answered questions with the qualifying phrase, "Not to the best of my knowledge." [35]

In spite of the wariness which frequently showed through in his testimony, Alger Hiss seems to have made a reasonably favorable impression upon the members of the committee at this first hearing. Representatives Mundt and Nixon both made statements toward the close of the hearing which indicated that they were at least entertaining the possibility that Chambers might be mistaken,[36] and at the close of the session Mundt, who had acted as chairman in Thomas'

[34] *Ibid.*, p. 647.

[35] *Ibid.*, p. 646. A further illustration of Hiss's wariness is seen in the following exchange:

"*Mr. Nixon:* Mr. Hiss, did you testify earlier that you did or did not know Mr. Ware?

"*Mr. Hiss:* I hadn't been asked the question. I did know Mr. Ware while I was in the Department of Agriculture." *Ibid.*, p. 652.

[36] "*Mr. Mundt:* It would seem that the testimony is diametrically opposed and it comes from two witnesses whom normally one would assume to be perfectly reliable. They have high positions in American business or organizational work. They both appear to be honest. They both testify under oath. Certainly the committee and the country must be badly confused about why these stories fail to jibe so completely.

"I think we have neglected to ask you, Mr. Hiss, one other possible clue to this situation. It could be that Mr. Chambers has mistaken you for your brother. Would you know if he would testify under oath whether your brother has ever belonged to any subversive organizations or is a Communist?" *Communist Espionage Hearings*, p. 650.

Representative Nixon suggested that a confrontation of the two men might reveal that this was a case of mistaken identity:

"*Mr. Chairman:* I think in justice to both of these witnesses and in order to avoid what might be a useless appearance on the part of Mr. Chambers, when arrangements are made for his being here, that the witnesses be allowed to confront each other so that any possibility of a mistake in identity may be cleared up. It may be that Mr. Chambers' appearance has changed through the years but

absence, stated: "The Chair wishes to express the appreciation of the Committee for your very co-operative attitude, for your forthright statements, and for the fact that you were first among those whose names were mentioned by various witnesses to communicate with us asking for an opportunity to deny the charges." [37]

Following these initial separate appearances of Chambers and Hiss, the committee held several further hearings in rapid order. The day after Hiss's first appearance a subcommittee again heard Chambers, this time in executive session. A week later, on August 16, Hiss was heard a second time, likewise in executive session. The next day in New York the two men were brought face to face for the first time, again in an executive session, and finally on August 25 occurred a public confrontation scene in Washington.[38]

The committee's purpose in the two separate executive sessions with Chambers and Hiss was to place each man under searching questioning concerning the area in conflict. At the session on August 7, Nixon subjected Chambers to quite rigorous cross-examination on the details of his alleged relationship with Hiss, and then on the sixteenth, Hiss was queried over much the same ground. The result was to re-establish the committee's confidence in Chambers' story, for he revealed a rather intimate knowledge of many aspects of Hiss's personal life which were later verified unconsciously by Hiss on the sixteenth. Among the points verified were the following:

1. Hiss was an amateur ornithologist and once saw a very rare prothonotary warbler.[39]

2. Hiss as a boy sold spring water in Baltimore.[40]

3. Timmy, Mrs. Hiss's son by an earlier marriage, was a difficult child.[41]

4. The Hisses had an "elderly Negro maid." [42]

5. The Hisses had an old Ford with a hand-operated windshield wiper. [43]

---

it is quite apparent that Mr. Hiss has not put on much weight. He must have been very thin before if he did.

"I think if there is mistaken identity on Mr. Chambers' part he will be able to recall it when he confronts Mr. Hiss." *Ibid.*, p. 651.

[37] *Ibid.*, p. 659.

[38] The testimony taken in the three executive sessions was made public by the committee on August 25 at the time of the public confrontation hearing.

[39] Chambers' testimony, *Communist Espionage Hearings*, p. 666; Hiss's verification, p. 961.

[40] *Communist Espionage Hearings*, pp. 668, 963.   [41] *Ibid.*, pp. 668, 943–944.

[42] *Ibid.*, pp. 665, 954. Partial verification only.   [43] *Ibid.*, pp. 666, 957, 959.

6. The Hisses acquired a new Plymouth.[44]

7. The Hisses took an auto trip through Pennsylvania with Chambers as a passenger.[45]

Among the other details of Hiss's private life recalled by Chambers, but not necessarily confirmed by Hiss, were the following: the Hisses had a cocker spaniel, a "very nondescript" library, ate only simple food, drank no liquor, had no piano, had a red leather cigarette box, had a double bed, Mrs. Hiss blushed easily, and Alger Hiss did not go to church.[46]

On the other hand, Chambers was not able to recall any of the pictures on the walls of the Hiss homes, any particular articles of furniture, or the patterns of the silverware or china. Moreover, Chambers did make certain positive statements that were not borne out by Hiss's testimony, and which seemingly have never been verified. The following discrepancies may be noted:

1. Chambers: Mr. and Mrs. Hiss were known within the family as "Hilly" and "Dilly." [47]

Hiss: Mr. Hiss was known as "Hilly," but Mrs. Hiss was known as "Pross" or "Prossy," never "Dilly." [48]

2. Chambers: The Hisses took Timmy out of an expensive private school and put him into a less expensive one so as to divert money Timmy's father was supplying for his education to the Communist Party.[49]

Hiss: Timmy was put into a more expensive school.[50]

3. Chambers: Hiss is deaf in one ear. ("*Mr. Mandel:* A picture of Hiss shows his hand cupped to his ear. *Mr. Chambers:* He is deaf in one ear. *Mr. Nixon:* Mr. Hiss is deaf in one ear? *Mr. Hébert:* Which ear? *Mr. Chambers:* I don't know. . . .") [51]

Hiss: Hiss is not deaf in one ear. ("*Mr. Stripling:* Are you hard of hearing in your left ear? *Mr. Hiss:* Not to my knowledge. *Mr. Stripling:* I noticed you had your hand up to your ear. *Mr. Hiss:* If I have

---

[44] *Ibid.,* pp. 666, 959.   [45] *Ibid.,* pp. 669, 964.

[46] *Ibid.,* p. 654 ff.   [47] *Ibid.,* pp. 664–665.

[48] *Ibid.,* p. 960. Chambers says in *Witness,* "In some instances his memory was better than mine as in the case of the name Dilly, which I presently realized he had not called his wife." (p. 580).

[49] *Communist Espionage Hearings,* p. 668.

[50] *Ibid.,* p. 962. Stripling ignored this failure of the Hiss and Chambers testimony to jibe completely when he later wrote, "Unknowingly, Hiss confirmed Chambers' assertion that he . . . had moved his stepson from one school to another. . . ." *The Red Plot,* p. 124.

[51] *Communist Espionage Hearings,* p. 668.

done that, it is only when I wanted to be sure I· was hearing.") [52]

It may also be noted that in the rigorous questioning to which Chambers was subjected on the seventh, almost no effort was made to have Chambers indicate evidence of any sort of close social or intellectual companionship between the two men. On one of the rare occasions when the questioning turned in this direction Chambers gave a rather weak answer:

Mr. Stripling: Did Mr. Hiss ever discuss with you his activities or his career at Harvard when he was an outstanding student?

Mr. Chambers: No; I don't think he did. He used to talk about the time when he was Justice Holmes' secretary.

Mr. Stripling: Do you remember anything he ever told you or said to you about his relationship with Justice Holmes?

Mr. Chambers: No, I am sorry. He told me a number of pretty good stories, but I can't remember good stories. He had several about the Justice.[53]

At the executive session with Hiss on August 16 an even more important development than Hiss's partial verification of Chambers' testimony concerning his personal life took place. This was Hiss's admission that he could conceivably have known Chambers under another name and that he had in mind a specific individual who had called himself "George Crosley," and who might prove to be the same man now calling himself "Whittaker Chambers." The Crosley story in Hiss's own words is as follows:

Mr. Hiss: I have written a name on this pad in front of me of a person whom I knew in 1933 and 1934 [54] who not only spent some time in my house but sublet my apartment. That man certainly spent more than a week, not while I was in the same apartment. I do not recognize the photographs as possibly being this man. If I hadn't seen the morning papers with an account of statements that he knew the inside of my house, I don't think I would even have thought of this name. I want to see Chambers face to face and see if he can be this individual. I do not want and I don't think I ought to be asked to testify now that man's name and everything I can remember about him. I have written the name on this piece of paper. I have given the name to two friends of mine before I came in this hearing. I can only repeat, and perhaps I am being overanxious about

[52] *Ibid.,* p. 958. Seemingly this point about Hiss's deafness was not checked further by the committee.

[53] *Ibid.,* p. 1261.

[54] Hiss, like Chambers, was prone to change some of the details of his story. He later placed George Crosley's first visit to his office in December, 1934, or January, 1935.

the possibility of unauthorized disclosure of testimony, that I don't think in my present frame of mind that it is fair to my position, my own protection, that I be asked to put down here of [sic] record personal facts about myself which, if they came to the ears of someone who had for no reason I can understand a desire to injure me, would assist him in that endeavor.

. . . . .

Mr. Hiss: . . . The name of the man I brought in—and he may have no relation to this whole nightmare—is a man named George Crosley. I met him when I was working for the Nye committee. He was a writer. He hoped to sell articles to magazines about the munitions industry.

I saw him, as I say, in my office over in the Senate office building, dozens of representatives of the press, students, people writing books, research people. It was our job to give them appropriate information out of the record, show them what had been put in the record. This fellow was writing a series of articles, according to my best recollection, free lancing, which he hoped to sell to one of the magazines. He was pretty obviously not successful in financial terms, but as far as I know, wasn't actually hard up.

Mr. Stripling: What color was his hair?

Mr. Hiss: Rather blondish, blonder than any of us here.

Mr. Stripling: Was he married?

Mr. Hiss: Yes, sir.

Mr. Stripling: Any children?

Mr. Hiss: One little baby, as I remember it, and the way I know that was the subleasing point. After we had taken the house on P Street and had the apartment on our hands, he one day in the course of casual conversation said he was going to specialize all summer in getting his articles done here in Washington, didn't know what he was going to do, and was thinking of bringing his family.

I said, "You can have my apartment. It is not terribly cool, but it is up in the air near the Wardman Park." He said he had a wife and little baby. The apartment wasn't very expensive, and I think I let him have it at exact cost. My recollection is that he spent several nights in my house because his furniture van was delayed. We left several pieces of furniture behind.

The P Street house belonged to a naval officer overseas and was partly furnished, so we didn't need all our furniture, particularly during the summer months, and my recollection is that definitely, as one does with a tenant trying to make him agreeable and comfortable, we left several pieces of furniture behind until the fall, his van was delayed, wasn't going to bring all the furniture because he was going to be there just during the summer, and we put them up 2 or 3 nights in a row, his wife and little baby.

. . . . .

Mr. Stripling: What kind of automobile did that fellow have?

Mr. Hiss: No kind of automobile. I sold him an automobile. I had an old Ford that I threw in with the apartment and had been trying to trade it in and get rid of it. I had an old, old Ford we had kept for sentimental reasons. We got it just before we were married in 1929.[55]

Previous to this admission Hiss had once more remained steadfast in his refusal to make positive identification of Chambers on the basis of photographs, although he was careful not to say that he had never seen or known the man whose picture he was being shown. The testimony concerning this matter was as follows:

Mr. Hiss: . . . Actually the face has a certain familiarity. I think I also testified to that.

It is not according to the photograph a very distinctive or unusual face. I would like very much to see the individual face to face. I had hoped that would happen before. I still hope it will happen today.

I am not prepared to say that I have never seen the man whose pictures are now shown me.

· · · · ·

Mr. Hiss: I don't want to suggest any innovations in your procedure, but I do want to say specifically that I do hope I will have an opportunity actually to see the individual.

· · · · ·

Mr. Hiss: . . . The face is definitely not an unfamiliar face. Whether I am imagining it, whether it is because he looks like a lot of other people, I don't know, but I have never known anyone who had the relationship with me that this man has testified to and that, I think, is the important thing here, gentlemen. This man may have known me, he may have been in my house. I have had literally hundreds of people in my house in the course of the time I lived in Washington.

· · · · ·

Mr. Hiss: Mr. Chairman, I hope you will not think I am being unreasonable when I say I am not prepared to testify on the basis of a photograph. On the train coming down this morning I searched my recollection of any possible person that this man could be confused with or could have got information from about me.

The Chairman: Then you are not prepared to testify on this subject from a photograph?

Mr. Hiss: I am not prepared to testify on the basis of a photograph. I would want to hear the man's voice.[56]

[55] *Communist Espionage Hearings,* pp. 948, 955–956, 957.
[56] *Ibid.,* pp. 940, 941, 946, 947.

There was plenty of drama at the private confrontation scene in New York on the seventeenth. Hiss entered the meeting in a definite state of irritation. In the first place, he was quite obviously provoked at being rushed, unawares, into a meeting with Chambers, for the committee had reached an agreement with him the day before that such a meeting would occur at a public session on August 25.[57] Secondly, the news of Harry White's death had just reached Hiss, and he clearly felt that the committee was responsible for this tragic event. Finally, he was annoyed that news concerning his session with the committee on the previous day had leaked into the press. On the sixteenth the committee had asked him whether he would be willing to submit to a lie-detector test. Hiss had demurred and asked for time to think it over. In spite of the fact that the committee itself had stressed the importance of keeping the proceedings confidential some member of the committee or of its staff had leaked the lie-detector story as well as other information concerning the hearing to the newspapers. It is just possible that the committee did its part to provoke Hiss's

[57] *Ibid.*, pp. 972, 973. The following exchange of remarks occurred at the beginning of the session on the seventeenth:

"*Mr. Hiss:* I was not notified by Mr. McDowell by wire or when he telephoned me that this would be the occasion of my having a chance to meet Mr. Chambers.

"*Mr. McDowell:* That is correct.

"*Mr. Hiss:* I had been told yesterday that the meeting would be in Washington on the 25th and that my opinion as to whether it should be public or not was of some interest to the committee, whether it would be a public confrontation.

"*Mr. McDowell:* That is correct. That is all part of the record."

.   .   .   .   .

"*The Chairman:* I want to say one thing. I think you knew yesterday when you began to tell about George Crosley that there was a very striking resemblance and you would probably be called in at a very early date.

"*Mr. Hiss:* That is a statement of your opinion for the record.

"*The Chairman:* Yes; naturally, for the record. You made your statement for the record.

"*Mr. Hiss:* Would you like me to say what my impression actually was?

"*The Chairman:* I am not interested in your impression. I am asking you if you didn't believe that you would be called much earlier than the 25th when you built up this Mr. Crosley?

"*Mr. Hiss:* I certainly did not. We talked about the 25th, Mr. Chairman, at the very conclusion of our meeting yesterday, and I think the record will so show."

.   .   .   .   .

"*Mr. Nixon:* Then you object to having had a confrontation? That is what you want the record to show?

"*Mr. Hiss:* I want the record to show the nature of the preliminary to this particular meeting. That is all." *Ibid.*, pp. 996, 997.

irritation on the theory that an angry man would let down his guard. Certainly Representative Nixon rushed into an exchange of angry remarks with Hiss at the first opportunity, and it was quite clear that the committee had decided that Hiss should be treated rather roughly at this session. Whether this was good investigating tactics is hard to say. The transcript of this Hiss-Chambers confrontation scene reads a bit like a Henry James story, for it is full of subtleties and ambiguities. On the substantive side some readers have found in the testimony convincing proof of Alger Hiss's basic innocence; others feel that there are unmistakable signs of a guilty man in Hiss's conduct. On the procedural side it is difficult to know whether the committee had carefully planned its tactics or whether it brought the two men together with no idea what would happen. In any event, attention was wholly concentrated on the personal side of the mystery.

When the two men were brought face to face, Hiss was seemingly prepared to identify Chambers as George Crosley immediately. He said almost at once, "I think he is George Crosley, but I would like to hear him talk a little longer." [58] Thereupon Chambers denied that he had ever been known as George Crosley, and Hiss began to hedge, saying, "I believe I am not prepared without further checking to take an absolute oath that he must be George Crosley." [59] And a little later he said, "If this man had said he was George Crosley, I would have no difficulty in identification. He denied it right here." [60] Then after a further exchange between the two men, Hiss was at last ready to make a positive identification: "Mr. Chairman, I don't need to ask Mr. Whittaker Chambers any more questions. I am now perfectly prepared to identify this man as George Crosley." [61] A few minutes later Hiss had become vehement in the certainty of the identification:

Mr. McDowell: Well, now, Mr. Hiss, you positively identify—
Mr. Hiss: Positively on the basis of his own statement that he was in my apartment at the time when I say he was there. I have no further question at all. If he had lost both eyes and taken his nose off, I would be sure.[62]

[58] *Ibid.,* p. 978. Nixon later described the actual instant at which the two men first came together in the same room: "During the time Mr. Chambers was entering the room, Mr. Hiss, who had said he would like to see this man who had made these charges against him, stared straight ahead. He did not turn around once to look at Mr. Chambers as he entered the room." 96 *Cong. Rec.* 1001.
[59] *Communist Espionage Hearings,* p. 979.
[60] *Ibid.,* p. 985.   [61] *Ibid.,* p. 986.   [62] *Ibid.,* p. 988.

Thereupon Hiss challenged Chambers to make the same accusations against him without privilege: "May I say for the record at this point, that I would like to invite Mr. Whittaker Chambers to make those same statements out of the presence of this committee without their being privileged for suit for libel. I challenge you to do it, and I hope you will do it damned quickly." [63]

At this point it is clear that the subcommittee regarded itself as a grand jury and that it was now prepared to return a true bill against Alger Hiss. It refused to request Chambers to answer Hiss's challenge, and for the remainder of the hearing the questions were directed almost entirely to Hiss and in a manner that was persistent and unfriendly.[64] The hearing ended on a sour note:

> *The Chairman:* Any more questions to ask of Mr. Hiss?
> *Mr. Nixon:* I have nothing.
> *The Chairman:* That is all. Thank you very much.
> *Mr. Hiss: I don't reciprocate.*
> *The Chairman:* Italicize that in the record.
> *Mr. Hiss:* I wish you would.[65]

The public confrontation scene on August 25 marked Alger Hiss's last appearance before the Un-American Activities Committee. Following the immediate identification of each man by the other, most of the day was devoted to careful questioning of Hiss concerning the details of his admitted relationship with "George Crosley," Chambers being questioned more briefly at the end of the day.[66] At the very beginning of the questioning Hiss protested the concern for detail which the questions revealed and insisted that the committee should deal with the larger issue as to whether he was a Communist.[67] And later

[63] *Ibid.*, p. 988. See note 31.

[64] *Ibid.*, pp. 988–1000. The reluctance of committee members to encourage Chambers to repeat his charges in an unprivileged forum is curious, to say the least. Later, even after Chambers had repeated his charges and had thereby set in motion the chain of events that was to lead to the production of the damaging documentary evidence that meant so much to the committee's case against Hiss, this reluctance persisted. As late as January, 1950, in a speech in the House of Representatives, Nixon was insisting that Chambers might properly have refused to repeat his charges, since by repetition in an unprivileged forum Chambers ran the risk of a libel suit. 96 *Cong. Rec.* 1001.

[65] *Communist Espionage Hearings*, p. 1001.

[66] The *Washington Post* (August 26, 1948) reported that Hiss was in the witness chair for six hours, and Chambers for one hour and forty minutes.

[67] "*Mr. Hiss:* The important issues, the important charges are not questions of leases, but questions of whether I was a Communist, and it was to try to get the issues raised that are the real issues—it seems to be topsy-turvy to be talking only

he indicated that he thought the committee should be searching his record as a public officer for substantive evidence of wrongdoing:

First, my record should be explored. It is inconceivable that there could have been on my part, during 15 years or more in public office, serving all three branches of the Government, judicial, legislative, and executive, any departure from the highest rectitude without its being known. It is inconceivable that the men with whom I was intimately associated during those 15 years should not know my true character far better than this accuser. It is inconceivable that if I had not been of the highest character, this would not have manifested itself at some time or other, in at least one of the innumerable actions I took as a high official, actions publicly recorded in the greatest detail.[68]

But the committee ignored these challenges and relentlessly queried Hiss on details, dwelling at length upon the weak spots in his story. This line of questioning revealed the committee at its efficient best. Its staff had obviously done a good detective job in running down the mechanical details of the Hiss story in the best FBI tradition. Moreover, the witness, Hiss, did not come out of this line of questioning in very good shape, for in the end he failed to explain away a number of discrepancies or weaknesses in his story. The following weaknesses may be noted:

1. Hiss's claim that on a strictly business-deal basis he leased an apartment to Crosley for several months in the summer of 1935 because he was moving to another place and the leases overlapped. Committee staff work revealed that the overlap was much briefer than Hiss had indicated and this tended to support Chambers' story that Hiss for personal reasons had housed him and his family for a brief period.

2. Hiss's claim that he threw in a 1929 Ford roadster as a part of the apartment deal in 1935 because he had acquired a new Plymouth as against Chambers' contention that Hiss later disposed of the Ford by arranging to have it given to some needy and deserving Communist. Committee staff work revealed that Hiss did not acquire the Plymouth until several months after the lease on the apartment expired and that a year later, in July, 1936, he sold the Ford to the Cherner Motor Company. Moreover, on the same day the Cherner

about leases, Mr. Nixon; in such a serious charge as this it seems to me we should be getting after the question of my record and what did people who worked closely and intimately with me think of me." *Communist Espionage Hearings,* p. 1088.
[68] *Ibid.*, p. 1162.

Motor Company transferred the car to William Rosen, who later refused to testify before the committee concerning the transaction on grounds of self-incrimination. Hiss's only explanation of this curious business in 1936 was that long after he had disposed of the Ford someone came to him and asked him to sign a transfer certificate and that he did so, having no reason to suppose that anything improper was taking place.[69] W. Marvin Smith, an attorney in the Department of Justice, who notarized the transfer certificate, committed suicide in October, 1948. Although no evidence has ever been brought to light that would suggest any connection between his death and the Hiss-Chambers case, Stripling asserts in his book that the car story "remains something of a mystery, deepened by the awful fact that the man who notarized the papers on the car's transfer either leaped or fell to a ghastly death from the top floor of the Justice Department in Washington." [70]

3. Hiss's inability then or later to name or find any other person who had ever known Chambers as "George Crosley."

4. Hiss's truculence about identifying Chambers by his photographs, when many other people agreed that they were reasonably good likenesses of the man. On the other hand, the committee's insistence on several different occasions that Hiss recognize Chambers —or George Crosley—from a photograph was from its own point of view a faulty procedure. An actual confrontation of the two men at the very first Hiss appearance before the committee would have been appropriate procedurally and would have made Hiss's evasive tactics concerning the photographs unnecessary and impossible.

5. The issue of how much Hiss told John Foster Dulles and others, about the charges against him at the time he was appointed president of the Carnegie Endowment for International Peace in December, 1946.

Hiss, at this hearing more than ever, qualified his answers. For example, on a point that was later to prove crucial to his interests, he testified as follows concerning the date of his last meeting with Crosley:

> Mr. Nixon: Mr. Hiss, when did you last see Crosley?
> Mr. Hiss: Are you talking about that individual there?

[69] Ibid., see pp. 1095, 1102–1107, 1122–1125.

[70] The Red Plot, p. 133. Drew Pearson has also stressed Smith's death, suggesting that, along with the deaths of Harry White and Laurence Duggan, it may have been related to the Hiss case. Washington Post, March 17, 1951.

Mr. Nixon: I am talking to you, and I am asking when did you last see Crosley.

Mr. Hiss: The man I knew as Crosley, I see over there now. What do you mean?

Mr. Nixon: Now, Mr. Hiss, I realize that you are trying to be facetious. It is a serious question. I am attempting to find out the terminal date of your acquaintanceship with Mr. Crosley. Now, when did you last see him during the thirties?

Mr. Hiss: Mr. Nixon, I have testified repeatedly that to the best of my recollection I think I must have last seen him sometime in 1935.

Mr. Nixon: In the fall of 1935?

Mr. Hiss: Whether it would be the fall or the summer, I am not absolutely confident of my recollection.

Mr. Nixon: Did you see him in 1936?

Mr. Hiss: Not to the best of my recollection, Mr. Nixon.

Mr. Nixon: Can you say positively that you did not see Crosley in 1936?

Mr. Hiss: It would be very difficult for me to say positively that I had not seen anybody in 1936. I do not believe I saw Crosley in 1936.

Mr. Nixon: But you are leaving open the possibility that you might have seen Crosley in 1936, do I understand you correctly?

Mr. Hiss: I think you understand me correctly.

Mr. Nixon: Now, how about 1937? Did you see Crosley in 1937?

Mr. Hiss: Not to the best of my recollection, and I would be confident that I did not. I would be absolutely confident that I did not see him at any time under the circumstances he has testified to.

Mr. Nixon: My question is: Are you positive you did not see Crosley in 1937?

Mr. Hiss: I am reasonably positive that I did not see or lay eyes on Crosley in 1937.

Mr. Nixon: Will you testify to the effect that you did not see him in 1937?

Mr. Hiss: I'll testify that to the best of my knowledge and recollection I did not.

Mr. Nixon: Then, you are leaving the implication that it is possible that you could have seen him in 1937.

Mr. Hiss: Mr. Nixon, it seems to me I must leave that implication. I cannot be sure that I did not see anybody—

Mr. Nixon: Did you see Crosley in 1938?

Mr. Hiss: I would like to reply exactly the same way to that. I feel confident I did not.

Mr. Nixon: But it is possible that you might have?

Mr. Hiss: It is certainly conceivable and possible.[71]

---

[71] *Communist Espionage Hearings,* pp. 1170–1171. There is a strong suggestion here that Nixon was trying to lay the basis for a perjury charge against Hiss.

Moreover, he showed a tendency to quibble and thereby to evade the main point of a dangerous question. For example:

> *Mr. Mundt:* When did you first conclude—because I was not present, I wasn't at that portion of the hearing—that instead of this Whittaker Chambers being a man about whom you knew nothing about, whom you had never seen, that perhaps he was a George Crosley with whom you had had a great many personal dealings? When did you first conclude that and why?
>
> *Mr. Hiss:* That question is, to say the least, a slightly loaded question. You talked about "a great many personal dealings."
>
> *Mr. Mundt:* Yes. You loaned him a car or gave it to him, and you loaned him your apartment or gave it to him, you loaned him money or you gave it to him, you entertained him in your home, you took him out to lunch. I think that stands as "a great many personal associations."
>
> *Mr. Hiss:* That is your privilege, Mr. Mundt.[72]

Notice should be taken of the testimony of one other witness who appeared before the committee during this first period. This is Adolf A. Berle, Jr., who had been Assistant Secretary of State at the time Chambers came to Washington in 1939 in an attempt to tell his story to governmental authorities. In general, Berle confirmed the main outlines of Chambers' story, which had also been corroborated by Isaac Don Levine, who had accompanied Chambers on his visit to Berle's home. But Berle's testimony disagreed with that of Levine in two important respects. In his appearance before the committee on August 18, the latter insisted that Chambers had made it clear to Berle in 1939 that the government employees, whom he named as members of a Communist cell, were actually members of the party and that they were engaging in espionage:

> *Levine:* . . . After dinner the three of us retired to Mr. Berle's study. It was a warm evening. We spent some time on the lawn talking. We returned back to the study, and Mr. Berle was making notes.
>
> I think probably between a half dozen and 10 sheets of notes were made by Mr. Berle while Mr. Chambers was opening up the insides of the State Department and various other departments in Washington where he had underground contacts who supplied him with documentary and confidential information for transmission to the Soviet Government.
>
> The picture which emerged by midnight was quite appalling to me,

---

In any case this exchange pointed the way for the later grand jury questioning of Hiss that did result in Hiss's indictment and trial for perjury.
[72] *Ibid.*, p. 1131.

and I think Mr. Berle was very much shaken by the various names of the Soviet agents that Mr. Chambers disclosed.

. . . . .

Mr. Nixon: Can you tell us whether the name of Alger Hiss was mentioned in that conversation with Mr. Berle?

Mr. Levine: Both Hiss brothers were mentioned. The name of Alger Hiss and the name of the other Hiss.[73]

Berle, on the other hand, gave the committee the impression that Chambers had told him only that these men were Communist sympathizers. He testified:

This was not, as [Chambers] put it, any question of espionage. There was no espionage involved in it. He stated that their hope merely was to get some people who would be sympathetic to their point of view. With that in mind apparently a study group of some sort had been formed of men who were interested in knowing something about Russia and Russian policy and the general Communist theory of life, and so on. . . .

He said that these men, it was hoped, would go, as they called it, "underground"; that is to say, that they would not appear as part of the well-known or open Communist group, but that they would simply be there and be sympathetic.

In one respect, what he told me omitted something that he has told you: He did not make the direct statement that any of these men were members of the Communist Party. They were apparently, from what I then gathered, men who were sympathetic to their general point of view and to whom they might have access and perhaps a sympathetic approach in case anybody brought a request there.

. . . . .

And I must add that Chambers did not state to me that he was a member of the Communist Party. . . .[74]

In his appearances before the committee during the August phase of the hearings Chambers never referred directly to any specific acts of espionage. In his first reference to the meeting with Berle he suggested only that he told Berle that Hiss and other government employees were Communists.[75] It was only in December that Chambers told the committee that he had definitely included the espionage angle in the story he told Berle in 1939.[76] The notes which Berle took on the 1939 meeting were introduced as evidence in the second Hiss trial, and they tend to suggest that Chambers had specifically accused

[73] *Ibid.,* pp. 1007, 1008.   [74] *Ibid.,* pp. 1293, 1297–1298.
[75] *Ibid.,* pp. 580–582.   [76] *Ibid.,* Part Two, p. 1422.

Hiss of party membership and that espionage had been mentioned during the course of the interview.[77] Berle's memory served him badly in another respect. In answering Stripling's question as to what he did about the information that Chambers had supplied him with, he stated that he checked on "the two Hiss boys, first," and that when Dean Acheson became Assistant Secretary of State and "Alger Hiss became his executive assistant," he checked with Acheson. Berle continued, "Acheson said that he had known the family and these two boys from childhood and he could vouch for them absolutely. I further checked and found that Mr. Justice Frankfurter would give them an exactly similar endorsement." [78] Actually, Alger Hiss was never Acheson's assistant. Acheson became Assistant Secretary of State in 1941, and Donald Hiss served as his assistant. Alger Hiss was, from 1936 to 1939, assistant to Francis Sayre, who was also an Assistant Secretary of State.

As a matter of hindsight the most striking point about these various accounts of the Berle-Chambers-Levine meeting in 1939 is the specific assertion by Levine before the committee on August 18 that Chambers told Berle that he had "had underground contacts who supplied him with documentary and confidential information for transmission to the Soviet Government." [79] Later in August, at a press conference in New York City, Levine was reported as stating that Chambers had told Berle "how confidential papers were taken from State Department files, microfilmed and returned, copies being then delivered by Mr. Chambers to New York for shipment to Russia or given to other Soviet couriers in Washington." [80] The committee may, perhaps, be pardoned for not having taken Levine with complete seriousness. As something of a professional anti-Communist, Levine had cried wolf so many times that committee members might properly have discounted his testimony. But, the fact remains that from the point of view of its own standards and goals the most serious shortcoming in the committee's handling of the August phase of the Communist espionage hearings was its failure to draw from its leading witness, Whittaker Chambers, information concerning the espionage angle of his relations with members of the Communist cell in Washington. Here on August 18 was a lead that the committee might well have tried to follow more carefully than it did. To be sure, the committee did set in motion a series of developments which was

[77] *U.S. v. Alger Hiss*, Transcript of Record, VI, 3325.
[78] *Communist Espionage Hearings*, p. 1294.
[79] *Ibid.*, p. 1007.   [80] *N.Y. Times*, Sept. 1, 1948.

to lead in December to the revelation of the Baltimore deposition papers and the Pumpkin Papers. But it is hard to avoid the conclusion that had Nixon, Mundt, and Stripling been as vigorous in their questioning of Chambers as they were of Hiss during the first phase of the hearings, Chambers would have found it difficult to remain silent about the espionage phase of his story.[81]

During the questioning of Berle on August 30 occurred one of the committee's few efforts to probe for substantive evidence that communism had influenced Alger Hiss's actions as a government officer. The following exchange between Stripling and Berle took place:

Mr. Stripling: . . . I am going to ask you if at any time when you were in the State Department, did Mr. Hiss ever do anything, whether it was on a policy level or on a minor level—did he ever do anything that would arouse any suspicion on your part as one of the two top administrators and officials of the Department of State which would lead you to believe that he might be either sympathetic to the Communist Party or that he might be, shall we say, serving the interest of the Soviet Union or the Communist Party?

I know that is a long statement, long question, but what I would like to know is: Were you ever at any time suspicious of Mr. Hiss?

Mr. Berle: A better way of saying it is: I was worried. I ought to say, begin by confessing a prejudice here so that you can discount whatever I say here.

As I think many people know, in the fall of 1944 there was a difference of opinion in the State Department. I felt that the Russians were not going to be sympathetic and cooperative. Victory was then assured, though not complete, and the intelligence reports which were in my charge, among other things, indicated a very aggressive policy and not at all in line

---

[81] It is interesting to reread Chambers' testimony on his first appearance before the committee on August 3 concerning his meeting with Berle with this problem of the unrevealed information about espionage in mind. Up to this point emphasis in the questioning of Chambers had been placed upon securing from him the names of the members of the Communist cell in the government service. When he mentioned the meeting with Berle he was being questioned by Nixon, and Nixon's first interest was in finding out whom Chambers had named to Berle as members of the group. At the point where it is just possible that a question might have been put to Chambers that would have begun to get at the issue of what he had told Berle his relation with these men had been, McDowell, in characteristic fashion, interrupted to ask whether this was "the A. A. Berle who became an Ambassador to one of the South American countries," and Chambers, perhaps sensing a feeling of antagonism on the part of McDowell and Rankin toward Berle, came to the latter's defense, insisting that he was "an anti-Communist." *Communist Espionage Hearings,* pp. 580–582.

with the kind of cooperation everyone was hoping for, and I was pressing for a pretty clean-cut show-down then when our position was strongest.

The opposite group in the State Department was largely the men—Mr. Acheson's group, of course, with Mr. Hiss as his principal assistant in the matter. Whether that was a difference on foreign policy—and the question could be argued both ways; it wasn't clean-cut—was a problem, but at that time Mr. Hiss did take what we would call today the pro-Russian point of view.

Now that was reason for worry. It is not necessarily a reason to draw the conclusion that he was a disloyal man because many people were quite loyal, including a good many of the Army officers who felt the Russian Army would be important in case of an invasion of Japan and that by consequence it was desirable not to raise any issues until later.

I say that in Mr. Hiss' defense, although I got trimmed in that fight, and, as a result, went to Brazil, and that ended my diplomatic career. I mention that, because I did have a biased view. . . .

Yet, in general it was true during that period Mr. Hiss was all for cooperation with Russia. This was also the policy during the war, and at the time when the question was raised as to whether we ought not to begin tightening up. He may have been right objectively. I don't know. I disagreed.[82]

On August 27, while participating in a radio program, Whittaker Chambers met Alger Hiss's challenge and repeated his charge that Hiss had been a member of the Communist Party while an employee of the federal government. Chambers stated, "Alger Hiss was a Communist and may still be one." By this action Chambers started a chain reaction that was to lead to the sensational second phase of the espionage hearings in December, 1948, and to culminate over a year later in.the conviction of Alger Hiss in a federal court for the crime of perjury. In spite of his challenge Hiss took several weeks making up his mind to sue Chambers for slander. It was not until September 27, after being prodded by such a friendly newspaper as the *Washington Post* for his inaction, that Hiss sued Chambers in the federal district court in Baltimore for $75,000.[83] Thereafter, as the attention of the American people turned to the impending presidential election, and while attorneys busied themselves in Baltimore with the taking of depositions the case dropped out of sight. Then

[82] *Ibid.*, pp. 1296–1297. The statement that Hiss was Acheson's principal assistant is the same point on which Mr. Berle was in error before, since, presumably, he is referring to Alger Hiss. Mr. Acheson's assistant was Donald Hiss.

[83] Editorial, Sept. 4, 1948. Hiss sued Sept. 27 for $50,000. On October 8 he sued for the additional $25,000 because of allegedly slanderous remarks made by Chambers at the time the suit was filed on the 27th.

came the sensational turn. On November 17, while being questioned by a Hiss attorney in Baltimore, Chambers was asked whether he had any evidence that would corroborate his charges against Hiss. Chambers is reported to have answered, "Only these" and to have produced a batch of papers which he said were copies of documents that had been stolen from the State Department by Hiss early in 1938 and given to Chambers for transmission to Soviet agents. The attorneys were so stunned by this development that they called in federal Judge W. Calvin Chestnut, and a decision was made to turn the papers over to the Department of Justice.[84]

There has been much speculation as to why Chambers took this sudden step of producing vital evidence which he had so long withheld. One widely accepted explanation is that the Hiss lawyers had subjected Mrs. Chambers to vigorous treatment during the pretrial hearings and that Chambers, angered, had reacted by producing the documents.[85] Bert Andrews, Washington correspondent of the *New*

[84] *N.Y. Herald Tribune*, Dec. 4, 1948. Story by Bert Andrews. Alger Hiss later stated that he "directed" his attorneys to "place" the documents "before the Department of Justice" (*N.Y. Times*, Dec. 4, 1948). See note 31. Chambers' nephew by marriage, Nathan L. Levine, told the committee, Dec. 10, that Chambers had given a sealed envelope to him for safekeeping some ten years earlier, and that about the middle of November, 1948, Chambers had come to him for the envelope. During the ten-year period it had remained untouched on top of a linen closet in a dumb-waiter shaft in Levine's mother's home. Levine testified that when Chambers opened the envelope "he uttered an exclamation to me which I don't remember the exact words—it was either 'holy cow' or some exclamation, 'I didn't think that this still existed,' or 'was still in existence.' " *Communist Espionage Hearings, Part Two*, pp. 1454, 1456.

[85] Stripling tells this version of the story as follows:
"Then a Hiss attorney, during a pre-trial examination of Mrs. Chambers in Baltimore, in which district Hiss had lodged his slander suits against Chambers, made a historic blunder.

"What he said to Mrs. Chambers may never be known. Whatever was said outraged Chambers, a man normally slow to anger. As he said later to Representative Nixon, a fellow Quaker:

" 'You will understand this. When I testified before the Committee last August I wanted to expose the Communist conspiracy, but I did not want to destroy the humans involved. I sat for a whole day in meditation, as to what I should do. Finally I came to the conclusion that I could go just so far, and achieve exposure without destroying the families of the people involved.

" 'But after my testimony they spread stories that I was insane and that I was a pervert.

" 'Then they called in my wife and were very rough with her. It made me angry. I know as a Quaker I must never act in anger. So I sat for another day, and I came to the conclusion that the only thing to do was to tell everything I

York Herald Tribune, who followed the Hiss-Chambers case very closely, has written, "Another part [of Chambers' motive in producing the documents] lay in the fact that he did not believe the revelations he had previously made were being studied on a non-political basis with the sole objective of getting at the truth." [86] Another explanation is that Chambers' failure to produce the papers earlier was part of his deliberate policy of telling only part of what he knew, either because of a sincere desire, as he himself put it, not to hurt people more than was necessary, or because of the necessity of protecting his own restored reputation. Confronted at last by the possibility that Hiss might win the slander suit, he was compelled to tell the whole story and produce corroborative evidence. In an executive session on December 5 Chambers made the following statement concerning his motives in withholding the documentary evidence for so long a time:

> I returned to New York after my conversation with Berle, believing that a full investigation would be pushed, that I would give all possible help to that investigation, and that the espionage angle would certainly be developed. I heard nothing more of the matter for at least 2 years.
>
> After that lapse of time another very important factor in an ex-Communist mind began to have full play, and I sought in my testimony to do two things: My one purpose was to destroy the Communist conspiracy or to stop its activities. My other purpose was to do no more injury than necessary to the human elements involved.
>
> Most of the men in the Communist underground apparatus were men of high type, some of them widely recognized for intelligence and ability. They had been my friends. I had been in their homes and knew their wives and children whose faces I could remember. Very important to an ex-Communist is the question of other Communists breaking with the Communist Party. Breaking with the Communist Party is not an easy matter. It takes strength of purpose, and it takes, above all, time for reversing the pattern of a lifetime and the consequences may be dire. Time is the essence of such a break, and I desired to give these people an opportunity to make their own break, damaged as little as possible by me.[87]

---

knew, to spare no one. This thing must be stopped. Look what they're doing in China and Eastern Europe. We've got to know what we're confronted with in this country.' " *The Red Plot,* pp. 140–141.

[86] *N.Y. Herald Tribune,* Dec. 8, 1948.

[87] *Communist Espionage Hearings, Part Two,* p. 1422. At the first Hiss trial Chambers testified that he produced the documents in the libel suit because his attorney said "that I had practically no other choice." *Washington Post,* June 9, 1949.

There was no immediate revelation to the public of this development. However, on the first day of December two contradictory stories appeared in the press. That day the United Press sent out a news story that the Justice Department was about to abandon its investigation of the Hiss-Chambers affair, which it had been conducting since the August developments. As carried in the *New York Times* the story ran, "The Justice Department investigation of the Hiss-Chambers affair is about to die for lack of evidence, it was disclosed today. Unless something new turned up soon, officials said, there would be little use going to a grand jury with the information obtained so far." [88] The same day a Washington columnist reported, "Since Alger Hiss sued Whittaker Chambers for libel, attorneys for both men have been taking detailed depositions from witnesses, including the two principals. Some very startling information on who is a liar is reported to have been uncovered." [89] In the meantime, according to Stripling, members of the Un-American Activities Committee staff had been receiving hints from friendly newspapermen, from Chambers' lawyers, and from Chambers himself, concerning these developments.[90] On December 1 Stripling questioned Chambers at his Maryland farm. Chambers seemingly told him that he had turned over evidence that "was highly important" but that "he would be in contempt of court if he discussed [with them] what he had submitted at Baltimore." [91] Early in the morning of December 3, using a subpoena that Nixon had ordered served on Chambers, staff members went to the latter's home, and he produced the famous microfilms which he had placed for safekeeping in a hollowed-out pumpkin on his farm in Maryland. The so-called Pumpkin Papers, which were the prints developed from these films, were entirely separate from the documents that Chambers had turned over to the lawyers at the pretrial hearing in Baltimore.[92] On

[88] Dec. 2, 1948 (UP). The entire text of the UP story as carried in the *Washington Daily News* (Dec. 1, 1948) is reproduced in the committee's final report, *Soviet Espionage, Second Rept.*, Dec. 31, 1948, p. 4.

[89] *Washington Post*, Dec. 1, 1948 (column by Jerry Kluttz, "The Federal Diary").

[90] See Stripling, *The Red Plot*, pp. 141 ff.

[91] *Soviet Espionage, Second Rept.*, Dec. 31, 1948, p. 5. Chambers has written in *Witness* that when Stripling came to his farm he asked him whether he still had some evidence that he had not presented in the libel suit. Chambers writes, "I shook my head," but he implies that he conveyed the opposite impression and that Stripling served a subpoena duces tecum on him the next day because [Stripling] had "read my eyes correctly the night before" (pp. 751–752, 754).

[92] In the end there were three types of documents: (1) photographs of original

December 4 the committee made public the facts about its possession of the microfilms, and the story was out. In its ultimate form this story was to the effect that, beginning in the early part of 1935 and continuing until April, 1938, Chambers had been receiving confidential government documents from his collaborators in the government service for microfilming and transmission to the Soviet Union. In its final report on the Communist espionage hearings the committee stated Chambers had testified "that during the 2 years previous to the receipt of this particular batch of documents [which represented 'only 1 week's supply of information and a very small proportion of the total volume which Chambers had transmitted to the Soviet Union'] he had been running a veritable espionage production line out of the State Department and other departments of the Government, the output of which was being funneled to Moscow by way of a skillfully run transmission belt." [93]

The House committee accomplished two things at this point: (1) It obtained from Chambers important corroborative evidence in addition to that already in the possession of the Department of Justice. Why the department had not taken steps to find out whether Chambers had any such additional evidence has never been explained. (2) It "broke" the story. There is no reason to suppose that the Department of Justice would not ultimately have taken some sort of action on the basis of the Baltimore deposition papers that had been turned over to it. Indeed, the action of the House committee in forcing the story out in the open may well have interfered with the department's investigations in the case. But the fact remains that the department had not succeeded in securing the additional microfilms, and there are those who will always suspect that the department was actually contemplating no action at all. [94]

State Department documents (the microfilms or "Pumpkin Papers"); (2) typewritten copies or paraphrases of original documents (Baltimore deposition papers typed on the Woodstock); (3) handwritten memoranda (Baltimore deposition papers in Hiss' hand).

At the Hiss trials the government contended that Hiss had first brought documents to Chambers for photographing but that this had later been abandoned for a system whereby Hiss took documents home overnight and Mrs. Hiss made typed copies of them for delivery to Chambers. The memoranda were alleged to be in Hiss' handwriting, and Hiss himself acknowledged that three of them "looked like his." See Cooke, A Generation on Trial, p. 111.

[93] Soviet Espionage, Second Rept., pp. 6–7.

[94] In his speech to the House of Representatives, January 26, 1950, Nixon made it clear that he was convinced of the existence of an administration conspiracy

In any case, things moved very fast thereafter. Nixon had departed on a trip to Panama by steamship. But with the sensational new developments he was removed from the ship in spectacular fashion by a Coast Guard plane and flown back to Washington, where he arrived on December 5. The next day, while both Hiss and Chambers were appearing before the grand jury in New York, Nixon held a press conference in Washington at which he read passages from the Chambers testimony given during the deposition proceedings in Baltimore in which Chambers charged that Hiss had supplied him with the State Department documents. Nixon added that three of

---

to suppress the fact that documentary evidence of the theft of papers from the State Department had been turned over to the Justice Department (96 *Cong. Rec.* 1005–1006). But this theory is a dubious one. How could the administration have expected that Chambers would remain quiet in the face of indefinite inaction by the Justice Department? And the existence of the documents must inevitably come out at the time of the libel trial.

The whole sequence of events at this point is curious, to say the very least. Chambers produces certain typed copies of State Department documents at the libel suit deposition but withholds the more damaging microfilm rolls which contained photographs of actual documents. The deposition papers are turned over to the Department of Justice, and it seemingly has no suspicions that there may be additional evidence in Chambers' possession. Word of these developments leaks to the House committee and it is instantly suspicious that Chambers can supply additional evidence. The query is obvious: Did Chambers deliberately withhold the microfilms so that he could give them to the House committee if it suited his purposes to reopen the investigative phase of his case against Hiss?

On this point Drew Pearson has written that Stripling telephoned Chambers following the appearance of the Kluttz column, Dec. 1, and asked Chambers to come to Washington to see him. Pearson states, "Chambers, an old friend, did so, and promised to get some additional documents for the Un-American Activities Committee." *Washington Post*, Dec. 16, 1948.

On the other hand, Cabell Phillips' version is as follows: "Members of the committee, however, did question Chambers about [the Baltimore papers]. A chance remark of his led to the suspicion that he had still more. When he refused either to admit or deny this the committee obtained a blanket subpoena—just on a hunch—and the microfilms were brought out of their pumpkin-patch hiding place." *N.Y. Times*, Dec. 19, 1948.

Chambers threw considerable light upon these obscure points when his autobiography, *Witness*, was published in May, 1952. He says that he withheld the microfilms when he submitted the typed documents to the lawyers at the deposition hearings because "at the level of conscious motive" he did not know what the films contained or whether they had any bearing on the Hiss case. He states that he planned to try to develop the films himself to see what they contained. But he adds:

"No act of mine was more effective in forcing into the open the long-smothered Hiss Case than my act in dividing the documentary evidence against

the Baltimore documents were in Hiss' handwriting and were now in the House committee's possession.[95]

On December 7 the House committee reopened its hearings, and on five days between December 7 and 14 it heard ten witnesses— three of whom were its own investigators. The committee had the microfilms and seemingly the Baltimore documents, too, but it lacked the main performers in the drama. Both Hiss and Chambers had immediately been placed under subpoena for new appearances before the federal grand jury in New York. There followed several days of bitter acrimony between the committee and federal law enforcement officials as to whether the proceedings before the grand jury should have priority or whether the committee might conduct hearings simultaneously. Nixon's action, on the sixth, in making public Chambers' deposition testimony charging that Hiss had given him the State Department documents was a most improper procedure, for it came close to usurping the function of the New York grand jury and prejudicing its findings.

The committee finally agreed to let the grand jury have access to the microfilms and to defer any effort to bring the principals in the case back to its witness stand until the grand jury had had a chance to take action. On December 5 a subcommittee had managed to gain possession of Chambers in New York and had taken further testi-

Hiss, introducing the copied State Department documents into the pre-trial examination (which, in effect, meant turning them over to the Justice Department), and placing the microfilms, separately, in the pumpkin. It was my decisive act in the Case. For when the second part of the divided evidence, the microfilm, fell into the hands of the Committee, it became impossible ever again to suppress the Hiss Case" (p. 742).

[95] *Washington Post*, Dec. 7, 1948. How Nixon obtained Chambers' Baltimore testimony and the Baltimore documents (or copies of them) is not entirely clear. The *Post* story on the 7th suggested that the testimony had been obtained from Chambers' lawyer by subpoena. The *New York Times* (Dec. 19, 1948) implied that Chambers had supplied the committee with the Baltimore documents. But these must have been copies of the originals, for the originals had presumably been turned over to the Department of Justice shortly after Chambers had produced them on November 17. Since Nixon had helped question Chambers in New York on the evening of December 5, the information he made public in the Washington press conference on the 6th may well have come to him from Chambers. At a committee hearing on December 7 Stripling also stated that the deposition data had been obtained by subpoena from Chambers' lawyer. *Communist Espionage Hearings, Part Two*, p. 1388. In *Witness* Chambers states that his lawyers had made photostats of the typed documents before introducing them at the deposition hearings (p. 738). Thus it would have been easy enough for Chambers to have supplied the committee with copies of the Baltimore papers.

mony from him in executive session. At this session Chambers named Henry Julian Wadleigh as a second State Department source from whom he had received documents and also indicated that some of the microfilm documents in the committee's possession might have come from Wadleigh rather than Hiss. This testimony as read into the record on December 9 during the questioning of Wadleigh in a public hearing ran as follows:

Mr. Nixon [addressing Chambers]: The documents you are now examining are all documents from the State Department, they bear the stamp "State Department, Assistant Secretary of State."

Mr. Chambers: Yes. I should think from the nature of these documents which I have examined they were turned over to me by Alger Hiss. . . . There was, however, another active source in the State Department, Mr. Julian Wadleigh, who was in the Trade Agreements Division of the State Department and it is possible some of these documents were from him.[96]

On December 9 Wadleigh appeared before the committee in Washington but refused to answer all questions pertaining to Chambers' accusation against him, on the ground of self-incrimination. However, Wadleigh shortly decided to confess, and, as he told the story in later syndicated newspaper articles, he appeared before the grand jury in New York the next day and verified Chambers' charges against him.[97] Wadleigh later appeared as a witness during the Hiss trials and testified that he had transmitted between 400 and 500 State Department papers to Chambers and another Soviet agent in 1936 and 1937. Chambers said he had also had a contact in the National Bureau of Standards and one in the Army Proving Ground at Aberdeen, Maryland (identified as Franklin V. Reno), who had supplied him with restricted data.[98] On December 20, Representative

[96] *Ibid.*, p. 1433. At the two Hiss trials Chambers denied that any of the Baltimore or microfilm documents had come to him from Wadleigh, although at the second trial he held open the possibility that one of them had been obtained from Harry White (Cooke, *A Generation on Trial*, pp. 319–321). Chambers' testimony at the second trial that one of the papers may have come from White was perhaps influenced by the discovery of an FBI typewriter expert that one of the Baltimore documents had not been typed on the Hiss Woodstock typewriter. See *N.Y. Times*, Dec. 8, 1949.

[97] The Wadleigh articles appeared in the *Washington Post*, July 24, 31, August 7 and 14, 1949.

[98] *N.Y. Times*, Dec. 20, 21, 1948, and June 10, 1949; *Washington Post*, June 10, 1949. On November 13, 1951, Reno was indicted by a federal grand jury in Baltimore on a charge of having concealed former membership in the Communist Party when he answered a federal loyalty questionnaire in November, 1948. *N.Y. Times*, Nov. 14, 1951.

Mundt, who served as acting chairman of the Un-American Activities Committee all during this second phase of the Communist espionage hearings (J. Parnell Thomas having been indicted on November 8 on the charge of having compelled members of his office staff to "kick back" their salaries to him in violation of federal law), announced that the committee would make no further effort to hold public hearings in the Hiss case. His statement made it clear that the committee at last saw the impropriety of conducting hearings paralleling criminal proceedings in a federal court. Mundt's concern was that the interests of the prosecution might be adversely affected. He said, "The committee has no desire to hold hearings which might prejudice the case. We recognize that when a case reaches the criminal stage, the evidence of the prosecution should not be pre-exposed. The defense should build its own case." [99]

On December 15, on the final day of its eighteen-month life, the grand jury indicted Alger Hiss for perjury on two counts, charging that in his testimony before it he had perjured himself when he denied turning over any documents to Chambers and when he said that he never saw Chambers after January 1, 1937. This action brought to an end any immediate possibility of further public hearings by the committee with Chambers or Hiss as witnesses. However, committee agents continued to question Chambers at length in private sessions. Just as the year ended it was reported that Mundt and Nixon had had a secret five-hour interview with Chambers and that he had given them new leads "sufficiently numerous to keep investigators busy for from six months to a year." [100]

In the meantime the committee had been squeezing the last ounce of publicity value out of the documentary evidence in its possession. On December 7 it called as witnesses Sumner Welles, who had been Under Secretary of State at the time the documents had been taken from the State Department, and John Peurifoy, currently Assistant Secretary of State in charge of administration. Both men were shown certain of the documents, and each testified concerning their great importance and indicated that in his opinion it would still be prejudicial to the nation's interest to make certain of them public. Both men also stated that possession of these documents by foreign agents would have enabled them to break the various codes in which they had originally been transmitted as dispatches.[101]

[99] *N.Y. Times,* Dec. 21, 1948.   [100] *Ibid.,* Dec. 30, 1948.
[101] For example:
"*Mr. Stripling:* I shall now ask Mr. Welles if he will read this document care-

In its first statements to the press the committee gave the impression that the contents of the Pumpkin Papers were so important and confidential that it was unlikely that many of them would ever be made public. For example, on December 8, Representative Mundt was reported as having stated, "Out of the ones we have studied out of more than two hundred documents we have not yet found a single one that can be published without impairing national security or interests. True, we have not yet had time to examine them all." [102] However, committee members were not above using the documents to suit their own political purposes. On the eleventh Nixon was reported as having "charged that one of the stolen government documents . . . indicated that in 1937 and 1938 certain decisions in foreign policy were influenced by considerations of political strategy in the approaching 1940 Presidential elections." [103] And the next day he was reported as having added that this document "reflects only the fact that the major consideration of foreign policy in 1937 and 1938 was the effect that it would have on the 1940 election." [104]

---

fully and tell the committee whether or not the national security would be violated in his opinion, by the reading of this document into the public record.

"*Mr. Welles:* Mr. Chairman, after reading this message, it is my conviction that without regard to the interests of any individual, or any other interest, the publication at this time of this message would be prejudicial to the Nation's interests." *Communist Espionage Hearings, Part Two,* p. 1387.

And:

"*Mr. Stripling:* Would the possession of the document as translated, along with the original document as it appeared in code, furnish an individual with the necessary information to break the code?

"*Mr. Welles:* In my judgment, decidedly yes." *Ibid.,* p. 1388.

Peurifoy's testimony on the code-breaking point was made in executive session. *N.Y. Times,* Dec. 8, 1948.

[102] *N.Y. Herald Tribune,* Dec. 8, 1948.   [103] *Ibid.,* Dec. 11, 1948.

[104] *Washington Post,* Dec. 12, 1948. Presumably Nixon is referring to "Exhibits 79 and 80" (following the numbering system used by the House committee in *Soviet Espionage within the United States Government: Second Report,* pp. 91–92). This is a long letter dated December 31, 1937, and addressed to Harry C. Hawkins, chief of the Trade Agreements Division of the Department of State, which was prepared by Charles F. Darlington, assistant chief of the same agency, and which comments on a German Aide Memoire submitted to the State Department in October, 1937. The Aide Memoire had indicated that Germany would like to enter into negotiations looking toward the drafting of a trade agreement with the United States. The Darlington letter looked with favor upon the undertaking of such negotiations but pointed out that the political effect of such relations with Nazi Germany might be bad in the United States and suggested that nothing be attempted until after the 1938 election. See *N.Y. Times,* Dec. 17, 1948.

The line that the documents were too important to be made public was not long adhered to by the committee. On the eleventh it was announced that twelve of the documents would be made public the following day and that the State Department had cleared sixty for further release. On the fourteenth the committee stated it would ultimately make public all but about four of the papers that had come into its possession. Thereafter, the papers were released in batches over a period of days. There can be little doubt that the committee used this piecemeal method of releasing the documents as a means of maximizing public attention upon its achievement in obtaining the documents in the first place. It has been widely predicted, following President Truman's spectacular victory in the November election, that the Un-American Activities Committee would be either abolished outright when the 81st Congress convened in January or allowed to wither on the vine.[105] Now the committee had scored a great coup in its running battle with the President, and it was clear that the members of the committee were determined to make the most out of this favorable turn of events. For example, on the thirteenth, after the first batch of documents had been released, Nixon was reported to have expressed confidence that the 81st Congress would support the committee: "He said that 'President Truman's first defeat in the new Congress will come January 3 when his people try to abolish the committee.'"[106]

In all, the committee finally released fifty documents, which covered in their original format 117 pages. Forty-three of the documents (sixty-five pages) were Baltimore deposition papers; seven documents (fifty-two pages) were microfilm Pumpkin Papers.[107]

In the opening words of its final report on Soviet espionage in the

---

No trade agreement with Nazi Germany was ever negotiated. (See also the story by Ferdinand Kuhn, Jr., *Washington Post*, Dec. 17, 1948.)

[105] For example, William S. White (*N.Y. Times*, Nov. 14, 1948), said, "The House Committee on Un-American Activities, as it is now known and as it has proceeded for two embittered years, was stricken, probably mortally, in the election returns."

[106] *N.Y. Herald Tribune*, Dec. 13, 1948.

[107] The documents are reproduced in photostat form in the report of December 31, 1948, *Soviet Espionage within the United States Government: Second Report*. The word "document" is used very loosely throughout all of the committee statements and news stories of this period. Seemingly, each page of the original deposition and Pumpkin Papers was viewed as a "document," although in many instances a document in the usual sense of the word consisted of two or

United States, the Un-American Activities Committee asserts, "Communist espionage has broken through the security forces of the United States Government and made off with secret information of both military and diplomatic character concerning our national plans, policies, and actions." [108] In this entirely accurate statement the committee points to its own achievement, for had it not been for the work of the committee it is doubtful that any such statement of fact ever could have been made. Marquis Childs, certainly no admirer of the committee, wrote in his syndicated column soon after the documents were released, "the overwhelming fact is that secret documents have been taken from the Government's files and the transmittal of these documents to a foreign power could have worked great harm to this country. If it had not been for the persistence of the committee, followed by the Hiss libel suit against Whittaker Chambers, the documents would not have come to light." [109]

On January 21, 1950, there could have been added to this recitation of the committee's accomplishments the conviction in a federal court of Alger Hiss on the charge of perjury. In all, this record of achievement is a very considerable one. However, in bringing the Hiss-Chambers story to light and in publicizing it in sensational fashion, the House committee was obligated as an arm of the American Congress to do more than it did. Content as it seemingly was to stress only the sordid side of the story, it encouraged the irresponsible wave of Red-hunting and of loyalty-impugning that was to culminate early in 1950 in the shocking and dangerous tactics of Senator McCarthy. Had the House committee been interested in fulfilling its responsibility to Congress and to the American people, it would not have been content with the mere exposure of Alger Hiss's wrongdoing—which in the end it seems to have made its one great purpose. Instead, it would have tried to put this story of treachery in its proper context. Was Alger Hiss unique in that he alone among those young men of promise who in the late thirties were beginning to rise to important posts in the government could have been corrupted by

---

more of these pages. Some 55 documents (125 pages) were introduced at the two Hiss trials. Forty-seven (69 pages) were Baltimore papers and eight (56 pages) were microfilm Pumpkin Papers.

For an interesting discussion of the content and importance of the documents see Cooke, *A Generation on Trial*, pp. 161–164, 317–318.

[108] *Soviet Espionage, Second Rept.*, p. 1.

[109] *Washington Post*, Dec. 22, 1948.

Communist agents such as Whittaker Chambers? Or were there other equally promising young men who might just as well have helped Chambers in his dirty business? It seems likely that the tragedy of Alger Hiss was personal and unique. To be sure, Chambers stated that he had had several other contacts in the federal service, including Henry Julian Wadleigh, who committed espionage for him. This perhaps suggests that isolated government employees were committing espionage or near-espionage during the war years. Nonetheless, it is a fact that the relentless search of recent years for subversive agents in the United States government has demonstrated beyond question the absolute loyalty of the overwhelming majority of the men and women who labored in the federal service during the war and postwar years. It seems reasonable to conclude that a democratic society as strong as our own can safely absorb the evil that the rare traitor may do. Granted that the people are entitled to have the facts about such a traitor and that every effort should be made to ferret him out and to punish him, it must be recognized that too much emphasis upon the flamboyant and sensational aspects of his story may threaten the perspective of the people as to the fundamental integrity of their society. If it be granted, for the sake of argument, that Alger Hiss was a weak, confused, or even sick young man, his story falls far short of demonstrating that American society or government was weak, confused, or sick. If there was even the slightest suggestion that Hiss was symptomatic of a corrupt strain in his generation, then the Un-American Activities Committee had a much larger responsibility to the American people which it never attempted to fulfill. That responsibility would have included the making of inquiries with respect to such issues as motivation, extent of the danger, and cure—a cure which could not even begin to be effected by sending one man to jail. One can read through the hearings and reports of the committee and learn almost nothing about the larger aspects of the threat offered by subversive agents in a democratic society in a world in revolution. In the final analysis, the story is in the best cops-and-robbers tradition and seldom suggests any interest in the social background against which its characters play their parts.

On the other hand, if the conclusion be accepted that it was Whittaker Chambers and Alger Hiss who were corrupt and not the generation or society of which they were parts, then it may be said that the Un-American Activities Committee allowed the sordid facts of a single story of treachery to confuse the American people and undermine their confidence in the strength and integrity of their way of life.[110]

The Condon Case

On March 1, 1948, a subcommittee "on National Security" published a report addressed to the full committee on Un-American Activities. The subcommittee consisted of three members, Representative Thomas, chairman, and Representatives Vail and Wood. At the moment Chairman Thomas was ill in a hospital, and it was reported that final approval had been given to the report by the three subcommittee members in a dramatic meeting at Thomas' bedside. The subcommittee's assignment had presumably been to undertake investigations within the area of point four of the eight-point program of investigation announced in January, 1947, at the beginning of the 80th Congress. Point four in the somewhat ungrammatical language which is common to statements and publications of the committee had promised that "those groups and movements who are trying to dissipate our atomic bomb know-how for the benefit of a foreign power will have the undivided attention of our committee agents, as well as those who are seeking to weaken other aspects of our national security." [111]

The report was identified as a "preliminary" one, and it was admitted that the subcommittee's "investigation is not yet completed." This, however, was the only report that the subcommittee ever made. The report was devoted entirely to one isolated subject—a "matter which is of such importance that it demands immediate attention." The matter was Dr. Edward U. Condon, director of the National Bureau of Standards. The report stated flatly that "from the evidence at hand, it appears that Dr. Condon is one of the weakest links in

[110] In his speech made in the House of Representatives at the time of Hiss's conviction for perjury, Nixon admitted that the personal side of the case had been unduly stressed. He said, "There has been too much of a tendency to look upon this case as simply a dramatic conflict between two striking and powerful personalities, Mr. Hiss on the one side and Mr. Chambers on the other." 96 Cong. Rec. 1002. He might have added that no one had done more to encourage this tendency than committee members themselves.

[111] Report to the Full Committee of the Special Subcommittee on National Security of the Committee on Un-American Activities, March 1, 1948, p. 1. Abbreviated hereafter to Rept. to the Full Committee.

our atomic security." There follow six pages of text "respectfully" submitted "in substantiation of this statement." [112]

This report of March, 1948, was not the first evidence that the Un-American Activities Committee under J. Parnell Thomas was interested in Condon. In March, 1947, there had appeared two articles in the *Washington Times-Herald*, a paper which has always had exceedingly close and friendly relations with the Un-American Activities Committee and which has often been used by the committee to send up trial balloons. These articles hinted that grave charges were pending against Condon and indicated that he would soon be investigated. In the June issue of *American* magazine and in the June 21 issue of *Liberty* magazine appeared two signed articles by J. Parnell Thomas in which Dr. Condon was attacked because of his connection with the American-Soviet Science Society, and the statement was made that he would shortly be subpoenaed. On July 17 a further article appeared in the *Times-Herald*, based upon a committee press release, attacking Dr. Condon once more.[113] In the meantime, on July 9 Dr. Condon wrote Chairman Thomas offering to appear voluntarily before the committee and to supply it with all of the information he possessed. When this letter was ignored, Condon on July 17 addressed a similar communication to every member of the Un-American Activities Committee. This was acknowledged by a few members, but nothing happened, and no public hearings by the full committee or any subcommittee were ever held.[114] Thus, while the committee's interest in Condon was well

[112] *Ibid.* The use of subcommittees by the Un-American Activities Committee has always been informal and erratic. The existence of this particular subcommittee on national security is not acknowledged in any other publication of the full committee. As a subcommittee report to the full committee it was theoretically not necessary to secure the approval of members of the full committee before releasing it. But it is hard to draw any other conclusion than that this procedural arrangement was a subterfuge which enabled the committee chairman to rush into print a highly controversial document that might just possibly have encountered objection from some members of the full committee had their approval been necessary for publication.

[113] This article was written by a James Walter. It was answered in detail by Representative Holifield of California in the House on July 22. See 93 *Cong. Rec.* 9770. Representative Holifield later asserted that "the charges [of the subcommittee report] are little more than regurgitations of the charges made in the Washington *Times-Herald* on July 17, 1947. . . ." 94 *Cong. Rec.* 2435 (March 9, 1948).

[114] Much of this chronological information has been derived from an excellent speech made by Representative Holifield in the House of Representatives on July 29, 1948. *Ibid.*, 9546.

known, the suddenness of the appearance of the subcommittee report in March, 1948, and the vehemence of its attack upon Condon created a furore, and the case quickly became a *cause célèbre.*

There has been much speculation concerning the pronounced and continuing interest of the Un-American Activities Committee, and of its chairman particularly, in Dr. Condon. In view of the complete failure of the committee ever to document its charges against Condon with serious or substantial evidence, one is forced to discard the theory that in Dr. Condon the committee was genuinely convinced it had found a truly dangerous government employee from a loyalty or security point of view, one so dangerous as to justify the unique, all-out attack made upon him. The subcommittee's own explanation of its interest in Condon is that there had come into its possession a letter addressed in July, 1946, to a member of Congress, at that time a member of the "Joint Committee on Atomic Energy of the Congress," written by an unnamed person who had "held a high post in the security division of the Manhattan project," and who was at the time of the report's issuance "a ranking official of the Atomic Energy Commission." The letter stated, "May I suggest that you demand Dr. Condon's record of the FBI. It would be enlightening." [115]

In a statement made by Dr. Condon the same day the subcommittee report was released, it is implied that Chairman Thomas' attack upon him was the result of the two men having been on opposite sides in the bitter controversy over civilian versus military control of atomic energy which had occurred before the adoption of the Atomic Energy Act in 1946. Condon speaks of "an undercover attempt to smear civilian control of atomic energy by smearing the scientists who assisted the development of the Atomic Energy Commission of 1946. In this connection, I was adviser to the Special Senate Committee on Atomic Energy under the chairmanship of Senator Brian McMahon." [116] Robert E. Stripling, in his book, *The Red Plot Against America,* which was published late in 1949 and which had appeared serially early in the same year in many newspapers, makes this same assertion as a flat statement of fact. He writes:

[115] *Rept. to the Full Committee,* p. 3. The Joint Committee on Atomic Energy did not exist in July, 1946. It was one of the agencies provided for by the Atomic Energy Act which became law on August 1, 1946. The Congressional committee was not organized until January, 1947.

[116] *N.Y. Times,* March 2, 1948.

Chairman Thomas and Dr. Condon first clashed when they stood on opposite sides of the Congressional debate over whether military men or civilians should control our post-war atomic energy and A-bomb program. In the course of his support of the military for this role, Thomas received a letter from a former security officer in the Manhattan Engineering District project (and now a ranking official of the Atomic Energy Commission) urging him to enquire into Condon's record.[117]

It is a fair inference that Thomas, like Dies before him and McCarthy after him, also saw the political advantage in an attack upon the loyalty of an important employee in the executive branch and did his best to exploit it. The timing of the release of the subcommittee report was probably designed to win support for a $200,000 Un-American Activities Committee appropriation, which was then pending in the House of Representatives and which was approved on March 9 by an overwhelming majority. This was the largest grant ever made to the committee.[118] The fact that Thomas was confined to bed in a hospital might well have delayed the release of the report had there not been a special reason for bringing it out at just that moment.[119]

The subcommittee report on Condon is a brief, loosely organized document of six and a half pages. The first paragraph, as has been indicated, states the charge against Dr. Condon and announces that the remainder of the report will substantiate the charge. There follow three sections entitled "Personal History and Education of Dr. Edward U. Condon," "Information regarding the National Bureau

[117] *The Red Plot*, p. 85. On April 14, 1948, Representative Douglas of California charged in the House of Representatives that the "attacks upon Dr. Condon seem to be part of a general strategy to undermine the McMahon bill [establishing the Atomic Energy Commission]; . . . The objective seems glaringly apparent: By discrediting the scientists responsible for atomic energy and the legislators and citizens active in the establishment of the McMahon bill, and then by subsequent overt attacks upon the Atomic Energy Commission, it is hoped that the McMahon bill will be revised or recanted and that a totally military bill will be substituted." 94 *Cong. Rec.* 4464 (April 14, 1948).

[118] See, for example, *Time*, March 14, 1948, which said: "New Jersey's Representative J. Parnell Thomas knows that a good headline, come appropriation time, can do more than months of hard work. Last week, as his Committee on Un-American Activities applied for a whopping $200,000 allotment from the House, Thomas dug deep. What he fetched up was an old file on Dr. Edward U. Condon. . . ."

[119] In *The Red Plot* Stripling says that he "objected" to the release of the subcommittee report on the ground that Condon should first have been granted a hearing (p. 86). Louis Russell, June 24, 1949, told the author that he also had opposed the release of the report.

of Standards," and "Conclusions and Recommendations." The report at best is a flimsy document, deficient both in its failure to touch upon much pertinent information pertaining to Dr. Condon and in its strange, and at times improper, use of the material it does present.[120]

In the second sentence of the section on the personal history and education of Condon is a statement which should put the wary reader on guard. The statement is that in 1922 Condon "married Emilie Hunzik, an American-born woman of Czechoslovakian descent." The more one ponders this statement the more curious its presence in the report becomes. Mrs. Condon is admitted to be of American birth, but attention is called to her European descent. Why? Presumably no less could be said of any American, save perhaps the Indians. Moreover, no reference is made to the number of generations between Mrs. Condon and her Czechoslovakian forebears. For all the report says, her ancestors might have come to this country in colonial days. Why, then, is attention called to the issue "of Czechoslovakian descent" save possibly to create an initial mood of suspicion or presumption of guilt against the Condons in the mind of the unwary reader—against Mrs. Condon because of her ancestry and against Dr. Condon because he married such a woman?

This biographical section also contains a number of inaccuracies. For example, Condon's titles in earlier positions at Princeton University and the Westinghouse Laboratories are incorrectly given.[121] This is a minor matter, but in their way errors of this type, which mar many of the publications of the Un-American Activities Committee, do reflect inadequate research on the part of the committee's staff.

The most serious objection to this biography of Condon lies in what it does *not* say. Condon's former jobs are mentioned, and the neutral observation is made that "Condon is principally regarded as a theoretical physicist which [*sic*] involves radar, nuclear physics, radioactive tracers, mass spectroscopy, and the elastic properties of metals." [122] But there is no suggestion at all that he is regarded "by his fellow scientists . . . as one of the world's leading authorities

[120] On March 9, 1948, Representative Holifield analyzed the subcommittee report at length in the House of Representatives (94 *Cong. Rec.* 2435). In the January, 1949, issue of *Harper's Magazine* there appeared an article, "The Ordeal of Dr. Condon." The author of this article uses a pen name, Louis Welborn, and is identified only as a "correspondent of a well-known news organization." Welborn draws heavily upon the Holifield analysis, and the present author has used both sources in preparing his own analysis of the report.

[121] See the March 9 Holifield speech.   [122] *Rept. to the Full Committee*, p. 2.

on quantum mechanics, microwave electronics, and radioactivity." [123]

A further illustration of the tendency of the subcommittee to tell less than the whole story is found in the following sentences: "On November 5, 1945, Dr. Edward U. Condon was appointed Director of the National Bureau of Standards. Dr. Condon was recommended by Henry A. Wallace, who was then Secretary of Commerce. The Bureau of Standards is a Bureau in the Department of Commerce." And again, "In this country [the Communists] haven't gotten as far as they have in Czechoslovakia, but they got pretty far, because they got a man as Vice President of the United States, and he is now their candidate for President, and he is the same man who recommended Dr. Condon as Director of the Bureau of Standards." [124]

Entirely apart from the implication of this passage that Vice-President Wallace was a Communist or an agent of the Communists, the committee's report fails to tell that Wallace did not know Condon until the time of the appointment and that the recommendation was made on the basis of the findings of a departmental committee which had been directed to find the best-qualified man for the job.[125]

A little over four of the six and a half pages of the report comprise the section entitled "Information regarding the National Bureau of Standards." After a brief résumé of the bureau's activities and of its services to the Atomic Energy Commission and to the Army and Navy, the keynote to the section is sounded in these words: "The Bureau of Standards is one of the most important national defense research organizations in the United States. Because of this, it has become the target of espionage agents of numerous foreign powers." [126] The remainder of the section is an attempt to document the ambiguous second sentence of the extract quoted and to show that Dr. Condon had been a tool, willing or unwilling, of the "espionage agents" in their efforts to reach their "target." The committee's efforts to document these conclusions may appropriately be examined point by point. How well does the subcommittee support its unrestrained and unqualified attack upon Dr. Condon?

Point One. The subcommittee states that it "has in its possession" a list issued at the end of November, 1947, of employees of the Bureau of Standards cleared by the Atomic Energy Commission "from a loyalty standpoint" to do work on atomic energy projects. Dr. Condon's name is "carried in a *pending status*." This situation

[123] "The Ordeal of Dr. Condon," *Harper's Magazine,* Jan., 1949.
[124] *Rept. to the Full Committee,* pp. 2, 7.   [125] "The Ordeal of Dr. Condon."
[126] *Rept. to the Full Committee,* p. 3.

is said to be a matter of "serious concern" when it is recalled that in 1941 Condon was a member of the Roosevelt Committee on Uranium Research and in July, 1946, was a member of the President's Evaluation Committee, formed to observe the effects of the Bikini atom bomb test.[127]

What particular clearance investigation is being referred to is not made clear. What "pending status" means is not stated. Whether this "pending status" still prevailed on March 1, 1948, when the subcommittee report was issued, is not said. Why a decision of the Atomic Energy Commission, which was not even established until 1946, to carry Dr. Condon on a "pending status" has any bearing upon Condon's activity in 1941 is left unexplained.

What is fact about Dr. Condon's standing with the Atomic Energy Commission is that on July 15, 1948, four and a half months after the publication of the subcommittee's report, the commission made public a report in which the conclusion is reached:

> On the basis of voluminous record before it, the members of the Commission are fully satisfied that, in the terms of [the Atomic Energy Act] Dr. Condon's continued clearance for the purposes stated above "will not adversely affect the common defense and security" of the United States. The Commission considers that his continued clearance is in the best interests of the atomic energy program.[128]

This was a "security" clearance and under the Atomic Energy Act was based upon consideration of Dr. Condon's character and associations as well as his loyalty. The Atomic Energy Commission had before it separate reports from the FBI based upon two intensive investigations of Dr. Condon, and it is quite clear no person has ever received a more searching scrutiny with respect to his loyalty than did Condon from the FBI. The decision of the AEC to give Dr. Condon an unqualified clearance was made even though the commission's Personnel Security Review Board, an advisory agency, had recommended that final clearance be delayed until the Un-American Activities Committee completed its consideration of the Condon

[127] *Ibid.*

[128] The full text of the AEC report may be found in 94 *Cong. Rec.* 9547. The phrase "purposes stated above" has reference to the fact that, as director of the Bureau of Standards, Dr. Condon would have access to certain types of restricted data but not to others (such as atomic-weapon production or stockpile data). Under the Atomic Energy Act it is the usual procedure to give security clearance only with respect to the area of a person's duties. Failure to give broader clearance in no sense implies an adverse judgment against an individual.

case. Moreover, in its report the AEC takes notice of certain adverse judgments of Dr. Condon. It first notes that "in the opinion of some persons Dr. Condon's tact, judgment, and discretion appear to be subject to some degree of criticism." But it also observes that "there are statements by persons who have been closely associated with Dr. Condon during his long work on classified information, which indicate proper care on his part in assuring that unauthorized persons should not obtain access to classified information." A second adverse observation is that "the file contains unfavorable information of a relevant character concerning persons with whom Dr. Condon and Mrs. Condon have from time to time had contacts." But the AEC report adds, "The file also shows that Dr. Condon is a man of wide associations, and that his associates include many highly reputable members of the scientific community who have great confidence in him."

The Un-American Activities subcommittee did not have the benefit of this AEC evaluation of Dr. Condon at the time it prepared its own report. But it surely knew that "pending status" meant that Dr. Condon was still under investigation by the AEC and that sooner or later under the normal routine prescribed by the Atomic Energy Act a final judgment would necessarily be made. Its own independent action on March 1 was not only an improper effort by a legislative body to usurp a duty, assigned by law to an administrative agency and in this instance in the process of being performed, but was also an attempt to turn the fact that the AEC had not yet completed its investigation of Dr. Condon or passed final judgment upon him into a finding of guilt against him.

Point Two. The subcommittee's report then states, "It is interesting to note" that when Condon reorganized the Bureau of Standards in May, 1947, and set up fourteen divisions, he appointed himself head of the Atomic Physics Division, even though he had not been cleared to work on atomic energy projects for the AEC.[129] Read carefully, this statement makes no adverse finding against Dr. Condon. It merely states what was seemingly the fact at the time. But it fails to call attention to Dr. Condon's pre-eminence as a nuclear physicist, or to his own close connection with atomic research previous to 1947, and once more it is the sort of statement that creates a mood of suspicion in the unwary reader.

Point Three. One of the most controversial points in the subcom-

[129] *Rept. to the Full Committee,* p. 3.

mittee's case against Dr. Condon is the use of a portion of a letter written in 1946 by an anonymous person, said to have held a high post in the security division of the Manhattan project, to an anonymous Congressman said to have been a member of the "Joint Committee on Atomic Energy." This letter has already been referred to, but its key sentences may be repeated. They are: "May I suggest that you demand Dr. Condon's record of the FBI. It would be enlightening." Neither of the anonymous persons has ever been officially identified. In *The Red Plot Against America* Stripling writes as though the Congressman were Thomas himself.[130] Thomas was never a member of the Joint Committee on Atomic Energy. However, he was a member of the House Military Affairs Committee which considered the atomic energy bill in 1946, and he was a member of the House-Senate conference committee on the bill—a joint committee of sorts. If Thomas was in fact the Congressman referred to in the subcommittee report, then the two sentences quoted were something less than completely candid.

In any case, the quoted passages of the letter are so barren of factual information and so obviously gossipy in tone that their inclusion in a six-page report that has set for itself the enormous task of proving that one of the nation's most eminent scientists is a weak link in our atomic security is highly questionable.

Point Four. The most controversial of all the points made against Condon in the subcommittee report is one depending upon a partially quoted letter written by J. Edgar Hoover to Secretary of Commerce W. Averell Harriman in May, 1947, which seemingly accuses Condon of having been in contact with Soviet espionage agents as late as 1947. The basic point itself is the old one of guilt by association. "The associations of Dr. Condon and his wife have been cause for great concern to the agencies charged with the security of the United States," says the report.

The Hoover letter is quoted "in part" as follows:

The files of the Bureau reflect that Dr. Edward U. Condon has been in contact as late as 1947 with an individual alleged, by a self-confessed Soviet espionage agent, to have engaged in espionage activities with the Russians in Washington, D.C., from 1941 to 1944.

Mr. and Mrs. Condon associated with several individuals connected with the Polish Embassy in Washington, D.C. Among those are Mrs. Joseph Winiewize, wife of the Polish Ambassador, Virginia Woerk, a clerk

130 *The Red Plot*, p. 85.

employee of the Polish Embassy, Helen M. Harris, secretary of the Polish Embassy and Ignace Zlotowski, former counselor of the Polish Embassy and presently a Polish delegate to the United Nations.

Helen Harris is identified as a former secretary to the American-Soviet Science Society during the time it was known as science committee [*sic*] of the National American-Soviet Friendship Society. She went to work for the Polish Embassy in the fall of 1946.

Zlotowski is identified as a nuclear scientist who studied under Joliet Curie, known member of the Communist Party. He was ex-secretary of the American Soviet Society. It is known that in February 1947, Zlotowski purchased 270 books on atomic energy which had been published by the Department of Commerce.

It is also known that Mr. and Mrs. Condon were in contact with several other persons closely associated with this alleged Soviet espionage agent. It is also reliably reported that in March 1947, Zlotowski offered the use of the Polish diplomatic pouch to scientific groups as a means of transmitting scientific material outside the United States, dissemination of which had to be restricted because of security reasons by military authorities.

Zlotowski was in contact with Anatole Cromov, first secretary of the Soviet Embassy who has since returned to Russia. Mrs. Emily Condon applied for passports for European travel in 1926, and passport for travel to Russia in 1945. Passports were withdrawn. Condon issued passport 276319 on October 11, 1946, to travel and study in Germany, France, Holland, Italy, Czechoslovakia, Great Britain, Denmark, and Switzerland. He applied for passport June 4, 1946, to Russia which was issued but was later canceled by the Army.[131]

How the subcommittee obtained a copy of this confidential letter from Hoover to Harriman is itself a controversial issue. Attorney General Tom Clark stated in May in a speech at the National Press Club that the Un-American Activities Committee had stolen a portion of the FBI loyalty report on Condon.[132] The official explanation as to how the letter was obtained was made by the House Committee on Interstate and Foreign Commerce in a report on House Resolution 522 directing the Secretary of Commerce to turn over to the House the full text of the Hoover-Harriman letter. In this report it is stated that in September, 1947, Thomas wrote a letter to "an employee" of the Department of Commerce asking him to furnish a committee investigator with any information concerning Condon that might be available; that the investigator was allowed to make a brief examination of a file of papers and documents which in-

[131] *Rept. to the Full Committee*, p. 4.   [132] *N.Y. Times*, May 14, 1948.

cluded the Hoover-Harriman letter; that he undertook to copy the letter, but that before he could finish he was requested to discontinue and did so.[133]

Soon after the publication of the subcommittee report on Condon it was discovered, apparently by a reporter for the *Washington Post,* that portions of the Hoover-Harriman letter favorable to Condon had been omitted. The first paragraph of the letter as published in the report—a paragraph stating that Dr. Condon had been in contact as late as 1947 with an individual alleged by a self-confessed Soviet espionage agent to have engaged in espionage activities with the Russians in Washington—failed to include this all-important qualifying sentence from the original letter: "There is no evidence to show that contacts between this individual and Dr. Condon were related to this individual's espionage activities." In the report there is no typographical indication that the portions of the letter printed are not complete. If the story concerning the copying of the original letter at the Department of Commerce by a committee investigator is correct, it is easy to understand how the text might have undergone abridgment, although the investigator's interest in damaging testimony against Condon and his lack of interest in information supporting Condon would then throw a good deal of light on the general frame of mind with which the committee's staff members approach their research tasks.

[133] The full text of the relevant passages of the report are:

"It is appropriate to inform the House as to how the Sub-committee on National Security was able to obtain the partial text of the letter referred to, and why it was unable to obtain the full text.

"On September 6, 1947, the following letter was addressed to an employee of the Department of Commerce by the chairman of the Committee on Un-American Activities:

" 'Dear Mr. ——: In connection with official investigation being conducted by the Committee on Un-American Activities, I would appreciate your furnishing Mr. William A. Wheeler, investigator for this committee, any information you have available on Edward U. Condon, Director of the Bureau of Standards. Your cooperation in this matter will be greatly appreciated.

" 'J. Parnell Thomas,
" '*Chairman*'

"In response to this request the investigator was permitted to make a brief examination of a file of papers and documents, among which was the letter written by Mr. Hoover, above referred to. The investigator undertook to make a copy of this letter, but before he was able to copy all of it he was requested to discontinue, and acceded to the request. The result was that the subcommittee had available for publication in its report only that part of the letter which the investigator had been able to copy." 94 *Cong. Rec.* 5862–5863 (May 14, 1948).

Chairman Thomas, when confronted with the evidence as to the less-than-complete text of the letter carried by the report, took the position that the omission was inadvertent and unfortunate.[134] There followed an attempt to get the full text of the original letter from the Department of Commerce. Chairman Thomas first caused a subpoena to be issued directing Secretary of Commerce Harriman to furnish the subcommittee with the letter. On March 4, Harriman, after obtaining advice from the Attorney General, wrote to Thomas refusing the request on the ground that under the principle of separation of powers the executive branch has the duty to exercise its own judgment in meeting requests for information from the legislative branch, and that in this case it was his judgment that releasing the letter would be prejudicial to the public interest. On March 13, President Truman issued his famous directive in the form of a "Memorandum to All Officers and Employees in the Executive Branch of the Government" ordering that all "reports, records, and files relative to the [loyalty] program be preserved in strict confidence" and that any requests by subpoena or otherwise for such materials, coming other than from persons in the executive branch entitled to have access to the materials, should be respectfully declined and referred to the Office of the President. Thereupon, the House of Representatives adopted on April 22, by a vote of 322 to 29, a resolution directing the Secretary of Commerce to transmit the letter. Two days later the Department of Commerce again formally declined to meet this request, giving the Truman directive of March 13 as the ground for its refusal.[135]

It is perhaps unfair to J. Edgar Hoover and the FBI to analyze or criticize the letter to Secretary Harriman in view of the fact that the full text has never been made public and that the partial text of the subcommittee report was a copied version prepared by an Un-American Activities Committee investigator. Moreover, it should be remembered that the information contained in the letter is of the typical raw-data type contained in FBI reports, no attempt having been made by the FBI to evaluate the information. Nonetheless, it would appear that the substance of the letter is not above criticism.

[134] In a letter to Thomas dated March 29, 1948, Condon's lawyers, Thurman Arnold, Abe Fortas, and Paul Porter, called attention to the fact that press statements also implied that language was inserted in the subcommittee version of the letter which was not found in the original. They did not cite the passages referred to. *Ibid.*, 4795 (April 22, 1948).

[135] It should be noted that Condon himself requested that the full text of the letter be made public. *N.Y. Times,* May 9, 1948.

For example, in his House speech on March 9 analyzing the subcommittee report, Representative Holifield stated that Condon had denied the assertion in paragraph two of the letter that he and his wife had "associated" with the wife of the Polish Ambassador and Virginia Woerk, a clerk in the Polish Embassy. Holifield also threw additional light on Condon's "association" with the Ignace Zlotowski mentioned in the letter. Holifield points out that Zlotowski was the Polish representative on the Atomic Energy Commission of the United Nations and that because of this Condon could hardly have avoided "associating" with him. Holifield adds,

It is interesting to note that one of the occasions on which Dr. Condon met Dr. Zlotowski was at Bikini, when the President's Evaluation Board, under the chairmanship of Senator Carl A. Hatch, gave a reception on the deck of the Navy vessel, the U.S.S. *Haven*, in honor of the official delegates of the United Nations to the atomic bomb tests at Bikini. I was there, as was Senator Hatch, and so were other Members of Congress and many other prominent Americans. Does this mean that our association with Mr. Zlotowski was improper or indiscreet? [136]

The data in the final paragraph of the Hoover letter with respect to the issuance of passports to the Condons and the withdrawal of passports for travel to Russia has been challenged as to accuracy.[137] It has been pointed out that the cancellation by the Army of Condon's passport to Russia was a much more innocent affair, at least from Condon's point of view, than the Hoover letter makes it sound. Condon did not apply for a passport to Russia in 1946. The reference is presumably to a passport granted to Condon in 1945. Various organizations had been invited to send delegates to a conference being held in Russia in celebration of the 200th anniversary of the Russian Academy of Sciences. Two organizations, the National Council of American-Soviet Friendship [138] and the American Institute of Physics, invited Condon to go as their delegate. Sixteen Americans, including two government officials, did actually make the trip, flying in a plane made available by the Army at the request of the President. Condon did not go, because the Army decided at the last moment that no nuclear physicists should make the trip, lest they be quizzed by the Russians concerning the then-secret experiments with atomic energy

[136] 94 *Cong. Rec.* 2440.
[137] See the Holifield speech of March 9, 1948, in *Cong. Rec.* 2435; also his speech of July 22, 1947, in 93 *Cong. Rec.* 9770.
[138] This was long before the NCASF was characterized by the Attorney General as a subversive organization.

being made in this country and find it embarrassing to make any sort of answer. Mrs. Ruth Shipley, chief of the Passport Division of the Department of State, wrote to Condon on June 18, 1945,

I desire to confirm to you the statement I made in asking that the passport be returned; namely, that in denying you permission to depart from the United States, neither the action of the military authorities, nor that of the Passport Division cast any reflection whatsoever on your integrity, your loyalty, or your character.[139]

Point Five. The subcommittee report then charges in a series of paragraphs that the Bureau of Standards has been visited "for a great many years" by the representatives of many foreign governments, that Condon had appointed one Demetry I. Vinogradoff, "a Russian-born scientist" who during the war years had been employed by the Westinghouse Electric Company and was in charge of liaison between that company and the Soviet Purchasing Commission, to accommodate foreign visitors to the bureau, and that from July, 1946, through March, 1947, visitors and delegates from foreign nations numbered 302 and that of these, 39 were Russians and 3 were Poles. It is then noted that after March, 1947, the number of Russians visiting the bureau declined substantially. This leads to the cryptic observation that "the reason for the decline . . . is unknown to the subcommittee." But it is added that in December, 1946, Vinogradoff, at the request of Condon, made arrangements with a Russian Embassy official in Washington "to discuss the problem of exchanging books, pamphlets, and other written material" and that "it was agreed" these discussions would be informal "because, otherwise it would be necessary to obtain a clearance from the State Department." Note is also taken of the knowledge that Vinogradoff "has been in close touch with" the assistant naval attaché of the Russian Embassy.

[139] The letter is quoted by Representative Holifield in his July 22, 1947, speech (93 *Cong. Rec.* 9770). Holifield also pointed out that the Army tried to keep Dr. Irving Langmuir, associate director of the research laboratory of the General Electric Company, from making the same trip, but that Langmuir insisted upon going. Langmuir later told the story in testifying before the Special Senate Committee on Atomic Energy on November 30, 1945, and offered as his opinion that this action by the Army in keeping both American and British physicists from attending the conference "resulted in giving the Russians the very information which the Army most wished to keep from them. Any sensible Russian scientist knowing of these facts (the sudden cancellation of the physicists' passports) would have believed that we were developing an atomic bomb and were keeping it secret from the Russians." Quoted by Holifield, *ibid.*, 9771.

What all of this adds up to is difficult to say. The subcommittee report fails utterly to distinguish between the Bureau of Standards as the governmental agency which maintains accurate standards of weights, measurements, and so forth, and as a research laboratory which engages in highly confidential experimental work for the armed services, the Atomic Energy Commission, and other governmental agencies. In its first capacity it readily makes available highly useful information to business and industry. Representatives of foreign governments often find this information of great value and are invited to seek access to it. In its latter capacity the bureau is, of course, a "sensitive" agency which must maintain absolute security in its operations. The information given in the report about foreign visitors to the bureau fails to make clear the purposes for which they went to the bureau, and, accordingly, the statements made, standing by themselves without further qualification, are meaningless.

Moreover, by its own statistics the committee acknowledges that among the foreigners visiting the bureau the number of Russians was not large and that the number declined after March, 1947. While Soviet-American relations were deteriorating during the period referred to, formally and officially the two nations continued to extend to each other full diplomatic recognition, and presumably we were not ready to single out the Soviet Union for such petty discrimination as denying its nationals access to the Bureau of Standards. Admittedly, the factual statements made in the subcommittee report could be background information supporting charges of known and specific espionage penetrating to the confidential and important scientific work being carried on within the bureau. But no such specific charges have ever been made, and by themselves the assertions of the report, carefully read, do not add up to a conclusion of the existence of nefarious activity. As though realizing this, the report goes quickly on to offer a gratuitous judgment as to the policy that the United States ought to be following with respect to the exchange of scientific information among nations:

> Your subcommittee would like to point out to the full committee that the exchange of scientific material with the Soviet Union is a one-way street, and that our Government is pursuing a dangerous and foolish policy of making scientific data available to the Soviet Union, since they will not permit us to inspect any of their bureaus, nor will they exchange any information with us.[140]

[140] *Rept. to the Full Committee*, p. 5. A little later the report quotes Dr. Condon as having said in a speech before the First Annual Scientific Institute in

146   THE HOUSE COMMITTEE

Point Six. The subcommittee emphasized as the final point in its case against Dr. Condon his identification with the American-Soviet Science Society. However, the material with respect to the ASSS is introduced by what is perhaps the most shocking irrelevancy in the entire report. "Your subcommittee," the report reads, "by a very diligent investigation, has determined that Dr. Condon has in the past 5 years been in personal contact and communication with a number of individuals who are American citizens, but who are members of the Communist Party. *There is no evidence in our possession that Dr. Condon is a member of the Communist Party, however. . . .*" [141] It is hard to see any justification for this wholly gratuitous negative assertion. Nothing that is presented elsewhere in the report suggests that Dr. Condon might be a member of the Communist Party, and accordingly this superfluous clearance suggests at least an unconscious intention on the part of the subcommittee that it might be well to call attention to the fact that, after all, Dr. Condon *could be* a Communist. "Louis Welborn's" comment on this is that not only is there no evidence Condon is a Communist but that there is "abundant evidence that he is a militant believer in democratic government, human dignity, the Bill of Rights, and other precepts of the American way of life to which Communism is uncompromisingly hostile." [142]

Having cleared Dr. Condon against such an inference, the subcommittee proceeds to say that "as a member of the executive committee of the American-Soviet Science Society, which is affiliated with the National Council of American-Soviet Friendship, Inc., and which was recently cited as a subversive organization by Attorney General Clark, he has lent his name and influence to one of the

March, 1946, "We must welcome [Russian] scientists to our laboratories, as they have welcomed ours to theirs, and extend the base of scientific cooperation with this great people. Of course, we must behave this way toward the scientists of all nations. I only mention Russia because she is right now the target of attack by those irresponsibles who think she would be a suitable adversary in the next world war."

The subcommittee adds the following comment: "This subcommittee is in possession of no evidence or information which indicates that the Soviet Government has in the past, or will in the future permit the scientists of the United States in their laboratories or to [*sic*] make available to them any information of any scientific importance. Any Government official who is not aware that the Soviet Union is bent upon the Stalinization of the world, is not qualified to hold a strategic position which affects the security of the United States." *Rept. to the Full Committee,* p. 6.

[141] *Ibid.,* p. 5. Italics added.   [142] *Harper's Magazine,* Jan., 1949.

principal Communist endeavors in the United States."[143] Here it is impossible to tell whether the subcommittee has been guilty of a deliberate and disgraceful distortion of the truth, or has merely come a cropper because of the shaky punctuation and grammar which are common to publications of the Un-American Activities Committee. The point is that it is the National Council of American-Soviet Friendship, Inc., and not the American-Soviet Science Society, that is on the Attorney General's list of subversive organizations. Dr. Condon's affiliation is admittedly with the latter organization. Yet if the sentences just quoted from the report are read carefully, the comma and the "and " which follow the qualifying phrase in which reference is made to the National Council certainly suggest that it is the ASSS itself that is on the Attorney General's list. That the subcommittee's "mistake" is a calculated one is suggested by the next three paragraphs of the report. A letter is reproduced in which Samuel Gelfan, for the membership committee of the ASSS, allegedly addresses "certain employees of the Bureau of Standards" inviting their membership in the ASSS at the suggestion of Dr. Condon. The subcommittee then asserts, "In response to this letter, 10 scientists of the Bureau of Standards *joined this subversive organization.*"[144]

Entirely apart from the subcommittee's improper and unwarranted reference to "this subversive organization," it gives a sinister cast to what was no more than a harmless drive for members. Soon after the publication of the subcommittee report Professor L. C. Dunn of Columbia University wrote in a letter to the *New York Times* that a letter similar to the one quoted in the report "went to several hundred scientists in many different universities and laboratories. Wher-

[143] *Rept. to the Full Committee,* p. 5.

[144] *Rept. to the Full Committee,* p. 6. Italics added. That the ASSS was not a "subversive organization" is suggested among other things by the fact the board of trustees of the Rockefeller Foundation (which included such men as Winthrop Aldrich and John Foster Dulles) made a grant of $25,000 to it in 1946 for the development of its program. "Welborn" points out that Condon joined the ASSS along with 400 other eminent American scientists, and that the ASSS's "only specific project was the translation of Russian scientific papers *into English* for distribution in this country." It should be added that the ASSS broke relations with the National Council when the latter organization was placed on the Attorney General's list. It may also be added that Professor L. C. Dunn of Columbia University stated in a letter to the *N.Y. Times,* March 19, 1948, that as of that date the society had been unable to utilize the Rockefeller grant by starting a journal or otherwise putting its program into action because the Department of the Treasury had after two years still failed to grant the society a certificate of tax exemption as a nonprofit, educational organization.

ever possible, we named a member of our society in the same laboratory or university from whom information about our society could be secured." [145] It should also be noted that in May an Un-American Activities subcommittee under Representative Vail as chairman was reported to have held a week of executive hearings at which it attempted to ascertain whether Dr. Condon had brought pressure upon employees of the Bureau of Standards to join the American-Soviet Science Society.[146] However, no further statement or report on this point was ever made by the committee.

The final section of the report, headed "Conclusions and Recommendations," is a brief one. It begins with several sound observations to the effect that the "ruthless rúsh of Stalin through Europe" necessitates a revision of American policy and thinking regarding communism; that our government is charged with preserving the security of our people and institutions; and that the Communists do not fight our way—they employ "the strategy of getting a few men in the Government and then a few more, and they [take] over the entire Government without firing a single shot or calling out a single regiment of soldiers." [147] But from these incontrovertible observations the subcommittee hastens on to the conclusion that it is the unanimous opinion of its members "that Dr. Condon should either be removed or a statement should be forthcoming from the Secretary of Commerce, setting forth the reasons why he has retained Dr. Condon, in view of the derogatory information which he has had before him." The subcommittee then adds that the full committee ought to call the attention of the President of the United States to "the fact that the situation as regards Dr. Condon is not an isolated one, but that there are other Government officials in strategic positions who are playing Stalin's game to the detriment of the United States" and that the evidence before the subcommittee "indicates very strongly that there is in operation at the present time in the United States an extensive Soviet espionage ring, and to permit this ring to continue, in view of the high atomic prizes which they are seeking, is folly, and can only lead to ultimate disaster." [148]

The trouble with these final observations is not that they were untrue. Indeed, later developments in the Fuchs case were to suggest they perhaps came quite close to the mark. The trouble with them is that the evidence presented in the subcommittee report does not support them and that the careful and impartial reader can only

[145] *N.Y. Times*, March 6, 1948.   [146] *Ibid.*, May 25, 1948.
[147] *Rept. to the Full Committee*, pp. 6–7.   [148] *Ibid.*, p. 7.

conclude that for reasons of its own the subcommittee is playing the old game of crying "wolf." Dr. Condon remained a respected and valued director of the Bureau of Standards until his voluntary resignation in the summer of 1951. When, on the other hand, in 1950 the FBI arrested an obscure scientist named Harry Gold, in Philadelphia, as an American who had during the war helped Klaus Fuchs turn over atomic secrets to the Russians, so cleverly had the true culprits hidden their activities that Gold's name was not to be found in the list of more than one million subversives of all nations that the Un-American Activities Committee had accumulated through the years. As the *New York Herald Tribune* put it the Condon report, "a masterpiece of unfair innuendo," utilizes methods that outrage "decent people and thereby tend to blind them to the real dangers which may exist, and which submerge all the facts—and there are important facts involved in these matters—in a sea of sensation that makes real knowledge and proper action all but impossible." [149]

The Un-American Activities subcommittee did not have long to wait for an answer to its demand that Dr. Condon either be dismissed from his government position or a statement be made by the Secretary of Commerce justifying his retention. Within a matter of hours after the release of the subcommittee report the Department of Commerce issued a statement that the department loyalty board by unanimous action had given Condon a loyalty clearance six days before, holding that "no reasonable grounds exist for believing that Dr. Condon is disloyal to the Government of the United States." [150]

J. Parnell Thomas and his colleagues were, however, unwilling to accept this statement as made in good faith. On March 2, Thomas stated that he could "not understand how the loyalty board could have cleared Dr. Condon in view of the evidence." He then added, "The committee has no evidence that Dr. Condon is disloyal, but it has ample evidence that he had been at least indiscreet in a position in which indiscretion could have serious consequences." [151] Apart from the fact that this statement shows a definite tendency on Thomas' part to back away from the more vigorous language of the subcommittee report, his words raise the question as to why there should be any difficulty about understanding a Department of Commerce finding that Condon was loyal, when Thomas himself admitted his committee had no evidence Condon was disloyal. At any

[149] March 3, 1948.   [150] *N.Y. Times,* March 2, 1948.
[151] *Ibid.,* March 3, 1948.

rate, Thomas was unwilling to let the case rest at this point. From his hospital bed he ordered committee subpoenas served upon officials of the Department of Commerce, directing them to produce all departmental records bearing upon Condon's loyalty clearance.

On March 4, Secretary Harriman announced that the subpoenas would not be honored. The angry Thomas then retorted, "This is just another example where an agency of the Government is attempting to flaunt the Congress and if they think they are going to get away with it they are mistaken. Our committee will hold public hearings on this case and we are going to summon . . . Dr. Condon, Secretary Harriman, and Attorney General Clark. . . . I am resolved to have a showdown." [152]

A week later three members of the Department of Commerce loyalty board appeared before the committee in executive session, but they refused to produce any departmental records or to testify concerning Condon's loyalty clearance by the department. Following this session committee members charged that the department had not cleared Condon six days before the issuance of the subcommittee report as it had claimed, but that Condon had been cleared only after the publication of the report. Secretary Harriman was reported to have reacted to this charge by saying that the committee's action was "un-American." [153] Thereafter occurred the attempts which have already been mentioned to secure the Hoover-Harriman letter and other departmental records in the Condon case by formal Congressional action. The Truman directive ordering the withholding of all loyalty records from Congress was issued on March 13. On April 22, the House passed a simple resolution requesting the Secretary of Commerce to surrender the letter. As has been stated, this request was refused, and President Truman was reported to have indicated at a press conference that his attitude was—the House has acted; now let it try to get the letter! On May 13 by a vote of 219 to 142 the House passed a bill sponsored by Representative Clare Hoffman that would have forced all executive agencies to produce information requested by Congress with a threat of jail terms for nonco-operative officials up to the level of Cabinet members. This bill was never acted upon by the Senate and in any case could not have become law without the President's signature or passage by a two-thirds vote over a veto.

In the meantime, Dr. Condon was vigorous in his own defense and was not lacking in widespread support. His immediate reply on

[152] *Ibid.*, March 5, 1948.   [153] *Ibid.*, March 11, 1948.

March 1 to the subcommittee report was a statement, "If it is true I am one of the weakest links in atomic security that is very gratifying and the country can feel absolutely safe for I am completely loyal, conscientious and devoted to the interests of my country, as my whole career and life clearly reveal." [154] He immediately renewed his demand that the Un-American Activities Committee hear him in a public hearing, and there ensued the on-again, off-again scheduling of such a hearing which ended finally in no hearing at all.

It is possible that the responsibility for the failure to hold public hearings in the Condon case does not rest entirely with the Un-American Activities Committee. There is no doubt that the committee was at fault at the beginning in making it possible for one of its subcommittees to issue such a controversial report as that dealing with Dr. Condon before having held any public hearings. With respect to the situation after the issuance of the report it is not easy to determine just why no hearings were ever held. Dr. Condon seems to have been anxious for such hearings. On March 5 he forced himself upon members of the committee at the close of a session and is reported to have asked for a hearing.[155] A day or so earlier he asked Senator Hickenlooper, chairman of the Joint Committee on Atomic Energy, to have his committee make an independent investigation for the purpose of "restoring conditions in which men of intelligence would be willing to work for their Government and not be constantly harassed and harried by irresponsible attacks upon their character." [156]

Later in March it was announced that the House committee would hold a public hearing in the Condon case on April 21. Thereafter, on March 29, Condon's lawyers, Thurman Arnold, Abe Fortas, and Paul Porter, addressed a long letter to Chairman Thomas in which they demanded certain "minimal procedural rights" at the April 21 hearing. In general, these demands were eminently reasonable, but one, at least, the right to cross-examine hostile witnesses, is a right that Congressional investigating committees have seldom if ever granted. On the other hand, the letter was not written in an adamant tone, and had the committee shown any willingness to compromise

[154] *Ibid.*, March 2, 1948.
[155] Representative Holifield on March 9, 1948. 94 *Cong. Rec.* 2443.
[156] *N.Y. Times*, March 4, 1948. The Hickenlooper committee took the Condon request under advisement, but it ultimately refrained from entering the case or holding any public hearings.

with respect to procedural matters there is no reason to suppose that Condon would have refused to appear unless all of his demands were met.[157] The committee took no public notice of the letter, and on April 14 it announced that the hearing was being postponed to a later date. In *The Red Plot Against America* Robert Stripling offers two reasons why no Condon hearings were ever held by the committee during the 80th Congress. One is that since the White House would not release the full text of the Hoover letter to Harriman an all-important means by which a final judgment could be formulated in the case was denied the committee. The other was that Thomas' continuing illness made it impossible for him to "get to Capitol hill to defend the Committee's action." As in previous situations, says Stripling, Thomas was unwilling to delegate his authority as chairman to any other member of the committee.[158]

When the Un-American Activities Committee was reorganized in the 81st Congress in 1949, it took the position that it would be glad to give Dr. Condon a public hearing if he asked for one. Presumably, Dr. Condon did not avail himself of this offer. "Louis Welborn" says that Condon failed to ask for a hearing because the new committee's seeming disinterest in his case meant that he "would probably be in the awkward position of having to act as both his own prosecutor and defense." [159]

It is possible that the Thomas committee was also overwhelmed by the volume and vigor of the public opinion in Dr. Condon's favor which took shape immediately after the release of the subcommittee report. Editorial treatment of the report in the press of the nation, apart from those few papers that could be counted on to support the committee regardless of the merits of a particular situation, was uniformly hostile to the committee.[160] The scientific profession of America rose almost to the man and in righteous indignation denounced the committee and reaffirmed its faith and confidence in Dr. Condon. Individual scientists and formal societies vied with each other in writing letters to the press, to Congressmen, and to the President of the United States, and in adopting resolutions and making public statements. It would have been a brave Congressional

[157] The full text of the letter is found in 94 *Cong. Rec.* 4795–4796 (April 22, 1948).

[158] *The Red Plot*, pp. 86–87.

[159] "The Ordeal of Dr. Condon," *Harper's Magazine*, Jan., 1949.

[160] For an excellent summary of editorial treatment of the Condon report, see the speech of Representative Douglas on April 14, 1948, 94 *Cong. Rec.* 4464.

committee, indeed, that would not have been somewhat taken aback by the eminence of the scientists who leaped to Condon's defense and the enthusiasm of the language used on his behalf.[161]

Perhaps more than at any other point in its history, the Un-American Activities Committee, in permitting the Thomas attack upon Dr. Condon, found itself opposed by an organized, responsible, and highly articulate segment of the American people. Faced with this opposition it is not surprising that the committee lost heart in continuing an attack which from the beginning had little or no justification in fact or logic.

The Duggan Case

The tragic death of Laurence Duggan on December 20, 1948, involved the Un-American Activities Committee in one of the most serious controversies of its entire career. Moreover, the episode is of considerable significance in the history of the committee because it illustrates in striking fashion a particular type of committee activity, one in which the committee plays an important role in the total absence of any public hearings or formal reports. The Condon case, as has been seen, was also marked by an absence of hearings, but it centered about the release of a printed subcommittee report. In the Duggan case, report as well as hearings were missing, for the committee played its part in the absence of both of these procedures traditional to Congressional investigations.

Laurence Duggan, director of the Institute of International Education, was killed in a fall from a window of his office on the sixteenth floor of an office building in midtown New York City. The institute, founded in 1919 by Duggan's father, has as its chief purpose expediting the exchange of students and teachers between the United States and foreign countries. Duggan's fall occurred at the end of the day, about 7 P.M., and was marked by several unusual circumstances. Still a relatively young man of forty-three years, married, and the father of four children, it seemed unlikely that such a man would take his life within a week of Christmas, particularly without leaving any word of explanation to members of his family. And yet the evidence surrounding the fall was such that the final police report listed the cause of death as "jumped or fell." [162] There was

---

[161] For an excellent summary of these statements, resolutions, etc., see the speech of Representative Douglas on April 15, 1948. *Ibid.*, 4553.

[162] The police were reported almost at once as satisfied that no crime had been committed and that Duggan had either committed suicide or had been suddenly

no evidence of a struggle or that anyone else had been in the room at the time of the fall. Duggan was evidently preparing to leave his office when he fell, for he had one galosh on, and the other was found beside the window from which he fell. Members of Duggan's family revealed that he had had an operation for ulcers several years earlier and that he had had a spinal disc removed a month before his death. His brother was reported as saying that he was in the habit of keeping a thermos bottle of milk in his office "to settle his stomach between meals," and he concluded, "the best guess we in the family can make is he may have had a spasm or nausea when he bent over to put on his galoshes, and then went to the window for fresh air." [163] One of his colleagues in the Institute of International Education added that Duggan was "a very tired man and ill for some time." [164] On the other hand, Sumner Welles at once made public the information that he had received a cheerful letter from Duggan within twenty-four hours of his death in which Duggan sought his assistance in a professional matter. Welles added that the letter convinced him that Duggan was prepared to wait patiently for an answer and that he was not contemplating suicide at the time it was written.

It was not these facts, tantalizing in their mystery though they were, that made the Duggan death a front-page story in the nation's press during the closing days of the year. Instead, it was the possibility that somehow Duggan had been involved in the sordid tale of Communist espionage told by Whittaker Chambers, which already included as one of its chief characters such a seemingly impeccable young man as Alger Hiss.

taken ill and fallen through a window he had opened to obtain air (*N.Y. Herald Tribune*, Dec. 22, 1948). On December 24, Police Commissioner Wallander reported to Mayor O'Dwyer as follows:

"I have this day received from Chief of Detectives George Mitchell a complete report of the investigation into the cause of the death of Laurence Duggan which occurred on December 20.

"From reading this report, which is the result of a very careful and searching inquiry to determine if a crime had been committed, it was found that everything about the room was in order and undisturbed.

"There were no signs or marks of a struggle within the (eight by fourteen-foot) room or on the (thirty-three-inch above the floor) window sill, which would tend to rule out that death came by violence. Apparently, he was in the room alone at the time of the occurrence. We have no witnesses to the incident.

"Unless other evidence develops that would indicate a necessity for reopening the case, we are concluding this investigation with the finding that Mr. Duggan either accidentally fell or jumped." *Ibid.*, Dec. 25, 1948.

[163] *Washington Post*, Dec. 22, 1948.   [164] *Ibid.*

To begin with, Duggan's career had in many ways paralleled that of Hiss. The two men were almost of an age, were good friends, and had known each other since both were students at Harvard University. Both had served in the State Department, and after leaving the government service both became heads of private institutions interested in the cause of international friendship and peace. Duggan had served in the State Department for a period of fourteen years and had for ten years been chief of the Division of American Republics when he left the department in 1944. Like Hiss, he was well known among scholars of international relations and enjoyed an excellent reputation in professional circles. Coming as it did just five days after Alger Hiss's indictment for perjury, Duggan's death might well have provoked comment as to the relationship between the two men. But there was not to be any need for speculation about the relationship, for within five hours of Duggan's death a statement was released to the press by Representative Mundt, acting chairman of the Un-American Activities Committee, which suggested that the dead man had been deeply involved in the espionage story.[165] In a midnight press conference at which Representative Nixon and Chief Investigator Stripling were also present, Mundt announced that, less than two weeks before, Isaac Don Levine in a closed hearing before a subcommittee had testified that Laurence Duggan was one of the names that Whittaker Chambers had given Adolf Berle at the 1939 conference of the three men when Chambers had first revealed the details of his espionage story to a government official. The following excerpt from Levine's testimony was given to the press by Mundt and Nixon:

Rep. Mundt: Mr. Levine, the purpose of this executive meeting following your public testimony is simply to enable you to give the committee all the names and all the leads that you can supply that you feel might lead to the information which would be helpful in trying to get to the culprit or culprits involved in the espionage case—the theft and disclosure of State Department records.

Mr. Levine: I take it for granted that this can be very brief. The six

[165] In the closing days of 1948 the Un-American Activities Committee was rapidly disintegrating. The impending meeting of the 81st Congress and the reorganization of the committee by the Democrats, the continuing illness of Thomas, and the indictment of Hiss following the sensational revelations concerning the Pumpkin Papers all combined to bring about this result. Mundt is identified in the news stories of the period as the committee's acting chairman. Representative Nixon was also present in Washington, as was seemingly Representative Rankin.

names in the State Department that were disclosed in the course of that evening (in Adolf Berle's house) were as follows: Laurence Duggan.

Mr. Mundt: May I interrupt to ask, discussed in what connection?

Mr. Levine: In connection with the transmission of papers which Mr. Chambers had, well, which Mr. Chambers was covering. He was covering the State Department which he mentioned as having at different times passed confidential information.

Mr. Mundt: That is what I wanted.

Mr. Levine: The first name is Laurence Duggan.[166]

The next day at a press conference in Washington a reporter asked Mundt who the other five persons were that Levine had named to the subcommittee in the closed session. It was reported that Mundt replied, "We will give them out as they jump out of windows." [167] Mundt was also reported as having said the day after Duggan's death that he believed there was "more than a slight possibility" that Duggan had been slain, adding, "If foul play is involved it might lead directly to the Communist conspirators." [168]

Further developments in the Duggan case now followed quickly. Thomas J. Donegan, Special Assistant Attorney General, promptly announced that the federal grand jury in New York which had indicted Alger Hiss had not heard Laurence Duggan as a witness. On the other hand, it was announced that an FBI agent had questioned Duggan on December 10, just ten days before his death. It was said that this interview was a "routine" one, after Duggan's name had been "mentioned." The FBI agent who made this announcement to the press refused to state who had done the "mentioning" of Duggan's name, saying, "It could have come from any possible source," but news stories suggested that the FBI interview was the direct result of Levine's secret testimony before the House committee on December 8.[169] On December 24, Attorney General

[166] *N.Y. Herald Tribune,* Dec. 23, 1948.

[167] *Washington Post,* Dec. 22, 1948.

[168] *N.Y. Herald Tribune,* Dec. 22, 1948.

[169] *Ibid.,* Dec. 22, 1948, and *N.Y. Times,* Dec. 23, 1948. This revelation that the FBI had questioned Duggan set off a minor controversy between the Department of Justice and the Un-American Activities Committee. The implication of the FBI agent's story was that the FBI had interviewed Duggan as the result of a "leak" from the House committee. Mundt immediately requested the head of the New York office of the FBI to explain why it had questioned Duggan just two days after Levine had given his name to the Un-American Activities Committee. The request was refused (*N.Y. Herald Tribune,* Dec. 24, 1948). Thereafter, on December 24, Attorney General Clark stated that Duggan "was interviewed by the FBI on December 10, 1948, ten days before his death, and

Clark announced that the FBI investigation of Duggan had produced no evidence of any kind linking Duggan with the espionage case or the Communist Party. "On the contrary," said Clark, "the evidence discloses that Mr. Duggan was a loyal employee of the United States Government." [170]

On the day after Duggan's death Whittaker Chambers cast a good deal of doubt upon the accuracy of the Levine testimony as released by Mundt at the midnight press conference on the day of Duggan's death. The transcript revealed Levine as having testified that Chambers mentioned Duggan's name to Berle "in connection with the transmission of papers." In an interview with newspapermen, Chambers now denied that he had ever said that Duggan had passed him any papers from the State Department. "It would be more proper," said Chambers, "to say that I mentioned six people. I mentioned Mr. Duggan, but I did not mention all these people as having turned over papers to me. I did not name Mr. Duggan as passing over papers to me." Chambers was also reported to have answered the question, "Was Mr. Duggan a Communist?" with the direct reply, "No, not to my direct knowledge," adding that he

---

after his name had been mentioned by a congressional committee." This statement angered Mundt, who immediately attacked the implication of Clark's words that the House committee had put the FBI on Duggan's trail as a spy suspect. Mundt said, "It [the Clark statement] is not correct if it is meant to imply that the FBI investigation was undertaken as a result of our committee giving out any information concerning Laurence Duggan prior to the night of the plunge which cost him his life. I would like to point out that the department statement does not specifically say that the FBI investigation came as a result of such information *coming* from our committee." *N.Y. Times*, Dec. 25, 1948.

[170] *Washington Post*, Dec. 25, 1948. The text of the Justice Department statement is as follows:

"In answer to many inquiries concerning Laurence Duggan, the Attorney General stated that while it is the policy of the Department of Justice not to comment upon the evidence in the files or upon interviews made by its agents, he was deviating from this rule in order to prevent an injustice being done to the family of a former employe of the Government.

"While the department had no derogatory information covering espionage on Laurence Duggan, he was interviewed by the FBI on December 10, 1948, 10 days before his death, and after his name had been mentioned by a congressional committee.

"In the course of this inquiry, as in any other investigation, the FBI interviews many loyal and patriotic citizens.

"The FBI investigation has produced no evidence of Mr. Duggan's connection with the Communist Party or with any other espionage activity. On the contrary, the evidence discloses that Mr. Duggan was a loyal employe of the United States Government." *Ibid.*

had never met Duggan. On the other hand, when asked, "Did you know him as a member of the Washington apparatus of the Communists?" Chambers merely replied, "No comment." And he was also reported to have made the gratuitous statement that he understood Duggan was "a gentle and sensitive man from what I have heard about him and how he was devoted to his family." [171]

Still further doubt was cast on the Mundt midnight press conference story when newspapermen finally reached Isaac Don Levine by telephone in Mexico City, where he was at the time of Duggan's death. Levine was reported to have denied categorically that he had ever testified before the House committee to the effect that Chambers in his 1939 session with Berle had said that Duggan had turned over classified documents to him. The *New York Herald Tribune* reported, "Mr. Levine did say, however, that Mr. Chambers claimed he had received 'confidential information' from Mr. Duggan." And it quoted Levine as saying, "At this distance, I should say that the man jumped—he couldn't face the music." A United Press story, however, had Levine saying, "It might have been another Masaryk affair . . . the technique of pushing people out of a window was tried on Masaryk with success." [172]

[171] *N.Y. Herald Tribune* and *N.Y. Times*, Dec. 22, 1948.

[172] *N.Y. Herald Tribune*, Dec. 23, 1948. When Levine returned to this country in January, he held a press conference at which he once more denied he had ever testified before the Un-American Activities Committee to the effect that Duggan had passed any State Department papers to Chambers. He insisted that he had said Duggan had passed confidential "information" not "papers," and he was quoted as telling reporters, "The point of my testimony was that Duggan had been mentioned in connection with the 'apparatus' handled by Chambers, who alone had first-hand knowledge of the exact nature of that connection." He then criticized the committee for making public testimony given in executive session. "The violation of confidence perpetrated by certain members of the committee defeats every purpose of bona fide investigation. Publication of such secret testimony is not only abhorrent to every sense of fair play but is bound in the future to seal the lips of responsible witnesses."

At this press conference Levine also intimated that the full story of Duggan's relations with Soviet espionage agents had not yet been told. While refusing to tell what the additional information was, he suggested Duggan had perhaps been "innocently victimized" by these agents and that he might have been used as a "contact" without knowing it. And he added that a good "contact" could be "the key that turns the lock" for the real spies. *N.Y. Times*, Jan. 6, 1949.

A few days later Levine wrote a letter to the *N.Y. Times*, taking it to task for its editorial of Dec. 23, 1948. In part his letter reads:

"As to your statement that Chambers had declared that he never received any papers from Mr. Duggan, the inference is made that I had said so. I never

Thereupon, Whittaker Chambers, in one of those ambiguities which are common to his telling of the espionage story and concerning which he has seldom been questioned intelligently or systematically, backtracked a bit and was reported as having told newspapermen the next day, "Too much emphasis has been placed on my statement that I personally never knew Laurence Duggan and that he never gave me documents. Practically overlooked is the fact that I found it necessary to give Duggan's name to Mr. Berle in 1939. I resent slaps at Isaac Don Levine. We are both making statements on the basis of information we do not wish to discuss at this time." [173]

Representative Mundt and Nixon were obviously taken aback by the partial repudiation by Chambers and Levine of the original story against Duggan which they had sponsored at the midnight conference; by the testimonials in support of Duggan's character and ability coming from such persons as Cordell Hull, Sumner Welles, Adolf Berle, and Francis Sayre; [174] and by the vehemence of the

---

did. Just as Mr. Mundt was hasty in drawing this inference from the transcript, for which you justly criticized him, so your editorialist was hasty in repeating the same inference.

"My statement in executive session before the House Un-American Activities Committee was that Mr. Chambers mentioned Mr. Duggan in connection with the apparatus in the State Department which Mr. Chambers was handling. A careful reading of my testimony, never intended for publication and designed merely to furnish a lead for further investigation, will bear me out." Ibid., Jan. 10, 1949.

[173] Ibid., Dec. 23, 1948. In Witness, Chambers flatly calls Duggan one of the "contacts" of the Hede Massing Communist "espionage apparatus" in Washington, although he also writes that he gave Duggan's name to Berle in 1939 "as someone whom I believed, though I was not certain, to be connected with a Soviet apparatus" (pp. 30, 334, 382).

[174] Sayre told newsmen: "I knew Mr. Duggan well and was a close friend of his in the State Department. He was a man who was very much trusted by Cordell Hull. He was greatly respected throughout South America and had much influence with the Latin-American peoples, as his work lay mostly in that field. He rendered great service to his country and was a lovable fellow who had many friends." Ibid., Dec. 22, 1948.

Welles issued the following statement:

"Laurence Duggan was for ten years one of my closest associates in the Department of State. As Chief of the Division of American Republics, and later as political adviser on inter-American relations, he rendered outstandingly able service to the United States and to the cause of hemispheric solidarity.

"He was one of the most brilliant, most devoted, and most patriotic public servants I have ever known. His death comes as a great shock and as a deep personal sorrow to me." N.Y. Herald Tribune, Dec. 22, 1948.

Cordell Hull is reported to have told former associates in the State Depart-

criticism which was soon directed against them and the Un-American Activities Committee from many directions. Following Chambers' first denial that Duggan had supplied him with State Department documents, Nixon stated on a television broadcast that Chambers' statement "clears Duggan of any implication in the espionage ring. That is the best evidence." [175] And even following Chambers' partial retraction of his statement clearing Duggan, Mundt took the position at a press conference on December 24 that the case is "a closed book as far as the committee is concerned." Asked whether he was now satisfied of Duggan's innocence he said, "Well, as far as the evidence before us is concerned. We have dropped the case." [176]

The day after the Duggan story "broke," Representatives Mundt and Nixon were denounced by two of their colleagues for their action in making public the transcript of the Levine testimony. From his home in New Orleans Representative Hébert called for a halt in the committee's practice of doing business "with one eye on today's evidence and the other on tomorrow's headlines." He added, "Headline happiness has always been one of the committee's obstacles. This is another example of that malady. It is incongruous that a committee which is denouncing leaks in the State Department and other Government agencies can't stop leaks within its own ranks." More specifically he charged, "The revelation that the name of Laurence

---

ment that in a message of condolence to Mrs. Duggan he "spoke highly" of Duggan and expressed faith in his "honesty" as a public servant, and that he had meant every word of a letter he had written to Duggan praising him when he retired from the State Department in 1944. *N.Y. Times,* Dec. 23, 1948.

In an editorial, Dec. 23, 1948, the *Washington Post* recalled that Duggan's retirement from the State Department in 1944 was due, at least in part, to a disagreement over United States policy concerning the recognition of the Villaroel regime in Bolivia which had come to power following a coup d'état in 1943. Duggan was said to have favored recognition even though there was evidence that Villaroel had Fascist and Nazi support, his argument being that recognition might woo Villaroel away from these supporters. According to the *Post,* Duggan's arguments prevailed, Villaroel was recognized, but this failed to weaken the Fascists and Nazis. A two-year reign of terror followed in Bolivia, until Villaroel was overthrown and killed in 1946. Said the *Post,* "Over several months in 1944 the Bolivian incident rocked the State Department and the Capitol." However, it added that Hull never gave any indication of doubt concerning Duggan's integrity, and that one of Duggan's associates who had been demoted for opposing the Duggan policy had telephoned the *Post* on the news of Duggan's death to say that "he would rather trust 'Larry' than himself."

[175] *N.Y. Times,* Dec. 23, 1948.   [176] *Washington Post,* Dec. 25, 1948.

Duggan . . . had been mentioned before the committee . . . in connection with the Hiss-Chambers affair was a blunder, a breach of confidence and a violation of agreed upon procedure." According to Hébert, committee members had agreed earlier in the month not to bring the name of anyone "into a public session before a closed session had been held and the person given an opportunity to defend himself." And then pointedly he said he was not criticizing the whole committee. "I am accusing only the guilty ones and they know who they are." [177]

Representative Rankin also attacked his colleagues and called their action "atrocious" and "unfortunate." He insisted that if he had been consulted he would have "protested" the releasing of the Levine testimony. "I am sure if the full committee had been consulted it would not have been given out. I would have tried to talk Mundt out of releasing it. Duggan was dead and nothing was accomplished by releasing it." [178]

Mundt replied immediately to these attacks by his colleagues. "I don't think it [releasing the testimony] was a blunder and I have no regrets about it," he told newsmen. "We said when we put it out that we did not imply either guilt or innocence to Duggan. We released it on the theory that no congressional committee should conceal information that might be helpful to the police in determining the cause of a tragic death." However, Mundt agreed that Hébert was correct in saying that the committee had voted to keep such testimony as that given by Levine confidential. But he insisted that the decision to depart from the agreement had been made by a majority vote of the subcommittee members still in Washington "on the theory that [the information] would be helpful to the police." But he was forced to add that this "majority vote" consisted only

---

[177] *N.Y. Times* and *Washington Post*, Dec. 23, 1948. On Dec. 31 Hébert issued another statement, again attacking his colleagues, taking them to task for what he called a "hysteria for newspaper headlines." He said, "It is rather peculiar that two members of the committee who have been such well-known transgressors of the principles from which these rules and regulations rise [Hébert is referring to proposals recently submitted by Mundt and Nixon for reform in committee procedures] should now appear in public as champions of the procedure. All the rules and all the regulations which the committee might adopt are not worth a tinker's dam if some members of the committee fail to practice what they preach and admonish others 'to do as I say, and not as I do.' " *Washington Post*, Dec. 31, 1948.

[178] *Washington Post*, Dec. 23, 1948.

of his own vote and that of Nixon. The only other member in town was Rankin, and Mundt said he was not contacted because of the late midnight hour when the decision was made.[179]

By the twenty-fourth the tide of criticism against the committee had risen to such proportions that Mundt and Nixon felt it necessary to issue two statements, in one of which Mundt, speaking for himself alone, endeavored to explain away his statement about counting espionage agents as they jumped out of windows, and in the other of which the two men jointly tried to justify their action in giving out to the press the transcript of the Levine testimony within a matter of hours after Duggan's death. In the first of these statements Mundt did not deny that he had made the remark attributed to him but implied that the remark did not accurately reflect his feelings in the matter and that in any case he had not expected newspapermen to use a flippant remark made in the nature of an aside. The text of his statement follows:

I recall being asked many questions by reporters as to when and whether we would release the other names mentioned by Mr. Levine. I told them it would be done only by committee action and only when and if further evidence was secured. I modified this statement by saying something to the effect that this would govern our policy unless something like this comes along again, and that circumstances and the vote of the committee would then determine that. I was correctly quoted in these words in some dispatches, and they accurately reflect my position as I intended it to be used, if at all, by those reporting that interview with the press.

I do not desire to get into any argument with the press over what I may or may not have said in offhand conversation with press people present but with no intention that it be made part of a press report reflecting the position of our subcommittee. The foregoing paragraph to the best of my memory reproduces exactly what I intended and expected the press would carry concerning our continued intention of keeping secret the other names mentioned by Levine until and unless a change in circumstances warrants their publication.[180]

The text of the joint statement justifying the midnight press conference is as follows:

Late Monday night newsmen called Congressman Mundt and Robert E. Stripling asking them the direct question, "has your committee had any testimony before it connecting Laurence Duggan with the espionage case?" Neither Mundt nor Stripling recalled definitely what if any testimony had been placed in the record in Mr. Duggan's connection, but when it

[179] N.Y. Herald Tribune, Dec. 23, 1948.   [180] Ibid., Dec. 25, 1948.

IN THE EIGHTIETH CONGRESS: 1948

was explained that an unsolved violent death had occurred in New York, they called Congressman Nixon and agreed to meet in the committee room to determine whether there was anything in the testimony which might help to throw light on this mysterious death.

Shortly before midnight, we located in the committee files the testimony that Mr. Levine had given in connection with Mr. Chambers' report to Adolf Berle in which Duggan's name appeared. We were then confronted with three possible choices: (1) We could tell the newsmen who by then had called us in great numbers that "there is no testimony on Duggan in the record." That would have been a bare-faced lie and a concealment of truth which we felt was unjustified. (2) We could simply have said, "no comment," which we decided against on the basis it would have left to every reporter's imagination the importance or non-importance of the testimony in the record and might well have been ballooned into something considerably larger and more damaging than the testimony itself. (3) We could release the exact transcript of the testimony itself in the hope it might be helpful to the public and the police in solving the cause and the circumstances of this violent death.

We selected the third alternative and in so doing perhaps warrant some honest criticism, but it is difficult to know what would be a wiser decision should we be confronted with such a perplexing problem again.

One other point should be made clear. In releasing this transcript we emphasized at the time we were doing so with the hope it would be helpful in clearing up the mystery surrounding this death. We made no statement implying the guilt of Mr. Duggan and said specifically, "this statement must stand on its own feet" with no elaboration from us. We have adhered to that position. We feel that Mr. Chambers' statements on this matter are the best source of direct information.[181]

Up to a point this statement is a persuasive one. Those critics of Mundt and Nixon who went so far as to argue that it was shameful that the Un-American Activities Committee should have shown any interest at all in such an honorable and blameless individual as Laurence Duggan clearly overstated the case against the committee. After all, Duggan did die a sudden and violent death under most unusual circumstances. And whatever may be the truth about what Isaac Don Levine did say, or intended to say, in his secret testimony before the committee on December 10, it is clearly established that he mentioned Duggan by name and in such a way that the committee might well have been expected to show further interest in him. After all, it was possible to suppose as of midnight on the day of his death that Duggan had met with foul play and that he had

181 *Ibid.*

been killed to prevent him from telling what he knew about Communist espionage in the government.

But the speed with which Representative Mundt moved was inexcusable. The story of the pressure put upon him by newspapermen who began calling him as soon as the word of Duggan's death was known is not completely convincing. How they should have had any suspicion that the committee had received "any testimony . . . connecting Laurence Duggan with the espionage case" is not explained. Here, Mundt must pay the price for the very close relations he and other members of the committee have maintained through the years with certain newspapermen and newspapers. Try to be impartial though he may, the neutral but informed observer of the committee cannot help wondering whether the calls did not come from certain of the committee's close friends among newspapermen and whether Mundt, Nixon, and Stripling were not all too willing to rush down to the committee's offices, check the files, and make a spectacular midnight announcement to the reporters present. And in any case it is clear that such an experienced and tough-skinned legislator as Mundt could easily enough have refused to make a statement that night, have insisted that the entire committee would have to be consulted, and have dismissed the newspapermen by telling them that a statement would be made at a later time. There was certainly no need for the mad dash by the three men on the night of December 20 to Capitol Hill, with reporters virtually breathing down their necks as they checked the files to see whether Laurence Duggan's name was there. An experienced Congressman could, if he had so wished, have insisted upon a more leisurely and dignified examination of the situation before making any statement, without prejudicing the case in the way in which Mundt and Nixon claim it would have been prejudiced had they not acted as they did.

A somewhat different explanation of the motives that influenced Representative Mundt in his actions is suggested in an editorial in the *New York Times*. This editorial may fairly be compared with the Mundt-Nixon statement. It reads in part:

Shortly after 6 o'clock Monday evening Laurence Duggan, Director of the Institute of International Education and formerly a trusted adviser of the State Department on Latin-American affairs, fell, leaped or was pushed to his death from the window of his sixteenth-floor office in a building in West Forty-fifth Street. Five hours later, before there had been more than a brief police examination of the circumstances, and certainly before any calm conclusion could have been drawn, Representative Karl

Mundt, acting head of the House Committee on Un-American Activities, issued in Washington the transcript of testimony given before that Committee in secret session twelve days previously which led to the appearance the next morning of a headline in this newspaper: "Fall Kills Duggan, Named with Hiss in Spy Ring Inquiry."

The inference subsequently drawn from Mr. Mundt's transcript was quite obviously what Mr. Mundt had intended, which was to show a connection between the death, under circumstances that still are not clear, of a former State Department official and the Committee's investigation of alleged Communist infiltration of that Department and other departments of the Government. There was probably not a newspaper reader anywhere in whose mind that thought was not planted.[182]

Mundt's assertion that the transcript of Levine's testimony was released as an aid "to the police in determining the cause of a tragic death" is not very persuasive. The committee could easily have transmitted a confidential report to the New York City police without making public the information in its possession.

In no other instance, save perhaps in the Condon case, were the Un-American Activities Committee and its members so vigorously condemned in the press. In particular, editorial comment in conservative and respected papers was blunt and distinctly unfavorable. For example, the *New York Herald Tribune* stated that Mundt and Nixon's handling of the Levine testimony "has caused a deep shock." And it added, "At a stroke it has undone months of genuine effort on the part of the Un-American Activities Committee to correct past excesses and bring its procedures within the limits of reason and fairness." [183] The *Washington Post* was even more outspoken. "The trigger-happy legislators who are ready at any moment to abandon their own rules in order to strike at a helpless victim, without waiting to assemble all the pertinent facts, have once more demonstrated their unfitness for the task they are trying to do." [184]

In the end the facts of the story of the Un-American Activities Committee's role in the Duggan case speak for themselves. If there remained by 1948 any doubt about the impropriety and lack of wisdom in a policy by which members of a Congressional committee conducting investigations in such a controversial field as subversive activity made use of press conferences and public statements as formal means of carrying on their work, the doubt was now dispelled once and for all.

[182] *N.Y. Times,* Dec. 23, 1948.   [183] Dec. 24, 1948.
[184] Dec. 28, 1948.

V: The Committee in the Eighty-first Congress: 1949-1950

FOR THE third time in five years, the Un-American Activities Committee received a new complement of members. Seven of the nine men who served on the committee throughout most of the 81st Congress were new to its ranks. Only John Wood and Richard Nixon carried over from the 80th Congress. Representatives Rankin and Hébert were forced off the committee by the Democrats themselves, who adopted informal rules excluding nonlawyers (Hébert) and chairmen of other House committees (Rankin) from committee membership. Wood resumed the chairmanship and was joined by an entire new group of Democrats: Francis Walter of Pennsylvania, Burr Harrison of Virginia, John McSweeney of Ohio, and Morgan Moulder of Missouri. Nixon's Republican colleagues were Francis Case of South Dakota, Harold Velde of Illinois, and Bernard Kearney of New York.[1]

In 1949 and 1950 the Un-American Activities Committee was busier than ever before. The printed hearings reveal that it held sessions on thirty-four days in 1949, and on seventy-four days in 1950.[2] This total of 108 days on which the committee conducted

---

[1] Nixon resigned from the committee late in 1950, and his place was filled briefly during the closing days of the 81st Congress by Donald Jackson of California. J. Parnell Thomas was carried as a member of the committee throughout 1949 until he resigned his seat in Congress in January, 1950. However, he attended no sessions of the committee. His place was taken by Bernard Kearney of New York.

[2] The piecemeal fashion in which the committee has published the record of hearings conducted in executive session suggests that there may well be additional hearings that have never been identified and testimony that has not been published.

hearings during the 81st Congress campares with a total of sixty-two days during the 80th Congress, and twelve days during the 79th Congress. The number of pages in the printed hearings for the 81st Congress is no less than 3,626, a number far above the figures for the 79th and 80th Congresses.[3] Eleven reports were published during the two-year period. These included an "annual" report each year, seven reports on alleged Communist front organizations, a report to the House of Representatives accompanying the internal security bill, and a report on the subject of atomic espionage.[4]

Some sense of the 1949–1950 record can be conveyed by suggesting that with Democratic recapture of the committee and the return of John Wood to the post of chairman, the committee mounted horseback and rode off in every direction. There were no single inquiries that dominated the scene as had the Hollywood hearings in 1947 or the Chambers-Hiss hearings in 1948. Instead, the committee's interests ranged widely, and it carried on a wide variety of investigations simultaneously.[5] This change in the general character of the committee's program had both its good and its bad sides. On one hand, the committee must be given credit for having consciously attempted to avoid the isolated, sensational lines of inquiry it had pursued in former years. The wide scope of the new program unquestionably reflected a desire to subject subversive activity in the United States to broad, systematic investigation. On the other hand, with few exceptions, the hearings of the period are marked by futility. They attracted little attention when held; on the whole the printed record of them makes dull reading, and they have seemingly had little influence. There are scattered indications that members of the committee's Republican minority regarded this busy concern for a great many small subjects as a more or less deliberate attempt to keep the committee preoccupied with harmless matters. A fairer explanation would be that a conscious effort was being made to do a thorough job of investigating all phases of the problem assigned to the committee.

Insofar as there is any rhyme or reason to the program of the committee during this two-year period, the hearings may be placed

[3] The hearings for the 81st Congress are numbered consecutively from p. 1 to p. 3626. Pages 775–796 seem to be unaccounted for.

[4] For the list of hearings, reports, and other publications of the committee in the 81st Congress, see Appendix, Table I.

[5] An indication of the varied nature of the hearings is to be seen in the fact that the transcript is published in thirty-five separate volumes.

in four categories. The most numerous and easily identifiable group of hearings carried forward the committee's researches into the nature of the Communist movement in the United States. The approach to this subject was a twofold one: geographical and functional. The first is seen in a series of hearings dealing with Communist activity in the District of Columbia, in western Pennsylvania, in the Cincinnati area, and in Hawaii. The second finds the committee continuing its inquiries into Communist infiltration of labor unions, the federal governmental service, and minority groups.

A second group of hearings attempted to advance the committee's search for information concerning Communist espionage in connection with the atomic bomb, particularly as centered in the Radiation Laboratory at the University of California. A third set of hearings was held on two "internal security" bills that were referred to the committee by the House of Representatives: the Wood bill, and the Nixon bill. Finally, a fourth, vaguely defined group of scattered hearings dealt with specific personalities. The central figures in these hearings were of different types. Some were ex-Communists, willing in varying degrees to tell the committee what they knew about the pattern of Communist activity in the United States. Witnesses of this type were General Izyador Modelski, former military attaché of the Polish Embassy in Washington; Paul Crouch, who as a member of the American Communist Party from 1925 to 1942 had had a varied career as a minor party functionary; and Lee Pressman, the former general counsel of the CIO, who, late in the summer of 1950, admitted that he had once been a member of the Communist Party, thus verifying the charge made against him by Whittaker Chambers in 1948. Some were "unfriendly witnesses," persons suspected of Communist activity, who when subpoenaed by the committee refused to answer its questions, usually on the ground of self-incrimination. In this category were Steve Nelson, the indefatigable Communist functionary whose name had appeared through the years in so many Communist hearings, and Philip A. Bart, general manager of the company publishing the *Daily Worker*. A third group consisted of persons seeking a hearing before the committee as a means of denying charges that they were Communists or members of subversive organizations. Such well-known personalities from the entertainment profession as Edward G. Robinson, Hazel Scott Powell, and Josh White fall into this group.

Certain general observations can be made concerning the 1949–1950 hearings. A surprisingly large number of them made public information already well known to the FBI. This was true of all the hearings dealing with Communist activity in certain sections of the country. Often the leading witness in such committee hearings was an undercover FBI agent who had infiltrated the Communist movement. It is quite apparent that these hearings were designed to serve the purpose of publicizing information in FBI files.

In general the hearings of this period reflected exceedingly careful preliminary work by the committee's staff. The very dullness of many of the hearings can be attributed to this factor; they had been so carefully rehearsed and there were so many details to be brought out that the proceedings often lacked spontaneity or drama. Moreover, the staff handled far more of the questioning of witnesses than ever before. In many of the hearings virtually all of the questions were asked by such staff members as Frank Tavenner and Louis Russell. Where committee members did participate in the interrogation process, they did so in an orderly, disciplined way, following exhaustive probing of the witnesses by the staff members. In general, the Republican members of the committee were quiescent. Now and again, Representatives Case, Nixon, and Velde attempted to stir things up, but generally they were satisfied to let the staff do the questioning and seemed often bored by the proceedings. Among the Democrats only Chairman Wood and Representative Walter took any regular part in the questioning, and their voices were heard far less often than had been the voices of majority members in the 80th Congress.

In general, the hearings were marked by adherence to fair and just procedures. Witnesses were allowed to enjoy the benefit of counsel, to make brief oral statements, and to file longer written statements with little or none of the quarreling that had marked the exercise of such rights before the committees of the 79th and 80th Congresses. Now and again, an unco-operative witness was badgered a bit, but there was little of the angry bullying that such men as Thomas and Rankin had once indulged in. The committee was faced with refusal by more than three-score witnesses to answer questions for one reason or another, mostly on the ground of self-incrimination. Ultimately some fifty-six of these witnesses were cited for contempt in what was proving by the middle of 1951 to be an abortive attempt by the committee to defend its authority in the courts against this form of nonco-operation. But while they were before the committee as witnesses, these persons were generally free from the rigorous treatment extended to unfriendly witnesses in earlier years. Any attempt to set forth even a brief summary of all of the hearings of the 1949–1950 period would be beyond the scope of this book. However, an adequate impression of the committee's interests and activities can be obtained by sampling the hearings in the four categories enumerated above.

Communism in Hawaii

Five members of the committee, with Representative Walter serving as chairman, and four staff assistants journeyed to Hawaii in April, 1950, to hold nine days of hearings regarding Communist activities in the Islands. These hearings had been well prepared in advance by the committee staff, and as the hearings unfolded it was clear that the story being told was one well known to the FBI.[6] In his opening statement on the first day of the hearings Chairman

[6] These hearings were published in three volumes, *Hearings regarding Communist Activities in the Territory of Hawaii—Part I, Part II, Part III.* Abbreviated hereafter to *Communism in Hawaii Hearings.*

The decision to hold public hearings in Hawaii was announced in February, 1950. At that time it was stated that committee investigators had been working in the Islands for six months preparing for the hearings. Two investigators were also sent to Hawaii six weeks before the opening of the hearings (*Washington Post*, March 1, 1950). FBI knowledge of Communist activity in the Islands is indicated by the following testimony of one of the witnesses who appeared before the committee:

"*Mr. Tavenner:* Now, I don't believe you have told us how you withdrew from the Communist Party, if you did withdraw from it. Did you withdraw?

"*Mr. Johnson:* Well, after resigning from the union in—let's see—I think it was in November—October—the latter part of October, I was unemployed there for a while. I began to think the thing over. It did not look too good, did not sound too good, so I got in touch with the CIB gentleman in Hilo.

"*Mr. Tavenner:* With whom?

"*Mr. Johnson:* The Counter Intelligence Bureau, I think it is. I cannot remember correctly. But its office is in the Federal Building in Hilo. I got in touch with him and talked to him about it, and he in turn got in touch with the FBI agents in Honolulu and a week later an FBI agent in Honolulu came down to Hilo. I talked to them and gave them all the information I had and showed them my membership card and everything. And they urged me to continue membership in the party, not to withdraw. And I have kept it up and every once in a while they would come back to Hilo, about every 2 months or 6 weeks, they would come back to Hilo and I would talk to them and tell them what I knew, or it may be that nothing new came up. So I finally turned in the card to Arakaki. As far as paying dues or anything like that, and that was the end of it." *Communism in Hawaii Hearings,* p. 1985.

Walter denied that the hearings were intended to "injure the campaign for statehood for Hawaii." [7] Probably there was no such conscious intention, certainly on the part of the committee's Democratic majority. In fact, the House of Representatives had already given its approval to the Hawaiian statehood bill on March 7, 1950.[8] Moreover, the hearings were fairly conducted, and in the end the extent of Communist activity revealed to exist in the Islands was about as small as could possibly have been expected to be the case. Nonetheless, coming as they did late in the life of the 81st Congress at a time when the issue of statehood was about to be decided, these hearings may well have contributed to the Senate's failure to act upon the bill. The very fact that a single member of the Communist Party could be found in Hawaii was certain to persuade some Senators— as it undoubtedly did—that the statehood bill should not pass. Upon his return to Washington, Representative Walter appeared as a witness before the Senate Committee on Interior and Insular Affairs which was considering the statehood bill and emphasized the limited amount of Communist activity in the Islands found to exist by his committee.[9]

The first half-dozen witnesses heard during the Hawaiian investigation were of the "friendly" variety. All were ex-Communists who testified freely concerning the Communist movement in the Islands. They told how they had been recruited into the party, set forth the details of its organization and program, and gave the names of scores of persons said to be party members. The testimony of these and twelve other ex-Communists who were heard later in the hearings lent support to the following conclusions:

1. The number of full-fledged party members in the Islands was

[7] *Communism in Hawaii Hearings,* p. 1354.

[8] *Cong. Rec.* (daily ed.), p. 2992. Of the five committee members who went to Hawaii, Representatives Walter, McSweeney, and Velde had voted for statehood, Harrison had voted against it, and Moulder was recorded as not voting.

[9] The Senate Committee on Interior and Insular Affairs submitted its report June 29, 1950, recommending that the statehood bill pass (81st Cong., 2d Sess., Senate Rept. 1928). The majority report calls attention to the slight amount of communism found in the Islands by the Un-American Activities Committee (p. 8). However, the minority statement filed by Senator Hugh Butler dwells at length upon communism in the Islands as a reason for opposing statehood and refers to the House committee's investigation in support of this position (p. 51). Two efforts were made to pass the statehood bill in the Senate by calling it on the Consent Calendar, but both times objection was registered and the bill was passed over (Sept. 13, *Cong. Rec.,* daily ed., p. 14918; Dec. 15, p. 14918). The bill was never called up in the Senate in the usual fashion.

never great—something over one hundred being the maximum figure.[10]

2. Virtually all of the identified Communists in the Islands had
been members of the International Longshoremen's and Warehouse-
men's Union, and many of them had held offices in the union.[11] Once
more, testimony before the Un-American Activities Committee did
serve the purpose of illustrating the seeming ease with which a small
number of Communists could play an influential role in the affairs of
a labor union.

3. Some of the identified Communists had been surprisingly active
and influential in the Democratic Party in the Islands. Two witnesses,
one of whom admitted past membership in the Communist Party,
and the other of whom refused to testify on ground of self-
incrimination, were revealed to be delegates to the Hawaiian state
constitutional convention which was in session at the same time that
the committee hearings were held. The former voluntarily resigned
his seat, and the latter was expelled by the convention.[12]

4. The Communists in the Islands had enjoyed a limited success
in infiltrating private organizations. The Hawaii Civil Liberties Committee was effectively demonstrated to have been a Communist front,
and the existence of a Communist faction in the island chapter of the
National Association for the Advancement of Colored People was
suggested.[13]

As had been true of the Hollywood hearings of 1947, the friendly
witnesses of the first days of the hearings were followed to the stand
by a series of distinctly "unfriendly" witnesses who refused to answer
all questions pertaining to Communist party membership or activity.
Unlike the recalcitrant Hollywood witnesses who had justified their
silence by reference to the First Amendment, only to discover that
this defense could not save them from later serving jail terms for
contempt, the nonco-operative Hawaiian witnesses justified their
refusal to testify on the ground of self-incrimination and thereby
probably protected themselves against punishment for contempt.

[10] Representative Walter told the Senate committee that there were never more
than 160 Communists in Hawaii and that the number had declined from that
maximum figure in 1946 to fewer than 100 in 1950.

[11] See *Communism in Hawaii Hearings*, pp. 1940, 1945, 1958, 1961, 1970,
1977, 1987, 2013, 2014, 2019, 2020, 2021, 2040, 2042, 2043, 2045, 2046, 2047,
2054, 2056, and 2058.

[12] *N.Y. Times*, April 22, 1950.

[13] References to the HCLC are frequent throughout the printed hearings. See
pp. 2066–2068 for the reference to the NAACP.

In the light of the testimony of the friendly witnesses and of the circumstances under which the unfriendly witnesses refused to testify, their continuing membership in the Communist Party might reasonably have been assumed. On the other hand, in the thirty-nine witnesses ultimately cited for contempt for failure to co-operate with the committee during these hearings, it seems likely that the committee had put its finger on most of the active Communists remaining in the Islands in April, 1950. The Hawaii hearings of the committee demonstrated beyond a doubt that the Communist movement in the Islands had never been other than weak and ineffectual. Even such a bitter partisan as Representative Velde was reported as saying at the end of the hearings that the inquiry showed communism to be no more of a problem in Hawaii than in any other part of the United States.[14]

Much the same conclusion can be drawn from the committee hearings on communism in the District of Columbia, in western Pennsylvania, and in the Cincinnati area. In all of these hearings the committee turned up unmistakable evidence of Communist activity, particularly in the labor movement. But in no instance did such evidence reveal that the Communist Party had made significant headway in recruiting members or in dominating important organizations or influencing major policies. Interesting as are the details of Communist intrigue brought to light, they are noteworthy finally for their petty, insignificant character.

The Atomic Espionage Hearings

It will be recalled that at the very end of the Hollywood hearings in October, 1947, the Un-American Activities Committee suddenly turned its attention away from the Red threat in the movie capital to examine a charge that Communist espionage agents had successfully penetrated to the heart of the nation's atomic bomb laboratories and installations. Thereafter, the committee maintained a continuing, if fitful, interest in this matter. As its 1950 program came to a close, almost the last matter that received the committee's attention, late in December, was a renewal of these hearings.

It is almost impossible to give a coherent account of the committee's atomic espionage hearings. They were never systematically planned, and they stretch over a four-year period. Some were public hearings; many were held in executive session, and only portions of

[14] *Washington Post,* April 21, 1950.

the testimony in the latter have ever been released. No fewer than twelve separate volumes of hearings touch upon atomic espionage in one way or another. There have been two special reports on the subject, one in September, 1948, and the other in September, 1949, and in addition, the subject receives attention in the annual reports for the years 1948, 1949, and 1950. Moreover, the committee deliberately compounded the confusion surrounding this line of inquiry by making periodic promises of "sensational" revelations to come (which never materialized) and by emphasizing an element of mystery in the investigation. For example, it persisted in referring to one person suspected of espionage as "Scientist X" long after his name was being freely used in newspaper stories of the case, and in such a way as to suggest that he was a master spy rather than one of many persons who had fallen under suspicion. Moreover, it is clear that in its hearings the committee was merely reworking ground that had long been carefully explored by the FBI, the Manhattan Engineering District, which was responsible for wartime atomic research, and the intelligence units of the armed services. At times the committee's dominant motive in thus duplicating the efforts of the executive branch of the government seemed to be to fulfill the informing function of Congress—to acquaint the American people with the details of atomic espionage in a way in which the FBI and the other detective or intelligence forces active in this field could not. But at other times its chief purpose seemed to be to duplicate or supplement the efforts of law enforcement agencies by prosecuting persons guilty of wrongdoing. Then again it seemed interested in ascertaining whether these agencies—in particular, the prosecutive arm of the Department of Justice—were properly performing their duties. It seems likely that the activity of the Canadian Royal Commission, which investigated atomic espionage in Canada in 1946 and which filed a monumental report in June, 1946, also influenced the Un-American Activities Committee to embark upon this undertaking, hopeful that it might enhance its prestige by duplicating the findings of the Royal Commission. This is not to suggest that there is any impropriety or inconsistency about these varying motives, but only to suggest that the committee's own seeming uncertainty as to what it was trying to prove by this line of inquiry does not make it any easier to understand the undertaking.

In the committee's first report on the subject, released on September 28, 1948, it is dogmatically asserted that as a result of espionage activity in the United States "certain vital information was actually transmitted to the Russian Government, and that this information has been and will be of assistance to the Russians in their development of the atomic bomb." [15] With this challenging assertion as a point of departure the possibilities in a search for concrete evidence to support such a finding were highly intriguing.

As this series of hearings progressed through 1948 and 1949 the committee's interest tended to center in two "cases," one known as the Hiskey-Chapin case, involving alleged espionage in atomic research laboratories at Columbia University and the University of Chicago, and the other known as the "Scientist X case," which involved alleged espionage in the Radiation Laboratory at the University of California.[16] The facts in the two cases were somewhat similar. In each instance an international Communist was allegedly given the assignment during World War II of contacting employees in atomic laboratories and of obtaining from them highly secret data concerning the progress being made in the United States toward the production of an atomic bomb. In each instance, a small cell of Communist Party members was seemingly formed among the scientists working in the laboratories in question, and there were strong indications that one or more members of each cell did supply the international Communist functionary with some measure of confidential data. However, it should be noted that, with one exception, the Department of Justice has never undertaken to prosecute any of the persons involved in the Un-American Activities Committee's investigations in this area, although the department has presumably been in possession of even more information concerning these cases than has the committee.[17] When the department did undertake to prose-

[15] *Report on Soviet Espionage Activities in Connection with the Atom Bomb,* Sept. 28, 1948, p. 161. Abbreviated hereafter to *1948 Atom Bomb Rept.*

[16] The first volume of hearings, covering sessions held in Sept., 1948, is concerned with a third case, as well. But the central figure in this case co-operated with the committee by answering its questions, denied any participation in espionage activity, and persuaded the committee he had "committed a serious act of indiscretion rather than an act of espionage." *Annual Rept.,* Dec. 31, 1948, p. 20.

[17] This in itself is a controversial point. The House committee repeatedly asserted that the Department of Justice possessed far more information about these cases than did the committee, demanded that the department undertake to prosecute the guilty, and in the face of the department's failure to do so implied that it was being derelict in its duty. See particularly the *1948 Atom Bomb Report,* pp. 161–162. Apparently, the Department of Justice has been deterred from

cute certain individuals for atomic espionage the persons involved had never figured in any House committee investigations.

One Arthur A. Adams played the role of the international Communist in the Hiskey-Chapin case. Adams, said by the committee to be "virtually a 'charter member' Communist of the Soviet Union," [18] remains a somewhat shadowy figure, since he disappeared from sight in 1945 after he discovered he had been placed under surveillance by the MED and the FBI, and was never questioned by the Un-American Activities Committee. But the committee obtained information indicating that Adams had shuttled back and forth between the United States and the Soviet Union during the twenties and thirties and that with the outbreak of war his career as an espionage agent began. According to the testimony of American intelligence agents given to the committee, Adams in the fall of 1942 succeeded in contacting one Clarence F. Hiskey, a scientist then at an MED laboratory at Columbia University who later moved on to the University of Chicago when the laboratory was shifted there in late 1943. In April, 1944, Hiskey was ordered to active duty in the Army, presumably because intelligence agents had discovered his association with Adams. Hiskey appeared as a witness before the Un-American Activities Committee on three separate occasions but refused to answer all significant questions on the ground of self-incrimination. When Hiskey was called to active duty in 1944 there is evidence that Adams got in touch with him and told him that he must "develop" another contact agent among the scientists in the laboratory. Hiskey apparently selected one John H. Chapin for this role. Chapin appeared as a witness before the committee and acknowledged that he had met with Adams, having been told by Hiskey that Adams was a Soviet agent, but denied that he had ever given Adams any restricted information. In the committee's own words, "Chapin was a very cooperative witness," and while it observed that he had seemingly entered into a criminal conspiracy with Hiskey (and the latter's wife) to divulge classified information concerning the atomic bomb project to a Soviet espionage agent, it concluded that he had not actually done so and that he was entitled to leniency: "When he appeared before the committee he was cooperative and apparently sincere in his answers to pertinent questions directed to him; . . .

---

seeking indictments in those atomic espionage cases in which the committee took an interest because some of the department's evidence was obtained by wire tapping.

[18] *1948 Atom Bomb Rept.*, p. 166.

Chapin impressed the committee as a person of deep sincerity who in a moment of weakness, had made a vital mistake." [19]

Upon being assigned to active Army duty in 1944, Hiskey was sent to Alaska. A witness, identified as a former security officer of the MED, told the committee that Hiskey's personal effects had been searched while he was en route to Alaska by another intelligence officer of the MED and that top-secret written matter was discovered and removed. That Adams did succeed in obtaining secret information from Hiskey or others is definitely asserted by the committee. Adams "experienced considerable success in securing data that he desired, for when his room and his effects were secretly searched in 1944 by Government agents, he was found to have in his possession highly secret information regarding the atomic bomb plant at Oak Ridge, Tenn. as well as other vital information regarding the development of atomic energy in other countries." [20] However, the exact nature of the data secured by Adams has never been made public. Here, the committee was obviously drawing upon information in the possession of intelligence agencies in the executive branch, and it is possible that not even the committee was told how extensive or serious the data was.

Steve Nelson, the Communist functionary in the Scientist X case, was a far more tangible figure than Arthur Adams, for his varied activities as a party figure over a long period of years were described at length by numerous witnesses appearing before the committee, and Nelson himself appeared before the committee in September, 1948, and April and June, 1949, although he proved on all of these occasions to be a distinctly "unfriendly" witness, refusing on the ground of self-incrimination to answer all questions of consequence.[21] In outline, the story of the Scientist X case was that Nelson had been given the assignment of developing a Communist cell consisting of five or six young physicists employed in the Radiation Laboratory at the University of California. In March, 1943, one of these scientists, ultimately identified as Joseph W. Weinberg, was reported by intelligence agents to have gone to the home of Nelson late at night and to have given him "a complicated formula" which he had obtained from the Radiation Laboratory. Thereafter, government agents had observed Nelson meet Peter Ivanov, the Soviet vice-consul in San Francisco, "in the middle of an open park," at which time he transferred to Ivanov "an envelope or package." Still later the third

[19] *Ibid.*, p. 147.   [20] *Ibid.*, p. 167.
[21] See, for example, *Hearings regarding Steve Nelson*, June 8, 1949.

secretary of the Russian Embassy in Washington was reported to have paid a visit to San Francisco and while there to have "paid Nelson 10 bills of unknown denominations." [22] Again it may be noted that no statement of the nature of the secret information that reached the Russians, or of its importance, has ever been made by the committee.

It was not until the publication of its annual report for 1949 on March 15, 1950, that the committee formally identified Scientist X as Joseph Weinberg. Apart from a desire to enhance the publicity value of its undertakings by thus emphasizing the factor of mystery, the committee presumably refrained from identifying Weinberg because of his own specific denial of the charges against him. Weinberg appeared as a witness before the committee on three occasions and specifically denied having furnished any information regarding the atomic bomb to Steve Nelson and, in fact, that he had ever even known Nelson. The committee notes that this denial was in direct contradiction to the testimony of other witnesses, including a former MED intelligence agent. The committee ultimately reached the conclusion that Weinberg had testified falsely, for in a report published on September 29, 1949, it recommended that the Attorney General undertake to prosecute Weinberg for perjury.[23] A federal grand jury did ultimately indict Weinberg in May, 1952, for perjury.

In both the Hiskey and Weinberg cases the Un-American Activities Committee extended its investigations well beyond the immediate principals and over a period of three years heard a long series of witnesses, some of whom were related to the two cases only in the most marginal way. In the California case, the committee had reason to believe that a meeting of a Communist cell had taken place at Weinberg's home in August, 1943. Present, according to report, were Nelson, another Communist functionary, Bernadette Doyle, and four employees of the Radiation Laboratory, Giovanni Lomanitz, Irving Fox, David Bohm, and Ken Manfred. All of these persons ultimately appeared as witnesses before the committee, and all refused to answer significant questions on the ground of self-incrimination. At the time of these appearances, Bohm was an assistant professor at Princeton University, Fox was a teaching assistant at the University of California, Lomanitz was an associate professor at Fisk University, and Manfred was an assistant professor

[22] *Report on Atomic Espionage*, Sept. 29, 1949, pp. 4, 5. Abbreviated hereafter to *1949 Atomic Espionage Rept.*
[23] *Ibid.*, pp. 1–11.

at the University of Puerto Rico, on leave to obtain his Ph.D. at the University of California. Admittedly, the committee was aware that these men were vulnerable because of their contemporary professional positions, and it did not hesitate to touch them in this sensitive spot. In view of the fact that the committee itself specifically acknowledged, when it released the printed record of their testimony, that there was no evidence that Lomanitz and Bohm had ever engaged in espionage,[24] it may be questioned whether it was not subjecting them to unfair treatment in publicizing their earlier activity. On the other hand, all of these men had been employed in the Radiation Laboratory, and there was evidence suggesting that they were close associates of Weinberg. All elected as witnesses before the committee to refuse to answer significant questions on the ground of self-incrimination. All, save Manfred, were ultimately cited for contempt by the House of Representatives and indicted by a federal grand jury in November, 1950.[25] Thus it may be said that in refusing to testify and in taking their stand on the right to be free from self-incrimination, all of these men consciously chose to risk their professional careers. It may also be said that in view of their relationship with men who apparently had engaged in espionage activity, the committee was not going out of its way in questioning them and publicizing their testimony.

But the committee ultimately went well beyond the questioning of persons who had seemingly been closely associated with persons suspected of actual espionage. Two examples may be given. On June 14, 1949, the committee heard Frank F. Oppenheimer and his wife, Jacquenette Oppenheimer, as witnesses. The former is a brother of J. Robert Oppenheimer, the great atomic physicist. Both witnesses testified readily as to membership in the Communist Party between 1937 and 1941, during their student days. Thereafter, Frank Op-

[24] *Hearings Regarding Communist Infiltration at Radiation Laboratory and Atomic Bomb Project at the University of California, Berkeley, Calif.—Vol. 1*, p. vi. Two volumes of these hearings are abbreviated to *1949 Radiation Lab. Hearings;* the third hearing is abbreviated to *Radiation Lab. Hearings, Vol. III* (Dec. 1950).

This is not to imply that Fox and Manfred were regarded by the committee as having engaged in espionage. They appeared before the committee several months later and their testimony is reported in Vol. II, which does not carry the same statement of exoneration by the committee found in the foreword to Vol. I.

[25] *1950 Annual Rept.*, p. 31. No member of the committee was present when Manfred testified. His testimony was heard only by members of the committee staff, and this presumably explains the failure to seek a contempt citation against him.

penheimer was employed as a research associate in the Radiation Laboratory at the University of California from 1941 to March, 1947. In the latter year he became an assistant professor at the University of Minnesota. During his period of employment with the Radiation Laboratory, he spent some time at both Los Alamos and Oak Ridge. In view of these facts, the House committee's decision to call Frank Oppenheimer as witness is not difficult to understand. At the same time the committee seemingly had no shred of evidence connecting the Oppenheimers with espionage or even with the Communist cell at the Radiation Laboratory. The committee showed the good grace and judgment to begin the Oppenheimer hearing in executive session, but before the day was over the committee voted, seemingly on the spur of the moment, to turn the hearing into a public one, and the full testimony of both witnesses was then made available for public scrutiny.[26] The committee's decision in this respect may have been influenced by Frank Oppenheimer's refusal to state whether certain persons named to him by the committee were known to him as members of the Communist Party. The witness's unwillingness to cooperate with the committee in this respect was justified in the following words:

> Dr. Oppenheimer: I might restate those reasons: That I would like to cooperate with this committee in helping you find out any acts which were inimical to the United States, and if I knew of such acts I would have reported them already. I know it is for your decision how to proceed in this matter, but I cannot discuss political affiliations and political thoughts of people here. I believe they have to be questioned on these themselves.[27]

Testimony concerning a meeting which occurred late in 1941 or early in 1942 at which Oppenheimer admitted he and Steve Nelson had both been present ran as follows:

> Mr. Velde: Was anyone with Steve Nelson when you met him?
> Dr. Oppenheimer: I met him at a social gathering where there were other people present.
> Mr. Velde: Did you meet with him on more than one occasion?
> Dr. Oppenheimer: On two occasions.
> Mr. Velde: And there were other people present at your meetings with Steve Nelson?
> Dr. Oppenheimer: On both occasions; yes.
> Mr. Velde: Will you state the names of the other persons present?
> Dr. Oppenheimer: No.

[26] 1949 Radiation Lab. Hearings, Vol. I, p. 362.   [27] Ibid., p. 359.

Mr. Velde: You do know the names of some of the people who were present?

Dr. Oppenheimer: I do.

Mr. Velde: And you refuse to answer?

Dr. Oppenheimer: Yes.

Mr. Velde: That is all.

Mr. Walter: Your meeting with Steve Nelson, I understand, was of a personal nature?

Dr. Oppenheimer: It wasn't even of a personal nature. It was of a social nature.

Mr. Walter: At that meeting you did not discuss Communist affairs?

Dr. Oppenheimer: Not to my recollection.[28]

It is hard to avoid the conclusion that the committee was primarily motivated by a desire to embarrass the Oppenheimers and through them, J. Robert Oppenheimer.[29] Investigations by the committee's staff had certainly made it clear to the committee that Frank Oppenheimer and his wife were innocent of anything other than youthful membership in the Communist Party, motivated exclusively by intellectual considerations. There was little reason to suppose that either witness could actually supply significant new information concerning Communist activity in the Radiation Laboratory during the war years, and any leads that they might have been able or will-

[28] *Ibid.*, pp. 369–370.

[29] Careful reading of the committee's publications reveals that through the years the committee concerned itself with the issue of J. Robert Oppenheimer's loyalty. There are several references to a curious event in the personal life of "one of the leading physicists engaged in the development of the atomic bomb," whose name is never given. The committee acknowledges that "an investigation" of this scientist disclosed that he had never "engaged in any subversive activities" and that his "loyalty has never been questioned by the Government" (*1949 Atomic Espionage Rept.*, pp. 3–4). This careful and commendable discretion of the committee in refraining from identifying Oppenheimer with respect to a personal matter that was seemingly of no consequence anyway came to an end early in 1951 when the committee published the testimony of Kenneth May, taken in executive session. In the course of the questioning of May, Representative Velde deliberately made it obvious that Robert Oppenheimer was the anonymous scientist, and then the decision of the committee to make public this testimony completed the process by which the discreet handling of this point was brought to an end. This episode also illustrates the careless manner in which the committee sometimes moves back and forth between public and executive sessions. Here the committee was either guilty of deliberately making public information that it had earlier thought desirable to keep confidential, or it was so offhand in its decision to release the executive session testimony that it did not even realize what one consequence of the decision would be. *Radiation Lab. Hearings, Vol. III*, Dec., 1950, p. 3500.

ing to supply could properly have been sought in executive session. For the committee to have forced Oppenheimer into making the difficult personal decision to refuse to identify past friends or associates as members of the Communist Party and to have insisted upon publicizing this refusal seems to have been a wholly unnecessary course of action.

Oppenheimer tendered his resignation at the University of Minnesota before coming to Washington to testify. He received word during the hearing that his resignation had been accepted.[30]

A similar example of a willingness by the committee to publicize former membership in the Communist Party by a college professor, for no other ascertainable reason then to subject him to the risk of present professional ruin because of past conduct, occurred late in 1950. Five days before Christmas the committee questioned in executive session David Hawkins, a professor of philosophy at the University of Colorado, and his wife. Their testimony was very similar to that of the Frank Oppenheimers. Husband and wife readily acknowledged membership in the Communist Party from 1938 to 1943, during which period both were in their twenties.[31] Hawkins

[30] N.Y. Times, June 15, 1949.

[31] Hawkins testified as follows concerning his voluntary action in joining the Communist Party in 1938 at the age of 25, while a graduate student at the University of California:

"Mr. Harrison: Would you mind telling me why you joined the Communist Party?

"Dr. Hawkins: Yes, sir; I would be very glad to tell you. In this period—this is somewhere near the time of Munich—I was very much alarmed, and I think I could say in this period I had become more interested in political matters. I had been pretty much absorbed in my activities as an undergraduate, and pretty unworldly in my attitude. I became concerned about what appeared to be the imminent drive toward war in Nazi Germany, and I felt that this was something—well, I think the first recollection I have of a strong interest in political matters was the civil war in Spain. I was very much afraid that this aggressive drive toward war of Nazi Germany would not be stopped by the policies of Chamberlain and Daladier, and this view to which I came was at that time held very strongly by the Communist Party.

"I think more than any other one factor was the feeling that this drive toward war could be stopped by a collective security policy and when I looked around to find people who strongly supported that policy, at least in California, the Communist Party seemed to be the principal group that was taking that position. I think this was the thing that got me interested and is the thing I kept falling back on if I had doubts about the Communist Party. This was one thing definite on which I felt one could work with these people for a good end. I

was identified as having held a post at Los Alamos under J. Robert Oppenheimer as an "administrative aide," beginning in May, 1943, at which point, he testified, his membership in the party or belief in communism had come to an end. Like Frank Oppenheimer, Hawkins was reluctant to identify former friends as known to him as Communists. When he was pressed to name the members of the San Francisco Communist group to which he belonged, which he insisted consisted chiefly of teachers, the testimony ran as follows:

Mr. Harrison: Your naming those people is not going to put them in the Atlanta penitentiary. We try to find out which ones of them are still active in the party and, therefore, dangerous to the country. I wouldn't say it isn't a reflection on a man's judgment that he belonged to the Communist Party in that period, but there is nothing sinister about it. It also has this bearing: We would like to know whether these people subsequently became employed by the Government, particularly on the atomic-bomb project.

Dr. Hawkins: I realize that. My hesitation arises from two things, mainly. I can assure you that none of these people had any connection whatever with the Radiation Laboratory or Communist Party affairs at Berkeley, and if your interest is centered there I can assure you that there is no connection I know of or can conceive of between these people and the Berkeley group. It was only this extreme separation between the Berkeley group and this group that made me desire to affiliate with it.

Mr. Harrison: Of course, there was another group that did deliver to

think I was at a stage of development—well, not all college professors are as remote from practical considerations of politics as I was, but I was pretty remote from that sort of thing.

"*Mr. Harrison:* I can't help but be impressed by how strong the appeal of communism was to so many of what we might call the intelligentsia.

"*Dr. Hawkins:* It may be true that at this particular time, at least in California, there was a kind of feeling of crisis in the air. This was the time of terrific strife in the valleys of California, labor strife, and on the waterfront. There was a general feeling that society was not all in one piece, that people were not participating together in the democratic process but were separating into warring camps; and that may have influenced persons like myself who had sympathies for people coming out of the depression. My wife was a kindergarten teacher and saw real suffering. Children would come to school with nothing to eat or bloated stomachs because they were eating only starch. I think I never had any particular romantic illusions about the Soviet Union. I understood they had decided to follow a path that was going to be very hard on any internal democratic process, but it was true that in this period the Soviet Union, in international affairs, seemed to stand for the things that would seem to lead to peace." *Radiation Lab. Hearings, Vol. III,* Dec., 1950, pp. 3425–3426.

the Soviet government every piece of scientific information they had from the Radiation Laboratory.

Dr. Hawkins: I know nothing about that.[32]

Later, while Mrs. Hawkins was testifying, the committee's case for holding this kind of hearing and seeking the names of the Hawkinses' associates was well stated by Representative Harrison:

Mr. Tavenner: What were their names?

Mrs. Hawkins: I wish you wouldn't ask me that question.

Mr. Harrison: Mrs. Hawkins, some of those people, like you, who joined the Communist Party at that time, were soon disillusioned and got out of it. Others perhaps didn't, and remained in an organization which you have described here tonight as a menace to the safety of our country. We are holding these closed hearings, from which newspaper people have been barred, so that we may have the opportunity to give further consideration to any names you may give in determining which of those names may be released for publication. That is the reason we have held these hearings all day behind closed doors, so that we may evaluate the testimony. You don't like to give the names of these people; and, on the other hand, the safety of our country is important.

Mrs. Hawkins: That is right.

Mr. Harrison: That is the reason we have closed hearings, so that we may evaluate the testimony and see which of those names should be released and which should not. Therefore, I want to ask that you cooperate with us and rely on us not to vilify these people unnecessarily, which we are not going to do.

Mrs. Hawkins: I appreciate your talking to me that way. If this group were a large group in which I had any doubt as to the basic loyalty and integrity of these people, then I would certainly have to answer with those names.

Mr. Harrison: Some of the people that come before us are the nicest

[32] *Ibid.,* p. 3422. Later, Hawkins stated:

"I have really no desire to inhibit or impede the investigations of your committee, sir; and if I knew of anything connecting individuals about whom I feel this hesitation with the radiation laboratory or with any crimes in which they might have been directly or indirectly involved, I would not feel any hesitation; but, not having such knowledge, I feel very deeply—and I am sure you will agree with this proposition—that there are certain fundamental relations of trust which tend to distinguish American society from other societies in the world today; and, unless this kind of question is to your knowledge directly or indirectly related to the subjects you are investigating, I would very much like to ask not to be asked such a question.

"If there is information of this sort that you would like to get, I would just ask whether there may not be more efficient or direct ways to get it, such as asking the question of the individual himself rather than of me" (p. 3428).

people you ever saw; they are some of the most pleasant people, and we have had experiences that would astound you. I again assure you we are not going to do anything to those people. We are not going to injure their reputations. But I must ask that you cooperate with us and not withhold information. Where people have been in the Communist Party and got out, we don't do anything to them. We didn't bring you all the way across the country for nothing. There are matters in which we think you could aid us, and I do most earnestly ask for your cooperation.

Mrs. Hawkins: I certainly do want to give my cooperation, Mr. Harrison, and I can only say that any reluctance I have in this is one which is very carefully weighed, and one which has certainly been thought out along the lines you have outlined.

Mr. Harrison: You mean you are certain they are now out of the party?

Mrs. Hawkins: I am absolutely certain that these people—well, it is as if, if I doubted their loyalty I would doubt mine, and that is impossible, because I know where mine lies.

Mr. Harrison: You will find among Communist Party members people you least suspect who were once in the Communist Party and who now make up the espionage organization of the party.[33]

Whether the committee's record in handling confidential information or in not injuring reputations bears out Mr. Harrison's reassuring words is somewhat doubtful. For example, during the same series of hearings in which the Hawkinses participated, the committee heard in executive session one Kenneth May, an associate professor of mathematics at Carleton College, also a self-admitted ex-Communist. May did tell the committee the names of his associates in the Communist movement, insofar as he could remember them, but this did not deter the committee from making his testimony public.

Apart from their refusal to identify other persons as Communists, the testimony of the two Hawkinses impresses the reader of the printed record as honest, sincere, and thoughtful. Seen through their testimony they are revealed as intelligent, well-meaning people who were doing their best to extricate themselves from a difficult dilemma without doing injury to others whom they believed to be essentially innocent. But as might have been expected, the publicity given to Hawkins' appearance before the committee jeopardized his position as a teacher. Following his appearance before the committee the board of regents of the University of Colorado directed the president of the university to prepare a series of allegations against Professor Hawkins. These allegations were presented to a standing committee of the university whose function it is to investigate any charges

[33] *Ibid.,* pp. 3455–3456.

made against members of the faculty and to recommend to the regents whether or not the faculty member should be retained. This committee unanimously recommended Hawkins' retention and the regents, by a vote of four to one, accepted the recommendation.[34]

The George Racey Jordan Hearings

Closely related to the atomic espionage hearings were the hearings held between December, 1949, and March, 1950, in which George Racey Jordan, an ex-major of the Army Air Corps, was the central figure.[35] On December 2, 1949, a sensational radio interview took place between Jordan and Fulton Lewis, Jr., in which Jordan charged that secret data concerning atomic research, as well as quantities of uranium, had been flown to Russia during the war under the Lend-Lease program.[36] Three days later, on December 5, Jordan appeared before the House committee, with four Democratic members in attendance, and repeated his story at considerable length. Jordan testified that he had served as Lend-Lease expediter of wartime air freight between the United States and the Soviet Union at an air base at Great Falls, Montana, in 1943 and 1944. On this job he became disturbed at the great amount of freight being flown to Russia in sealed suitcases under diplomatic immunity and eventually took it upon himself to break the seals and open certain of the containers. In them he discovered maps and diagrams of important American industrial plants, transportation lines, the Panama Canal, documents of the State Department and of other governmental agencies, and restricted information pertaining to atomic research. In particular, he said he found material concerning Oak Ridge, including a map, accompanied by a handwritten note on White House stationery bearing Harry L. Hopkins' printed name, which read: "Had a hell of a

[34] Information supplied to the author by an officer of the University of Colorado. See also Carey McWilliams, "The Case of David Hawkins," The Nation, March 10, 1951.

[35] These hearings were published under the title, Hearings regarding Shipment of Atomic Material to the Soviet Union during World War II. Abbreviated hereafter to Hearings regarding Shipment.

[36] Life magazine (Dec. 19, 1949) charged that Jordan had been trying to peddle his story for some time and that he had offered it to Life as early as November 16. Life stated: "Our domestic news editor, our science editor and one of our best reporters, a man with long experience in military and security matters, heard the story and carefully examined the 'evidence' offered in support. Life's editors and reporter found that Jordan did not substantiate his story." See also Life, Jan. 9, 1950, pp. 2, 4.

time getting these away from Groves. H. H." He identified these initials as those of Harry Hopkins. Jordan also stated that several shipments of uranium and of heavy water had gone to Russia and that Harry Hopkins had talked with him by long-distance phone and had urged him to expedite these shipments.[37] Jordan told the committee that he had gone to Washington early in 1944 to report on his findings and to find out whether the Russians were making improper use of their diplomatic immunity in making these shipments. But in Washington, Jordan testified, he had been brushed off and had been told to go back to Montana and mind his business.[38]

A day after his appearance before the House committee Jordan further embellished his story during a press conference in New York City. He told reporters that he had ripped radar equipment out of four Russia-bound planes, but that another plane with such equipment had managed to get through to the Soviet Union because it did not stop at the Great Falls base.[39]

The point of the Jordan story, thus gradually unfolded, seemed to be that Russian agents in the United States had succeeded during the war in sending to Russia much restricted information concerning the American industrial and communications systems and atomic research, as well as quantities of uranium, either with the knowledge and approval of government agencies or as a result of their carelessness. Thereafter, the House committee endeavored to pin down responsibility for these shipments. It appeared that the government had been fully aware of the uranium shipments, and, indeed, had granted three different export licenses for them. At one point or another in the testimony of Jordan and subsequent witnesses, several government agencies were identified as having shared responsibility

[37] Jordan's testimony is on pp. 908–933 of *Hearings regarding Shipment.* Specific references to Hopkins are on pp. 918, 926.

[38] "*Mr. Tavenner:* Will you tell us your experience with the State Department? I understand you reported the matter to the State Department.

"*Mr. Jordan:* Well, I went to Washington on that trip and walked up and down the corridors of the State Department trying to find somebody who would tell me they had diplomatic immunity. I was passed from one room to another. The impression I got from the State Department was that I was being too officious, and I would be better off if I helped expedite the movement and did not spend so much time in Washington. So I decided to go back to Great Falls and let the matter rest." *Ibid.,* p. 914.

Jordan's memory for specific detail was explained by the fact he had kept a diary during the period in question in which he had entered numerous notes pertaining to his discoveries.

[39] *N.Y. Times,* Dec. 7, 1949.

for permitting these shipments. These were the armed services, the State Department, the Office of Lend-Lease Administration, the War Production Board, the Board of Economic Warfare, and the Manhattan Engineering District. It ultimately appeared that formal responsibility for the licenses rested with the Board of Economic Warfare, then headed by Henry Wallace, but that the Office of Lend-Lease Administration was, in fact, the agency that had most to do with approving them.[40]

Actually, there was little that was new about the uranium shipment story. Representative McDowell had described the shipments in a speech in the House of Representatives as early as August 6, 1948, and the committee's staff had given intermittent attention to the subject since that time.[41] Indeed, it was this continuing interest in the uranium shipments that the committee pointed to in justifying the prompt attention it paid to such a bizarre witness as Jordan, as contrasted, for example, with the failure of the Joint Senate-House Atomic Energy Committee, under Senator McMahon's chairmanship, to call him as a witness.[42] Two days after Jordan's testifying, Lieutenant General Leslie R. Groves, wartime head of the Manhattan Engineering District, appeared before the House committee, and his testimony made it clear that there had been nothing irregular about the granting of the export licenses for the uranium shipments. There were some ambiguities in Groves's testimony as to whether he had approved or disapproved the licenses, but it was made plain that the United States had had good reason for permitting the shipments. Presumably the Soviet Union had other access to uranium, and there was reason to believe that the attempt to purchase uranium in this country was calculated to reveal whether the United States was engaged in atomic research (the presumption being that if it was, the exportation of uranium would not be allowed). If that in fact was what had been back of the Russian attempt to obtain uranium, then it had behooved the United States to outguess the Russians by allowing uranium to be exported.[43] General Groves testified that by granting an export license for "uranium metal," which was

[40] See the testimony of James P. Hoopes, *Hearings regarding Shipment,* pp. 1100–1118.

[41] 94 *Cong. Rec.* 10106–10107 (August 6, 1948). The House committee had also heard testimony concerning these shipments in executive session in June, 1948. *Hearings regarding Shipment,* pp. 902–904. McDowell stated that over thirty witnesses had been heard on this subject. Their testimony has never been released.

[42] *Ibid.,* p. 901.   [43] *Ibid.,* pp. 906, 940.

seemingly a scarce commodity, the MED was enabled to see whether the Russians could find a commerical source of it in the United States, something that MED very much wanted to do itself without calling attention to the fact that it was interested in purchasing such a commodity.[44] General Groves also denied that either Harry Hopkins or Henry Wallace had put any pressure on him to supply the Soviet Union with any information or materials pertaining to Oak Ridge or atomic research.[45]

The Jordan story immediately became the subject of bitter controversy. Antiadministration newspapers seized upon the references to Hopkins and Wallace and suggested that sensational new evidence of espionage in the New Deal was about to be disclosed.[46] Democratic members of the Un-American Activities Committee indicated skepticism concerning Jordan's testimony.[47] Republican members of the committee were prompt to charge that the majority was trying to "whitewash" the Jordan charges. They asserted that the Jordan hearing had been arranged on three hours' notice and that only a gesture of notifying them had been made. (Velde was in Puerto Rico, Case in South Dakota, and Nixon in California.) General Groves, apparently displeased because newspaper headlines concerning his testimony suggested that he had contradicted the Jordan story, was reported by the Associated Press as asserting on December 8 that his testimony should not be construed as completely refuting Jordan.[48] On December 9, the *New York Times* reported that in a telephone interview General Groves stated he had deliberately withheld reports on atomic developments from Vice-President Wallace after the fall of 1943, and when asked whether he had any special reason for not showing reports to Wallace he gave the cryptic reply, "I preferred not to." [49]

Toward the end of January, 1950, the House committee resumed

---

[44] *Ibid.*, pp. 941 ff., 1116.   [45] *Ibid.*, pp. 946 ff., 955.

[46] See "Seven-Day Wonder," *Time*, Dec. 19, 1949, p. 33.

[47] See *N.Y. Times*, Dec. 8, 1949. Representative Walter was reported as telling newspapermen, "Personally, I think there are so many discrepancies it is highly improbable that many of the things Mr. Jordan said occurred did occur." And Representative Harrison was reported to have added, "I will go further. Mr. Jordan's story is inherently incredible."

[48] *N.Y. Times*, Dec. 9, 1949. The *Times* headline on Dec. 8 concerning the Groves testimony had run: WALLACE, HOPKINS ABSOLVED BY GROVES OF USING PRESSURE TO GIVE ATOM DATA TO SOVIET—JORDAN IS DISPUTED.

[49] See "Wheezy Pinwheel," *Time*, Dec. 19, p. 8, for a story strongly critical of General Groves's vacillation concerning the Jordan charges.

its hearings and received testimony from both government officials and businessmen concerning the uranium shipments and the export licenses authorizing them. On January 26, Henry Wallace voluntarily appeared before the committee and, in a session marked by numerous angry exchanges between the witness and committee members, denied that he had known anything about atomic research after the earliest days of the war or had had anything to do with the export licenses. Wallace was particularly angry because of General Groves's remarks to newsmen implying that he had been unwilling to trust Wallace with information concerning the progress of atomic research during the war.[50]

On March 3, Major Jordan was called back to the stand, at the request of the Republican members of the committee who were obviously very anxious to see his story vindicated. Immediately preceding Jordan, however, the committee heard as a witness one of its own investigators, Donald T. Appell, who reported the results of a careful, detailed study he had been making of the Jordan charges since December. The Appell testimony was rather curious and had somewhat the same ambivalence that had marked General Groves's testimony on his first appearance. Actually, Appell had tried to check each point in the Jordan story, and his findings tended to verify some of Jordan's assertions and to cast doubt upon others.[51] Rep-

[50] Representatives Wood and Case argued, in rather petulant fashion, that the accusations concerning Wallace's trustworthiness had not been made before the committee and that accordingly he should not be allowed to use the committee as a forum to answer them. But Wallace was allowed to proceed with his statement (*Hearings regarding Shipment*, p. 1084). The ill will existing between General Groves and Wallace had been indicated when Groves told the committee that on the one occasion he had delivered a report on atomic research to the Vice President he had "had to wait quite a while to see him, which was very annoying, because I had an appointment, and I didn't think the people he was seeing were very important to the war effort" (p. 956). Wallace returned the insult rather effectively when he appeared before the committee: "I know that the man in my office immediately preceding General Groves was a Latin-American diplomat. My secretary knew nothing about the Manhattan project, knew nothing about General Groves, and she couldn't tell by looking at General Groves that he was a very important figure, any more than General Groves could tell by looking at the Latin-American diplomat, when he came out of my office, that he was an important figure" (p. 1076).

[51] The ambiguity of Appell's testimony is indicated by the fact that the *Washington Post* headlined its story on his appearance, "House Probe Fails to Back Up Jordan Story on Harry Hopkins." The first paragraph of the *Post* story ran: "An investigator of the House Un-American Activities Committee testified yesterday he was unable to find any evidence substantiating the more

resentative Nixon in his questioning of Appell made it clear that he thought Jordan's testimony had been almost wholly accurate and that, like Whittaker Chambers, Jordan had found it necessary to tell his story many times before people were persuaded that he was telling the truth.[52]

Jordan's second appearance before the committee was largely utilized by the Republican members of the committee to give him a further chance to substantiate his story. Jordan himself admitted that there were certain minor errors in his original testimony.[53] On the other hand, he continued to insist upon the accuracy of his main charges. However, like Whittaker Chambers, he proved to be

lurid of the charges of former Air Force Maj. George Racey Jordan" (March 3, 1950). On the other hand, the *N.Y. Times* story on the Appell testimony was headlined, "Russia Got Secret War Plant Data in '44, House Investigator Asserts," and its general tone was to the effect that Appell had found Jordan's testimony to be generally accurate. One paragraph in the *Times* story read: "Mr. Appell's testimony appeared to support much of the Jordan story. The testimony was built upon official records of Government departments and agencies" (March 3, 1950).

[52] See *Hearings regarding Shipment*, pp. 1124, 1146 ff. Nixon insisted that Appell's investigations revealed that Jordan's story stood up on four out of five points: (1) that Jordan had tried to report information concerning the Russian shipments to his superiors at the time they were being made; (2) that he had ripped radar equipment out of planes going to Russia; (3) that he had opened suitcases and found they contained secret material that should not have been going through under diplomatic immunity; and (4) that uranium had been shipped to Russia.

Nixon conceded that Jordan's story about the Hopkins memorandum seemingly did not stand up because Appell's investigations had revealed that Hopkins always signed his memoranda "H.L.H.," never "H.H.," and had never used White House stationery with his name printed on it (pp. 1136–1138, 1167–1172). But Nixon glosses over other difficulties: (1) Not all of the details of Jordan's claims that he had protested to higher authorities in 1943 and 1944 had held up. He claimed, for example, that he had gone to Washington and protested personally to John Hazard, an official in the Foreign Economic Administration. Hazard told Appell he had never seen or talked with Jordan (p. 1135). (2) Verification of the radar story was only partial at best (pp. 1134–1135). (3) Jordan's claim that Hopkins had talked with him on the telephone and urged him to expedite the uranium shipments was not verified and remained somewhat incredible. But see pp. 1170–1171 for Jordan's testimony on this point during his second appearance.

[53] For example, he had claimed that the telephone conversation with Hopkins had taken place in 1944. Jordan's critics had pointed out that Hopkins was seriously ill at this time and could not have talked with Jordan. Jordan now claimed that the conversation had occurred in May, 1943. This corrected assertion at least coincides with the time when the uranium shipments were actually made.

the kind of witness who had an important new detail to add with each successive telling of his story. This time Jordan claimed that among the folders containing copies of government documents he had found when he had broken into the sealed suitcases were some from the State Department. These were arranged "in rows with elastic bands around five or six folders, and in the front would be a white piece of paper with 'From Hiss' and the next batch 'From Sayre' and so on." [54] This new claim illustrates the essential weakness in the Jordan story. Atomic research was presumably unknown to Jordan in 1943 and 1944, the importance of uranium could not have been apparent to him, and Alger Hiss (and even Francis Sayre) were such obscure bureaucrats that it is difficult to believe that their names would have caught Jordan's attention and that he would have bothered to note them down in his diary. On the other hand, it is at least conceivable that, as an Army Air Force Major, he did keep such a diary and that he placed in it many small details which at the time did not seem to him to have much meaning. If, as ultimately had happened to Whittaker Chambers and Elizabeth Bentley, Major Jordan had found it necessary to repeat and support his testimony in a court of law, the authenticity of his diary would almost certainly have become a crucial issue.

But it is unlikely that Jordan will ever serve as a witness for the government in a criminal proceeding, for if the complete truth of his story be accepted it reveals little more than that the Soviet Union had been permitted to buy uranium in this country in 1943 and that Russian agents were sending information and materials of many kinds to the Soviet Union by a privileged air-freight route. Some of these materials may have been the fruits of espionage, but if so, the Jordan story merely throws light on how such material was sent home and not how it was obtained. [55] To be sure, the full implications of the reference to Hopkins are that he secured documents

[54] Hearings regarding Shipment, p. 1160.

[55] In its annual report for 1950 the committee's claims with respect to the Jordan hearings are very modest. It is stated that Jordan's testimony revealed "laxity of controls over shipments to the Soviet Union . . . under the lease-lend program" and that by this route Soviet agents had been able to ship uranium, heavy water, and data pertaining to the industrial strength and know-how of the United States. It is also stated that testimony by Victor Kravchenko given in connection with the Jordan hearings revealed that all Soviet representatives in the United States, whether diplomatic, military, or economic, were (and are) potential spies, carefully trained in espionage (Annual Rept., Jan. 2, 1951, pp. 5–6.)

concerning Oak Ridge and sent them to the Russians. But this is the weakest part of the Jordan story, and it is doubtful whether even the Republican members of the committee believed that Hopkins had been guilty of such treachery to the United States.

"Internal Security" Legislation

During an eleven-day period in March, April, and May, 1950, the committee held hearings on "legislation to outlaw certain un-American and subversive activities." [56] The committee had before it two bills which had been referred to it as a legislative committee by the House of Representatives for consideration. These were H.R. 7595, known as the Nixon bill, which was a revised version of the controversial Mundt-Nixon bill that had passed the House of Representatives in the 80th Congress, and H.R. 3903, a much shorter bill, known as the Wood bill, which would have made it a criminal offense for a government employee or any person employed on national defense contract work to be a member of, or contribute funds to, the Communist Party or any organization designated as subversive by the Attorney General. Ultimately, the committee reported favorably upon a new bill, H.R. 9490, which was not dissimilar to the Nixon bill. This bill was passed by the House of Representatives and was absorbed into the McCarran bill in the Senate, which was enacted into law over a veto by President Truman in September, 1950.

The 1950 hearings on these bills were not unlike the legislative hearings conducted under Representative Nixon's chairmanship in February, 1948. The committee heard some twenty witnesses and received and printed statements from about an equal number of additional persons. Virtually all of the persons testifying or submitting statements represented organizations. These included the American Bar Association, the Chamber of Commerce of the United States, the American Federation of Labor, the Congress of Industrial Organizations, all of the veterans' organizations, the American Civil Liberties Union, Americans for Democratic Action, the Civil Rights Congress, the Socialist Party, the Progressive Party, and the Communist Party. Opponents of the bills before the committee outnumbered supporters by a ratio of two-to-one. As had been true of the 1948 legislative hearings, these hearings were conducted fairly and calmly, and the

[56] *Hearings on Legislation to Outlaw Certain Un-American and Subversive Activities.*

testimony is a rich source of excellent analysis, favorable and unfavorable, of the bills under consideration.

The McCarran, or Internal Security, Act, which became law late
in 1950, is an omnibus piece of legislation that includes a variety
of provisions aimed at suppressing subversive activity. The extent
to which the name of the chairman of the Senate Judiciary Committee has been associated with this law obscures the extent to which it
is a product of the Un-American Activities Committee. Important
parts of the law—in particular, sections 18 through 31 of Title I and
all of Title II—were added in the Senate. These provisions amend
the criminal code and the immigration and naturalization laws. Title
II, to which is given the title, "Emergency Detention Act of 1950,"
provides authority under which in time of emergency the executive
branch may order the detention of all persons concerning whom there
is reasonable ground to believe that they would engage in espionage
or sabotage activities. But the other provisions of the law, which require the registration of Communist organizations with the Attorney
General, set up a subversive activities control board to designate
Communist organizations, forbid the employment of members of
Communist organizations in federal jobs or in defense industry jobs.
forbid the granting of passports to such members, deny the use of the
mails or the radio or television to Communist organizations except
for communications and programs clearly labeled as Communist,
and so forth, are all derived from the bill reported favorably by the
Un-American Activities Committee in August, 1950, and can, in
fact, be traced back quite readily to the Mundt-Nixon bill of the 80th
Congress.

The Remington Hearings

As already suggested, a great many hearings during the 1949–1950
period were centered in specific personalities. Several of these may
be noted. The committee has always been interested in listening to
the ex-Communist-turned-informer. There can be no denying the
value of the specific information that these persons have been able
to supply the House committee. On the other hand, the individual
who can within the space of a few years travel all the way from membership in the Communist Party to identification with reactionary
organizations and publications is not likely to be very stable or dispassionate, or wise in his opinions and his understanding of social

problems. Certainly, one ought to be on guard in listening to such persons and maintain at least a slight skepticism toward them. That, the House committee has seldom been able or willing to do, when an ex-Communist has appeared before it as a "friendly witness." Witnesses of this type heard during the 81st Congress included General Izyador Modelski, onetime military attaché of the Polish Embassy in Washington, Paul Crouch, an important functionary in the American Communist movement between 1925 and 1942, and Victor Kravchenko, long a member of the Russian Communist Party and in 1943 and 1944 an economic attaché to the Soviet Purchasing Commission in the United States. Like the Budenzes and Chamberses before them, these men were able to provide the committee with important factual information concerning the details of the Communist movement, but the questioning of them was never sufficiently shrewd or penetrating to remove from the impartial reader's mind lingering doubts as to their accuracy or their dispassion.

Perhaps the most significant hearings concerning an individual during this period were those in the Remington case. It will be recalled that in the summer of 1948 Elizabeth Bentley, a confessed ex-Communist courier, told the Senate investigating committee headed by Senator Ferguson that one William W. Remington had supplied her during the war years with restricted information drawn from federal agencies with which he was employed. In 1948, at the time of the Bentley testimony, Remington occupied an important post in the Office of International Trade in the Department of Commerce. Under President Truman's loyalty program Remington was brought under scrutiny by the Department of Commerce and was suspended in August, 1948. However, in February, 1949, the Loyalty Review Board ordered him reinstated on the ground that the evidence against him did not establish reasonable ground for a belief that he was then disloyal. There is reason to believe that Elizabeth Bentley's unwillingness to appear before the board to restate her charges against Remington played an important part in the board's decision to clear Remington. In the meantime Remington had filed a libel suit against Miss Bentley, since she had repeated her charges against him on a radio program. The National Broadcasting Company and General Foods Corporation, sponsor of the program, were codefendants in the suit. In February, 1950, this suit was settled out of court, and Remington was reported to have received a sum of money in settlement of the case. Miss Bentley later insisted that this settlement was arranged over her objection and that she did not participate in the payment made Remington.[57]

Late in April, 1950, the House committee called Remington and other witnesses before it in a series of hearings that closely fore-shadowed the subsequent prosecution and conviction of Remington in a federal court on the charge that he had perjured himself before a federal grand jury in denying membership in the Communist Party. In its annual report for 1950, released in January, 1951, the House committee flatly claims credit for the reopening of the Remington case and for the discovery of the evidence that led to his conviction. The committee states:

At the time the Remington case was reopened, no investigative agency of the executive or legislative branch of the Government had in its files any information which would establish Remington's membership in the Communist Party. . . .

Convinced that the testimony of Bentley was true and that Remington was a member of the Communist Party, not only during the time of his association with Bentley but even during the days of his employment by the Tennessee Valley Authority, the committee conducted a full investigation of Remington's activities.[58]

As the result of this investigation, which, as described in the report, was remarkably persistent and ingenious, it was discovered that Remington had received mail in 1936–1937, when he worked for the Tennessee Valley Authority as a youth of nineteen, through a post office box which he shared with four other men, three of whom were known to the House committee as having been members of the Communist Party at that time. A prolonged search for the four men followed. It was learned that one had died. The other three were found and subpoenaed; they testified before the committee in executive session. One, Merwin S. Todd, refused to answer all questions with respect to the Communist Party on the ground of self-incrimination; one, who is not identified by name, admitted that he had been a member of the party but stated that he did not know whether Remington had been a party member; [59] the third, Howard

[57] *Hearings regarding Communism in the United States Government—Part I,* 1950, pp. 1849 ff.

[58] *Annual Rept.,* Jan. 2, 1951, pp. 1–2.

[59] The testimony of this witness was not printed in the published record of these hearings. On the surface this would appear to be unfair to Remington and indicate a discriminatory policy on the part of the committee: only that testimony that supports its theses receives emphasis.

A. Bridgman, in 1950 an assistant professor of economics at Tufts College, testified that both he and Remington had been members of the same Communist Party cell in Knoxville, Tennessee.[60] Still another witness, Kenneth McConnell (known also as Malcombre and Malcolm), who identified himself as a former Communist Party organizer, although not a member of the cell that Remington was said to have belonged to, testified that he had known Remington as a party member in TVA days.[61]

Armed with this information the House committee subpoenaed Remington and he appeared before it in public sessions on May 4 and 5, 1950. Remington once more denied having been a member of the Communist Party at any time in his life,[62] although he admitted having known and associated with Todd and Bridgman during his TVA days. Indeed, he acknowledged having roomed with Todd for two months toward the end of his stay in Tennessee, but he denied that Todd was even known to him as a Communist.[63] On the other hand, Remington denied ever having known McConnell.[64] The committee also questioned Remington at length concerning his later relations with Elizabeth Bentley during the war years in Washington.

Immediately after his appearance before the committee, Remington was called before a federal grand jury in New York, and on June 8, 1950, he was indicted for perjury on the charge that he had falsely denied membership in the Communist Party. He was brought to trial early in 1951, and convicted. However, this judgment was later set aside by the federal Court of Appeals and a new trial ordered.[65]

On its face, this sequence of events reflects great credit upon the House committee, for, as in the Hiss case, the committee was seemingly responsible for the action that led ultimately to Remington's conviction in a federal court—a conviction that seemingly stamped him as a Communist as well as a perjurer. Both the Hiss and the Remington cases seem to show the committee and its staff of investigators beating the FBI and the executive branch of the govern-

[60] *Hearings regarding Communism in U.S. Government—Part I*, pp. 1753 ff.
[61] *Ibid.*, pp. 1697 ff. On the other hand, McConnell while stating that he had known Bridgman for many years, added that he could not say and did not believe that Bridgman had been a party member (p. 1700). Bridgman, in turn, stated that he had known McConnell (under the name of Malcombre) as a member of the party (pp. 1758–1759).
[62] *Ibid.*, pp. 1777 ff.   [63] *Ibid.*, p. 1786.   [64] *Ibid.*, p. 1792.
[65] *United States v. Remington*, 191 F. 2d 246 (1951).

ment at the latter's game—the enforcement of the law and the prosecution of violators of the law. But, as in the Hiss case, the confident and unrelenting manner with which the committee set out upon the task of demonstrating Remington's guilt has disturbing implications. Granted that the Department of Justice was falling down on the job in failing to prosecute Remington, is it desirable that a Congressional committee should take up such a case and see to it that a guilty man is punished? This action suggests the dreaded bill of attainder of seventeenth-century English history. Admittedly, a Congressional committee may appropriately investigate the failure of the law enforcement process with a view to recommending remedial legislation. But apart from claiming credit for the reopening of the case against Remington, there is not a word in the 1950 annual report of the committee criticizing the Department of Justice for the way in which it handled the Remington case.[66]

The Pressman Hearings

The 1950 hearings concerning Remington are published by the committee under the title, *Hearings regarding Communism in the*

[66] It is impossible not to avoid the suspicion that the House committee received help from the outside in its decision to reopen the Remington case and in its search for evidence against him. One possibility is that the FBI or the Department of Justice "leaked" information to the committee. In view of the very bad relations that prevailed between the committee and the department in the Hiss case, this seems unlikely, although the fact that the committee in the 81st Congress was once more controlled by the Democrats might suggest a closer relationship with the FBI, or even the Justice Department. Another very real possibility is that in preparing her defense against Remington's libel suit Elizabeth Bentley had discovered some leads respecting Remington's record in TVA days, and that, annoyed by the out-of-court settlement of the suit and the attendant publicity that seemed to suggest that she had "bought off" Remington, she turned her information over to the committee. This theory finds some support in the printed record of Miss Bentley's testimony before the committee on May 6, 1950, when she reappeared as a witness. In the course of explaining the out-of-court settlement of the libel suit, Miss Bentley submitted a letter that she had received from her lawyer, Godfrey P. Schmidt, dated May 5, 1950. In this letter Schmidt states: "Some time prior to your examination before trial [by Remington's lawyers], I had discussed with Mr. Barry [one of the lawyers representing a bonding company which had insured NBC and General Foods against libel] the possibility of investigating certain leads provided by the inconsistent testimony of Mr. Remington before a congressional committee. Also, I sent my associate, Mr. Egan, to Tennessee to consult certain persons who asserted that they had evidence of Mr. Remington's membership in the Communist Party at one time. *I was particularly pleased with the results of Mr. Egan's in-*

United States Government. Also under this title is found the record of the testimony given before the committee in the late summer by several well-known persons who Whittaker Chambers had charged in 1948 were members of the Communist Party in the 1930's when he had served as a party courier. The first such witness, heard on August 28, 1950, was Lee Pressman. His reappearance before the committee, almost two years to the day after he had refused to tell the committee during the Hiss-Chambers hearings whether he had been a Communist or had known Alger Hiss as a Communist, was the result of an interesting series of developments. In August, 1950, following close upon Henry Wallace's break with the Progressive Party, Pressman, too, had publicly resigned from the American Labor Party, the Progressive Party's alter ego in New York State. It appears that Representative Nixon then took the lead in persuading the House committee to subpoena Pressman on the theory that he might be willing to "tell all" or could be badgered by the committee into providing some of the missing links in the Hiss espionage case. On August 27, the day before Pressman was to appear before the committee, Bert Andrews, a newspaperman who had enjoyed exceedingly close relations with Nixon, ran an "inside story" account of the affair in the *New York Herald Tribune*. Andrews stated that Pressman would reveal that he had been a member of the Communist Party in 1934, that he would refuse "to put the finger" on friends or associates who had also been Communists, and that committee

---

vestigation." *Hearings regarding Communism in U.S. Government*—Part I, p. 1851. Italics added.

The following exchange also took place between Miss Bentley and Frank Tavenner, the House committee's counsel:

"*Mr. Tavenner:* Miss Bentley, while this suit was pending, and up until the present time, did you turn over any leads for investigation, or any investigative leads, to this committee or any member of its staff?

"*Miss Bentley: I don't believe so.* I don't believe this committee asked me for them. As I recall it, when I testified here in August 1948 the Senate was investigating Mr. Remington, and wasn't it decided that in view of that this committee would not go into it? *I don't believe you asked me for them. I don't think so*" (p. 1852; italics added).

It may be true that the House committee's investigators and Miss Bentley's investigators were working the Tennessee ground independently of each other. If so, they must have had a hard time keeping out of each other's way! If, indeed, there was co-operation between the two forces, then it would appear that Remington's libel suit against Miss Bentley boomeranged and set in motion the developments that led to his conviction for perjury. The parallel here to the Hiss case is quite startling.

members—chiefly Nixon—would do their best, under threat of a contempt citation, to compel him to tell the full story. Said Andrews, in a passage that is most revealing concerning Nixon's motivation:

The Pressman story, plus the testimony of others who will be called, may finally crack the iron ball of secrecy within which have nestled so many colleagues with knowledge which they thought they would never have to disclose.

It may make the Alger Hiss case look not like a small potato—but like one of the many big and hot potatoes. It may implicate persons who have never been mentioned before. It may have a big bearing on the outcome of the 1950 Congressional elections.

There is not the slightest doubt that the Republicans will try to make hay and that the Democrats will fret about things that happened while they were in power. . . .

The same day that Andrews' story appeared, and perhaps angered by it, Pressman released a statement to the press in which he admitted that he had "joined a Communist group in Washington, D.C., about 1934." He stated that his "participation in such group extended for one year" and that when he had left the government service late in 1935 to re-enter the private practice of the law he had "discontinued any further participation in the group." He then specifically stated that he had "no knowledge regarding the political beliefs or affiliations of Alger Hiss," and he added, "I do know that for the period of my participation he was not a member of that group." He also denounced members of the Communist Party as "the supporters and apologists for an aggressive war" in Korea.[67]

After this advance publicity Pressman's appearance before the House committee was something of an anticlimax. He restated his admission of Communist Party membership in 1934 and added that he had been a member of a small Communist cell in the Agricultural Adjustment Administration. But he did his best to avoid identifying any of his associates in this cell. He further admitted, under committee questioning, that his final and complete ideological break with communism had come only recently.[68] There was a good deal of somewhat ridiculous fencing between the committee and the witness, with the latter intimating that he would name his associates if the committee demanded that he do so, and with Chairman Wood replying that the committee would not direct the witness to reply to

[67] N.Y. Times, August 28, 1950.
[68] Hearings regarding Communism in U.S. Government—Part II, pp. 2861–2866.

its questions, but implying that he might be cited for contempt if he failed to do so.[69] Ultimately, Pressman in effect stated that Nathan Witt, Charles Kramer, and John Abt had also been members of the Communist cell.[70]

The questioning of Pressman was prolonged but in the end rather fruitless. Beyond his reluctant admission that the three men already named had been Communists, he was either unwilling or unable to throw any new light upon the story of Communist infiltration of the government service that Whittaker Chambers had told. Pressman did deny any personal involvement in, or knowledge of, espionage activity by Communists in the government. Moreover, he did demonstrate rather effectively that there were minor inaccuracies in Chambers' testimony.[71]

[69] "*Mr. Wood:* The committee does not direct you to answer anything.
"*Mr. Pressman:* I refuse to decline to answer. I am not being jocular.
"*Mr. Wood:* Suppose you answer it, then.
"*Mr. Pressman:* Is that a direction from the chairman?
"*Mr. Wood:* It is a suggestion. A person can't decline and acquiesce at the same time.
"*Mr. Pressman:* I find myself in a very peculiar position, because it has been my experience, in terms of understanding a committee's work, that when an individual or a witness is asked a question and the witness indicates there is a problem in connection with the question, he is entitled to ask the committee if he is directed to answer the question, and, please, I ask if I am directed.
"*Mr. Wood:* It would be a strange anomaly if a member of the committee asked a question and did not want an answer to it.
"*Mr. Pressman:* I don't know what the reluctance of the committee is to tell me yes or no whether it is directing me to answer.
"*Mr. Wood:* There is no reluctance, Mr. Pressman. It is not in the province of the committee to direct you to answer.
"*Mr. Pressman:* I say I do not want to be in a position of declining to answer a question.
"*Mr. Wood:* Suppose you go ahead and answer it, if you do not decline to answer it." *Ibid.,* p. 2878.
[70] *Ibid.,* pp. 2853, 2876–2879.
[71] "*Mr. Pressman:* . . . Secondly, to show you how inaccuracies can develop, on page 576 of the record of the proceedings of this committee you will find an exchange between Mr. Chambers and Mr. Hébert. Mr. Chambers I quote first: 'After I had been in Washington a while it was very clear that some of the members of these groups were going places in the Government.'
"And I quote Mr. Hébert: 'What year is this?' Mr. Chambers: 'I would think about 1936. One of them clearly was Alger Hiss, and it was believed that Henry Collins also might go farther. Also was Lee Pressman.'
"And there is some more comment, and he says they decided to separate some of these people, and so on.
"Now, get that. In 1936, as a matter of public record, Lee Pressman was

Thereafter the committee recalled as witnesses the three men acknowledged by Pressman to have been Communists, and also Abraham George Silverman, another of the 1948 witnesses who had refused to testify on grounds of self-incrimination. Once more, all four witnesses were unco-operative and persisted in their refusal to answer the committee's questions on the ground of self-incrimination.

The Lowenthal Hearing

The final witness in this series of hearings published under the title, *Hearings regarding Communism in the United States Government*, was Max Lowenthal. This witness had absolutely no connection with either the Remington or the Pressman case with which the printed hearings under the above title are otherwise exclusively concerned. Indeed, the inclusion of Lowenthal's testimony in a volume bearing this title is an act of sheer irresponsibility by the House committee. Lowenthal is the author of a critical study of the FBI, published in 1950.[72]

Lowenthal appeared before the committee on September 15, 1950, in response to a subpoena and testified in executive session, but his testimony was made public shortly thereafter with the publication of the printed record. There is no doubt that this action by the committee was part of a calculated attempt on the part of the FBI's friends in Congress to embarrass and discredit, if possible, a man who had been so bold as to write critically concerning the FBI. Lowenthal's professional career as a lawyer and public servant is a distinguished one. He had been a law clerk to federal Judge Julian

---

in the city of New York. Chambers has me going high in Government places, and Lee Pressman is in the city of New York, having left Washington and the Government service a year before.

"*Mr. Wood*: Let us not labor the point, Mr. Pressman. I think your answer was responsive to the question. Any further questions?" *Ibid.*, p. 2858. See also pp. 2884, 2896–2897, 2900.

[72] *The Federal Bureau of Investigation* (New York: William Sloan Associates, 1950). Although the Lowenthal book had many bitter critics, it was favorably reviewed in many responsible journals. Cabell Phillips, a member of the *N.Y. Times* Washington staff, reviewed it for the *Times*. Cabell said, in part: "This is a thoughtful and important book that too few people will take the trouble to read. It is a thoughtful book because of the immense research and careful documentation that went into its writing. It is important because it dares, almost for the first time, to pull aside the self-righteous cloak in which the F.B.I. has wrapped itself. And it is a heretical book that is sure to stir up the dogs of controversy." *N.Y. Times Book Section*, Nov. 26, 1950.

W. Mack (1912), secretary of the President's Mediation Commission (1917), assistant to the chairman of the War Labor Policies Board (1918), assistant secretary to the President's Industrial Conference (1920), executive secretary of the Wickersham Commission (National Commission on Law Observance and Enforcement—1929), counsel to the Senate Committee on Interstate Commerce (1935), member of the staff of the Board of Economic Warfare (1942), and a consultant under General Clay in connection with the administration of occupied Germany (1946).[73] Former Senator Burton K. Wheeler, with whom Lowenthal had worked during his period of service with the Senate Committee on Interstate Commerce, appeared with him before the House committee as his counsel.

The committee's questioning of Lowenthal was unfriendly and even presumptuous. He was asked whether he owned stock in WQQW (a radio station in Washington long suspected of being Communist-dominated), whether he had advised Bartley Crum during the Hollywood hearings in 1947 (he had), whether he knew such persons as Alger Hiss, Lee Pressman, Nathan Witt, John Abt, and so forth (he acknowledged having known all of them in varying degrees), and he was quizzed closely concerning his membership in and resignation from the National Lawyers Guild. Questioning also brought out that Carol King, a lawyer who frequently represented Communists in recent years, had worked in 1920 for a period of three months for a law firm with which Lowenthal was identified.[74] He was even asked whether he had been associated with the Twentieth Century Fund, the question being asked in such a context as to suggest that the organization was regarded by the committee as a subversive one.[75]

That the committee had any legitimate basis for questioning Lowenthal even in executive session is doubtful, in view of the questions actually put to him; that it had any justification for making public his testimony, beyond a desire to tar him as a person who had been investigated by the Un-American Activities Committee, is in no way apparent.

That the House committee in the 81st Congress, for all of its efforts to improve upon the much-criticized methods of its predecessor committees, could have its own irresponsible moments is further illustrated by this same series of hearings. In the printed record of the

[73] *Hearings regarding Communism in U.S. Government—Part II*, pp. 2960–2961.
[74] *Ibid.*, pp. 2980–2982.   [75] *Ibid.*, p. 2977.

hearings there is published an "Appendix" which is stated to contain "information from the files of the Committee on Un-American Activities regarding *the Communist record and activities*" of some of the persons named during the hearings.[76] Among the persons subjected to this treatment are Bartley C. Crum and Robert W. Kenny, who had served as counsel for the unfriendly witnesses in the Hollywood hearings, Thomas I. Emerson, professor of law at Yale University, and Shad Polier, a New York attorney and an officer of the American Jewish Congress. Whatever the liberal or radical activities of these men, no shred of evidence has ever been produced suggesting that any one of them has a "Communist record" or has engaged in "Communinst activities." The data which is printed in the "Appendix" for these men consists largely of undigested odds and ends of information drawn from the committee's files. As usual, generous use is made of the guilt-by-association technique. For example, the statement under Bartley Crum's name includes such items as: "one of the attorneys for the 10 Hollywood Communists"; the *Daily Worker* once listed him "as one of the signers of a protest against outlawing the Communist Party" (the House committee itself has repeatedly warned that "outlawing" the Communist Party would be an unwise move); his book, *Behind the Silken Curtain,* was favorably reviewed by the *Daily Worker;* in 1943 he was president of the San Francisco chapter of the National Lawyers Guild, and has been vice president of it since 1946; he has "been associated with" such "Communist-front organizations" as the Veterans of the Abraham Lincoln Brigade, the American Slav Congress, the American Committee for Spanish Freedom, the Joint Anti-Fascist Refugee Committee, and the American Committee of Jewish Writers, Artists, and Scientists.[77] As usual with such organizational listings in House committee publications, no attempt whatsoever is made to indicate the exact character of Crum's "association" with these agencies.

The Powell Hearing

The appearance of Hazel Scott Powell before the committee in September, 1950, illustrates the type of hearing in which a person whose loyalty to the United States has been attacked is allowed to appear before the committee as a voluntary witness and to assert his or her 100-per-cent Americanism. The committee has from time to

[76] *Ibid.,* p. 2987. Italics added.　　　　[77] *Ibid.,* pp. 2989–2990.

time taken great pride in the claim that it is thus available as a public forum to enable innocent persons to free themselves from any subversive taint. Actually, the number of people who have taken advantage of this opportunity is very small,[78] and as often as not they appeared in an attempt to answer charges against them that the committee had permitted other witnesses before it to make or that had been made by the committee itself or its members.

Mrs. Powell's appearance was due ostensibly to an attack upon her in the publication, *Red Channels*, issued by a private organization of ex-FBI agents which publishes a weekly leaflet known as *Counterattack*. Chairman Wood, in opening the hearing, stated that the committee did not recognize any obligation to allow persons to appear before it to clear themselves against charges made by private organizations and that Mrs. Powell was being allowed a hearing because she was "the wife of one of our colleagues." [79] However, the House committee twice listed Mrs. Powell in its 1947 *Report on Civil Rights Congress as a Communist Front Organization*. Moreover, the House committee has been one of the chief sources of the data utilized by the *Counterattack* group in their irresponsible campaigns against a wide variety of liberals and radicals, Communist and non-Communist alike. During the course of Mrs. Powell's testimony, Representative Harrison made a most ingenious attempt to defend *Counterattack*. Mrs. Powell was denying the accuracy of certain organizational affiliations listed in *Red Channels*. Harrison observed that certain of these listings had been drawn from the reports of such an agency as the California Un-American Activities Committee and then insisted that a private agency such as *Counterattack* was above criticism if it had obtained its data from such an official source. Both Harrison and Wood seemed to suggest that it was most unfair of Mrs. Powell to attack *Red Channels* for publishing false information and that she should have instead attacked the California committee. Harrison makes it plain that he feels *Counterattack* had no obligation whatsoever to evaluate data obtained from

[78] Other persons who have taken advantage of this "opportunity" include Yelverton Cowherd (see *Annual Rept.*, March 15, 1950, pp. 46 ff.), Josh White (see *Hearings regarding Communist Infiltration of Minority Groups—Part III*, Sept. 22, 1950), and Edward G. Robinson (see *Testimony of Edward G. Robinson*, Oct., Dec., 1950). Several persons, such as Alger Hiss, Lauchlin Currie, and Harry White, asked to be heard during the Communist espionage hearings in 1948 so that they might deny charges against them.

[79] *Testimony of Hazel Scott Powell*, p. 3611.

such a source as the California committee before using it to attack a person as a subversive. The exchange of remarks is worth quoting at some length because it illustrates how one member of the House committee balances in his mind the interests of the individual accused (perhaps falsely) of subversive conduct against the right of organizations (governmental and private) to make such accusations:

Mr. Harrison: You have made an attack on this publication [*Red Channels*].

Mrs. Powell: That is right.

Mr. Harrison: Of false listings unaccompanied by official action, I believe?

Mrs. Powell: Yes.

Mr. Harrison: On the other hand, if they have made correct copies from official documents which they have published in a book without comment, I don't agree with you it is a false listing.

Mrs. Powell: If you were in danger of losing your job because of this you would agree with me.

Mr. Harrison: If this is a correct listing from official documents, that is one thing. If it is a false listing, as you have said, it is another thing.

Mrs. Powell: I haven't said that. I have said that they made an error in listing people. Their purpose, as stated in the beginning of the book, is to show how Communists and pro-Communists have infiltrated the entertainment field. They say they have checked.

Mr. Harrison: I have read what they have said, and they have said that many innocent people have allowed themselves to be duped into these organizations. What I am trying to get at is whether or not the statements made by Counterattack are true. They are true if they correctly quote their source, and they are not true if they don't. Do you follow me?

Mrs. Powell: Yes. I don't see any possible way of answering you without reading my prepared statement.

Mr. Harrison: The next thing they say is that the House Un-American Activities Committee, in Appendix 9, page 347, lists you as being the guest of honor at a dinner on April 17, 1943, given by the American Committee for the Protection of the Foreign Born. Can you state whether or not the House Un-American Activities Committee so lists you?

Mrs. Powell: May I ask you a question? If any committee, an official committee, lists me as having two heads, does that make me have two heads, and does that give Red Channels a right to publish I have two heads?

Mr. Harrison: Would you deny the right to reprint from official records without comment?

Mrs. Powell: They say they want to protect innocents.

Mr. Harrison: They make no bones of the fact they do not evaluate the listings.

Mrs. Powell: They simply prepare a blacklist.

Mr. Harrison: I don't agree with you. . . .

. . . . .

Mr. Harrison: They do nothing that I see in here but simply quote from official records.

Mrs. Powell: But, don't you see, if those records are false, how can you prove it?

Mr. Harrison: If they are false, they were false in the original sources.

Mrs. Powell: Exactly.

Mr. Harrison: Then the publication is not false.

Mrs. Powell: It is at fault for printing false reports without verifying them.

Mr. Harrison: That would leave to a private individual the duty of evaluating official records.[80]

[80] *Ibid.,* pp. 3616–3618.

VI: The Committee's Personnel

THE UN-AMERICAN Activities Committee has never been a closely knit, systematically organized agency. Congressional committees, in spite of the important part they play in the legislative process, are not characterized by cohesion or order, but the disunity and disorder of the Un-American Activities Committee have been outstanding. Two special conditions have contributed to this situation. One is the agency's status as an irregular type of Congressional committee; the other is the very high turnover in the personnel of the committee and its staff during the first six years of its existence as a permanent body.

The Un-American Activities Committee is an anomaly among Congressional committees. Although it possesses a limited measure of jurisdiction over bills, thus qualifying as a "legislative" committee, its function is almost exclusively an investigative one. As a permanent investigating committee it is a unique body in the House of Representatives.[1] Moreover, where the average House committee has twenty-five or more members, the membership of the Un-American Activities Committee is fixed at nine. Similarly, the committee is one of the few in the House that is exempted from operation of the rule that a Representative may serve on but one standing committee. In other words, every member of the committee serves on another House committee, and in every instance the latter is his regular committee assignment, service on the Un-American Activities Committee being in the nature of an "extra." For example, during the period from 1945 to 1950 members of the committee had such other committee

[1] Alone among the standing committees of the House the Un-American Activities Committee is given a permanent subpoena power and is also authorized to sit while the House is in session.

assignments as the following: Wood and Nixon were members of the Education and Labor Committee, Rankin was chairman of the Veterans' Affairs Committee (in 1945 the Committee on World War Veterans' Legislation), Mundt, was on the Foreign Affairs Committee, Thomas and Hébert were on the Armed Services Committee, Walter was a member of the Judiciary Committee, and Case a member of the Appropriations Committee. Often these assignments were viewed as more important than service on the Un-American Activities Committee. Even the Representatives who have served as chairman of the latter committee have had major interests as members of other committees. For example, John Wood's name was actively associated with a proposed bill to amend the Taft-Hartley Act which was considered by the Education and Labor Committee in 1949.

The statistics concerning the turnover in personnel reveal that the committee's membership has been anything but stable. Indeed, it is proper to say that between 1945 and 1950 there were three quite separate and different un-American activities committees. Twenty-two different Representatives served on the nine-member committee during the 79th, 80th, and 81st Congresses.[2] During this period the committee had three chairmen, and at least two "acting" chairmen, and its staff had four chiefs. At the beginning of each of the three Congresses in 1945, 1947, and 1949, wholesale changes were made in the committee which were only partly explained by the fact that party control of the House of Representatives passed from Democratic in the 79th Congress to Republican in the 80th Congress and back to Democratic in the 81st Congress. When the standing committee was organized in 1945 seven of its nine members had had no connection with the Dies committee of the 78th Congress. In the 80th Congress four new members were appointed to the committee, and in the 81st Congress seven of its members were again new to the body. Only one man, John S. Wood, was continuously a member of the permanent committee throughout the first six years of its existence. No other standing committee of either house of Congress saw such frequent and thoroughgoing changes in personnel during this period.

The Un-American Activities Committee has not been famed among Congressional committees for the high quality of its membership. Some of its members have admittedly been able men, but, in the main, respected and intelligent Representatives have not sought sev-

[2] For the membership of the committee, 1938–1950, see Appendix, Table II.

ice on this committee. For example, rumor had it late in December, 1948, that members of both parties were dodging service on the committee in the 81st Congress. It was reported that the prospective Speaker of the House, Sam Rayburn, had received letters from 101 new Democratic members and from more than fifty carry-over Democratic members expressing their committee preferences and that not one had asked for service on the Un-American Activities Committee, even as a second choice.[3] Moreover, this condition existed at a moment when the committee had just scored a great coup in bringing to light the Pumpkin Papers and in thereby demonstrating the validity of its espionage investigation.

In terms of their appointment to the Un-American Activities Committee its members have fallen generally into three categories. There has been a small group that has willingly accepted membership. Such men as Rankin, Thomas, and Mundt fall into this category and it seems fair to say that with few exceptions these men have either been strongly motivated by a conservative point of view and an enthusiasm for hunting subversives and mere liberals as well, or have sought membership on the committee as a means of securing political advancement—with a seat in the Senate as the most frequent goal.[4] A second group includes those members who have quite obviously accepted service upon the committee only as a result of pressure brought upon them by party leaders and friends that such service be viewed as a duty. The committee's first chairman, Edward J. Hart, and such members of the committee in the 81st Congress as Francis E. Walter and John McSweeney, fall into this group. It is in this group that many of the most sober and able members of the committee have been found, although the men in this group have not always been among the most active members of the committee and some have attempted to get off it at the first opportunity. Finally, there is a third group that has seemingly accepted membership with neither enthusiasm nor distaste and has not brought to the committee's labors any marked interest or vitality. Outstanding among the members in this category has been John S. Wood. In spite of the fact that he served as the committee's chairman during nearly four

[3] *N.Y. Herald Tribune*, Dec. 30, 1948. One Democrat was reported to have said privately that new members "seem to regard the Un-American Activities Committee as a Jonah—a jinx." A Republican was reported to have said that service on the committee was not viewed with favor "because it takes up an awful lot of time that you ought to be spending on your district."

[4] Dies, Rankin, Mundt, Nixon, and Case have all sought election to the Senate following membership on the committee, the latter three, successfully.

of its first six years, Wood's attitude toward the committee has not been far above indifference. It is also fair to say that it is this third group that has supplied the committee with many of the nonentities and mediocrities that have frequently appeared upon its roster.

The membership of the Un-American Activities Committee in the 81st Congress was the best the committee enjoyed up to that time. Almost without exception its members were able and respected Representatives. And yet, with this striking improvement in the caliber of its personnel, the committee moved into a quiet, unspectacular, and, in the end, largely futile and meaningless two-year period of activity. In terms of the usual standards of activity—number of days devoted to hearings, publication of reports, development and use of its files—this committee was busier than any of its predecessors. But its work attracted little public attention, and it was seemingly content in a period of high interest in problems pertaining to loyalty and subversive activity to allow other agencies, such as the Tydings subcommittee of the Senate Foreign Relations Committee, to take over the main burden of investigation and control in this area. In other words, the indication is that when its talent was at a peak, the Un-American Activities Committee lost some of its zest for hunting subversives.

These preliminary observations suggest a thesis: the use of the Congressional power of investigation is apt to be hampered in the field of subversive activity because of chronic difficulties in staffing a committee to undertake such an investigation. There is seemingly a basic dilemma which cannot be escaped. Those men who have enthusiasm for such an undertaking are apt to be the reactionaries and professional Red-baiters, if not the crackpots, of Congress. When an attempt is made to press into service some of the more responsible members of the national legislature much of the spirit seems to go out of such an investigation.[5]

It is desirable that this general analysis of the personnel of the

[5] The Tydings subcommittee of the Senate Foreign Relations Committee in the 81st Congress was obviously an exception to the rule, for its personnel was, with one or two exceptions, excellent. But the charges of Senator McCarthy concerning Communists in the federal service which led to the subcommittee's creation were so irresponsible and so crassly political in motivation that Senate leaders had powerful motives for finding an able group of men to investigate these charges, and these men had good reason to make careful use of the power granted to them. However, Senator Tydings' defeat in the 1950 election is not apt to encourage other Congressmen of his high caliber to accept such assignments in the future.

committee be supported by a further examination of some of the specific individuals who have served as members of it. Any such examination is bound to be a more or less personal one. Judgments of Congressmen are apt to be affected by the judge's politics and his general scheme of values. Nonetheless, the Un-American Activities Committee has inevitably been affected by the men who have served upon it. Its twenty-two members have left their imprint upon the committee for better or worse, and if its record is to be properly understood attention must be given to the manner of men who were and are the committee.

The Un-American Activities Committee has had three chairmen since 1945. They are Edward J. Hart of New Jersey, who served for the first half of 1945; John S. Wood of Georgia, who succeeded Hart and served for the remainder of the Democratic 79th Congress and who returned to the same post in 1949 in the 81st Congress; and J. Parnell Thomas of New Jersey, who was chairman in 1947 and 1948 in the Republican 80th Congress.[6]

Under the rules and procedures of the House of Representatives and the Senate, the chairmen of all Congressional committees possess very considerable power. Moreover, arbitrary exercise of this power is traditional. The chairmen of the Un-American Activities Committee have not departed from this tradition. Since 1945 the personality of the committee has depended as much upon its chairmen as upon any other single factor. This has merely been a continuation of the situation that existed during the long Dies regime. No one of Dies's successors perhaps ever quite turned the committee into the one-man agency that he did, but all were conscious of the tradition he had established.[7] The available evidence suggests that the chairman, assisted by the head of the committee's staff, has largely determined the committee's policies and guided its activities. An indication

[6] John E. Rankin was an unofficial "acting chairman" for a brief period following Hart's retirement in 1945, and Karl Mundt was "acting chairman" in the closing weeks of 1948 when Thomas' indictment compelled him to withdraw from active service.

[7] Ogden suggests that the Dies committee was virtually a one-man organization from 1941 on. He writes, "Somewhere between the fall of France and 7 December 1941 the Committee, as far as the public record indicates, had disappeared. Its place had been taken by a one-man agency which could not properly be called administrative and yet could not be called legislative. The information gathered by the investigators was utilized by the Chairman who, to all intents and purposes, had become the Committee." *The Dies Committee*, p. 249.

of the importance of the chairman's position is also seen in the loyalty given him by members of the committee's staff and in their tendency to look to him for orders.[8] This is a natural relationship, and it should be added that the chairman of a Congressional committee almost always controls the selection and work of the members of the committee's staff. However, the policy of recent years to make provision for one or more staff members to be selected by and responsible to the minority members of a committee has not been followed by the Un-American Activities Committee. In the 81st Congress the committee functioned as a responsible, collective group perhaps more than it had in previous Congresses. Its chairman, John Wood, was not an aggressive person; its other members were collectively more vigorous and intelligent than their predecessors had ever been; and the natural result was that the committee's program by and large reflected the joint wishes of its members.

Edward Hart was a quiet, unobtrusive Representative who began his service as a member of Congress in 1935 and was still a member at the time of writing. Characteristically, his biography in the *Congressional Directory* is a four-word statement revealing only that he is a Democrat, a lawyer, and that he comes from Jersey City. It seems probable that he was named chairman in January, 1945, because he was a loyal party member and staunch supporter of the Roosevelt administration who might be expected to keep a watch over the unpredictable Rankin. The latter could almost certainly have claimed the chairmanship himself had it not been that he was already chairman of the Veterans' Affairs Committee and thus rendered ineligible because of a House rule limiting members to a single chairmanship. It was soon apparent, however, that Hart had no liking for his assignment and that he was unwilling or unable to control the extremists within the committee and its staff. A careful reading of the OPA hearings, held in June, 1945, shows Hart's unhappiness about the antics of some of his colleagues. It seems likely that Hart's early resignation in July, 1945, from the chairmanship and the committee was caused in good part by distaste for the assignment.[9] However, in his letter of resignation submitted to

[8] Louis Russell told the author (June 24, 1949) in an interview that so far as he was concerned Chairmen Thomas and Wood were "the law." He said, "I do what they tell me to do."

[9] At the time of his retirement there were news reports that he had been wrangling with Rankin for some time. See, for example, *N.Y. Herald Tribune*, July 1, 1945.

Speaker Rayburn he stated merely that his physician had given him "definite instructions to diminish substantially" his activities. Representative Mundt also denied on the floor of the House that Hart's resignation was the result of dissention among members of the committee.[10]

At the other extreme from Hart was the committee's Republican chairman in the 80th Congress, J. Parnell Thomas. Noisy, arrogant, and opinionated, he, more even than John Rankin, was responsible for the bad name that the Un-American Activities Committee came to enjoy among thoughtful and impartial Americans. Thomas had served continuously since 1938 as a member of the Dies committee and of the Un-American Activities Committee and was such a strong candidate for the chairmanship on the basis of seniority that it would have taken far more willingness to ignore seniority than either political party has ever shown to pass over him in 1947. Yet in the end he was to prove a terrible liability not only to the committee but to the Republican Party—above all a liability to those conservatives who wished strongly for the success of the Un-American Activities Committee. There is no better illustration in modern times of the utterly irresponsible way in which both houses of Congress choose their committee chairman than the Thomas appointment.

J. Parnell Thomas—born John Parnell Feeney in Jersey City in 1895—was first elected to the House of Representatives in 1936 and during his first term became a member of the Dies committee at the time of its creation in 1938. His previous record was that of a small-town businessman and politician, and of a World War I soldier with a strong continuing interest in veterans' affairs.[11] Apart from his charter membership on the Un-American Activities Committee, it would be hard to imagine a person less qualified to hold the chairmanship of such a delicate, complicated undertaking as the Un-American Activities Committee. Throughout his two-year term as chairman, Thomas' deep initial prejudices were always apparent. He was seemingly incapable of undertaking an investigation without

---

[10] 91 *Cong. Rec.* 7142, 7186 (July 2, 3, 1945).

[11] Thomas was a member of the American Expeditionary Force during World War I and was discharged with the rank of captain. He was elected to the Allendale, New Jersey, borough council in 1925 and was elected mayor of Allendale in 1926 and 1928. In 1935 he was elected to the New Jersey legislature. He was at one time vice commander of the Bergen County American Legion and was also a member of the Veterans of Foreign Wars; he was an insurance broker.

simultaneously indicating his judgment that un-American activity would be uncovered.[12] Similarly, his speeches in the House of Representatives and elsewhere and his magazine writings all reveal deep-seated prejudices, a habitual use of flamboyant language, and an utter irresponsibility in making charges in the absence of supporting evidence. For example, after a brief trip to Panama early in 1948 Thomas published an article in *Liberty* magazine, entitled "Reds in the Panama Canal Zone," in which he did not hesitate to draw a detailed picture of extensive Communist infiltration and espionage in all phases of the life of the Zone. Typical of the article are such unsupported and reckless charges as the following: "The University of Panama is a hotbed of Communist and extreme leftist sympathizers. The head of the University himself is far left of center, and perhaps three-quarters of the faculty are leftist sympathizers." "A leading woman leftist, who is strongly suspected of being a Communist, is married to a man who holds a responsible job in the Zone." And Thomas viewed criticism of the "gold" and "silver" classifications, which serve as the basis of racial segregation in the Zone, as the work of "Communist agitators," in spite of the fact that every responsible student of race relations who has investigated conditions in the Canal Zone has condemned the use of these symbols.[13]

Thomas' ready inclination to voice his prejudices on a wide variety of subjects was frequently apparent during the conduct of committee hearings. For example, he eagerly told the commander-in-chief of the Veterans of Foreign Wars when he appeared as a witness during the 1947 hearings on bills to curb the Communist Party, "I am 100 per cent with you on the transfer of the atomic bomb back to the

[12] The following comment by Thomas during the course of the 1947 hearings on communism in labor unions is a typical illustration of this weakness: "We are not going to fail, we are going to succeed as no committee of Congress has ever succeeded before in this respect. That is, to expose the un-American activities, not only in unionism but in other fields, education, the films, government. We are going to expose them like they have never been exposed before. We are going to do a job of teaching the American people the dangers from these inroads based on their foreign connections." *1947 Hearings regarding Communism in Labor Unions,* p. 11b.

[13] Thomas writes, "Communist agitators exploit as racial discrimination such distinctions as the gold and silver classifications which grew out of early payment of United States citizens in gold and others in silver." Thomas was assisted in the writing of the article by Stacy V. Jones. The article appeared in the May, 1948, issue of *Liberty* and was read into the *Congressional Record* by Thomas. 94 *Cong. Rec.* A2657 (April 21, 1948).

military. If we put the atomic bomb in the hands of a group of 'milk toasts' we can be certain that we can just hurry the day when the bomb is going to be used against us." [14]

Not the least serious of Thomas' faults was his complete lack of dignity as the committee's presiding officer. Seldom has an important Congressional agency been so handicapped by the vulgarity of its leader. At a time when representative institutions in democratic lands sorely needed respect, Thomas' raucous, coarse manner was a fearful liability not only to the committee but to the Congress of the United States. Again and again Thomas conducted committee hearings as though he were a cheap comedian or a participant in a street-corner political harangue. He was fond of making such observations as that Frank Sinatra was "sort of a Mrs. Roosevelt in pants," to win the "laughter" indicated in the printed hearings, or that "a great man like General Eisenhower would not ever think or dream or stoop to ever being a low-down Communist," to win the "loud applause" similarly indicated.[15] Attention should also be called to the petulant manner in which Thomas reacted to recalcitrant witnesses or to criticism of himself or of the committee. Again and again, he matched the vehemence or truculence of a witness with angry or petty responses. He seemed constitutionally incapable of conceding that the committee's opponents might be speaking in good faith or asserting what were to them sound arguments. Instead, such efforts were always met by him with ridicule, or, what is worse, by an effort to impugn the motives behind them. Thus, any argument that the contemptuous witnesses in the Hollywood hearing might have constitutional support for their conduct was' dismissed by Thomas in a speech in the House of Representatives as "a concerted effort on the part of the Communists, their fellow-travelers, their dupes, and paid apologists to create a log of fog about constitutional rights, the First Amendment, and so forth." [16]

It is probable that Thomas is to be correctly understood as a small, vain, stupid man rather than as one who was consciously mean or evil or motivated by a reactionary or native Fascist philosophy. At the same time it is clear that he hated the New Deal and all of its works with every fiber of his being and that he welcomed every

[14] *Hearings on H.R. 1884 and H.R. 2122*, March 24–28, 1947, p. 281.

[15] *Investigation of Un-American Propaganda Activities in the United States* (*Gerald L. K. Smith*), Jan. 30, 1946, p. 46; *Hearings regarding the Communist Infiltration of the Motion Picture Industry*, 1947, p. 388.

[16] 93 *Cong. Rec.* 10771 (November 24, 1947).

opportunity that came to the committee to discredit the Roosevelt-Truman program by discrediting its supporters.

In fairness to Thomas it should be pointed out that there are moments in the hearings when a sort of elementary decency asserts itself in him and he reacts adversely to the more shameful conduct of a Rankin, Mundt, or Stripling. For example, he was capable of defending the National Association for the Advancement of Colored People against an effort by Rankin to get a witness to call it a Communist front,[17] of protecting a witness against an irrelevant line of questioning by Mundt concerning his private business affairs,[18] and of preventing Stripling from directing a witness to name certain labor union officers who chanced to be sitting in the audience at one of the committee's hearings.[19]

[17] "*Mr. Steele:* I think I have already answered the question, anyhow, that I haven't found the national organization as a whole is a Communist front. I have found locals and local officers connected with the other Red front movements.

"*The Chairman* [*Thomas*]: Did you know the national association had passed a resolution at its recent convention condemning communism?

"*Mr. Steele:* I didn't know that; no, sir.

"*Mr. Rankin:* Do you know it passed one the other day condemning this committee?

"*Mr. Steele:* Yes, I knew that.

"*Mr. Rankin:* And for the destruction of this committee.

"*Mr. Steele:* I knew of that, sir.

"*Mr. Rankin:* Because of its fight against communism.

"*The Chairman:* There are a lot of other people condemn this committee, but that doesn't mean they are Communists." *Testimony of Walter S. Steele regarding Communist Activities in the United States*, pp. 98–99.

[18] "*Mr. Mundt:* You handle contracts with such companies as American Tobacco Co. or General Motors?

"*Mr. Miller:* Those don't happen to be our clients; no.

"*Mr. Mundt:* Could you name a few of your clients?

"*The Chairman* [*Thomas*]: I don't think you should name them.

"*Mr. Mundt:* If it isn't confidential; if it is, that is different.

"*The Chairman:* If he names his contracts, he just opens up the firm." *Communist Espionage Hearings*, p. 799.

[19] "*Mr. Stripling:* Would you care to name them for the record?

"*Mr. Nixon:* You mean of the local union?

"*Mr. Julianelle:* No.

"*Mr. Stripling:* The international.

"*Mr. Julianelle:* Of the international.

"*The Chairman* [*Thomas*]: No. These people are entitled to the same consideration as others in the audience.

"*Mr. Julianelle:* All right. . . ." *1947 Hearings regarding Communism in Labor Unions*, p. 150.

It is hardly necessary to dwell at length upon Thomas' conviction in a federal court on charges growing out of his acceptance of "kick-backs" from persons on his office staff on the salaries paid them by the government.[20] His subsequent resignation from Congress and the ruin of his career as a public servant have nothing directly to do with his role as chairman of the Un-American Activities Committee. They do, however, provide a further commentary upon the kind of man whom Congressional and party leaders were willing to see assume the chairmanship of such a committee. Thomas' ultimate disgrace could not have been foreseen by those who permitted him to go upon the Dies committee in 1938 or who sanctioned his chairmanship in 1947 under the seniority rule. But evidence that he was small, narrow-minded, petty, emotional, vindictive, and blindly partisan was available from the start. That he should have ended his career branded as a criminal was in a sense an anticlimax—a perverse, almost incredible turn of fate by which he was made to suffer the same torture he had inflicted upon some of his own victims.[21]

John S. Wood of Georgia, who served as chairman of the Un-American Activities Committee for nearly four of its first six years, was an accident in that post. He first became chairman in July, 1945, following the resignation of Chairman Hart, at a time when no majority member of the committee had acquired any seniority worthy of note. Although he had served two terms in the House of Representatives in the early thirties, Wood had returned to Congress only six months before his appointment as chairman. Wood's voting record in the House from 1945 through 1950 places him well down toward the bottom of the list of Democrats with respect to party regularity. He is a conservative Southerner who has usually voted against administration measures, particularly those of the New Deal or Fair Deal variety. A veteran of World War I and a lawyer, Wood

---

[20] The charge that Thomas had compelled members of his office force to "kick back" their salaries to him was originally made in the summer of 1948 by Drew Pearson. See his columns in the *Washington Post*, August 4, 7, 10, and 17, 1948.

[21] That Thomas should have refused, Nov. 4, 1948, in his appearance before the federal grand jury investigating the charges against him to testify on advice of counsel on the ground that he might incriminate himself was surely one of the supreme ironies of American politics. Coming within a matter of weeks after a long line of witnesses accused by Whittaker Chambers and Elizabeth Bentley had refused to testify before the Thomas committee on the same ground of self-incrimination, it is difficult not to regard this turn of affairs as a cosmic judgment upon the entire Un-American Activities Committee undertaking.

had served both as a state's attorney and judge in Georgia before
his election to Congress. William S. White of the *New York Times*
has written of Wood that he "has none of the aggressive temperament
of Mr. Thomas and, moreover, has had considerable training in the
law. A rather gentle, passive man who was long on the judicial
bench. . . ." [22] On the other hand, Wood was the subject of a series
of charges of wrongdoing by Drew Pearson in the summer of 1950
in the latter's widely syndicated newspaper column.[23]

It is difficult to characterize Wood's service upon the committee
or his role as chairman. The most impressive thing about his record
is its negative quality. Wood is a quiet, unaggressive person who
seldom asserts himself. As presiding officer at committee hearings
his remarks rarely go beyond the bare minimum required of such
an officer. He has never taken a leading role in the questioning of witnesses, and his statements to the press or other informal utterances
are rare and sparsely worded.

Wood was a minority member of the committee during the 80th
Congress, but his attendance record at committee sessions was far
and away the worst of any of the nine members. For long periods he
did not appear at any public hearings. During both of his periods
as chairman, Wood was reasonably regular in attendance at committee sessions and went through the appointed rounds of his office
in faithful fashion, but there is little or no evidence that he was much
interested in his work or felt deeply about the necessity of investigating un-American activities. Insofar as he has revealed any feelings
in the matter they were certainly conservative and orthodox in character. At the same time he has been generally fair and circumspect
in his treatment of witnesses and the general conduct of hearings.
He has shown a certain quiet irritation when confronted with an
unco-operative witness, but he has almost never allowed this to lead
him to the use of flamboyant language or to browbeat the witness.
On the other hand, his record is not above criticism in this respect.
For example, he was one of the three members of the Subcommittee
on National Security that released the Condon report in March,
1948. It is possible, even probable, that Wood took no active part
in the work of this subcommittee. But it is also unlikely that he had
any strong disapproval of Thomas' action in releasing the report, and,
in any case, such inactivity would illustrate his most serious short-

[22] Nov. 14, 1948.
[23] See the Pearson columns in the *Washington Post,* June 12, 13, 20, and 22,
1950.

coming: a negative acquiescence in the Congressional tradition of hunting subversives through a loosely organized investigating committee oriented strongly in a witch-hunting direction. To put it somewhat differently, Wood has perhaps revealed a quiet decency and a basic honesty in the day-by-day conduct of the affairs of the committee, but he has seemingly had no deep understanding of the risks inherent in the investigation of anything so nebulous as un-American activity, and he has certainly never been willing, or perhaps able, to use his power as chairman to guide his committee in a systematic, intelligent manner. It is easy enough to say that Wood's committee in the 81st Congress was far and away the best of all the un-American activities committees since 1938. But it was best only in the sense that its record was largely free from shameful action. The record was otherwise a largely futile one, and at the moment when the threat of communism to democracy was at its peak the committee's contribution to an understanding of the threat was not a substantial one.

Although he was never a member of the Dies committee and served upon the permanent committee for only four years, John Rankin is perhaps more closely identified in the mind of the average person with the Un-American Activities Committee than any other individual. It is difficult to know whether to dismiss Rankin as a cruel but meaningless joke in the annals of the committee, or to take him seriously and subject his character and his record to systematic analysis. It is probable that, as a symbol of all that is dark and evil in the committee's record, Rankin's importance has been overestimated. At times during the 79th Congress, either as acting chairman or because of the free rein given him by the easy-going Wood, Rankin ran amok and did real damage. But during the 80th Congress, while upon occasion he was permitted to voice his incredible prejudices and irrelevances, he had little real influence and in the end played an inconsequential part in the making of the record during the most important period in the committee's history. On the other hand, Rankin almost singlehandedly was responsible for the creation of the permanent committee in 1945, and it is his basic notion of what constitutes un-American activity that has dominated the work of the committee even in its most calm and fair-minded moments.

Rankin appeared in the House of Representatives in 1921 as a member of the 67th Congress. He was a veteran of World War I and a lawyer and had served as a prosecuting attorney in Mississippi. As a member of Congress, Rankin has had four consuming interests:

the development of governmentally owned electric power projects, the enhancement of war veterans, the protection of white supremacy in the South, and the suppression of communism.

Rankin's conduct at the public hearings of the Un-American Activities Committee was incredible. At his most harmless he sat in his chair, seemingly obsessed with his own thoughts, and broke in with irrelevant interruptions. An example of his absent-mindedness occurred during the second phase of the Communist espionage hearings in 1948. Rankin argued one day at some length that the original copies of the documents stolen from the State Department and turned over to Chambers for microfilming had been turned over to Russian agents, in spite of the fact that the testimony of Chambers and others showed that the documents had been carefully returned to State Department files after having been photographed. The exchange of remarks ran as follows:

Mr. Rankin: Mr. Hébert, may I correct you on one thing? We did not get the originals of these documents. The originals probably went into the hands of the Russian agents. We merely got the microfilm of them that were [*sic*] taken at the time.

Mr. Hébert: Oh, Mr. Chairman, the originals are back, we hope. They are checking the State Department files now to ascertain that.

Mr. Rankin: But the files they took out, we haven't even got the copies. We got the microfilm. But the copies that were stolen were turned over to Russian agents.

Mr. Hébert: But the mechanics of this, which I understand are well known already, that this traitor or traitors in the Department of State—how many there are, or whichever level they are—took from the files of the State Department these important documents—

Mr. Rankin: And had them copied.

Mr. Hébert: Brought them to Chambers, who in turn had a Communist photographer photograph or microfilm these documents. Then the microfilm was given to the Russian agent to be dispatched to the Kremlin, and the documents themselves were returned to the State Department files.

Mr. Rankin: That is not my understanding. My understanding is that they made these copies and turned the copies over to Mr. Chambers. Mr. Chambers had those copies microfilmed and the copies themselves were turned over to somebody else.

Mr. Mundt: I will ask the chief investigator to correct me if I am wrong, but I think Mr. Hébert has described the mechanics of this operation exactly correct. . . .[24]

[24] *Communist Espionage Hearings,* pp. 1424–1425. A random selection from the hearings of a four-month period in 1947 of irrelevant interruptions by Rankin includes the following references: *Josephson Hearing,* March 21, pp. 39, 45, 46,

In his more dangerous moments Rankin gave free voice to his monumental prejudices against the Jews, the Negroes, and various other objects of his hatred, and he was capable of flying into towering rages in which he bullied witnesses and made dire threats against them. The following excerpts are typical of his many attacks upon the Jews and Negroes:

Mr. Rankin: . . . Isn't it true that communism . . . is a racial fight, and isn't it a fact that practically every leader in Russia belongs to a racial minority, every Communist leader, that is the 14 top-flight men, practically every one of them belong [*sic*] to a racial minority? [25]

. . . . .

Mr. Rankin: In other words, [communism] is nothing but a system of abject slavery, dominated by a racial minority that has seized control, as members of the Politburo; is that correct?
Miss Bentley: I am not clear about the racial minority.
Mr. Rankin: I am. . . .[26]

. . . . .

Mr. Stripling: Mr. Chairman, I have a document here which shows the employment history of Lee Pressman.
Mr. Mundt: Will you identify the document, please?
Mr. Stripling: It is Who's Who.
Mr. Rankin: Who's Who in American Jewry, isn't it?
Mr. Stripling: Yes; Who's Who in American Jewry. . . .[27]

On the floor of the House, Mr. Rankin said: "It is not a disgrace to be a real Negro. As I said on this floor before, if I were a Negro, I would want to be as black as the ace of Spades. I would then go out with Negroes and have a real good time." [28] Other objects of his hatred ranged all the way from *Time* magazine (because of its attacks upon him) [29] to the United States Senate (because of its

---

49; *Hearings on H.R. 1884 and H.R. 2122*, March 24, pp. 3–6, 27, 29; *Bullitt Hearing*, March 24, pp. 19–23; *Dennis Hearing*, April 9, pp. 13–14; *Kravchenko Hearing*, July 22, p. 11; *1947 Hearings regarding Communism in Labor Unions*, July 23–24, pp. 62, 67–69, 126; and *Hanns Eisler Hearings*, Sept. 25, pp. 90, 105, 167.

[25] *Hearings on Proposed Legislation to Curb or Control the Communist Party*, Feb., 1948, p. 206.

[26] *Communist Espionage Hearings*, July 31, 1948, p. 544.

[27] *Ibid.*, p. 567.   [28] 93 *Cong. Rec.* 1131. (Feb. 18, 1947).

[29] When Representative Nixon read into the record statements from *Time* magazine concerning the resignation of Whittaker Chambers as senior editor, Rankin protested: "From the vicious and unwarranted attacks that Time maga-

"persecution" of Bilbo).[30] He was particularly vehement against Mrs. Roosevelt [31] and fair employment practices legislation.[32]

Rankin's all-abiding fear of communism and the incredible lengths to which he went in seeing evidence of the threat of communism were never more evident than in the following remarks which he made on the floor of the House of Representatives on July 18, 1945:

> Communism . . . hounded and persecuted the Savior during his earthly ministry, inspired his crucifixion, derided him in his dying agony, and then gambled for his garments at the foot of the cross. . . .
>
> These alien-minded communistic enemies of Christianity, and their stooges, are trying to get control of the press of the country. Many of our great daily newspapers have now changed hands and gone over to them. . . .
>
> They are trying to take over the radio. Listen to their lying broadcasts in broken English and you can almost smell them.[33]

zine has made on me, I don't think a Communist on their editorial staff would embarrass them, and I just object to reading this defense of it into the record." *Communist Espionage Hearings, Part Two*, p. 1460.

[30] During the early phase of the Communist espionage hearings, when the Un-American Activities Committee decided to let the Ferguson committee in the Senate have first call on William Remington as a witness, Rankin protested: "Now, the Senate, the majority of the Members of the Senate, at that time participated in that lynching of Senator Bilbo, and I am not willing to turn over to a Senate committee the prerogatives of this committee to investigate people on the Federal payroll who are known to be Communists and plotting the overthrow of this Government." *Ibid.*, p. 535.

[31] See, for example, the *Hanns Eisler Hearings*, p. 90, where Rankin called an article by Mrs. Roosevelt, "the most insulting, communistic piece of propaganda that was ever thrown in the faces of the women of America."

[32] The following are examples of Rankin's references to FEPC:

"*Mr. Rankin:* You understand, Mr. Chairman, in the State of New York under their present FEPC law you can't ask a man who applies for employment what his name was before it was changed or where he came from, so that it is a veritable storm cellar for people of that character." *Communist Espionage Hearings*, p. 570.

"*Mr. Rankin:* I know that the Senate is busy now nagging the white people of the South, and all of the FEPC, and all this communistic bunk." *Ibid.*, p. 548.

"*Mr. Rankin:* . . . The Communists seem to have got their hands in this FEPC in the State of New York and all over the country and it is just the same old pattern." *Ibid.*, p. 632.

For other references by Rankin to FEPC in the *Communist Espionage Hearings*, see pp. 571 and 579. See also the *Josephson Hearing*, pp. 45, 49.

[33] 91 *Cong. Rec.* 7737 (July 18, 1945). During the Communist espionage hearings the following exchange of remarks between Rankin and Hébert occurred:

"*Mr. Rankin:* What I am trying to say is that we have a world of Communist

Rankin's tendency to bully witnesses was well illustrated during the Joint Anti-Fascist Refugee Committee hearing in 1946. He warned one witness, Jacob Auslander, who had refused to answer certain questions put to him by the committee, "Do you realize that you are violating your oath of citizenship when you show contempt for this committee, and are likely to have that citizenship canceled?" And he told another witness, Manuel Magana, "You are rubbing your nose right up against the gates of the penitentiary here." [34]

At times, Rankin's reactions to witnesses and their testimony might seem amusing, were they not so unpredictable and violent. For example, he seems to have a tender spot in his heart for the Scottish people. He grew angry during the Communist espionage hearing at the attack upon Lauchlin Currie and at one point told the witness, Elizabeth Bentley:

> You certainly have an unlimited credibility. If you would take the word of any Communist, Silverman or Silvermaster, or both of them, and I believe you named another one, whom you relayed it through, who was also a Communist, if you take that testimony as to what this man Currie, as I said, a Scotchman, has said about the Communists—it just looks to me as if we have gone pretty far afield here to smear this man by remote control, instead of getting someone who heard him or who knew that he had made any statement. [35]

And after a reference to Alger Hiss' post as head of the Carnegie Endowment for International Peace, he remarked: "Right at that point, don't you think Mr. Carnegie, the rich Scotchman that developed this foundation, would turn over in his grave if he knew that kind of people were running the foundation?" [36]

There was also a bit of wry humor in the dilemma in which Rankin frequently found himself because of his desire to remain at a public hearing of the committee and his wish to be present also on the floor of the House of Representatives. For example, he said one day in leaving a session of the hearing on communism in labor unions: "The 15-minute bell has rung. I am going to have to leave. The Bible says, 'Watch as well as pray,' and there is a good deal to be watched on the floor of the House at this time. But there is one question I would

---

professors in our educational system, and they are poisoning the minds of the young students of this country.

"*Mr. Hébert:* This is absolutely correct. . . ." *Communist Espionage Hearings*, p. 551.

[34] *Joint Anti-Fascist Refugee Committee Hearing*, pp. 6, 63.

[35] *Communist Espionage Hearings*, p. 558.   [36] *Ibid.*, p. 579.

like to ask the witness—." [37] Rankin is a clever parliamentarian and on the floor of the House he has always watched like a hawk for attacks upon the Un-American Activities Committee. If the critics of the committee use language that is in the slightest degree unparliamentary Rankin is quick to invoke House rules and to demand that the words "be taken down" and to move that they be stricken from the record. For example, a mere reference by Representative Koppleman in a one-minute speech given on April 16, 1946, to "unlawful prying" by the committee brought Rankin into action, and his motion to strike the offending language was adopted by the House.[38] The readiness with which the House supports Rankin in these sallies against Representatives for language that seems colorless in comparison with his own is difficult to explain. A particularly shocking illustration of Rankin's influence with the House in this respect occurred in February, 1946. Representative Sabath, chairman of the Rules Committee, had written a letter to Chairman Wood in which he called the committee the "Un-American Committee" and otherwise used vigorous language in condemning it. He had then asked for and received permission to insert this letter in the Appendix of the *Congressional Record*. When Rankin spotted the letter in the *Record,* he moved to have it expunged. Debate on this motion was prolonged, and the House's inclination to give Rankin free rein was shocking. In his own remarks Rankin wandered far afield. At one point he read at length from testimony given by William Z. Foster, the Communist leader, before the Dies committee many years earlier. Representative Marcantonio objected to this maneuver under a House rule which forbids members to read documents without the consent of the House, but such consent was promptly given. At the end of his speech, Rankin took advantage of House rules to move the previous question in an effort to prevent Sabath from presenting his side of the story. In spite of the patent unfairness of this action the House by division voted 139 to 80 to order the previous question. The yeas and nays were then demanded and in the subsequent record vote Rankin's motion to close debate lost by the narrow margin of 161 to 185. Sabath then asked unanimous consent to delete the offending language from the *Record,* and Rankin withdrew his motion to expunge.[39]

Much of the work of carrying out the program of the Un-American

---

[37] *1947 Hearings regarding Communism in Labor Unions,* pp. 149–150.
[38] 92 *Cong. Rec.* 3761 (April 16, 1946).   [39] *Ibid.,* 1727 ff. (Feb. 27, 1946).

Activities Committee during the 80th Congress fell upon Representatives Mundt and Nixon. Thomas' incompetence, his chronic illness, and his indictment late in 1948 all served to bring about this result. As the senior Republican on the committee next to Thomas, Mundt occupied a position of strategic importance and served throughout much of 1948 as the committee's acting chairman. Nixon, while a first-term member of the committee, possessed a good deal of drive and ability, and by the close of the 80th Congress had become the most influential member of the committee. Certainly he was the dominant member throughout the Hiss-Chambers hearings.

Karl E. Mundt of South Dakota was elected to the 76th Congress in 1938 and served continuously as a member of the House of Representatives until January, 1949, when he became a United States Senator. Mundt's professional background is a varied one: at the time of his election to Congress he had served as a schoolteacher and a magazine editor and writer, and had had business interests in real estate, insurance, and farming. He was appointed to the Dies committee in 1943 and, with Thomas, became a charter member of the permanent committee in 1945.

In his farewell speech to the House of Representatives on August 7, Mundt labeled himself "a country boy from South Dakota." This was sheer cant. Mundt is a born investigator and a clever one. More almost than any other man who ever served on the committee he seemed to enjoy searching for evidence of "un-American activity." [40]

[40] At one time or another the vigor and enthusiasm with which Mundt approached the problem of controlling subversive activity and the serious view he takes of the danger offered by subversives have been indicated by his language. At a 1947 hearing he said: "I think it would be a wonderful thing if every State in the Union had a little Dies committee, as it were, or a little committee on un-American activities, because they have the intimate contacts and knowledge which a national committee such as ours cannot possibly have." *Hearings on H.R. 1884 and H.R. 2122*, p. 252. At the 1948 hearings of the Nixon subcommittee on legislation to curb the Communist Party he described a bill he had introduced as one designed "to bring out of the black night of seductive secrecy the operations and activities of those conspiring to change the American way of life by stealth." *Hearings on Proposed Legislation to Curb or Control the Communist Party of the United States*, p. 5. Later, at the same hearings he said, "Our committee holds that organizations shall be under continuous process of investigation." *Ibid.*, p. 30.

During the debate in the House of Representatives in 1946 over the resolution submitted by the Un-American Activities Committee asking the House to cite some sixteen officials of the Joint Anti-Fascist Committee for contempt, Mundt again indicated the vigor of his stand. It was found that the resolution was faulty because only one of the sixteen officials had actually been subpoenaed.

Certainly no other member of the committee, not even Thomas, was more concerned about his personal publicity than was Mundt. More significantly, Mundt brought to the committee a series of strong prejudices and a bitter sense of partisanship. Like Thomas, he did not hesitate to indicate a bias or even a fully formed judgment at the beginning of a hearing, and he never lost an opportunity to attack the Democratic administration. Among his ready biases were a strong disapproval of the State Department, of the United Nations, and of American postwar foreign policy generally.

A good example of Mundt's bias is found in the record of the Communist espionage hearings for August 3, the day of the first appearance of Chambers before the committee. After Chambers had made his initial statement and had made his first charges against Alger Hiss—but before Hiss had had any opportunity to reply, and long before the details of Chambers' accusation against Hiss had been obtained or analyzed—the following dialogue between Mundt and Chambers occurred:

Mr. Mundt: Mr. Chambers, I am very much interested in trying to check the career of Alger Hiss. I know nothing about Donald Hiss; but as a member of the Foreign Affairs Committee [of the House of Representatives], the personnel committee, I have had some occasion to check the activities of Alger Hiss while he was in the State Department.

There is reason to believe that he organized within that Department one

---

It was obvious that the House, which has almost never refrained from giving the committee anything it asked for, was here reluctant to cite these individuals until they had been formally served with subpoenas by the committee and given an opportunity to purge themselves of their implied contempt of the committee. In fact, Chairman Wood finally offered an amendment withdrawing all of the names save that of Dr. Barsky. Subsequently, the others were subpoenaed, they persisted in their refusal to testify, a second resolution was introduced in the House, and the entire group was cited for contempt. But the House's reluctance to take this action when first requested to do so by the committee infuriated Mundt, and in an angry speech, he said:

"Now is as good a time as any in the course of an election year for the Members of Congress to stand up and be counted on this issue of whether they believe the American way of life should be defamed or defended.

"A vote against this privileged resolution is a vote to give aid and comfort to the defamers of America. A vote to approve this resolution is a clear-cut, on-the-record vote to defend America and to serve notice that those who would defy and defame Congress and discredit its Committee to Investigate Un-American Activities are not mightier than the Government nor the Constitution of the United States which so few of them revere except when they hope some technicality from it may be invoked to induce a wobbly minded court to protect them in their sinister, secret acts." 92 *Cong. Rec.* 2749 (March 28, 1946).

of the Communist cells which endeavored to influence our Chinese policy and bring about the condemnation of Chiang Kai-shek, which put Marzani in an important position there, and I think it is important to know what happened to these people after they leave the Government. Do you know where Alger Hiss is employed now?

Mr. Chambers: I believe Alger Hiss is now the head of the Carnegie Foundation for World Peace.

Mr. Mundt: That is the same information that had come to me and I am happy to have it confirmed. Certainly there is no hope for world peace under the leadership of men like Alger Hiss.[41]

On the first day of the Communist espionage hearings Mundt asked Stripling for a full employment record of all the persons named by Elizabeth Bentley, saying, "I am interested, Mr. Stripling, in getting their employment records down to date, because our experience on another committee of the House has been that, especially where Communists have been employed in the State Department and then removed because of loyalty charges, they have gravitated to the United Nations." [42]

Mundt was one of the two or three most intelligent members of the committee. He was regular in his attendance at committee sessions, he followed the development of a hearing carefully, and his questioning of witnesses, or his conduct of hearings when serving as acting chairman or subcommittee chairman was generally competent. At times, however, his ability revealed itself as mere cleverness, and unlike his colleague, Nixon, he was occasionally careless about facts.[43]

Mundt was politically ambitious. He received the Republican nomination for the Senate in South Dakota and was elected to the Senate in November, 1948. During his service on the committee he overlooked no opportunity to gain publicity for himself out of its activities. During his period as acting chairman in 1948 he held a number of press conferences and took obvious enjoyment in his place in the limelight. For example, early in December, 1948, from his home in South Dakota he released the story that Chambers had turned over the Pumpkin Papers to the committee.[44] Later that month he and Nixon released the Levine testimony against Laurence Duggan.[45]

[41] *Communist Espionage Hearings,* p. 579.   [42] *Ibid.,* p. 519.
[43] See *ibid.,* pp. 643, 647, 1135–1137.
[44] Stripling, *The Red Plot,* p. 148; *N.Y. Times,* Dec. 4, 1948.
[45] *N.Y. Times,* Dec. 21, 1948. For report of a similar press conference in which

Richard M. Nixon was elected to the House of Representatives from California in the Republican landslide of 1946, defeating Jerry Voorhis, the Democrat who had been holding the seat. A graduate of Whittier College and the holder of a law degree from Duke University, he had practiced law for five years in California, and had served briefly with the Office of Emergency Management in Washington before going into the Navy late in 1942. He was discharged from the Navy early in 1946 and within a matter of months was elected to Congress.

Nixon became a member of the Un-American Activities Committee at the beginning of his first term in 1947 and before the end of the 80th Congress had become the most competent member of the committee. It is hard not to overpraise Nixon, for he brought to the committee enthusiasm, a willingness to work hard, ability as a lawyer, and a reasonable detachment and sense of fairness, qualities that have been rare among the committee's members. Nonetheless, at several points he was guilty of bad errors of judgment, and as time went on he showed increasing signs of partisanship and personal ambition.

During 1947 Nixon was a relatively quiet member of the committee. He did not, for example, play a vigorous role in the Hollywood hearings. As a matter of fact, he showed a mild inclination to defend the motion picture industry against the attack of Thomas, Stripling, and others. When Stripling questioned the director, Sam Wood, concerning the making of pictures in Hollywood which portrayed "the sordid side of American life," Nixon came to Wood's aid:

Mr. Nixon: As a matter of fact, isn't it true that there are many pictures which point out the weak features of our own American system which have been made by people whose loyalty, insofar as Communism is concerned, is absolutely unquestioned? In other words, people who are anti-Communist have made and will continue to make, pictures which point up weaknesses in our American system?

Mr. Wood: Yes, sir; if it is a good subject, they make it.[46]

Early in February, 1948, a subcommittee under Nixon's chairmanship conducted public hearings on proposed legislation to curb the Communist Party. These hearings were well planned, and the wit-

Mundt undertook to speak for the committee, see the *Washington Post,* August 28, 1948. See also his speech in the House of Representatives, Jan. 29, 1947, in which he charged the Amtorg Trading Corporation with engaging in "legal" espionage. 93 *Cong. Rec.* 675 (Jan. 29, 1947).

[46] *Mot. Pict. Ind. Hearings,* p. 64.

nesses included a number of eminent lawyers and scholars. The testimony and questioning were a bit aimless at times, and it may be said that the hearings were never sharply focused upon the intricacies of the problem—statutory control of the Communist Party. Nonetheless, they are among the most intelligent hearings ever conducted by the committee, and the printed volume of testimony remains a remarkable source of information and opinion about the threat of communism and ways and means of meeting the threat. Nixon must be given credit for having participated in the planning of these hearings and for having conducted them with dignity and intelligence. Moreover, since his name was joined with that of Mundt in the introduction of the ultimate bill which took shape out of these hearings, it must be presumed that he played an important part in formulating this bill. The Mundt-Nixon bill became the center of much controversy and was bitterly resisted by many loyal and intelligent Americans. But it was a far more carefully drawn piece of legislation and a much more defensible proposal than were any of the bills originally submitted to the Nixon subcommittee for consideration.

Nixon was seen at his best during the Communist espionage hearings in 1948. However, it was also in this connection that he revealed his growing sense of partisanship and at times showed a tendency to use some of the more vigorous methods for which the committee has always been condemned by fair-minded observers. That Nixon had prepared himself for these hearings with great care and was paying close attention to developments became apparent during the first days when he was exceedingly effective in handling such witnesses as Silvermaster, Perlo, Ullmann, and Silverman. In particular, he exposed the inconsistency between the prepared statements of these men in which they denounced Elizabeth Bentley's charges against them as "false and fantastic" and their refusal to answer specific questions concerning her charges on the ground of self-incrimination.[47] By such means Nixon revealed the worthlessness and dishonesty of the witnesses' prepared statements, and what is more, thereby indicated the value from the committee's point of view of allowing witnesses, however "unfriendly" they might be, to read such statements.

Nixon's questioning of Hiss was able, discerning, and persistent. More than any other member of the committee, more perhaps even than Stripling, he sensed the weak spots in Hiss's story and then

[47] *Communist Espionage Hearings*, pp. 594 ff., 604 ff., 693 ff., 768 ff., 844 ff.

exerted relentless pressure upon the witness. Mundt, in his interrogation of Hiss, was inclined to be prolix, uncertain of his facts, and too ready to let his prejudices get in the way of intelligent questioning. Nixon was remarkably clever in questioning Hiss about his disposal of the Ford roadster and the discrepancies between his story and the official records of the transaction.[48] Another illustration of Nixon's ability to pounce upon the weaknesses in Hiss's testimony

[48] It is difficult to convey by brief quotations from the printed record of the hearings a full sense of the quality of the questioning. However, the following long excerpt gives some sense of Nixon's agility in questioning Hiss about the car:

"*Mr. Nixon:* Now, is your testimony then that you did give Crosley the use of the car?

"*Mr. Hiss:* That is my testimony, Mr. Nixon.

"*Mr. Nixon:* On that point you are sure?

"*Mr. Hiss:* As sure as I can be of any of these details of 14 years ago, Mr. Nixon.

"*Mr. Nixon:* Mr. Hiss—

"*Mr. Hiss:* Have you ever had occasion to have people ask you continuously and over and over again what you did on the night of June 5, 1934 or 1935? It is a novel experience to me, Mr. Nixon.

"*Mr. Nixon:* Mr. Hiss, I will answer the question. I will tell you this: That if I had given anybody the use of a car for a period of 2 months, I would remember.

"*Mr. Hiss:* Well, I have testified to you that I do recall that.

"*Mr. Nixon:* All right. Now, your testimony is that you did give Crosley the car for a period of 2 months. When did that occur?

"*Mr. Hiss:* My best recollection is that it coincided with the sublease. I am not positive that it occurred then, rather than in the fall or some other time.

"*Mr. Nixon:* And you do not know whether it occurred at the time of the sublease in connection with that transaction?"

"*Mr. Hiss:* My recollection is that it occurred because it is fixed in my memory in a rather vague way as connected with the lease. Whether it preceded or followed or was simultaneous, I am afraid I am not able to testify with exactness.

"*Mr. Stripling:* Mr. Chairman—

"*Mr. Nixon:* Just a moment. Mr. Hiss, it is not likely that you would have given the car to Crosley after he failed to pay the rent, is it?

"*Mr. Hiss:* I do not recall the details of when I concluded he was a fourflusher.

"*Mr. Nixon:* Well, now, you have testified that he went—

"*Mr. Hiss:* It was sometime—not after this.

"*Mr. Nixon:* Your testimony was that you had seen Mr. Crosley after he failed to pay the rent.

"*Mr. Hiss:* Yes; I feel quite confident I saw him some time after the sublease transaction.

"*Mr. Nixon:* Now, do I understand you to say that you might have loaned Crosley a car for a couple of months after he failed to pay the rent?

"*Mr. Hiss:* I might have, if I had considered that his reasons for not paying were as plausible as his reasons had been for not paying back small loans, be-

occurred on August 25 at the public confrontation scene between Hiss and Chambers. Hiss claimed that his identification of Whittaker Chambers as George Crosley at the earlier private confrontation scene on August 17 had depended in part upon an admission Cham-

cause the rent was not a major consideration in my mind. Of that I feel quite confident.

"*Mr. Nixon:* When were the small loans made?

"*Mr. Hiss:* Again, Mr. Nixon, I am testifying from the best of my recollection, which I have certainly in the course of the last few days done my very best to go over and over again. I think I loaned Crosley a total, in small amounts, of $25 or $30. Whether they were made prior to the sublease, some of them after the sublease, I just frankly do not recall with exactness. But at some stage I reached the conclusion that this had better be terminated, that I was being used, that my kindness was being abused.

"*Mr. Nixon:* And your testimony then is that the car—that you are not sure that the car was tied in to the rental transaction; you think it might not have been.

"*Mr. Hiss:* It could have been tied in toward the end, it could have been tied in toward the beginning. My best recollection is that there is a connection between the two transactions.

"*Mr. Nixon:* Could it have taken place several months after the rental transaction?

"*Mr. Hiss:* Mr. Nixon, it could have.

"*Mr. Nixon:* You mean several months after he had refused to pay the rent?

"*Mr. Hiss:* After he failed to pay the rent.

"*Mr. Nixon:* Well, didn't you ask him for the rent?

"*Mr. Hiss:* Mr. Nixon, I don't recall at any time his ever refusing, ever saying, 'I just am not going to pay.' Quite the contrary, he was going to pay at some time.

"*Mr. Nixon:* How long after he moved out of his apartment did you decide he was a dead beat?

"*Mr. Hiss:* Mr. Nixon, I am not able to testify with exactness on that.

"*Mr. Nixon:* But you think it is possible that you loaned him a car or gave him a car after he failed to pay the rent?

Mr. Hiss: I may very well have given him the use of the car even though he had not paid the rent at that particular time.

"*Mr. Nixon:* And your testimony is that this man was simply a casual acquaintance.

"*Mr. Hiss:* This man was an acquaintance. Under the circumstances this man was an acquaintance, under the circumstances to which I have testified.

"*Mr. Nixon:* You said he was not a guest in your home. You objected when Mr. Stripling used that phrase.

"*Mr. Hiss:* That is correct.

"*Mr. Nixon:* You objected when there was any suggestion that Mr. Crosley was a friend of yours, and you are now testifying that is is possible that you gave him a car after he failed to pay the rent.

"*Mr. Hiss:* Yes, Mr. Nixon.

"*Mr. Nixon:* All right." *Communist Espionage Hearings,* pp. 1104–1106.

bers made that day that he had once told Hiss a story about his being a day laborer on a Washington street railway construction job. Nixon was quick to point out to Hiss that Chambers had not gotten around to this story on the seventeenth until *after* Hiss had finally agreed that Chambers and Crosley were the same man.[49] It may be noted that Nixon stated on a radio broadcast that Bert Andrews, Washington correspondent of the *New York Herald Tribune,* co-operated closely with the committee during the Communist espionage hearings.[50] There is reason to believe that he aided Nixon in developing the line of questioning that the latter followed in interrogating Hiss.

It may be said that these examples of Nixon's ability as an inquisitor merely demonstrate that as an able lawyer he could function effectively in the best Un-American Activities Committee tradition of hunting guilty individuals and that they do not show that he had any great understanding of the larger problem of disloyalty among government servants or any deep interest in finding out why such servants became disloyal or what might be done to prevent such disloyalty. But again it must be pointed out that this latter approach to the problem of un-American activities is one in which the committee has never shown much interest. In other words, within the framework offered by the committee Nixon was an exceedingly effective member. To show that there were Communists in the federal service, to see them punished, to see those who permitted them to gain their public posts discredited, to see the laws changed if existing ones provided an inadequate basis for punishing the wrongdoers —these were Nixon's interests. Seldom, if ever, did he show interest in such questions as how and why such a man as Alger Hiss had seemingly become a Communist, whether that demonstrated a weakness in American democratic traditions, and what might be done to strengthen those traditions against the aberrations of intelligent, potentially loyal and useful, young Americans.[51]

[49] *Ibid.,* p. 1130.   [50] *N.Y. Herald Tribune,* Jan. 22, 1950.

[51] In a long speech which he delivered in the House of Representatives, Jan. 26, 1950, reviewing the Hiss case in great detail, Nixon seemed to attribute the tragedy of Hiss to the failure of the American educational system. He said,

"The tragedy of this case is that men like Alger Hiss who come from good families, are graduates of our best schools, and are awarded the highest honors in Government service, find the Communist ideology more attractive than American democracy.

"This is a serious reflection on our educational system, and it is essential that we remedy the situation if we are to survive as a free people. The statement of Mr. John Foster Dulles when he commented upon the Hiss verdict last Saturday

In the second session of the 80th Congress, Nixon became a vigorous critic of the Truman administration. In part, this merely reflected the deepening sense of antagonism that had developed between the committee and the administration as the Hiss-Chambers case unfolded. But Nixon became increasingly politically minded and, with Mundt, lost no opportunity to denounce the President and his subordinates. He accused the President, the Justice Department, and the federal officials presenting evidence in the espionage case to the New York grand jury of laxity and also seized every new chance to attack the executive branch and thus to widen the breach between the committee and the administration. These attacks continued after the November election in 1948 and reveal how deep-seated the conflict betwen the administration and such a committee member as Nixon had become. For example, following the arrest of Judith Coplon early in 1949 Nixon publicly demanded an investigation of the Justice Department, saying, "In my opinion this case shows why the Department may be unfit and unqualified to carry out the responsibility of protecting the national security against Communist infiltration." [52] A month or so later, the escape of Gerhart Eisler from the country led Nixon to demand a "public accounting" by the Justice Department, and he added, "The Eisler escape certainly indicates laxity on the part of the Justice Department. It would seem obvious that a man who has been termed the No. 1 Communist agent in the United States has not been kept under proper surveillance. [53]

In July, 1949, when the jury in the first Hiss trial was unable to agree upon a verdict, Nixon bitterly denounced the administration and the trial judge. He was reported as charging that "the entire Truman Administration was extremely anxious that nothing bad happen" to Alger Hiss, as challenging Judge Samuel H. Kaufman's "fitness to serve on the bench," and as stating, "When the full force of the conduct of this trial is laid before the nation, I believe the people will be shocked." [54]

Nixon's political motivation reached full development in January, 1950, when in a long speech in the House of Representatives which

---

is particularly pertinent: 'The conviction of Alger Hiss is human tragedy. It is tragic that so great promise should have come to so inglorious an end. But the greater tragedy is that seemingly our national ideals no longer inspire the loyal devotions needed for their defense.' " 96 *Cong. Rec.* 1003 (Jan. 26, 1950).

[52] *Washington Post*, March 6, 1949.   [53] *Ibid.*, May 15, 1949.
[54] *Ibid.*, July 10, 1949.

commanded great interest he reviewed the Hiss case in detail and laid great stress upon the incompetent manner in which the administration had handled the case.[55] By now Nixon had determined to seek a seat in the United States Senate from California, and since victory could only be won in a strictly party struggle his increasingly strong sense of politics is readily understood. This is not to say that Nixon was not as much entitled, in terms of training, ability, and experience, to think of himself as a likely candidate for the Senate as was anyone else. It is, however, unfortunate, that a young man who had only appeared in Congress in 1947 and who, in a short two-year period had become an able and effective member of the Un-American Activities Committee, should so quickly have been compelled by circumstances to think of claiming a reward for his labors and have been turned so completely into a strict partisan. It is true that such has been the tradition with those Congressmen who have in modern times achieved sudden fame through participation in a sensational investigation. Few have been able to resist the temptation to accept the quick glory and rewards which such activity sometimes offers. This is perhaps as legitimate a basis for political advancement in a democracy as any other. At the same time, one cannot help feeling that the serious business of evolving a satisfactory national policy with respect to the problem of subversive activity deserved better of such an able worker as Nixon than that he should so quickly have given himself over to the task of realizing personal political ambitions.

Among the Republican members of the committee in the 80th Congress, attention may finally be given to John McDowell of Pennsylvania. It is difficult not to speak ill of McDowell, because he represents so well one of the things that has been wrong through the years with the personnel of the Un-American Activities Committee. The plain truth is that McDowell was a complete nonentity among members of Congress, a man of exceedingly limited ability, and, what is worse, one who was unable to remain silent or to play the quiet role of a follower which so many men of mediocre talents have wisely selected for themselves.

McDowell was an obscure newspaperman from Wilkinsburg, Pennsylvania, who was swept into Congress in the Republican landslide of 1946.[56] The Un-American Activities Committee has always

[55] 96 *Cong. Rec.* 1000 ff. (Jan. 26, 1950).

[56] He had served one previous term in the House as a member of the 76th Congress.

had its share of such freshmen members of Congress, and the way in which they have handicapped the committee, particularly where, as political accidents they proved to be one-term members of Congress, is well illustrated by McDowell's service on the committee. McDowell was a man of deep prejudices and an exceedingly narrow horizon. His questioning of witnesses and his frequent interruptions of the proceedings at public hearings to make personal observations were almost always painful in character. At best, his comments provided moments of unconscious humor; at worst, they brought the Congress of the United States into contempt and ridicule. The caliber of McDowell's comments upon the problem of controlling subversive activity is well illustrated by the following observation which he made during the course of the 1947 hearing on legislation to curb the Communist Party:

I would like to put in one statement. . . . A great American, who probably knows as much about world conditions as any other figure, told me last week that if America wants to do something about communism, there are two places that America can do something about communism. This striking at the fingers of communism in the various places that they occur may never accomplish what we are trying to do. One is in America, and the other one is in Moscow. That is all.[57]

During the espionage hearings, when Representative Mundt made a reference to Chambers' charge that Hiss was a member of the Communist Party, McDowell interrupted to ask, "Mr. Chairman, in that connection so much has been said in the last 4 days that I have forgotten entirely what charge was made by Mr. Chambers. Would the chief investigator enlighten me?" [58] McDowell completed his very brief questioning of Duncan Lee, one of the witnesses heard during the espionage hearings, with the plaintive comment:

Well, now, Mr. Chairman, here, for, I believe the first time since the conspiracy of Aaron Burr, a high officer of the Army has been accused publicly of the violation of the Articles of War, which he must certainly realize the penalties of and the punishment. The questions which are flooding my mind at this moment, I feel, should not be given here. I have no further questions now.[59]

During the Hanns Eisler hearing McDowell accused Eisler of having written music to accompany a song "opposing the prohibition of abortions." This avenue of questioning was quickly shut off by

[57] *Hearings on H.R. 1884 and H.R. 2122*, p. 44.
[58] *Communist Espionage Hearings*, p. 646.   [59] *Ibid.*, p. 749.

Chairman Thomas, who interrupted to say, "I would suggest that we don't get very deep into the question of abortion." [60]

McDowell's ability to employ strange figures of speech was phenomenal. During the espionage hearings he commented on the testimony of Elizabeth Bentley by saying, "Mr. Chairman and members of the committee, here is an American citizen who delved into this business, and now has the courage to walk through the valley of the shadow of publicity that she is doing now, and I want to commend

[60] *Hanns Eisler Hearings*, p. 59. Harry White in his tragic, embittered appearance before the Un-American Activities Committee took great delight in baiting McDowell:

"*Mr. McDowell:* Dr. White, I am almost ashamed to say that up until Miss Bentley mentioned your name I had never heard of you.

"*Mr. White:* Well, it is nothing to be ashamed of. May I ask your name?

"*Mr. McDowell:* McDowell.

"*Mr. White:* I did not mean to be facetious. I heard your name, but I just did not connect the face with the name.

.   .   .   .   .

"*Mr. McDowell:* In making myself acquainted with you, Dr. White, I have been told that you were the author of the famous Morgenthau plan. I presume that is true; is it?

"*Mr. White:* Did you also hear I was the author of the famous White plan, by chance?

"*Mr. McDowell:* Yes.

"*Mr. White:* You did. Apparently you did hear of me. No; I would not quite say that. I would say that I participated in a major way in the formulation of a memorandum which was sent to—which was given to the President, I suppose, to the proper authorities, and might I comment on that?

"*Mr. McDowell:* Well, no.

"*Mr. White:* Or would you rather I would not?

"*Mr. McDowell:* I would rather you would not. It is immaterial.

"*Mr. White:* What is immaterial?

"*Mr. McDowell:* I would like to ask you—

"*Mr. White:* I thought you asked a question. You would not ask immaterial questions.

"*Mr. McDowell:* Sometimes I do.

"*Mr. Hébert:* Mr. Chairman, I suggest you instruct the witness that it is obvious that he is a great wit, that he is a great entertainer, and would undoubtedly be a great entertainer socially, but I would ask you to instruct the witness to answer the questions. He is well able to take care of himself.

"*The Chairman* [*Thomas*]: Mr. White, please be responsive to the questions; leave out the side remarks, and I would like to say this to other people in the room. You are the guests of the committee. We are conducting a public hearing; we have got very important questions to ask, and we are attempting to get the answers. The Chair would appreciate it if you would not applaud. Proceed, Mr. McDowell." *Communist Espionage Hearings*, pp. 903–904.

her. . . ." [61] And again he referred to the questioning of William Rosen with respect to the disposition of Alger Hiss's old Ford roadster as follows: "If such be the case, Mr. Chairman, Mr. Rosen is engaged here in a conspiracy to deceive this committee. In other words, he is engaged here in a conspiracy to drive us down an alley of blind ownership of a car which, apparently and obviously, he had nothing to do with. . . ." [62]

McDowell's use of extravagant language to praise each friendly witness who appeared before the committee is indicative of his utter lack of critical judgment. Thus, during just one set of hearings, those on Hollywood, he commented on witnesses as follows: "In addition to being a great American" Adolph Menjou is called "one of the greatest American patriots I ever met." McDowell told Menjou, "Of all the thousands of people I have discussed communism with you have the most profound knowledge of the background of communism I have ever met [sic]." Of Lela Rogers, he said that "she has become, in my opinion, one of the outstanding experts of communism in the United States." Oliver Carlson is told, "I have been an amateur student of communism and Communist activity and its history for more than 20 years, and I doubt very seriously if any witness that ever came before this committee . . . has expressed such a profound knowledge of this phenomena [sic] as Mr. Carlson." [63]

At times, McDowell's native shortcomings got him into serious trouble. In September, 1948, he held a press conference and seemingly identified himself as "acting chairman" of the Un-American Activities Committee. He charged that "100 or more" American military secrets had fallen into Russian hands during the war, attacked the Department of Justice, and demanded the impeachment of Attorney General Clark if he continued to resist demands by the committee for the indictment of five wartime espionage agents. As though this were not enough, he reportedly asserted that the "indictments" of the eleven Communists under the Alien Registration Act by the federal grand jury in New York had been "deliberately" drawn up "in such a way that they won't stick." [64]

---

[61] *Ibid.*, p. 559.   [62] *Ibid.*, p. 1337.

[63] *Mot. Pict. Ind. Hearings*, pp. 102, 103, 237, 251.

[64] *N.Y. Times*, October 1, 1948. The *Times* reports McDowell as saying, "I have knowledge of the fact that the indictments of twelve prominent Communists in New York were drawn in such an unusual legal fashion that competent constitutional lawyers who have examined the indictments are of the opinion that the twelve indicted persons are not only practically certain of not being

United States Attorney John F. X. McGohey was quick to react to this charge. He asserted that McDowell, in effect, had charged the existence of a conspiracy to obstruct justice "by me and the other lawyers who, with me, drafted the indictments." And he called upon McDowell to appear before the grand jury and support his charge with evidence.[65] There followed a series of exchanges in which McDowell gradually backed down hill and as a result of which McGohey abandoned his efforts to force the Congressman to appear before the grand jury.[66]

Representative F. Edward Hébert of Louisiana was appointed to the Un-American Activities Committee in January, 1948, to fill the vacancy created by the resignation of Representative Bonner of North Carolina. Hébert served on the committee only one year, since he was forced off against his will in the 81st Congress through the adoption by the Democrats of an informal rule that Democratic members of the committee should all be lawyers.[67] He was, however, one of the most active members of the committee during the Communist espionage hearings.

Hébert was first elected to Congress in 1940 as a member of the anti-Long faction of the Democratic Party in Louisiana. He had been a newspaperman of some prominence in New Orleans for a number of years prior to his entry into politics. As a member of the Un-American Activities Committee, Hébert is not easily classified. He was clearly above the committee average in ability. His participation in the Communist espionage hearings was on the whole vigorous and intelligent. He was obviously a hard worker and he brought a good deal of interest and enthusiasm to the conduct of the hearings. Moreover, Hébert showed a good deal of concern that the hearings

---

punished for their crimes against the American people but that future decisions on this matter may endanger the entire security of the nation by destroying some of the necessary law that it now has."

[65] N.Y. Times, Oct. 2, 1948.

[66] See the N.Y. Times, Oct. 6, 7, 9, and 10, 1948. McDowell ultimately denied that he had ever used the "deliberately" or "won't stick" phraseology. It is true that his formal statement at the press conference Sept. 30 did not contain such language, although it implied the same result. Following this denial the Associated Press and the United Press both distributed stories repeating their original versions of what McDowell had said and insisting that the reported language had been used by McDowell orally in supplementing his written statement.

[67] There is little doubt that this maneuver was aimed at Hébert. He had become increasingly antiadministration in his work as a member of the committee, and with the coming of Democratic control of the 81st Congress, party leaders took steps to eliminate the antagonism between the committee and the administration.

should be fairly conducted and that witnesses should not be bullied and badgered. He was the only Democratic member of the committee in the 80th Congress who made any effort to resist the cruder partisan antics of such Republicans as Thomas and Mundt.

Hébert's sense of fairness is seen in his insistence throughout the Communist espionage hearings that if friendly witnesses were to be allowed free rein in introducing into the record the names of persons not hitherto identified with subversive organizations or activity, the persons so named should be guaranteed the right to reply. On the very first day of the hearings, while Elizabeth Bentley was on the witness stand, he stated,

> If anybody puts in jeopardy an individual who is charged with being a Communist, I think, in fairness, that this individual should be allowed his day in court here in public hearing as well. Now, if you were in a secret session or in executive session, and these names were used, then we owe them no obligation, but the minute that we allow a witness on the stand to mention any individual, that individual has a right to come before this committee and have his day in court, and every man or woman mentioned here this morning has a right to be subpenaed to come here.[68]

At the very end of the Communist espionage hearings, in December, Hébert's attitude in this respect stiffened, and he even went so far as to assert that witnesses should not be allowed to mention any new names except in testimony given in executive session.[69] But by this time the damage had been done, for the witnesses already heard had been freely allowed to mention the names of scores of persons whom they accused of subversive activity, and Hébert proved little by his last-minute insistence upon this point.

Hébert several times indicated his dissatisfaction with the publicity methods used by certain of his colleagues. He was critical of Thomas for the latter's action in releasing the Condon report, and he was vigorous in his condemnation of Mundt and Nixon for their action in making public the secret testimony of Isaac Don Levine concerning Laurence Duggan.[70]

On the other hand, it is easy to cite instances of Hébert's own deep-seated prejudices and of unfair treatment of witnesses by him.

[68] *Communist Espionage Hearings*, p. 537.

[69] See *Communist Espionage Hearings, Part Two*, pp. 1400 ff. While Isaac Don Levine was testifying, Hébert stated, "If he intends to bring any new names in, as I expressed myself before, I will immediately move for an executive session."

[70] See pp. 160–161.

He had an implacable hatred of communism, which unquestionably led him to take a distorted view of the prevalence of Communists and of the seriousness of the threat they offered. For example, he was convinced that American colleges and universities were overrun with Communists. It was obvious that he distrusted Alger Hiss and similar witnesses because of their university backgrounds. Early in the Communist espionage hearings he said, "I am from Tulane, and to my chagrin there are more Communists who infest that place than Americans." [71] And when he learned that Whittaker Chambers had gone to Columbia University he said, "It is interesting to note that every time we talk about communism we hear about Columbia University." When Chambers retorted that he had known no Communists at Columbia at that time and that he had become a Communist after he left Columbia, Hébert persisted, and asked, "How about communism in that institution now?" to which question Chambers had the good grace to reply, "I am not qualified to discuss it." [72]

Hébert's tendency to see Communists everywhere was again illustrated in a speech he made in the House of Representatives on May 5, 1948, in which he accused the Federal Communications Commission of granting a broadcasting license to a person who had engaged in "communistic activities." Subsequently he wrote Chairman Thomas a letter asking that the Un-American Activities Committee investigate the FCC, adding, "I have heard numerous complaints about how other people, real Americans, whose Americanism has never been challenged, are kept cooling their heels in the halls of the Commission, while fellow travellers get all the courtesies and results. As one individual expressed it to me: 'You can't get a permit unless you are a commissar.'" [73]

Hébert, more almost than any other member of the committee, seemed to have complete confidence in Whittaker Chambers and Elizabeth Bentley and repeatedly defended them against the charge that, as ex-Communists, their testimony was necessarily suspect. Indeed, Hébert went so far as to depict both witnesses as "reformed saints." When Alger Hiss grew angry that Hébert should profess impartiality between Hiss and Chambers, "a confessed former Communist and traitor to his country," Hébert replied:

Show me a police force with a poor record, and I will show you a police force without a stool pigeon. We have to have people like Chambers

[71] *Communist Espionage Hearings,* p. 552.   [72] *Ibid.,* p. 583.
[73] 94 *Cong. Rec.* 5326 ff. (May 5, 1948).

or Miss Bentley to come in and tell us. I am not giving Mr. Chambers any great credit for his previous life. I am trying to find out if he has reformed. Some of the greatest saints in history were pretty bad before they were saints. Are you going to take away their sainthood because of their previous lives? Are you not going to believe them after they have reformed? [74]

Hébert could also be grossly unfair in the questioning of a witness. For example, when the committee heard Duncan Lee, during the Communist espionage hearings, Hébert persisted in trying to show that Lee's connection with Russian War Relief during the war somehow marked him as a subversive. Hébert was either highly ignorant of the respectable status enjoyed by Russian War Relief during the National War Fund era, or, knowing better, he did not hesitate at such a late date as 1948 to imply that anyone who had been closely identified with this Russian "society," as he insisted upon calling it, must have been Communist-inclined.[75]

[74] *Communist Espionage Hearings,* p. 952.

[75] *"Mr. Hébert:* Now, this Russian society of—what do you call it, that business that you were counsel of?

"Mr. Lee: Russian War Relief.

"Mr. Hébert: Yes. What kind of a society or an organization was it?

"Mr. Lee: It was a private relief organization.

"Mr. Hébert: Who sponsored it?

"Mr. Lee: A great many people. I can submit for the committee, if it does not already have the information, the members of its board of directors and sponsors, and so on. I do not have that information with me. I can merely say this, that they were, to the best of my knowledge, all extremely respectable conservative people.

"Mr. Hébert: What was the purpose of that organization?

"Mr. Lee: To raise money for Russia.

"Mr. Hébert: Then, to raise money for Russia—

"Mr. Lee: Yes, sir. Russia was at that time carrying, I think, most people felt, the brunt of the war. This was in 1941 and 1942. A great deal of money was raised for Russia.

"Mr. Hébert: And how was that money expended?

"Mr. Lee: Sir, I do not think that is something that I am in a position to testify to.

"Mr. Hébert: Well, during your services in the high executive position—

"Mr. Lee: I would merely say this, that there were public reports made to the President's Committee on Relief Organizations and other competent authorities, and those reports are available.

"Mr. Hébert: This was in 1941 or 1942 that you were associated with them? Well, the early part of the war.

"Mr. Lee: I think it was organized in 1941, Congressman, and I continued my association until I left New York in 1942.

In the end, it is not unfair to say that while Hébert tried hard to dissociate himself from the methods and purposes of Thomas, Mundt, and Rankin, his own obsessions about communism were so strong that no witness before the committee could count upon him for fair, dispassionate treatment.

The personnel of the committee in the 79th Congress included five men in addition to those who have been named: J. Hardin Peterson of Florida, J. W. Robinson of Utah, John R. Murdock of Arizona, Herbert C. Bonner of North Carolina—all Democrats—and Gerald W. Landis of Indiana, a Republican. Peterson remained a member of the committee throughout the 80th Congress, and Bonner served during the first session of the 80th Congress, resigning from the committee in December, 1947. The other three served on the committee only during the 79th Congress. No one of these men made much of an imprint upon the committee. At times Robinson and Murdock indicated mild displeasure with the antics of Rankin and were in general inclined to defend the Democratic administration against its critics on the committee. But their major interests in Congress were obviously elsewhere, and there is no evidence that they ever seriously concerned themselves about the work of the committee.

"*Mr. Hébert:* In your duties then you came in contact with many Russian people, undoubtedly.

"*Mr. Lee:* Not very much; no, sir.

"*Mr. Hébert:* You did not?

"*Mr. Lee:* No, sir.

"*Mr. Hébert:* Did you come in contact with any Communists?

"*Mr. Lee:* I would not know, sir. Most of the people I came in contact with were either Wall Street bankers or Wall Street lawyers. [Laughter.]

"*Mr. Hébert:* That would be in your general duty. I mean in your duties as an executive of the Russian society.

.   .   .   .   .   .

"*Mr. Hébert:* But after you got into the OSS, were you not instructed in the ways and means of sort of recognizing Communists or spies or espionage agents, or was that not in your field?

"*Mr. Lee:* I was doing administrative or legal work, sir. I was not an agent in that field, and had nothing to do with operations until considerably later.

"*Mr. Hébert:* But you came in contact with a great many individuals in OSS who were well schooled in that art.

"*Mr. Lee:* Yes, sir. And there was careful—

"*Mr. Hébert:* From being exposed to contact with them, didn't you discuss Russian agents and Communists and espionage agents?

"*Mr. Lee:* At that time, sir, we were more inclined to discuss German agents."
Ibid., pp. 745–746.

The personnel of the committee in the 80th Congress was rounded out by Representative Richard B. Vail, Republican, of Illinois, and Representative J. Hardin Peterson, just mentioned. As members of the committee during its most important two-year period both men were complete nonentities, and so far as the public record is concerned, played no roles of any significance whatsoever in its work. While neither man can be criticized for the use of the questionable tactics frequently employed by their more active colleagues, there is no evidence that either man ever lifted his voice in protest against the wrongdoings of the Thomas committee.[76]

In the 81st Congress the Un-American Activities Committee contained seven new members. The only carry-overs were Wood and Nixon.[77] The seven new members of the committee included four Democrats—Francis E. Walter of Pennsylvania, Burr P. Harrison of Virginia, John McSweeney of Ohio, and Morgan M. Moulder of Missouri; and three Republicans—Francis Case of South Dakota, Harold H. Velde of Illinois, and Bernard W. Kearney of New York. Walter, McSweeney, and Moulder were all administration Democrats whose voting records in the House showed high party regularity. Harrison's voting record, on the other hand, showed rather low party regularity. The appointment of the three loyal Democrats to the committee was obviously intended to and did bring to an end the administration-committee irritation and conflict which had prevailed during the 80th Congress and even during the 79th Congress. On the other hand, Case, Velde, and Kearney were all staunch Republicans.

Several of the new members of the committee in the 81st Congress

[76] Vail's general attitude toward the threat of subversive activity was perhaps indicated by one of his rare questions which he asked a witness during the 1948 hearings of the Nixon subcommittee on legislation. His question was: "You mentioned that you had in your district talked to a number of schools and colleges and it has been a matter of concern to this committee that our youth has been subjected to a type of thought control and direction along far too liberal, if not genuine communistic, lines. Do you think we are justified in that concern?" *Hearings on Proposed Legislation to Curb or Control the Communist Party of the United States,* Feb., 1948, p. 396. The witness was a fellow Congressman, so it may be presumed that Vail's question was a rhetorical one.

[77] Thomas remained a member of the committee until his resignation from Congress in January, 1949, when he was replaced by Bernard W. Kearney of New York. However, he attended no sessions of the committee and took no part in its deliberations after the close of the 80th Congress.

were well-known and respected legislators. Walter was one of the leading Democrats in the House. He was chairman of the Democratic Caucus, and, next to Chairman Celler, the ranking Democrat on the Judiciary Committee. He had played a prominent role in the enactment of the Administrative Procedure Act of 1946 and was "viewed as having one of the soundest legal minds in the House." [78] He began his service as a Congressman in 1933, having previously practiced law and served as a county solicitor in his home state. Walter was a member of the armed forces during both World Wars. McSweeney returned to Congress in January, 1949, having served four nonconsecutive terms in the House during the twenties and thirties. He was an attorney, a veteran of both wars, and well known in Ohio as an able public servant in both federal and state government. Case, a veteran of World War I, had been a member of the House since 1937, and was perhaps best known as sponsor of the Case Labor Relations Bill passed by Congress and vetoed by President Truman in 1946. Velde, a newly elected Representative, was a veteran of World War II, and an attorney who had served for three years in the Sabotage and Counter-Espionage Division of the FBI and also as a county judge in Illinois. As an FBI agent he had developed a strong interest in the efforts of wartime espionage agents to obtain atomic energy secrets, particularly in West Coast laboratories. The committee had investigated atomic espionage in the 80th Congress, and it continued to give its attention to this subject during the 81st Congress. Velde was vigorous in his insistence that this line of investigation should be continued. Perhaps alone among the members of the reconstructed committee, Velde was inclined to use some of the tactics in public hearings which had brought the committee so much criticism in the two preceding Congresses. Velde joined Nixon in the bitter attack made upon Judge Kaufman at the close of the first Hiss trial. He charged Kaufman with "bias bordering on judicial misconduct" and demanded that Congress investigate the judge's conduct of the trial.[79]

It would be too much to say that the members of the committee in the 81st Congress lost their importance as individuals. Nonetheless, the committee functioned more impersonally during this Congress than at any time in its previous history. As has been seen, apart from Wood and Walter the members did very little of the question-

[78] C. P. Trussell in the *N.Y. Times,* May 1, 1949.
[79] *N.Y. Times,* July 11, 1949.

ing during the hearings. The record of the hearings during the two-year period is largely free from episodes involving flamboyant conduct by individual members. Statements to the press or speeches on the floor of the House concerning the affairs of the committee by individual members, if they did not disappear completely, became much more infrequent than in earlier years.

VII: The Committee's Staff

It is impossible to exaggerate the importance of a permanent, professional staff to the work of an agency like the House Un-American Activities Committee. Committee members have such a broad range of interests and responsibilities and are by training and experience so seldom acquainted in any professional or technical sense with many of the problems confronting them that they are highly dependent upon the assistance rendered them by professional staff assistants. In particular, a staff can offset the distracting and divisive forces that tend to destroy the morale and efficiency of a committee. Perhaps more than any other force a competent staff can give a Congressional committee stability and continuity.

It has long been recognized that the staff facilities enjoyed by Congress have been inadequate. This is true of the individual Congressman, committees, and the House or the Senate as a whole. All students and agencies interested in recent years in Congressional reform and reorganization have given a great deal of attention to this staff problem. The most noteworthy result of this interest to date has been the Legislative Reorganization Act of 1946, which made provision for increased staff facilities at all levels of Congressional activity. It is too early to judge the results of this legislation, but it is generally agreed that they have been mixed. At the committee level, in particular, it is evident that some Congressional committees have made real progress toward the building up of permanent non-political staffs of experts to aid them in their work, whereas others have not been able to escape from the traditions of partisanship and patronage in the utilization of funds for staff purposes.

The importance of a staff to a Congressional committee is, if anything, accentuated when the chief function of that committee is the

247

making of investigations by means of public hearings. Unless such hearings are planned with great care, the background to the subject under investigation thoroughly explored, and the potential contribution of each witness carefully estimated, an investigation is apt to prove aimless and fruitless. Occasionally, one or more Congressmen identified with an investigation make themselves masters of the subject under inquiry and either on their own, or by working closely with members of a professional staff, make a great personal contribution to the success of the undertaking. More often, however, the Congressional members of an investigating committee depend upon their staff assistants for the spade work in preparation of public hearings, for the actual conduct of such hearings, for the writing of reports, and, indeed, in some instances for the setting of the whole tone and direction of an investigation. An excellent example of this is found in the so-called Wall Street Investigation of 1933 conducted by a subcommittee of the Senate Banking and Currency Committee. This inquiry is often referred to as the Pecora investigation, taking its name from Ferdinand Pecora, who was the committee's counsel and chief investigator. Many Senators made real contributions to this investigation, which was one of the most successful inquiries of modern times in terms of the central purpose of the undertaking— the enactment of remedial legislation to correct abuses in the marketing of securities and the operation of stock exchanges. Nonetheless, Pecora dominated the investigation, and he more than any other single individual was responsible for its successful conduct and excellent results.

The staff of the Un-American Activities Committee has been at the same time an asset and a liability to the investigation of subversive activity. This particular Congressional investigating committee has depended heavily upon a professional staff for assistance. Even where such committee members as Thomas, Rankin, Mundt, and Nixon have played vigorous and significant roles in the actual conduct of the investigation, they have worked closely with the staff, utilizing in substantial degree the data supplied by it and following closely the directions recommended by it. Perusal of almost any volume of the published hearings of the committee since 1945 reveals the extent to which the task of questioning witnesses and developing the main lines of a particular inquiry has been turned over to staff members. At no time has any committee member or group of members been prepared to assume chief responsibility for the planning and execution of a program. Without the contribution made by the committee's staff, the investigation of un-American activities would most likely have died a-borning. It is doubtful whether even such a fanatic as John Rankin, with his major interests in other directions, could have given the investigation sufficient attention to keep it going on anything but a fitful, unproductive basis.

The textbook affair provides a good illustration of the respective roles played by the chairman, the members, and the staff of the Un-American Activities Committee. On June 8, 1949, Chairman Wood announced that the committee had sent letters to some seventy-one state boards of education, colleges, and high schools asking them to supply lists of the textbooks they were using, and that the committee was interested in finding out whether any textbooks were written from a Communist slant.[1] It was also announced that the committee was undertaking this new line of inquiry as the result of a petition received from the National Sons of the American Revolution containing "serious allegations" about textbooks in use in American schools and colleges.

Wood's announcement provoked a short-lived but violent controversy. The committee was denounced by college presidents, by the press, and ultimately even by five of its own members.[2] Wood had seemingly not cleared the letter with the committee, and when some of its members saw the vehement public reaction provoked by the letter they were publicly critical of Wood's action.[3] From inter-

[1] N.Y. Times, June 9, 1949. The text of the letter was reproduced in the Washington Post, June 14, 1949, as follows:

"The Committee on Un-American Activities is desirous of obtaining lists of text books and supplementary reading with the names of authors in use in our educational institutions throughout the country in the fields of American literature, geography, economics, government, philosophy, history, political science and any other of the social science group.

"We have immediate need for the material and the committee would very much appreciate your cooperation in making this material available to us at the earliest possible date."

[2] See N.Y. Times, June 12, 14, 18, 19, 21, 1949.

[3] Ibid., June 19, 1949. Wood was reported as saying that the committee had made "no formal decision" in the matter but that "it never occurred to me anyone would object." However, he added that the members had discussed the subject and suggestions had been made that "we get what information we could on it." Following criticism by committee members a second letter was sent to the recipients of the first letter. The N.Y. Times described the content of the second letter as follows:

"The letter today assured educators that the earlier request for textbook lists should not be construed as having the slightest unfavorable reflection or criticism on your school or any person connected therewith.'

views with Chairman Wood and with members of the committee's staff, the writer gained the following impressions of the affair. An interest in the textbooks used in American schools and colleges, with an eye toward their "subversive" content, has been a perennial one with the committee. Everything suggests that it was the staff that kept the interest alive, that through the years it carried on research and investigation in the field, and that it always had available in its files a certain amount of data that could quickly be used as a starting point for a vigorous, full-fledged investigation in this direction. The petition from the Sons of the American Revolution came at a moment when the committee was not particularly busy and the staff was seemingly anxious to proceed with such an inquiry. The matter was discussed at an executive session of the committee, there was no disapproval of the idea, and, with this tentative backing of the committee, Chairman Wood sent out the letter without submitting it to other committee members for their approval. The text of the letter was largely the work of staff members. Thus, it may fairly be said that the initial impetus in the affair was provided by the staff, that the chairman gave the move his complete and positive approval, and that some of the committee's members knew vaguely about the undertaking and did not disapprove it. In this last respect the chairman and the staff were doing no more than committee chairmen and staffs frequently do—they were initiating a new study on the assumption that the full committee membership did not disapprove and that it would have a later opportunity to consider and approve further developments. In this instance, when news of the affair was unfavorably received by the public, members of the Un-American Activities Committee took advantage of the vague and informal pro-

---

"It said that if the request involved too much work the committee would be willing to pass up supplemental material and get along with just 'the title and author of the principal text books now in use' in the fields the committee mentioned.

"The letter, taking note of complaints that the committee objects to the teaching of the principles of Karl Marx and other founders of communism, said:

" 'It is of no concern to the committee if the Communist Manifesto or any other book or document containing the tenets of communism is being studied. for comparative purposes in our educational institutions.'

"The committee said that it did take the Sons of the American Revolution petition at face value and was trying to determine the amount of work involved in proving or disproving its allegations. It added that the committee had 'no preconception of what might be found, if anything at all.' "

cedure customary in such matters to disown the undertaking and force the chairman to accept full responsibility for it.[4]

The committee's staff has faced difficulties not of its own making and beyond its control. For example, the size of the staff has varied considerably as appropriations given the committee by the House have fluctuated widely.[5] On the other hand, staff salaries have not been inadequate as government salaries go, particularly since 1948. In 1950 the committee's payroll revealed that eleven of its staff employees received salaries of $8,000 or more. In part, inability to build a stable, permanent staff has merely reflected the continuing uncertainty of Congress as to the scope and role of legislative staffing generally. In part, it has reflected the uncertainty of the House as to the desirability of investigating un-American activities. Again, three shifts in party control of the House of Representatives between 1945 and 1950 helped make the creation of a truly professional staff difficult. But when all such allowances are made, the fact remains that the committee's staff has been unimpressive, inadequate to the enormously difficult business of discovering and evaluating subversive activity in the United States.

Perhaps the outstanding point to be made about its staff practices has been the committee's final failure or inability to tap the nation's best sources of professional talent in the field in which it has been active. It is true that there are few real experts on subversive activity. Certainly there is no formal class of trained students of the subject.

[4] It is significant that when the Republican minority members of the committee issued a formal public statement condemning Wood's action they by no means disapproved the idea of searching for evidence of Communist influence in "our educational system and our school textbooks." Instead, they took the position that such a search should be conducted by an impartial, nonpolitical commission of educators (N.Y. Times, June 21, 1949). Representative Wood told the author that in sending out the request for data he had had in mind that the staff would make a preliminary analysis of the returns and that the committee might then have called upon an impartial commission of educators to evaluate the evidence. Interview on June 24, 1949.

[5] The appropriations granted to the committee by the House of Representatives since 1945 are as follows: 1945, $50,000; 1946, $75,000; 1947, $100,000; 1948, $200,000; 1949, $200,000; 1950, $150,000. Ogden lists the following appropriations for the Dies committee: 1938, $25,000; 1939, $100,000; 1940, $110,000; 1941, $150,000; 1942, $110,000; 1943, $82,500; 1944, $75,000.

Beginning with the 80th Congress all committees have had to make biannual reports of the personnel of their staffs and of their staff payrolls. The data reported by the Un-American Activities Committee will be found in the Appendix (Table III).

Nonetheless, there are many academicians and lawyers—to mention just two groups—who have either given much thought to the problem of safeguarding a democratic society against the twin revolutionary threats of the modern era, fascism and communism, or who have had actual experience in prosecuting and defending persons charged with subversive activity under laws dealing with treason, espionage, sedition, conspiracy, and sabotage. So far as is known, no serious effort has been made by the Un-American Activities Committee to place upon its staff any person from these groups. The closest that the committee has come to obtaining the services of persons with any sort of professional training or experience in areas relevant to its interests and tasks is the employment of ex-FBI agents or of ex-Communists or ex-fellow travelers. This is not to say that such persons do not have both ability and experience that may be of great value to the committee. But the evidence suggests that when such persons have been employed by the committee, they were not known for their outstanding records at the time of employment. And as often as not, even the ex-FBI agent has been passed by when appointments were being made. For example, such well-known and important members of the committee's staff as Robert Stripling and Ernie Adamson came to the committee originally with no recognizably relevant talents or experience whatsoever.

It may be conceded that the committee might well have had great difficulty persuading persons of recognized ability and integrity to accept employment with it, in the light of the bad name acquired by the committee during the seven years of the Dies regime. In any case, it is clear that the committee has never aimed high in recruiting its staff members. When in the 81st Congress able Representatives were persuaded to serve on the committee, the corresponding effort to improve the committee's staff was nothing like as vigorous as it might have been. In its new counsel, Frank Tavenner, Jr., the committee obtained perhaps the best-qualified and most dispassionate assistant it ever had. But almost nothing was done to raise the level of the remainder of the staff.

The staff of the Un-American Activities Committee has been loosely organized into three divisions: investigations, research, and files. It is difficult to get a clear picture of the separate functions of these divisions or of the lines of communication which connect them to each other and to any central authority. The threefold division of responsibility has taken shape through the years, and specific duties have depended at any given moment upon the availability of personnel and upon the abilities and inclinations of the division heads.

The investigative unit has always been the most important part of the staff. The committee's staff heads—Adamson, Stripling, and Tavenner—have been closely identified with the work of this unit. Many of the committee's most famous investigations, such as those dealing with the motion picture industry and with Communist espionage, have been largely planned by this division. It has been responsible not only for the extensive field work which has had to be performed before public hearings could be held, but also for the actual conduct of these hearings. Members of the division, such as Louis Russell, have often joined Adamson, Stripling, or Tavenner in the questioning of witnesses, with particular reference to specific points which have been under examination by them.

The research unit has two primary responsibilities: feeding new materials into the committee's files by maintaining a careful watch of newspapers, periodicals, and other sources for information concerning organizations and individuals considered to be inclined toward subversive activity; and preparing certain of the committee's written reports—in particular, those dealing with private organizations alleged to be Communist fronts, such as the Southern Conference for Human Welfare or the Congress of American Women.

The files unit, from the point of view of administrative organization, has had a purely ministerial function—that of maintaining the committee's extensive records in such physical condition that they are readily available to those who have authority to use them. The personnel of this unit has thus attracted little attention and has never been involved in controversy. But the files themselves have been the center of vigorous and persistent controversy. Indeed, no phase of the work of the Un-American Activities Committee has been more bitterly criticized than has its policy with respect to its files. The criticism has been twofold. First, it has been argued that the committee has shown little discretion or responsibility as to the kind of information or material it has allowed to be placed in its files, and second, the committee has been attacked for the irresponsible manner in which it has allowed its files to be used. There is much justification for both criticisms.

The files are a voluminous mass of miscellaneous, undigested materials and information pertaining to thousands of organizations and perhaps one million individuals.[6] Physically, the file material is

[6] It is difficult to be accurate about such estimates. Committee spokesmen and publications have at one time or another used various figures in describing the

of two types: a card index consisting of hundreds of thousands of entries, and a very much smaller number of folders containing exhibits and source materials. A typical card carries the name of a person and makes a brief reference to some activity or organizational affiliation viewed as suspicious or questionable by the research or investigative divisions of the staff. At the time the author interviewed the head of the files section in June, 1949, there chanced to be present upon her desk a number of these cards, all bearing the name of Owen Lattimore, each of which contained a brief reference to some writing or activity or affiliation of Mr. Lattimore. It would appear that Lattimore is merely one of an incredibly large number of Americans whose day-by-day activities are carefully watched by the staff. Every time such a person makes a speech, publishes a book or article, lends his name as sponsor to some organizational activity, signs a petition, or engages in some similar activity which is reported in the press or otherwise comes to the attention of the committee staff *and seems significant to them*, another entry is added to the card file. If a file dossier is maintained for an individual or organization and the new development involves documentary material, this material is presumably added to the dossier.

That a Congressional committee should follow, and maintain a record of, the activities of thousands of persons and hundreds of organizations is a shocking thing. In the committee's defense it may be said that most of the information placed in its files is seemingly limited to the raw facts of an event. A has given an address at the annual banquet of the League of American Women for Constitutional Government; B has signed a petition to the Mayor of New York asking him to investigate police conduct during a May Day parade; C is listed as a member of the executive board of the Atlantic Federation of Cooperatives; D has published an article in *The New Nation* analyzing the Communist victory in China.[7] While such

extent of the files. The statement that one million individuals are referred to in the committee files has been made repeatedly. For example, Stripling has written, "In the decade that followed we were to expand to many rooms, to agencies in leading U.S. cities, a staff of 75, and 600 filing cases containing more than 1,000,000 names, records, dossiers and data pertaining to subversion" (*The Red Plot*, p. 23). It is probable that the estimate of 1,000,000 names is an exaggerated one.

[7] The *Washington Post* reports Stripling as saying that "every card in the file is based on a document. . . . There is no card which says simply that a particular individual was seen at a Communist Party headquarters, but if that in-

bits of information may be put to a distorted or unwarranted use in later hearings or publications of the committee, or in statements made by its members or by others who have enjoyed access to the files, it does appear that the files themselves are largely free from editorializing about, or evaluation of, the basic, raw data. On the other hand, the decision to include or exclude a basic fact does involve a good deal of editorial discretion. A has addressed the League of American Women for Constitutional Government, an organization viewed by the committee as a Communist front. But the facts that his subject was "The Importance of Supporting the United Nations' Appeal for Children" and that the speaker also addressed the New York State Chamber of Commerce and the Middle Atlantic Presbyterian Youth Conference on the same subject may well not be recorded by the committee. Clearly, these additional bits of information are highly relevant if the committee's files are intended to tell a full and accurate story of a person. Moreover, although maintaining that the files contain no material based solely upon hearsay or gossip, Louis Russell told the author that items based "upon sworn testimony that has not been refuted" are included. In other words, accusations made by such committee witnesses as Walter Steele, Louis Budenz, Elizabeth Bentley, and Whittaker Chambers are regarded as proper bases for file entries unless the accused person manages by one means or another to "refute" them. That many such accusations have little more than a "hearsay or gossip" basis is apparent to anyone who reads the testimony of such witnesses before the committee. Moreover, the "opportunity-to-refute theory" has little validity with respect to the committee's files, since their restricted status means that the average person concerning whom data is assembled is probably totally unaware that the committee has a file on him, let alone acquainted with its content. Only as use is made of this file by one having access to it, a use that comes to the attention of the person in question, is any opportunity to refute obtained.

The investigative unit of the staff maintains a file of its own, apart from the general files of the committee. This file is very much smaller than the latter and is presumably a working file limited to information about individuals and organizations under direct investigation by this staff unit. Material in this file is drawn upon for the committee's hearings and publications, but it is not available—at least for-

dividual wrote a Communist article or made a Communist speech, these would be in the file." August 27, 1948.

mally—to the large number of people who have access to the general files.

An excellent example of the kind of information placed in the general files concerning individuals in whom the committee has a keen interest was brought to light during the Hollywood hearings. The long lists of activities, organizational affiliations, writings, and similar information concerning each of the "unfriendly witnesses" which were read into the record by Louis Russell were drawn directly from the committee's files.[8]

Access to the files of the committee and use of the information contained therein is restricted, but the number of persons enjoying such access is so large that the possibilities of the information pertaining to a particular person being put to an irresponsible use are very great. In the main, only Congressmen and members of government agencies properly concerned with loyalty and subversion issues have been permitted to use the files, but Stripling has estimated that the number of such "accredited agents" who have actually used the files is "about 20,000." Moreover, by indirect if not direct means, private persons and organizations have obviously had access to the committee's files.

It is quite clear that members of Congress have not hesitated to use their access to the committee files for political reasons or at times to supply constituents with requested information about individuals whom they suspect of subversive activity. For example, on August 2, 1946, Representative H. C. Fuller of New York rose in the House of Representatives to attack "one Clifford T. McAvoy . . . described as the director of the Political Action Committee of the UE-CIO" because McAvoy had "visited" Fuller's Congressional district "for the express purpose of telling the people there how to vote in the fall election." Fuller reported that he had asked the Un-American Activities Committee whether McAvoy had "ever been cited" by it and that he had received an answer listing thirty-seven "citations." In the list as revealed by Fuller were such curious or ambiguous items as the following:

Organization	Participation	Source of Information
School for Democracy	Guest lecturer	Catalog & Program, Jan. 1942
United Nations Ball	Participant	Daily Worker, Jan. 11, 1943, p. 3.

[8] Some of this information may have been drawn from the more limited and restricted files maintained in the offices of the investigative staff.

Organization	Participation	Source of Information
Consumer-Farmer Milk Cooperative	Consumer director	"Why a Milk Cooperative?" (back cover)
New York State Conference on National Unity	Member	Program leaflet, Dec. 6, 1941 [9]

Granted that such items, or others of the thirty-seven not here mentioned, may show identification in one way or another with Communist or Communist front organizations, this use by a Congressman of data to say that a person opposing him for re-election "has been cited 37 times by the House Committee for his un-American activities" is irresponsible, and the Un-American Activities Committee is guilty of irresponsibility in maintaining files that can be so used.

The use of the committee's published listings and of its file data by private agencies is well illustrated by the activities of American Business Consultants, Inc. This is an organization of ex-FBI agents which has done much to encourage the growth of a vigilante spirit in the United States. Its weekly newsletter, *Counterattack,* and its notorious booklet, *Red Channels,* have drawn heavily upon committee sources for their data. *Red Channels* has become a sort of bible for persons and organizations opposed to communism and determined to bar any persons suspected of even the mildest fellow-traveler sympathies from employment in the radio or television industries. Jack Gould, radio editor of the *New York Times* has described the influence of *Red Channels* in these words:

> The way the policy operates now is this: the sponsor or advertising agency simply does not hire a person listed in "Red Channels" or does not renew a contract upon its expiration. The individual is not even told in so many words that the "Red Channels" listing is responsible. Any number of perfectly normal excuses—a change of cast, etc.—suffice. The individ-

[9] 92 *Cong. Rec.* A4942 (August 2, 1946). A similar use of files material occurred June 17, 1948, when Representative Nodar of New York interrupted debate in the House on the Selective Service Act of 1948 to read a report he had received from the files division of the Un-American Activities Committee concerning the *Queensbridge Home News,* a free newspaper distributed to tenants of a federal housing project in his district. The report indicated that the names of six of the fifteen members of the editorial board and staff of the paper were found in the committee's files. Individuals, so cited, had written letters to the *Daily Worker,* spoken for an organization on the Attorney General's list of subversive agencies, run for Congress on the Communist Party ticket, and signed Communist election petitions.

ual is just out of a job. To be sure, there are some exceptions among employers who still have regard for fair play, but they are distressingly few and far between.

The vicious "controversiality" policy in effect has circumvented all the traditional safeguards of due process and fair hearing. The person named in "Red Channels" is "controversial" per se; his innocence or guilt is now beside the point so far as many—if not most—prospective employers are concerned. If he speaks up or if he says nothing he still has not lost the tag of being "controversial." His basic and fundamental rights have disappeared into thin air.[10]

Again, for a period of months in 1950 and 1951 the public school system in the District of Columbia followed a policy of not permitting any outside speakers whose names were contained in House committee listings to address student assemblies. While this rule was in effect such well-known non-Communists as Pearl Buck and Marquis Childs were prevented from speaking merely because their names happened to be present in "unappraised" or "unevaluated" files of the committee.[11]

The committee has taken great pride in its files—in particular, in the fact that they contain the names of so many individuals and organizations, and in the fact that they are used regularly by so many Congressmen and other government officers. Indeed, the committee has reported at regular intervals on the extensive use of its files.[12] In its report of December 31, 1948, the committee included a long statement concerning the character of its files and the uses to which they are put. In view of the controversy over these files and

[10] "Conspiracy of Silence," *N.Y. Times*, April 22, 1951.

[11] See the *Washington Post*, Jan. 26, 30, Feb. 7, 9, 1951.

[12] Thus Representative Wood reported to the House on May 29, 1947, that between January 22 and May 27 of that year 512 "callers" had checked the files with respect to 8,529 names. 93 *Cong. Rec.* A2546 (May 29, 1947).

For a similar period in 1948 it was reported that 1,087 requests had been received from members of Congress for information about 6,374 individuals and 1,163 organizations. In addition, there had been 3,198 visits to the files by government agents. 94 *Cong. Rec.* A3475 (May 26, 1948).

Since the Truman loyalty program in the executive branch of the government officially authorized use of the Un-American Activities Committee files as a source of information concerning government employees, visits to the files increased greatly as the program got under way. In its report of August 28, 1948, the committee stated, "This year alone security officers and loyalty board representatives of the executive departments have paid over 14,000 official visits to our file rooms." *Interim Report on Hearings regarding Communist Espionage in the United States Government*, Aug. 28, 1948, p. 14.

the difficulty of securing precise information about them, it is appropriate to quote at length from this statement:

The files of the Committee on Un-American Activities constitute a vast and unexcelled storehouse of information concerning subversive individuals and organizations in the United States. The committee's collection of information covers 10 years of diligent investigation and inquiry into subversive activities.

Numerous witnesses have testified in public and executive hearings before the committee and submitted evidence in support of that testimony. In the course of its widespread investigations, the committee has amassed records of individuals, histories of organizations, reports, pamphlets, periodicals, photostats, photographs, documents, and books. Its files include information and documentary material obtained from regional offices which were maintained in Chicago, Los Angeles, and New York, records turned over to the committee by other agencies, and information compiled by law-enforcement agencies in many States.

The volume of this valuable collection of basic informational material covering un-American activities can be measured by the fact that it would fill 200 file cabinets. It is one of the most voluminous collections of its kind in existence.

.   .   .   .   .

From June 20, 1946, to December 22, 1948, reports on 25,591 individuals and 1,786 organizations were compiled by staff members at the request of Members of Congress.

.   .   .   .   .

Indexes to public hearings and committee publications contain 48,221 references to individuals and 8,593 references to organizations. These indexes and the committee's card files are consulted daily by authorized personnel from numerous Government agencies in connection with loyalty or security investigations. During the period January 22, 1947, to December 21, 1948, accredited representatives of Government agencies made 5,975 visits to the committee file room to secure information.

.   .   .   .   .

Government investigators have made constant use of the consolidated card records, a collection of 300,000 card references to activities and affiliations of individuals. Eight cabinets are devoted to these references which are an index to source material in committee files.

In addition to the consolidated card records, which contain references to thousands of individuals, files are maintained on the activities of some 3,040 persons. Five cabinets are devoted to information concerning these individuals, many of whom are top leaders in subversive groups or prominent fellow travelers of the Communist Party. These collections are a valuable guide to the activities of various subversive groups as well as individuals.

The Committee has compiled lists of signers of Communist Party election petitions for various years in 20 States, showing 363,119 signatures.

. . . . .

Since subversive forces try to infiltrate other organizations while working through their own, the committee has acquired a vast store of information concerning thousands of organizations in the United States. Its scope can be illustrated by the fact that files contain information concerning 380 organizations with names beginning with the letter "A."

. . . . .

Some 8,553 issues of 644 periodicals serve as valuable sources of information. These periodicals reveal the motives and policies of hundreds of subversive groups and the activities of their leaders. The collection, dating back to 1923, contains irreplaceable copies of publications issued by Japanese, Fascist, and Nazi groups. It includes publications of labor unions, religious and racial groups, anti-Fascist, and anti-Nazi, and anti-Communist publications.

. . . . .

The committee has in file hundreds of reports compiled by staff investigators. These reports, dating from 1939 and paralleling committee investigations, cover a wide range of subjects and contain references to thousands of subversive individuals. The card index shows that reports of investigators contain references to 15,825 organizations. Many contain documentary evidence which is useful as exhibit material.

The committee has collected numerous books dealing with subversive activities in the United States for use as reference material, copies of hearings held by other groups investigating subversive activities, and necessary general reference books.

Each day brings a huge amount of valuable new material to committee files: News clippings, pamphlets, and literature of subversive organizations, reports of Communist activities here and in foreign countries, and material pertinent to the work of the committee. This material is classified, indexed, and added to the growing specialized collection.

This ever-expanding storehouse of information has been a valuable tool in exposing enemy agents, alien subversives, those who promote un-American ideologies—those who seek to destroy our Government by force and violence. It is a valuable tool in furnishing information to the American people about such individuals and the organizations they create—information which the American people demand in self-defense.[13]

[13] *Annual Rept.*, Dec. 31, 1948, pp. 21–24. See also *Annual Rept.*, March 15, 1950, pp. 18–21, and *Annual Rept.*, Jan. 2, 1951, pp. 40–43.

In the final analysis, the committee's enthusiastic claims concerning the usefulness and value of its files must be tested by results. Have these files proved their value by providing essential and otherwise unavailable information concerning persons involved in episodes of undoubted subversive activity, as the latter have come to light? Does such demonstrated value outweigh the liability which may properly be attributed to the committee's files because of improper uses to which they have been put in attacks upon individuals and organizations innocent of any true subversive activity? It is impossible to answer such questions accurately. There is no way of knowing with any degree of certainty, for example, how useful these files have proved to loyalty boards and officers charged with the administration of the Truman loyalty program. At the same time, enough information concerning the use of the files is available to make it doubtful whether they have proved an important depository of information concerning persons identified with the truly dangerous subversive activity of the postwar period. When Elizabeth Bentley and Whittaker Chambers made their sensational disclosures in 1948 concerning Communist cells in the federal service, there is no indication that information already available in the files was of any particular usefulness. The names of Bentley and Chambers themselves were presumably not present in the files. The names of certain of the persons accused by them may well have been in the files, but there is nothing to suggest that the data accompanying these names had any high degree of pertinency to the stories unfolded by the two witnesses. Again when the British scientist, Klaus Fuchs, was revealed to be an espionage agent and the trail led to his American accomplices, Harry Gold, Julius and Ethel Rosenberg, Morton Sobell, and David Greenglass, the indications are that the Un-American Activities Committee files were completely useless as a means of obtaining information about these persons. It was announced at the time of the arrest of Harry Gold, the Philadelphia chemist, that his name was not to be found among the one million individuals listed in the committee files!

The lines of authority within the staff have varied considerably. In the 79th Congress the head of the staff was Ernie Adamson, and he was listed in the committee's publications and records as "counsel." He was replaced in the 80th Congress by Robert Stripling, who was known as "chief investigator." The committee had no counsel while Stripling was head of the staff. In the 81st Congress Stripling retired, and top authority was transferred back to the office of counsel, which was filled by Frank S. Tavenner, Jr.[14] It is not clear how much authority each of these three chiefs actually wielded over the separate units of the staff. In each instance it appeared that the chief's primary responsibility was to plan the public hearings of the committee and to take charge of the actual questioning of witnesses, rather than to direct in any very detailed fashion the work of the separate staff units. In other words, it seems correct to say that the staff has never had a true "director" with the necessary authority, ability, and inclination to plan and administer the committee's research, investigation, and publication programs in systematic fashion.

Further information concerning the structure, authority, and duties of the staff units can best be presented by an examination of the actual personnel of the staff, for the working arrangements used from time to time have depended more upon the personalities and abilities of the people employed than they have upon any effort to blueprint an efficient staff organization.

Ernie Adamson, the first staff chief, was a shadowy figure about whom there is little to be said. Representative Hart told the writer that Adamson had been recommended to him in 1945 by a Georgia Congressman and that he had been favorably influenced by the fact that Adamson was the son of the Congressman who had fathered the Adamson Railway Labor Act in 1916. Hart stated that the younger Adamson was an attorney interested in transportation problems and that the appointment had been made with full knowledge that Adamson was totally lacking in background or experience in the field of the committee's endeavors. It is obvious that this appointment, so casually made, was a most unfortunate one. Adamson proved to be exceedingly reactionary in his views and generally incompetent in his administration of the committee's business. The first judgment is borne out by his strong prejudices, which were frequently revealed during the conduct of hearings in 1945 and 1946, and, in particular, by the letters he wrote to various individuals and organizations in which he implied that since the United States was a republic and not a democracy the use of the word democracy was suggestive of subversion.[15] Adamson's incompetence is apparent in virtually

[14] Tavenner was not employed until the late spring of 1949. In the meantime Louis J. Russell, who acquired the title of "Senior Investigator" in the 81st Congress, was the top authority on the staff.

[15] See p. 282. For copies of such letters see 92 *Cong. Rec.* 1230, 1299, A701, A872 (Feb. 11, 13, 1946). A letter from Adamson to Drew Pearson included

every hearing held by the committee during the 79th Congress. These hearings, almost without exception, were poorly planned and badly conducted. Entirely apart from issues as to the propriety or desirability of investigating the particular subjects selected for public hearings, or as to the fairness of the procedures used in these hearings, it is quite plain that the hearings of this period were conducted in very inefficient fashion. They are characterized by opportunism and expediency, the questioning is often purposeless, and the results highly inadequate even from the point of view of the committee's own standards.[16]

Robert E. Stripling is perhaps the most significant person identified with the Un-American Activities Committee since its origin in 1938, either as a member or a staff employee, with the possible exception of the temporary committee's long-time chairman, Martin Dies. While totally unprepared in training and experience for the important post he occupied with the committee on and off during a ten-year period, and while he shares much of the responsibility for the low esteem in which the committee came generally to be held, there is no denying Stripling's great ability as an investigator and inquisitor. Recognition of this ability has ranged all the way from the admission by one of his leading critics, Drew Pearson, that he was the "real brains of the Un-American Activities Committee" [17] to such flattering estimates as that of Frank Conniff of the *New York Journal-American* (Hearst) that Stripling was "probably the most unappreciated patriot of the day." [18] The comment on Stripling made by the Un-American Activities Committee itself at the time of his retirement in December, 1948, is worth quoting, for, coming as it does from the Thomas committee, it reveals the complete confidence that the committee had in Stripling and suggests the important part he played in its activities.

---

the following statement: "Several people have called to my attention the closing line of your Sunday night broadcast, 'make democracy work.' I should like very much to have your definition of the word 'democracy' as you are using it over the radio. If you will be good enough to supply this information, I will give the matter further consideration to determine whether it should be called to the attention of the members of the committee for such action as they deem proper."

[16] At the close of the 79th Congress committee members were reported as angered by an unauthorized release of a report by Adamson. Thomas was said to have stated that his first official act as chairman of the committee in the 80th Congress would be to fire Mr. Adamson. *N.Y. Times,* Dec. 28, 1946.

[17] *Washington Post,* Dec. 10, 1948.

[18] From the foreword to Stripling's book, *The Red Plot Against America,* p. 7.

It is our studied opinion that Bob Stripling has become one of the best informed men in the United States on the identities, the tactics, and the end objectives of the Communist conspiracy. He has few equals and no superiors in his knowledge of the treacherous methods of disloyal, un-American elements in this country.

At considerable sacrifice to himself and family, he has for more than a decade suffered the carping criticisms of the Communist clique in this country and the uninformed attacks of honest citizens who have been misled by irresponsible reports of his activities and motives. He has been a bulwark in the fight to maintain freedom in America. It will be a task of unrivaled difficulty to find a replacement for him. Both in private life and as a soldier in the late war, Bob Stripling has been a splendid exemplification of the type of patriotic, clear-thinking, and unselfish young men upon whom America must depend and whose devotion to public service and duty is a credit to our way of life.[19]

Stripling was a charter member of the staff of the original Dies committee. He came to Washington from Texas as a youth of college age in 1932 to take a low-salaried patronage job that Dies had obtained for him in the House folding room. He had attended both Texas A. and M. College and the University of Texas before coming to Washington, although he had apparently not obtained a degree from either. He subsequently studied law at National University and the Washington College of Law but never obtained a law degree. When the Dies committee was created in 1938, Stripling reports that Dies was discouraged because the initial appropriation given the committee by the House was only $25,000. Stripling takes great credit for having persuaded Dies to swallow his disappointment and proceed with his plans. Stripling writes, "In my small way I persuaded Dies to carry on. I offered to serve as secretary of the committee for no pay. . . . Dies gave me a desk in his outer office. I borrowed an empty file case from his secretary, and the House Un-American Activities Committee began to breathe—slightly." [20] Stripling's conceit, indicated in the passage just quoted, was often apparent. When he returned to the committee in 1946 after eighteen months of service in the Army,[21] he reports,

[19] *Soviet Espionage within the United States Government, Second Report,* Dec. 31, 1948, pp. 11–12.

[20] *The Red Plot,* pp. 22–23.

[21] Stripling insists that he was "shanghaied" into the Army by the enemies of the committee. He writes, "There was something ludicrous about [the] insistence that I, a somewhat sedentary type, be dispatched to bolster an Army which by that time possessed about 10,000,000 men." *Ibid.,* p. 50.

Drew Pearson, in his later columns attacking J. Parnell Thomas, published

As for the House Un-American Activities Committee, it had fallen into a depressing state. I got a taste of what a lot of returning servicemen suffered when the Committee's new counsel [presumably Adamson] offered me two days' work at $10 a day, ". . . if I cared to return."

I had worked too hard to turn away in disgust. I brought up the question of the GI Bill of Rights, and soon was back in my job as chief investigator. There was a lot of work to do . . . as well as some work to undo.[22]

Stripling was not an attractive person in appearance or in manner. Almost universally, impartial observers at committee hearings saw in him a sinister quality. While this feeling was in part encouraged by Stripling's physical characteristics, his personality was that of a dedicated and fanatical man.[23]

There is no denying the large and important role played by Stripling in both the development and execution of the committee's program. The *Washington Post,* no admirer of the Un-American Activities Committee or of Stripling, said of him, "He functions as a unique combination of master of ceremonies, chief counsel, main interrogator, and front-running guide through the labyrinths of subversive organizations." [24]

Thomas and Stripling obviously got along together exceedingly well; so much so, that it is difficult to be certain of the respective

a letter allegedly written by Thomas to a businessman in Paterson, N.J., November 16, 1944, seeking a defense job for Stripling so that he could avoid the draft. Pearson also asserted that it was Thomas who got Stripling out of the Army in 1946. *Washington Post,* Nov. 5, 1948.

[22] *The Red Plot,* p. 57. Chairman Wood seemingly made an unsuccessful attempt to get Stripling out of the Army at an earlier date. Stripling writes:

"At committee headquarters the new chairman, Rep. John S. Wood (D., Ga.), and Rep. Thomas were deploring the manner in which the latest investigations had failed to produce fruitful information. Wood was very friendly.

" 'There's no reason in the world why you should be kept in the Army, doing nothing, when we need you,' he said. 'I'm going to get you out immediately.'

"That suited me" (p. 54).

[23] A description of the impression given by Stripling at public hearings, which is perhaps unfair in its emphasis upon Stripling's purely physical characteristics, but which is nonetheless perceptive, was written by Edward A. Harris in the *St. Louis Post-Dispatch.* Stripling is described as "a tall, thin young man who wears horn-rimmed glasses, has slicked-down black hair, a sallow, drawn face and a habit of constantly pursing his thin lips together, as if continually revolting at something." Oct. 21, 1947.

[24] August 27, 1948, "People in the News." This article also commented upon Stripling's photographic memory. "This shows in his technique in public hearings today. He goes before the committee with few documents. He carries most of his prepared material in his head, and deals his questions with quick informality—'shoots them from the hip,' he says."

contributions of each man, or to tell who was the dominant figure during the period of the Thomas committee. However, it is a fair guess that while Stripling gave Thomas his complete loyalty, as he had Dies before, he was the leader rather than the follower. Although the views and temperaments of the two men were such that they usually saw eye to eye, the evidence suggests that new ideas and the impetus to carry them out were supplied by Stripling more often than by Thomas.

Thomas is reported to have said of Stripling, "He and I have worked together in combatting un-American activities for the past 10 years. I doubt if there is a person in the United States more able to fight un-American activities than is Stripling." [25] Stripling has indicated the freedom that the committee permitted him to exercise. With reference to one episode he writes, "I prepared the difficult Gerhart Eisler case without informing a single member beyond Chairman Thomas, until the night before the witness was called and gave his remarkable performance on the stand. The Eisler case went like clockwork. . . ." [26]

Although Stripling was an effective head of the committee's investigative staff and a clever, relentless interrogator, his strong bias and his essentially naïve concept of the Communist threat were constantly apparent in his work. The Communists were viewed as wicked, diabolically clever men who were forever on the verge of poisoning American public opinion or seizing control of the country. His estimate of the damage that the Communists might do through control of the motion picture industry is typical of his point of view:

If the Communist Party could seize the motion picture industry as completely as it has seized a number of supposedly impregnable U.S. unions and other organizations, it could hasten by many years its long-range plan to communize the country.

About 75,000,000 Americans attend movies each week. Most of the patrons believe what they see. [27]

Stripling resigned his post with the committee in December, 1948, and when the 81st Congress convened in January, 1949, it was reported that the committee was seeking an eminent lawyer to serve as the head of its staff. [28] Eventually, Frank S. Tavenner, Jr., was

[25] *Washington Post,* August 27, 1948.   [26] *The Red Plot,* p. 24.
[27] *Ibid.,* p. 70.
[28] Bert Andrews wrote in the *N.Y. Herald Tribune* (Jan. 26, 1949) that Representative Walter was supporting a "plan to obtain a highly experienced and

selected to fill the vacancy. Tavenner hardly qualified as the eminent man the reports suggested the committee was searching for, but he possessed qualifications for the post which had been sadly lacking in his predecessors. He had served for some fifteen years, first as assistant United States attorney, and then as United States attorney, in the Virginia federal district. At the close of the war he was loaned for a period of two and a half years to the Department of the Army and was acting chief counsel in the Tojo trial. In direct contrast with Adamson and Stripling, Tavenner was a quiet, unspectacular person. Under his direction committee hearings were in the main carefully planned and fairly conducted. At times, the hearings of 1949 and 1950 seemed almost purposeless and in general they attracted little attention, but they usually showed evidence of having been calmly and thoroughly prepared. Tavenner seemingly approached his tasks with no sense of pressure. For example, when he took office early in 1949 one of the most important issues facing the committee was what to do about recalcitrant witnesses who refused to testify on grounds of self-incrimination. The problem was a difficult one, and there were no definitive court rulings to follow. Tavenner at once placed the problem under study, but it was not until the middle of 1950 that a decision was made to force the issue by asking the House of Representatives to cite several score witnesses for contempt because of their refusal through the years to testify on the ground of self-incrimination.

Next to the staff chiefs—Adamson, Stripling, and Tavenner—Louis Russell has been the committee's most important employee. Moreover, his service with the committee has been coterminous with its existence as a permanent body, for his employment began in May, 1945. Through the years Russell's assignment has been directing and conducting the actual work of field investigation. In his own background of training and experience, and in his attitudes toward the committee's work, Russell has been typical of the kind of man who has served upon the committee's investigative staff.[29] At the time of his appointment, Russell had had ten years of service as an FBI agent. Earlier he had been a professional baseball player, playing, to

reputable lawyer, who would serve as counsel and would have charge of the committee's investigators."

[29] The credentials of other members of the committee's investigative staff have been placed in the record from time to time. See *Hanns Eisler Hearings*, p. 78; *Mot. Pic. Ind. Hearings*, pp. 4–6; *Communism in Hawaii Hearings, Part I*, p. 1475; *ibid., Part II*, p. 1656.

use his own words, "in all leagues but the majors." He had qualified for employment with the FBI by training as an accountant.

The indications are that in his immediate work as an investigator —running down evidence in the field, such as in the Hiss case, and assembling information for use in the questioning of witnesses— Russell has been efficient, hard-working, and conscientious. But when it comes to an understanding of the larger significance of the committee's work, or of the implications of an undertaking by a democratic government to control subversive activity, it is not unfair to say that Russell is an unsophisticated person. In conversations with the author he used the word "liberal"·as though it were synonymous with "radical" and made it clear that he did not like either type of person. He called attention to the number of well-known liberals who have acquired wealth by inheritance or marriage, and, as a man who came up the hard way himself, it was clear he had little use for men who had not had to work hard for their wealth, particularly if they were unorthodox in their politics or economics. Communists were readily identified in Russell's thinking simply as "bad" men to be discovered and exposed. That a democratic society might be faced with a larger problem of discovering why some of its members develop a loyalty to a way of life utterly alien to its own principles and traditions and of finding ways and means of strengthening its own appeal seemed not to interest Russell. Like Adamson and Stripling, Russell showed no understanding of or sympathy for the idea that one way of fighting communism is to perfect the social and economic institutions of a democratic society. On the other hand, unlike Adamson and Stripling, Russell showed no traits of fanaticism— of dedication to the task of destroying those who hold radical views. Moreover, he revealed a certain basic sense of fair play.

A little-known, but important, member of the committee's staff was Benjamin Mandel, director of research, who left the committee in 1951 to join the staff of the newly organized subcommittee on internal security of the Senate Judiciary Committee. An ex-Communist, Mandel was an employee of the committee from 1939 to 1951, save for a two-year period toward the close of the war when he was with the State Department. Whittaker Chambers has identified Mandel as "the former business manager of the *Daily Worker*" who was known in his party days as "Bert Miller." Curiously, it was Mandel who issued Chambers his first "party book" when the latter joined the Communist Party.[30]

[30] *Witness*, pp. 207, 536.

There was something of the zealot and dogmatist in Mandel's devotion to the committee and its tasks. Like his staff colleague of Dies committee days, J. B. Mathews, he brought to the task of fighting Communists all of that determination and unity of thought and purpose possessed by those who once found communism itself attractive. Moreover, like others who have turned away from the Communist movement, he took a very serious view of the threat of communism and was inclined to see evidences of communism at work where most people did not. It is not surprising then that he viewed the function of the Un-American Activities Committee as of prime importance. Above all, he saw the committee as the one agency that was in a position to educate the nation concerning the dark evils and dread threat of communism.

The research unit of the committee's staff, as has been indicated, was largely synonymous with Mandel, since apart from him its personnel never exceeded two or three "research clerks" working under his direction. There is no doubt about Mandel's familiarity with the intricacies of the Communist movement. Its personnel, its "front organizations," its publications, and its techniques were well known to him. Accordingly, he was able to feed into the files on a day-by-day basis published evidences of Communist activity. At the same time, it is quite clear that he did not always succeed in distinguishing carefully between genuine communism and the non-Communist left. Moreover, as his own direct familiarity with communism receded further into the past, his knowledge of the present-day party, its leaders, and its method developed obvious gaps.

Mandel's good and bad points are clearly revealed in those committee publications which were largely his responsibility. The half-dozen or so reports that deal with Communist front organizations and the two reports on the Communist Party itself are valuable sources of information. But their data are often undigested and badly organized. Virtually all of these reports are exceedingly difficult to read, and they contain so many obvious errors and grossly unfair attacks upon persons of undoubted non-Communist standing that it is often difficult to single out or evaluate the authentic information about Communists and Communist activity that they contain. Mandel seems to have been largely responsible for the consistent use in these reports of tables, charts, and textual analyses of the organizational affiliations of long lists of persons who are either directly or by implication accused of subversive activity. Indeed, as has already been indicated, the material in the committee files consists in good part of just such information, and it is this emphasis upon the importance of the organizational affiliations of persons attacked by the committee which has been described by the committee's critics as a technique of "guilt by association." There is little doubt that Mandel was overwhelmingly convinced of the importance of these bits of information that were laboriously collected and fed into the committee's files over a period of years and that he was largely responsible for having persuaded the committee to place such great importance upon them.

VIII: The Planning and Conduct of Investigations

THE PROGRAM of most standing committees of Congress is largely determined for them by the number, kind, and importance of bills referred to them for consideration. This has never been true of the Un-American Activities Committee. As has been seen, it does possess a certain measure of substantive jurisdiction over a particular legislative area,[1] but very few bills have ever been referred to it and it has not functioned primarily as a "legislative" committee. Instead, the committee has had to devise an investigating program of its own in order to keep busy. This it did in varying ways in each of the three Congresses between 1945 and 1950. In the 79th Congress, devising was held at a minimum, and as a result the committee was almost wholly inactive. In the 80th Congress, an extensive program was devised and the committee concerned itself with many matters of considerable significance. In the 81st Congress, the committee thought up a great many things to do, and kept quite busy, but its work attracted little attention, for in the main it was not concerned with important issues in which the public was deeply interested.

[1] The language of the 1945 resolution, by which the permanent committee was established, and of the Legislative Reorganization Act of 1946, which defines the jurisdiction of all Congressional committees, is somewhat vague on this point and does not clearly indicate that the Un-American Activities Committee possesses legislative jurisdiction. Moreover, jurisdiction over bills dealing with espionage is clearly granted to the House Judiciary Committee. Nonetheless, the Un-American Activities Committee has functioned as a legislative committee and bills have been referred to it.

271

The Committee's Own View of Itself

The Un-American Activities Committee's own view of itself has been marked by confusion. In part, at least, this is understandable. Insofar as it was and is primarily an investigating committee rather than a legislative committee it has necessarily been bothered by the uncertainties and lack of a common tradition that have always troubled all such committees. Secondly, as a committee charged with the assignment of discovering and exposing subversive activity it has occupied no enviable position, for the subject matter with which it deals is exceedingly nebulous. Nonetheless, the committee's views of itself have been remarkably varied, and at times some of its members have gone far afield in their conceptions of the committee's purposes.

As has already been suggested, Congressional investigating committees have traditionally been regarded as having three proper functions: they may seek information that will enable Congress to legislate wisely; they may undertake to check administrative agencies, with particular respect to the enforcement of law or the expenditure of public funds; and they may attempt to influence public opinion. The Un-American Activities Committee has certainly shown an interest in all of these functions—an increasing interest in the order in which the functions are named. The committee's search for information that might lead to the enactment of laws—either the revision of existing laws dealing with espionage and sedition or the passing of entirely new statutes in this area—has been the slightest of all its interests through the years. Occasionally its interest in checking the work of administrative agencies, particularly that of the Department of Justice, has been substantial. But always its interest in public opinion has been paramount. Always the committee has been concerned lest the American people fail to share its understanding of the nature of subversive activity and the many forms it may take, or appreciate the seriousness of the threat offered by this activity to the "American way of life" as seen by itself.

In addition to these three functions the committee has tried to exercise two others. First, it has tried in a nonstatutory way to define subversive or "un-American" activity and thereby to set the standards of American thought and conduct with respect to orthodoxy and heresy in politics.[2] Second, it has tried in varying ways to

[2] In his speech in the House of Representatives, May 26, 1948, reviewing ten years of activity by the Un-American Activities Committee, Thomas took great

take over the function of administrative or judicial agencies in the *enforcement* of public policy with respect to subversive activity.

It is difficult enough to frame wise and workable statutes dealing with such specific and traditional forms of antisocial conduct as espionage, sabotage, sedition, and treason. But when it comes to defining by exposure and illustration the norms of proper thought and conduct in a democratic society, the undertaking becomes almost hopeless. Certainly, the charter of authority and instructions under which the Un-American Activities Committee functions does not help matters very much. To tell a committee that its concern shall be "the extent, character, and objects of un-American propaganda activities in the United States" and "the diffusion within the United States of subversive and un-American propaganda that is instigated from foreign countries or of a domestic origin and attacks the principle of the form of government as guaranteed by our Constitution" is to give it an exceedingly difficult assignment. The committee's jurisdictional assignment is such that any attempt by it to set informal patterns of thought and conduct for the American people in this area, while not impossible of fulfillment, is almost certain to produce unfortunate results. From time to time the committee has concerned itself with such matters as the content of Hollywood films, the programs of radio news commentators, and the textbooks used in American schools. In most of these instances the committee's chief purpose has seemed to be the establishment of patterns of American, as against un-American, activity which would be controlling in the development of our national life, public and private.

The committee's efforts to usurp the functions of administrative and judicial agencies have taken many forms but almost always have grown out of its desire to put the accusing finger on specific individuals whom it deems guilty of subversive activity. At times the committee has regarded itself as a detective agency, and it has paralleled the work of the Department of Justice, and of the FBI in particular, in trying to apprehend law violators and to procure evidence against them. This view of itself was certainly shown in its interest in Alger Hiss, William Remington, and other specific persons accused by Whittaker Chambers and Elizabeth Bentley of having engaged in espionage, in its interest in the Hollywood "ten," and in its interest in

pride in listing as one of the five outstanding achievements of the committee the fact that it had "pioneered in establishing standards by which Federal, State, and local governments [might] judge Communist and Communist-front organizations and their members." 94 *Cong. Rec.* A3471 (May 26, 1948).

Joseph Weinberg, Clarence Hiskey, and others accused of having committed espionage while working as scientists in atomic energy laboratories. Of course, it may be argued that these individuals were merely incidental to the larger problems which they illustrated— such as espionage in the public service—and that the committee's true (and proper) interest was in the latter. But it is hard to avoid the conclusion that it was tracking down the individual culprit that interested the committee and that in putting the accusing finger on such a person as Alger Hiss it felt that it was rendering a valuable (and proper) service to the public welfare. The investigative arm of the committee's staff has always regarded itself as a "little FBI." Ex-FBI men have provided part of its personnel, and its methods and interests have been comparable to those of the FBI. Moreover, it is this kind of work that the committee's staff has performed most successfully. In unearthing the details of the disposition of Alger Hiss's Ford roadster or of John Howard Lawson's organizational interests and activities the staff has shown its greatest efficiency.

The incongruity of a Congressional committee operating as though it were a detective agency has at times occurred even to members of the committee. During the last phase of the Communist espionage hearings in 1948, Representative Hébert made the following observation:

I . . . direct attention also to the fact that this committee is not the Department of Justice, nor a detective agency. We are not charged with the responsibility of apprehending the criminal. We are charged with the responsibility of bringing to the attention of the proper authorities the fact that a crime has been committed. Then it becomes incumbent upon and the responsibility of the proper agency of the Government to apprehend that criminal when they know a crime has been committed and to prosecute him to the fullest extent of the law.[3]

But even this statement shows a concern for the specific (pointing out that a crime has been committed), rather than the general (in this instance the extent and seriousness of Communist infiltration of the federal service). The general may properly be illustrated by the specific, but it is the former and not the latter that should be the central concern of a Congressional investigating committee.

Early in 1945 a brief memorandum entitled *Suggested Standards for Determining Un-American Activities* was prepared by the Brookings Institution for the Un-American Activities Committee at the

[3] *Hearings regarding Communist Espionage in the United States Government —Part II*, p. 1424.

latter's request.[4] There is no evidence that this memorandum was ever consciously employed by the committee in determining either its goals or its methods. However, it is significant that four of the five "objectives" recommended to the committee emphasized investigation and exposure of *individuals* suspected of engaging in un-American activities. The statement of objectives is as follows:

1. To determine the adequacy of existing law with respect to un-American activities and whether further legislative action is desirable.

2. To publish the results of investigation so that the people of the United States may have accurate and comprehensive information regarding un-American activities of individuals and associations and act in the light of these facts.

3. To inform legislative and executive officers of the un-American activities of persons who are engaged in them and are attempting or may attempt to influence governmental action.

4. To disclose fully un-American activities of persons who are or may become candidates for public office, whether by election or appointment.

5. To detect and give the people of the United States accurate and reasonably complete information of un-American activities of any person holding any public office.[5]

It is true that the Brookings memorandum then warned the committee that it ought not "to try, prosecute, or punish any individual or group for any crime or misdemeanor," or "to persecute an individual or group for un-American activities," but the latter warning was softened by the statement that it "should not be construed to prevent the Committee from presenting to the American people facts regarding the un-American activities of such individual or group." Thus from the beginning the committee had the moral support of such an eminent organization as the Brookings Institution in the emphasis it has placed upon individuals in its investigations.

At times the committee has moved forward one step through the traditional law enforcement process and has regarded itself as having a grand jury function. This view of its role is to be seen in certain of its public hearings where it has listened to evidence suggesting wrongdoing by an individual (evidence usually gathered and presented to the committee by members of its own staff), has then given some sort of opportunity to the suspect to explain away the evidence against him, and has subsequently "indicted" or cleared him in a

---

[4] This memorandum was published as a pamphlet and placed on public sale by the Brookings Institution.

[5] *Suggested Standards*, p. 8.

printed report upon the proceedings. The grand jury analogy has actually been used by committee members in so many words. For example, Rankin was fond of calling the committee "the grand jury of America." [6]

Throughout the eighteen-month life of the federal grand jury (June, 1947, to December, 1948) that indicted Alger Hiss and twelve members of the Communist Party hierarchy, the Un-American Activities Committee was attempting to cover much the same ground as the grand jury. Many of the same witnesses were heard by both groups. In December, 1948, after Whittaker Chambers had produced the Pumpkin Papers, competition between the two groups was particularly keen. For example, the *New York Times* observed in its news columns on December 11, "The Department of Justice and the House group remained belligerently at loggerheads over jurisdiction over witnesses appearing before the Committee and the special Federal grand jury in New York which is investigating Communist activities. Their race for first call on witnesses continued, with the jury apparently winning two heats during the day." And on the 13th the *Washington Post* took the committee to task for letting the grand jury see its microfilms only "after a week of resistance."

In December, 1948, Representative Mundt protested against the suggestion that there was anything improper in the House committee's activity paralleling that of the grand jury and insisted that the committee would continue its efforts to track down and punish those who had delivered the State Department documents to Chambers. He said:

It is utterly silly for two coordinating branches of the Government to get involved in a running debate over who is going to talk to a witness. As far as this committee is concerned there is just one big unsolved question left:

Who stole these documents from the State Department which we know were delivered to Mr. Chambers at the time he admits he was a paid Communist agent? This committee is not going to permit any source to squelch our efforts to answer that question.

We are giving and will continue to give full cooperation to all Government agencies by making available to them all evidence coming into our possession. While we regret that this reciprocal attitude is apparently not to be a two-way street, we shall continue to try to discover, to dis-

[6] See 91 *Cong. Rec.* A4456 (Oct. 22, 1945) and 93 *Cong. Rec.* 1131 (Feb. 18, 1947), and *Communist Espionage Hearings*, p. 537.

close and to punish disloyal employees who stole secret documents with the purpose of delivering them to foreign Communist agents.[7]

Representative Nixon also attempted to justify the committee's encroachment during this period upon the grand jury's province by pointing out that, due to the running of the statute of limitations, the grand jury might not be able to return any indictments and that accordingly the committee had a "solemn responsibility" to find out who the guilty persons were.[8] However, this position involved prejudgment of the difficulties that the grand jury might encounter and is a rationalization that would justify unlimited encroachment by a Congressional committee upon the jurisdiction of a grand jury under almost any circumstances.

The sense that the Un-American Activities Committee was functioning as a grand jury was so strong that in a presentment handed down in April, 1949, the successor grand jury directed an implied criticism against the committee. In complaining about the large number of witnesses before it who refused to testify on the ground of self-incrimination, the grand jury said, "This, such witnesses have unquestionably done because they have been alerted through the publicity given by other investigating bodies to the circumstances which the grand jury must examine in secrecy." And it added, "Having seen at firsthand the difficulties in arriving at the truth concerning espionage violations when witnesses have been alerted by publicized charges and countercharges, the grand jury recommends that all investigating bodies conduct their inquiries into espionage in secret." [9]

At other times committee members have seemingly viewed the committee as a final court of justice sitting in judgment on individuals accused either of specific offenses against the law or of more

[7] *N.Y. Times,* Dec. 11, 1948.

[8] *Communist Espionage Hearings,* p. 1420. He said, "They may not even be guilty of technical crimes due to the lapse of the statute of limitations, in which case the grand jury has no right whatever to hear their case, and in that case this committee has a solemn responsibility, despite the efforts of the administration to silence this committee and keep the facts from the people—and I say that, not because of any political implications, because this is bigger than politics—this committee has the responsibility to continue its investigation and to call every witness before it until we find who was responsible for bringing this information to Mr. Chambers, and to see whether or not those people are still engaged in that kind of activity."

[9] From the text of the presentment as printed in the *N.Y. Times,* April 27, 1949.

general offenses against the public good or safety. During the Communist espionage hearings Representative Hébert told one witness, "you are now before the greatest open court in this country." A little later he said, "Miss Bentley has made these charges. . . . Now, you have your opportunity in open court [to reply to them]." And again, "You asked for an open court. I am giving it to you." [10] Mundt also referred at one point to the fact that a witness had had "his opportunity, in the best court of this country, which is the court of public opinion." [11] And again, while admitting that the committee was not a court, he said this was "unfortunate." [12] It may readily be admitted that in these statements committee members were using the word, court, very broadly and did not intend to suggest that they regarded themselves as a court of law. Nonetheless, their very use of the word, in however broad a context, reveals a tendency to think of a hearing as being primarily concerned with establishing the guilt or innocence of particular individuals who are charged with specific offenses.

It is not suggested that because an issue has been actively brought within the jurisdiction of the courts, legislative committees are barred from simultaneous examination of the issue. The United States Supreme Court tended to sanction that position in 1881 in *Kilbourn v. Thompson.*[13] But the Kilbourn decision has been much criticized and in its more recent rulings upon Congressional investigations the court has insisted upon no such extreme separation of functions between the courts and investigating committees. The trouble with the Un-American Activities Committee is not only that it has been active in the same field as has the judiciary, but that it has actually tried to usurp the judicial function, i.e., the trial and punishment of transgressors against the law. The committee might properly in 1948 have concerned itself with the espionage problem at the same time as did the federal grand jury. But its concern should have been with the broader aspects of the problem—the extent and seriousness of the evil, the adequacy of existing statutes protecting against the evil, and the adequacy of the record being made by administrative and judicial agencies in the enforcement of these statutes. Of course, the House committee in its Communist espionage hearings was concerned with these broader aspects. But it is clear from the record that this kind of concern was always secondary to a greater interest in

[10] *Communist Espionage Hearings,* pp. 846, 847.
[11] *Ibid.,* p. 892.   [12] *Ibid.,* p. 926.   [13] 103 U.S. 168.

finding and exposing guilty individuals.[14] Similarly, the committee has concerned itself with the adequacy of existing statutes and has from time to time made recommendations for their revision or for the enactment of new laws. But these recommendations have seldom gone beyond the generalization stage. The Mundt-Nixon bill is the only carefully worked out piece of legislation ever proposed by the committee.

And finally, there is no doubt that the committee has concerned itself with the adequacy of law enforcement machinery. But in the Communist espionage hearings, which have been singled out as an example, this concern was not particularly helpful. A political antagonism between the committee and the Department of Justice was apparent from the start, and the committee lost no time in making a virtual declaration of war against the department. Subsequently, the oral statements of committee members and the printed passages

[14] In its *Interim Report on Hearings regarding Communist Espionage in the United States Government*, published August 28, 1948, there is an interesting analysis of the relative roles of the FBI, the grand jury, and the Un-American Activities Committee. It is said that "the FBI is a fact-finding and investigating agency and not an exposure agency. Its duties are to find and record the facts so they will be available to police officers, law-enforcement officials, and the prosecuting agencies of Government. It is not a vehicle for reporting to the public on the extent of nefarious activities." With respect to the grand jury it is asserted that its methods of fact finding involve secrecy and that it rests with the Attorney General to determine what evidence is submitted to it, and what verdicts will be asked for. "At best, the grand jury is not a vehicle for reporting to the public on the extent of un-American activities in a free republic." And then in a lengthy analysis of the role of the House committee the report states:

"As contrasted with the FBI and the grand jury, the House Committee on Un-American Activities has a separate and a very special responsibility. It functions to permit the greatest court in the world—the court of American public opinion—to have an undirected, uncensored, and unprejudiced opportunity to render a continuing verdict on all of its public officials and to evaluate the merit of many in private life who either openly associate and assist disloyal groups or covertly operate as members or fellow travelers of such organizations. It is as necessary to the success of this committee that it reveals its findings to the public as it is to the success of the FBI that it conceal its operations from the public view.

"The functioning of the Communist espionage rings in Government provides a dramatically vivid illustration of the functions of the three foregoing public institutions in their rendering of the service they are created to perform.

"The FBI functions to find and assimilate all of the facts available to that organization and to make them available to the prosecuting agencies of the Federal Government. The Federal grand jury functions to consider the evidence

in its reports referring to the Department of Justice were all so shrill and venomous that they had virtually no value in providing a basis for calm, intelligent evaluation of the department's efforts, successful or unsuccessful, to ferret out espionage agents in the federal service.

Planning of the Committee's Agenda

At no time has any member of the Un-American Activities Committee or of its staff had the interest or the understanding to try to map out a systematic program of investigation or a workable scheme of carrying out such a program. Instead, the committee has held itself in readiness to jump this way or that depending upon day-to-day developments, upon the political atmosphere of the moment, or upon the mere whim of the chairman or of staff members. It is true the committee has had its perennial interests. Staff work has been carried on in certain fields more or less continuously. For example, communism in education is a subject that has always been on the committee's agenda, and its staff has periodically looked for evidence of subversive content in textbooks used in schools and colleges. But this concern has been an aimless one. It has never been brought to a head in public hearings or in the publication of a formal report.

The "eight-point" program of research and investigation an-
_____
selected from these facts by the Attorney General and to pass judgment upon whatever verdicts it is asked to make by the Attorney General. The House Committee on Un-American Activities functions to alert the public concerning the existence and operation of these espionage practices, and to point up and propose the necessary new legislation to provide our country with greater safeguards and to enable it to protect itself against the constantly changing tactics and practices of world-wide and world-dominated communism and its American ramparts (pp. 1–2)."

In 1947 in a radio speech following the Hollywood hearings Thomas took notice of "a current campaign of vilification" directed against the committee and made the following statement concerning the committee's functions:

"The Committee on Un-American Activities is a fact finding body. We are not a court. We subpena persons to testify before us under oath, in order that we may get all the available accurate information on subversive or un-American forces at work in this country. If certain legislative action is needed to cope with the situation, according to the evidence, we must report the fact to the House.

"The chief function of the committee, however, has always been the exposure of un-American individuals and their un-American activities. This is based upon the conviction that the American public will not tolerate efforts to subvert or destroy the American system of government once such efforts have been pointed out. The Congress' right to investigate and expose undemocratic forces is as established and untrammeled as our Constitution." 93 *Cong. Rec.* A4277 (Nov. 20, 1947).

nounced by Chairman Thomas early in 1947 did range rather widely. But it was little more than a hasty listing of certain subjects that had been of perennial interest to the committee. The individual items were spotty in character and showed an all-consuming concern with the threat of communism. In January, 1948, in a radio speech Thomas stated that he was "recommending" a "twelve-point" program to the committee for the coming year. Five of the points proposed continuation of the perennial investigations into communism in education, labor unions, Hollywood, the federal civil service, and atomic research. The other seven points were as follows: (1) "Submit to the House as soon as practicable a series of bills designed to break up the Communist conspiracy in the United States." (Thomas announced that hearings on such bills would be conducted by a subcommittee under the chairmanship of Representative Nixon.) (2) "Full public hearings of the activities of those . . . who . . . spread antiracial and antireligious propaganda." (Thomas announced that these hearings would be conducted by a subcommittee under the chairmanship of Representative McDowell.) (3) "Public hearings by the full committee, beginning on March 1, on a number of Communist aliens who are illegally in the United States." (In a characteristic attitude of prejudgment Thomas added, "Our committee has a complete record on these individuals and will demand their deportation.") (4) Hearings in February before the full committee "on the extent of subversive influence seeking to exploit the Negro population of the United States." (Thomas added that a report prepared by a Negro investigator was "now ready to be submitted to the committee and 30 witnesses have been scheduled to appear.") (5) The holding of an inter-American conference of delegates from the legislatures of the American hemisphere to work out "a hemispheric unity of purpose" in legislating against the spread of communism. (6) The committee to recommend legislation strengthening the authority of the government to deal with espionage. (7) Preparation by the committee's staff of reports for "public consumption" on "all Communist-front organizations operating in the United States." [15]

Many of the projects announced by Thomas were not carried out during the year. The reference to a subcommittee under McDowell which was to look into racial and religious prejudice is an interest-

[15] 94 *Ibid.* A65 (Jan. 8, 1948). There is no evidence that the committee itself ever formally approved this twelve-point program. However, April 6, 1948, the committee apparently approved at an executive session a very similar program. This latter program also proposed investigation of Gerald L. K. Smith and his associates and "the state of security in Panama." *N.Y. Times,* April 7, 1948.

ing one. Seemingly, this is the same subcommittee which was referred to from time to time as a subcommittee on fascism.[16] There is no evidence that this subcommittee ever functioned. Certainly it held no public hearings, and it published no reports.

When the Democrats reorganized the committee in the 81st Congress, it was announced that the "eight-point" program was being abandoned. Thereafter, the committee remained as busy as it had ever been, but the random character of its program of hearings and publications became even more pronounced than it had been under the Thomas regime.

Two indications of the *ad hoc* manner in which the committee picks subjects for investigation are seen in its use of the "fishing expedition" and its sensitivity to requests for committee activity submitted by outside organizations. The committee's staff has engaged in a more or less continuous checking of private organizations on the chance that now and then one of them may be found to be engaging in subversive activity and thus warrant the committee's closer attention. This casting of a wide net to catch an occasional fish was particularly evident during the 79th Congress when Ernie Adamson was head of the committee's staff. Adamson wrote a series of letters to numerous organizations demanding that they submit various records and papers to the committee for examination. The text of a letter addressed to the Veterans against Discrimination was read into the *Congressional Record* by Representative Ellis Patterson. The letter dated January 29, 1946, was as follows:

GENTLEMEN:

Would you please be good enough to send me a list of your officers and your managing committee?

Several of your circulars have been sent to us by citizens of your city and I note that you refer to democracy several times. I wonder if you are sufficiently familiar with the history of the United States to be aware that this country was not organized as a democracy and that section 4 of article 4 of the Constitution reads in part as follows:

"The United States shall guarantee to every State in this Union a republican form of government."

Is it your purpose to ask for an amendment of the Constitution or do you propose to conduct a propaganda campaign against the administration of the provisions of the Constitution?

Yours very truly,
ERNIE ADAMSON,[17]
Chief Counsel

[16] See note 26.   [17] 92 *Cong. Rec.* A508 (Feb. 5, 1946).

It is probable that the committee's interest in the Joint Anti-Fascist Refugee Committee grew out of such fishing expedition methods. On December 8, 1945, the latter organization received a letter from Ernie Adamson which read, "In the interest of saving time, I suggest that you permit one of our investigators to make a preliminary investigation of your organization to determine whether or not this committee is interested in your organization." [18] Two days later its records were subpoenaed by the committee, and it was resistance by the organization's officers and directors to these efforts to obtain its records that led ultimately to the imprisonment of more than a dozen persons for contempt of Congress.

The committee has several times indicated that it will honor any request from respectable individuals or organizations that it pursue a particular line of investigation. For example, a 1946 report of the committee stated, "The committee has formulated the policy of investigating complaints received from American citizens who have the interests of the United States foremost in their hearts and minds." And it added, "Any organization which advocates the establishment of the fascist system of government in the United States will be investigated by the committee upon receipt of information that such an organization does exist." [19] When the committee in 1949 requested American colleges and universities to submit lists of the textbooks and readings used in certain courses, the excuse was offered that the committee had been requested to make such a survey by the National Council of the Sons of the American Revolution and that it could not very well ignore this request from such an eminent and respected organization.

It is unlikely that any investigation has actually been undertaken solely because it was requested by an outside organization. For example, the committee's staff had shown a perennial interest in textbooks, and the request for action from the National Council of the Sons of the American Revolution was in all likelihood little more than a convenient peg upon which Chairman Wood decided to hang his go-ahead order to the staff. In the end the committee has done

---

[18] The letter is reproduced in *ibid.* A263 (Jan. 28, 1946). It was placed in the *Record* by Representative Celler of New York.

[19] Report of June 7, 1946, p. 2. In a radio speech given in June, 1946, Representative Landis said, referring to the Un-American Activities Committee and justifying its controversial action in calling for the radio scripts of certain news commentators, "As a public agency we are compelled to respect a reasonable request from substantial citizens." 92 *Cong. Rec.* A3149 (June 3, 1946).

what it has wanted to do and has refrained from doing those things it did not want to do.

Procedure in Hearings

The Un-American Activities Committee in the six years of its existence as a permanent committee had not developed a systematic body of procedures in the conduct of its hearings. This is apparent when the committee's practice is checked on the following points: use of open and closed hearings; use of the full committee and of subcommittees for the conduct of hearings; techniques used in the questioning of witnesses; rights accorded witnesses.

In fairness to the Un-American Activities Committee it should be pointed out that the issue of open hearings versus closed hearings in the conduct of a legislative investigation is a perennial one that has never been really settled. The open hearing is frequently attacked on the grounds that if it has not been preceded by closed hearings or by careful spadework on the part of a committee's staff it is likely to prove an aimless and fruitless proceeding, and that it permits irresponsible witnesses to slander innocent people by suddenly introducing their names into the testimony without warning. For these reasons it is argued that the real search for information by an investigating committee can most successfully be made in closed sessions and that public sessions, if held at all, should be little more than carefully staged performances in which a committee gives publicity to information which it feels the people should know about.[20] On the other hand, closed hearings are frequently attacked as "star chamber" proceedings. It is argued that in such sessions witnesses are easily browbeaten and denied essential rights and are then helpless against

[20] In an interview with the author, William P. Rogers, chief counsel during the 80th Congress of the investigations subcommittee of the Senate Committee on Expenditures in the Executive Departments—the "Ferguson committee"—took this position. He laid great stress upon the use of executive hearings to screen testimony, to prevent the publicizing of unwarranted charges, and to give a committee a chance to decide the directions in which it wants to move. He said, for example, that when the Ferguson committee heard Elizabeth Bentley and William Remington in public hearings in 1948, all seven members of the subcommittee understood and agreed upon the purpose the public hearings were to serve: providing an answer to the question as to how a person like Remington, concerning whom charges of disloyalty had been lodged with the proper authorities as early as 1945, could make progress in the government and gain a post of great responsibility under the President's loyalty program. Interview, June 28, 1948.

the later use a committee may make of their testimony in stories "leaked" to the press or in published reports.[21]

The trouble with the Un-American Activities Committee is not so much that it has used open hearings or closed hearings as it is that it has used both types freely and frequently without having had any clear understanding of the proper use of either or any consistent policy as to their use. While no record has ever been made public of the number or kind of closed hearings conducted by the com-

[21] A very interesting passage from testimony given in an executive session, later made public, in which the issue of closed vs. open hearings was discussed, is found in *Excerpts from Hearings regarding Investigation of Communist Activities in Connection with the Atomic Bomb* (pp. 13, 14, 15):

"*Dr. [Martin] Kamen:* Now it seems to me that at this point I should say I am not going to testify in a secret session. I want a public hearing on this. Anything involving the Manhattan project. I am not in a position to discuss atomic energy matters unless I am given clearance from the Atomic Energy Commission.

"*Mr. Stripling:* The committee will not ask you any questions which involve secrets.

"*Dr. Kamen:* I have nothing whatever to speak about which is secret.

"*Mr. Stripling:* Dr. Kamen, it is not up to you to decide whether a committee of Congress will sit in executive or open session.

"*Dr. Kamen:* I realize that.

"*Mr. Stripling:* The committee subpenaed you to appear in a closed session, and under the authority of this subpena and under the laws of the United States you are to testify. You are not the one who will set the conditions upon which you will testify.

"Now the committee is endeavoring to get the facts regarding this matter, which is very important to you.

"*Dr. Kamen:* Yes.

"*Mr. Stripling:* More important to you than to anybody else, I know, involved. Now we have questions here, all of which are pertinent, and all we want from you is the answers to these questions.

"*Dr. Kamen:* I would like to know why I can't answer these questions in a public hearing.

"*Mr. Stripling:* The committee does not see fit to ask you questions in a public hearing at this time.

"*Dr. Kamen:* On the advice of my attorney, I have been told that I can ask for a public hearing. I do not have to testify in a secret hearing, and that is all I know.

"*The Chairman [Thomas]:* I would like to say your attorney has advised you very badly on that score. We have been holding executive sessions for some 2 weeks, more than 2 weeks. We have had three to seven witnesses in a day, and this committee has decided to continue the sessions until we complete our current investigation.

"Whether we will hold public hearings later on this subject depends entirely upon what we learn in these executive sessions. So proceed, Mr. Stripling."

.   .   .   .   .

mittee, enough is known to support the statement that it has made extensive use of both types. Occasionally a hearing which has been started as a closed one has been turned into a public session; or, vice versa, the audience has been dismissed and a public hearing has been turned into an executive one.[22] Again, the record of a closed hearing has in many cases been made public after the passage of time. Such developments were common in 1948 during the Com-

---

"*Dr. Kamen:* I think I will be very happy to answer those statements in a public hearing.

"*Mr. Stripling:* Well, is there any reason why you won't answer them in a closed hearing?

"*Dr. Kamen:* There is no reason except my past experience from what has happened to me in the past 2 weeks, it appears that I have no protection with regard to what kind of quotes come out from the committee to the press. Maybe the press is at fault—I think they are—but in any case it seems to me there is less chance of the whole truth not being told in a public hearing than in a private hearing.

"None of us here apparently has the power to prevent misquotes; whereas, in a public hearing, at least, there is a minimizing. I only ask it for my own protection. I have every desire to cooperate with the committee, I have nothing but the highest respect for the committee, and I want to see something done because particularly if something can be gotten which will disclose that there has been an atomic spy ring working, it will exonerate me because I have had no connection with an atomic spy ring to my knowledge. So if some evidence is gotten by the committee, it will help me.

"*The Chairman:* I think that this whole session can help you and help you much more in an executive session first than if we went right into a public hearing. I am going to tell you if we should go into a public hearing right now with the record that has been presented to us, it wouldn't be advantageous to you. You have got a chance to clear yourself of some testimony that has been given to us in this executive session.

· · · · ·

"*The Chairman:* You have got a chance now to do a good job at clearing your name of any testimony that has been given to us that is derogatory to you. So proceed.

"*Mr. Stripling:* Dr. Kamen, are you now or have you ever been a member of the Communist Party?

"*Dr. Kamen:* No."

[22] The committee started to hear both Whittaker Chambers and Elizabeth Bentley in executive sessions in their initial appearances but voted to open the sessions to the public after they were under way. As Stripling tells the story the decision to turn the Chambers hearing into a public session was taken as casually as follows:

"After 15 minutes of [Chambers'] story one of the members interrupted.

" 'Hell,' said the member, 'why is this in executive session? This should be in the open.' " *The Red Plot*, pp. 92, 100.

munist espionage hearings. At one point during these hearings, Representative Mundt, who was acting chairman at the moment, tried to state the committee's policy in the following words:

It is an established policy of the House Committee on Un-American Activities that whenever possible, and in the public interest, public business shall be conducted publicly. We have adopted the policy, therefore, of taking the public into our confidence whenever that can be done in hearings of this type, without injury to anybody's individual character, or without injury to the public interest.[23]

This was a sound enough generalization, but there is little evidence that the actual choice between open and closed hearings at that time was being made on the basis of this policy statement alone. During the August phase of the Communist espionage hearings the committee seemingly used the closed hearing upon occasion for the sensible reason that it did not quite know where it was going or what would come out of the testimony of witnesses. There was always the possibility that the Bentley-Chambers story of Communists in the federal service would blow up in the committee's face. Accordingly, it is not surprising that such a session as the first Chambers-Hiss confrontation scene was held privately in a New York hotel room on August 17. The transcript of this session was made public on August 25.

During the December phase of these hearings the committee adopted a rule, under the prodding of Representative Hébert, that it would not permit witnesses to submit any new names in connection with charges of espionage except in executive sessions. This was a bit like closing the barn door after the horse had been stolen, but the rule was followed on December 8 when, after hearing Isaac Don Levine in public session, the committee suddenly went into an executive session to permit Levine to give it the names of six additional persons that Chambers was said to have turned over to Adolf Berle in 1939 as members of a Communist ring in the federal government. However, the light attitude taken toward such confidential information became apparent a few days later when Representatives Mundt and Nixon took it upon themselves to give out one of the names to the press, that of Laurence Duggan at the time of his sudden death.

When the committee was reorganized in the 81st Congress in 1949, it was announced that greater use would be made of executive

[23] *Communist Espionage Hearings*, p. 1386.

sessions.[24] The indications are that this policy has been carried out and that most of the public hearings since 1949 either have followed executive hearings in which the ground has already been explored or have been based upon more careful and systematic staff studies than had been made in previous years. On the other hand, the decision to move back and forth from executive to public sessions is still made upon occasion in rather casual fashion.[25]

The committee's use of subcommittees has been most informal, and it is difficult to generalize about it beyond saying that there is no systematic or logical pattern. At no time since 1945 has a careful attempt been made to break up the total jurisdiction of the committee into logical segments and to create subcommittees to facilitate an across-the-board approach to the committee's assignment. There have been substantive subcommittees. For example, in the 80th Congress the committee made use of a subcommittee on national security under Chairman Thomas which issued the Condon report, a subcommittee on fascism under Chairman McDowell which seemingly

[24] Late in April, 1949, Chairman Wood stated: "Because of the nature of certain phases of the espionage hearings, the committee will find it necessary to hold a large number of executive sessions. This does not mean that the evidence will not be made public. The committee has found it necessary to hold these executive meetings in order to develop certain leads which could not be fully developed at public hearings." N.Y. Times, May 1, 1949.

In an interview with the author, June 27, 1949, Frank S. Tavenner, Jr., the committee's counsel, emphasized the desirability of using preliminary executive hearings and of making thorough preparations before holding public hearings. He said that it was even desirable that executive hearings should sometimes be conducted by one-man subcommittees so that the confidential character of the testimony could be preserved.

[25] For example, a decision to turn the executive hearing on June 14, 1949, at which Frank Oppenheimer was being heard, into a public session was made in the following fashion:

"Mr. Wood: For the benefit of those who were not here this morning, we had as the witness Dr. Frank Oppenheimer, whose testimony was not concluded.

"Mr. Harrison: Is there any reason why the press could not have the testimony he gave this morning? I think it would be very interesting for the public to read it.

"Mr. Wood: Is it the sense of the committee that the hearing is in open session now?

"Mr. Velde: I believe it should be in open session.

"Mr. Harrison: And with the understanding they can have the earlier testimony if they want it.

"Mr. Wood: It is so ordered. Very well, you can open the doors." Hearings regarding Communist Infiltration at Radiation Laboratory and Atomic Bomb Project at the University of California, Berkeley, Calif.—Vol. I, p. 362. See above, p. 181, note 29.

did nothing,[26] and a subcommittee on legislation under Chairman Nixon which conducted hearings on the Mundt-Nixon and related bills. But these subcommittees were apparently created by the chairman of the full committee on the spur of the moment and functioned as *ad hoc* committees. At no time in its entire history has the committee ever listed or identified its subcommittees in a printed document.

A much more common use of subcommittees is seen in the day-by-day conduct of the committee's hearings, public and executive. Many of the committee's most widely publicized hearings were actually conducted by subcommittees, at least on certain days of the hearings. This was true even of the Hollywood hearings and of the Hiss-Chambers hearings.[27] The explanation has presumably been the inability to muster a quorum (five members) of the full committee. To avoid subsequent legal complications in such a situation the practice has been to announce that a hearing is being conducted by a subcommittee, which is sometimes as small as one man and sometimes large enough to qualify as a session of the full committee. Attendance of committee members at hearings has always been spotty. It is difficult to say whether the committee's record in this respect is any worse than the practice among Congressional committees generally, for while it is well known that attendance at committee hearings is often poor, statistical information on this point is scanty. Be that as it may, it is clear that the attendance record of the Un-American Activities Committee has not been good. It is fair to take the Communist espionage hearings of 1948 as a test in this respect, for certainly no hearings ever held by the committee attracted more interest from its members. During the two phases of these hearings,

[26] There are only scattered references to this subcommittee. For example, there is a letter in 93 *Cong. Rec.* A2837–2838 (June 13, 1947) from McDowell to Representative Sabath, thanking the latter for suggestions covering the work of the subcommittee, and stating that work has been started drafting "the various parts of a report" on fascism. No such report was ever published. See *N.Y. Times,* Jan. 12, 1948, for another reference to this subcommittee.

[27] The printed record of the Communist espionage hearings suggests that the first hearings in August and the *Interim Rept.* of August 28 were the responsibility of the full committee. However, the volume in which the text of the December hearings was published and the *Second Rept.* of December 31 both carry a reference to a "Subcommittee" consisting of six members (all of the members of the full committee except Thomas, Wood, and Peterson) with Mundt as chairman. The jurisdiction of this subcommittee is not mentioned. However, even during the August phase of the hearings many sessions were actually conducted by subcommittees which were sometimes as small as one man.

the committee held sessions on twenty-seven different days.[28] On only seven of these days were the hearings conducted by the committee itself, the sessions on the other twenty days having been conducted by various subcommittees. Representative Wood was never present at any hearing throughout the entire period from July 31 to December 14. Representatives Peterson and Vail were absent a good deal of the time. Representative Rankin was present during the first few days of the hearings but was absent during most of the month of August and was not a member of any subcommittee except during December when five of the twenty-seven days of hearings occurred. Chairman Thomas missed three of the seven days of hearings by the full committee and was present on only eight of the twenty days of subcommittee hearings. Only four of the nine members of the committee—Mundt, Nixon, McDowell, and Hébert —were regular in their attendance at sessions during the Communist espionage hearings.[29]

The Un-American Activities Committee's treatment of its witnesses has ranged widely. To begin with, it has often observed a distinction between "friendly" and "hostile" witnesses. Friendly witnesses have been allowed to ramble at length and to tell their stories in their own words. They have seldom been asked embarrassing questions and often have been asked few questions of any type. On the other hand, hostile witnesses have often been denied the right to make prepared statements or to testify informally at any length, and the committee has frequently subjected them to vigorous, penetrating cross-examination.

In the long run a very substantial share of the questioning of witnesses has been done by staff members such as Robert Stripling, Louis Russell, and Frank Tavenner, Jr., although certain committee members have also participated freely in the questioning. In general, the committee has followed the traditional and sensible plan of letting a staff member initiate the questioning of a witness and develop the main lines of testimony which the committee seeks from the witness, with committee members joining in the questioning as the hearing proceeds. But adherence to such a systematic mode of procedure has depended upon the care with which a hearing has been prepared, upon rapport between staff and committee members,

[28] This reference is to the sessions that were public and to those executive sessions the record of which was ultimately made public. The committee held a number of additional executive hearings which were never made public.

[29] See Appendix, Table IV.

and upon the idiosyncrasies of particular Representatives. It was always difficult to restrain Representative Rankin so as to allow an orderly development of testimony. In the 79th Congress Rankin was often allowed to proceed at will, and he disrupted more than one hearing by his irrational and prejudiced questioning of witnesses. In the 80th Congress Chairman Thomas, and in his absence such men as Mundt and Nixon, kept Rankin pretty well suppressed. But at all times the committee has had more than its share of incompetent and irresponsible legislators as members, and this has had a pronounced effect upon the questioning of witnesses.

Examples of every possible type of treatment of a witness and of techniques of questioning are readily found in the committee hearings. Monologues by witnesses, intelligent cross-examination, bitter and unfair questioning, half-hearted questioning, ineffective questioning, are all easily illustrated. The committee has been particularly prone to let ex-Communists indulge in monologues. The possibility that intelligent, persistent questioning of such a friendly witness might be just as effective in producing results as in the treatment of an unfriendly witness seems not to have been recognized by the committee. When Louis Budenz appeared before the committee in 1946 he was allowed to talk at great length, and almost no effort was made by the committee to guide him. He was allowed to develop in great detail his thesis that there is a "conspiratorial apparatus" that lies back of the regular Communist Party organization. His testimony had the ring of sincerity and accuracy, and it unquestionably dealt with a highly significant aspect of the Communist movement. But his presentation was long-winded and disorderly, and the committee showed itself largely unable to direct his testimony on to topics that should have been of great interest to a Congressional body anxious to acquaint itself concerning all phases of Communist organization and tactics.[30] The committee has also made the mistake of allowing ex-Communists, such as Budenz, Chambers, and Bentley, to tell their stories in piecemeal fashion and to reveal significant bits of information as they happened to think of them or as suited their purposes. It is perhaps using the advantage of hindsight and demanding of members of the Un-American Activities Committee an intelligence and sophistication which few people possessed at the time to suggest that in the period 1946–1948 the committee did not make the most of its opportunity to query these witnesses vigorously and systematically. The committee was always somewhat awed by

[30] See pp. 35–36.

the Budenzes and Chamberses, and it allowed itself to be maneu-
vered into the position of regarding these men as "committee witnesses" upon whom it depended substantially for the development of
its hearings concerning espionage in the public service, in atomic
laboratories, and so forth. At times the committee was seemingly
afraid to question these witnesses vigorously for fear that their usefulness as witnesses for the prosecution might be impaired. Had the
committee questioned Chambers as vigorously as it questioned Alger
Hiss during the first phase of the Communist espionage hearings, it
might well have compelled Chambers to produce the Pumpkin
Papers months before he did, or it might have uncovered significant
bits of information concerning espionage in the government service
that came to light only much later during the two Hiss trials.

Half-hearted or otherwise poor questioning is readily illustrated.
For example, the questioning of Donald Hiss and Mrs. Alger Hiss in
1948 was very half-hearted. The committee had indicated great
interest in hearing Mrs. Hiss and had seemingly gone to great lengths
to arrange a session at which she could be present and testify. But,
when the hearing was finally held, only one member of the committee, Nixon, was present, and his questioning was exceedingly brief
and perfunctory. The entire printed record of the hearing occupies
less than two pages.[31]

The committee's failure to press Hiss and other witnesses for information pertaining to Hiss's actual record as a State Department
official would also seem to illustrate poor questioning. This policy
may have been deliberate, i.e., the committee may have been afraid
that it would discover no evidence of wrongdoing by Hiss as a public
servant and that such a line of questioning might boomerang in his
favor. Or it may have felt that as an alleged espionage agent Hiss
would have been careful not to let his Communist sympathies affect
his day-to-day work so that as a man above suspicion he could function more effectively as an espionage agent. But such explanations
are not quite adequate. The espionage angle did not loom large
until the December phase of the hearings. At first the Chambers
testimony merely stressed the idea that Hiss was a Communist
who had risen to a high post in the government. Moreover, as a staff

[31] Communist Espionage Hearings, pp. 928–933, 942–943, 955, 1011–1013.
Nixon later admitted to the author that persistent questioning of Mrs. Hiss at
this point might have elicited significant testimony from her. As it was, Mrs. Hiss
was exceedingly vague, could remember almost nothing, and Nixon apparently
gave up questioning her as a bad job almost at once.

member of the United States delegation to the Yalta Conference, as Secretary General of the San Francisco Conference, and as chief of the State Department Office of Special Political Affairs, Alger Hiss offered a splendid target for questioning concerning the substance of his ideas and his policies. The committee's relative lack of interest in developing this line of questioning is not easily explained.[32]

Again, the questioning of the hostile witnesses during the Hollywood hearings does not impress one as having been shrewd or intelligent. The committee allowed the witnesses to set the tone of the proceedings, matched their truculence and emotionalism, and, by pressing the question concerning membership in the Communist Party, seemed content to let them refuse to answer questions and to run the risk of punishment for contempt, when a more patient approach might have encouraged them to be more articulate on points of real significance to the subject under examination. At times, even the goal of contempt citations was endangered, for the questioning got out of hand to such an extent that the committee seemed to be forgetting the necessity of establishing a clear factual showing that the witnesses were refusing to answer pertinent questions.

Every Congressman who participates in committee hearings sooner or later runs the risk of appearing ridiculous by asking a silly question or making an absurd remark. But such blunders have been so common to Un-American Activities Committee hearings that it may fairly be said that they indicate a general lack of sophistication on the part of committee personnel with respect to the subject matter with which they are dealing. For example, the following passage from the 1948 Communist espionage hearings, amusing though it is, illustrates more than just a passing moment of foolishness or maladroitness on the part of a committee member, and unfortunately it is too easily matched with similar examples. (The committee was questioning one Robert Miller, a former State Department employee, who had been mentioned by Elizabeth Bentley in her testimony.)

[32] There were exceptions. At one point, Representative Mundt asked a series of questions which obtained from Hiss the information that he had helped draft portions of the Yalta agreement, that he had opposed the idea of giving three votes to the Soviet Union in the United Nations Assembly, that he had had nothing to do with the formulation of the State Department China policy in 1945, and that he had played a part in determining the veto provision of the United Nations charter. *Ibid.*, p. 657.

Mr. Hébert: How did [your wife] get to Russia? Why did she go there?

Mr. Miller: She went there during the depression because she was interested in dancing. She considered the Russians had the best ballet in the world.

Mr. Hébert: Would that be associated with the Academy of—Mr. Stripling, what is the name of that science academy?

Mr. Stripling: Academy of Science.

Mr. Hébert: The Academy of Science. What is that in Russia?

Mr. Miller: I frankly know very little about it. It is, I suppose, an organization where guidance is given in all kinds of scientific procedure.

Mr. Hébert: Was she a member of that academy?

Mr. Miller: Lord, no. The ballet had nothing to do with that.

Mr. McDowell: I didn't get the answer.

Mr. Miller: I said, no; she certainly had nothing to do with that. Some people would say that the ballet is a science, but I don't think she would.

Mr. Hébert: Did she have any connection at all with the Academy of Science?

Mr. Miller: No, sir.

Mr. Hébert: Do you know what the Academy of Science in Russia is?

Mr. Miller: Only as a name which I assume means an organization which is something like the one we have in this country where leading men in science are employed to give guidance and that sort of thing all over the country. I don't know a damned thing about it.

Mr. Hébert: In your two and a half years in Russia, you mean your inquisitiveness as a newspaper reporter wouldn't lead you to find out what everything means in Russia, what is going on in Russia?

Mr. Miller: Good gracious, sir; it is a big country. I applied myself quite diligently, I think, to learning as much as I could. I just didn't happen to hit the Academy of Science.[33]

There has been continuous controversy over the issue of the rights to be enjoyed by persons appearing before the committee. In part, this controversy reflects the absence of an established pattern for the conduct of hearings by Congressional committees generally. Moreover, many of the specific criticisms directed against the Un-American Activities Committee could almost as easily have been made against virtually every investigating committee which has dealt with controversial subject matter. There has been a tendency to take all such committees to task for their failure to grant to witnesses the procedural rights which are customarily extended in the criminal courts. The need for procedural reform in the conduct of Congressional investigations is undeniable. But the fact remains that up to the present there has been no general agreement as to the rights that

[33] *Ibid.,* p. 796.

a Congressional committee should extend to its witnesses, and few if any specific committees have ever gone so far as to grant their witnesses the same status they would enjoy in a courtroom.

Nonetheless, the Un-American Activities Committee has had more than its share of difficulty over procedural issues, and this almost certainly reflects an unusual degree of carelessness or irresponsibility on the part of the committee. It is perhaps unfair to lay too much stress upon the remark made by Chairman Thomas in an unguarded moment when he told an obstreperous lawyer who was serving a witness before the committee as counsel, "The rights you have are the rights given you by this committee. We will determine what rights you have and what rights you have not got before the committee." [34] And yet Thomas' angry remark is not too far away from the truth, at least with respect to the particular committee which he headed. In *The Red Plot Against America*, Stripling recognized that upon occasion the committee with which he was identified used vigorous methods in the treatment of its witnesses. But he insists that this was really the fault of the witnesses who "provoked" committee members to the use of controversial methods. He writes, "The Committee hears, by and large, a type of witness completely foreign to other Congressional committees in search of information. More often than not it is faced with subversives and fellow travelers who are superbly well trained and well advised in the incitement of public sentiment. The reactions of some members [of the Committee] to their type of testimony have been provoked very artfully." [35]

There has been more controversy over the right of witnesses before the committee to enjoy the assistance of counsel than over any other single procedural issue. Throughout the six-year period of the 79th, 80th, and 81st Congress, the Un-American Activities Committee showed itself reluctant to recognize this right on anything but a very narrow base. While there were moments when the committee seemed to be close to denying a witness any right to counsel,[36] it

[34] *Ibid.*, p. 1310.   [35] *The Red Plot*, p. 160.
[36] For example, in 1945 during the Communist Party hearings the following exchange took place between the committee and a witness, Jacob A. Stachel:
"*Mr. Adamson:* Mr. Stachel, will you be sworn?
"*Mr. Brodsky:* May I move my chair up closer to Mr. Stachel, so I can advise with him?
"*Mr. Thomas:* No.
"*Mr. Brodsky:* It would save a lot of time, because if he wants to consult with me you would simply have to wait till he comes back to me.
"*The Chairman* [*Wood*]: The policy of this committee, with all due regard,

was generally willing to allow a witness to be accompanied by counsel if he insisted upon it. But it extended this right very grudgingly in many instances; it frequently cast reflections upon witnesses because of their insistence upon enjoyment of the right; it attempted to discredit particular attorneys appearing before it; and it confined counsel to the narrow role of advising a client only with respect to his constitutional rights.[37]

The committee's general irritation with witnesses who insist upon being accompanied by counsel has been many times indicated.

is to never recognize counsel in these hearings." *Communist Party Hearings,* p. 36.

Again in 1946 during the abortive hearings on the Joint Anti-Fascist Refugee Committee the Un-American Activities Committee was very reluctant to let witnesses be accompanied by counsel, stating that it was not its policy to allow counsel in executive sessions. The following exchange of remarks took place with the first witness, Dr. Jacob Auslander. (The witness was duly sworn by the chairman.)

"*Dr. Auslander:* Mr. Chairman, may I ask my counsel to come in?

"*The Chairman* [*Wood*]: No; we do not have lawyers in here with the witnesses.

Dr. Auslander: May I ask you for permission, then, to consult with counsel if I believe I need to?

"*The Chairman:* You can confer with him at any time in answer to any questions that may be asked you." *Joint Anti-Fascist Refugee Committee Hearing,* p. 1.

Later the chairman made the following statement to another witness: "Mr. Lustig, during these hearings the committee policy has uniformly been that we do not permit lawyers in the committee room during executive sessions. If during the course of your examination any matter arises involving legal questions about which you desire to consult your counsel, you can go out and consult him." *Ibid.,* p. 27.

[37] When Hanns Eisler appeared as a witness in September, 1947, the following remarks were made relating to the issue of Eisler's enjoyment of the right to counsel:

"*The Chairman* [*Thomas*]: Well, first of all, is there any objection on the part of any member of the committee that Mr. Eisler be permitted counsel?

"*Mr. Rankin:* Mr. Chairman, I think the investigation should be conducted by the investigators, without outside interference.

"*The Chairman:* The investigation will be conducted by the investigators, and there will be no outside interference, I can assure you of that. Is there any objection that Mr. Eisler be permitted counsel? [No response.]

"*The Chairman:* Then, Mr. Eisler, you will be permitted counsel." *Hearings regarding Hanns Eisler,* p. 2. Later, Thomas said: "Mr. Eisler, it has been the custom of this committee to permit witnesses to have counsel, but the counsel can only advise the witness as to his constitutional rights. . . . You cannot, however, go beyond that. And if you do go beyond it, then the Chair will have to ask you to leave the witness table." *Ibid.,* p. 3.

When, for example, Alger Hiss in his fourth appearance before the committee was, for the first time, accompanied by counsel, there was an unmistakable undertone of displeasure on the part of committee members that the witness should have availed himself of this privilege. While Hiss was testifying, "an unknown person" conferred with Hiss's counsel, and Chairman Thomas abruptly interrupted the proceedings and demanded identification of this person.[38] When Thomas was quizzing Hiss as to whether he should or should not have been able to recognize a photograph of Whittaker Chambers at an earlier hearing, Hiss's lawyer tried to break into the exchange of remarks and was bluntly told by Thomas, "Never mind, you keep quiet." [39] Another time he was silenced by Mundt, who said, "I object, Mr. Chairman. I want Mr. Hiss to finish his statement without any interruption by counsel. You may speak afterwards." [40] Earlier, during the Communist espionage hearings, Mundt congratulated Lauchlin Currie for having appeared before the committee without counsel. He said, "I would like to have the record show that Mr. Currie, in addition to having answered questions in a forthright manner, came here without benefit of counsel to whisper in his ear the answers he should give to the committee. I think that is very commendable." [41]

[38] *Communist Espionage Hearings*, pp. 1082–1083. See also Chambers, *Witness*, pp. 635–636.

[39] *Communist Espionage Hearings*, p. 1143.   [40] *Ibid.*, p. 1161.

[41] *Ibid.*, p. 875. During Abraham George Silverman's appearance before the committee in the course of the Communist espionage hearings in 1948, the issue of counsel's participation in the proceedings was discussed as follows:

"*Mr. Nixon:* I raise the specific point that counsel can advise the witness on his constitutional rights, but counsel is not here to tell the witness what answers to make to the questions. Both of the last times counsel was giving the witness the answer to the question. From now on he should advise the witness as to his rights in each case.

.   .   .   .   .

"*The Chairman [Thomas]:* I would like to say, Mr. Counsel, let the witness answer these questions. Don't whisper in his ear every time that he wants to answer.

"*Mr. Jaffee:* I have no intention of doing that. I was simply advising him.

"*Mr. Mundt:* Regardless of your intention, you have been doing it. I have been watching what you said and the witness has parroted everything you said. Wait until the witness consults you" (pp. 842, 845).

During the testimony of Clarence Hiskey, a witness before the committee during the atomic espionage hearings in September, 1948, the following exchange took place:

"*The Chairman [Thomas]:* I might say to the counsel that it is proper for

The committee has also upon a number of occasions shown considerable interest in the private communications between a witness and his counsel and has not hesitated to encroach upon what is generally recognized, in judicial procedure at least, to be a confidential relationship. For example, both Mundt and Hébert showed great interest in Henry Julian Wadleigh's dealings with his counsel. Wadleigh appeared before the committee without counsel, stating, in response to a question, that by mutual agreement he and his counsel had parted company that morning. Mundt and Hébert were both interested in finding out how Wadleigh had first engaged his attorney and why he had later decided to dispense with his services.[42]

him to advise the witness on constitutional questions and only constitutional questions.
    "*Mr. Colloms [counsel for Hiskey]*: I am aware of that, Mr. Thomas.

                      .   .   .   .   .

    "*The Chairman:* Now, the record will show that the witness, after almost every question, has referred to his counsel, and I say to both the witness and to counsel that we have got a great many questions to ask. We will expect answers, and the witness can answer of his own free will and accord. He doesn't have to get advice on every single question.
    "*Mr. Hiskey:* Well, this particular question involves a matter of security." *1948 Atom Bomb Hearings,* pp. 3–4.
    And during the Hollywood hearings, Oct., 1947, the following exchange took place between Eric Johnston, Stripling, and Thomas:
    "*Mr. Stripling:* Mr. Johnston, are you represented by counsel?
    "*Mr. Johnston:* I am.
    "*Mr. Stripling:* Do you desire counsel?
    "*Mr. Johnston:* Mr. McNutt has been hired by the Motion Picture Association. He is here with me.
    "*Mr. Stripling:* As a witness, do you desire counsel?
    "*Mr. Johnston:* As a witness, I do not need counsel.
    "*Mr. Stripling:* For what purpose will Mr. McNutt serve?
    "*Mr. Johnston:* Mr. McNutt represents the association. I think it is wise for him to stay here with me.
    "*Mr. Stripling:* You are the witness.
    "*Mr. Johnston:* That is right.
    "*Mr. Stripling:* And you don't desire counsel yourself?
    "*Mr. Johnston:* No.
    "*The Chairman:* Well, if he would feel any better by having Mr. McNutt next to him, why, it will be all right for Mr. McNutt to sit next to him.
    "*Mr. Johnston:* He may need to hold my hand, Mr. Stripling." *Hearings regarding the Communist Infiltration of the Motion Picture Industry,* pp. 304–305.
    [42] "*Mr. Russell:* Mr. Wadleigh, you have consulted an attorney, have you not?
    "*Mr. Wadleigh:* I have consulted an attorney, but I am not now represented by one.
    "*Mr. Russell:* Do you desire counsel?

During the Hollywood hearings the committee frequently indicated its displeasure with the role being played by counsel, particularly during the appearance of the unfriendly witnesses upon the stand. At one point the questioning of Albert Maltz was interrupted, and Robert W. Kenny, who with Bartley Crum had appeared with Maltz as his counsel, was suddenly called to the stand and sworn. The committee then proceeded to question him at some length concerning an article that had appeared in the *Washington Times-Herald* the same day to the effect that Kenny was advising all of the unfriendly witnesses to refuse to say whether they were members of the Communist Party. Kenny refused to say whether he had advised his clients not to answer the question concerning party

---

"Mr. Wadleigh: I would have preferred to come here with counsel.

"Mr. Mundt: Why couldn't you bring counsel with you?

"Mr. Wadleigh: In consultation with my attorney this morning it was mutually agreed that he would no longer represent me.

"Mr. Mundt: What was the name of that attorney?

"Mr. Wadleigh: Herman Greenberg.

"Mr. Mundt: Of what firm?

"Mr. Wadleigh: Greenberg—

"Mr. Russell: Forer and Rein.

"Mr. Wadleigh: Forer and Rein, that is correct.

"Mr. Mundt: The Chair has a question of our committee counsel at this stage. Has Mr. Greenberg, or any member of his firm, the firm of Greenberg, Forer, and Rein, appeared before a committee previously to testify or support the testimony of a witness?

"Mr. Russell: They have.

"Mr. Mundt: Who?

"Mr. Russell: Gerhart Eisler and numerous subjects who were mentioned during the course of the Bentley hearings.

"Mr. Mundt: The same firm has represented those witnesses as the one consulted by Mr. Wadleigh?

"Mr. Russell: That is true.

"Mr. Mundt: Proceed with your questioning.

"Mr. Rankin: Now, Mr. Chairman, I think the record ought to show at this point that those witnesses you referred to who were found to be members of the Communist Party [*sic*].

"Mr. Mundt: That is correct.

. . . . .

"Mr. Mundt: Mr. Wadleigh, the Chair would like to refer for a moment to the statement you made earlier that in consultation this morning with Mr. Greenberg it was mutually agreed that he would not represent you at these hearings. I think I have quoted you correctly, have I not?

"Mr. Wadleigh: That is correct.

"Mr. Mundt: I would like to ask you whether you were contacted by any third

membership, pleading that the committee was encroaching upon the privacy of the client-counsel relationship. Thereupon, Thomas proceeded to read Kenny the federal conspiracy act, implying that Kenny and his clients might have committed a criminal offense if they had deliberately agreed that the latter as witnesses should place themselves in contempt of the committee by refusing to answer its questions.[43]

Perhaps the most serious conflict between the committee and its witnesses over the issue of counsel took place during the Communist espionage hearings in 1948 when the committee was hearing William Rosen and his wife. Chambers had accused Hiss of having disposed of a 1929 Ford roadster by giving it to a member of the Communist Party, instead of lending or giving it to him as claimed by Hiss. Committee investigators discovered from the records of the Department of Motor Vehicles in the District of Columbia that Hiss had transferred title to the car to the Cherner Motor Company in July, 1936, and that on the same day the company had transferred title to a William Rosen. As a witness before the committee, Rosen

---

party, any third party at all, suggesting to you that you terminate your connections with Mr. Greenberg in connection with this case?

"*Mr. Wadleigh:* Nobody made any such suggestion to me.

"*Mr. Mundt:* Was the termination of your consultation with Mr. Greenberg as a result of your suggestion or his?

"*Mr. Wadleigh:* That is a matter which developed in discussions between counsel and client, sir.

"*Mr. Mundt:* You do not care to inform the committee?

"*Mr. Wadleigh:* I understand that it is my right not to divulge what took place in such consultations.

"*Mr. Mundt:* You do not have to, I am simply asking you whether you cared to give that information to the committee, or not. You are not required to do so.

"*Mr. Wadleigh:* I would prefer not to do so without consulting Mr. Greenberg first." *Communist Espionage Hearings*, pp. 1432, 1438. See also pp. 1444–1445.

[43] *Mot. Pict. Ind. Hearings*, pp. 367 ff. Kenny ultimately took the position that the newspaper article was not entirely accurate. Thereupon, the following exchange took place between Thomas and Kenny:

"*The Chairman:* I will tell you, Mr. Kenny, as chairman, I want to let you know that you squirmed out of this one temporarily, but if the committee should determine that is a violation of this Conspiracy Act, then the committee will take under consideration referring the matter to the United States attorney.

"*Mr. Kenny:* That is right, Mr. Thomas. I might say that the committee has squirmed out of one too, because I am sure that committee did not intend to invade the sacred province of relationship between attorney and client.

"*The Chairman:* Oh, no; and neither would you want to commit conspiracy" (p. 369).

refused to answer all significant questions on the ground of self-incrimination. The hearing was an acrimonious one, and Rosen's counsel, Maurice Braverman, interrupted the questioning a number of times. Finally, Stripling demanded that Braverman be sworn so that the committee could question him. Braverman refused to be sworn, on the grounds that as Rosen's counsel it was improper for the committee to seek to turn him into a witness and also that he was entitled to obtain his own counsel if he were going to appear as witness.[44] In the face of this resistance by Braverman the committee backed down. But a little later, when Mrs. Rosen was on the stand, much the same situation developed again:

Mrs. Rosen: I refuse to answer this question on the ground that any answer I give may tend to incriminate me.

The Chairman [Thomas]: I am getting pretty sick of this refusing to answer questions on the ground that it might incriminate you, when some of the questions haven't got anything to do with whether or not this person is a member of the Communist Party. You will have to be more responsive.

Mr. Stripling: Mr. Chairman, perhaps counsel can explain to the committee why the witness is answering in this manner.

Mr. Braverman: Are you asking me?

Mr. Stripling: Yes.

Mr. Braverman: I merely advised my client as to what I think are her constitutional rights.

[44] "*Mr. Stripling:* . . . I would suggest that the chairman swear counsel. I have a few questions I would like to ask counsel.

"*Mr. McDowell:* Stand up and raise your right hand.

"*Mr. Braverman:* I will stand up, but I refuse to be sworn in as a witness in this case. I am counsel.

"*Mr. McDowell:* Get a subpena.

"*Mr. Braverman:* Mr. McDowell, will you permit me to call counsel?

"*Mr. McDowell:* Well, no; there has been no action taken yet. Wait a minute.

"*Mr. Braverman:* I would like to call counsel before I am subpenaed.

"*Mr. McDowell:* There has been no subpena yet. Just wait a minute until you need counsel.

. . . . .

"*Mr. Stripling:* I ask you now: Will you take the oath?

"*Mr. Braverman:* No; I won't.

"*Mr. Stripling:* Why?

"*Mr. Braverman:* For the simple reason that I am here representing Mr. Rosen. I think any attempt to put me under oath is an attempt to intimidate my client and hurt my professional relations between attorney and client. I have a perfect right to appear as attorney for my client, and I think the committee has no right to ask questions regarding relations between me and my client." *Communist Espionage Hearings,* pp. 1215–1216.

Mr. Stripling: Will you tell the committee why answering whether or not she is a member of the Communist Party will incriminate her?

Mr. Braverman: I feel I have a right to advise my client to the best of my ability, Mr. Stripling.

. . . . .

Mr. Stripling: And that is your answer?

Mr. Braverman: That is my answer.

Mr. Stripling: And you intend to appear here with further witnesses?

Mr. Braverman: As long as I have the right to practice law and unless I am barred by this committee. I don't know on what grounds that could be.

Mr. Stripling: I think counsel coming before this committee should come here in good faith, and I think the committee should now consider whether you are here in good faith.

Mr. Braverman: I believe I am here in good faith.

. . . . .

The Chairman [Thomas]: Mr. Counsel, will you stand and be sworn? Please stand and be sworn, because we want to ask some questions about this matter and it is very important and we want sworn testimony.

Mr. Braverman: Mr. Thomas, I will state as I stated before, that I am not here as a witness. I am here as counsel.

The Chairman: From now on you are here as a witness.

Mr. Braverman: Before I appear as a witness I would like the privilege of consulting counsel and being represented by counsel before this committee.

The Chairman: Is your counsel present now?

Mr. Braverman: No.

The Chairman: Do you refuse to be sworn?

Mr. Braverman: I refuse to be sworn and appear as a witness until I have the right of counsel. I want counsel present to advise me.

The Chairman: I will have to insist that you be sworn now. Raise your right hand or I will hold you in contempt.

Mr. Braverman: I am sorry, I do not want to be in contempt of this committee, but if I am sworn as a witness I want the right to consult counsel.

The Chairman: We want to ask you two or three simple little questions and we think the testimony should be sworn testimony, so if you will just please oblige the committee by raising your right hand—

Mr. Braverman: If this committee will allow me the right to have counsel present when I am here as a witness, I will be happy to be sworn as a witness.

Mr. Stripling: The witness has just given the committee a dissertation

of his familiarity with the rights and privileges of witnesses. I don't think
he needs counsel.

The Chairman: Do you have questions you want to ask him?

Mr. Stripling: Yes.

The Chairman: I think it should be sworn testimony.

Mr. Stripling: I do, too.

Mr. Braverman: Mr. Thomas, I can repeat I have a right to be represented by counsel, if I appear here as a witness. I have not been subpenaed. I appear here as counsel.

The Chairman: The rights you have are the rights given you by this
committee. We will determine what rights you have and what rights you
have not got before the committee. I insist you be sworn at the present
time. So please raise your right hand.[45]

In spite of this threatening language by Thomas, Braverman still
refused to be sworn and once more the committee backed down.
However, it now proceeded to subpoena Braverman in the usual
manner, and on the next day he appeared as a witness accompanied by
his own counsel. Braverman was then asked pointblank whether he
was a member of the Communist Party and whether he had been
put in touch with Rosen through the party. Braverman refused to
answer these questions on the grounds that they encroached improperly upon the client-attorney relationship and also encroached
upon his rights under the First and Fifth amendments.[46]

During the 1949 hearings regarding communism in the District
of Columbia, Representative Velde, in a seeming effort to discredit
a witness's counsel, went so far as to imply that Clifford Durr, who
represented the witness, John Anderson, as counsel, had perhaps
earlier used his post as a member of the Federal Communications
Commission to render an improper favor to a business enterprise in
which the witness was interested:

Mr. Velde: How long have you known your attorney, Mr. Durr?

Mr. Anderson: I have known Mr. Durr about a year, I guess.

Mr. Velde: Did you know him at the time you got this stock in WQQW?

Mr. Anderson: I didn't know Mr. Durr. If I had met Mr. Durr, I would
not have known who he was. I knew there was a Mr. Durr, but I didn't
know him.

[45] *Ibid.,* pp. 1308–1310.

[46] *Ibid.,* pp. 1342–1346. For other instances of committee efforts to discredit
particular attorneys appearing before it see: *Hearings regarding Hanns Eisler,*
p. 158; *1947 Hearings regarding Communism in Labor Unions,* pp. 109, 122–
123.

Mr. Velde: Did you know he was on the Federal Communications Commission at that time?

Mr. Anderson: I saw his name as a Government official from time to time.

Mr. Velde: Do you know if he assisted in getting a license for Station WQQW?

Mr. Anderson: I don't know that.

Mr. Durr: Congressman, if you want to go into the question of my connection with Station WQQW, I will be glad to appear before this committee at any time.

Mr. Velde: That is up to the committee. That is all.[47]

It may be admitted that in certain of the instances where the committee came into conflict with counsel there was some reason to believe that attorneys representing witnesses were themselves members of the Communist Party or had expressly advised Communist clients to utilize the self-incrimination ground as a means of avoiding testimony. But this was obviously not true in all such situations, and in any case it is exceedingly doubtful whether the committee had sufficient provocation to concern itself with counsel to the extent that it did. In refusing to testify on the ground of self-incrimination or on other grounds, witnesses were running a considerable risk. As it turned out, in several hearings, notably the Hollywood one, numerous witnesses ultimately went to jail for their failure to answer questions. This would seem to constitute a sufficient hazard for a nonco-operative witness without the necessity of threatening his attorney because of advice given a client. Thomas' action in bullying Robert Kenny by reading him the text of the conspiracy act remains one of the low points in the history of the committee's procedures.

Attention should be given to the role that counsel has been permitted to play during committee sessions. In general, counsel has remained silent, and this is very much a part of the tradition of Congressional investigations. Occasionally, counsel has tried to play the more active role common to attorneys in judicial proceedings. For example, in the Hollywood hearings there occurred an interesting attempt to use the motion to quash the proceedings. Three attorneys representing nineteen clients notified Chairman Thomas by wire that when the hearings opened on the first day they would move to quash the subpoenas on the ground that the investigation constituted an unlawful attempt "to control the content of motion

[47] *Hearings regarding Communism in the District of Columbia—Part I,* p. 713.

pictures through censorship and political intimidation." [48] When the hearings opened Thomas refused to let Kenny or Crum argue their motion orally, but the committee did accept a written brief. When the first unfriendly witness, John Howard Lawson, was heard a week later, Kenny renewed his efforts, and the committee in effect allowed him to make a short oral argument and to present "two additional evidences" of the illegality of the proceedings based upon the proceedings of the previous week, namely, that the committee was trying to dictate to producers the content of films and to induce them to maintain a blacklist. Kenny asserted, "Both of these . . . indicate an unconstitutional purpose . . . to invade the domain protected by the first amendment. . . ." [49] Upon hearing this oral argument Chairman Thomas announced that the committee would go into executive session to consider the issue. It did so and reconvened shortly, at which time the chairman announced "the decision on the brief" in the following words:

No committee of Congress has the right to establish its own legality or constitutionality. A committee of Congress cannot disqualify itself from the provisions of the law. We operate under Public Law 601. We cannot set aside this law to suit the convenience of certain witnesses or their counsel. As a former attorney general of California you certainly know that your remedy, if any, is in the courts. [50]

From time to time attorneys appearing before the committee have asked for permission to question their clients or to cross-examine other witnesses, but invariably these requests have been denied. [51] During the Communist espionage hearings the lawyer representing

[48] *N.Y. Herald Tribune*, Oct. 20, 1947.

[49] *Mot. Pict. Ind. Hearings*, p. 288. In the written brief it was argued that the Un-American Activities Committee was illegal and unconstitutional "both in the manner in which the authority given to it by the Congress has been executed, and by the terms of that authority itself."

[50] *Ibid.*, p. 289. During the Hollywood hearing, Paul V. McNutt as counsel for the Motion Picture Association asked for, and was given, permission to read a statement protesting statements made by Chairman Thomas while Eric Johnston, president of the MPAA, was testifying before the committee, that Johnston or his assistants had brought pressure on the committee to call off or postpone the Hollywood hearings (pp. 360–363).

[51] For example, during the Hollywood hearings, when John Howard Lawson was called as a witness, his attorney, Bartley Crum, requested the right of crossexamination and asked the committee to call back some ten witnesses who had testified during the first week of hearings so that they might be cross-examined. Thomas immediately denied the request. *Ibid.*, p. 289.

a witness, Alexander Koral, was in effect allowed to enter objections to one or two questions asked his client, but these objections were overruled, and Chairman Thomas soon put a stop to the procedure, insisting that counsel had no right to enter objections.[52]

In the final analysis, an attorney representing a witness before the Un-American Activities Committee can do virtually nothing for him beyond advising him what his chances are of avoiding a successful prosecution for contempt if he refuses to answer certain questions put to him. It should be repeated again that virtually the same statement can be made about attorneys and witnesses appearing before any Congressional committee. But because the Un-American Activities Committee has personalized its hearings to a degree seldom reached by other committees of Congress, the inability of counsel to render to a witness the kind of assistance he could give were his client a defendant in a court trial becomes a serious matter.

There has been much argument through the years over the right of witnesses before the Un-American Activities Committee to make prepared statements. The committee has never recognized a general right on the part of witnesses to make oral statements. On the other hand, the committee has usually been willing to receive from a witness and place in the record a written statement, provided the substance of the statement is regarded as pertinent to the matter under investigation, and provided the witness has co-operated with the committee by answering its questions or has not otherwise irritated or angered it. This policy was illustrated during the 79th Congress when the committee heard Gerald L. K. Smith in January, 1946. Smith asked to submit a rather long statement to which he had given the flamboyant title, "A Petition for Redress of Grievances and for an Investigation into Promoted Terrorism, Denial of Civil Liberty, Conspiracy against Freedom, Organized Character Assassination, Corrupt Practice, Organized Rioting, Etc." It was accepted for printing in the published volume of the hearing. This, however, did not satisfy Representative Rankin and the following exchange of remarks took place:

[52] *Communist Espionage Hearings*, pp. 704–711. Thomas was characteristically rude in silencing Koral's attorney. The record bristles with such phrases as, "You keep quiet a few seconds," "You will please be quiet," "I just want you to be quiet." Granted that the attorney was seeking to play a role seldom, if ever, granted attorneys representing witnesses before Congressional committees, Thomas, here as elsewhere, seemed unable to control the proceedings in a manner befitting the dignity and tradition of an agency of the Congress of the United States.

Mr. Smith: I appeal for the right to make a 15 minute statement in this committee.

Mr. Thomas: No, I have asked a simple question. He has been charged with being anti-Semitic, and I want to know whether he thinks he has been anti-Semitic or not. That can be answered very quickly.

Mr. Smith: I insist on answering that with my statement, because I have prepared the answer to your question, Mr. Congressman, deliberately, knowing that such a question would be raised, and I prefer—rather than to speak extemporaneously, I prefer to speak for the record from the manuscript I have prepared for the purpose of answering this very question.

The Chairman [Wood]: Your statement, Mr. Smith, is in the record that you hold in your hand.

Mr. Rankin: Mr. Chairman, if this man wants to read his statement or make a statement to the committee under these charges, I think he should be permitted to do so. [Applause.]

The Chairman: There will be no applause in this hearing.

Mr. Rankin: Everyone we have brought here who did not resist the subpena of this committee—everyone we have brought since I have been a member of this committee has been permitted to make a statement, every single one of them.

The Chairman: On the contrary, since I have been connected with the committee there has been no statement submitted to be read to the committee, and I see no reason to deviate from the rule. I have held that this statement may be placed in the record.[53]

As it turned out, Representatives Thomas and Rankin continued to insist that they wanted to hear Smith's statement, and before the hearing was over he was allowed to read long sections of it.[54]

At the first public hearing conducted by the committee during the 80th Congress, Chairman Thomas told the witness, Gerhart Eisler, "It is not the policy of this committee to permit witnesses to make a statement. After you have completed your testimony, if you desire to make a statement, the committee will permit you to put it in the record at the conclusion of your testimony." [55] Thereafter, Eisler refused to be sworn by the committee. As a result he gave no testimony, and the committee did not receive his statement, although it was apparently distributed to newsmen in the committee room by his attorney.[56]

[53] *Gerald L. K. Smith Hearing,* pp. 23–24.   [54] See *ibid.,* pp. 38 ff.
[55] *Hearings on Gerhart Eisler,* p. 2.
[56] *Ibid.,* p. 4. Another example of the committee's practice in 1947 with respect to statements is seen in the following exchange of remarks which took place during the hearings concerning communism in labor unions:

There have been many exceptions to the general policy outlined in the preceding paragraph. During the Hollywood hearing in 1947, the committee vacillated greatly with respect to the making of statements. Many of the friendly witnesses had no statements. Those who did, such as Sam Warner and Louis Mayer, were usually permitted to read their statements at the beginning of their testimony.[57] Paul McNutt and Eric Johnston were permitted to read statements highly critical of the committee at the beginning of their testimony.[58]

When it came time to hear the ten unfriendly witnesses the committee was seemingly unable to decide upon and follow any con-

---

"*Mr. Stripling:* I have questions I want to ask him, but he has asked permission to make a statement. I was going to ask him if his statement is in written form.

"*Mr. McCrea:* Yes, sir; it is.

"*Mr. Stripling:* Would you care to submit it to the chairman first? The procedure of the committee, Mr. McCrea, is to ask questions, then if the witness has a statement the committee will consider having him read it. [The statement referred to was handed to the chairman.]

"*Mr. Stripling:* Mr. Chairman, I suggest that the witness be permitted to read the statement.

"*The Chairman:* Any objection? [No response.]

"*The Chairman:* All right, Mr. McCrea; you may read the statement.

"*Mr. Stripling:* Mr. McCrea—

"*Mr. Nixon:* May I ask a question?

"*The Chairman:* Mr. Nixon.

"*Mr. Nixon:* The copies of the statement are already in the hands of the committee, and I think, for the record, that we shall have an understanding as to the procedure; the statement is in order because it relates to the facts which have been brought out in this investigation, and it is an attempt by the witness to refute those facts. That is the reason that it is being read.

"*The Chairman:* The Chair agrees.

"*Mr. Stripling:* Is your statement the same as this press release which was distributed this morning?

"*Mr. McCrea:* Yes.

"*Mr. Bonner:* I would like to ask one question before the statement is read. Mr. McCrea, I am in favor of your reading the statement. After you read the statement, are you going to submit yourself to questions about this matter?

"*Mr. McCrea:* Yes; I would be glad to.

"*The Chairman:* All right; proceed." *1947 Hearings regarding Communism in Labor Unions,* pp. 116–117.

[57] *Mot. Pict. Ind. Hearings,* pp. 9, 70. In the case of Roy Brewer, a friendly witness who testified concerning the Communist influence in Hollywood labor unions, he was told at the beginning of his testimony that everything in the statement could be substantiated through questioning. However, at the end of his testimony he was permitted to read the statement (pp. 343, 356).

[58] *Ibid.,* pp. 305, 360.

sistent policy. Each of the ten men had a prepared statement which he asked permission to read as soon as he took the witness chair. It may be presumed that all of the statements were highly critical of the committee and contained vigorous language. In each instance the chairman asked to see the statement, and a cursory examination of it was made by him and other committee members before he ruled on the witness' request. The first of the unfriendly witnesses, John Howard Lawson, was denied permission to read his statement. After a brief examination of it Thomas stated, "I don't care to read any more of the statement. The statement will not be read. I read the first line. . . . I refuse you to make [sic] the statement, because of the first sentence in your statement. That statement is not pertinent to the inquiry." [59] Dalton Trumbo, the second of the unfriendly witnesses, was similarly treated. However, with Albert Maltz, the third witness, the committee suddenly reversed its policy and permitted him to read his full statement at the beginning of his testimony, even though it showed bitter opposition to the committee.[60] Maltz was followed by Alvah Bessie, who was permitted to read the opening and closing paragraphs of his statement, the remainder being received and incorporated in the printed record of the hearings.[61] Having made this generous gesture to two of the unfriendly witnesses, the committee once more about-faced, and the next four witnesses were all refused permission to read or submit their statements, the refusal being justified in each instance because the statement contained "vilification" and/or was not pertinent to the inquiry. The next-to-the-last of this group of witnesses, Ring Lardner, Jr., was told he could read his statement after the completion of his testimony, but he promptly got into the same squabble with the committee over refusal to answer the question as to membership in the Communist Party as had his colleagues, and he was dismissed from the stand without further reference to the statement.[62] The last member of the group, Lester Cole, was denied permission to read or submit his statement.

During the Communist espionage hearings in 1948 the committee adhered to a somewhat more consistent policy. Elizabeth Bentley, the first witness, had no prepared statement and submitted at once to questioning. The second witness, Whittaker Chambers, had a

[59] *Ibid.*, p. 290.   [60] *Ibid.*, p. 364.   [61] *Ibid.*, p. 383.
[62] *Ibid.*, pp. 480 ff. Thomas indulged in some rather childish bargaining with Lardner. When the latter began to balk at answering the committee's questions, Thomas said, "Now, Mr. Lardner, don't do like the others, if I were you [sic], or you will never read your statement. I would suggest—."

statement which he was allowed to read almost immediately after he took the witness chair.[63] The third witness was Nathan Gregory Silvermaster, who had been named by Miss Bentley as the leader of a group of Communist espionage agents in the federal government. Upon being sworn, Silvermaster immediately asked for permission to read a statement. The statement was received and examined by the committee, and it appeared that Stripling and Rankin had objections to parts of it, although Mundt, who was acting as chairman, announced it might be read "at the proper time." [64] Almost immediately, however, Stripling informed the chairman that he would like to have the witness read his statement and this was done. In the course of this rather brief statement, Silvermaster said, "The charges made by Miss Bentley are false and fantastic. I can only conclude that she is a neurotic liar." [65] Thereafter, Silvermaster refused to answer most of the questions put to him, including one as to whether he had ever known Miss Bentley, on the ground of self-incrimination. Representative Nixon in very telling fashion then proceeded to tax the witness concerning an inconsistency between his calling Miss Bentley's charges "false and fantastic" and his refusal to say whether he knew Miss Bentley or to say whether her specific charge that he had maintained a photographic laboratory in his home was true or not.[66] It may well be that Stripling and Nixon saw the advantage of letting Silvermaster read his statement at an early stage in the hearing because of its flat repudiation of the Bentley charges and in effect set a trap for him, knowing that he was going to refuse to answer specific questions on the ground of self-incrimination. In any case, this episode showed the advantage from the committee's own point of view of first letting a witness read a prepared statement and then subjecting him to questioning over the ground covered in the statement. Had this same technique been used during the Hollywood hearings it is entirely possible that, by allowing the unfriendly witnesses to read their statements when they first took the witness

[63] *Communist Espionage Hearings*, p. 564.
[64] "*Mr. Mundt:* The statement is perfectly pertinent to the inquiry and may be read at the proper time.
"*Mr. Rankin:* Let me call attention to a discrepancy there.
"*Mr. Mundt:* We will go into the discrepancies at a later time.
"*Mr. Stripling:* There is one portion I would like to call attention to, Mr. Chairman.
"*Mr. Mundt:* I think we probably should take the statement as a whole and not out of context. We had better wait until the proper time." *Ibid.*, p. 587.
[65] *Ibid.*, p. 590.   [66] *Ibid.*, pp. 594, 604.

stand, a basis would have been laid for questions which the witnesses would have found it difficult not to answer, or which, if not answered, would have placed them in a less enviable light than they actually occupied.

In the espionage hearings this technique was used effectively on William Ullmann and Abraham Silverman. Both made more or less categorical denials of the Bentley charges in their prepared statements, but both refused to answer questions as to the truth or falsity of specific charges made by Miss Bentley, on the ground that they might incriminate themselves in replying.[67] Virtually all of the other witnesses who testified during the espionage hearings who wished to read prepared statements were permitted to do so either immediately upon taking the witness chair or shortly thereafter.[68] A notable exception occurred on August 25 when the public confrontation between Alger Hiss and Whittaker Chambers took place.. Soon after taking the stand in the morning Hiss asked to be allowed to read a statement. Thomas rather petulantly inquired whether the statement was the same as a letter which Hiss had sent to Thomas and had also released to the press. Stripling then advised Thomas to defer the reading of the statement. Hiss renewed his request several times, but it was not until the end of a long day's session, after Hiss had been subjected to prolonged and searching questioning, and after Nixon and Mundt had both made long statements of their own summarizing the Hiss-Chambers case to date and drawing conclusions from the evidence submitted up to that point, that Hiss was allowed to read his statement.[69] This petty treatment of Hiss was certainly not fair under the circumstances. What is more important, the statement, if introduced early in the day, might well have provided a basis for more intelligent questioning. In view of the spectacular developments in the Hiss-Chambers case that were to come months later, there is always the possibility that a different line of questioning might have resulted in an earlier denouement in the case. In his statement, Hiss challenged the committee to explore his record as a public officer carefully for evidence of wrongdoing. The failure of the committee ever to do this in systematic fashion remains

[67] *Ibid.*, pp. 774, 844.

[68] In addition to those already mentioned, prepared statements were read by: Alger Hiss, *Communist Espionage Hearings*, p. 642; Victor Perlo, p. 699; Duncan Lee, p. 723; Henry Collins, p. 805; Lauchlin Currie, p. 852; Harry White, p. 878; Bela Gold, p. 907; Sonia Gold, p. 913; Frank Coe, p. 916; and Donald Hiss, p. 928.

[69] *Ibid.*, pp. 1077, 1124, 1126, 1147, 1149, 1157, and 1160.

a weakness in its handling of the case. In this statement Hiss also asked permission to have certain questions put to Chambers. This permission was granted, but, perhaps because this development took place toward the end of a long and tiring day, Chambers was not pressed very hard to give full answers to some of the questions.[70]

In 1949 during the course of the hearings concerning communism in the District of Columbia, the committee reverted to its earlier policy of not permitting the making of statements by witnesses who otherwise failed to co-operate with the committee. For example, Rose Anderson was denied permission to make a statement because she had "not condescended to answer any of [the committee's] questions." [71]

The record which the Un-American Activities Committee has made since 1945 in squabbling with numerous witnesses over the making of prepared statements is outstanding for its futility. It may be granted that virtually all of the statements that were barred were marked by vilification and distortion. Nonetheless, in refusing permission to certain witnesses to make such statements the committee allowed itself to be drawn down to the level set by the truculent witnesses and opened itself to the charge of unfair treatment of them. In almost every instance, banned statements were released to the press, and while they were seldom carried in full by many papers their content was certainly not effectively suppressed by the committee's action in refusing to allow them to be read or received for the record. It is difficult to see what possible harm could have been done in any instance by allowing a statement to be read publicly

[70] For example, one of the questions asked Chambers was for a full bibliography of all of his writings under every name he had used. Virtually no effort was made to get Chambers to answer this question, which was surely a significant one. *Ibid.*, pp. 1177, 1188. Nixon, who was putting the questions to Chambers, stated that Chambers should submit such a bibliography to the committee at a later date, but there is no evidence that he ever did so, and if he did submit a list of his writings it was never made public.

[71] *Hearings regarding Communism in the District of Columbia*—Part I, p. 698. The record on this point is as follows:

"*Mrs. Anderson:* Can I make a statement now?

"*Mr. Wood:* You can leave it with the reporter for the benefit of the record.

"*Mrs. Anderson:* May I read it?

"*Mr. Walter:* In view of the fact the witness has not condescended to answer any of our questions, I don't think we should accord to her any privilege of making a statement.

"*Mr. Harrison:* I am in agreement with that, Mr. Chairman.

"*Mr. Wood:* If the witness wants to leave a statement for the reference of the Committee, she may do so."

and placed in the printed record. At the worst, committee members might have had to listen to outbursts of bombast and propaganda, but they could have done so in the knowledge that witnesses who resorted to extreme language in their statements often condemned themselves far more effectively than the committee itself could do. At best, the reading of the statements might have provided a basis for telling questioning of a witness, as was true in the cases of Silvermaster, Ullmann, and Silverman during the Communist espionage hearings.

The Un-American Activities Committee has never recognized in any formal sense the right of cross-examination. In refusing this right the committee has had the precedents on its side so far as the practice of Congressional investigating committees is concerned. Nonetheless, the issue continues to be raised from time to time. During the Hollywood hearings, it came up repeatedly. At the very beginning of the hearings, Bartley Crum claimed the right for his clients:

Mr. Crum: May we ask if we have a right to cross-examine?

The Chairman: You may not ask one more thing at this time. Please be seated.

Mr. Crum: Certainly American [sic].[72]

A few minutes later Paul McNutt got a more definitive ruling on the same point:

Mr. McNutt: . . . I should like to make a request to be permitted to cross-examine witnesses.

The Chairman: You will not have that permission. It is not the policy of the committee to permit counsel to cross-examine witnesses. You will only have the right, the solemn right, to advise your client, the witness, on his constitutional rights. Nothing else. You are no different from any of the other attorneys who have appeared before this committee this year in the many hearings we have had. . . .[73]

On the second day of the hearing, while John Moffitt, motion picture critic for *Esquire* magazine, was testifying, a "Mr. Katz," who announced that he represented a number of persons who had been subpoenaed, interrupted the proceedings, asked for permission to cross-examine Moffitt, and was ejected from the room.

Mr. Stripling: . . . Now, Mr. Moffitt, as a writer in Hollywood and as a critic, could you name for the committee any writers that you consider to be Communists who are employed in the motion-picture industry?

[72] *Mot. Pict. Ind. Hearings,* p. 4.   [73] *Ibid.,* p. 7.

Mr. Katz: Mr. Thomas, I represent a number of persons who have been subpenaed—

The Chairman: I am very sorry. You are out of order. We have a witness on the stand, so please go back and sit down.

Mr. Katz: You have said—

The Chairman: I said you are out of order.

Mr. Katz: You have said you want a fair hearing. Cross-examination is necessary.

The Chairman: Will you take this man out of the room, please? Put him out of the room.

Go ahead with the testimony.

We must have order in these chambers, or we will be inclined to clear the room of the audience.[74]

Again at the beginning of the second week of hearings, Robert Kenny asked permission to recall a number of witnesses for cross-examination, and the request was abruptly denied.[75]

During the Communist espionage hearings the following year, an interesting exchange of remarks took place between the committee and one of its witnesses on the subject of cross-examination. The witness was Frank Coe, who had been named by Elizabeth Bentley as a member of one of the Communist groups in the federal service with which she said she had been in touch as a Communist courier. Coe denied all of Miss Bentley's charges against him and answered all questions put to him by the committee. In his prepared statement, which he was allowed to read, Coe said:

One of the members of this committee has been reported as saying that these hearings would leave the decision to public opinion. If public opinion is to decide, surely the committee ought to hear witnesses on behalf of the accused. Such witnesses should be heard and cross-examined, and Miss Bentley should likewise be cross-examined. The public would not find such testimony as exciting as the original accusation, but at least all the facts would be available.

I understand that this committee has previously decided against using such procedures on the ground that, though they may be incumbent on a court, they are not desirable for a legislative committee. It seems to me, however, that this committee does in fact function as a criminal court. Before this committee there are accusers and accused, just as in a court. The accused are punished. The grave and sensational charges which are made here are given wide publicity, and that is a cruel punishment. It hurts the accused, his family, and his friends and associates.

The peculiarity of this court is that all who are accused before it are

[74] *Ibid.*, pp. 118–119.   [75] *Ibid.*, p. 289.

punished—the innocent and the guilty alike. Under the present methods of the committee, that result is inevitable. As the committee knows, these views are held by many people. I hope they will be given consideration. . . .[76]

A little later Coe renewed his request: "Mr. Chairman, I have a request to make. If Miss Bentley is here, I would like to ask her some questions." Mundt, who was acting as chairman, replied:

> The position of this committee has been—and you explained it very clearly in your statement—that we are not functioning as a court, don't have the power, unfortunately, that a court does have, and so we have not made it a policy to cross-examine witnesses or to permit counsel to do so.
>
> Had we the full authority of a court, certainly it would be easier to get down into the disputed evidence in this particular case. Since we do not have, we cannot adapt ourselves to part of the rules of the court without having the authority that goes with being a court. Unfortunately, we cannot accept your request.[77]

Thereupon Coe asked permission to read the questions he would have asked Miss Bentley had he been permitted to cross-examine her. At first, Mundt seemed inclined to grant this permission. But Stripling protested that such a procedure had never been followed by a Congressional committee and that granting the permission requested would establish a precedent. Thereupon, the committee went into one of its characteristic "ornery" spells and refused even to let Coe make a further statement incorporating what he said were the correct factual answers to the questions he would have put to Miss Bentley. He was told he had already made one statement and that if he wanted to add to that statement he would first have to put it in writing. Finally Mundt stated that the committee could not "hear stump speeches by anybody." [78] As has already been indicated, the committee did later permit Alger Hiss to submit a list of formal questions which it then proceeded to put to Whittaker Chambers, although whether the committee pressed for adequate answers is debatable.

Closely related to the right to cross-examination is the right to reply to adverse testimony given by other witnesses. Controversy over this latter right has been chronic in connection with the investigations of the Un-American Activities Committee because of its

[76] *Communist Espionage Hearings,* pp. 916–917.   [77] *Ibid.,* p. 926.
[78] *Ibid.,* p. 927.

pronounced tendency through the years to allow certain of its witnesses great freedom in bringing the names of other persons into their testimony. The issue is really a double one: what can or should be done to prevent witnesses from naming other persons in a derogatory context, and what right should persons so named have to reply?

In no year since its creation in 1945 has the committee had a clean record in preventing witnesses from indulging in the irresponsible naming of other persons. Indeed, there is hardly a hearing in the six-year period covered by this study in which there are not to be found shocking instances of "character assassination." [79] In particular, there are numerous instances of a failure on the part of the committee to honor the "right of reply." A flagrant example is found in the Hollywood hearings. One of the charges against the motion picture industry widely publicized by the committee, even in advance of the hearings in Washington in October, 1947, was that the Roosevelt administration had brought improper pressure upon the industry to make pro-Soviet films. In particular, the charge was developed that Lowell Mellett used his authority as a high OWI official to compel Robert Taylor to play a part against his will in the film, *Song of Russia*.[80] Mellett denied this charge and repeatedly requested the committee to grant him a hearing. Mellett was particularly bitter when the committee adjourned its Hollywood hearings without letting him testify and asserted, "The committee deliberately avoided letting me give them the truth." [81]

Another type of difficulty arising out of irresponsible testimony, for which the committee must share at least partial responsibility, is the wide publicity that is given to statements that are clearly factually erroneous and which might properly have been challenged at the moment they were made by witnesses. For example, one of the friendly witnesses during the Hollywood hearings was Walt Disney. He testified that Communists had been responsible for labor troubles in his studio and asserted that among the Communist front organizations which, following these troubles, had tried to "smear" him and to encourage boycotting of his pictures was the League of Women Voters. This was a reckless error by a confused witness, for the fact

[79] This assertion is easily documented, as any careful reader of the committee's printed hearings will quickly discover. Strong as is the temptation to provide a definitive and systematic list of examples, the author is deterred from doing so by a desire not to give any further publicity to the people whose names have been so used.

[80] *N.Y. Times*, May 15, 1947; *Mot. Pict. Ind. Hearings*, pp. 166–167.

[81] *Washington Post*, Oct. 31, 1947.

is that the organization which seemingly had participated in such a boycott campaign was the League of Women Shoppers.[82] The Un-American Activities Committee cannot be expected to correct all of the factual errors made by its witnesses. But the committee has always prided itself on its expert knowledge concerning allegedly subversive organizations. Identified as present at the hearing the day Disney testified were such staff members as Robert Stripling, Louis Russell, and Benjamin Mandel. It is inconceivable that when they heard Disney refer to the League of Women Voters they did not know that this was an organization against which no charges, however ludicrous, had ever been made, or that Disney probably meant the League of Women Shoppers.[83] Yet not only did they and committee members fail to query Disney more closely at the moment when he made the original error, but they failed to note the error the next day when Disney in a wire to the committee began to realize that some sort of error had been made. On November 3, 1947, Disney addressed a letter to the committee in which he corrected his error. He wrote:

Since returning to my office in Burbank, California, I have had an opportunity to carefully review my files pertaining to this subject matter. I can now definitely state that while testifying as above I was confused by a similarity of names between the two women's organizations. I regret that I named the League of Women Voters when I intended to name the League of Women Shoppers.

The text of this letter was carried as an exhibit in the appendix of the volume of hearings published in January, 1948. But as always in such situations the correction of the error did not receive the same publicity that the original charge did, and it is probable that the League of Women Voters suffered a measure of damage in this situation which has never been fully undone.[84]

[82] That it was not just a slip of the tongue on Disney's part was made clear the next day when Stripling read into the record a telegram received from Disney in which he endeavored to reply to the protest which was already being made over his irresponsible reference to the League of Women Voters. In this telegram Disney began to backtrack, but he still identified "several women" who had presumably been responsible for the boycott efforts as representing themselves as members of the League of Women Voters. *Mot. Pict. Ind. Hearings,* p. 329.

[83] For example, in the pamphlet, *Citations by Official Government Agencies of Organizations and Publications Found to be Communist or Communist Fronts* (p. 62), published by the Un-American Activities Committee, Dec., 1948, there is no reference of any kind to the League of Women Voters. The League of Women Shoppers is listed as having been cited twice: by the Dies Committee in 1944 and by the California Committee on Un-American Activities in 1943.

[84] *Mot. Pict. Ind. Hearings,* pp. 534 ff.

Perhaps the most vigorous attempt during the life of the committee to curb irresponsible testimony and to guarantee a right of reply was made by Representative Hébert in 1948 during the Communist espionage hearings. While the first witness, Elizabeth Bentley, was testifying Hébert insisted that the persons whom she named should have a public hearing.[85] But he was not particularly successful in his efforts. The committee's two star witnesses, Elizabeth Bentley and Whittaker Chambers, were given a free rein and were permitted to name persons without restraint and seemingly without any previous checking. Indeed, at times they were even encouraged by committee members or investigators to drag in additional names.[86] On the other hand, the committee did apparently allow every person named by Bentley or Chambers to appear before the committee and deny the charges, if he wished to do so. In fact, the committee itself subpoenaed a number of these persons, only to have many of them refuse to confirm or deny the charges, on the ground of self-incrimination.[87]

The generally equivocal attitude of the committee on this issue of the right of reply was never made clearer than in the following statement in the committee's *Interim Report* of August 28, 1948, on the Communist espionage hearings:

It is the established policy of this committee to protect in every feasible manner the reputations and the sensibilities of innocent citizens. It is also an established fact that in conducting public hearings—and this committee deplores the use of star-chamber, secret sessions unless public necessity requires them—an occasional mention of some innocent citizen in con-

[85] See p. 240.

[86] For example:

"*Mr. Stripling:* Did you ever meet Aubrey Williams?
"*Mr. Chambers:* No I never did.

.   .   .   .   .

"*Mr. Stripling:* Did you ever hear Aubrey Williams' name discussed at any . . . meetings?
"*Mr. Chambers:* I can't say definitely that I did, but I have heard Communists mention Williams as a friend of the Communist Party."
And again, to Mr. McDowell's question, "Do you know Vera M. Dean?" Mrs. Marion Bachrach replied, "No." *Communist Espionage Hearings,* pp. 545, 576, 1474.

[87] There were a number of persons named by Bentley or Chambers who were not subpoenaed and did not appear as voluntary witnesses. Whether anyone in this category made an effort to be heard and was denied an opportunity to testify by the committee is not clear from the record. It seems likely that every person who made an active effort to be heard was granted a hearing.

nection with a nefarious practice will inevitably occur. When it does, we provide every opportunity for those mentioned to clear themselves of all suspicion in the same forum before the same publicity media as in the case of the original allegations. In addition we have frequently inserted memoranda in our files to protect those innocently accused elsewhere from unjust attack or suspicion.

At times, however, your committee is confronted with the necessity of running the risk that a few innocent people may be temporarily embarrassed or the risk that 140,000,000 innocent Americans may be permanently enslaved. When necessary to resolve the relative merits of two such risks as that, your committee holds to the position that its primary responsibility is to that great bulk of our American population whose patriotic devotion to our free institutions deserves the greatest diligence in being protected against those who would utilize our Bill of Rights and our American freedoms to destroy permanently these great safeguards of personal liberty and human dignity.[88]

[88] *Interim Rept.*, p. 3.

IX: The Committee's Publications

A STEADY stream of publications has issued from the Un-American Activities Committee through the years.[1] The distribution of these publications, with a few notable exceptions, has been limited, and they have not attracted wide public attention or interest. Nonetheless, a considerable part of the impact of the committee upon the government and the people has been felt through them. This is largely due to the nature of their circulation. They have gone, in the first place, to the members of Congress and to Congressional staff agencies. They have gone also to newspapers and periodicals. In both instances they have had to compete for attention with the tremendous flood of publications flowing constantly from other Congressional committees and government agencies. That they have done quite well in this competition is indicated not only by the careful attention they have received at the time of issuance but also by the fact that they have been kept on file and are used regularly as a standard source of information concerning subversive activity, alleged or otherwise, in the United States. Finally, the committee's publications have gone to private individuals and organizations interested in the threat of communism, real or imaginary, and have served these people and agencies as an authoritative reference source upon subversive activity.

Broadly speaking, the publications of the committee fall into two series—hearings and reports. The hearings contain what purports to be a verbatim account of the testimony of the witnesses who have appeared before the committee. In general, only the testimony given at the *public* hearings of the committee is included in these pub-

[1] See Appendix, Table I, for lists of the committee's publications from 1945 through 1950.

320

lications, although from time to time the committee has authorized the publication of testimony given in executive session.

Careful examination of the published hearings of the committee since it became a permanent agency in 1945 leads to the conclusion that these documents provide a generally accurate record of what actually transpired at the sessions of the committee. So far as can be ascertained, no witness has ever complained that his testimony was not fairly reported by the committee.[2] On the other hand, it is quite clear that 100-per-cent accuracy has not been achieved. The testimony is recorded at the hearings by a stenotypist, and minor deviations in the printed record are bound to exist where this method is used. An interesting illustration of such a deviation is found in the testimony of Whittaker Chambers given before the committee in 1948. The printed hearing shows Chambers stating that he once had supper with the Hisses when they were living on a "Dent Place" in Washington.[3] At the first Hiss trial Chambers denied that he had ever so identified the street and insisted that he had correctly identified it as Volta Place. Thereafter, the prosecution called as a witness the stenotypist who had reported the committee hearing, and he testified that he was responsible for the error. He had failed to catch the word, had made a tear in the stenotype paper as was his custom when he was uncertain, and had later checked with someone and had inserted, "Dent Place." [4]

It also appears that the editing and proofreading of the hearings by the committee's staff leave something to be desired. For example, proper names are frequently misspelled. Thus, when Whittaker Chambers was asked whether he knew Owen Lattimore, the record shows Owen Latimer.[5] Still and all, the record seems to be generally accurate, and these minor discrepancies do not affect the substance

[2] Interview with Mrs. A. S. Poore, staff editor of the committee, June 30, 1949. Mrs. Poore stated that in general witnesses are not allowed to edit their testimony. An exception was made in the case of the witnesses who testified on the Mundt-Nixon bill before the legislative subcommittee. Committee members are given an opportunity to edit their remarks.

[3] *Hearings regarding Communist Espionage in the United States Government,* p. 1190.

[4] See Alistair Cooke, *A Generation on Trial* (New York: Alfred A. Knopf, Inc., 1950), pp. 136, 174.

[5] *Communist Espionage Hearings,* p. 575. In the same volume (pp. 786, 840) the well-known Columbia University professor, Leo Wolman, becomes Leo Wohlman. Carl B. Spaeth, formerly in the State Department, and now dean of the Stanford Law School, becomes Carl B. Spate.

of the testimony. At the same time one could wish that the committees of the Congress of the United States might achieve the same high standards in the editing and publication of their records that are maintained by the federal judiciary. Attention should also be called to the exceedingly unattractive format which Congress has prescribed as the standard for all of its publications. As a result Congressional documents are poorly designed and are printed in unattractive type on poor-quality paper. No casual reader's attention is ever drawn to such a document by its format.

The "reports" issued by the committee during the six-year period between January, 1945, and December, 1950, fall roughly into several categories. First, a general division can be made between those reports that are based primarily upon the committee's hearings and reflect the evidence supplied by witnesses and those based primarily upon the research activities of the committee's staff. There is a certain amount of overlapping here, but the committee has carried on a considerable amount of research quite independently of, and unrelated to, its hearings, and certain reports reflect this independent research activity.

Reports based upon hearings are of two types. First, there are five so-called annual reports which attempt more or less systematically to describe the committee's activities, findings, and conclusions, with particular emphasis upon the hearings. Second, there are reports based upon specific hearings. For example, two of these resulted from the hearings on the Mundt-Nixon bill and similar legislative proposals in 1947 and early 1948, two grew out of the Communist espionage hearings in 1948, and two set forth the results of the atomic espionage hearings conducted intermittently from 1947 on.

Reports based upon research are also of two types. One of these is a continuing series of reports on the Communist Party and alleged Communist front organizations. By 1950 there were some eleven titles in this series. Two of these reports deal with the Communist Party of the United States as an "agent of a foreign power" and as an "advocate of overthrow of government by force and violence." In addition there are separate reports on the following alleged Communist front organizations: American Youth for Democracy, Southern Conference for Human Welfare, Civil Rights Congress, Scientific and Cultural Conference for World Peace, American Slav Congress, Congress of American Women, Hawaii Civil Liberties Committee, the National Lawyers Guild, and the National Committee to Defeat the Mundt Bill. The other category of research reports is a miscellaneous one into which may be put such items as the brief 1946 report on *Sources of Financial Aid for Subversive and Un-American Propaganda,* the Condon report of 1948, a 1950 report on the Communist *Peace Petition Campaign,* and two 1948 publications entitled *Citations* and *Index II* which contain listings of individuals and organizations either regarded as subversive or whose names have figured in the committee's work.

This attempt to set forth the nature of the committee's reports over a six-year period is perhaps misleading in that it gives the impression that the committee has been following a more systematic publications program than has in fact been the case. Reports have come from the committee in exceedingly helter-skelter fashion, and it is only as the six-year product is examined carefully that any sort of pattern can be discerned. Nonetheless, the total impact of the publications upon both governmental policy and public opinion has been very substantial, and a full understanding of the committee's record necessitates a careful examination of the different types of report that have been mentioned.

The Annual Reports

The first of the five general reports of the committee in the six-year period is dated June 7, 1946.[6] The second one appeared less than six months later, on January 2, 1947, and together the two purport to tell the story of the Hart-Wood committee in the Democratic 79th Congress. The third report did not appear until two years later. It is dated December 31, 1948, and covers the full two-year program of the Thomas committee in the Republican 80th Congress. The fourth report is dated March 15, 1950, and covers the first year of the 81st Congress committee, which was again under the chairmanship of Representative Wood. The fifth report is dated January 2, 1951, and covers the committee's activity during 1950.

As a group these five documents are exceedingly inadequate summaries of the work of the committee. They are poorly written and almost totally lacking in systematic organization. They wander along in incredibly informal fashion. Here and there a paragraph or a section is encountered which is succinctly written and contains a significant evaluation of, or defensible conclusion concerning, a matter

[6] The first three of these publications bear the title *Report of the Committee on Un-American Activities.* The fourth and fifth ones are entitled *Annual Report of the Committee on Un-American Activities.*

that has been under investigation by the committee. But there is no orderly discussion of all phases of the committee's work. Some important matters are ignored entirely, and others are only briefly touched upon. On the other hand, some matters of seeming unimportance are given considerable attention. Similarly, the passages embodying reasoned, defensible conclusions are interspersed among other sections in which the committee's penchant for giving expression to unsupported accusations and the rankest kinds of prejudices enjoys free rein. These shortcomings are perhaps most apparent in the earlier reports in this series, while the last two reports are relatively free from them.

The major subject dealt with in the first report is the investigation of the Joint Anti-Fascist Refugee Committee. In addition, attention is given to such miscellaneous matters as the radio broadcasts of certain unnamed liberal commentators, communism in labor unions, the distribution by the War Department of an allegedly subversive pamphlet, and the collection and disbursement of money for subversive purposes, particular emphasis being given in the latter instance to an agency known as the Sound View Foundation, Inc., and certain organizations affiliated with the National War Fund. The section on the liberal radio commentators is incredibly prejudiced. A dispassionate reader is hard-pressed to find here any evidence of "subversive" activity. Instead he encounters such uncritical or prejudiced judgments as the following:

The analysis of many scripts has given us a general picture of a trend.

From the review of the scripts of several news commentators it appears that several of the so-called "liberal" commentators are all receiving information from the same source, inasmuch, as practically all of them night after night discuss the same subjects and with very little difference in their interpretative language.

.   .   .   .   .

Most of our real 100 per cent American commentators are free from subversive influence. It would be safe to say that 95 per cent of the native born commentators, who have not changed their names, are loyal and sincere. . . .

Many individual Members, and Congress as a whole, are slandered, maligned, and ridiculed by certain commentators in what appears to be a well-organized campaign to break the confidence of the American people in our elective system and representative form of government. Some of these loud-mouthed trouble makers can hardly speak English. America has given them refuge and they in return seek to destroy our constitutional form of government.[7]

In addition to the fact that they have criticized Congress and its members, evidence that these commentators are pro-Communist and pro-Russian is found in the fact that they have attacked "the American State Department," "presidential appointees," "certain sections of the American press," "the governments of European and Latin-American countries," and "General MacArthur and Chiang Kai-Shek."

The 1946 report contains a bitter attack upon the War Department because of a pamphlet it published on March 24, 1945, and "tried to force down the throats of American soldiers." The pamphlet was labeled "Army Talk—Orientation Fact Sheet No. 64" and was designed for use by instructors in an Army educational program. It met with condemnation by the House committee because it condemned Fascists and not Communists, contained "verbatum [sic] extracts from the Soviet Constitution, together with very friendly comments and words of explanation" (which are not cited), contained a long section on "How can we identify native American fascists at work?" warned against persons who claim to be "100 percent American, anti-Jew, anti-Negro, anti-labor, anti-foreign-born, anti-Catholic," and used "sly comparisons" (unspecified) "which, by inference condemn our representative form of government and recommend . . . the Soviet form. . . ." The committee's final criticism of the pamphlet is: "When Fact Sheet No. 64 was published, the files and records of this committee were available for use by the War Department. . . . However, the group of officers who were responsible for this communist propaganda sheet made no effort to ascertain from our records what the facts were." [8]

The section of the report dealing with the Joint Anti-Fascist Refugee Committee is long and discursive. The JAFRC is examined as an agency engaged in the collection and disbursement of money for subversive purposes, and a certain amount of evidence indicating that the agency was in fact a Communist front is presented. But the

---

[7] *Annual Rept.*, June 7, 1946, pp. 9–13.

[8] *Ibid.*, pp. 14–16. The 1945 pamphlet in question has not been examined by the present author. It may, in fact, have been written by persons sympathetic to communism. The important point is whether the pamphlet has here been subjected to fair, dispassionate analysis by a Congressional committee. It is difficult to see how any impartial reader of the committee report could avoid the conclusion that the condemnation of the pamphlet depends on innuendo, phrases quoted out of context, and the asking of loaded questions.

House committee is never content to develop its case calmly and systematically or to let the evidence speak for itself. Again and again it digresses to voice irrelevant and shocking prejudices. For example, having explained the JAFRC's unsuccessful effort to gain certification as a National War Fund agency, the report, in wholly gratuitous fashion, uses data the committee had obtained from the files of the President's War Relief Control Board as a basis for an attack upon eleven organizations that did participate in the National War Fund. These data are presented "to show, first, the vast sums of money being collected from the American people and sent abroad, and, secondly, the great difference in administrative costs as between different types of organizations." The report adds, "It should be borne in mind that during the war there was a restriction upon the export of money, which seems to have been ignored insofar as these money-collecting agencies were concerned. It should also be borne in mind that the American Red Cross was functioning very well all during this period, that our Lease-Lend program was in full operation, and it appears that some of these money-collecting organizations may have been quite unnecessary and were operated primarily for political purposes." [9]

The utter lack of continuity in the report is illustrated when, in an analysis of the alleged Communist front agencies interested in the Spanish refugee problem, the reader suddenly finds the committee attacking the Department of Justice for failure to prosecute the persons "responsible for the communist sponsored strikes held at Allis-Chalmers and North American Aviation" and then in irrelevancy compounded encounters the statement, "This same agency did find time to prosecute some 30 or 40 native Americans who were charged with sedition, and a trial covering 8 months and costing hundreds of thousands of dollars was conducted to convict these persons." [10]

Throughout the section on the Spanish refugee problem there are constant indications that the committee regarded the Spanish Civil

[9] *Ibid.*, p. 23. The eleven organizations were: Ambijan Committee for Emergency Aid to the Soviet Union; American Field Service; American Friends Service Committee; American Jewish Joint Distribution Committee, Inc.; Front Line Fighters Fund of the International Workers Order; Hadassah, Inc. (Women's Zionist Organization of America and Hadassah Medical Relief Assn., Inc.); Hebrew Sheltering and Immigrant Aid Society; National Refugee Service; Refugee Relief Trustees, Inc.; Russian War Relief, Inc.; and United Palestine Appeal (pp. 24–26).

[10] *Ibid.*, p. 32.

War as a struggle between the forces of communism and Satan on one side and the forces of sweetness and light on the other. There is a reference to the "3,000 American boys who were induced by various illegal and deceptive methods to participate in the Communist-Loyalist War in Spain." Also, the committee lends its support to "the tablet Catholic Weekly" [sic], published in Brooklyn, N.Y., in the latter's attack upon the State Department because of a letter sent by the department to Bishop Lewis O. Hartman of Boston containing the following passage:

The Department recognizes and shares fully the feeling of the American people that there should be established in Spain forms of government which would give to the Spanish people the opportunity to achieve their political aspirations. The question of how to use our influence, in the best and most effective manner, and to aid in the achievement of these objectives in an orderly and peaceful way, is receiving constant study by officers of the Department.[11]

The 1946 report is not totally without merit. Mixed with the irrelevancies, the *non sequiturs,* the innuendoes, the unwarranted attacks, and the unsupported conclusions is a certain amount of factual information on the nature of international communism and the organization and techniques of the Communist underground movement and of Communist front agencies. But the impartial reader finds himself repelled by the good as well as the bad, because of the incredible prejudices and irrelevancies with which the report is burdened.

The report of January 2, 1947, shows a slight improvement upon its predecessor of six months before. The committee is still overly fond of making such prejudiced and gratuitous judgments as the following:

During the crucial 2 years of the Seventy-ninth Congress, with which this report deals, we witnessed the military defeat of the "totalitarian right" but we also witnessed a world-wide onslaught from the "totalitarian left." Most of Europe has succumbed to it—England is en route.

· · · · ·

Real democracy as our American fathers knew it was a rule of personal conduct; it has never worked as a national form of government.[12]

The report is largely confined to a brief but systematic analysis of the Communist Party of the United States and of its connections with the international Communist movement. The temptation to

[11] *Ibid.,* pp. 29, 46.   [12] *Annual Rept.,* Jan. 2, 1947, pp. iii, iv.

digress is held to a minimum. Some of the judgments of the American Communist movement, read in the light of the evidence that has accumulated in the years since this report was released, reveal a shrewd accuracy. For example:

For many years American Communists have endeavored to dupe gullible people and to masquerade their totalitarian objectives as "liberal" or "progressive," whereas, in fact and in practice, the procedures of communism, wherever they have ever [sic] dominated the government of any country, are virtually identical with the procedures of fascism. . . .

Plainly speaking, the entire history of the so-called Duclos letter provides a chain of evidence that definitely links the Communist Party of the United States to the Communist International and to those who control it. . . .

The American Communist Party can make no more than a superficial claim that it is a "political party" in the sense in which the American people understand those words. It is, on the contrary, a constituent member of the Communist International, which still exists, and is its agent in the United States. The Communist International in turn is completely dominated by the Communist Party of Soviet Russia.[13]

The report of December 31, 1948, is the only effort which the Thomas committee made to issue a systematic, "annual" type of report. Although it does review briefly the activities and achievements of the committee during the preceding two-year period, it is loosely organized, poorly written, and repetitive of other reports. Ten of its twenty-five pages are devoted to a review of the contempt proceedings against some thirty witnesses who had refused to testify or otherwise co-operate with the committee. The report also contains a section entitled "Opposition to the Committee," which is notable because of its assertion that the committee's opponents are limited "in the main" to "Communists and their close fellow travelers," "those who have been duped or compromised by the Communists and who seek to cover up their own gullibility," and "those who are too naive to believe that there is a serious Communist menace to our way of life." [14] The section which reviews the committee's hearings on legislative proposals such as the Mundt-Nixon bill contains a sound paragraph with which few readers would quarrel:

Confronted as we are with a problem entirely new in our history, it is fully understandable that little attention has been paid in the past to the difficult task of drafting legislation to curb the activities of the Communist fifth column. How to check the machinations of a conspiracy

[13] *Ibid.*, pp. 1, 10, 11.   [14] *Annual Rept.*, Dec. 31, 1948, p. 3.

inspired and directed by a foreign power and involving many thousands of individuals including some native-born Americans, without at the same time infringing upon the rights guaranteed by the Constitution, is a task which our forefathers could scarcely have envisaged over 150 years ago. It is a task which will tax the genius of our most brilliant legal minds in the years ahead. Upon its successful solution may well depend our preservation as a democratic nation.[15]

The two reports of the Wood committee in the 81st Congress show considerable improvement over their predecessors. They are largely free from violently prejudiced language and attempt in a reasonably businesslike way to describe the committee's activities during 1949 and 1950. On the other hand, they have some of the defects of their predecessors in that they range widely, include considerable material of decidedly secondary importance, and fail in the end to demonstrate to the impartial reader the existence of a serious subversive threat to the integrity or security of the American nation. The leading sentences of the various sections into which the report for 1949 is divided are here reproduced. Brought together within brief compass in this fashion they reveal the philosophy, findings, and recommendations of the Wood committee of the 81st Congress concerning the danger presented by subversives to the well-being of America.

ESPIONAGE

The committee believes that espionage is one of the most deadly weapons in the hands of the American Communists at the present time. . . .

The major part of the committee's attention during 1949, therefore, was devoted to unearthing additional evidence of Communist activity in this field. The following is a summary of some of the testimony heard by the committee in connection with its espionage investigations.

· · · ·

Gen. Izyador Modelski

Evidence of current Communist espionage was presented to the committee by Gen. Izyador Modelski, former military attaché of the Polish Embassy, who broke with the Communists late in 1948. Armed with a mass of official Polish Government documents, General Modelski appeared before the committee on March 31 and April 1, 1949, and described the operations of a spy ring working from the Polish Embassy in Washington, D.C., with the aid of the Russian Embassy.

· · · · ·

[15] *Ibid.*, p. 17.

Nicholas Dozenberg

Conclusive evidence that a Communist espionage apparatus existed in the United States as early as 1928 was presented to the committee last year through the statement of Nicholas Dozenberg, self-confessed former agent of Soviet Military Intelligence in this country.

. . . . .

Jet Propulsion and Aircraft

Attempts of a Soviet espionage agent, Andrei V. Schevchenko, to obtain secret information regarding aeronautical developments at the Bell Aircraft Corp. and Westinghouse Electric Co. during World War II were revealed through the testimony on June 6, 1949, of three witnesses who had been contacted by Schevchenko.

. . . . .

Mary Jane and Philip O. Keeney

Committee hearings held on May 24 and 25 and June 9, 1949, exposed the associations of Mr. and Mrs. Philip O. Keeney, former United States Government employees, with persons previously identified with Communist espionage rings in the United States.

. . . . .

Paul Crouch

A comprehensive picture of Communist underground activity was offered in the testimony of Paul Crouch on May 6, 1949.

. . . . .

COMMUNIST INFILTRATION OF RADIATION LABORATORY AND ATOMIC ESPIONAGE

Communist espionage in the vital field of atomic energy continued to get special attention in committee investigations during the year 1949.

. . . . .

Nelson-Weinberg Case

By pursuing investigations begun back in 1947, the committee was able to offer the American public a comprehensive picture of the operations of a Communist cell in the wartime atomic project at the radiation laboratory, University of California, Berkeley, Calif.

. . . . .

Hiskey-Adams Case

The committee had developed the case of Clarence Francis Hiskey, Arthur Alexandrovich Adams, and John Hitchcock Chapin in 1948. This dealt with an atomic espionage group operating through the Metallurgical Laboratory at the University of Chicago. . . . In 1949, it pursued this inquiry still further, and produced additional evidence regarding the Hiskey-Adams case.

. . . . .

Jordan Hearing

On December 5, 1949, the committee received the testimony of George Racey Jordan regarding alleged shipments of Government documents and uranium to the Soviet Union by way of a United States Army airport at Great Falls, Mont., during the war.

. . . . .

LABOR

A primary Communist objective is the penetration and control of the labor movement in the United States. The international Communist "apparatus" has supported local Communists in this objective. The Committee on Un-American Activities, therefore, has felt obligated to expose the machinations of the Communists in the labor field.

United Electrical, Radio, and Machine Workers of America (CIO)

Testimony heard by the committee regarding the United Electrical, Radio, and Machine Workers of America (CIO) resulted in partial exposure of the Communist control which has been exercised over the national union organization, District Council 6, and local 601.

. . . . .

COMMUNIST PARTY, U.S.A., AND THE INTERNATIONAL COMMUNIST MOVEMENT

On August 9, 1949, Joseph Zack Kornfeder, former member of the central executive committee of the Communist Party, U.S.A., who had also served on the official staff of the Communist International and a student of the Lenin School in Moscow, outlined for the committee the nature of Joseph Stalin's international Communist "apparatus."

. . . . .

COMMUNIST ACTIVITY IN THE DISTRICT OF COLUMBIA

Hearings in June and July 1949 dealt with the operations of a Communist group within the Nation's Capital. While this group does not include Government employees, it was considered worthy of special attention by the committee in view of the fact that Communists working outside the Government have been known in the past to aid subversive agents within the Government.

. . . . .

MINORITY GROUPS

The Communist Party, U.S.A., has consistently sought to create the impression that it is genuinely interested in furthering the welfare of our Negro population. . . . To permit this false impression to stand unchallenged would have been unfair to the millions of loyal Negro Americans. The committee, therefore, arranged a series of hearings to which were invited outstanding members of our Negro community.

· · · · ·

COMMUNIST-FRONT ORGANIZATIONS

From its inception the committee has devoted considerable attention to the exposure of Communist-front organizations. As a result, a number of these organizations were rendered ineffectual and in some cases were dissolved.

[There follow paragraphs on the Scientific and Cultural Conference for World Peace, the American Slav Congress, the Congress of American Women, and the Southern Conference for Human Welfare.]

IN RETROSPECT

The committee would like to remind the Congress that its work is part of an 11-year continuity of effort that began with the establishment of a Special Committee on Un-American Activities in August 1938. The committee would also like to recall that at no time in those 11 years has it ever wavered from a relentless pursuit and exposure of the Communist fifth column. In many instances in the past, however, the positions taken by the committee on certain questions were not immediately supported. The committee had to wait upon the course of history for some of its findings to be legally substantiated. We would herewith list some of these instances as applied to 1949.

[There follow sections on Twelve Communist Leaders, Harry Bridges, Joint Anti-Fascist Refugee Committee, Gerhart Eisler, the Hiss Conviction, and Communist-Dominated Unions, and sections describing the Files of the Committee and the Distribution of Publications.]

RECOMMENDATIONS

Looking back upon 4 years' experience as a standing committee of the House of Representatives and almost 7 years as a special committee, we feel more than ever impressed with the insidiousness and vastness of the ramifications of the Communist movement and the urgent necessity for unflagging efforts to expose and curb its machinations. To further the effectiveness of these investigations and to curb the subversive activities of the Communist Party, United States of America, its agents and its dupes, the committee recommends the following action by the incoming House of Representatives. . . .

The recommendations included these:

"The statute of limitations in espionage cases must be amended."

"The legal definition of treason [should] be broadened to cover a period like the present cold war."

The Communist espionage and propaganda that has been focused in the embassies of Communist-dominated countries in this country "should be limited by proper safeguards sternly enforced."

A pending bill "providing safeguards against the employment of subversive individuals in defense plants should be adopted."

A bill "providing for the supervision and detention of undeportable [Communist] aliens should be enacted into law. . . ."

Legislation should be enacted "creating a presumption of law that a committee quorum, once established, continues to exist."

"Effective action against the well-coordinated, interlocking Communist network requires . . . the fullest cooperation between legislative and executive arms of the Government. . . ." Modification (unspecified) of the executive loyalty program is recommended.

The co-operation recommended in the preceding paragraph should take the form of Justice Department prosecution of those "subversive elements" that deny their Communist affiliations before the National Labor Relations Board or in filling out civil service forms, and then refuse to affirm or deny such affiliations before Congressional committees.

Legislation should be enacted subjecting officers of national labor unions having bargaining contracts with companies that have contracted to do secret and classified defense work for the armed forces or the AEC to "the same security standards" required of "members who have access to secret or classified material." [16]

The Reports on the Communist Party

The two reports issued by the committee since 1947 on the Communist Party of the United States and the nine on allegedly Communist front organizations constitute one of the most systematic efforts ever made by the committee to investigate subversive activity. The Communist Party reports are perhaps the most meritorious publications ever issued by the committee. Dealing with the party "as an agent of a foreign power" and "as an advocate of overthrow of government by force and violence," their aim is an orderly, detailed exposition of the history of the party, its philosophical commitments,

[16] *Annual Rept.*, March 15, 1950, pp. 1–23.

its goals, and its methods. The purpose of the first volume is stated to be "a documented refutation" of the "misconception" that the Communist Party of the U.S. "is a domestic political party . . . operating within the democratic framework of our Constitution." [17] More specifically it is said that the report seeks "to establish from documentary sources" four points about the the party, namely, that it (1) operates "under centralized discipline subordinated to the Communist Party of the Soviet Union"; (2) is "a section of a World Communist Party controlled by the Communist Party of the Soviet Union"; (3) has as its basic aim the "abolition of our present economic system and democratic form of government and the establishment of a Soviet dictatorship in its place"; and (4) uses "deception, evasion, illegal methods, violence, and civil war" to secure its revolutionary ends.[18]

Similarly, it is said in the second volume that it will show that (1) Marx, Engels, Lenin, and Stalin taught the use of force and violence; (2) the Communist Party of the Soviet Union which serves as a model for the American party, used force and violence to achieve its ends; (3) international communism, which dominates the American party, used force and violence in many countries; (4) the leaders of the American party are on record as advocating the use of force and violence; (5) the American party has encouraged and supported Communist parties in other lands in the use of force and violence to overthrow governments in these lands; and (6) the lower federal courts of the United States have made judicial findings that the American party advocates the use of force and violence.[19]

At their best these two reports provide seemingly accurate, factual information about the Communist movement and perceptive insights into its character and purposes. The following are examples:

The Communist movement is primarily a combative organization dedicated to the struggle against those whom it looks upon as class enemies. It, therefore, operates on strict military lines. Indoctrination serves this army, as it does any other, as a cohesive factor. Its professed idealistic aims tend to glorify the movement and build up the morale of its followers. Communist theory exalts and perpetuates the authority of its leaders,

[17] *The Communist Party of the United States as an Agent of a Foreign Power*, April 1, 1947, p. iii. Abbreviated hereafter to *1947 Communist Party Rept.*

[18] *1947 Communist Party Rept.*, p. 1. See the similar analysis of the Communist Party found in Justice Jackson's opinion in *American Communications Assn. v. Douds*, 339 U.S. 382, 422 (1950).

[19] *Report on the Communist Party of the United States as an Advocate of Overthrow of Government by Force and Violence*, May 11, 1948, pp. 1–2. Abbreviated hereafter to *1948 Communist Party Rept.*

for it claims to present a body of unassailable scientific principles of which the Communist leader is the sole authorized spokesman and interpreter. Any deviation from the principles of Marxism-Leninism-Stalinism, as most recently interpreted by the leader, is subject to severe penalties all the way from censure and expulsion to physical liquidation.

. . . . .

The Communists propose to substitute for the democratic, capitalist system under which ownership and control of industry is diffused among millions of individuals, a system under which industry, banks, newspapers, railroads, radio networks, films, and the government itself, are all controlled by a one-party dictatorship of the Communists. Under the so-called dictatorship of the proletariat, which is actually the rule of a small group at the head of the Communist Party led by an all-powerful dictator, the great mass of the people would be deprived of those freedoms which we have learned to enjoy as naturally as the air we breathe, namely, the right to take a new job; the right to work or not to work; the right to own and operate an automobile; the right to travel freely from place to place without police passport; the right to have a private telephone without interference; the right to criticize freely public officials and remove them, if necessary; the right to hear and read opposing opinions on the radio and in the press; the right to vote an opposition ticket; the right to a fair trial under a system of law emphasizing the innocence of the accused unless proven guilty; freedom from personal surveillance by janitors and other agents in the employ of the police; freedom of speech, press and assembly; freedom of workship [sic]; freedom of research.

. . . . .

Having had no previous experience with a centralized world party of this new type, Americans find it difficult to grasp its essential character. We are prone to judge the Communist Party in terms of other American political parties which are bound by no international ties but are inherently devoted to this country, which are loose in their discipline and tolerate wide differences of opinion, parties which serve as vehicles for the aspirations and demands of multifarious American groups and are wholly indigenous.[20]

At their worst the reports are badly organized and poorly written. Both contain a great deal of undigested material that is presented in a disorderly manner. The second report, in particular, contains a great mass of quotations from the writings of individual Communists, from Marx to Foster, and from party documents of all types which are not always directly in point, or do not always quite prove what

[20] *1947 Communist Party Rept.*, pp. 7, 12–13, and 27.

they are supposed to. Many of the conclusions arrived at are defensible, if controversial. Although largely free from the grossly prejudiced language of many of the committee's other publications, these reports do contain some passages that are, to say the least, uncritical. For example, it is stated that "the Communists organized and led" the riot at the Republic Steel plant in Chicago in May, 1937, in which ten persons were killed. According to the report, "A coroner's jury investigation disclosed that the riot had been carefully prepared by the Communists even to the extent of provision for Red Cross supplies and motion-picture cameras. The entire Communist press then proceeded to place the blame upon the Republic Steel Corp. and the Chicago Police force." [21] The only authorities cited in the report for this controversial judgment on a controversial episode are the *Chicago Tribune*, the *Chicago Daily News*, and the (Hearst) *Chicago Evening American*.

In the end both reports almost certainly overstate the danger offered by American communism. For example, the first one asserts,

In the light of our own highly integrated and sensitive society, it is well within the bounds of practical possibility, that if the present potentialities of the American Communist movement were fully mobilized for a supreme subversive effort, if these potentialities were given substantial aid from a strong foreign power, they could seriously dislocate our economic and social life and even the effectiveness of our armed forces.[22]

And this is echoed in the second report:

Modern society has become so intricate that it is conceivably possible for a comparatively small, closely knit, and determined group, located in strategic and sensitive points and dedicated to the use of force and violence, to create serious confusion, to dislocate and perhaps even paralyze the machinery of our economic and social life. It has been established that the American Communists have for years concentrated on infiltrating strategic areas of our economy, especially at the vital parts of the American military machine.[23]

No one can deny that it is "conceivably possible" (although an informed person might doubt that it is "within the bounds of practical possibility") that the American Communist movement might do grave harm to the established order in America *if* it were to realize its "potentialities" to the full and *if* it were to receive "substantial"

[21] *1948 Communist Party Rept.*, p. 78.
[22] *1947 Communist Party Rept.*, p. 2.
[23] *1948 Communist Party Rept.*, pp. 2–3.

foreign aid. But such a speculative assertion stacks the cards in wholly unwarranted fashion. The issue that has been facing the country since 1945 is whether evidence as to the immediate danger offered by Communists in the United States is sufficiently serious to warrant the severe program for the control of domestic propaganda and Communist political activity that the Un-American Activities Committee has constantly advocated. To be sure, the committee finds the threat offered by American Communists not only "potentially" great, but also currently dangerous. In the first of these reports it says, "In 1947 . . . we find this totalitarian bridgehead [the Communist Party of the United States] firmly entrenched in the labor movement, the Government, political parties, the press, radio and films, the schools and colleges, the churches and social organizations." [24] But the committee has certainly never succeeded in documenting this extremely lugubrious view of the actual headway made by communism in the United States.

The Southern Conference for Human Welfare Report

In June, 1947, the Un-American Activities Committee issued a report on the Southern Conference for Human Welfare. The report was issued on the eve of a political rally in support of Henry Wallace sponsored by the Southern Conference in Washington and was seemingly timed to embarrass the sponsors of this meeting. Moreover, the report barely antedated the final death of the conference and probably contributed to its demise. The report may properly be examined closely because it is quite typical of all of the committee's reports dealing with organizations. Each of these reports seeks to set forth the story of Communist enterprise either in influencing the original establishment of an organization or in "capturing" it at a later date. Each seeks to show that the organization in question faithfully follows the American Communist Party line and that to a greater or lesser extent it is tied to some sort of parent international Communist body. Each uses a "box score" method in an attempt to show the interlocking record of Communist-line activity by many persons active in the organization under examination. With minor exceptions, the information contained in these reports was assembled without benefit of any public hearings concerning the organizations reported on.

It must be conceded that these reports deal with organizations

[24] *1947 Communist Party Rept.*, pp. 1–2.

which as a matter of actual fact did sooner or later show unmistakable signs of Communist influence. But each is grievously marred by a loose and rambling organization, by factual inaccuracies, and by curious digressions and irrelevancies. The loose, rambling character of these reports is largely explained by the fact that they are little more than a hasty throwing together of material in the committee's files, almost no effort having been made to systematize the presentation. In this respect, they follow very closely the pattern of the 1944 "Appendix Nine," which described over one hundred private organizations and was admittedly a hasty printing of a large portion of the material in the Dies committee's files, which were allegedly threatened with destruction.[25]

The Southern Conference for Human Welfare was organized in

[25] "Appendix Nine" was published in seven volumes numbering just under 2,000 pages. It was prepared in the closing days of 1944 by the so-called Costello subcommittee of the Dies committee, presumably to preserve the files of the latter committee, which were thought to be threatened with destruction. Seven thousand sets were published at a cost of $20,000, and were delivered to the committee. When the publication came to the attention of the full committee early in 1945, it was ordered restricted and the existing copies destroyed. However, a number of sets had already been sold by the Government Printing Office to private subscribers. Others had been distributed by the committee to government agencies. Sets are reported to have remained in the possession of the Civil Service Commission, the FBI, the State Department, Army and Navy Intelligence, and the Legislative Reference Service of the Library of Congress. The volumes carry the title, *Communist Front Organizations with Special Reference to the National Citizens Political Action Committee.* There is no introduction to the volumes, and they carry no explanatory statement concerning their purpose or use. The first six volumes are divided into 245 sections, in which alleged Communist front organizations (or groups of organizations) are examined. In each of these sections the organization is described in a series of introductory paragraphs which are followed by a series of "exhibits" consisting of miscellaneous documents taken from the Dies committee files. Benjamin Mandel told the author that these exhibits are "a fair cross-section of our files today." (The Dies committee files were not destroyed but were turned over to the permanent committee in 1945.)

The seventh volume in the set is an index which contains some 22,000 names, chiefly of individuals. An examination of this list immediately reveals that many of the persons named are neither Communists nor fellow travelers. Mandel admitted to the author that this was so and said he regretted that the volumes did not carry an explanatory note warning users that the presence of a name in the index did not necessarily mean that the person was a subversive. He also stated that many of the persons suspected in 1944 of being fellow travelers may have subsequently proved their loyalty. In any case, the continuing use of these volumes by intelligence officers or by private individuals can only lead to dangerous and irresponsible results. It is quite clear that attacks by private

1938 and seems to have become defunct about the end of 1947. It had a permanent secretariat in which Clark H. Foreman was the dominant figure. Frank P. Graham, then president of the University of North Carolina, was the organization's honorary president during much of its life. Beginning in 1938, and every two years thereafter, with the exception of 1944, the conference held a formal meeting or convention in a southern city which was attended by one thousand or more delegates. A periodical known as *The Southern Patriot* was published regularly by the conference.[26]

The Un-American Activities report on the Southern Conference has been subjected to a unique and penetrating analysis by Professor Walter Gellhorn of the Columbia Law School. In an article in the October, 1947, issue of the *Harvard Law Review*, entitled "Report on a Report of the House Committee on Un-American Activities," Professor Gellhorn sets forth in detailed fashion the inadequacies of the committee report from the point of view of careful and impartial scholarship.[27] Professor Gellhorn makes it clear that his purpose is not to whitewash the Southern Conference or to demonstrate that it was not in fact a Communist front organization. Instead, his purpose is "to determine whether, upon the facts and arguments [the Committee's Report] contains, fair-minded men, striving dispassionately to arrive at the truth, could reach the conclusions it states." [28] Much of the analysis of the committee report which follows is based upon the Gellhorn article.

persons and organizations upon specific individuals are the result of access which these organizations have had to "Appendix Nine."

When the author attempted to query Representatives Wood and Nixon about the continuing use made of "Appendix Nine" each man professed complete ignorance about the publication and its contents. Interviews with Mandel and Wood, Jan. 31, 1950. Interview with Nixon, Feb. 2, 1950.

[26] This magazine continues to be published by an organization known as the Southern Conference Educational Fund, Inc., which was established by the Southern Conference for Human Welfare before the latter's demise.

[27] The Gellhorn article attracted much favorable attention, and so far as this writer knows none of its points has been successfully refuted. In interviews with members of the House committee staff the writer asked whether they had ever attempted to formulate a systematic reply to the article or had discovered any serious errors in it. Benjamin Mandel, the committee's director of research, made a brief and evasive answer to this question, referring, as he talked, to a copy of the Gellhorn article which had been underlined and which contained marginal notes. I came away from the interview with the impression that the staff either was not interested in replying to Gellhorn or had not been able to find any serious errors in his article.

[28] 60 *Harvard Law Review*, 1194.

The central thesis of the committee report on the Southern Conference is set forth in its first sentences:

The Southern Conference for Human Welfare is an organization which seeks to attract southern liberals on the basis of its seeming interest in the problems of the South. . . . Careful examination of its official publication and its activities will disclose that the conference actually is being used in devious ways to further basic Soviet and Communist policy. Decisive and key posts are in most instances controlled by persons whose record is faithful to the line of the Communist Party and the Soviet Union.[29]

The committee report is not divided in orderly fashion into chapters or sections, but in the light of the headings used and the actual substance of the report it is fair to say that it deals with the following subjects:

Origin. It is the thesis of the report that Communists played a large, if not a dominant, role in the organization of the Southern Conference in 1938: "In reporting to its constituents, the conference is extraordinarily vague as to the exact origin of the organization. . . . Its claim to represent any significant proportion of southern opinion is . . . entirely self-assumed." "The Communists were using the conference as a specific application of the so-called popular-front policy in the South. This line had been adopted by the Communist International at its seventh congress in Moscow in 1935. . . . The honest liberals drawn into the conference were merely the most convenient guinea pigs." [30] The scanty fashion in which these assertions are documented is illustrated by the final paragraph of the section on the conference's origin:

Evidence before our committee indicates that the central committee of the Communist Party was intimately concerned with the affairs of the conference from its very inception. William Weiner, former treasurer of the Communist Party, testified that a subsidy of $2,000 had been paid to the Communist Party of Alabama in 1938, when the Southern Conference for Human Welfare was founded, that this conference had been discussed with Robert F. Hall, when he was in New York, and that it had also been discussed by the central committee of the Communist Party. Mr. Browder publicly admitted that the Communist Party had "suffered great hardships to maintain the growing southern movement." [31]

[29] *Report on Southern Conference for Human Welfare*, June 16, 1947, p. 2. Hereafter cited as *Southern Conference Rept.*
[30] *Ibid.*, pp. 2, 3.   [31] *Ibid.*, p. 3.

Professor Gellhorn's analysis shows the irrelevancy of these observations. Where Browder did his public admitting is not stated but one may guess he was referring to the growth of the Communist Party in the South and not the Southern Conference. The content of the discussion with Hall and the Central Committee is unrevealed. For one organization to discuss another does not reveal a connection between the two. The payment of $2,000 to the Alabama Communist group does not by itself indicate any relationship between the payment and the Southern Conference.[32]

Communist Manipulation. This loosely organized section is largely concerned with named individuals who were active in various capacities in the Southern Conference and who are alleged to have been Communists, Communist-sympathizers, or persons "who show [ed] a predilection for affiliation to various Communist-inspired front organizations."[33] The committee finds signs of subversive activity in an article in *The Communist* written by Robert F. Hall, a delegate to the 1938 meeting, in which it is stated "that the main work of the conference was carried out through sections or panels and that resolutions adopted in the panels were usually adopted by the conference as a whole."[34] Mr. Gellhorn points out that this is the customary way of conducting large conventions or conferences, and he criticizes the committee for making such a procedure sound sinister by indicating that its information on this point was obtained from Hall.[35]

The report names the twenty-two members of the resolutions committee at the 1938 conference and condemns them because no record exists in the proceedings of the conference that they objected to the activities of five named Communist delegates among the 2,000 delegates in attendance, and further condemns them for having "adopted the following Communist party line resolutions: Demand for the release of the Scottsboro boys, endorsement of the Communist-dominated Congress of Mexican and Spanish-American Peoples, and condemnation of the Dies Committee."[36] In analyzing this charge Mr. Gellhorn, while stating that he knows nothing about the Congress of Mexican and Spanish-American Peoples, points out that this "seemingly minor resolution" was one among a very large number adopted by the resolutions committee which dealt with such diverse subjects as freight-rate differentials, farm tenancy, credit,

[32] 60 *Harvard Law Review*, 1201.   [33] *Southern Conference Rept.*, p. 6.
[34] *Ibid.*, p. 4.   [32] 60 *Harvard Law Review*, 1201.
[36] *Southern Conference Rept.*, p. 4.

social security, penal reform, public health, and so forth, "none of which was indicated in the Committee Report." He adds:

As for freeing the Scottsboro boys, the history of that unsavory rape case is still fresh enough to render unnecessary the reminder that many enlightened persons believed at the time and still believe that justice was withheld from the defendants; the time is not yet here, one may hope, when protestants against injustice must be deemed "fellow-travelers" merely because the Communists may chance to be protesting against the same injustice.

And as for the reference to the resolution condemning the Dies committee, he says:

Many men of good will and deep faith in Americanism have believed that the Dies Committee "was guilty of using unfair and inefficient methods," that it "had demonstrated its inability to present the complete truth," and that "if we use undemocratic means to preserve our democracy, we, in the act of so doing, destroy that very democracy." [37]

Foreign Policy. Here is the most serious charge against the Southern Conference:

The most conclusive proof of the Communist domination of the Southern Conference for Human Welfare is to be found in the organization's strict and unvarying conformance to the line of the Communist Party in the field of foreign policy. It is also a clear indication of the fact that the real purpose of the organization was not "human welfare" in the South, but rather to serve as a convenient vehicle in support of the current Communist Party line.[38]

The brief attempt of the report to document this assertion is little more than ludicrous, for the record of the Southern Conference during the years of its existence overwhelmingly supports Gellhorn's conclusion that "the Southern Conference . . . concerned itself but little with foreign affairs." [39] The report tries hard to show that the Southern Conference followed the variations of the Communist Party line from 1938 on. But this leads to such ridiculous indications of sympathy for the Communist position as the fact that in 1938 when the Communists were following a popular front line, "a letter of greeting from President Roosevelt brought 2,000 conference delegates to their feet cheering," and that in 1942 when the Communists,

[37] 60 *Harvard Law Review,* 1205. In the passage dealing with the Dies committee, Gellhorn is quoting from Ogden, *The Dies Committee,* pp. 108, 294, 296.
[38] *Southern Conference Rept.,* p. 8.   [39] 60 *Harvard Law Review,* 1225.

naturally enough, were supporting the war effort "wholehearted agreement marked the sessions of the conference . . . devoted to 'the South's part in winning the war for democracy' " and "the Convention demanded that all 'join in a great offensive now, to work, to produce, to sacrifice, to win.' " [40] Only with respect to the 1940 meeting of the Southern Conference does the report present any evidence of a real attempt to commit the conference to the Communist International line, which at the time was antiwar. That meeting was apparently marked by a real battle between Soviet sympathizers and independent liberals. The former were able to put through a resolution in which the delegates declared themselves "unalterably opposed to loans to the Allies and other belligerents" and opposed defense appropriations "at the expense of the welfare of the American people at home." [41] The report grudgingly admits that the liberals in the conference were able to put through a resolution condemning aggression by "Nazis, Communists, or imperialists." However, the committee insists that this resolution was a "mild" one granted by the Communists to their opponents as a "convenient sop." Whether this is a fair characterization of the resolution can best be decided by the reader. The resolution is quoted in its entirety by Gellhorn as follows:

We deplore the rise of dictators anywhere, the suppression of civil liberties, the persecution of minorities, aggression against small and weak nations, the violation of the neutral rights and the democratic liberties of the peoples by all fascist, nazi, communist and imperialist powers alike which resort to force and aggression instead of to the processes of law, freedom, democracy and international cooperation.[42]

In this section is found one of the most incredible examples of the use of the guilt-by-association technique ever employed by the Un-American Activities Committee. Reference is made to a 1947 dinner meeting of the Washington chapter of the Southern Conference at which a speaker "flayed President Truman's foreign policy in Greece and Turkey." Then there occurs one of those paragraphs, occasionally found in the publications of the committee, which is so stupid in its irrelevancy that it tends to reduce the entire report to a ludicrous level:

Entertainer at the Washington meeting was Susan Reed, employed by Cafe Society, a night club owned by Barney Josephson, brother of Leon

[40] *Southern Conference Rept.*, pp. 8, 9.   [41] *Ibid.*, p. 8.
[42] 60 *Harvard Law Review*, 1227.

Josephson, leading Communist, Soviet Secret Service operative, charged with passport frauds. Mrs. Leon Josephson also owns an interest in this enterprise. Barney Josephson has been a supporter of the New York branch of the Southern Conference.[43]

Interlocking with Communist Causes. Three pages of this seventeen-page report are devoted to a box score on sixty-two persons identified with the Southern Conference, which score purports to show their propensity to affiliate with Communist organizations and causes. Through the years this has been one of the chief means by which the House committee has sought to demonstrate the extent and depth of Communist influence in the organizational life of the American people. Admittedly, organizational affiliations are not without significance in this respect. If specific individuals can be identified as Communists and it can then be shown that they have been active in considerable numbers or in important ways in various organizations, a basis has been provided for a suspicion that such organizations are Communist fronts. But the House committee has never been content with any such careful or limited use of this technique. Instead, its method has been to take the names of persons active in a non-Communist organization, which may be called A, to show that they have also been identified with organization B which is alleged to be Communist-controlled, and to conclude that they have necessarily acquired a Communist taint from B, that they have necessarily transmitted this taint to A, and that the taint has ultimately touched all members of A, even those who have had no association with B. These latter members of A are then ready to be used in new box scores to show that organization C with which they are identified has acquired the taint.

Even this analysis does not fully suggest the shocking manner in which the committee has sometimes used the guilt-by-association technique. The members of organization A, selected for box-score treatment by the House committee, are often a small minority of the organization's total membership. The nature of their affiliation with A is not always carefully set forth. Indeed, upon investigation one often discovers that they are not even *members* of the organization; they have only attended a dinner sponsored by it, spoken at one of its meetings, or signed a petition circulated by it. Neither is the nature of the identification of these people with organization B clearly set forth, nor is the fact that B is a Communist-controlled organization always convincingly demonstrated.

[43] *Southern Conference Rept.,* p. 10.

These generalizations are borne out by an examination of the box score in the report on the Southern Conference. The report asserts that "a *significant number* of the *leading lights* of the Southern Conference" [44] have ties to Communist organizations or causes. But out of the thousands of persons who have been identified with the Southern Conference through the years only sixty-two individuals are so named. Their identification with the Southern Conference is in many instances explained only by the use of the single word "sponsor" or "supporter." That in presenting only sixty-two persons the committee has limited itself to naming dyed-in-the-wool Communists in the Southern Conference is quickly disproved when the presence on the list is noted of such names as Joseph E. Davies, Frank P. Graham, Lester Granger, Mrs. J. Borden Harriman, William H. Hastie, Harold L. Ickes, Freda Kirchwey, Eduard C. Lindeman, Lillian Smith, Channing Tobias, and Henry A. Wallace. The sixty-two persons are then checked in the box score on five points: (1) "Statement defending Communist Party," (2) "Support of defense of individual Communists," (3) "Organizations defending Communists," (4) "Pro-Soviet relief or propaganda organizations," and (5) "Organizations defending Soviet foreign policy." What "statement defending the Communist Party" is referred to the reader is left to guess. The nature of the "support" given individual Communists is identified only by the listing of the names of the alleged Communists defended. Listed are such persons as Angelo Herndon and Harry Bridges, who in their struggles with the law certainly received the support of many non-Communists interested in seeing to it that American justice lives up to the high tradition of our history. The identification of the sixty-two persons with the organizations under headings three to five is in no way specified as to either time or character, nor is the subversive nature of the organization in any way indicated. Although many of the organizations are ones that have appeared on various lists of allegedly subversive agencies, others, such as Russian War Relief, do not necessarily impress the reader as falling within the dangerous category.

Conclusion. In a brief concluding section, the report makes what is in effect an apology for its failure to present a more factual or persuasive case in support of its thesis. It is asserted, "The Southern Conference for Human Welfare is perhaps the most deviously camouflaged Communist-front organization." But having thus momentarily wavered, the committee regains its courage and insists that

[44] *Ibid.,* p. 13. Italics added.

"when put to the acid test" the organization "reveals its true character," namely, that:

1. It shows unswerving loyalty to the basic principle of Soviet foreign policy.

2. It has consistently refused to take sharp issue with the activities and policies of either the Communist Party, USA, or the Soviet Union.

3. It has maintained in decisive posts persons who have the confidence of the Communist press.

4. It has displayed consistent anti-American bias and pro-Soviet bias, despite professions, in generalities, of love for America.[45]

Entirely apart from the issue of fact as to whether the Southern Conference was "captured" by Communists it must be immediately apparent to any fair-minded reader of the report that it contains little or no tangible evidence in direct support of any one of the four points of the Conclusion. And the apology for lack of evidence implied in the assertion that the Southern Conference is "the most deviously camouflaged Communist-front organization" is suggestive of the kind of inverted reasoning which those who begin by searching for subversives are apt to end up using. There is a parallel between this reasoning of the House committee and the argument used by Louis Budenz in 1950 in his appearance before the Tydings subcommittee of the Senate Foreign Relations Committee: that if a person accused of being a Communist sues his accuser for libel he thereby proves the truth of the charges, for such libel suits are part of the Communist technique.

Many of the procedural shortcomings and unfair tactics which have at one time or another characterized so much of the work of the Un-American Activities Committee are illustrated in this report on the Southern Conference:

1. *Suppression of Relevant Facts.* The report on the Southern Conference demonstrates that the Un-American Activities Committee is not always interested in telling the whole factual story about an organization or individuals, including the good and the bad, so that the American people may evaluate charges pertaining to subversive activity in their full context. There is more to the story of the Southern Conference than is set forth, or even implied, in the committee report. For example, readily available evidence shows that the origin of the conference in 1938 did directly reflect a growing concern among liberals and thoughtful Southerners concerning the social problems of the South.

[45] *Ibid.*, p. 17.

2. *Coloring the Facts.* To bolster its charge that the Southern Conference was more interested in supporting Soviet foreign policy than it was in promoting human welfare in the South, the committee is guilty of coloring the facts. For example, the report refers to an issue of the Southern Conference's journal, *The Southern Patriot,* in which an anonymous "leading conference spokesman" is quoted as saying he did "not want to be a party" "to gang[ing] up on the Russians" and as thinking that the people of America, of the Big Three, and of the Soviet Union wanted to avoid war.[46] Gellhorn has observed that apart from the fact that "this does not immediately strike the uninitiated as necessarily revolutionary dogma" there is a good deal of fact coloring in this reference. Gellhorn's research revealed that the unidentified person was Senator Claude Pepper, who while on occasion a speaker before the Southern Conference was never a "spokesman" of it, that the quoted remarks came from speeches made by Pepper on the floor of the United States Senate, and that they were included in an issue of the *Patriot* in which special tribute was being paid by the conference to Pepper.[47] Or again, the report asserts that at the 1946 meeting of the conference in New Orleans "the chief speaker devoted most of his talk to a defense of Russia as a 'misunderstood' government which will continue to remain at peace with the United States." [48] In this instance Gellhorn's research revealed that the "speaker" was again Senator Pepper, that newspaper reports of the New Orleans meeting made it clear that Pepper's references to Russia were made not in his speech to the conference but in an interview with newspapermen held "outside the convention and not in connection with the Southern Conference at all." [49]

3. *Misleading Use of Quotations.* The Un-American Activities Committee has been more than ordinarily careless about removing quotations from their context and using them to support a point or thesis which is not warranted by the full text of the source. For example, in the Southern Conference report it quotes from an article by Robert F. Hall in *The Communist* in such a way as to give the impression that the language, "In strengthening this movement, our party has before it a great task," refers specifically to the Southern Conference. Gellhorn demonstrates that the full paragraph in *The Communist* from which this sentence came makes it clear that the

---

[46] *Ibid.,* p. 9. [47] 60 *Harvard Law Review,* 1230–1231.
[48] *Southern Conference Rept.,* p. 10.
[49] 60 *Harvard Law Review,* 1231–1233.

"movement" to which Hall referred was not the conference specifically, but "the progressive movement in the South" generally.[50]

4. *Use of Irrelevant Information.* Gellhorn has also pointed out that in the Southern Conference report the Un-American Activities Committee is prone to use irrelevant odds and ends of information "which have no capacity to prove anything about the Southern Conference but which tend to create a mood in the unwary reader to whom the report is addressed." For example, the report names Paul Crouch as one of the five Communist Party delegates to the 1938 meeting of the Southern Conference and adds that he "was convicted for treasonable activities within the armed forces of the United States in Hawaii on June 8, 1925," and also that "he subsequently made a pilgrimage to Moscow where he paraded in a Red Army uniform (*Daily Worker*, May 1, 1928, p. 5).[51] With reference to the latter item of information Gellhorn asks, "What possible light could this shed on the Southern Conference, which came into being ten years after the alleged pilgrimage?"[52]

5. *Loaded Use of Sources.* Throughout the report the activities of the Southern Conference are invariably described by reference to news stories and articles in the *Daily Worker* and other Communist publications. As Gellhorn puts it, "This tactical choice by the Committee is seemingly intended to leave the reader with the impression that the Southern Conference must be Communist because its proceedings are reported in a Communist newspaper." And he adds, "In analyzing the Committee's report, the author has found fuller accounts of the Southern Conference's proceedings in the *New York Times* and in the *Christian Science Monitor* than in the *Daily Worker*, while, of course, the Conference's own published proceedings are the fullest accounts of all."[53]

[50] *Ibid.*, 1199. The complete paragraph in *The Communist* is as follows: "The Southern Conference for Human Welfare has given a strong impetus to progressivism in the South. The fruition of its purpose depends on the greater strengthening of the progressive movement in the South. In strengthening this movement, our party has before it a great task." Hall, "The Southern Conference for Human Welfare," 18 *The Communist* (1939), pp. 57, 65.

[51] *Southern Conference Rept.*, p. 4.

[52] 60 *Harvard Law Review*, 1202 n. It might be added that the name of Paul Crouch is a recurring one in the annals of the Un-American Activities Committee. In 1949 he appeared before the committee as a friendly witness. By now an ex-Communist, he had joined the ranks of those informers whose word is trusted and prized by the committee. See hearings, *Testimony of Paul Crouch*, May 6, 1949.

[53] 60 *Harvard Law Review*, 1204. At one point Gellhorn's research reveals

6. *"Insupportable Innuendo"* against individuals. The Un-American Activities Committee has repeatedly been guilty of failure "to give a rounded body of information about a person it denounces," and the Southern Conference report provides several illustrations of this practice.[54] An example is found in the attack upon Yelverton Cowherd. In a section labeled "Communist Manipulation," the report states that "Yelverton Cowherd, signer of a resolution against the Dies committee in 1939, who appeared before the La Follette committee in 1937 to defend the case of Joseph Gelders [who is elsewhere described in the same section as another implied "Communist Manipulator"] was a member of the nominating committee at the first conference, according to its official proceedings." [55] Gellhorn's research reveals the following essential information about Cowherd:

1. He is an attorney for the United Mine Workers of America, "which does not admit Communists to simple membership let alone to responsible office."

2. The resolution which he signed against the Dies committee, while not specifically identified by the report, was probably one which carried the names of more than one hundred members of the bar, including a number of law professors.

3. The La Follette committee subpoenaed Cowherd to appear before it as a witness "not as a supporter of Gelders, but as former chairman of the Americanization Committee of the . . . [Birmingham] Post of the American Legion . . . to discover whether the work of these committees was financially supported by a certain individual who had been implicated in [an] attack upon Gelders." Cowherd's testimony had then proved to be favorable to Gelders.[56]

It is quite possible that the House committee fell into error in this use of Cowherd's name in the Southern Conference report because of an inherent weakness in its own file system. While the com-

---

that the committee's report actually uses the language of a *Daily Worker* article verbatim without quotation marks or any other acknowledgment. This passage is as follows: "The thousand delegates denounced war and 'pro-Allied propaganda,' as threatening America with war. They declared themselves 'unalterably opposed to loans to the Allies and other belligerents' and denounced war appropriations 'at the expense of the welfare of the American people at home.'" *Ibid.*, p. 1226; *Southern Conference Rept.*, p. 8; *Daily Worker*, April 17, 1940, p. 4, col. 1.

[54] The quoted phrase is Gellhorn's, 60 *Harvard Law Review*, 1211.

[55] *Southern Conference Rept.*, p. 5.

[56] 60 *Harvard Law Review*, 1207–1208.

mittee has protested to the contrary, the very presence of a name in the files tends to suggest that the person is a subversive. Here the committee perhaps found Cowherd's name in its files as a signer of a resolution against the Dies committee and as a witness before the La Follette committee and, without checking further, jumped to the conclusion that he was a subversive. In 1949 the committee tried to make amends for the unfair context in which it had placed Cowherd's name in the report on the Southern Conference. It allowed Cowherd to appear before it in executive session on October 5, 1949, and to protest against the committee's implied charge that he was a "Communist Manipulator." His testimony at this session is reproduced in an appendix to the committee's annual report for 1949. But here the committee's traditional carelessness (or its more deliberate deviousness) results in a further injustice to Cowherd. In spite of the fact that this appendix (numbered II) is limited to the Cowherd testimony it is given a brief introduction in which it is stated that the committee "is cognizant" that Communist Party members and Communist front supporters "become disillusioned" and it is stated to be "an objective of the committee to hasten such disillusionment and reeducation." It is then noted that "the committee endeavors in its files and reports to record such repudiation wherever possible, and wherever there seems to be convincing evidence of genuine sincerity." All of this has nothing whatsoever to do with Cowherd who was in no sense appearing before the committee as a "disillusioned" or "re-educated" ex-Communist. Nonetheless, in spite of the fact that the committee also notes, much more briefly, its desire "to amend its records in order to avoid any injustice" where it "may have erred in reference to an individual or an organization," these introductory paragraphs can only serve to give the unwary reader the impression that the committee was graciously allowing Cowherd a day in court as a repentant Communist.[57]

Professor Gellhorn's final conclusion concerning the Southern Conference report is bluntly stated: "The report demonstrates, not that the Southern Conference is a corrupt organization, but that the Committee has been either intolerably incompetent or designedly intent upon publicizing misinformation." [58] This is strong language, but it is difficult for any calm, dispassionate person to measure the committee's report against Professor Gellhorn's analysis of it without agreeing with his conclusion.

[57] See *Annual Rept.*, March 15, 1950, pp. 46 ff.
[58] 60 *Harvard Law Review*, 1233.

The Other Reports on Communist Front Organizations

Neither space nor the reader's patience will permit a detailed analysis of the other eight reports which deal with organizations alleged to be Communist fronts. But their strong and weak points may be summarized.

On the debit side, all are poorly organized and badly written. Only the reader who perseveres is apt to reach the end of one of these reports. Although its purpose may be stated with reasonable precision on page one, the mass of miscellaneous data, the irrelevant digressions, and the ridiculous prejudices are likely to discourage the dispassionate reader before he has proceeded very far. The "scare" technique is used, and the danger is almost always overstated. Some of the organizations, such as the Southern Conference for Human Welfare and the National Lawyers Guild, had largely lost whatever importance they once had by the time the House committee focused its spotlight upon them. Others, such as the Congress of American Women, never achieved much importance or influence. Indeed, one of the charges made by the House committee against certain of these organizations is that they have grossly exaggerated their membership. Yet in virtually every instance the committee also suggests that the organization is a dangerously subversive one which is making serious inroads upon American life. For example, the opening pages of the report on American Youth for Democracy tell the reader that "forces hostile to American democracy and seeking its destruction are penetrating our schools and colleges in an effort to subvert the great body of American students," that "the specter of communism stalks our college campuses masked under the cloak of the American Youth for Democracy," and that there is "a determined effort to disaffect our youth and to turn them against religion, the American home, against the college authorities, and against the American government itself." [59]

Again and again in these reports the committee succumbs to the temptation to reach beyond the agencies under examination and to impugn the motives of, or to insult, persons or organizations in no way identified with them. Thus the American Civil Liberties Union is gratuitously insulted in the report on the Civil Rights Congress. In spite of the fact that it suits the purposes of the House committee to use the American Civil Liberties Union's dispassionate estimate

[59] *Report on American Youth for Democracy*, April 17, 1947, pp. 1–2. Hereafter cited as *AYD Rept.*

of the postwar civil rights situation in the United States as a means
of emphasizing "the incendiary character" of the Civil Rights Congress' propaganda, it attacks the American Civil Liberties Union
for having "gone so far in its preoccupation with civil liberties as
to defend both Communists and Fascists, sometimes with an almost
complete disregard for considerations of national security involved." [60] Again, in the report on the Congress of American Women,
Vera M. Dean of the Foreign Policy Association is subjected to a
totally irrelevant and slanderous attack. The only excuse for mentioning Miss Dean, who seemingly never had any connection with
the Congress of American Women, is that she addressed a 1946
meeting in New York arranged by a "group of well-known American
non-Communist women," which meeting, according to the House
committee, suffered from "boring from within" by Communists who
wanted to make certain that it would not lead to the creation of a
rival agency to the Congress of American Women. The report states
that Miss Dean "arrived in this country from her native Russia in
1919"; *Plain Talk* magazine is cited as authority for the assertion
that Miss Dean is a great friend of the USSR; and she is then quoted
as having urged "the assembled women to 'whittle away their conceptions of national sovereignty' and [having] called upon them to
pull themselves out of the 'ancient grooves of nationalism.'" [61]

This attack upon Miss Dean also illustrates the strong tendency
of all these reports to wander from one subject to a second one only
slightly related to the first and then by making a tenuous point respecting the second to lead the unwary reader to conclude that a
point has been scored with respect to the first subject. For example,
in the report on American Youth for Democracy it is asserted without proof that the AYD spawned a series of subsidiary subversive
organizations. An organization known as Sweethearts of Servicemen is said to have been one of these, and evidence of its nefarious
character is found in the fact that it sent seventy-five young women
to Washington "to petition Congress 'to give their soldier boy friends
and husbands the chance to vote in the 1944 Presidential elections.'" [62] Another organization mentioned in a similar way is the
World Federation of Democratic Youth, whose subversive character

[60] *Report on Civil Rights Congress as a Communist Front Organization*, Sept.
2, 1947, p. 9.
[61] *Report on the Congress of American Women*, Oct. 23, 1949, p. 109. Hereafter cited as *CAW Rept.*
[62] *AYD Rept.*, p. 12.

is indicated by the fact it "concerned itself with the question of Franco Spain, condemnation of the 'reactionary' Greek Government, and support for Marshal Tito," and which showed its "marked anti-American" bias by adopting a resolution to call on Secretary of State Byrnes when he was in Paris in 1946 to condemn the " 'lynch atrocities and the rising tide of Fascist terror which are being perpetrated against the Negro people in Georgia, Mississippi, and the southern part of the United States.' " [63]

Often the introduction of irrelevant detail has only a ludicrous result. Thus in the report on the Congress of American Women the reader is told that one of the homes of the Rumanian Communist leader, Anna Pauker, has "a garden and needle showers" and that "the Committee on Un-American Activities is in possession of four affidavits which show that in 1937 and 1938 Susan B. Anthony decorated the walls of her apartment at 1742 P. Street, N.W., Washington, D.C., with hammers and sickles." [64]

The utterly irrelevant character of the data introduced in support of a charge against an organization is frequently shocking from the point of view of the rules of sound scholarship. For example, the National Lawyers Guild is accused of having waged "a vicious campaign of opposition" to the Federal Bureau of Investigation. This charge is supported by a completely unidentified quotation, presumably derived from a National Lawyers Guild source, to the effect that the FBI is a "gestapo" or "political police" whose "practices and policies . . . violate our laws, infringe our liberties, and threaten our democracy"; by a reference to action taken at the 1941 Guild convention calling for the removal of J. Edgar Hoover and opposing FBI appropriations; and by the testimony of J. Edgar Hoover given before a Congressional committee in 1950, in which he is said to have stated that the Guild had vociferously denounced the FBI since 1940 and quoted an unnamed Guild member as having said at a 1940 meeting of the organization that continued criticism of Hoover and the FBI would ultimately "weaken the power of the FBI and hamper them very effectively." Then, as if realizing that these supporting data are not very damaging to the Guild, the committee report goes on to assert, "There is no doubt in the opinion of the committee that the National Lawyers Guild attacks on the Federal Bureau of Investigation are part of an over-all Communist strategy aimed at weakening our Nation's defenses against the international Communist conspiracy." This unproved assertion of a connection between the

[63] *Ibid.*, p. 13.　　　　[64] *CAW Rept.*, pp. 39, 102.

Guild and "over-all Communist strategy" made, the report immediately adds that the Guild's propaganda "is a duplicate of the line put out by Moscow," which is then illustrated by two long quotations, one from a "Soviet Home Service short-wave network" broadcast and the other from a *Daily Worker* editorial.[65]

The improvements noted elsewhere in the 81st Congress committee over its predecessors in the conduct of hearings is not borne out in the further reports on alleged Communist fronts issued by it. That on the National Lawyers Guild, September 17, 1950, follows the pattern of the earlier reports and contains most if not all of their faults. For example, the brief concluding paragraphs of this report provide one of the most flagrant illustrations that can be given of the committee's tendency to regard itself, not as an agency of Congress seeking information for legislative purposes, but as an arm of the law enforcement branch of government seeking to ferret out wrongdoers and to pronounce sentence upon them:

> The Committee on Un-American Activities recommends that the National Lawyers Guild be placed on the Department of Justice subversive list and that it be required to register as an agent of a foreign principal.
>
> It recommends further that members of the National Lawyers Guild be barred from Federal employment and that the American Bar Association consider the question of whether or not membership in the National Lawyers Guild, a subversive organization, is compatible with admissibility to the American bar. It calls on decent lawyers and those sincerely interested in the liberal principles of American justice to warn the younger members of the bar of the real nature of the guild, as an arm of the international Communist conspiracy.[66]

In all fairness it must be acknowledged that these reports on organizations do have their calm and dispassionate moments and do contain some informative, significant information. For one thing,

---

[65] *Report on the National Lawyers Guild—Legal Bulwark of the Communist Party,* Sept. 17, 1950, pp. 6–7. Hereafter cited as *NLG Rept.* For a reply to this report, see *The National Lawyers Guild—Legal Bulwark of Democracy,* reprinted from the *Lawyers Guild Review,* X, no. 4 (Fall, 1950). This eighteen-page pamphlet is patterned somewhat after Professor Gellhorn's analysis of the Southern Conference report and attempts to refute the House committee in point-by-point fashion. Entirely apart from the issue as to whether there has or has not been Communist influence in the Lawyers Guild, this reply is an impressive document. As is true of the Gellhorn article it demonstrates beyond a doubt the shoddy, careless, grossly unfair research and writing that have gone into reports of the House committee.

[66] *NLG Rept.,* p. 21.

scattered through the different volumes in the series one finds significant discussions of the tactics of international communism. Back of
many of the American agencies described in these reports is stated
to exist some parent Communist body organized by the Soviet Union
as a means of advancing Communist interest internationally. Thus
the American Youth for Democracy is said to be related to a World
Federation of Democratic Youth and an International Union of Students; the American Slav Congress to an All-Slav Congress in Moscow; the Congress of American Women to a Women's International
Democratic Federation; and the National Lawyers Guild to an International Association of Democratic Lawyers. Each of these international bodies is alleged to be a specific instrument of the international Communist movement. However, the absence of detailed
evidence concerning the true character of these latter agencies and
of the exact relationship between the American organization and
the international body seriously weakens the committee's charges in
this respect. Nonetheless, a partially convincing blueprint of the
structure of international communism is supplied and the existence
of ties between Communist fronts in the United States and Russian-
controlled international bodies is strongly suggested.

Secondly, these reports do supply American liberals with a certain
amount of information concerning the "boring from within" methods
used by Communists who are seeking to capture organizations in
which liberals are members. However, in passing it should be noted
that the constant tendency of the committee to decry the liberal as
"gullible" is not entirely borne out by the committee's own admission that the membership lists of the organizations under study are
often severely padded. When the committee reports, as it does, that
the Lawyers Guild could claim only 3,891 members on June 1, 1950,
and that some of these were no longer paying dues,[67] it would appear
that in this one instance, at least, liberals had not waited for the
committee's advice before resolving the issue against the organization. At the same time there is admittedly much in these reports on
nine organizations that should prove informative to liberals who
have not always recognized the extent of Communist influence in
agencies in which they have been members.[68] There are many illus-

[67] *Ibid.*, pp. 20–21.

[68] Recognition of this Communist influence in an organization does not necessarily lead to the conclusions expressed or implied in these committee reports.
Liberals in some instances have early recognized the Communist influence but
have chosen to remain members and to fight the Communists for control of an

trations showing how the Communist sympathizers within these organizations have attempted to keep organization programs consistent with the frequent changes in the Communist Party lines. Similarly, there is revealing information concerning the successful tactics used by Communists to kill off rival organizations, to dominate parliamentary proceedings, or to divert an organization from its traditional or logical area of activity into other areas closer to Communist interests.

In the end it is difficult to avoid the conclusion that these nine reports fall wide of the mark at which they are aimed. They are concerned with organizations which almost certainly have been, or are, subject to strong Communist influence. It may be that it is a proper function of a Congressional committee to acquaint the American people with the devious behind-the-scenes tactics which Communists employ either to organize Communist fronts or to gain control of established non-Communist organizations. But these reports are so poorly written, are based upon such shoddy research, and are so irresponsible in their frequent attacks upon non-Communist liberals that the fair-minded reader is almost certain to be repelled by them. Indeed, it is likely that the adverse reactions experienced by some readers of these documents have led them to the conclusion that the organizations in question, having been so unfairly attacked, must be entirely innocent of the charges made against them. Once more, there is good reason to suppose that the House committee has done real harm by so irritating and repelling fair-minded Americans as to lead them to reject valid evidence concerning Communist activity along with the invalid and thus to confuse them concerning the undeniable threat offered by Communists. It is a tragic thing when much-needed liberal organizations, such as the Southern Conference for Human Welfare or the National Lawyers Guild, are destroyed, in part at least, as the result of Communist efforts to turn them into "fronts" for the Communist Party. Fortunately, non-Communists have slowly learned the necessary lesson, and more than one famous and valuable organization has been saved against this Communist assault. But it is doubtful whether the House committee reports have helped very much in the achievement of these victories. Indeed, by repelling and confusing fair-

organization. This was true of the forces led by Frank Graham in the Southern Conference for Human Welfare. On the other hand, in the organizations which are the subjects of these House committee reports, it must be confessed that this fight by liberals was often a losing battle.

minded persons it is probable that they have actually handicapped non-Communists in the struggle within organizations against Communists and have made victory harder to win.

These House reports have also done unquestionable harm in discouraging Americans from establishing or joining organizations. It is all very well for the committee to state in one of these reports: "It would indeed be unfortunate if any significant body of American women were persuaded to join or lend themselves to the purposes of this organization simply because it has adopted so deceptive a name as the Congress of American Women. It is the purpose of this report to offset any such eventuality." [69] But the committee surely has an obligation, which it has not met, to make clear that not all organizations with innocent-sounding names are Communist fronts; indeed, that only a very small percentage of American organizations have ever been subjected to even a minor assault by Communists. It is impossible to measure the harm done in this respect. Probably most Americans are not easily or permanently intimidated in a matter like this, and their tendency to join organizations is so strong that it is not apt to be permanently weakened by the committee-encouraged apprehension that almost any organization may turn out to be a Communist front. At the same time, there exists today a very general reluctance to join organizations or, indeed, to have anything to do with either persons or organizations within a very broad zone of controversiality. The habit of trust which has been a characteristic of American life seems well on its way to being replaced by a habit of suspicion. The House committee must assume part of the responsibility for this changing attitude toward organizations. The ease with which a Walt Disney confuses the League of Women Voters for the League of Women Shoppers and attributes to the former the Communist taint of the latter merely illustrates the handicap which honorable organizations now have to overcome as a result of the committee's activities.

"100 Things You Should Know about Communism"

The six pamphlets of the "100 Things You Should Know about Communism" series, issued in 1948 and 1949, are so crudely written and so superficial in content that one is tempted to refuse to take them seriously. But this would be a mistake, for they clearly represent a well-planned attempt by the committee to reach and influence the

[69] *CAW Rept.*, p. 1.

mass mind. It appears that better than one million copies of these pamphlets have been sold or given away, and it is probable that they have been widely read.[70]

These pamphlets consist of brief questions and answers written in a catchy and at times vulgar style. At their best, they provide the general reader with a certain measure of seemingly accurate, but overly simplified, information about Communist activity in the government service, the labor movement, and so forth. At their worst, they exaggerate the threat of domestic communism to the established patterns of American life beyond any bounds supported by evidence. An impression of the content of the six pamphlets can be obtained from a random sample of each one. First, from *100 Things You Should Know about Communism in the U.S.A.*:

These booklets are intended to help you know a Communist when you hear him speak and when you see him work.

If you ever find yourself in open debate with a Communist the facts here given can be used to destroy his arguments completely and expose him as he is for all to see.

1. What is Communism?
A system by which one small group seeks to rule the world.

·   ·   ·   ·   ·

48. Why do people become Communists then?
Basically, because they seek power and recognize the opportunities that Communism offers the unscrupulous.

But no matter *why* a particular person becomes a Communist, every member of the Party must be regarded the same way, as one seeking to overthrow the Government of the United States.

·   ·   ·   ·   ·

76. Where can a Communist be found in everyday American life?
Look for him in your school, your labor union, your church, or your civic club. Communists themselves say that they can be found "on almost any conceivable battlefront for the human mind."

From *100 Things You Should Know about Communism and Religion*:

[70] It is never easy to obtain accurate statistics on the distribution of government publications. It appears from the reports of the House committee that in the two years, 1948 and 1949, 850,000 copies of the pamphlets were distributed free of charge by the committee itself, and that in 1949 nearly 320,000 copies were sold by the Government Printing Office.

14. Would I be allowed time off for religious holidays and celebrations as now?
Not a chance.

. . . . .

27. Was Marx crazy?
Perhaps. But Marx was not the first evil and crazy man to start a terrible world upheaval, nor was he the last. Hitler was like that, too, but look at what he did.

. . . . .

72. Are there Communist clergymen?
Unfortunately, yes.

. . . . .

75. Are they important?
Not as important as the others who have joined the Communist fronts which the Attorney General and this committee have declared to be "subversive."

. . . . .

80. But is Communism a "real" danger inside our churches?
Here's J. Edgar Hoover on the subject:
"I confess to a real apprehension, so long as Communists are able to secure ministers of the Gospel to promote their evil work and espouse a cause that is alien to the religion of Christ and Judaism."

. . . . .

86. Is the YMCA a Communist target?
Yes. So is the YWCA.
Also, church groups such as the Epworth League.

From *100 Things You Should Know about Communism and Education:*

2. Is it [Communism] aimed at me?
Right between your eyes.

. . . . .

96. Do many of our teachers play the Communist game?
The files of our Committee, running back over a ten-year period, show that the Communists have always found the teaching group the easiest touch of all the professional classes for actual Party zealots and fellow travelers.

From *100 Things You Should Know about Communism and Labor:*

1. Is this pamphlet an attack on the unions?
No. Read it through and see for yourself.

. . . . .

23. *Is everybody a Communist who criticizes the United States?*
Of course not, but Communists and their dupes made a career of it.

24. *Is everybody a Communist who defends Russia?*
Oh, no. Some of the loudest Russia lovers are only fellow travelers and members of Communist fronts.

· · · · ·

96. *What's a good program for an American union man against Communism?*
Here is one given by James B. Carey, secretary-treasurer of the CIO: Full exposure of the Communists, plus a strong progressive policy "far in advance of the bogus progressivism of the Communists." Swift, flexible infighting that defeats the Communists at their own game within the union.

From *100 Things You Should Know about Communism and Government:*

28. *And you say some Communists have sneaked into our Government, as it is today?*
Yes. And we repeat, nobody knows how many.

· · · · ·

65. *Do Communists ever try to fix elections?*
As in every other field, they lay a poisonous hand on the ballot box.

· · · · ·

66. *Any proof?*
For example, in the 1940 Presidential election year, this committee made a special inquiry into Communist voting tactics.

Surveys in Maryland, West Virginia, Pennsylvania, Kentucky, and Ohio all unearthed wholesale frauds.

More than 100 indictments were brought on the basis of evidence the committee disclosed and between 50 and 60 convictions followed.[71] But that did not end the problem. Communists still try to corrupt the ballot box at every opportunity.

· · · · ·

87. [After relating the testimony of Elizabeth Bentley, Whittaker Chambers, and General Groves, concerning Communists in the government

[71] The committee does not further identify these cases, and the author has not been able to discover any evidence to support the committee's assertion. The cases certainly were not federal ones. It seems doubtful that any such prosecutions were based exclusively or even primarily "on the basis of evidence the committee disclosed" or that they were directed primarily against "Communist voting tactics."

service] *And that sort of character has been living off my tax money?*
Has been, still is, and still will be, until YOU force every Communist
out of power.

From *Spotlight on Spies* (The questions and answers in this pamphlet are unnumbered):

Would anyone but a fool be willing to spy for Russia?
  No. But you'll find "fools" in pretty HIGH places.
  Soviet spy rings contain well-educated and able Americans who are
looked up to by their fellow men. They may be scientists, lawyers, professors, writers, Government career workers, and even successful businessmen
who have been filled with Communist poison.

⋅   ⋅   ⋅   ⋅   ⋅

Are spies after our Government secrets RIGHT NOW?
  You can be sure of it.

⋅   ⋅   ⋅   ⋅   ⋅

All this is pretty serious, isn't it?
  Very, very serious.
  But in the case of much important information, Russian agents haven't
had to steal it. We have GIVEN it away.
What do you mean?
  For one thing, we have tried to be friendly to Russia and as a result
Russian officials have been able to collect a lot of our industrial and mili-
tary inventions just by buying patents for the inventions from our Govern-
ment Patent Office. This is done right out in the open with our permission.

⋅   ⋅   ⋅   ⋅   ⋅

What else have we GIVEN away?
  During the war, because they were our allies, Russian visitors were
invited to inspect our country and its defense industries. One of the
results was that the Russians betrayed our friendship and printed a thick
book which can easily be used as a handbook for bombing and sabotage
against the United States.
What does this book show?
  In pictures, maps, and words, the location and lay-outs of our Nation's
large power dams and power plants, aircraft and auto factories, plants
dealing with metals, bridges, railroads, and important communications.
Is America doing anything to protect herself from Soviet spies?
  Yes. The world's finest investigative agency is on the job—the FBI. It
is aided by Military and Naval Intelligence.
Isn't this enough?

Far from it. Every patriotic American must be on the alert and report all suspicious activities brought to his or her attention to either the Federal Bureau of Investigation, the Army or Navy Intelligence services, local police departments, and/or the Committee on Un-American Activities.

This is particularly important since the spy network is growing bigger because of new sources for spies.

The pamphlets of this "100 Things You Should Know about Communism" series represent an attempt to bring the work of the Un-American Activities Committee to the attention of large numbers of readers. The committee's wish to get away from the unattractive format and style of regular Congressional publications is understandable and commendatory. But it is difficult to avoid the conclusion that these pamphlets cheapen the national legislature. One can readily agree with Woodrow Wilson as to the importance of the "informing function" of Congress, but these pamphlets are written in such an informal style, are so biased in tone, and so generally lacking in documentation of their illustrative data that they are reduced to the level of cheap propaganda.

The Authorship of Committee Reports

Who writes the reports of the Un-American Activities Committee? This question is always difficult to answer with complete accuracy concerning the publications of any government agency. It is almost always safe to assume that others than those whose names are formally appended to a government document have had a hand in its writing. That this is so is not necessarily reason for alarm or condemnation. Provided public officers have determined in advance the main lines of the substance, the policy statements, and the conclusions of a formal document, have then carefully checked its content before publication, and are prepared to accept full responsibility for it, there is no reason why they should not enjoy assistance, particularly from their own staff employees, in its writing. Certainly this is a well-established practice among the committees of Congress. The best evidence suggests that the Congressmen who have been members of the Un-American Activities Committee have not personally done much of the writing that has gone into the committee's reports. In particular, it is wholly unlikely that its chairmen, John Wood and J. Parnell Thomas, have served as the actual draftsmen of the reports. Instead, it seems clear that the committee has depended very largely upon its professional staff to do its writing.

To what extent have committee members scrutinized and revised the drafts of reports prepared by others before signing them? The indications are that the so-called annual reports have been subjected to more or less rigorous examination by the committee but that such publications as the reports on the Communist Party and alleged Communist front organizations have received only cursory attention before being released.[72] The indications are, also, that the first drafts of the "annual" reports have been prepared by the nominal head of the staff—the chief investigator or the counsel. During the period of Stripling's services with the committee, preparation of these reports was seemingly his responsibility. On the other hand, the reports on the Communist Party and alleged Communist front organizations were probably written by the staff research unit under Benjamin Mandel's direction. There is also evidence that the first drafts of certain reports have been prepared by persons having no official connection with the committee. Stripling bluntly asserts in *The Red Plot Against America* that the "100 Questions" pamphlets were prepared "with the considerable aid of Frank Waldrop, editor of 'The Washington Times-Herald'—a staunch and courageous friend of the Committee in many of its darkest hours." [73] And again, Representative Nixon told the writer that the *Atomic Espionage Report*, dated September 29, 1949, was written by an "able attorney in private practice" and that in his opinion it was "the best report the Committee had ever issued." [74]

[72] From time to time indications of committee participation in the writing of reports, or the absence of such, appear in the press. For example, the *N.Y. Herald Tribune* reported, Jan. 15, 1949, that it was doubtful whether a report covering the committee's 1948 activities, "written largely" by Stripling would ever be released. It added that Representative Hébert was objecting vigorously to sections dealing with the Condon case and with Elizabeth Bentley's testimony. This story presumably referred to the final report of the Thomas committee, which is dated Dec. 31, 1948, but which was not actually released until Jan. 27, 1949.

At about the same time the press reported that Hébert and Peterson had forced the deletion of the names of twenty-seven former government employees named by Bentley and Chambers as members of Communist cells from the pamphlet, *100 Things You Should Know about Communism and the Government. N.Y. Star*, Jan. 6, 1949.

[73] Stripling, *The Red Plot*, p. 167.   [74] Interview, Feb. 2, 1950.

x: Press Treatment of the Un-American Activities Investigations

Publicity has been essential to all Congressional investigations. The investigating committee, of modern times at least, which has not depended heavily upon front-page press coverage of its activities as a means of effecting its purposes has been rare, indeed. Even the committee which has had as its chief purpose persuading Congress to enact legislation recommended by it has not been able to ignore the opportunity to create a favorable public opinion through the wide reporting of its work. But publicity is the very lifeblood of the committee that has only a secondary interest in legislation and is first of all anxious to influence directly patterns of social thought and conduct.

From the first days of the Dies committee in 1938 the story of the un-American activities investigation has been kept continuously in the forefront of the news, and no other phase of the work of Congress during this period has received better coverage in the press. Interestingly enough, the Dies committee was at first seemingly unaware of its great news potentiality. Ogden writes that the committee started off in circumspect enough fashion, but that it promptly had its eyes opened when one of its early witnesses, John P. Frey, an AFL official, made sensational charges concerning the presence of Communists in the CIO, and the "headlines began to scream." [1]

That the headlines have been screaming ever since has been due to two things: the committee's continuing awareness of the news value of its doings, together with its increasing ability to obtain

[1] *The Dies Committee*, pp. 52–56.

maximum publicity for them; and the press's own enthusiasm to tell the committee's story. In the narrow sense, the committee's labors have been performed in the city of Washington, where most of its hearings have been held, sometimes in executive session, often in the presence of a mere handful of spectators, and never before more than a few hundred people, and where the record of these hearings and its reports have been published, usually in limited editions of a few thousand copies. In the larger sense, however, the press and magazine, the newsreel, and the radio have provided the committee with a national audience. Its hearings have been brought in graphic detail to millions of newspaper readers and movie-goers. Its reports have been analyzed by scores of newspaper columnists and radio commentators for these same millions. In the end, it is fair to say that the process by which the committee's labors and findings have been reported to the American people by the press, magazine, radio, and motion picture has become an integral and essential part of the investigation itself. This fact has clearly been recognized by members of the committee and its staff, and they have planned and executed the committee's program accordingly.

Although committee members have from time to time made significant use of such devices as radio speeches and magazine articles to bring various aspects of the committee's work to the attention of large audiences, the newspaper has been the all-important agency which they have depended upon for publicity. Of course, a good part of the news about the committee carried in the press has consisted of normal reporting of public hearings, analysis of the committee's official publications, and accounts of press conferences held by committee members. But relations between the committee and the press have gone well beyond this. Members of the committee and its staff have endeavored with great success to establish close, informal ties with particular newspapers and newspapermen. Confidential information has leaked in both directions between the press and the committee; anonymous or unofficial statements have been planted in the press which have had much the same effect as though they bore the official imprint of the committee, but which have been readily disowned or repudiated if the need arose; and the committee has provided a steady flow of publicity concerning sensational things to come—"surprise" hearings to be held, "mystery" witnesses to be heard, and "shocking" findings to be revealed—which has been enthusiastically utilized by many papers. The result has been that a good deal of the news about the committee printed by the press has had no basis in official action and has gone well beyond the mere reporting of events as they have taken place. That many of the rumors, predictions of coming sensations, and similar gossip stories have not been borne out by actual developments has often escaped the attention of newspaper readers.

Press-Committee Co-operation: Communism in Cincinnati

In July, 1950, the House committee conducted several days of public hearings on the subject of Communist activity in the Cincinnati area.[2] The two chief witnesses, a husband and wife, were identified as undercover informers for the FBI, who had joined the Communist Party in 1940 and had reported to the FBI on Communist activity in Cincinnati for something over one year. The testimony of these witnesses follows closely the pattern set in all of the hearings of this period in which the committee investigated Communist activity in certain geographic areas. Scores of persons were specifically named by the witnesses as having been members of the Communist Party, and their tactics and strategy in the Cincinnati area, with particular reference to the labor movement, were set forth.

What makes this series of hearings particularly interesting is that earlier, in February and March, 1950, the *Cincinnati Enquirer* had run a series of six feature articles in its Sunday issues which purported to set forth in systematic fashion the story of Communist activity in the city. Although the articles were highly sensational in character and alleged that party members were to be found in all walks of life in the community, including newspapermen, labor union officials, businessmen, radio announcers, and a member of the University of Cincinnati faculty, the *Enquirer,* presumably deterred by fear of libel suits, refrained from naming specific persons as Communists.[3] However, as the articles appeared the *Enquirer* was subjected to increasing pressure to name the persons referred to, and ultimately its series was vigorously criticized by the other Cincinnati newspapers, which charged that the author of the articles had derived much of his data from a "turncoat Communist" who had once been a patient in a mental institution. At some point along the way,

[2] *Hearings regarding Communist Activities in the Cincinnati, Ohio, Area—Part I.*

[3] I have relied for information about this episode on an article, "Cincinnati's Phantom Reds," by James A. Maxwell, *The Reporter,* Sept. 26, 1950. See also "The Cincinnati Reds," *Time,* March 27, 1950.

it seemingly occurred to the *Enquirer* that if the names of the alleged Communists could be presented to a Congressional committee in a public hearing the information could then readily be printed without fear of libel suits. For several weeks, the *Enquirer* printed a petition on its front page which it urged its readers to sign. The petition asked that "the names of Cincinnati Communists be exposed before the proper investigating authority in Washington." A reported ten thousand signatures were obtained and taken to Washington by the author of the articles. Shortly thereafter, the House committee hearings took place. The reporter did not testify, but the committee is said to have listened in executive session for several days to his informant. This latter testimony has never been made public by the committee.[4] On the other hand, the four witnesses of the "friendly" variety whose testimony was heard in public session gave the *Enquirer* a sound legal basis for publishing the names of more than one hundred alleged Communists.

There is no direct evidence that the House committee knowingly co-operated with the *Cincinnati Enquirer* in providing it with what one reputable Cincinnati observer has called a "libel-proof sounding board."[5] Indeed, it apparently refused to hear the author of the articles and his informant in March when they had asked to be allowed to testify while the articles were appearing. Nevertheless, the committee did hold hearings soon after the articles were published, and in so doing it did, consciously or unconsciously, enable the *Enquirer* to document its charges without fear of being taken into court in a series of libel actions. This is not to say that it is not a proper function of either a newspaper or a legislative committee to concern itself with the nature and scope of Communist activity in an American community. But the libel laws have historically been designed to prevent just such unsupported charges against named individuals as the *Enquirer* was seemingly unwilling to make until a Congressional committee gave it the necessary immunity bath. In the end, the question whether the newspaper and the committee consciously co-operated in this undertaking is not so important as the fact that their separate actions did dovetail very effectively. The *Enquirer* set the stage, at least so far as the interest of Cincinnatians was concerned, the committee took over the actual performance of the drama, and both paper and committee then took credit for the

---

[4] The published volume of hearings is labeled *Part I*, which suggests that the committee contemplated publishing further testimony.

[5] James A. Maxwell in the article referred to in note 3.

entertainment provided. Perhaps no other incident in the history of the committee shows quite so directly the closely intertwined roles inevitably played by the committee and the press as the search for evidence of "un-American activity" is pushed forward.

Press Coverage of Committee Hearings: The Hollywood Hearings

The desire to put on a good "show" and thereby to influence public opinion or to bring direct pressure upon a part of the nation to mend its ways motivated the Un-American Activities Committee about as strongly in the 1947 Hollywood hearings as in any project it ever undertook. The realization of this desire depended upon the co-operation of the press. The committee's expectations that the press would report such hearings in sensational fashion were not disappointed. Throughout the last two weeks of October, 1947, the Hollywood hearings remained a front-page story in virtually every daily newspaper in the country, in spite of the fact that the story had to compete with such spot news developments as the Bar Harbor fire and a great airplane disaster. Accordingly, the treatment given by the press to this set of hearings may properly be examined rather closely as a case study, with certain questions in mind. As the story was reported day by day, what among the welter of witnesses and confusion of detail did the press regard as most significant? Was any effort made by the press to maintain a proper balance between testimony suggesting that Hollywood was subject to a strong Communist influence and the testimony suggesting that it was not? To what extent were the merely flamboyant or grotesque items in the testimony singled out for emphasis? How successful was the press in maintaining any thread of continuity in its reporting of the story as it unfolded? Did it keep the reader's attention fixed upon the larger significance of the undertaking, upon the main points which the committee itself said would be developed, or was it content to report mere details? Finally, was there any uniformity among different newspapers in the way they reported the story, or do wide divergencies in the content of headlines and lead paragraphs suggest that reporting of the episode reflected the varying prejudices of newspapers or inability to agree as to the significance of the testimony?

In an attempt to answer such questions an analysis has been made of the way in which the Hollywood hearings were reported by six newspapers: the *New York Times,* the *New York Herald Tribune,*

PM (New York), the *Washington Post,* the *St. Louis Post-Dispatch,* and the *Chicago Tribune.* Admittedly, this is not a well-rounded sample of American newspapers. *PM* might be expected to report the story with a strong leftist bias, the *Chicago Tribune* with a vigorously reactionary bias, and the other four papers to achieve varying degrees of impartiality, accuracy, and completeness in their stories. Certainly, however, these six papers collectively might reasonably be expected to rise somewhat above the national average in bringing fairness and understanding to their reporting of the hearings.[6] Therefore, it may safely be assumed that any shortcomings in the manner in which they handled the story was more than matched in the press of the nation generally.

The reporting of the hearings was generally given front-page attention by all six papers throughout the two-week period. In a few instances, the hearings for particular days got banner headlines, but more generally the stories, while prominently displayed, had only the usual one- or two-column headlines. Most of the papers assigned top reporters to cover the hearings, and their stories carried by-lines. The *New York Herald Tribune* stories were written by Carl Levin, the *Washington Post* stories by Mary Spargo, the *Chicago Tribune* stories by Willard Edwards, and the *PM* stories by Quentin Reynolds. The *New York Times* used three different reporters from day to day: Samuel A. Tower, Anthony Leviero, and Joseph A. Loftus. The stories in the *St. Louis Post-Dispatch* carried no by-line.

First Day (October 20).[7] On the first day of the Hollywood hearings the chief witnesses were Jack Warner and Louis Mayer, powerful motion picture producers, and Sam Wood, an eminent director. The testimony of these men ranged widely. They asserted their belief that Communists and fellow travelers had infiltrated the motion picture industry and had tried to introduce subversive prop-

---

[6] *Hearings regarding Communist Infiltration of the Motion Picture Industry,* Oct. 20–24, 27–30, 1947.

Any attempt to make a broad survey of the reporting of the Hollywood hearings by an adequate sample of American newspapers and to use the techniques of content analysis would quickly become a major research undertaking in itself. Such a project was beyond the means and purpose of the present study. However, it did seem that the manner in which the story was handled by the six papers selected (with a combined circulation of nearly two and a half million) would be a significant thing to ascertain in its own right.

[7] The *Times, Herald Tribune, Post, Tribune,* and *PM* were all morning papers, and accordingly each day's hearing was reported by them in the issue of the following day. The *Post-Dispatch,* being an afternoon paper, reported on each hearing in its issue of the same date.

aganda into films. Wood, in particular, emphasized the extent of Communist influence in Hollywood. But they testified also concerning their successful efforts to thwart the Communist threat. Warner and Mayer defended their studios, at length, against the charge that in making such pictures as *Mission to Moscow* and *Song of Russia* they had allowed Communist propaganda to dominate their products.

Almost without exception the headlines and lead paragraphs of the six papers emphasized the angle of Communist penetration of the motion picture industry. The *New York Times* headlines began, FILM MEN ADMIT ACTIVITY BY REDS. This was offset by the immediate acknowledgment, HOLD IT IS FOILED.[8] Wood got first attention in the *Times* headline—SAM WOOD LISTS WRITERS BY NAME AS COMMUNISTS AND SAYS GROUP SEEKS RULE. On the other hand, the first words of the *Times* story were to the effect that the Communists in Hollywood had been successfully checkmated and that the industry was overwhelmingly patriotic. The *Herald Tribune* headlines stressed only the Communist threat: 18 IN MOVIES HELD PRO-RED BY PRODUCERS—14 WRITERS, 4 DIRECTORS NAMED BY MAYER, WOOD, WARNER IN U.S. INQUIRY. The first paragraphs of the *Herald Tribune* story stressed the naming of Communists in the industry, although the following paragraphs pointed out that the witnesses had testified that these Communists were known and that their propaganda was being carefully excluded from pictures.

The *Chicago Tribune* headline proclaimed, REDS INVADE MOVIE COLONY, PROBERS TOLD—CLAIM ORDERS CAME FROM MOSCOW. The first paragraphs of the *Tribune's* story were exclusively concerned with developing the two points set forth in the headline. Similarly, the *St. Louis Post-Dispatch* headlines gave an unrelieved picture of subversive activity in the movie industry: UN-AMERICAN IDEAS PUT IN MOVIE SCRIPTS BY SOME WRITERS, SAYS PRODUCER—HOUSE GROUP TOLD REDS GOT $87,000 AT MEETING; "NOT FOR BOY SCOUTS"—MOVIE MAN SAYS KATHARINE HEPBURN APPEARED AT SESSION—EFFORT TO GAIN UNION CONTROL CHARGED. Likewise, the first part of its story dealt only with the naming by witnesses of Communists who were

---

[8] It is impossible to reproduce newspaper headlines with graphic accuracy. The headlines cited varied widely with respect to type size and style, spacing, and so forth. Usually the latter portions of the headlines accompanying a story were set in smaller type and thus did not have the same impact as did the first statement or two.

"seeking to gain control of unions and guilds in the movie capital." Not until the sixteenth paragraph did the emphasis change and was reference made to the fact that one of the producers had testified concerning successful countermeasures taken by the industry to thwart Communist tactics.

The *Washington Post* headline was a relatively balanced one, although the first thing mentioned was "Red" activity: RED EFFORTS TO SUBVERT VIA SCREEN DESCRIBED—PRODUCERS REPORT ANTI-PROPAGANDA GAINS; WOOD URGES PARTY BE OUTLAWED. The first paragraph of the *Post's* story was of the scare variety: "Top Hollywood producers told Congress yesterday that Communists have been trying for years to use motion pictures to put subversive propaganda across to millions of Americans every day." An effort to offset this frightening assertion was made in the second paragraph, which reported that in the main Communist propaganda had been kept out of pictures and that more care in this respect was now being exercised.

PM's headline first proclaimed the identity of its special correspondent covering the hearings, namely, Quentin Reynolds, added his observation that FILM MAGNATES, ON STAND, PLAY ROLES AS THOUGH COACHED, and concluded on an ambiguous note, HOLLYWOOD WRITERS NAMED AT QUIZ. *PM's* story on the first day of the hearings, like those that followed, revealed a tendency to ignore or play down the actual testimony while emphasizing trivialities. The first five paragraphs told of the disappointment of a member of the audience, one Mrs. Joseph Geiger, because no big film stars had testified.

Second Day (October 21). Three witnesses testified on the second day of the hearings. Adolph Menjou and Rupert Hughes made detailed, highly personal, and bitter attacks upon alleged Communists and fellow travelers in Hollywood. The third witness, J. C. Moffitt, motion picture critic for *Esquire* magazine, also vigorously denounced many persons in the industry as Communists. At the end of his testimony, pressed by Stripling as to whether any of these persons had ever engaged in espionage or similar activity, Moffitt stated that a prominent official of an agency which sold story material to the movies and to magazines had once tricked an Army test pilot, named Slick Goodlin, into preparing a rough draft of a magazine article in which he unconsciously revealed secret information about a supersonic plane he had been testing. Moffitt asserted

that this official had been sent to Hollywood by Communist headquarters in New York.[9]

Two newspapers, the *Chicago Tribune* and the *Washington Post*,
featured the supersonic plane story. As the *Tribune* saw it: PROBERS
LEARN DATA ON PLANE WAS OBTAINED—TEST PILOT VICTIM OF
PLOT, WRITER SAYS. The first paragraph of the *Tribune* story reported that this tale of Communist espionage in Hollywood had
shocked the Un-American Activities Committee. The *Washington
Post* headline was even more lurid: MOVIE AGENT GAVE REDS PLANE
PLANS, HEARING TOLD—TEST PILOT TRICKED, WITNESS TESTIFIES;
LAWYER EJECTED BY HOUSE COMMITTEE. Moreover, in the lead paragraph of her story Mary Spargo asserted that the secret of a supersonic military plane went straight to Communist Party headquarters
from the hands of a prominent literary agent. Actually, a careful
reading of the printed record of Moffitt's testimony reveals that he
made no direct assertion that the literary agent had passed Goodlin's
data on to Communist headquarters.

Two papers, the *Times* and the *Post-Dispatch*, gave first attention
in their headlines to Adolph Menjou. The *Times* headline stated,
MENJOU TESTIFIES COMMUNISTS TAINT THE FILM INDUSTRY—ACTOR
SAYS "MISSION TO MOSCOW" AND "NORTH STAR" WERE FILMS CARRY-
ING PROPAGANDA. The gist of the *Times*'s lead paragraph was that
Menjou and two other witnesses had said that the industry was
"deeply tainted" by communism, but that it was also "increasingly
alert to the dangers." The *Times* headline and story also called at-
tention to a sensational assertion by Moffitt that 44 out of 100 plays
produced on Broadway between 1936 and 1946 supported the "Com-
munist line." The first part of the *Post-Dispatch* headline dealt with
Menjou. HOLLYWOOD A MAIN CENTER OF RED ACTIVITIES IN U.S.,
ADOLPH MENJOU TESTIFIES—"WE HAVE MANY, MANY DANGEROUS
DIRECTORS AND ACTORS," HE SAYS. Thereafter, the headline touched
on the Goodlin affair, WITNESS SAYS LEFTISTS GAVE ARMY TEST
PILOT'S DATA ON SUPERSONIC BOMBERS TO COMMUNISTS. In similar
fashion, the first paragraphs of the *Post-Dispatch*'s story dealt with
Menjou's testimony, and the following paragraphs with the super-
sonic plane affair.

The *Herald Tribune* gave first attention in its headlines to the
ejection of a lawyer from the hearing: LAWYER EJECTED FROM HEAR-
ING ON MOVIE REDS—MENJOU AND RUPERT HUGHES TESTIFY; PEPPER
ADVISES DEFIANCE OF COMMITTEE. The first paragraph of Carl Levin's

[9] *Hearings Mot. Pict. Ind.,* pp. 126–127.

story reported that Menjou and Hughes "gave . . . further reams of testimony of Communist intrigue and influence" in Hollywood. The supersonic plane story was played down, and a denial which the story agent had issued on hearing about Moffitt's allegation was carried.

PM's headline reported, MOVIE PROBERS CARRY ON ALMOST THE WAY HITLER's COURTS DID—LAWYERS FIND THE LAW DOESN'T COUNT AND ONE GETS BOOTED; MENJOU STARS. The first paragraphs of Quentin Reynolds' story dealt with the ejection of the lawyer— "diffident, quiet Mr. Katz heard Chairman Parnell Thomas cry, 'Throw him out.' He heard a newspaper columnist shout, 'Get a blackjack and slug him.'" The supersonic plane affair was completely ignored in Reynolds' story, although it was referred to in a separate, inside-page story.

Third Day (October 22). On the third day of the hearing four more "friendly" witnesses were heard. They were Robert Taylor, the actor; J. K. McGuinness, a script editor at MGM; Howard Rushmore of the editorial department of the New York *Journal American* and a former member of the Communist Party who had once served as film critic for the *Daily Worker;* and Morrie Ryskind, a stage and film writer.

Three papers, the *Tribune,* the *Post,* and the *Post-Dispatch* gave first attention to Robert Taylor. The *Tribune* headline had Taylor urging a LAW TO CLEAN OUT REDS and telling of his FIGHT TO AVOID PRO-SOVIET ROLE. Its story developed these two points, and by way of providing a bit of color reported that "feminine sighs and cries rose in volume as the black haired actor uttered his vigorous testimony. Chairman Thomas (R., N.J.) finally called on police to maintain order." The *Post* headline was brief: BOBBY SOXERS AND MOTHERS: WOMEN CHEER ROBERT TAYLOR AS HE URGES BAN ON REDS. Its story reported that "Robert Taylor, famed screen lover, yesterday asked Congress to outlaw the Communist Party while hundreds of women wildly cheered him on." The *Post-Dispatch* headline told: ROBERT TAYLOR TESTIFIES TO INCREASING SIGNS OF HOLLYWOOD RED ACTIVITY and then, more accurately than had the *Tribune's* headline, reported, DENIES HE WAS FORCED TO MAKE "SONG OF RUSSIA" BUT OPPOSED IT. The lead paragraphs of the story carried out the first theme of the headline: "Taylor . . . told congressional investigators . . . that he had seen 'more indications' of Communist activity in filmland in the last four or five years than previously."

The *Herald Tribune* gave first attention in its headline to the testi-

mony of McGuinness: MOVIE REDS CALLED ALIEN FIFTH COLUMN—
M.G.M. OFFICIAL TESTIFIES TINY GROUP OF LEFTISTS SERVES FOREIGN
IDEOLOGY. Thereafter, its headline touched upon an announcement
by Chairman Parnell Thomas that a list of seventy-nine Communists
in Hollywood would soon be made public; upon Taylor's advice to
the committee that all Communists be deported; and upon a statement by Paul McNutt, counsel for a portion of the motion picture
industry, denouncing the committee on the ground that it was trying
to dictate the content of films.

The *Times* headline was also of the omnibus variety: 79 IN HOLLY-
WOOD FOUND SUBVERSIVE, INQUIRY HEAD SAYS—EVIDENCE OF COM-
MUNIST SPYING WILL BE OFFERED NEXT WEEK—THOMAS DECLARES
TAYLOR URGES PARTY BAN. *PM's* headline ignored the proceedings
of the third day and featured Ronald Reagan as the star of the
impending fourth-day hearing.

An amusing aspect of the stories on the third-day hearing was the
inability of reporters to agree upon the color of Robert Taylor's ap-
parel. The *Tribune* story referred to "Taylor, clad in a suit described
as mauve with a green stripe." The *Post's* Mary Spargo reported that
"Taylor wore a brown suit with red and white pin stripes." And as
the *Herald Tribune* saw it, Taylor was "attired in a cocoa-colored
double-breasted suit with red and gray stripes."

Fourth Day (October 23). On the fourth day the committee
heard seven writers, directors, and actors, all of whom fell into the
"friendly witness" category. The testimony ranged rather widely
and it is perhaps not surprising that the headlines were varied and
confused. In three papers the dominant note was that the witnesses
had testified concerning the presence of Communists in Hollywood
but had definitely minimized the "Red menace." The *Times* headline
was: HOLLYWOOD COMMUNISTS "MILITANT," BUT SMALL IN NUMBER,
STARS TESTIFY. The lead paragraph reported, "Three Hollywood
stars, leaders in the Screen Actors Guild, stated today that their profession contained a 'militant, well-organized, well-disciplined minority' of Communist leanings. They declared the group was tiny
and had made no headway."

The *Post-Dispatch* headline was, REDS MORE NOISY THAN INFLU-
ENTIAL, SAY MOVIE STARS, and as *PM* saw it, WITNESSES OPPOSE
COMMUNISM BUT DOUBT MENACE. However, the *Tribune* and the
Post both featured Gary Cooper and a grotesque story which a
committee investigator had told while Cooper was on the stand to
the effect that Communist propaganda in Europe featured Cooper

as an American Communist. The *Tribune* headlined: COOPER TELLS OF REJECTING "PINKO" SCRIPTS—ACTOR "SHOCKED" BY RED PROPAGANDA. Its lead paragraph said that Cooper had learned that he was being exploited in Europe as a Soviet leader in the United States. The *Post* headline was WITHOUT THEIR KNOWLEDGE HOLLYWOOD STARS' NAMES USED IN EUROPEAN RED PROPAGANDA—GARY COOPER IS CALLED "COMRADE" HE LEARNS DURING MOVIE HEARING. The first nine paragraphs of the *Post* story developed the European propaganda angle.

The *Herald Tribune* headline featured the stars' attack upon the Communists in Hollywood, without noting that they had also minimized the threat. However, it did call attention to the resistance encountered by the committee to its suggestion that Hollywood should make more anti-Communist pictures. The headline was: FILM ACTORS ACCUSE REDS AT INQUIRY—BUT INQUIRY TAKES A NEW TURN AS STARS INSIST ON RETAINING CIVIL RIGHTS—McCAREY OPPOSES ALL "ANTI" MOVIES—MONTGOMERY, COOPER AND OTHERS STRESS HOSTILITY TO ALL TOTALITARIAN RULE. A fair criticism of the reporting of the fourth-day hearing was the general failure of the six papers to pay more attention to Ronald Reagan, who as president of the Screen Actors Guild gave a most intelligent and discerning account of the Communist threat in Hollywood as he saw it, and who offered the calm, sensible advice that the United States should not allow its fear of communism to lead it to compromise with any of its own democratic traditions. On the other hand, every paper managed to find space to report the following innocuous bit of testimony:

Mr. Stripling: How did [*Going My Way* and *The Bells of St. Marys*] do in Russia?
Mr. McCarey: We haven't received one ruble from Russia on either picture.
Mr. Stripling: What is the trouble?
Mr. McCarey: Well, I think I have a character in there that they do not like.
Mr. Stripling: Bing Crosby?
Mr. McCarey: No; God.[10]

Fifth Day (October 24). Three witnesses were heard on the fifth and last day of the first week of hearings. They were Walt Disney, Lela Rogers, mother of Ginger Rogers, and an obscure student of propaganda named Oliver Carlson. These witnesses had to com-

[10] *Ibid.*, p. 225.

pete for the attention of the press with the Bar Harbor fire story and also with an airliner crash in Utah which had taken fifty-two lives. Virtually every paper gave prominence to Disney's assertion that the Communists had tried to take over his studio. The *Post-Dispatch* headline said: DISNEY TESTIFIES REDS TOOK OVER ARTISTS AT STUDIO—QUOTES UNION LEADER AS SAYING HE USED NLRB AS IT SUITED HIS PURPOSE. The *Post* version was REDS TRIED TO RUIN HIM, DISNEY SAYS—WORLD-WIDE SMEAR CAMPAIGN FOLLOWED THREAT, ARTIST TESTIFIES. The *Tribune* reported: DISNEY REVEALS RED BATTLE TO RULE HIS STUDIO—TELLS THREAT BY SORRELL, ATTACKS BY *PM*. And the *Herald Tribune* said, DISNEY TESTIFIES REDS TOOK OVER ARTISTS IN STRIKE—FAVORS OUTLAWING PARTY IF IT IS UN-AMERICAN, HE TELLS HOUSE INQUIRY.

Only the *Times* and *PM* departed from the pattern. The *Times* devoted the first part of its headline and the first paragraphs of its story to a statement made by Representative Vail denouncing the press for its criticism of the Un-American Activities Committee. Its headline was: CRITICS OF FILM INQUIRY ASSAILED: DISNEY DENOUNCED "COMMUNISTS." And *PM*'s headline proclaimed that the FILM PROBERS were ON DEFENSIVE, would TRY COMEBACK, and that HOSTILE WITNESSES would TAKE STAND IN COMING WEEK.

Second Week: Sixth Day (October 27). Whereas virtually all of the witnesses during the first week had been of the "friendly" variety, the second week of hearings was devoted very largely to a parade of "unfriendly" witnesses to and from the stand. As has already been told, this parade quickly settled into a monotonous pattern: the witness was sworn in; was refused permission to make a prepared statement; he in turn refused to answer questions—particularly concerning membership in the Communist Party; the witness was dismissed with the statement that the committee would cite him for contempt; and Louis Russell, committee investigator, was called to the stand to read into the record a dossier of the allegedly Communist affiliations and activities of the recalcitrant witness.

On the first day of the second week the committee heard two witnesses: Eric Johnston, president of the Motion Picture Association of America, and John Howard Lawson, screen writer, and first of the unfriendly witnesses. Johnston testified at some length in defense of the industry's policies, and several rather vigorous exchanges took place between him, Stripling, Thomas, and other committee members. Lawson was an intractable witness, and his brief appearance before the committee was violent and disorderly. Three papers focused their headlines upon Johnston, three upon Lawson. In the first group, the *Post-Dispatch* headline read: SOUGHT TO BAR REDS IN MOVIES JOHNSTON SAYS—PRODUCERS REJECTED PROPOSAL, HE TESTIFIES, and then noted, COMMITTEE VOTES WRITER IN CONTEMPT. The first seven paragraphs of its story developed the Johnston aspect of the hearing.

The *Tribune* reported: FIERY SESSION SEES THOMAS, JOHNSTON Row, and added, referring to an item in Johnston's testimony, MOVIE CHIEF ADMITS AID WAS COMMIE. The opening paragraphs of the *Tribune's* story were evenly divided between Lawson's refusal to testify and Johnston's admission that he had once had a Communist assistant.

The *Herald Tribune* headline noted first: JOHNSTON REJECTS ANY DICTATION TO HOLLYWOOD BY GOVERNMENT—VOICES INDUSTRY'S STAND AT RED FILM INQUIRY, and then added: LAWSON WON'T SAY IF HE IS COMMUNIST: ORDERED OFF STAND, HE FACES CONTEMPT CITATION. The *Herald Tribune's* lead paragraphs ranged widely. The first one was devoted to Johnston's demand that the government refrain from dictating to the motion picture industry; the second called attention to an announcement by Thomas that the committee would soon investigate communism in the fields of labor and education; and the third stated that Lawson's refusal to testify had laid a foundation for a court test of the committee's powers.

In the second group, the *Times* headline was an omnibus one: FILM INQUIRY SEEKS CONTEMPT CITATION ON DEFIANT WRITER— HOUSE GROUP ACTS AS LAWSON FAILS TO ANSWER QUESTION ON WHETHER HE IS A RED—JOHNSTON HITS INQUIRY—URGES COMMITTEE NOT TO PUT THE FINGER OF SUSPICION ON INNOCENT PERSONS. The first two paragraphs of the *Times* story dealt with the Lawson and Johnston appearances in the same order as had its headline.

The *Post* headline proclaimed: LAWSON CITED IN CONTEMPT AS AUDIENCE CHEERS, BOOS—WRITER CHALLENGES COMMITTEE POWERS: JOHNSTON CLASHES WITH CHAIRMAN. In its story the *Post* first dealt with Lawson's refusal to testify, next noted the presence among spectators at the hearing of members of the "Committee for Preservation of the First Amendment," and then went on to Johnston's testimony. *PM*, in a thoroughly depersonalized headline, merely noted: MOVIE PROBE OPENS WAY FOR COURT TEST OF CIVIL RIGHTS. Its story dealt first with the Lawson fracas and then went on to Johnston's appearance before the committee.

Seventh Day (October 28). On the seventh day the committee cited for contempt three more witnesses who refused to answer questions; heard Roy M. Brewer, an official of the Stage Employees and Motion Picture Machine Operators Union, testify concerning alleged Communist activity in Hollywood labor disputes; and called to the stand Robert W. Kenny, counsel for the unfriendly witnesses and queried him concerning a news story which reported that he was advising his clients to refuse to testify. There was an ugly moment during Kenny's appearance, for when he protested that the committee was encroaching upon the privacy of the counsel-client relationship, Thomas read him the federal conspiracy statute and threatened him with a criminal prosecution.

Four papers gave first attention in their headlines to the additional contempt cases, three of them noting nothing else. The *Times* stated in its headline, THREE MORE FILM WRITERS FACE HOUSE CONTEMPT CITATIONS, and devoted the first four paragraphs of its story to this subject. It turned then to a public reply Paul McNutt had made as an attorney for the industry to an assertion by the committee that film leaders were doing their best to kill the inquiry.

The *Post-Dispatch* headline ran: CONTEMPT ACTION AGAINST 3 MOVIE WRITERS IN INQUIRY ON REDS—DALTON TRUMBO, ALVAH BESSIE AND ALBERT MALTZ REFUSE TO TELL HOUSE GROUP WHETHER THEY ARE COMMUNISTS. The first five paragraphs of its story deal with the contempt action, and the story then turned to an assertion made by Parnell Thomas that the committee had discovered more communism in Hollywood than any other place investigated.

The *Washington Post* headline began with a tease phrase, THEY WON'T SAY YES OR NO, and then explained, THREE MORE FILM WRITERS CITED FOR CONTEMPT FOR DEFYING HOUSE QUIZ ON COMMUNISM —TRUMBO, ALVAH BESSIE, AND MALTZ REFUSE TO TELL AFFILIATIONS. The *Post*'s story first gave the details concerning the three recalcitrant witnesses and then turned to Kenny's clash with the committee.

Alone among the six papers the *Herald Tribune* managed to find room in its headline for a passing reference to the Kenny episode: MOVIE INQUIRY CITES 3 MORE FOR CONTEMPT—TRUMBO, MALTZ AND BESSIE ARE ORDERED OFF STAND—COUNSEL GETS JAIL THREAT. The *Herald Tribune*'s story treated the new contempt citations rather briefly and then set forth in some detail Kenny's row with the committee over the issue of his advice to his clients.

The *Chicago Tribune* was the only paper which made even an oblique headline reference to the file data being read into the record by Louis Russell. It stated, BARED AS REDS AFTER BALKING AT QUESTIONS and then called attention to Thomas' attack upon Hollywood:

HOLLYWOOD IS WORST YET: THOMAS. The *Tribune's* story began by dealing with the two items in its headline in the same order used there.

PM ran an editorial headline, MOVIE PROBE UNMASKS ITSELF AS POLITICAL TRIAL, and its Quentin Reynolds story began by suggesting that Stripling had probably been lightly scolded by Thomas the night before, because the former had thoughtlessly "spilled the beans" by saying to Alvah Bessie, "You have been charged, etc.," thus revealing that the committee regarded itself as a prosecuting body.

Eighth Day (October 29). On the next to the last day of the Hollywood hearings the committee heard four more recalcitrant witnesses, and also Emmet Lavery, screen writer and president of the Screen Writers' Guild, and Dore Schary, then executive in charge of production at the RKO studios. It is not clear whether the committee expected Lavery to join the list of unfriendly witnesses. At any rate, he quickly dissociated himself from this group, stated flatly that he had never been a member of the Communist Party and went on to make a courageous and eloquent defense of the motion picture industry. In view of the monotonous routine now being followed by both the contumacious witnesses and the committee, Lavery's appearance was clearly the most significant development of the day. Nonetheless, four papers gave first attention in their headlines to the additions to the unfriendly list, and only two featured Lavery's testimony, although two papers in the first group managed to devote secondary headline attention to Lavery. As the *Chicago Tribune* saw it: HOUSE PROBERS EXPOSE 4 MORE AS MOVIE REDS—CITE WITNESS FOR CONTEMPT. The *Post-Dispatch* reported: FOUR MORE MOVIE FIGURES CITED FOR REFUSAL TO TELL IF THEY ARE REDS—ADRIAN SCOTT, SAMUEL ORWITZ, EDWARD DMYTRYK, HERBERT BIBERMAN BRING NUMBER ACCUSED OF CONTEMPT TO 8. Both of these papers devoted the lead paragraphs of their stories to the new contempt cases.

The two papers that found secondary headline space for the Lavery testimony were the *Times* and the *Post*. The *Times* headline ran: HOUSE CONTEMPT IS CHARGED TO FOUR MORE FILM FIGURES—NUMBER DECLINING TO TELL INQUIRY WHETHER THEY ARE COMMUNISTS RISE TO 8—HEAD OF WRITERS GUILD DENIES RED INFLUENCE. And the *Post* headline: FOUR MORE HOLLYWOOD FIGURES CITED IN CONTEMPT—SCREEN WRITERS' PRESIDENT DENIES THAT COMMUNISTS DOMINATE UNION. The stories in these two papers were rather more balanced than were their headlines and brought out the contrast between conduct of the contemptuous witnesses and that of Lavery.

The two papers which gave first attention to Lavery's testimony were the *New York Herald Tribune* and *PM*. The *Herald Tribune* headline was: Lavery Denies Reds Dominate Screen Writers— Guild Head Says He Is Not a Communist; 4 More Cited for Contempt. It then devoted the first half-dozen paragraphs of its story to Lavery's assertion that he was not a Communist and that the Screen Writers Guild was not Communist-dominated.

PM's headline was: Movie Probers Left Reeling by Writer— Emmet Lavery, the Underdog, Throws Punches and Makes 'Em Like It. The first paragraph of its story depicted Lavery as a conquering hero.

Ninth Day (October 30). On the ninth and last day the committee heard two more contemptuous witnesses, bringing the total in this category to ten. It heard also Berthold Brecht, a German writer, who had clearly been expected by the committee to join the unfriendly witness group, but who stated that since he was "a guest in this country" and did "not want to enter into any legal arguments," he would answer questions. He then stated flatly that he had never been a member of the Communist Party. The last witness of the day, before the Hollywood hearings were abruptly adjourned, was Louis Russell. For several days the committee had widely advertised the news that it would soon hear a mystery witness who would tell a sensational and shocking story. The mystery witness proved to be Russell, and the shocking story, which seemingly had no connection with the motion picture industry beyond a California setting, concerned alleged Communist espionage in the Radiation Laboratory at the University of California.

Without exception all six papers stressed Russell's espionage story, although several also noted the abrupt termination of the hearings. The *Times* headline was wordy but well balanced: Film Inquiry Reveals Move by Soviet Agents to Obtain Atom Research Data in 1942—Expert Balked It—Dr. Oppenheimer Called Step "Treasonable" Investigator Says—Two More Writers Hit—Lardner, Jr. and Lester Cole Face Contempt Action as Hearings Halt Abruptly. The *Herald Tribune* managed to introduce a disloyal "professor" into its headlines, and Louis Russell became an ex-FBI agent as he did also in the *Post-Dispatch* headline. The *Herald Tribune* headline ran: Russian Attempt to Get Atomic Secrets in 1942 Revealed to Committee—Ex-F.B.I. Agent Asserts Oppenheimer Rejected Plea as "Treasonable"—Says Bid Was Made by

U.S. PROFESSOR—FILM INVESTIGATION CITES LARDNER JR., LESTER COLE, THEN QUITS INDEFINITELY. And the *Post-Dispatch:* TESTIFIES SOVIET AGENT TRIED TO GET A-BOMB FROM SCIENTIST—FORMER F.B.I. MAN TELLS HOUSE GROUP THAT DR. OPPENHEIMER REJECTED PROPOSAL IN 1942 AS TREASONABLE. The *Washington Post* contented itself with a much shorter headline, which reported: HOLLYWOOD QUIZ RECESSED, and added, SOVIET AGENT TRIED TO CONTACT ATOM SCIENTIST, HEARING TOLD. *PM* proclaimed gleefully: A-BOMB "PLOT" FIZZLES, THOMAS CALLS HALT TO MOVIE PROBE—TWO MORE WRITERS CITED, BUT INQUISITORS FAIL TO COMPLETE LIST. And the *Chicago Tribune* was remarkably restrained: BARE RED'S BID FOR SECRETS OF A-BOMB EXPERT—FILM PROBERS GET STORY OF PLEA TO OPPENHEIMER.

In general, the leading paragraphs of the stories on the last day of hearings followed the headlines closely. All six papers discussed the espionage story, although several noted its irrelevance to the Hollywood hearings. The *Post* pointed out that the committee "produced no evidence to show that any movie stars, writers or other Hollywood personalities were connected in any way with the reported 'espionage attempts.' . . . Nobody on the staff could explain what [the espionage story] had to do with the committee's inquiry into communism." The *Times* was a bit more careful and admitted that "a few minor cinema figures were mentioned to show the exploitation of social relationships for alleged espionage purposes." All of the papers, save the *Tribune* and the *Post-Dispatch,* stressed the abrupt adjournment of the hearings early in their stories. *PM* expressed the general surprise. "No one knows why Chairman Thomas concluded the hearing so abruptly. There had been no intimation that they were nearing an end and witnesses who had been subpenaed had about made up their minds to dig in for the winter." The *Herald Tribune* was more specific about the cause for surprise. "The adjournment left several of the accused film personalities, including several under subpena, uncalled as witnesses. It left undisclosed Communist records which Thomas had promised to make public on seventy-nine prominent Hollywood persons. It left Lowell Mellett, newspaper columnist and former administrative assistant to the late President Roosevelt, angry at the committee's failure to call him on his repeated request, to reply to allegations in which he was named."

So far as news coverage of the Hollywood hearings is concerned it is difficult to avoid the conclusion that the six papers collectively did no better than an average job of reporting the story. These papers gave the story prominent billing and devoted a good deal of space to it. But in the end most of them left their readers with a confused and somewhat distorted picture of what had taken place in the committee's hearing room. Here, as in the case of other committee hearings—notably the Communist espionage hearings of 1948—the reader who goes to the printed record of the hearing finds that newspaper accounts have given but a fleeting, indistinct glimpse of the total picture.

In defense of the treatment given the Hollywood hearings by newspapers, it must be admitted that they had difficult material to work with, that the hearings were conducted in a seemingly disorderly and unsystematic way, and that it was not always easy to fathom the committee's purposes in its questioning of witnesses or to estimate the significance of the random episodes that occurred along the way. And yet there was a rough pattern to the hearings. During the first week the committee heard a series of friendly witnesses whom it quite obviously expected to substantiate three charges: (1) Communists had penetrated to the heart of the industry and occupied important posts as writers, directors, and actors; (2) many films contained specific Communist propaganda; (3) the Roosevelt administration had intervened during the war to persuade Hollywood to make pro-Soviet films. The second week was devoted in the main to hearing a series of unfriendly witnesses whom the committee expected to expose as Communists or fellow travelers either by their own testimony, or, as proved to be the case, through reading into the record data from the committee's files.

In general the press failed to note or emphasize this pattern. The basic contrast between the witnesses of the first week and those of the second week was made clear enough. Likewise, the committee's charge that there were Communists in the industry—and the degree of success it enjoyed in proving this charge—were well covered. But the committee's almost complete failure to substantiate either of its other two charges was largely ignored by the press, at least in headline and lead-paragraph treatment of the hearings. The successful defense made by industry representatives of such pictures as *Mission to Moscow* and *Song of Russia,* and the utter failure of the committee ever to produce a list of films allegedly containing subversive propaganda received little or no attention. The same thing was true of the charge pertaining to White House intervention. When Robert Taylor clearly repudiated the story that he had been forced to play in *Song of Russia* against his will, this significant admission did not receive the major attention it deserved. At the same time Taylor's rather casual affirmative answer to the committee's routine question, asked of all the friendly witnesses, as to whether he favored outlawing the Communist Party was given prominent attention by several papers. Or again, as has already been noted, Ronald Reagan's calm and reassuring estimate of the nature and extent of the Communist danger in Hollywood was generally overlooked.

Moreover, during the second week of the hearings the press failed generally to catch the importance of the dossier material on each of the recalcitrant witnesses which was read into the record by Louis Russell. This material was diffuse, disorderly, uneven, and often highly questionable in character. But its total impact was such as to prove rather conclusively that the witnesses were either members of the Communist Party or so generally sympathetic to communism and to the cause of the Soviet Union that the issue of actual membership in the party was not of first importance. In other words, Russell's testimony did document in rather decisive fashion the committee's assertion that there were Communists in Hollywood—whatever might be the significance of this demonstration. Yet the press did not underscore the Russell testimony or the specific content of the dossier material in its stories during the second week of hearings. In the papers examined one finds, for example, almost no reference in headlines or lead paragraphs to the facsimiles of the Communist Party registration cards produced by Russell.

As it turned out the unfriendly witnesses were able to gain the sympathy of many Americans for the stand they had made against the committee in support of their principles. Careful reading of their testimony and careful examination of Russell's dossier material concerning them rob them of much of their heroic quality. The committee itself must be held responsible for the early tendency of many people to give these witnesses more sympathy than they deserved, for by its perennial maltreatment of witnesses it had persuaded many Americans to believe that any witness who came into conflict with it must necessarily be in the right and entitled to sympathy and help. But the press, too, can be criticized in this instance, for it failed generally to give a clear picture of the raucous and arrogant manner of the unfriendly witnesses while they were on the stand, and it failed to convey an adequate impression of the truly damaging character of much of the data in the dossiers which was read into the record by Russell. Even if the alleged Communist Party registration cards were completely discounted, the remaining evidence established rather conclusively that the men in the group had become intellectual hostages to the Communist movement and that their presence in important writing and directoral posts in the motion picture industry was, at the very least, a fact that the public was entitled to have knowledge of. The press allowed both the committee and the witnesses to distract its attention from this fact.

It is true that newspaper articles published after the close of the hearings, such as those appearing in Sunday editions, were often more reflective and discerning in their efforts to interpret the significance of the Hollywood hearings than had been the original news stories. But it is likely that the great mass of readers are dependent upon spot reporting for both their initial and their lasting impressions of such an event as these hearings. Accordingly, it is unfortunate that the day-by-day reporting of the Hollywood hearings was not better than it was.

Press Coverage of Committee Reports: The Condon Report

The great majority of the committee's formal reports have not received extended press coverage. A handful of metropolitan papers, led by the New York Times, have faithfully analyzed these reports as they have appeared and have described their content in some detail. But in most instances a committee report has been briefly noted by the average paper, only the most sensational passages of the report being reproduced. But this does not mean that the reports have not been highly influential in the long run. Many of them have contained large segments of material from the committee's files and, as they have been read and preserved in newspaper offices, in the headquarters of professional patriots' groups, or by loyalty-testing agencies, public and private, they have had a continuing significance which has undoubtedly been very great. Certainly this has been true of all the reports denouncing specific organizations as Communist fronts. In all subsequent newspaper stories concerning such organizations it has been standard practice to call attention to their subversive status as determined by the House committee (and/or the Attorney General under the loyalty program).

One publication of the committee that did receive immediate and widespread attention in the press was the famous Condon report, released by the subcommittee on national security in March, 1948. For some six months thereafter the "Condon case" was a subject of bitter public debate and was the center of controversy as much as any matter that ever concerned the Un-American Activities Committee, save perhaps the Hollywood hearings of 1947 and the Hiss-Chambers hearings of 1948. The only official actions in the case were the release of the report by the subcommittee and certain subsequent efforts made by the committee and the House of Representatives to obtain access to material concerning Condon in the files of the executive branch of government. There were no hearings, executive or public, and the committee as a whole took no formal action on the subcommittee report and did not release any statement or publication of its own. Instead, the case was "tried in the newspapers." That this is what the committee intended to happen is quite clear. Accordingly, the way in which the press, consciously or unconsciously, permitted itself to play such an essential part in the development of the case is worthy of attention.

It will be recalled that the subcommittee report stated that Condon appeared to be "one of the weakest links in our atomic security" and that it leaned heavily upon excerpts from a letter written by J. Edgar Hoover to Secretary of Commerce W. Averell Harriman in May, 1947, in which it was stated that the files of the FBI reflected that Condon had "been in contact as late as 1947 with an individual alleged, by a self-confessed Soviet espionage agent, to have engaged in espionage activities with the Russians in Washington, D.C., from 1941 to 1944." [11] Simultaneously with the issuance of the Thomas report the Department of Commerce announced that the department loyalty board had unanimously given Condon a clean bill of health. There immediately developed a battle between the Un-American Activities Committee and the executive branch of the government over the right of the former to have access to the FBI file on Condon. Late in April the House of Representatives passed a resolution directing the Department of Commerce to furnish the committee with the full text of the Hoover-Harriman letter. This request was promptly refused under the Truman directive forbidding executive agencies to release any materials in their loyalty files. In July the Atomic Energy Commission announced that it was giving Condon security clearance after an elaborate investigation of his record. During this same period and on into the early fall these official developments were prominently reported by and discussed in the press. Similarly, much attention was given to the perennial issue as to whether Condon

[11] *Report to the Full Committee of the Special Subcommittee on National Security of the Committee on Un-American Activities,* March 1, 1948, p. 4. See above, p. 139 ff.

would be given a hearing before the Un-American Activities Committee. Much space in the press was also devoted to numerous gestures made by eminent scientists and scientific organizations on behalf of Condon.

Fortunately, the scientific technique of "content analysis" has been used to study the treatment given the Condon case between March and October, 1948, by the nine general daily newspapers then being published in New York City. The study was made at the request of six eminent scientists and *Scientific American* magazine by the Bureau of Applied Social Research of Columbia University. An article by Joseph T. Klapper and Charles Y. Glock, entitled "Trial by Newspaper," containing the findings of the study, was published in the February, 1949, issue of *Scientific American*. The discussion which follows is largely based upon this article.

"Content analysis" has been described as the means by which newspaper "material is classified according to objective criteria and thus rendered susceptible of statistical description." [12] The over-all purpose of the Columbia University Bureau of Applied Social Research in subjecting the press treatment of the Condon case in New York City to content analysis was to determine the bias shown by the nine papers in their straight news reporting on the case. To do this an attempt was made to find and analyze every news story in each one of the nine papers referring to the Condon case which was published during the period covered by the study. These news stories were then divided into separate "statements" each of which consisted of a "single complete idea" or factual reference. A total of 4,589 such statements was discovered in 306 separate news articles. Six hundred and eighty of the statements were "neutral statements of identification" (such as, "Dr. Condon is director of the National Bureau of Standards") and were eliminated from the analysis. The remaining 3,909 statements all involved some element of choice in newspaper writing and reflected a favorable or unfavorable view of Dr. Condon. To keep the analysis itself impartial, elaborate categories were worked out before the 3,909 statements were evaluated. For example, on the favorable side such categories were established as references to the clearances of Condon by the Commerce Department and the Atomic Energy Commission, to statements made in his behalf by eminent scientists, or to denials of the charges by

[12] Klapper and Glock, "Trial by Newspaper," *Scientific American*, Feb., 1949, p. 17. Quotations from the *Scientific American* are used by permission of the publishers.

Condon and others. On the unfavorable side, the categories contained references to such things as the "weakest link" passage in the subcommittee report or the charge that Condon had associated with Soviet espionage agents. These specific categories were later grouped together in more general fashion to produce finally a basis for a straight pro or con count.[13]

The general finding of this study was that, taken as a whole, the press of New York City had been more sympathetic to Dr. Condon than unsympathetic, for of the 3,909 statements which lent themselves to such evaluation, 745 or 19 per cent were unfavorable to Condon, whereas 971 or 25 per cent were favorable.[14] However, since virtually no New Yorkers were reading all nine papers for their impressions of the Condon case, the breakdown of the analysis paper by paper is more significant. Here the range was great, and the percentages ran all the way from a 65 to 35 split in Condon's favor in the *New York Times* to a 18 to 82 unfavorable split in the Hearst paper, the *Journal American*.[15]

Four of the nine papers fell on the pro-Condon side of the line, four on the unfavorable side, and one was right on the line. Those that favored Condon were the *Times*, the *Herald Tribune*, the *Star* (formerly *PM*), and the *Post*. Those whose treatment of the case was predominantly unfavorable to Condon were the *News* (Patterson), the *Mirror* (Hearst), the *Sun*, and the *Journal American* (Hearst). The *World Telegram* (Scripps Howard) was the paper on the fence.

[13] "A statement was classed as unfavorable to Dr. Condon if it criticized him directly or reflected on him indirectly by supporting the Un-American Activities Committee's treatment of the case. An example of the first type of statement is: 'Dr. Edward U. Condon . . . accused by a Thomas subcommittee . . . of associations with Soviet spies.' An example of the second type: 'McDowell insisted that the Committee's previous labeling of Condon stands as an "almost perfect description." ' Similarly, a statement was classed as favorable to Dr. Condon if it supported him directly (e.g., 'Dr. Condon . . . whose integrity and patriotism have been fully recognized by his scientific peers'), or criticized the Committee (e.g., 'The . . . Committee's attack on Dr. Edward U. Condon was condemned today as "irresponsible" by 200 leading scientists')." *Ibid.*, p. 18.

[14] The report states, "Of the rest, a surprisingly large group—some 15 per cent of all statements—concerned the struggle between Republican Congressmen and the administration over the release of the FBI letter. The remaining 41 per cent of the statements in the case were classified as descriptive background of a neutral character." *Ibid.*, p. 19.

[15] The percentages for all nine papers (*ibid.*, p. 19) were: PRO—*Times*, 65; *Herald Tribune*, 64; *Star* (*PM*), 63; *Post*, 57; *World-Telegram*, 50; *News*, 49; *Mirror*, 47; *Sun*, 43; *Journal-American*, 18; and CON (in the same order): 35, 36, 37, 43, 50, 51, 53, 57, 82.

Further analysis of the favorable and unfavorable categories revealed many interesting things. The favorable categories ranged widely, including, for example, statements in Condon's behalf made by several executive agencies of the government, many scientists and scientific societies, and even entire departments of leading universities. On the other hand, the unfavorable categories had a very narrow range and were limited almost entirely to references to the subcommittee report or to statements made by members of the House committee. Since all nine papers published some items that were favorable and some unfavorable to Condon, the varying use which each paper made of statements falling into different categories was examined. It was discovered, for example, that the four papers that were generally favorable to Condon made relatively great use of pro-Condon statements made by scientists and scientific societies. Twenty-one per cent of all their pro-Condon items fell into this category. On the other hand, the five papers generally neutral or unfavorable to Condon made sparing use of such material. Only 4 per cent of their statements favorable to Condon came from such sources. "Indeed, it appears that those five dailies all but ignored the multitude of meetings, letters and statements in defense of Condon by reputable scientists and institutions. As a result, 77 per cent of the case for Condon as presented to the readers of those papers came from Dr. Condon himself, from representatives of the Administration, or from unnamed sources." [16]

Another discovery was that the pro-Condon statements were generally new, that is, throughout the eight-month period of newspaper treatment of the case covered by the study, successive items favorable to Condon were generally being printed for the first time. On the other hand, many of the successive unfavorable statements were reprintings of items that had been published earlier. For example, "The newspapers repeated general denunciations of [Condon] six times as often as they repeated general statements in his support." [17] Indeed, it was discovered that if none of the papers had ever reprinted an item more than two days after the event or occurrence to which it referred, statements directly naming Condon would have numbered 416 in his favor and 301 against him. Actually, because of the reprinting of "old" unfavorable items the count was 695 to

[16] *Scientific American*, Feb., 1949, p. 20.

[17] *Ibid.*, p. 21. All told, 66 per cent of the pro-statements were new, and 34 per cent were of the "revived" variety. On the other hand, only 43 per cent of the anti-Condon statements were new, and 57 per cent were revived.

631 the other way. In other words, the majority of new news developments, which the nine papers might have been expected to report, during the eight-month period favored Condon, but the reuse of old material kept the balance weighted against him.

The authors of the *Scientific American* article are themselves very cautious about drawing conclusions. In the end they are willing to say only that their study produced the following findings:

> The nine New York papers showed wide variations in their news treatment of the case, although all were reporting the same story. Some presented a picture predominantly favorable to Dr. Condon, some predominantly unfavorable. As reported in all papers, the charges against Dr. Condon were vague. The width of the support of Dr. Condon received substantial attention in the *Times, Tribune, Star* and *Post* but very little attention in the other five papers. The background material revived for use in the running news stories had the effect of building up the case against Dr. Condon but did not build up his defense to anywhere near the same degree. All the papers reported the Committee's promise to give Dr. Condon a hearing far more often than they reported its failure to do so.[18]

A bolder critic might say that again, as in its treatment of the Hollywood hearings, the press made a positive contribution of its own to the harm being done by the Un-American Activities Committee in the Condon episode. Some papers with a reactionary bias almost certainly adopted a conscious policy of anti-Condon, pro-committee news reporting. Others, perhaps unconsciously, failed to give the story adequate coverage. They used the original "weakest link" charge repeatedly by way of giving background to day-by-day news stories, thus giving support to the case against Condon even though this case received almost no new supporting arguments or data as the story unfolded. On the other hand, they failed to stress the many new points in Condon's favor that did take shape as time went by. To put it somewhat differently, the press failed to give the story balanced treatment by largely ignoring such *factual* aspects of the case as: the failure of the committee ever to hold a single hearing on the case; the failure of the full committee ever to take any action on the report of its subcommittee; the ultimate vindication of Condon by other government agencies and his continuing presence in an important government post. In the end the press allowed the story to peter out without pointing vigorously to the obvious fact that this in itself represented a victory for Condon and a defeat for the committee, since the original attack upon Condon was now revealed in

[18] *Ibid.,* p. 21.

the total absence of support or follow-up as a shocking, irresponsible action.

Press Coverage of Committee Members

Service on the Un-American Activities Committee has meant that a member of the House of Representatives has enjoyed ready access to the front pages of the newspapers of America. He has had only to call a press conference, or even to engage in a passing conversation with a newspaperman, to have his remarks reach tens of millions of readers across the land. It has made little difference that his remarks were sometimes strictly his own, that he was not always an important member of the committee, or that he enjoyed no backing, official or unofficial, from the committee as a whole. It has made little difference that his remarks were sometimes incredible or even downright silly.[19] Indeed, the more flamboyant or incredible the remark the wider the press coverage it has received.

This ease with which any member of the committee has found it possible to obtain almost unlimited attention in the press for his remarks, whether casual or calculated, has been made possible by several conditions. In the first place, it reflects the obsession of the American people during the last decade with the subject of sub-

[19] For example: the N.Y. Times (Sept. 7, 1948) stated that Representative McDowell had told reporters, "The House Committee on Un-American Activities is trying to find out why a group of scientists has chosen a part of Africa, rich in uranium to set up a $9,000,000 astronomical laboratory. We are not undertaking this check-up as an attack on science, but in these days it is essential to learn such things as the source of the financing and who is behind the whole business." On the same day the Washington Post added that McDowell had told reporters that "he had run across an obscure item in a newspaper reporting that nine million dollars had been provided for establishing an observatory in the highlands of the eastern Congo. He said he has asked a committee investigator to find out the source of the money and all other details."

A few weeks later McDowell had another session with newspapermen and "in commenting on a story copyrighted by the Scripps-Howard newspapers which asserted the Russians had picked up and sent home at least 89 top-level secrets from the United States . . . estimated . . . that a Soviet spy ring has gotten hold of '100 or more' American secrets including atomic information. But he also said he 'felt sure' the Russians have not obtained complete information on how to make an atomic bomb" (Washington Post, Oct. 1, 1948). The Post story added, "The Pennsylvanian said the Russians have acquired American secrets involving atomic information, jet propulsion, radar, germ material, chemicals, State Department policy documents, defense and detective devices, new explosives and airfield locations."

versive activity. We have had so little confidence in our own national integrity and strength and such a morbid fear of the Soviet Union and communism that we have stood ready to give our close attention to any story, however ridiculous or unsupported by factual evidence, suggesting that the "Reds" are undermining our institutions or corrupting our people. Secondly, it has been made possible by the irresponsibility of the committee as a formal body. That the committee has been unable or unwilling to discipline its individual members and its staff and to prevent them from operating as self-designated spokesmen for it has been demonstrated again and again. Finally, it has been helped by the irresponsibility of an important part of the American press, which, either because it could not resist the opportunity to use a cheap, sensational story, or because it was thereby furthering its own prejudices, was unable to distinguish between an authoritative statement of an official spokesman and the mere babblings of a single member.

That members of the committee and its staff have been careful through the years to cultivate close relations with certain newspapers and newspapermen is well known to those who have followed the work of the committee closely. The resulting relationships have been two-way in character. Newspapermen have supplied the committee with leads, helped it gather evidence for use in hearings, and assisted in the preparation of reports and other publications. In turn they have received from the committee advance information of its plans and frequently have been able to publish stories containing "inside" information. Members of the committee and its staff have not even bothered to conceal the existence of these close relations with segments of the press. As already stated, Stripling has written that the "100 Things You Should Know about Communism" pamphlets "were prepared with the considerable aid of Frank Waldrop, editor of 'The Washington Times-Herald.'" Again he states that he had "newspaper friends of the Committee" make inquiries at the Department of Justice concerning the latter's plans in the Hiss case at the time when a newspaper story reported that the department was about to drop the case.[20]

[20] The Red Plot Against America, pp. 142–143, 167. Louis Russell in an interview with the author, June 24, 1949, said that Attorney General Clark had sought to secure his dismissal from the committee staff, charging that Russell had accepted two bottles of whisky from a newspaperman in payment for a story that Russell had "leaked" to him. Russell denied the bribe part of the story, asserting that he had given the story to the newspaperman at the direct order of Chairman Thomas. Representative Nixon in talks with the author frequently

THE HOUSE COMMITTEE

It should immediately be added that there is nothing wrong per se in the existence of a friendly relationship between newspapermen and government officials. Enterprising newspapermen in Washington have always sought to establish such relationships, and it is a fact that much of the reporting of news concerning the federal government is made possible by the intimate relations that have been established. At the same time, the intimacy which has existed between the committee and certain newspapers has at times been disquieting. With few exceptions the newspapers enjoying these close contacts have been reactionary journals, and the record makes it clear that they have aided and abetted the committee in some of its most sensational and flamboyant undertakings.[21]

referred to the close relations he maintained with Bert Andrews of the *N.Y. Herald Tribune*. It is a fact that Andrews' stories on the committee in the *Herald Tribune* frequently contained information that could only have been obtained through close and friendly contacts with members of the committee or its staff. See, for example, Andrews' story of August 27, 1950. In *Witness*, Chambers says it was Andrews who suggested the use of the lie-detector to the committee in the Hiss-Chambers hearings (p. 648 n.).

[21] The committee has had particularly cordial relations with the *Washington Times-Herald*, a member of the McCormick-Patterson newspaper axis. An exception to the statement that the committee's closest contacts have been with reactionary papers is seen in the relationship with Bert Andrews of the *N.Y. Herald Tribune*. Among New York papers, the *World Telegram* and the *Sun* (now combined) also had close relations with the committee. Outstanding among newspapermen close to the committee and its staff was Edward Nellor who worked for both the *N.Y. Sun* and the *Washington Times-Herald*, and has more recently been employed by Fulton Lewis, Jr., the radio commentator. Stripling gives Nellor some of the credit for having brought the committee in touch with Whittaker Chambers. He writes, "One day Ed Nellor, then Washington correspondent of the *N.Y. Sun*, asked me what I knew about a senior editor of Time who lived on a farm at Westminster, Md., and was to be questioned by a N.Y. Grand Jury. Nellor had inquired about him at the Justice Department, but had been asked to 'lay off.' " *The Red Plot*, pp. 95–96. The *N.Y. Sun* itself took credit for having started the whole business of the Bentley-Chambers espionage charges before Congressional committees. It asserted (Aug. 12, 1948):

"The opening wedge was driven into Russia's tightly organized spy networks by Edward Nellor, of the *Sun*'s Washington Bureau, who, in a series of exclusive stories, revealed the nature of the investigation by the special New York Grand Jury, told of the shocking contents of an affidavit made by Whittaker Chambers, revealed the story of the woman who had served as an espionage courier between Washington and New York, and broke the news that the twelve top American Reds would be indicted. . . . He disclosed for the first time on Dec. 9, 1947, that a well-educated woman, who had acted as a courier between Washington and New York for the Communists, had told her story to the Federal authorities. After several months, during which Nellor had made repeated references to her,

That committee and staff members have leaked confidential information to newspapermen and that the latter have reciprocated by supplying the committee with tip-offs concerning impending developments is widely accepted as true. Marquis Childs, a widely respected newspaperman, has written, "Favored reporters have their private leaks from committee members. These reporters make themselves champions of individuals and the particular theses of individual committee members." [22] Stripling himself admits this in his book, *The Red Plot Against America,* and speaks of the committee's "chronic inability to keep secret matters secret." He adds:

> The chairman of our committee during the Alger Hiss investigation on one occasion asked the members to take an oath that they would not divulge what had taken place in a secret session. They all took the oath.
> Within two hours the story was on the front pages of afternoon newspapers throughout the country.[23]

As a matter of fact, the Hiss-Chambers hearings were marked by the leaking of much information in both directions. It is possible that the hearings would never have been held had not newspapermen supplied the committee with leaks concerning the proceedings before the federal grand jury in New York.[24] On the other hand, committee or staff members quickly leaked information to the press concerning developments at the executive hearings in New York at which Hiss and Chambers were first questioned separately and then brought together in a confrontation scene. For example, the news that Hiss had been asked at an executive session on August 16 to

---

another newspaper retold her story as firsthand news [the reference is presumably to a series of stories which appeared in the *New York World Telegram* in the summer of 1948]. It was revealed later by the Thomas Committee that she was Miss Bentley." Quoted by A. J. Liebling, *Mink and Red Herring* (New York: Doubleday & Co., Inc., 1949), pp. 189–190.

If the *Sun's* claim is accepted as valid it is obvious that Nellor enjoyed the benefit of leaks from the federal grand jury in New York, whose proceedings were, of course, secret. And if Nellor's information was one of the things that stimulated the Ferguson and Thomas committees into action in the summer of 1948, then it follows that the resulting Congressional investigations were based upon information that had been improperly leaked from the grand jury proceedings in New York and that the press had played an important part in stimulating this rival activity by Congressional agencies.

For an account of another episode in which Nellor was revealed as playing a prominent role in the development of a story that atomic bomb secrets had been stolen from Oak Ridge, see Liebling, *Mink and Red Herring,* pp. 23 ff.

[22] *Washington Post,* Dec. 9, 1948. [23] *The Red Plot,* p. 24. [24] See note 21.

submit to a lie-detector test was reported in detail in the morning newspapers the next day. The *Washington Post* story ran in part:

> The proposal *it was learned* was made by the Committee to Hiss during a three-hour executive session. . . . Hiss' immediate reaction to the proposal was that he considers the lie-detector an unreliable instrument which measures emotions, rather than veracity, *it was said.* However, he agreed to give the Committee a formal answer by Wednesday morning.[25]

And the morning after the secret confrontation scene the *Washington Post* reported, "Stripling, who was present at the dramatic hotel room meeting, described it to reporters yesterday and related what steps had been taken since." [26]

In his book, *A Generation on Trial*, which is a study of the Hiss case, Alistair Cooke, himself a newspaperman, is more critical of the press than he is of the House committee. He writes:

> It is only fair, I think, to the Committee to recognize, as a full reading of its printed record shows, that in spite of its evangelical attack and the jingoism and scurrility of some of its members, the crimes of putting people into discreditable associations, and presuming guilt before innocence can be proved, were committed far more by the press than by the Committee. Very often innocent people were harmed by the mere act of reinterpreting the Committee's testimony in the newspapers. But the worst indignities were done by the headline-writers, whose slap-happy professional immunity is something that can be cured not by lamentation but by law. It was the feature writers who did a serious disservice to the motives and even to the legitimate procedures of the Committee, and such irreparable damage to Hiss that by the time he came to court an acquittal could be only the first step towards a distant prospect of vindication.[27]

A favorite practice of the committee, which perhaps falls short of the bald leaking of confidential information, has been the stimulation of unofficial stories concerning plans for the future or of speculative accounts as to developments that have taken place at executive hearings. Frequently, nothing comes of the rumors of future action,

[25] August 17, 1948. Italics added.

[26] August 19, 1948. Evidently this was not really a leak, for the subcommittee apparently decided to make an official announcement that Hiss and Chambers had been brought face to face and that Hiss had identified Chambers as George Crosley. But the eagerness with which those involved in the New York hearing immediately released the story to the press, without waiting for the public confrontation of the two men which took place a week later, is at least suggestive of their enthusiasm for publicity.

[27] Page 65. Cooke is the chief American correspondent of the *Manchester Guardian.*

but in the meantime the committee has enjoyed additional publicity. Moreover, the effect of the advance stories has often been so substantial that the failure of the actual event to live up to its publicity passes unnoticed.

A few random examples of stories stimulated by the committee concerning impending developments which never quite measured up to expectations may be noted. In August, 1948, two or three days after Whittaker Chambers' first appearance before the committee, the committee announced to the press that it had uncovered a mystery witness whose testimony "would crack wide open the whole Soviet Spy case." [28] That no such witness ever testified with such startling effect is obvious from the record of the Communist espionage hearings. A month later the committee announced that disclosures concerning a new Communist spy ring allegedly involving government employees would be made in hearings in October. The *New York Times* commented that "the timing will bring the hearing into the thick of the Presidential election campaign," and it added,

Chief Investigator Robert E. Stripling told reporters that, in addition to the new spy inquiry, the House Committee would look into:
1. Communism in Hollywood—a resumption of the hearings which began nearly a year ago.
2. Communist inroads among Negroes.
3. Entry of Communists into the U.S.[29]

No such hearings were held in October, no new spy ring was revealed, and the Hollywood hearings were not resumed.

In December, 1948, Representative McDowell arrived in New York City, identified himself as a one-man subcommittee about to hold some hearings, and asserted that he had dug up some "highly important" new evidence involving "the matter of espionage in Government affairs." [30] Since McDowell's term of office was to expire in a matter of days it is perhaps unfair to attribute any significance to this feeble effort to attract attention.

Press Coverage of Executive Hearings

A significant illustration of the committee's remarkable ability to obtain unlimited publicity in the press by releasing statements concerning impending developments which may or may not materialize occurred in September, 1948. At this time a subcommittee consisting of Representatives Thomas, McDowell, and Vail returned to a mat-

[28] *Washington Post*, Aug. 6, 1948. Story by Mary Spargo.
[29] Sept. 4, 1948. [30] *N.Y. Herald Tribune*, Dec. 18, 1948. See also note 19.

ter which had received attention at the close of the Hollywood hearings in 1947—the alleged infiltration of espionage agents into atomic laboratories, in particular, the Radiation Laboratory at the University of California—and held a series of executive hearings. These hearings were accompanied by a barrage of press releases to the general effect that the hearings would shortly be opened to the public and that sensational revelations would be made. Two preliminary points about this episode may be noted. First, the development took place at the same time that the committee was deeply involved in the sensational Hiss-Chambers case. The committee had a perfect right, and even duty, to make a simultaneous investigation into an entirely different matter, if the facts seemed to warrant it, but in view of all the publicity the Hiss-Chambers case had brought the committee, it might be supposed that the committee would have concluded it had no need to seek further publicity through an entirely different line of investigation, at least until it was ready to get down to business by holding public hearings or releasing actual findings. Second, this additional line of investigation was not a fresh one, for its subject matter had been fairly well indicated eleven months before when Louis Russell had testified at length concerning atomic espionage in California on the last day of the Hollywood hearings. The mystery with which the committee now surrounded its renewed approach to the subject led that inimitable student of the foibles of the press, A. J. Liebling, to assert that the committee and the press were engaging in a "re-de-secretization" operation. He observed, "Nothing has more news value than the revelation of a secret, and the only way to freshen a revelation for further use is to make it a secret again." [31]

At any rate, the flood of publicity which accompanied the September, 1948, executive hearings ran somewhat as follows. On the first day of the month the press announced that the committee would shortly begin a series of hearings on espionage committed by atomic scientists for the benefit of the Soviet Union. The *New York Times* stated, "The committee will seek to show the inadequacy of atomic security measures by publicizing the cases of the U.S. scientists who were discharged from Manhattan Project jobs only after there was reason to believe that they had already given away atomic secrets." [32] A week later Chairman Thomas was reported as announcing that "between 20 and 25 persons" would be subpoenaed and that public hearings would begin on the fifteenth. At the same time, the irrepressible Representative McDowell gave out his own statement

[31] *Mink and Red Herring*, pp. 199, 204.   [32] Sept. 1, 1948.

and "disclosed" that Major General Leslie R. Groves would be a key witness at these public hearings. McDowell was reported by the *Washington Post* as stating that "the hearings will bring out the story of a Russian-born French citizen, who apparently tried to beat the United States government to the punch in buying up uranium-bearing lands in the west during the war. McDowell said the man, now living in Paris, bought rights to land principally in Colorado, adjacent to the property which the Government planned to mine for atomic ores." [33] On the eleventh the press had a "leak" story on the testimony of General Groves made at an executive session the day before. According to the *Washington Post* he had testified "that if Russia got refined uranium from this country during the war he didn't know about it." He was said, however, to have "dropped a hint" to reporters that "atomic secrets might have leaked out of his Manhattan District to the Soviets despite all security precautions." [34]

By the twelfth the version of what Groves had testified was assuming more ominous proportions. The *Washington Post* had it that "Congressional spy investigators said yesterday that an Army expert on atomic energy is 'certain' Russian agents stole some wartime atom bomb secrets." It added,

Vail [now identified as one of the "Congressional spy investigators" doing the "saying"] did not name the officer. . . . Obviously he meant Lieutenant General Leslie R. Groves. . . .

"This statement," Vail said, "was a direct contradiction of Truman's contention that Communists were not involved in wartime espionage." [The reference was presumably to a Truman press conference statement ten days before that the Russians had been our allies during the war and that the Germans and Japs were the real spies.]

Vail said it would appear from facts obtained by the House Committee that "the President was either unaware of the true wartime espionage

---

[33] Sept. 8, 1948. In a story on the same day the *N.Y. Times* had a somewhat different "authoritative" account of what was about to transpire:

"As plans for the new investigation progressed, it was indicated authoritatively that the committee was setting out to prove true or show false reports reaching it to the effect that

"1. Uranium 235, prime ingredient of the atomic bomb, went to Soviet agents in undisclosed quantity from the Manhattan Project.

"2. Some of this U-235 reached Dr. Allan N. May, British scientist, convicted of Russian espionage in Canada.

"3. Soviet espionage operations in the United States were supervised by an 'inspector general' alleged to be working under the direction of Alexander Stevens, now under deportation proceedings in New York."

[34] Sept. 11, 1948.

situation or is desperately endeavoring to shield his Administration through such a generalization from justified public censure." [35]

At a press conference on the thirteenth Chairman Thomas announced that public hearings were being once more postponed. But, lest speculation concerning developments at the executive sessions lag, he added, "All that we can divulge at this time is that the committee is obtaining facts regarding the espionage operations of one of the most important Soviet agents. He is Arthur Adams. His assignment was the procurement of atomic and radar secrets." [36] On the fourteenth Thomas announced that the subcommittee conducting the hearings was bringing contempt proceedings against Steve Nelson, a veteran Communist Party organizer, because of his refusal to answer questions at an executive session the day before. Two days later he announced that the committee had thus far heard eighteen witnesses and that it had ten or twelve more to go. In the press reports of this announcement, as in preceding ones, the names of the witnesses being heard were freely revealed. For example, John H. Chapin, former chemical engineer with the Manhattan Project, had been heard on the sixteenth, and Thomas was reported as describing his testimony as "of most vital importance to the committee" and as shedding a "very illuminating" light on the whole atomic espionage issue.[37]

A committee "announcement" on the seventeenth took on a more aggressive note. According to the *Washington Post* the committee stated that "in spite of Mr. Truman, Mr. Lilienthal and a few misguided scientists, the American people will continue to get the facts from this committee and in the next few days, we shall reveal a shocking chapter in Communist espionage in the atomic field." [38] On the twentieth Representative McDowell was again engaged in his favorite pastime of "telling reporters." He stated that a witness at the executive sessions, Louise Bransten Berman, had refused to testify on grounds of self-incrimination, but he was reported as indicating that this did not matter very much, since the committee already had much testimony "linking Mrs. Berman and her Communist associates to vigorous activity in behalf of the ring of espionage conspirators." [39]

[35] Sept. 12, 1948.   [36] *N.Y. Times*, Sept. 14, 1948.

[37] *Washington Post*, Sept. 17, 1948. Seemingly, the committee itself readily revealed the names of witnesses at executive sessions to the press, or it made no effort to conduct these hearings in such a way as to prevent newspapermen from discovering very easily who the witnesses were.

[38] Sept. 18, 1948.   [39] *Washington Post*, Sept. 21, 1948.

Again, on the twenty-first, McDowell was talking to the press. This time, according to the *Washington Post*, he was "prepared to recommend prosecution of three persons on charges of wartime atomic energy espionage." The *Post* also stated that he "told reporters he is sure the committee has much more information on the cases than the Justice Department." In the same story the *Post* added that it had been "disclosed" that the committee was debating "whether to issue a report like that of the Royal Commission in the Canadian spy case or hold public hearings on evidence gathered so far in closed sessions." In any event, said the *Post*, the committee had promised "full and complete" revelations shortly on a "shocking chapter" in the story of wartime espionage.[40]

On the twenty-third McDowell was once again holding a "discussion" with reporters and dropping hints as to the identity of the three men whom the committee would urge be prosecuted.[41] And on the twenty-fourth Thomas announced that the committee had voted to hold no public hearings "in the interest of national security," but he asserted that the executive hearings had been devoted to "the gravest matter the committee has gone into" and that the committee would soon release a report patterned after that of the Candian Royal Commission.[42]

There now followed a brief but flamboyant build-up for the report, which was actually issued on the twenty-eighth. On the twenty-fifth, according to the *New York Times*, "an official close to the House Committee on Un-American Activities said . . . that its forthcoming report on atomic espionage would 'shock' the public. 'And the facts, the testimony will shock them.' . . . It will state, the official declared, that Presidents Roosevelt and Truman and Attorney General Tom C. Clark 'had all the facts' on a Russian spy ring that got atomic bomb secrets and did nothing about it. . . . He also said so far as he knew, there would be nothing in the report not already known to Government agencies."[43]

To bring to a close this account of the committee's efforts to obtain maximum publicity out of a series of executive hearings that might well have been kept confidential until the committee was ready to

---

[40] Sept. 22, 1948.   [41] *N.Y. Times,* Sept. 24, 1948.
[42] *Washington Post,* Sept. 25, 1948.
[43] Sept. 26, 1948. In the same story Representative Vail was reported as having stated that "the report will say that some scientists working with the super-secret Manhattan Atomic bomb projects at the University of Chicago made attempts to steal atomic secrets. We are inclined to believe they were successful."

make a definitive report on them, and of the readiness with which the press co-operated with the committee in providing such publicity, the general character of the report may be noted. The report was twenty-four pages long and was accompanied by a seventy-nine-page document giving the testimony of only three of twenty-five witnesses heard during the series of hearings. While well-written, the report shows signs of having been hurried, for it is peppered with references to loose ends that the committee would eventually pursue further. The report flatly states, "It has been established . . . that certain vital information was actually transmitted to the Russian government, and that this information has been and will be of assistance to the Russians in their development of the atomic bomb." [44] Inasmuch as neither the report nor the accompanying volume of hearings contained any evidence or data substantiating this sensational assertion, it is impossible to judge whether or not the committee in this particular inquiry was actually on the trail of specific means by which atomic secrets were given to the Soviet Union. Moreover, it is admitted in the report that the committee had discovered nothing not known to the investigative agencies of the government, and that, indeed, the latter unquestionably had additional information not known to the committee.

In its main outlines the report describes the committee's relations with the executive branch of the government in the matter, attacking the latter on two scores—its failure to have taken action on the basis of the evidence it had had in its possession for five years, and its obstruction of the committee's efforts to make an inquiry in the field— and then outlines three alleged cases of atomic espionage. The report recommends the prosecution of five persons involved in these cases —two scientists, the ex-wife of one of these men, and two Communist Party functionaries.

The sensationalism which marked this particular undertaking was deplorable, and both the committee and the press must share the responsibility for the lurid way in which this investigation into a delicate subject was publicized. It is just this sort of flagrant disregard for the importance of secrecy in an espionage investigation which has lent support to the oft-repeated assertions of the Department of Justice that the Un-American Activities Committee has

[44] *Report on Soviet Espionage Activities in Connection with the Atom Bomb,* Sept. 28, 1948, p. 161. It should be emphasized that this assertion had no reference whatsoever to the Fuchs-Rosenberg-Gold-Greenglass spy ring, the existence and activities of which was in 1948 completely unknown to the committee.

hindered rather than helped the apprehension and punishment of the espionage agents who were active in the United States during the World War II period. Again, the one legitimate excuse that a Congressional investigating committee might have had for concerning itself with the details of specific espionage cases under scrutiny by the law enforcement branch and still in the pre-prosecution stage would have been a desire to ascertain the adequacy of existing criminal legislation with respect to espionage or the vigor with which the Department of Justice was attempting to enforce such legislation. The use of the Congressional investigating power to educate public opinion in such an area almost certainly should have awaited the completion of the work of investigation and prosecution by law enforcement agencies. Admittedly, the committee's report did raise a serious question as to why the Department of Justice had been so tardy in seeking the indictment of certain of the people named in the report.[45] At the same time, espionage prosecutions are at best difficult undertakings, and those charged with the responsibility for law enforcement must be allowed a substantial measure of discretion to weigh such factors as adequacy of evidence, the harm that may be done in revealing the sources of evidence during the course of a public trial, or the adverse effect even a successful espionage prosecution may have upon the nation's security, before deciding to go into open court and publicly prosecute persons accused of espionage. It is far more important that the Department of Justice maintain continuing surveillance of present espionage activity than it is that it seek to send the guilty to jail for past acts of espionage. If the latter can be accomplished only by hazarding the success of the former, it had better be left undone.[46]

[45] When its report was released, the committee received editorial support on this point. The *N.Y. Times*, while stating that the report was hardly the "shocking" exposé of feverish spy activity that the public had been led to expect, did say that it raised "grave doubts" as to whether the Justice Department had been sufficiently energetic in seeking indictments. It said, "It is time for an announcement that action is under way to expose the guilty and clear the innocent of suspicion." Sept. 29, 1948.

The *Washington Post*, Oct. 2, 1948, in an editorial entitled "Red but Not Herring," criticized Attorney General Clark for his prompt rejection of the committee's demand for prosecution of the guilty, saying that while the committee might have been motivated by politics, the effort of the Truman administration to dismiss the whole business was "equally disingenuous and dictated by political expediency." See also note 17, ch. v, pp. 175–176.

[46] There is always the possibility that the Department of Justice continued to refrain from the prosecution of the persons named in the report for political

While the larger responsibility for the inadequacies of the story that has reached the American people certainly rests with the committee itself, the press has not distinguished itself in its reporting of the story. It is all very well to say that the story of the Un-American Activities Committee was there to tell, and that the press has merely done a straight reporting job in telling it. But anyone familiar with the Washington scene knows that the operation of the federal government is accompanied by scores of such stories, only a part of which can be told by the press in any great detail. Newspapermen do have a great deal of discretion in selecting the stories that they think are worth telling and also in deciding how vigorously and persistently they will dig for the many details of such stories which are by no means on the surface merely waiting to be published.[47] By and large, even the more respected and responsible papers have not been able to resist the temptation to emphasize the lurid aspects of the story, or to stress the testimony that suggested wrongdoing, while playing down the testimony that suggested the absence of wrongdoing. Nor have they taken the initiative in pointing out the obvious biases and errors in the testimony of irresponsible witnesses or even been able to avoid the introduction of new errors in their own reporting.[48]

---

reasons, i.e., that it feared a successful prosecution of such persons for espionage would do the Democratic administration harm because the public would conclude that a vigorous government would have prevented espionage before it could occur. But this is an unlikely thesis. No one of the persons named in the committee report had even the remotest connection with the Truman or Roosevelt administrations. A successful prosecution of them might have led the public to question the adequacy of the Manhattan District's personnel procurement policies, but it is not likely that the Department of Justice has feared the political repercussions of such questioning.

[47] A good illustration of this discretion in operation concerns Senator McCarthy. On August 1, 1950, the Senator read to the Senate an affidavit by one Willy Foerster alleging that in 1938 he brought a letter to Owen Lattimore from a man in Japan who was later executed by the Japanese as a Russian spy. When the Associated Press did not bother to put this item of "news" on the wire, McCarthy wrote a letter to every daily newspaper in the country complaining about the Associated Press's action (or inaction). The AP replied that it had given coverage to "all newsworthy aspects" of the Senator's campaign, but "in this case it was concluded the Senator's statement lacked news value." This illustration is drawn from an account in the New Republic, August 21, 1950. One could wish that the press had shown similar restraint in its handling, for example, of some of Representative McDowell's statements to newspapermen.

[48] Adequate documentation of these generalizations would, of course, require an elaborate and systematic analysis of press coverage of the committee and the presentation of a substantial amount of evidence. The author has not made such

It should be added that the editorial treatment of the House Un-American Activities Committee by the more respected and responsible newspapers of the country has in general been excellent. Again and again such papers have called attention to the procedural shortcomings of committee hearings, and, what is more, have subjected the committee's activities to careful analysis from the point of view of the requirements of democracy and civil liberty. Editorials on the committee in such papers as the *Washington Post,* the *New York Herald Tribune,* and the *New York Times* have often been discerning, wise, and couched in moving language. Unfortunately, coverage of the committee in the news columns of even these papers has not always matched their editorials in perspective, balance, or understanding. This is not to suggest that these papers should have allowed

---

an analysis and is depending upon his own cumulative impressions after wide reading of newspaper accounts of committee activity. One or two illustrations may be given:

The lead sentence in an AP story printed in the *Washington Post* on August 31, 1948, ran: "Whittaker Chambers testified today he used Communist influence to get a $6,000-a-year 'boondoggling' job with the Government in 1937." Representative McDowell promptly informed the press that this was an error and that the correct salary had been $2,000. The correction got very little attention in the press. Even the *N.Y. Times* inserted this information in the last sentence of a long story dealing with the testimony of a new witness before the committee.

Many of the *Washington Post's* stories on the Thomas committee were written by Mary Spargo, who was once an employee of the committee. While her stories were generally fair and accurate, they were more flamboyant in tone than one would expect *Washington Post* stories on the committee to be, and they were not entirely free from errors. For example, she certainly did her part, along with a considerable portion of the press, to build Alger Hiss up as a much more important public officer than the facts indicated he was. On August 4, 1948, she wrote that Hiss was a "top policy making official of the Roosevelt-Truman Administration" (which he never was), that he "rose to a top policy level in the State Department" (which he never did: the highest post he ever occupied in the State Department was Director of the Office of Special Political Affairs, which is below "the top policy level"); that "at Dumbarton Oaks and other preliminary conferences leading up to the United Nations conference in San Francisco, Hiss was in a position to exercise great influence on the language of the draft charter presented to the conference for consideration and revision"; and that "at this time, Hiss was chief American draftsman of the charter." There is certainly no evidence that Alger Hiss was *at any time* the "chief American draftsman of the charter." Again, when Alger Hiss finally admitted at a closed hearing in New York, August 17, 1948, that Whittaker Chambers was the man he had known as George Crosley, Mary Spargo shortened this into the flat assertion that "Alger Hiss . . . admitted he knows Whittaker Chambers." Issue of August 18, 1948.

their editorial views to creep into their straight news reporting of the committee story. Moreover, day-by-day reporting of the factual moves of such an erratic body as the Un-American Activities Committee is no enviable task for even such experienced newspapermen as those who make up the Washington news corps. A generous allowance must be made for mistakes in judgment in winnowing out each day the significant parts of a news story that has often been confusing and overwhelming in its total detail. Nonetheless, it must be admitted that even the best papers have all too frequently played up sensational witnesses, however irresponsible their testimony, have failed to report adequately the testimony of calmer witnesses or the replies of those who have been attacked, and have opened their columns too readily to the most trivial, ridiculous, or incredible musings, speculations, and predictions of committee members.

It must be added that press treatment of the committee's work underwent considerable change during the 81st Congress. With an increased sense of responsibility on the part of the committee came an increasingly responsible handling of the story by the press.[49] As the committee approached its tasks in a reasonably calm and unemotional manner, the press seemingly found it easier to gain perspective on the committee and to report its doings with balance and detachment.

The contrast between the Un-American Activities Committee of the 81st Congress and that of the 80th Congress, and the contrasting

[49] Early in 1949 Chairman Wood announced that the new committee in the 81st Congress had voted unanimously to exclude news photographers, television cameras, and radio recorders from all hearings (*N.Y. Times*, Feb. 1, 1949). This sweeping regulation was immediately protested. For example, such a responsible radio commentator as Edward R. Murrow, who had made use of recordings of the sessions of public agencies in his broadcasts, stated, "I would maintain that a public hearing is a public hearing, and that to deny the use of microphones and cameras to reporters who normally use them is the equivalent of saying to newspaper reporters: You may attend the hearing, but you may not bring either pencil or pen with you." *N.Y. Times*, Feb. 6, 1949.

Murrow ignores the fact that the just and efficient operation of a public body sometimes necessitates a limitation upon photographic or broadcasting activity which may well interfere with its work far more than does a pencil in the hand of a reporter, and that the courts, for instance, do traditionally maintain such a limitation without encroaching unduly upon the reporting of their sessions.

It is to the committee's credit that when it resumed its Hollywood investigation in April, 1951, immediately following the spectacular (and highly questionable) televising of the Kefauver crime committee hearings in New York City, it refrained from the use of newsreel, radio, or television to publicize its hearings.

ways in which the press reported their work, suggest that the press can be blamed too much for the Roman holiday quality it gave to the story of the Thomas committee. A flamboyant Congressional investigation probably makes flamboyant reporting inevitable. In reporting this particular investigation in the manner it did, the press perhaps merely reflected the same influences and pressures in American life that explain the existence of such a committee and the tremendous interest of the people in its doings.[50] But it is important to recognize that the press is not likely to rise above the level of such an undertaking or to help save the people against the ever-present temptation to search out and persecute nonconformists or heretics. The press is what it is, and when a society insists upon hunting witches and doubting its own integrity, it is only wise to assume that its press will play along with such insistence and doubts and give the people what they seemingly want to read, and give it to them in colorful style and generous quantity.

[50].Alistair Cooke does not let the press off quite so easily. It is his judgment that "the Committee was goaded by the press to become its own worst enemy." *A Generation on Trial*, p. 47.

XI: The Un-American Activities Committee and the Courts

No Congressional investigating committee has ever had its work subjected to such a large measure of judicial review as has the House Un-American Activities Committee. Since its establishment as a permanent committee in 1945, it has been engaged in almost continuous conflict with its witnesses. This conflict in turn has resulted in a steady flow of cases to the courts raising legal questions as to the committee's authority and procedures. Between 1946 and 1950 some nine such cases reached the federal appellate courts. These cases aroused the hopes of many of the committee's critics that it might finally find its nemesis in the courts. Having failed to persuade the House of Representatives to abolish the committee or to limit its authority or procedures, the committee's opponents transferred the struggle to the courts and counted heavily upon favorable judicial rulings to curb the committee's worst abuses, if, indeed, they did not expect the judiciary to declare the committee unconstitutional and outlaw it completely. But these hopes and expectations were not to be realized, for not a single final judicial ruling adverse to the interests of the committee has yet been made.[1] Moreover, it is significant that the United States Supreme Court has shown great reluctance to review the cases that have raised the most serious constitutional

[1] One witness, Richard Morford, who was prosecuted in the courts and found guilty on the charge of contempt, gained temporary relief when the Supreme Court ruled that he was entitled to a new trial on the ground that legal error, prejudicial to his interests, had occurred in the first trial. But upon being tried again he was found guilty a second time, and the appellate courts let this verdict stand.

issues concerning the work of the committee and has seemingly been content to let the federal courts of appeals render final decisions upon these issues.

That Congressional investigations should be subject to any judicial supervision whatsoever may well occasion surprise. It is one thing for the federal courts to invalidate the substance of a Congressional statute on the ground that it conflicts with the Constitution; it is quite a different thing for the judicial branch to review the procedural activities of the legislature. Whether the jurisdiction granted to one of its committees by the House or Senate is proper constitutionally might well be viewed as a "political question" to be decided by Congress itself. With respect to committee procedures, it may at first thought seem that private persons appearing before a Congressional committee are entitled to protection under the Bill of Rights and to relief in the courts when their procedural rights are encroached upon. But examination of the Bill of Rights suggests that such familiar procedural requirements as avoidance of unreasonable searches and seizures, allowing an accused person immunity against testifying against himself, making provision for the assistance of counsel, and trial by jury are all closely associated with criminal proceedings in a *court*. When the Sixth Amendment to the Constitution says, "In all criminal prosecutions the accused shall enjoy the right . . . to be confronted with the witnesses against him; to have compulsory process for obtaining witnesses in his favor, and to have the assistance of counsel for his defense," it may well be asked how a provision, so worded, can have any possible bearing upon the rights of a witness before a committee of Congress or how it can possibly serve as a basis for judicial review of the proceedings of such a committee.

As a matter of fact, for almost one hundred years the Congressional investigation "flourished virtually free from judicial supervision or control." [2] Then in 1881, in what is still an exceedingly controversial decision, *Kilbourn v. Thompson,* the Supreme Court brought this activity of the national legislature under a very substantial measure of control by the courts and for the first and only time declared that

[2] Gerald D. Morgan, "Congressional Investigations and Judicial Review: Kilbourn v. Thompson Revisited," 37 *Calif. Law Review* (Dec., 1949), 556. One authority on Congressional investigations points out that there was disagreement in Congress from the beginning as to whether the Bill of Rights had any bearing upon Congressional proceedings. Ernest J. Eberling, *Congressional Investigations* (New York: Columbia University Press, 1928), pp. 251, 283–288, 319.

a specific Congressional inquiry was an improper one.[3] In spite of the fact that *Kilbourn v. Thompson* has not fathered subsequent Supreme Court decisions holding other Congressional investigations improper, it has never been repudiated by the Court, and it has encouraged successive generations of critics to hope that the Congressional "witch hunts" of the moment may be suppressed through judicial intervention. It is significant that liberals and conservatives have taken turns supporting and condemning judicial supervision of Congressional investigations, as the inquiries themselves have ranged from liberal to conservative in motivation and character. During the 1920's and 1930's the inquiries were generally in the hands of liberal Congressmen and found staunch defenders in liberal commentators, whereas conservatives recalled *Kilbourn v. Thompson* and suggested the need for judicial intervention. In articles in learned journals and popular magazines alike, such liberals as James M. Landis and Felix Frankfurter deplored the *Kilbourn* case and warned that the courts should "keep hands off" Congressional investigations. On the other hand, such a conservative lawyer as Frederic R. Coudert gave to his article for a learned journal the title, "Congressional Inquisition vs. Individual Liberty," and was not unwilling to see the courts curb what Walter Lippmann was calling "that legalized atrocity, the Congressional investigation." [4]

---

[3] 103 U.S. 168 (1881).

[4] Among the articles protesting either expressly or by implication against judicial intervention were:

James M. Landis, "Constitutional Limitations on the Congressional Power of Investigation," 40 *Harvard Law Review* (Dec., 1926), 153.

John H. Wigmore, "Legislative Power to Compel Testimonial Disclosure," 19 *Ill. Law Review* (1924), 452.

Charles S. Potts, "Power of Legislative Bodies to Punish for Contempt," 74 *Univ. of Penn. Law Review* (May, June, 1926), 691, 780.

Felix Frankfurter, "Hands Off the Investigation," 33 *New Republic* (May 21, 1927), 329.

The position of the above authorities is well expressed by the assertion of Potts: "Public policy would seem to require that only in the clearest cases of want of jurisdiction and of oppression should the courts interfere with the legislative investigations" (p. 829).

Among the articles attacking the use of the investigating power by Congress and looking with favor upon the possibility of a judicial check to the use of the power by Congress were:

Frederic R. Coudert, "Congressional Inquisitions v. Individual Liberty," 15 *Virginia Law Review* (April, 1929), 537.

Charles Loring, "Powers of Congressional Investigation Committees," 8 *Minn. Law Review* (June, 1924), 595.

A generation later the shoe was on the other foot. The Un-American Activities Committee and other Congressional committees with a conservative orientation had liberals sadly disturbed and inclined to look to the courts for help, whereas conservatives found it convenient to argue that it would be unfortunate were the courts to attempt to check these committees. One cannot avoid a sense of amazement at coming upon a law review article by a bitter, and once implacable, critic of judicial review, Louis B. Boudin, in which he enthusiastically supports a judicial check on Congressional committees as a means of safeguarding personal rights.[5] On the other hand, Gerald D. Morgan, former assistant legislative counsel for the House of Representatives, has recently renewed the attack upon *Kilbourn v. Thompson*, asserting that the effect of this Supreme Court decision "was to treat the Senate and House of Representatives, when exercising an inherent power at the very threshold of the legislative process, as having a status analogous to that of an inferior court of limited or special jurisdiction." Morgan reminds his readers of Justice Holmes' words that it "must be remembered that legislatures are ultimate guardians of the liberties of the people in quite as great a degree as the courts" and of Justice Frankfurter's assertion that "interference by the courts is not conducive to the development of habits of responsibility," and comes to the conclusion that we should "return the workings of the legislative process to the exclusive jurisdiction and control of the legislature."[6]

Review by the courts of the work of the Un-American Activities Committee must be examined against this background of alternate distrust by liberals and conservatives of judicial interference with the investigative function of Congress. Moreover, the actual record of the committee's relations with the courts can be understood and evaluated only if the court-promulgated rules of constitutional law

[5] "Congressional and Agency Investigations: Their Uses and Abuses," 35 *Virginia Law Review* (Feb., 1949), 143. Another recent article in support of judicial supervision of Congressional investigations is "Constitutional Limitations on the Un-American Activities Committee" (unsigned note), 47 *Columbia Law Review* (April, 1947), 416.

[6] "Congressional Investigations," p. 556. The Holmes quotation is from the Court opinion in *Missouri, Kansas, and Texas Ry. v. May*, 194 U.S. 267, 270 (1904) and the Frankfurter quotation from the Court opinion in *Federal Communications Commission v. Pottsville Broadcasting Co.*, 309 U.S. 134, 146 (1940). Another article which looks generally with disfavor upon the prospect of judicial supervision of Congressional investigations is Henry W. Ehrmann, "The Duty of Disclosure in Parliamentary Investigation: A Comparative Study," 11 *Univ. of Chicago Law Review* (Dec., 1943; Feb., 1944), 1, 117.

concerning the investigating power of Congress are kept in mind.

It is now clearly established by decision of the Supreme Court that Congress possesses implied power to seek factual information through committee investigations to enable it to exercise its lawmaking powers. The decision of the Court in the *Kilbourn* case seventy years ago was but a temporary check to the establishment of this rule. In that case the Court held that the House of Representatives had exceeded the limits of its power in authorizing one of its committees to inquire into the failure of the banking house, Jay Cooke and Company, even though the Secretary of the Navy had made "improvident deposits" of federal funds with the company. In the resolution authorizing the inquiry the House had failed to point out that the findings of the committee might result in the enactment of remedial legislation, and the Court concluded that the investigation was a "fruitless" undertaking.[7] The Court found its position strengthened by the fact that the failure of the banking house had already become the subject of litigation in the courts, and also by its feeling that the Congressional committee had encroached improperly upon the privacy of witnesses called before it.

The use of the investigating power as a means of obtaining information essential to the enactment of legislation was expressly approved by the Supreme Court for the first time in 1927 in the well-known case of *McGrain v. Daugherty*. In an opinion for a unanimous Court Justice VanDevanter said:

We are of opinion that the power of inquiry—with process to enforce it —is an essential and appropriate auxiliary to the legislative function. . . .

A legislative body cannot legislate wisely or effectively in the absence of information respecting the conditions which the legislation is intended to affect or change; and where the legislative body does not itself possess the requisite information—which not infrequently is true—recourse must be had to others who do possess it.[8]

[7] The Court commented upon the resolution as follows: "It contains no hint of any intention of final action by Congress on the subject. In all the argument of the case no suggestion is made of what the House of Representatives could have done in the way of remedying the wrong or securing the creditors of Jay Cooke and Company, or even the United States. Was it simply to be a fruitless investigation into the personal affairs of individuals? If so, the House of Representatives had no power or authority in the matter more than any other equal number of gentlemen interested for the government of their country. By 'fruitless' we mean that it could result in no valid legislation on the subject to which the inquiry referred." 103 U.S. 168, 195 (1881).

[8] 273 U.S. 135, 174–175 (1927).

Moreover, the Court held that a Senate inquiry to determine whether or not the Department of Justice was properly performing its duties was a valid one, even though the Senate had neglected to make specific reference in the resolution authorizing the inquiry to the possibility that legislation might result from it.

There has never been a specific Supreme Court decision upholding the investigative power of Congress as a means of achieving the two other purposes which have in practice figured so prominently in many investigations: checking the administrative branch of the government and influencing public opinion. As a matter of fact, there has been no real need for the Court expressly to lend its approval to the use of the investigatory power for these purposes, for in practice no investigation in which either of these motives is present is ever utterly devoid of legislative possibilities. It has always seemed enough to the courts that a specific inquiry might result in legislation; speculation as to other motives or results has seemed superfluous. Moreover, since 1881 no specific inquiry has been disapproved by the Supreme Court on the ground that it was a "fruitless" one that could not result in legislation. While the range of subject matter that has sooner or later been brought within the scope of its inquisitorial power by Congress has indeed been wide, it is doubtful whether Congress has ever conducted an investigation that could not possibly have supplied information for some kind of legislation of undoubted constitutionality.[9] Accordingly, the principle that a Congressional investigation must be a potentially fruitful one has not had much meaning in practice, and it may be doubted whether the courts will ever find occasion to use it as the basis for a ruling that a specific inquiry is unlawful because of its subject matter.[10]

[9] In the Jay Cooke investigation the legislative possibilities were obvious. To mention only one possibility, a law might have been passed to prevent subsequent "improvident deposits" of federal funds by government officials.

[10] It should be added that the Supreme Court has approved the use of the investigative power by Congress for other purposes than supplying information for legislation. Congress may also seek information essential to a "wise" decision as to the expulsion of a member or the impeachment or conviction of a public officer. See In Re Chapman, 166 U.S. 661 (1897) in which the Court held that the Senate might properly authorize an investigation into charges that certain Senators "were yielding to corrupt influences in the consideration of . . . legislation." The Court has also approved the use of the investigating power to scrutinize campaign expenditures in a Congressional election looking toward a possible refusal to seat the winning candidate. Barry v. Cunningham, 279 U.S. 597 (1929).

The Supreme Court has ruled that a Congressional investigating committee is limited in its examination of witnesses to the asking of questions pertinent or relevant to the matter under inquiry. In particular, the Court has reiterated the point that a witness need not answer a question that has no other purpose than to probe into his personal or private affairs. And yet, apart from the *Kilbourn* case, the Court has never ruled that the particular questions asked a witness before a committee were impertinent; nor has it ever ruled that a particular inquiry encroached improperly upon a witness's privacy. But the Court has frequently warned against these forbidden practices. In the *McGrain* case the Court said that "a witness rightfully may refuse to answer where the bounds of the [investigatory] power are exceeded or the questions are not pertinent to the matter under inquiry." [11] Two years later, in 1929, in *Sinclair v. United States*, it added, "It has always been recognized in this country, and it is well to remember, that few if any of the rights of the people guarded by fundamental law are of greater importance to their happiness and safety than the right to be exempt from all unauthorized, arbitrary, or unreasonable inquiries and disclosures in respect of their personal and private affairs." [12] But in both of these cases, after having uttered these inspiring generalizations, the Court went on to hold that the actual inquiries and questions involved were proper.[13] Indeed, it may be asked whether the ruling of the Court that an investigating committee is limited to the asking of pertinent questions can have much vitality in practice. The operation of the rule is such that a substantial burden is placed on the witness who refuses to answer

---

On the other hand, the Court has held that Congress' power to punish private persons for contempt does not extend to a situation where a libelous attack is made on a Congressional agency in a newspaper and there is no indication of a resulting immediate obstruction of the legislative process. *Marshall v. Gordon*, 243 U.S. 521 (1917).

[11] 273 U.S. 135, 176 (1927).

[12] 279 U.S. 263, 292 (1929). In *Kilbourn v. Thompson* the Court had said, "We are sure that no person can be punished for contumacy as a witness before either House, unless his testimony is required in a matter into which that House has jurisdiction to inquire, and we feel equally sure that neither of these bodies possesses the general power of making inquiry into the private affairs of the citizen." 103 U.S. 168, 190 (1881).

[13] In the *Sinclair* case the witness appeared before a Senate committee but refused to answer certain questions. The Court ruled that the questions were pertinent and should have been answered. Daugherty refused to appear before the Congressional committee that had subpoenaed him, thus there was no actual issue of the pertinency of questions in that case.

questions. He takes a large risk, for, unless he is sustained by the courts in his assertion that the questions are impertinent, punishment for contempt will be his fate. This is a risk that most witnesses will be reluctant to take, particularly if the stubborn fact is brought to their attention by their attorneys that there are virtually no cases in which the courts have ruled that a committee has actually exceeded the bounds of its authority by asking improper questions.[14]

Constitutional law with respect to the procedure of Congressional investigations is less easily stated than is the law concerning their substance. In spite of the fact that the actual language of the Constitution suggests otherwise, it has long been accepted that some, if not all, of the procedural guarantees of the Bill of Rights do apply to Congressional investigations. But an accurate statement of the specific guarantees that do apply and of the effect or extent of their

[14] A possible exception to this is found in *In Re Pacific Railway Commission*, 32 Fed. 241 (1887). In this case a federal circuit court refused to help the Pacific Railway Commission, which had been created by act of Congress to conduct an investigation of certain railroads, compel Leland Stanford to answer certain questions. But see Charles B. Nutting, "Freedom of Silence: Constitutional Protection against Governmental Intrusions in Political Affairs," 47 *Mich. Law Review* (Dec., 1948), 181. This author holds "the so-called limitation of pertinence has been reduced to almost complete insignificance" (p. 216). The general inclination of the courts to grant legislative committees very considerable leeway in fixing the bounds of pertinency is illustrated by the opinion of the Court of Appeals for the District of Columbia in the case of *Townsend v. United States*. Dr. Townsend appeared before a House committee which was investigating old age pension plans but took offense at the proceedings and walked out of the committee room. He was then charged with contempt and convicted. In its decision upholding this conviction the Court of Appeals said: "A legislative inquiry may be as broad, as searching, and as exhaustive as is necessary to make effective the constitutional powers of Congress. . . . A judicial inquiry relates to a case, and the evidence to be admissible must be measured by the narrow limits of the pleadings. A legislative inquiry anticipates all possible cases which may arise thereunder, and the evidence admissible must be responsive to the scope of the inquiry, which generally is very broad. Many a witness in a judicial inquiry has, no doubt, been embarrassed and irritated by questions which to him seemed incompetent, irrelevant, immaterial, and impertinent. But that is not a matter for a witness finally to decide. Because a witness could not understand the purpose of cross-examination, he would not be justified in leaving a courtroom. The orderly processes of judicial determination do not permit the exercise of such discretion by a witness. The orderly processes of legislative inquiry require that the committee shall determine such questions for itself. Within the realm of legislative discretion, the exercise of good taste and good judgment in the examination of witnesses must be entrusted to those who have been vested with authority to conduct such investigations." 95 F. 2d 352, 361 (1938).

application is very difficult to make. On one hand, there is not the slightest suggestion in any court ruling that the Sixth Amendment guarantee that an accused person "shall . . . have the assistance of counsel for his defense" requires a Congressional committee to permit witnesses to enjoy such assistance. On the other hand, although there is no clear-cut ruling to this effect, the courts have intimated that the ban of the Fourth Amendment against unreasonable searches and seizures does bind such committees as well as ordinary law enforcement officers.[15]

Much of the argument concerning the applicability of the procedural guarantees of the Bill of Rights to Congressional investigating committees has centered in the self-incrimination clause of the Fifth Amendment, which says, "No person . . . shall be compelled in any criminal case to be a witness against himself." On its face this language would seem to have no bearing whatsoever upon the status of a witness before a legislative committee. Indeed, read literally, the clause would seem to restrict the right solely to the *defendant* in a *criminal* case actually under way.[16] However, tradition and precedent have long given the right to be free from self-incrimination a broader application than is suggested by the language of the Fifth Amendment. It is now generally recognized that the right may be

[15] There is no ruling by an appellate court that the Fourth Amendment controls Congressional committees. In *Strawn v. Western Union Telegraph Company* (1936) a District of Columbia Court granted an injunction to restrain the Western Union Company from handing over to a Senate committee all copies of telegrams sent or received by the plaintiff during a ten-month period on the ground that the subpoena duces tecum issued by the committee violated the Fourth Amendment. 3 *United States Law Week* 646. See also *N.Y. Times,* March 12, 1936; M. Nelson McGeary, *The Developments of Congressional Investigative Power* (New York: Columbia University Press, 1940), pp. 106–108; and *Hearst v. Black,* 87 F. 2d 68 (1936).

[16] Edward S. Corwin has written, "Considered in the light to be shed by grammar and the dictionary, the words of the self-incrimination clause appear to signify simply that nobody shall be compelled to give oral testimony against himself in a criminal proceeding under way in which he is defendant." "The Supreme Court's Construction of the Self-Incrimination Clause," 29 *Mich. Law Review* (1930), 1 and 191. Reprinted in *Selected Essays on Constitutional Law* (Chicago: The Foundation Press, Inc., 1938), II, 1398, 1399.

E. M. Morgan has written, "If this language were to be construed as fixing the limits of the privilege without regard to the existing precedents, it would be difficult to contend that it could be legitimately claimed in a civil action in law or equity, or in any proceeding which was not to be used as a foundation for a criminal prosecution." "The Privilege against Self-Incrimination," 34 *Minn. Law Review* (Dec., 1949), 1, 23.

claimed by witnesses as well as the defendant in a criminal case, by parties and witnesses in civil cases, and by witnesses in nonjudicial proceedings to justify a refusal to give any testimony that might later be used as a basis for criminal proceedings against them.[17] Moreover, it was long ago asserted that the right might be claimed by a witness before a Congressional committee. Indeed, as early as 1857, Congress endeavored to remove the threat to legislative inquiries, which repeated assertion of the claim might entail, by enacting legislation granting witnesses absolute immunity against prosecution for any crimes revealed by their testimony and in turn compelling them to testify.[18] It took this step even though there was no Supreme Court ruling that the right not to testify against oneself could be claimed by a witness before a Congressional committee. In fact, there has been no such flat ruling from the court even to this day, although, as one authority has pointed out, there are Supreme Court opinions whose "fair inference . . . is that the privilege as

[17] John H. Wigmore, the great authority on evidence, says the protection of the privilege against self-incrimination "extends to all manner of proceedings in which testimony is to be taken, whether litigious or not, and whether 'ex parte' or otherwise. It therefore applies in . . . investigations by a legislature or a body having legislative functions, and in investigations by administrative officials." 8 *Evidence* § 2252 (c). Supreme Court cases in which broad protection of the privilege has been recognized are: *Counselman v. Hitchcock,* 142 U.S. 547 (1892) and *Blau v. United States,* 340 U.S. 159 (1950) (privilege applied to grand jury proceedings); *McCarthy v. Arndstein,* 266 U.S. 34 (1924) (privilege applied to bankruptcy proceedings); *Boyd v. United States,* 116 U.S. 616 (1886) (privilege applied to statutory proceedings for forfeiture of goods); *Brown v. Walker,* 161 U.S. 591 (1896) (privilege assumed to apply to Interstate Commerce Commission proceedings).

[18] 11 Stat. 155. Chief Justice Vinson has stated that the 1857 statute was "designed on the one hand to compel the testimony of witnesses and on the other hand to protect them from prosecution for crimes revealed by their testimony." *United States v. Bryan,* 339 U.S. 323 (1950).

The Supreme Court has held that Congress may withdraw the privilege against self-incrimination by granting a witness before the Interstate Commerce Commission complete immunity against any prosecution on account of any transaction to which he might testify. That the statute could not also shield him against personal disgrace or opprobrium was held immaterial. *Brown v. Walker,* 161 U.S. 591 (1896). See also *Hale v. Henkel,* 201 U.S. 43 (1906). In the latter case the Supreme Court said, "If the criminality has already been taken away the [5th] amendment ceases to apply. The criminality provided against is a present, not a past, criminality, which lingers only as a memory, and involves no present danger of prosecution. . . . It is here that the law steps in and says that if the offense be outlawed or pardoned, or its criminality has been removed by statute, the amendment ceases to apply" (p. 67).

established in the Fifth Amendment protects witnesses in Congressional investigations as fully as in judicial proceedings." [19] At any rate for at least a century Congress seems to have recognized the right of witnesses to refuse to testify before its committees on this ground, and it either has attempted to compel testimony by granting immunity or has allowed witnesses to assert the right without challenge, even though the right rests on no more than "assumptions and intimations" in Supreme Court decisions.[20]

The legislative grant of absolute immunity against later prosecution for crime given by Congress in 1857 to witnesses before its committees was allowed to stand for only five years. In 1862 this provision of the Act of 1857 which had been passed by overwhelming majorities in both houses was unanimously repealed on the

[19] E. M. Morgan, "Self Incrimination," p. 31. Professor Morgan points out that there are square rulings in the state courts to the effect that state legislative committees are bound by the self-incrimination clauses in state constitutions. See *Emery's Case*, 107 Mass. 172 (1871), and *Matter of Doyle*, 257 N.Y. 244 (1931).

[20] E. M. Morgan, "Self Incrimination," p. 33. Actually Congress seems to have gone even further than have the courts in recognizing the right:

Recently the Court of Appeals for the Tenth Circuit stated, after analyzing earlier federal rulings, "We conclude the rule to be that the witness is not the sole judge as to whether his answer will tend to incriminate him; that when the question arises, it is for the court to determine from all the facts whether the question is of such a nature as might reasonably be expected to incriminate the witness, depending upon the answer thereto. If there is reason to believe that the answer might tend to incriminate the witness, he cannot be compelled to answer; neither can he be required to state why the answer might tend to incriminate him, because that would in itself to some extent constitute giving testimony against himself. Furthermore, a witness may not be required to give an answer which furnishes a link in a chain which would enable the Government to obtain the facts showing his guilt of a crime." *Rogers v. United States*, 179 F. 2d 559, 562 (1950). See the Supreme Court's decision in the same case, 340 U.S. 367 (1951).

And in a recent case the Supreme Court has stated, "The witness is not exonerated from answering merely because he declares that in so doing he would incriminate himself—his say-so does not of itself establish the hazard of incrimination. It is for the court to say whether his silence is justified, and to require him to answer if 'it clearly appears to the court that he is mistaken.' " *Hoffman v. United States*, 341 U.S. 479 (1951). See also *Blau v. United States*, 340 U.S. 159, 332 (1950).

At other times the courts have suggested that a witness may arbitrarily refuse to answer only those questions which *on their face* appear to call for incriminating answers, and that he must assume the burden of proof with respect to other questions and justify refusal to answer them by showing that he has substantial reason to believe his answers will be incriminating. See *United States v. Rosen,*

ground that it had "cheated justice of its dues more often than it had aided its administration, and its existence had come to be a crying evil." [21] It was stated in debate that the provision had operated in practice to induce criminals to appear before Congressional committees in order thereby to gain a general pardon for all offenses which they might mention in the course of their testimony. Reference was made to specific instances in which this result had prevailed during the five-year period the act had been in effect.[22]

In repealing the grant of absolute immunity Congress substituted for it a grant of relative immunity which has remained in effect to the present time. The substitute provides only that the actual testimony given by a witness shall not be used against him as evidence in any subsequent criminal proceeding. It does not protect the witness against prosecution for a crime that may be disclosed in his testimony where law enforcement officials can find other evidence than the witness's own testimony as a basis for a case against him. Moreover, official papers or records produced by a witness are specifically exempted from the ban on subsequent use as evidence in a criminal proceeding. As found in the present *United States Code,* this provision is as follows:

Title 18, § 3486

No testimony given by a witness before either House, or before any committee of either House, or before any joint committee established by a joint or concurrent resolution of the two Houses of Congress, shall be

---

174 F. 2d 187, 188 (1949) and *Alexander v. United States,* 181 F. 2d 480, 482 (1950).

It would appear that some if not all Congressional committees have allowed the witness himself to judge whether his testimony, if given, would prove incriminating, and there does not appear to have been regular insistence upon testimony being given where the statute of limitations has run concerning any crime that might be disclosed.

[21] 12 Stat. 333, 37th Cong., 2d Sess., *Cong. Globe,* pp. 364, 430.

[22] See Eberling (n. 2 above), pp. 319 ff. Eberling quotes Senator Wade as stating during debate over the repealer in the Senate: "I have not dared to enter upon certain investigations before a committee of which I am a member, for the reason that the law as it is now, exculpates great rascals from the responsibility they owe to the government, and gives entire immunity to any man touching any matter you see fit to inquire of him about. I wonder how such a law was ever passed. I never should have believed that such a law was on your statute book if it had not been suggested to me, and I had not found it. I was astonished to find a law in existence providing that if you inquired of any witness in regard to any delinquency that had arisen, he should be exculpated from that moment from the consequences of his crime" (322–323).

used as evidence in any criminal proceeding against him in any court, except in a prosecution for perjury committed in giving such testimony. But an official paper or record produced by him is not within the said privilege.[23]

There has been a good deal of doubt about the constitutionality of this arrangement. A somewhat similar statutory arrangement with respect to testimony given in judicial proceedings was declared unconstitutional by the Supreme Court in 1892 in *Counselman v. Hitchcock*. The Court held that the right established by the Fifth Amendment might be claimed by a witness before a grand jury and that a statutory attempt to withdraw the right by offering a witness immunity only against the use of his own testimony in a subsequent criminal proceeding against him could not meet the test of constitutionality.[24]

By analogy the legislation pertaining to witnesses before Congressional committees has seemed to have the same deficiency,[25] and accordingly, Congressional committees have been reluctant to insist that a witness must testify when he offers self-incrimination as an excuse for remaining silent. Of course, it should be recognized that a witness who offers this excuse usually discredits himself in the eyes of the

[23] As amended June 25, 1948, ch. 645, 62 Stat. 683. Derived from Acts Jan. 24, 1857, ch. 19 § 2, 11 Stat. 156; Jan. 24, 1862, ch. 11, 12 Stat. 333.

Attention may also be called to Title 2, § 193: "No witness is privileged to refuse to testify to any fact, or to produce any paper, respecting which he shall be examined by either House of Congress, or by any joint committee established by a joint or concurrent resolution of the two Houses of Congress, or by any committee of either House, upon the ground that his testimony to such fact or his production of such paper may tend to disgrace him or otherwise render him infamous." As amended June 22, 1938, ch. 594, 52 Stat. 942. Derived from Act of Jan. 24, 1862, ch. 11, 12 Stat. 333.

[24] 142 U.S. 547 (1892). See the discussion in Eberling, pp. 401 ff. The statutory provision involved in the *Counselman* case was § 860 of the Revised Statutes of 1874 which read as follows: "No pleading of a party, nor any discovery or evidence obtained from a party or witness by means of a judicial proceeding in this or any other foreign country, shall be given in evidence, or in any manner used against him or his property or estate, in any court of the United States, in any criminal proceeding, or for the enforcement of any penalty or forfeiture: *Provided,* That this section shall not exempt any party or witness from prosecution and punishment for perjury committed in discovering or testifying as aforesaid." § 860 is comparable to the present § 3486 of Title 18 of the *United States Code*. Indeed, the latter provision of law is derived from § 859 of the *Revised Statutes* where it was definitely a companion to § 860.

[25] Chief Justice Vinson's opinion in *United States v. Bryan*, 339 U.S. 323 (1950), implies the unconstitutionality of this legislation.

public, for in effect he admits he has been guilty of wrongdoing.

The way in which the courts have gained the opportunity to review the record of investigating committees, both with respect to substance and procedure, should be noted. With rare exceptions such cases have come to the courts as a result of the exercise of the contempt power by Congress. When witnesses have refused to cooperate with investigating committees, conviction for contempt of Congress has traditionally been the price such witnesses have paid. Such a conviction, in turn, has often afforded a witness the opportunity to challenge in the appellate courts the propriety of the subject matter of an investigation or of the procedures the committee making the investigation has employed. When such challenges have been made, the courts have, since 1881 at least, been ready to subject the investigation to the full measure of judicial review, although, having insisted upon the right to scrutinize this activity of a collateral branch of the government, they have then consistently ruled against the witness and for the Congress.

The right of Congress to punish a private person for conduct deemed contemptuous of it was recognized by the Supreme Court as early as 1821 in *Anderson v. Dunn*. In that case the Court upheld the power of the House of Representatives to arrest and punish a private person who had attempted to bribe one of its members. The Court declared this was an implied common law power essential to the effective exercise of Congress's express powers.[26] Until 1857 the procedure in such cases was to bring the accused individual before the bar of the Senate or the House where he was, in effect, tried. If a finding of guilt resulted, punishment might be imposed, ranging from a mere reprimand, as in Anderson's case, to imprisonment at the hands of the House or Senate Sergeant at Arms for the remainder of the session. In the 1857 legislation already referred to, Congress defined contempt of Congress as a statutory offense against the United States, thus making it possible to turn a contumacious person over to law enforcement officials for prosecution in the courts. This step was taken not so much to provide a statutory definition of contempt of Congress which all could see, as to establish a greater and more effective penalty, since the Supreme Court had inferred in the *Anderson* case that Congress itself could not imprison a person, declared by it to be guilty of contempt, beyond the duration of the current session.[27] The Act of 1857 made contempt of Congress a misdemeanor

[26] 6 Wheaton 204 (1821).
[27] See Eberling, pp. 302 ff. The Supreme Court had observed in *Anderson v.*

punishable by a fine of not more than $1,000 nor less than $100 *and* imprisonment for not more than one year nor less than one month. The text of this portion of the act, which has now become Section 192 of Title 2 of the *United States Code* is:

Every person who having been summoned as a witness by the authority of either House of Congress to give testimony or to produce papers upon any matter under inquiry before either House, or any joint committee established by a joint or concurrent resolution of the two Houses of Congress, or any committee of either House of Congress, willfully makes default, or who, having appeared, refuses to answer any question pertinent to the question under inquiry, shall be deemed guilty of a misdemeanor, punishable by a fine of not more than $1,000 nor less than $100 and imprisonment in a common jail for not less than one month nor more than twelve months.[28]

After the *Dunn* case in the 1820's, most of the cases in which private persons were held to be in contempt of Congress concerned unco-operative witnesses before investigating committees. Although the Act of 1857 made it possible to turn such persons over to the courts for trial, the two houses of Congress continued in many instances to deal with and punish such persons directly. One reason for this was that as long as Congress retained an unco-operative witness in its custody, there was always the chance he would change his mind and agree to testify, whereas once he was handed over to the courts this chance came to an end. In other words, imprisonment for contempt by Congress itself may be used more readily for its coercive effect, whereas imprisonment following a court trial is largely punitive in its effect.[29]

The constitutionality of the Act of 1857 was upheld by the Supreme Court in 1897 in *In Re Chapman*.[30] Chapman appeared in response to a subpoena as a witness before a Senate committee which was investigating charges that certain Senators had yielded to corrupt influences in the consideration of tariff legislation. He then refused to answer specific questions as to whether a brokerage firm of which he was a member had bought or sold sugar stocks for any Senator.

Dunn: "A period is imposed by the nature of things since the existence of the power that imprisons is indispensable to its continuance; and although the legislative power continues perpetual, the legislative body ceases to exist on the moment of its adjournment or periodical dissolution. It follows, that the imprisonment must terminate with that adjournment." 6 Wheaton 204, 231 (1821).

[28] As amended June 22, 1938, ch. 594, 52 Stat. 942. Derived from Act of Jan. 24, 1857, ch. 19, § 1, 11 Stat. 155.

[29] See Eberling, pp. 316 ff.   [30] 166 U.S. 661 (1897).

As the result of this refusal to testify he was successfully prosecuted under the Act of 1857. Chapman was the first person ever to be indicted for contempt of Congress under the Act of 1857, passed some forty years earlier.[31] In reviewing the case, the Supreme Court held that Congress might properly define refusal of private persons to testify before its committees as a misdemeanor. It also held that this statutory offense did not take the place of the common law offense recognized in the *Anderson* case, but was merely a supplement to it. Indeed, the Court implied that, were Congress to attempt by statute to vest in the courts exclusive power to try witnesses before its committees for contempt, the result would be an unconstitutional delegation of legislative power to the judiciary. The Court also stated that, were Congress first to punish a contumacious witness itself and then turn him over to the courts for prosecution and possible punishment, such procedure would not violate the double jeopardy clause of the Fifth Amendment.[32]

In recent years the House and Senate have depended heavily upon proceedings under the Act of 1857 as a way to compel private persons to co-operate with their investigating committees and have seldom invoked their own power to punish contumacious witnesses directly. It should be noted that while the statute states that when the facts concerning a contumacious witness are reported to either house, the President of the Senate or the Speaker of the House *shall* certify the case to the district attorney for the District of Columbia for presentation to the grand jury, the custom has been for the presiding officers to wait until the Senate or House by majority vote directs them to take this step.

Because a review of proceedings in contempt cases has been almost the only method by which the courts have gained the opportunity to pass generally upon the propriety of Congressional investigations, the means has always been available to Congress to avoid judicial supervision of this activity merely by refraining from

[31] Asher C. Hinds, *Precedents of the House of Representatives* (Washington: Government Printing Office, 1907), II, § 1613, p. 1076.

[32] On this point the Court said, "It is improbable that in any case cumulative penalties would be imposed, whether by way of punishment merely, or of eliciting the answers desired, but it is quite clear that the contumacious witness is not subjected to jeopardy twice for the same offense, since the same act may be an offense against one jurisdiction and also an offense against another; and indictable statutory offenses may be punished as such, while the offenders may likewise be subjected to punishment for the acts as contempts, the two being *diverso intuito* and capable of standing together." 166 U.S. 661, 672 (1897).

contempt proceedings against recalcitrant witnesses. On the other hand, unless Congress takes steps to punish at least an occasional unco-operative witness, its investigating committees might ultimately be faced by a wholesale refusal of witnesses to testify.

The Constitutional Case against the Un-American Activities Committee

In carrying their case against the Un-American Activities Committee to the courts, the committee's opponents have raised virtually every constitutional point that has ever been made against any earlier Congressional committee and have also devised several new arguments. As has been true of previous attacks upon the investigatory power, the arguments have fallen into two categories: one including attacks upon the committee's substantive authority to investigate subversive activity; and the other, attacks upon the committee's specific policies and procedures. Unfortunately, consideration of these arguments by the courts has not been systematic, nor has it resulted in a series of clear-cut legal rulings. There has been a good deal of disagreement between different courts hearing the same case and even between the justices of a single court. Moreover, the opinions, majority and dissenting alike, have been more than ordinarily discursive, and it is not easy to set forth their substance in orderly fashion.

In a two-and-a-half-year period between December, 1947, and April, 1950, five cases growing out of the work of the Un-American Activities Committee were decided finally at the court of appeals level and four more reached the Supreme Court for decision.[33] The cases that did not go beyond the courts of appeals raised the more

[33] The cases in the first group were: United States v. Josephson, 165 F. 2d 82 (C.A. 2d 1947); certiorari denied, 333 U.S. 838, 858 (1948); 335 U.S. 899 (1948). Barsky v. United States, 167 F. 2d 241 (App. D.C. 1948); certiorari denied, 334 U.S. 843 (1948). Eisler v. United States, 170 F. 2d 273 (App. D.C. 1948); certiorari granted, 335 U.S. 857 (1948); dismissed as moot, 338 U.S. 189 (1949). Lawson v. United States, 176 F. 2d 49 (App. D.C. 1949); certiorari denied, 339 U.S. 934, 972 (1950). Marshall v. United States, 176 F. 2d 473 (1949); certiorari denied, 339 U.S. 933, 959 (1950).

The cases in the second group were: United States v. Bryan, 339 U.S. 323 (1950); see the same case below: 174 F. 2d 525 (App. D.C. 1949). United States v. Fleischman, 339 U.S. 349 (1950); see the case below: 174 F. 2d 519 (App. D.C. 1949). Dennis v. United States, 339 U.S. 162 (1950); see the same case below: 171 F. 2d 986 (App. D.C. 1948). Morford v. United States, 339 U.S. 258 (1950); see the same case below: 176 F. 2d 54 (App. D.C. 1949).

basic issues concerning the law of Congressional investigations. The Supreme Court was seemingly content to let the lower courts settle these issues since it refused to review any of these cases.

Three of the cases grew out of the committee's investigation of the Joint Anti-Fascist Refugee Committee in 1946, two were the results of investigations of the National Council of American-Soviet Friendship and the National Federation for Constitutional Liberties, also in 1946, three were the result of the committee's somewhat disorganized investigations in 1947 into the Communist Party and the comings and goings of certain international Communists, and one was the product of the Hollywood hearings later in 1947. As yet, the spectacular Communist espionage hearings of 1948 have resulted in no litigation in which the authority of the House committee has been at issue, although a decision by the House of Representatives in 1950 to order the prosecution of certain witnesses who refused in 1948 to testify on the ground of self-incrimination may ultimately produce such a result.

The three most important cases of this period were perhaps *United States v. Josephson,* which was decided by the Court of Appeals for the Second Circuit in 1947, *Barsky v. United States,* which was decided by the Court of Appeals for the District of Columbia in 1948, and *Lawson v. United States,* decided by the latter court in 1949.

The Un-American Activities Committee subpoenaed Leon Josephson to appear before it in New York in March, 1947, presumably because it had reason to believe he could supply it with information concerning the methods by which Eisler and other international Communists had been able to enter and leave the United States with great ease. However, upon his appearance he refused either to be sworn or to give testimony. At the request of the committee the House of Representatives cited Josephson for contempt. He was then indicted and convicted in the federal district court in New York for violation of § 192 of Title 2 of the *United States Code.* This conviction was affirmed by the Court of Appeals by a two-to-one vote. The majority consisted of Judges Swan and Chase, Judge Charles E. Clark being the dissenter.

Dr. Edward K. Barsky, chairman of the Joint Anti-Fascist Refugee Committee, was subpoenaed together with Helen Bryan, executive secretary of the organization, and fifteen members of its executive board, to appear before the House committee in February and April, 1946, and to bring with them the organization's books and records relating to the receipts and disbursements of money and correspondence with persons in foreign countries. All of the subpoenaed persons appeared, but none produced the requested documents. Thereupon, at the request of the committee all of the witnesses were cited for contempt by the House, and all were ultimately tried and convicted in the courts under § 192. Barsky and others appealed to the Court of Appeals for the District of Columbia, which affirmed the verdicts by a two-to-one vote. The majority consisted of Judges Prettyman and Bennett Champ Clark, Judge Edgerton being the dissenter.

John Howard Lawson and Dalton Trumbo were two of the ten Hollywood witnesses who refused in October, 1947, to answer questions put to them by the House committee, including the now classic one, "Are you now or have you ever been a member of the Communist Party?" All ten were cited for contempt by the House, but only Lawson and Trumbo were tried immediately under § 192 in a District of Columbia court, the trials of the other eight being postponed by agreement until the validity of the prosecution of Lawson and Trumbo could be tested in the appellate courts. The two men were tried and convicted separately, but their appeals were heard jointly by the Court of Appeals for the District of Columbia. The latter court affirmed the verdicts unanimously. Thereupon, the other eight men were convicted by a three-judge court, the defendants having waived their right to a jury trial at the time of the postponement.

Does the Un-American Activities Investigation Have a Valid Purpose? It has repeatedly been argued that the Un-American Activities Committee's enabling resolution and/or the actual record made by the committee demonstrate that the committee is not concerned with discovering factual information that may serve as a basis for legislation, but that instead its purpose is to influence public opinion or to expose allegedly subversive people to public condemnation.[34] This argument implies that the committee's general authority has been granted or used for a purpose or purposes not hitherto recognized as valid by the courts. The argument was specifically rejected by the majority in the *Josephson* case. Judge Chase stated, "we have no occasion now to decide whether a Congressional investigation may have exposure as its principal goal. . . . It is sufficient to say that the authorizing statute contains the declaration of Congress that the information sought is for a legislative purpose and that fact is thus established for us. . . ." The court, calling attention to the express Congressional powers to "provide for the common Defence," "to

[34] See p. 431 for the text of the committee's enabling resolution.

raise and support Armies," "to provide and maintain a Navy," "to make Rules for the Government and Regulation of the land and naval Forces," "to make all Laws which shall be necessary and proper for carrying into Execution the foregoing Powers," to guarantee to every state a republican form of government, and to protect the states against invasion and domestic violence, suggested that the exercise of these powers might be facilitated by the findings of an un-American activities investigation. It also took notice of the many types of legislation that might grow out of the committee's findings, quoting with approval the following passage from a ruling of a federal district judge:

That the subject of un-American and subversive activities is within the investigating power of the Congress is obvious. Conceivably, information in this field may aid the Congress in legislating concerning any one of many matters, such as correspondence with foreign governments (U.S.C.A. Title 18, § 5); seditious conspiracy (Id. § 6); prohibition of undermining the morale of the armed forces (Id. § 9); suppression of advocacy of overthrow of the Government (Id. § 10); the registration of organizations carrying on certain types of propaganda (Id. §§ 14 and 15); qualifications for entering and remaining in Government service; the authorization of Governmental radio broadcasts to foreign countries; and other innumerable topics. Similarly such information may be helpful in appropriating funds.[35]

In spite of the fact that legislative recommendations have not been a conspicuous feature of the reports of the committee to the House and also that very little actual legislation can be traced to the work

[35] 165 F. 2d 82, 89–90 (1947). The quoted passage is from a ruling by Judge Holtzoff in *United States v. Bryan*, 72 F. Supp. 58, 62 (D.D.C. 1947).

In the *Morford* case the Court of Appeals for the District of Columbia took notice of the argument that "when the subpoena was issued against the defendant the Un-American Activities Committee had already passed judgment on the National Council of American-Soviet Friendship and was seeking to obtain names of persons participating in its activities and supporting it financially and otherwise, for the sole purpose of adding such names to its black-list and to facilitate the committee's efforts to destroy the effectiveness of the National Council of American-Soviet Friendship in its advocacy of American-Soviet Friendship by placing undue burdens upon such continued advocacy," and that this meant "the committee was not acting in furtherance of a legislative purpose. . . ." The court rejected this argument, holding "that a legitimate purpose is presumed when the general subject of investigation is one concerning which Congress can legislate, and when the information sought would materially aid its consideration." It added, "That presumption arises here, and it cannot be rebutted by impugning the motives of the individual members of the Committee." 176 F. 2d 54, 58 (1949).

of the committee, it is most unlikely that the courts can be persuaded to hold that the committee's grant of authority or its exercise of that authority is unconcerned with the search for information in aid of legislation.[36]

Does the Committee's Substantive Authority Bring It into Conflict with the First Amendment? A more promising attack upon the House committee has been that the specific authority granted to it brings it into conflict with the First Amendment. But this attack, too, has thus far failed in the courts. The argument that the committee has encroached upon the freedom of speech, press, and assembly guaranties of the First Amendment has been formulated in various ways. It has been argued that Congress's authority to undertake an investi-

---

[36] There is, of course, always the possibility that a particular line of inquiry might be held deficient in the sense that no legislation could result from it. But varied and unpredictable though the committee's interests have proved to be, it is doubtful whether the courts would hold that any of them lay completely outside the scope of legislative possibilities. For example, in undertaking to investigate the methods by which the Joint Anti-Fascist Refugee Committee raised funds and the nature of its contacts with persons in foreign lands it might seem as though the committee had both exceeded the limits of the authority granted to it and moved beyond the limits of permissible Congressional interest. But the Court of Appeals took notice of the existence of such official bodies as UNRRA and the President's War Relief Control Board and held that they "clearly justified Congressional inquiry into the disbursement abroad of private funds collected in this country avowedly for relief but reasonably represented as being spent for political purposes in Europe." *Barsky v. United States,* 167 F. 2d 241, 244 (1948).

Again in the *Morford* case it was argued that the committee's investigation of the National Council of American-Soviet Friendship was "not pertinent to any matter of inquiry committed to the Committee by Congress." The Court of Appeals for the District of Columbia rejected the argument and stated, "The National Council's unstinted praise of the communistic regime in Russia, and its comparison of Soviet official behavior with that of the United States to the disparagement of the latter, led logically to the Committee's conclusion that here was such strong indication of an attack on the *principle* of our form of government as to justify inquiry" under the committee's enabling resolution. 176 F. 2d 54, 56–57 (1949).

In the *Eisler* case the Court of Appeals for the District of Columbia affirmed Eisler's conviction under § 192 by a two-to-one vote. The dissenting judge, Prettyman, stated that a judgment of acquittal should have been directed on the ground the government had failed at Eisler's trial to show that he had been summoned by the House committee to testify on a matter falling within its authority under its enabling resolution. Prettyman added, "This record does not show, and we do not yet know, what it was that the Committee wanted appellant to testify about." 170 F. 2d 273, 284 (1948). The majority does not appear to have given any consideration to this point.

gation of subversive activity is limited by the clear and present danger doctrine. According to this doctrine Congress may not curb freedom of expression or related rights except when there is evidence that the exercise of such rights is creating a clear and present danger of a substantive evil that Congress has authority to prevent.[37] More specifically, it has been argued that the investigating power is subject to the same limitations as the legislating power and that in the absence of evidence that the nation is endangered by subversive activity the House committee may not undertake a program of thought control by such means as exposure and publicity where legislation attempting the same thing would most certainly be held to violate the First Amendment. A totally different line of argument under the First Amendment has been that the amendment establishes a right of privacy, or a right to remain silent, particularly as to an individual's political beliefs or affiliations; and this right has been violated by the committee's oft-repeated demand that its witnesses state whether or not they are members of the Communist Party.

However formulated, arguments based upon the First Amendment

[37] The first formulation of the clear and present danger doctrine was by Justice Holmes in the Court opinion in *Schenck v. United States*, 249 U.S. 47, 52 (1919): "The most stringent protection of free speech would not protect a man in falsely shouting fire in a theatre and causing a panic. It does not even protect a man from an injunction against uttering words that may have all the effect of force. The question in every case is whether the words used are used in such circumstances and are of such a nature as to create a clear and present danger that they will bring about the substantive evils that Congress has a right to prevent."

In *Whitney v. California*, 274 U.S. 357, 376–378 (1927), Justice Brandeis in a concurring opinion said, "To justify suppression of free speech there must be reasonable ground to fear that serious evil will result if free speech is practiced. There must be reasonable ground to believe that the danger apprehended is imminent. There must be reasonable ground to believe that the evil to be prevented is a serious one. . . . No danger flowing from speech can be deemed clear and present, unless the incidence of the evil apprehended is so imminent that it may befall before there is opportunity for full discussion. . . . Moreover, even imminent danger cannot justify resort to prohibition of these functions essential to effective democracy, unless the evil apprehended is relatively serious. . . . The fact that speech is likely to result in some violence or in destruction of property is not enough to justify its suppression. There must be the probability of serious injury to the State."

In *Bridges v. California*, 314 U.S. 252, 263 (1941), Justice Black in the Court opinion observed, "What finally emerges from the 'clear and present danger' cases is a working principle that the substantive evil [that the legislature seeks to prevent by statute] must be extremely serious and the degree of imminence extremely high before utterances can be punished."

have consistently been rejected by the courts. In both the *Josephson* and *Barsky* cases the majorities held that a Congressional committee may properly investigate the propaganda activities of political groups to determine whether there does exist a clear and present danger to American democracy that Congress may wish to meet through legislation. The majority judges in both cases refused to concede that the Un-American Activities Committee was itself attempting to meet the threat through exposure and publicity, or to decide whether this threat was sufficiently serious to constitute a clear and present danger. Instead, they implied that any such direct action by the committee was incidental to its main purpose—securing information that would enable Congress to decide whether remedial legislation was needed. And the judicial position in these two cases was that the search for information must necessarily be allowed to reach wider limits than can be encompassed by legislation itself. The reasoning in the majority opinions runs somewhat as follows: A statute restrictive of speech or political activity is valid only when aimed at a clear and present danger. But the questioning of witnesses before a Congressional committee concerning their political or propagandist activities must necessarily be broad when the purpose is to discover whether such activity does in fact create a clear and present danger. It will be time enough to consider whether a statute growing out of the investigation perchance violates the First Amendment, when such a statute is passed. In the meantime, the courts must presume that Congress will not be encouraged by the investigation at hand to pass unconstitutional legislation.[38]

---

[38] In the *Josephson* case the majority states, "The power of Congress to gather facts of the most intense public concern, such as these, is not diminished by the unchallenged right of individuals to speak their minds within lawful limits. When speech, or propaganda, or whatever it may at the moment be called, clearly presents an immediate danger to national security, the protection of the First Amendment ceases. Congress can then legislate. In deciding what to do, however, it may necessarily be confronted with the difficult and complex task of determining how far it can go before it transgresses the boundaries established by the Constitution." 165 F. 2d 82, 91 (1947).

In the *Barsky* case the majority states,

"In our view, it would be sheer folly as a matter of government policy for an existing government to refrain from inquiry into potential threats to its existence or security until danger was clear and present. And for the judicial branch of government to hold the legislative branch to be without power to make such inquiry until the danger is clear and present, would be absurd. How, except upon inquiry, would the Congress know whether the danger is clear and present? There is a vast difference between the necessities for inquiry and the

Similarly, the courts have rejected the notion that there is any absolute right under the First Amendment to remain silent as to one's political affiliations or activities. Insofar as such affiliations or activities may affect the public welfare, Congress may properly seek information as to their nature and extent, and private persons must co-operate with such a search. In the *Lawson* case the Court of Appeals for the District of Columbia observed that it is "beyond dispute that the motion picture industry plays a critically prominent role in the molding of public opinion," took notice of "the current ideological struggle between communistic-thinking and democratic-thinking peoples of the world," and concluded, "It is absurd to argue . . . that questions asked men, who, by their authorship of the scripts, vitally influence the ultimate production of motion pictures seen by millions, which questions require disclosure of whether or not they are or ever have been Communists, are not pertinent questions." And for good measure, the court added, "Indeed, it is hard to envisage how there could be any more pertinent question" where a committee of Congress is investigating un-American propaganda activities.[39]

It has also been argued that the committee's enabling resolution violates the First Amendment under the rule that a statute which impinges on rights protected by the amendment is void on its face if it is worded so broadly as to permit the punishment of conduct clearly protected by the amendment.[40] But the courts have been

necessities for action. The latter may be only when danger is clear and present, but the former is when danger is reasonably represented as potential.

"There was justification here, within the bounds of the foregoing restriction, for the exercise of the power of inquiry. The President . . . has announced to the Congress the conclusion that aggressive tendencies of totalitarian regimes imposed on free peoples threatens the security of the United States, and he mentioned the activities of Communists in that connection. . . . These culminations of responsible governmental consideration sufficiently demonstrate the necessity for Congressional knowledge of the subject and so justify its course in inquiring into it." 167 F. 2d 241, 246–247 (1948).

[39] 176 F. 2d 49, 53 (1949). In the *Josephson* case the majority says, "Surely matters which potentially affect the very survival of our Government are by no means the purely personal concern of anyone. And investigations into such matters are inquiries relating to the personal affairs of private individuals only to the extent that those individuals are a part of the Government as a whole. The doctrine of *Kilbourn v. Thompson* . . . is, then, not here involved." 165 F. 2d 82, 89 (1947).

[40] This rule finds expression in *Winters v. New York* in the Court opinion by Justice Reed: "It is settled that a statute so vague and indefinite . . . as to permit within the scope of its language the punishment of incidents fairly within

unwilling to apply this stringent rule to the resolution or statute by which a Congressional investigation is authorized. There is no case concerning the Un-American Activities Committee in which the majority has given this argument careful consideration. But in the *Barsky* case, having noted the argument, Judge Prettyman asserted, "There is a difference between the particularity required in the specification of a criminal act and that required in the authorization of an investigation. . . ." [41]

Do the Committee's Activities Encroach upon Rights Safeguarded by the Fifth Amendment? At least three arguments against the activity of the House committee have been based upon the Fifth Amendment. The first, and perhaps most serious, is that since the resolution establishing the committee defines the area of its investigative powers in exceedingly vague and nebulous terms, any attempt to use criminal statutes to punish persons who fail to co-operate with the committee is unconstitutional on the traditional ground that proscribed criminal conduct must be "set forth with clarity, so that the person to whom it applies may determine what conduct is legal and what is not." [42] Persons subpoenaed to appear as witnesses before Congressional committees are clearly entitled on the basis of Supreme Court decisions in the *Kilbourn, Daugherty,* and *Sinclair* cases to refuse to give testimony if the subject matter of the investigation lies outside the scope of Congress's legitimate interests, and they are entitled to refuse to answer specific questions which are

---

the protection of the guarantee of free speech is void, on its face. . . ." 333 U.S. 507, 509 (1948).

See also *Stromberg v. California,* 283 U.S. 359, 369 (1931); *Herndon v. Lowry,* 301 U.S. 242, 258–259 (1937); and *Thornhill v. Alabama,* 310 U.S. 88, 97–98 (1940).

On the other hand, the Supreme Court has sometimes upheld statutes, whose broad wording raised doubts about their constitutionality, as long as they were being narrowly applied in the cases bringing them to the Court's attention. For example, in the *Chapman* case the Court noted the argument that because the statute defining contemptuous conduct by a witness before a Congressional committee as a misdemeanor referred to "any" matter under inquiry it was "fatally defective because too broad and unlimited in its extent," but rejected this argument, preferring instead to follow the rule "that statutes should receive a sensible construction, such as will effectuate the legislative intention, and, if possible, so as to avoid an unjust or an absurd conclusion. . . ." 166 U.S. 661, 667 (1897).

[41] 167 F. 2d 241, 248 (1948). Judge Edgerton in his dissenting opinion gave this argument more careful and sympathetic consideration. See below, pp. 442 ff.

[42] *United States v. Josephson,* 165 F. 2d 82, 97 (1947).

not in fact pertinent to the legitimate subject matter of an inquiry. It has been argued that the subject matter of the un-American activities investigation is so vaguely defined that a witness has no basis for estimating his responsibility to co-operate by appearing or answering questions if he is to avoid prosecution for crime.

The committee's enabling resolution authorizes it to investigate:

(i) the extent, character, and objects of un-American propaganda activities in the United States,

(ii) the diffusion within the United States of subversive and un-American propaganda that is instigated from foreign countries or of a domestic origin and attacks the principle of the form of government as guaranteed by our Constitution, and

(iii) all other questions in relation thereto that would aid Congress in any necessary remedial legislation.

In trying to determine whether he may properly refuse to answer a question as not pertinent, a witness before the House committee might well find it difficult to know: (a) what "un-American propaganda" or "subversive and un-American propaganda" is; (b) whether the committee is authorized to investigate all "subversive and un-American propaganda . . . instigated from foreign countries," or only that subversive and un-American propaganda, foreign or domestic in origin, that "attacks the principle of the form of government as guaranteed by our Constitution"; (c) what "the principle [note the emphasis upon *one* principle] of the form of government as guaranteed by our Constitution" is; (d) what ground is covered by "all other questions in relation thereto."

The courts have conceded that this first argument under the Fifth Amendment is a serious and substantial one, but in the end they have rejected it in those specific situations in which it has been raised. For example, in the *Josephson* case the majority held that since the witness had refused to be sworn or to answer any questions at all he was precluded from raising this defense.[43]

---

[43] In the decision in the *Josephson* case the court added, "At the very least the language of the authorizing statute permits investigating the advocacy of the idea that the Government or the Constitutional system of the United States should be overthrown by force, rather than modified by the peaceful process of amendment. . . . The vice of vagueness in that language, if any, lies in the possibility that it may authorize, though we do not decide that it does so, investigations relating to the advocacy of peaceful changes. 165 F. 2d 82, 88 (1947).

More specifically, in the *Barsky* and *Lawson* cases, the Court of Appeals for the District of Columbia held that under that portion of the committee's enabling act which authorizes it to investigate "the diffusion within the United States of subversive and un-American propaganda that is instigated from foreign countries or of a domestic origin and attacks the principle of the form of government as guaranteed by our Constitution," the pertinency of a specific query as to a witness' membership in the Communist Party is made clear. In the *Lawson* case Judge Bennett Clark stated that it would be hard to imagine a more pertinent question to an inquiry into un-American activity as defined in the resolution creating the committee in view of the holding (of the *Barsky* case) that communism "is antithetical to the principles which underlie the form of government incorporated in the Federal Constitution and guaranteed by it to the States." [44]

A second argument under the Fifth Amendment which has been raised against the committee is that the implied right to the equal protection of the laws under the amendment has been violated by the committee because of the highly discriminatory fashion in which it had investigated some types of propaganda activity while ignoring others. In rejecting this argument in the *Josephson* case the court was content to refer to "the well-established principle that the legislature need not strike at the whole of an evil, but only at a part" and

---

In the decision in the *Barsky* case the court inferred that, standing by itself, subclause (i) of the resolution might be regarded as so vague as to be unconstitutional. But it concluded that subclause (ii) "is definite enough." And it added, "It conveys a clear meaning and that is all that is required. The principles which underlie the form of the existing government in this country are well-enough defined. . . ." In his dissenting opinion Judge Edgerton chided the majority for putting "a plural where Congress puts a singular," and added, "To me it is not obvious how much Congress meant by 'the principle,' or how much the court means by 'the principles.'" 167 F. 2d 241, 247–248, 262 (1948).

In the *Morford* case the Court of Appeals for the District of Columbia made a rather petulant reply to the argument that the enabling resolution is defective because of vagueness. It stated, "The Resolution authorized investigation into propaganda which attacks the principle of our constitutionally-guaranteed form of government. It is difficult to imagine how the standard could be further particularized, or how the test could be misunderstood. The National Council's literature either did or did not attack the principle of our form of government. It was not necessary to justify inquiry that there be an attack on our government, or an advocacy of its violent overthrow; enough if the *principle* of our form of government were attacked." 176 F. 2d 54, 57 (1949).

[44] *Lawson v. United States,* 176 F. 2d 49, 52, 53 (1949). *Barsky v. United States,* 167 F. 2d 241, 244, 248–249, 250 (1948).

to add that in this respect "the Congressional power to investigate is as flexible as its power to legislate." [45]

The third argument under the Fifth Amendment concerns the privilege against self-incrimination. The classic problem outlined earlier in this chapter has not yet reached the appellate courts, largely because the House committee, until recently, has allowed witnesses to refuse to answer questions when they were willing to pay the price of pleading self-incrimination to purchase the privilege of remaining silent. [46] Prior to 1950 all of the committee's witnesses actually prosecuted for contempt had justified their refusal to answer questions on some other ground. For example, in the Hollywood hearings, refusal to answer the question concerning membership in the Communist Party was based upon an alleged right under the First Amendment to remain silent as to one's political affiliations. In 1950, the committee did reverse its policy concerning the self-incrimination issue, and, at its request, the House of Representatives voted to order the prosecution of a number of witnesses who had refused to testify on the ground of self-incrimination, but the appellate courts have not yet passed upon the legal issues involved in these proceedings.

This sudden reversal of policy by the committee may result in its first setback by the appellate courts, for the soundness of its legal case against these unco-operative witnesses is far from clear. [47] There are many uncertainties about the law of self-incrimination, but the following relevant points may be noted:

1. The Fifth Amendment expressly establishes the privilege not

[45] 165 F. 2d 82, 92 (1947). See also the decision in the *Barsky* case, 167 F. 2d 241, 251 (1948).

[46] Refusal of witnesses before the Un-American Activities Committee to testify on grounds of self-incrimination occurred at the very beginning of the Dies committee hearings when Earl Browder and William Z. Foster used this excuse to refuse to answer the committee's questions. See Ogden, *The Dies Committee*, pp. 135, 143, 148, 196, 202.

[47] The case of *United States v. Rosen*, 174 F. 2d 187 (1949), bears out this statement. Rosen appeared before a federal grand jury in New York City in March, 1949, and refused on the ground of self-incrimination to answer many of the same questions that he had earlier refused to answer before the Un-American Activities Committee concerning the disposition of the Ford roadster Alger Hiss claimed to have given Whittaker Chambers. He was adjudged in contempt, but the Court of Appeals for the Second Circuit reversed the judgment on the ground that Rosen "was justified in believing that he was in a precarious situation" and that "he had the right to refuse to answer questions which might connect him with the Ford car. . . ."

to be a witness against one's self as a *federal* right. Nonetheless, the Supreme Court, in consistently refusing to extend the right into the area of *state* criminal procedures, has denied that the right is a basic or fundamental one—one "implicit in the concept of ordered liberty," an "immutable principle of justice," one necessary to "a fair and enlightened system of justice," or as "of the very essence of a scheme of ordered liberty." [48] Since this attitude has been expressed in cases where the right has seemingly been denied to *defendants* in state *criminal* cases, it is unlikely that the Court will show much enthusiasm for a *broad* application of the right to witnesses before Congressional committees.

2. Nonetheless, it seems likely that the Court will hold that the Fifth Amendment right, as such, does extend to witnesses before such committees, at least in its narrower sense.

3. It seems likely that the Court will hold that the immunity statutes (2 U.S.C. § 193 and 18 U.S.C. § 3486) are inadequate and do not withdraw the constitutional right from witnesses before Congressional committees.[49]

[48] This attitude of the Court toward the right is expressed in cases in which the Court has refused to hold that the Fourteenth Amendment carries freedom from self-incrimination over into the area of state criminal procedure. *Twining v. New Jersey*, 211 U.S. 78 (1908); *Adamson v. California*, 332 U.S. 46 (1947). See also *Palko v. Connecticut*, 302 U.S. 319, 325 (1937).

[49] Congress could presumably meet this difficulty by amending the present immunity statute (Title 18, § 3486) so as to restore the absolute immunity that was granted by the Act of 1857. As the *Washington Post* put it in an editorial (Sept. 14, 1948), the problem is to devise an immunity statute adequate to withdraw from witnesses before Congressional committees the privilege against self-incrimination but not so sweeping as to prevent the prosecution of a Fall or Meyers following his appearance before such a committee. The *Post* suggests that committees of inquiry be given discretionary power to grant complete immunity to witnesses on a selective basis, for "in the case of many witnesses subpoenaed before congressional committees the value of having their stories told in public far exceeds the public interest in their possible prosecution for some crime that might be uncovered."

The problem has been elsewhere posed in the following language: "An adequate immunity statute would give to legislative committees the power to require testimony of witnesses, but the question arises as to the wisdom of enacting such a statute. Clearly, immunity as broad as that required by the Supreme Court should not be granted unless the benefit to be derived from the possible increased efficacy of legislative investigations is sufficient to outweigh the social loss implicit in legislative largesse to admitted criminals. In England, the benefit derived from legislative investigations has been deemed to justify such immunity for over one hundred and fifty years. Whether the possibility of increasing the effectiveness of congressional committees similarly justifies the granting of such

4. The recent decision of the Supreme Court in the *Blau* case indicates that a witness before a Congressional committee may rightfully refuse on the ground of self-incrimination to answer the specific question, "Are you now or have you ever been a member of the Communist Party?" [50]

5. Many witnesses before the House Un-American Activities Committee have used the self-incrimination ground in seemingly improper and even irresponsible fashion to refuse to answer questions, when their answers could not possibly incriminate them, either because they are not related to criminal conduct or because the statute of limitations has run with respect to any criminal conduct that might be revealed. Perhaps the most ridiculous assertion of the right occurred during the 1948 Communist espionage hearings when Henry Collins used this ground to refuse to answer the question, "Do you belong to the American Legion?" [51]

6. A careful reading of the printed hearings suggests that the committee has not in all cases established a satisfactory basis for a prosecution under § 192 of those witnesses who have refused to testify on grounds of self-incrimination, since it has not always informed witnesses that they were using the ground improperly or directed them to answer questions. In a judicial proceeding it is customary for a judge to follow such a policy before holding an uncooperative witness in contempt of court. As a matter of fact, the printed hearings reveal statements by committee members to the effect that the committee recognizes and accepts the use by witnesses of the self-incrimination ground to refuse to answer questions.[52]

---

a broad immunity is a question for serious congressional deliberation." "Applicability of Privilege against Self-Incrimination to Legislative Investigations" (unsigned note), 49 *Columbia Law Review* (Jan., 1949), 87.

[50] *Blau v. United States,* 340 U.S. 159 (1950). See also *Blau v. United States,* 340 U.S. 332 (1951), and *Rogers v. United States,* 340 U.S. 367 (1951).

[51] *Hearings regarding Communist Espionage in the United States Government,* p. 807.

[52] *Communist Espionage Hearings,* pp. 591 (Mundt), 695, 1026 (Nixon). In the second instance Representative Nixon told the witness, Victor Perlo, "You have the right to plead self-incrimination on any particular matter, and you will note that the committee has never questioned that right. . . ." On the other hand, there are instances where the committee has seemingly rejected the ground, ordered a witness to answer questions, and warned him that further refusal to testify might result in contempt proceedings against him. For example:

"*Mr. Nixon:* Now, Mr. Rosen and counsel, I want you to listen carefully. You may refuse to answer questions on the ground of self-incrimination. It is possible that the answer given might involve you in a crime, but this committee is

One case growing out of the Joint Anti-Fascist Refugee Committee hearings that reached the Supreme Court did raise a secondary issue of self-incrimination. This was *United States v. Bryan* (339 U.S. 323, 1950). Helen Bryan, executive secretary of the JAFRC, was found guilty of contempt for refusing to produce the organization's records before the committee and to answer the question whether the organization's executive board supported her action in this respect. At her trial in the district court the transcript of the proceedings before the committee, including the defendant's testimony, was accepted as evidence. On appeal, Bryan argued that this had, in effect, forced her to be a witness against herself. In the majority opinion of the Supreme Court, Chief Justice Vinson admitted that the literal language of 18 USC § 3486, which grants immunity to witnesses before Congressional committees against the use of their testimony in any subsequent criminal proceeding against them, except in a prosecution for perjury committed in giving such testimony, seemingly had been violated in this case. But the majority held that thus to apply the statute in this case "would subvert the congressional purpose in its passage" and lead "to absurd conclusions." In effect, the majority asked how a recalcitrant witness could be prosecuted for contempt without the introduction as evidence of a transcript of the committee proceedings to demonstrate the contemptuous conduct of the witness?

In a vigorous dissenting opinion Justices Black and Frankfurter insisted that Congress had revealed a clear intention in the statute to make only one exception to the prohibition against the use of testimony in a Congressional hearing in a later criminal proceeding against a witness—that of a prosecution for perjury—and they accused the majority of "judicial law-making." Moreover, they insisted that a strict interpretation of the statute would not lead to absurd conclusions, because it would be perfectly possible in a contempt case for the prosecution to call witnesses who could testify as to the defendant's contemptuous conduct before a Congressional committee, thus making it unnecessary to introduce as evidence a transcript

---

unable to see how any answer concerning whether or not you purchased a 1929 automobile could involve you in a crime, particularly since any crime that could be involved in the purchase of such a car would now be outlawed by the statute of limitations.

"I will instruct you further that if you refuse to answer a question concerning a 1929 automobile on the grounds of self-incrimination and if the committee comes to the conclusion that no crime could be involved, that it will be the duty of this committee to cite you for contempt of Congress." *Ibid.*, pp. 1209–1210.

of the accused's own testimony (or refusal to testify). This seems like hairsplitting on the part of the dissenters, for it is hard to understand the reasoning by which an official transcript of what transpired at a Congressional hearing should be excluded while the word of persons present in the committee room should be admitted. It is perhaps significant that the two dissenters were not prepared to say that the statute, as interpreted by the majority, violated the self-incrimination clause of the Fifth Amendment. Instead they were content to argue that the Court was misinterpreting the statute.

Has the Committee Inflicted Punishment upon Its Witnesses, thus Violating the Constitutional Prohibition against Bills of Attainder? It has been argued that the House committee has tried certain individuals on the charge of subversive activity, has found them guilty, and has then subjected them to punishment by stirring up public opinion against them and in some instances causing them to lose their jobs. The result has been, the argument continues, to deprive such persons of their right to trial by jury under the Sixth Amendment. Much the same argument is seen in the claim that the punitive effect which certain committee hearings have had upon witnesses amounts to a bill of attainder in violation of section nine, Article I of the Constitution. In terms of traditional constitutional law it is difficult to take this particular argument seriously. The bill of attainder and trial by jury clauses of the Constitution have generally been thought of as concerning only the individual who is accused of *criminal* conduct. Clearly, the committee has not in any such formal sense been trying its witnesses for crimes. It is true that in 1946 in *United States v. Lovett* a divided Supreme Court did hold that action by Congress in an appropriation act ordering that no funds should be used to pay the salaries of three named federal officers amounted to a bill of attainder and was thus unconstitutional. The Court said:

Section 304, thus, clearly accomplishes the punishment of named individuals without a judicial trial. The fact that the punishment is inflicted through the instrumentality of an Act specifically cutting off the pay of certain named individuals found guilty of disloyalty, makes it no less galling or effective than if it had been done by an Act which designated the conduct as criminal. No one would think that Congress could have passed a valid law, stating that after investigation it had found Lovett, Dodd, and Watson "guilty" of the crime of engaging in "subversive activities," defined that term for the first time, and sentenced them to perpetual exclusion from any government employment. Section 304, while it does not use that language, accomplishes that result. The effect was to inflict punishment without the safeguards of a judicial trial and determined by no previous law or fixed rule. The Constitution declares that that cannot be done. . . .[53]

The decision in the *Lovett* case has undoubtedly encouraged witnesses who have been prosecuted for contempt of the House committee to raise the bill of attainder argument in their defense, and the issue has actually received some consideration at the appellate court level. In the *Eisler* case the Court of Appeals for the District of Columbia ruled that the trial court had properly refused Eisler permission to introduce evidence showing that the committee's real purpose in calling him as a witness had been to harass and punish him for his political beliefs. The Court of Appeals stated that Congress' power to compel private persons to appear and give testimony in aid of the legislative function is beyond question and that the courts have "no authority to scrutinize the motives of Congress or one of its committees." [54]

Actually it would be a considerable step from the *Lovett* decision to a Supreme Court holding that the Un-American Activities Committee has violated the bill of attainder clause of the Constitution by holding one of its witnesses up to public opprobrium or causing him to lose his job with a private employer. In the *Lovett* case there was no doubt whatsoever that the loss of job was the direct result of deliberate Congressional action. Congress deliberately enacted a statute imposing this penalty, because it was convinced of the disloyalty of the three men dismissed. For the Court to call this action a bill of attainder represented a step beyond established constitutional law on the subject, but its decision was supported by the facts in the case. The facts supporting the often-made charge that the House committee is more interested in seeing certain of its witnesses suffer loss of reputation or job than it is in obtaining factual information as a basis for the enactment of legislation by Congress are far less clear. This is not to say that the committee has not been so motivated. But for any court to isolate the evidence suggesting that this has been so, while simultaneously ignoring the interest shown by the committee, however slight, in facts as a basis for legislation, and then to conclude that the Constitution has been violated would be an act of judicial arrogance.[55]

[53] 328 U.S. 303, 316 (1946).   [54] 170 F. 2d 273, 279 (1948).

[55] The Hollywood hearings, already mentioned, provide perhaps the strongest basis for such a judicial finding. Ten witnesses lost their jobs in the motion pic-

In another sense, however, the bill of attainder argument raises an issue that cannot be easily dismissed. There can be little doubt that certain witnesses before the Un-American Activities Committee have suffered and been punished in just as realistic a sense as though they had been placed on trial in a criminal court and traditional criminal sanctions had been invoked against them. Professor John Frank has written: "Our own generation is finding more sophisticated ways of . . . putting economic instead of criminal sanctions on persons whose speech is offensive. These sanctions ought to be recognized as mere variants of criminal sanctions, and ought to be subject to the same tests." [56] Here the degree to which the hearings of this Congressional committee have been personalized establishes a real threat to the future of Congressional inquiries as fact-finding, legislative-aiding agencies. If, in fact, these committees are to be

ture industry as the result of their refusal to answer the House committee's questions. To say that this development pleased the committee would be gross understatement. Moreover, the committee showed so little interest in possible legislative action based upon the investigation that it did not even bother to file a formal report of its findings with the House of Representatives. At the same time, a court decision which accepted the conclusion that the committee was interested in seeing its witnesses punished and disinterested in legislation would necessarily be based upon rumor, inference, and conjecture. For the courts to attempt to check the legislative process at the committee stage on any such uncertain basis would be deplorable.

A further argument against judicial supervision of Congressional investigations is the difficulty the courts might have in enforcing decisions adverse to the Congressional interest. One may doubt whether rulings in the *Barsky* or *Josephson* cases that the Un-American Activities Committee was an unconstitutional body would have brought an end to the committee. All that was before the courts was the legality of the convictions of Barsky and Josephson under § 192. The courts could have seen to it that the two men did not go to jail, but it is a fair guess that the committee would have gone right on with its program and that the House of Representatives would have supported it. Moreover, to provide a sanction to compel witnesses to co-operate with the committee the House could have reverted to the early practice of bringing recalcitrant witnesses before its own bar to be tried for contempt, instead of turning them over to the courts for trial under § 192. It is true that the courts have, from the time of *Anderson v. Dunn*, claimed the right to review such proceedings. But there has never been a showdown with the courts on the issue of which branch has the ultimate authority in this situation. If a witness were tried before the House, found guilty, and ordered imprisoned by the House Sergeant at Arms for the duration of the session, would not the House hold the upper hand if it simply refused to recognize the validity of any court ruling ordering the prisoner set free, and if it protected its Sergeant at Arms against any reprisal by the courts?

[56] "The United States Supreme Court: 1949–50," 18 *Univ. of Chicago Law Review* (Autumn, 1950), 1, 32.

used increasingly as the means of exposing and "punishing" individuals deemed dangerous to the public welfare by committee members, then we shall have no choice, if we wish to preserve the most basic traditions of Anglo-American criminal procedure, but to subject such agencies to drastic controls—controls that may well hamper their effectiveness as fact-finding agencies. But that such control should now be achieved by encouraging the courts to see bills of attainder in committee treatment of witnesses would seem to be an exceedingly dubious way of dealing with this problem.

Miscellaneous Constitutional Arguments against the House Committee

A number of miscellaneous arguments have been raised against the Un-American Activities Committee, no one of which has received much support from the courts. One of the most ingenious of the arguments attacks the committee through its personnel on the ground that the election of such Southerners to the House of Representatives as John Rankin has taken place in violation of the Fourteenth and Fifteenth Amendments. Their illegal election by an electorate from which Negroes have been unlawfully excluded is said to taint the Congressional actions in which they have participated, including their committee activities.[57] The argument obviously proves too much, and no judge has given it serious consideration.

In the *Eisler* case the Court of Appeals for the District of Columbia considered the argument that, because the House committee had denied Eisler's request that he be granted three minutes in which to state legal objections to the hearing before he was sworn, a conviction for *willful* default because of failure to obey a subpoena summoning him to appear and give testimony could not stand. The trial judge had not allowed Eisler an opportunity to present evidence that he had merely wanted to state such legal objections. By a two-to-one vote the court rejected this argument. In the majority opinion Judge Bennett Clark says that in asking for a few minutes Eisler had not told the committee that he wanted to state legal objections to the hearing. Clark accepts the Un-American Activities Committee's version of the episode—that Eisler had held in his hands a lengthy

[57] For example, one of the reasons given by Lee Pressman for his refusal to answer questions put to him by the committee August 20, 1948, was the following: "The committee is unlawfully constituted by reason of the presence thereon of one John Rankin, who holds an alleged seat as a Member of Congress from Mississippi." *Communist Espionage Hearings,* p. 1023.

mimeographed statement he intended to read before being sworn and that the document would have taken much more than three minutes to read. In his dissenting opinion Judge Prettyman states that he thinks Eisler should have been allowed at his trial to try to show that his purpose in asking the committee for time had been merely to state legal objections to the proceedings, for, in Prettyman's opinion, such evidence would have been significant in showing that Eisler had not willfully defaulted.[58]

The validity of certain of the contempt proceedings growing out of the Joint Anti-Fascist Refugee Committee hearings was challenged before the Supreme Court in 1950 on the ground that the presence of a quorum of the committee members at the time the alleged contemptuous conduct occurred had not been proved. The Court rejected this argument, holding that the statute that declares a witness who willfully defaults when subpoenaed to produce papers before a Congressional committee guilty of a misdemeanor does not require that a quorum of the committee be present when the contempt occurs.[59]

United States v. Fleischman, a companion to the *Bryan* case, raised an additional issue to those passed upon by the Supreme Court in the latter case. Fleischman, one of sixteen members of the board of directors of the Joint Anti-Fascist Refugee Committee, had been found guilty of contempt for her part in the collective failure of the board to produce the organization records before the House commit-

[58] *Eisler v. United States,* 170 F. 2d 273 (1948). The Supreme Court agreed to review the case, but when Eisler fled the country in May, 1948, a majority of the justices, in a per curiam opinion, held that the case should be removed from the docket, pending the return of the fugitive. Chief Justice Vinson and Justice Frankfurter indicated in a dissenting opinion that they favored dismissing the case outright for want of jurisdiction. On the other hand, in separate dissenting opinions, Justices Murphy and Jackson stated their belief that the Court should have proceeded to decide the case on its merits, Eisler's flight notwithstanding. Alone among the justices, Jackson indicated how he would have decided the case. He would have affirmed the conviction of Eisler. *Eisler v. United States,* 338 U.S. 189 (1949).

[59] *United States v. Bryan,* 339 U.S. 323 (1950); and *United States v. Fleischman,* 339 U.S. 349 (1950). In 1949, by a five-to-four vote, the Supreme Court had set aside a conviction for perjury committed before a Congressional committee on the ground that a quorum of the committee had not been present at the time of the perjury. However, the decision rested on the ground that in the absence of a quorum such a committee was not a "competent tribunal" as required by the perjury statute under which the prosecution had taken place. *Christoffel v. United States,* 338 U.S. 84 (1949). The contempt statute in the Bryan and Fleischman cases did not contain this same phraseology.

tee. It was argued before the Supreme Court that at her trial the government should have been required to prove that as a single member of the board she had had it within her power to take some effective step toward collective action by the board to produce the records. The Supreme Court majority rejected this argument and held that the burden of the proof had properly been placed on the defendant to show that she had done all she could to get the board to produce the records. The evidence indicated that she had done nothing toward that end.[60]

Some of the Un-American Activities Committee cases that have reached the appellate courts have raised issues as to trial court procedures which have had nothing to do directly with the authority or procedures of the committee. For example, in *Dennis v. United States*, it was argued that when Dennis was tried under § 192 for contempt of the House committee the trial court had erred in failing to sustain Dennis' challenge for cause of all prospective jurors who were employed by the federal government on the ground that they could not help showing bias because of the existence of the federal loyalty program. By a five-to-two vote the court rejected the argument.[61] On the other hand, during the same term the Supreme Court in a per curiam opinion in *Morford v. United States* held that the defendant's right to an impartial jury had been infringed where the trial court had refused to allow him to interrogate prospective government employee jurors concerning their ability to render a just verdict in the face of their own troubles under the loyalty program. Morford was granted a new trial and was then found guilty a second time.[62]

The Dissenting Opinions of Judges Clark and Edgerton

In the *Josephson* and *Barsky* cases the verdicts of guilty were affirmed at the court of appeals level by two-to-one votes. In the

[60] 339 U.S. 349 (1950). Justices Black and Frankfurter dissented, and Justices Douglas and Clark did not participate. Justice Black stated in the dissenting opinion: "Refusal [under § 192] to comply with a subpoena to produce papers can be punished only if the witness has power to produce. It is a complete defense for him to show that the papers are not in his possession or under his control. . . . A command to produce is not a command to get others to produce or assist in producing."

[61] 339 U.S. 162 (1950).

[62] 339 U.S. 258 (1950). The judgment in the second Morford trial was sustained by the Court of Appeals for the District of Columbia and the Supreme Court refused to grant certiorari. 184 F. 2d 864 (1950); 340 U.S. 878 (1950).

Josephson case Judge Charles E. Clark dissented, and in the *Barsky* case Judge Henry W. Edgerton dissented. Each of these judges wrote a long dissenting opinion in which the constitutional arguments against the House committee are examined in systematic fashion and in which certain of these arguments receive vigorous, unqualified approval. Each is an eminent judge. Clark was once dean of the Yale Law School and Edgerton was a professor at the Cornell Law School. Accordingly, the careful, detailed statements of these men that the Un-American Activities Committee does violence to the Constitution of the United States should receive respectful attention, even though the Supreme Court was seemingly so little impressed by their stands that it refused to grant certiorari.

Both judges would accept the argument that the House committee's enabling act is unconstitutional because it encroaches upon rights safeguarded by the First Amendment, both would hold that the enabling act is so vague that when coupled with a criminal statute to punish witnesses for failure to co-operate with the committee it comes into conflict with the Fifth Amendment, and Judge Edgerton would also hold the enabling act invalid as a bill of attainder.

In considering the argument under the First Amendment, Judge Clark draws heavily upon an unsigned note entitled, "Constitutional Limitations on the Un-American Activities Committee," which appeared in the *Columbia Law Review* in 1947.[63] He picks up two points that are suggested somewhat tentatively in this article, namely, that Congress cannot undertake a completely unlimited inquiry in the area of the First Amendment, and that it cannot accomplish by publicity what it cannot do by legislation, and lends both his support. His own reasoning runs somewhat as follows:

The investigative power of Congress can be no broader than the extreme limits of its legislative power. In matters affecting speech and press the legislative and investigative powers are both limited by the clear and present danger test. If a statute sought to restrict speech and press in words as broad and vague as those used in the committee's enabling resolution it would certainly be declared unconstitutional. This being the case, the resolution itself is unconstitutional, for Congress may not do by investigation what it is forbidden to do by legislation. If the resolution were worded in the pattern of the Alien Registration Act of 1940 to the effect that the House committee is directed to investigate propaganda advocating

[63] See note 5.

the overthrow of the government by force or violence it could be held constitutional, just as the 1940 act has been.[64]

To put it somewhat differently, Judge Clark agrees that Congress may properly conduct an investigation to discover whether there are facts suggesting the existence of a clear and present danger to the well-being of the state, which it may then seek to curb by legislation. But such an investigation must be limited to a search for information concerning the kind of clear and present danger that can be met by legislation if it is found to exist. As it is, even if the Un-American Activities Committee does discover unmistakable evidence of the diffusion within the United States of propaganda of a domestic origin attacking "the principle" of the form of American government, Congress cannot constitutionally seek to suppress such propaganda by legislation. Thus the resolution is broader than it needs to be and for this reason it is unconstitutional.

Judge Clark, and Judge Edgerton as well, reject the further argument on behalf of the House committee that since in the cases at hand it was staying within proper bounds, in that it was actually seeking information pertaining to the program of international communism, the enabling resolution should not be held to violate the First Amendment on the ground it contains language that would permit the committee to go beyond proper bounds. Edgerton says on this point, "Even if the views the House Committee sought to elicit from these appellants had been of a sort that Congress might properly restrain, by investigative or other action aimed specifically at such views, the appealed convictions would have to be reversed. 'The statute, as construed and applied, amounts merely to a dragnet which may enmesh anyone who agitates for a change of government.' " [65]

Judge Edgerton is also impressed by the fact that the Alien Registration Act has been law since 1940 and that it goes about as far in curbing un-American propaganda as any constitutional act can, i.e., it outlaws propaganda advocating the overthrow of government by force and violence. This leads him to the conclusion that the House of Representative's purpose in setting up the Un-American Activities

[64] At the time Judge Clark wrote his opinion the 1940 act had been declared constitutional by the Court of Appeals for the Eighth Circuit in *Dunne v. United States*, 138 F. 2d 137 (1943). It was subsequently upheld by the Court of Appeals for the Second Circuit in *United States v. Dennis*, 183 F. 2d 201 (1950), and by the Supreme Court, 341 U.S. 494 (1951). See above, p. 17.

[65] 167 F. 2d 241, 258 (1948). The quoted passage is from the opinion in *Herndon v. Lowry*, 301 U.S. 242, 263 (1937).

Committee was exposure of certain propaganda activities much less specific or dangerous than this, and not a search for factual information as a basis for further legislation. Thus, again the House appears to be seeking to accomplish by exposure what cannot be done by legislation.

Judge Edgerton also holds that the First Amendment establishes the right of a person to remain silent as to political beliefs and affiliations and that the resolution establishing the committee has encroached upon that right.

Little need be added to what has already been said about the Fifth Amendment argument. Both judges are of the opinion that the key word in the resolution authorizing the committee to investigate certain types of propaganda is "un-American," that this word is so vague that no witness before the committee can possibly know when he is entitled to refuse to co-operate, and that thus any attempt to punish an unco-operative witness under such a criminal statute as § 192 violates the due process clause of the Fifth Amendment.[66]

On the bill of attainder point, Judge Edgerton holds that the committee's enabling act, as construed and applied by the committee, creates an offense against the United States, "delegates to the Committee the ascertainment of individuals to be punished and the infliction of punishment; provides no standard of guilt; compels the individual, in the committee's discretion, to testify against himself; deprives him of the right to testify in his own defense; and deprives him also of the right to counsel, the right to call witnesses, and the right to cross-examine opposing witnesses." [67] He holds that the committee has intentionally inflicted punishment on certain persons by bringing about their "dismissal from employment" and by subjecting them to "publicity and opprobrium." He then quotes with approval the holding of the Supreme Court in the Lovett case that no "congressional action, aimed at . . . named individuals, which stigmatize[s] their reputation and seriously impair[s] their chance to earn a living" can be sustained.[68]

Judges Clark and Edgerton have undoubtedly made the most of the constitutional case against the House committee and at times their

---

[66] Judge Clark concludes: "Since this is a penal statute we are called upon to enforce, standards so vague and doubtful should be adjudged insufficient under the settled requirements that prohibited conduct must for criminal purposes be set forth with clarity, so that the person to whom it applies may determine what conduct is legal and what is not." 165 F. 2d 82, 97 (1947).

[67] 167 F. 2d 241, 260 (1948).   [68] Ibid., p. 260.

arguments are quite persuasive. But when everything is considered, it is difficult to avoid the conclusion that the measure of judicial review of the investigating power of Congress which their stand entails would give to the courts a dangerous degree of power to check the legislative branch of the government. Although he takes the highly dubious stand of the Supreme Court in the *Kilbourn* case as his point of departure, Judge Clark ends his opinion with an acknowledgment that the Congressional investigation has been "so productive of good in so many instances in our history, that no one would wish to hamper it improperly." He agrees also that "the force of public opinion and the expression of the electorate at the polls must remain its main source of control." But he nonetheless asserts that in "the narrow, though important, field of constitutional liberties, more control is desirable," and he finds a rationalization for a judicial check upon the House Un-American Activities Committee in the thought that the committee's exercise of the investigative power is endangering the standing of this all-important power in the minds of a liberty-loving people and that accordingly "the application of a proper restraint" will prove "a source of strength in the long run, rather than the reverse." [69]

It seems wisest to abandon the hope that the Un-American Activities Committee may be curbed or even destroyed through judicial intervention. It seems apparent that the courts, least of all the Supreme Court, have no intention of exercising the power of judicial review to the point where serious constitutional defects will be found in the committee's authority or procedures. Only once in history has the Supreme Court challenged a Congressional investigation as to its basic constitutionality, and it seems likely that, while the Court has never said so in so many words, it is now of the opinion that this decision was a mistake. It is, of course, perfectly possible for Congress to violate the Constitution by authorizing an investigation whose subject matter lies beyond the limits of Congressional power. But since an investigation does not in itself amount to a statement of public policy to which all citizens must conform but is instead a means by which the legislative process is carried on, there is considerable weight to the argument that the duty to see that no violence is done the Constitution by such an investigation rests with Congress itself and not with the judiciary.

[69] 165 F. 2d 82, 100 (1947).

It is true that where the issue of the constitutionality of a Congressional investigation reaches the courts in a case involving personal liberty—where, perhaps, a person faces a jail term because of failure to co-operate with an investigating committee about whose constitutionality there may be doubts—a strong argument exists for judicial activism rather than judicial self-restraint. The issue of the constitutionality of a Congressional investigation does not come before the courts in abstract fashion; it comes in cases in which there are very real opposing interests or rights and where refusal of the courts to accept jurisdiction will result in automatic victory for the Congressional interest as against the interest of private individuals. One is strongly tempted to favor vigorous use of judicial power to protect those individuals who have been subjected by a Congressional committee to harsh or arbitrary treatment. Where that can be done without the necessity of simultaneous judicial scrutiny of the propriety of an investigation or of procedures essential to its success, resort to the courts by wronged individuals may readily be encouraged. Unfortunately, the price that would have to be paid for court assistance to such individuals would often necessarily be substantial interference with the Congressional inquisitorial power itself. Moreover, it is apparent from the record of Congressional inquiries that the great majority of witnesses who have been prosecuted for contempt have invited the result. They have carefully calculated the risks and, for reasons that seemed sufficient to them, have deliberately challenged the power of Congress and have willfully refused to co-operate. Almost never has a witness who was merely naïve, bewildered, or foolishly assertive of an extreme view of individualism gone to jail for contempt. Certainly the witnesses who have tangled with the Un-American Activities Committee knew what they were doing; often they were arrogant, dogmatic, and vituperative. It is hard to find in the record of the hearings much support for a view of them as innocent, grievously wronged citizens who were defending the cause of liberty and democracy against a too-pervasive arm of the state. This is in no sense to defend the Un-American Activities Committee—its purposes, its methods, or its record. But it cannot be denied that its recalcitrant witnesses fall readily into the tradition of the Daughertys, the Sinclairs, and the Dr. Townsends—men who willfully defied the inquisitorial arm of the national legislature and invited the consequences that they experienced. We have to choose, and it does not appear that the harm done such persons who have been punished for contempt would justify the threat to legislative power which a vigorous judicial supervision of investigations would entail.

In his opinion in the *Eisler* case, Justice Jackson said, "I think it would be an unwarranted act of judicial usurpation to strip Congress of its investigatory power, or to assume for the courts the function of supervising congressional committees. I should . . . leave the responsibility for the behavior of its committees squarely on the shoulders of Congress." [70] In the end it seems a sound conclusion that the answer to the Un-American Activities Committee is not to be found in the courts; it must be found within Congress itself.

[70] *Eisler v. United States,* 338 U.S. 189, 196 (1949). This was a dissenting opinion, but the majority justices would not necessarily have disagreed with Jackson's feeling as expressed in these words. In an article, "Standards for Congressional Investigations," 3 *Record of the Association of the Bar of the City of New York* (March, 1948), 93, 105, Federal Judge Charles E. Wyzanski, Jr., has written:

"If it be conceded that it is desirable that there should be a continuance of the practice of compelling private persons to testify before Congressional committees on matters upon which legislation may be adopted, the question remains as to what reforms should be instituted.

"Should there be a wider ambit of judicial review? . . . This and indeed any other broadening of judicial review seem to me ill-advised remedies. . . . Moreover, the suggestion of a broadened judicial review of legislative investigations is founded upon a not universally shared view that the power of judges should be extended because they are ultimately the surest guardians of our liberty. After all it was a judge who told us 'it must be remembered that legislatures are ultimate guardians of the liberties and welfare of the people in quite as great a degree as the courts.' "

XII: The Committee's Record Evaluated

On BALANCE the good things the Un-American Activities Committee has done are outweighed by the bad. Any government agency must finally be judged by the record it has made, and, after six years of operation, it is fitting and proper that the committee should be held to an accounting. Admittedly, the Un-American Activities Committee has certain achievements to its credit. The record is not as black as some of the committee's critics have claimed it is. But the committee has made fearful mistakes, and there are many things in its record which cannot be reconciled with the proper role of a legislative agency in a democratic society. What are its achievements? And what are the shortcomings for which it may properly be held responsible?

The Case FOR the Committee

Among the committee's achievements attention must first be called to the undeniable contribution it has made to the American people's understanding of the character and purposes of *international* communism. As one rereads today the record of the Browder-Foster hearings in 1945, the Budenz testimony of 1946 and later years, and the committee reports on the Communist Party published in 1947 and 1948, it must be acknowledged that the committee was shedding light upon the revolutionary aims of international communism at a time when many Americans were inclined to believe that the Communists were content to confine their experiment to the Soviet Union and that communism and democracy could live together peacefully in the same world. At the same time, the committee made this information available to the American people in such a disorderly and, at times, irresponsible way that the impact of its findings upon public opinion was much less strong than it might have been. Moreover, in the final analysis, it was desirable and probably inevitable that the pressure of world events should have been allowed to make clear the true character of international communism to the American people. It seems proper that in the years following World War II we should have disregarded the advice of those who prophesied an inevitable showdown with the Soviet Union and have made every effort to build peaceful and harmonious relations between the Communist and non-Communist worlds. As a democratic nation we had to let the Soviet Union make its record of obligations dishonored and of nations defiled before we could with justice and honor regard international communism as an implacable enemy. Nevertheless, it has to be admitted that certain of the committee's hearings and reports read today do reveal that the warning was there and that it was in many ways an accurate one.

Secondly, the committee has helped to educate the American people concerning the purposes and methods of our own domestic Communist movement. Through the years the committee hearings and reports have revealed much factual information concerning the tactics used by Communists in establishing cells in the government service, in obtaining important business posts such as in the motion picture industry, in infiltrating and controlling labor unions, in establishing Communist front organizations, or in capturing other organizations originally non-Communist in character. But again, more often than not, the committee presented this information in such careless and irresponsible fashion that it failed to persuade honest men of the impartiality and importance of its findings. Moreover, other forces have been at work in producing an understanding of the nature of the threat offered by the American Communists. For example, it seems likely that the expulsion of the Communist unions from the CIO which took place late in 1949 was based primarily upon the CIO's own experience with Communists in its midst and its own growing awareness of the damage they were doing. If the House committee's findings had any influence at all upon the CIO's course of action it is probable that they delayed rather than hastened the final house cleaning.

Thirdly, the committee has undoubtedly played a part in the exposure of the espionage activities of Communist agents in the United States. It is seemingly true that neither Alger Hiss nor William Remington would ever have been prosecuted had it not been for the investigations of the committee, although it should also be noted that in each instance the prosecution was for perjury rather than espionage. Moreover, the Department of Justice was at work in the same field as the committee, seeking to ferret out and prosecute espionage agents. Had the Un-American Activities Committee never existed, Hiss and Remington might not have been prosecuted. But the Rosenbergs, Greenglass, and Gold most certainly would have, and, all things considered, it seems clear that the latter were far more dangerous enemies of American security than was Alger Hiss. It is possible that the House committee put the Department of Justice on its mettle and thereby stimulated it to achieve the successful results that it did in prosecuting espionage agents. But the committee's criticism of the department's enforcement of the espionage laws was at times so partisan and vituperative that it probably succeeded only in antagonizing the department. There is little in the record to reveal that the committee ever successfully performed the traditional role of Congressional investigating committees by revealing shortcomings in the law enforcement program of the executive branch or by helping the latter to overcome these shortcomings. Moreover, at times the committee's own efforts to investigate espionage activity unquestionably hampered the department's simultaneous law enforcement activity in this field.

Fourthly, the Un-American Activities Committee may justly claim a major share of the credit for the passage by Congress of the Internal Security Act of 1950, in spite of the fact that the law takes its popular title from the name of the chairman of the Senate Judiciary Committee, Pat McCarran. The committee may say that its labors since 1945 have finally resulted in the enactment of one of the most far-reaching laws dealing with subversion in the history of the nation. Thus the committee may claim that it has not functioned solely as an informing committee, interested only in publicity and in influencing public opinion.

But what kind of statute is this offspring that the committee helped to sire? It is much too early to try to estimate the significance of the McCarran Act in American life. But at the moment it is one of the most criticized statutes in legislative history. Informed and impartial persons believe that it is an ill-considered statute, many of whose provisions seriously endanger our fundamental freedoms.[1] By and large the McCarran Act is aimed at the danger offered by domestic rather than international communism. Whatever the effect of the act upon our traditional civil liberties may prove to be, it seems fair to conclude that the Un-American Activities Committee did not, between 1945 and 1950, demonstrate the existence of a sufficiently serious threat of internal subversion to warrant the adoption of such an extreme policy of regulation and suppression as finds expression in this law.

The Case AGAINST the Committee

Perhaps the most serious shortcoming in the committee's record is the way in which it has always insisted upon *personalizing* its undertakings. This tendency has created an exceedingly serious threat to the Anglo-American concept of criminal justice. For centuries we have believed that no man shall be accused of an offense against society unless that offense has previously been carefully defined by law. We have further believed that an accused person shall be considered innocent until proved guilty and that the state must assume the burden of the proof in demonstrating his guilt. Finally, we have believed that the state's attempt to demonstrate the accused's guilt must take place in a court of law where the accused is allowed to enjoy such procedural rights as trial by jury, assistance of counsel, compulsory process for obtaining witnesses in his favor, and cross-examination of the witnesses against him.

It is quite clear from the six-year record of the committee between 1945 and 1950 that one of its leading purposes has been to demonstrate the "guilt" of certain persons for offenses not always defined in law and to see them punished in the sense of the destruction of their reputations and the loss of their means of livelihood. It is true that such committee witnesses as Alger Hiss and William Remington did ultimately have judicial trials. But there will always be reason to believe that the committee had so influenced public opinion and so prejudiced the standing of each man before either was brought into court that their right to fair court trials was seriously jeopardized. At the very least, the committee usurped the grand jury function and insisted upon "indicting" Hiss and Remington. Moreover, in usurping

[1] See, for example, Arthur E. Sutherland, "Freedom and Internal Security," 64 *Harvard Law Review* (Jan., 1951), 383. For a somewhat more sympathetic analysis see "The Internal Security Act of 1950" (unsigned note), 51 *Columbia Law Review* (May, 1951), 606.

the grand jury function the committee disregarded one of the prime characteristics of grand jury proceedings—secrecy. Grand juries operate behind closed doors and are scrupulously careful to avoid coloring the atmosphere in which a criminal trial is to take place.

Not the least shocking illustration of the committee's interference with traditional court procedures in criminal cases is seen in the denunciations by Representative Nixon and other committee members of the judge who presided at the first Hiss trial. At a time when the accused was yet to stand trial a second time these committee members did not hesitate to give the impression that any judge who failed to take a stern view of the accused's position would be suspected by them of improper conniving to procure the defendant's acquittal.

Other witnesses before the House committee, unlike Hiss and Remington, never enjoyed the right to a court trial, yet they lost their jobs and reputations as the result of "trials" before the committee. This was true of many of the witnesses who appeared during the Hollywood hearings of 1947, and it was also true of certain of the college professors who appeared before the committee through the years in the course of its atomic espionage investigation.[2] The record of these hearings makes it quite clear that the committee was by no means exclusively concerned with demonstrating that these men had actually succeeded in introducing Communist propaganda into motion pictures or had stolen scientific secrets and turned them over to the Russians. It also had the much more simple goal of driving such men from their jobs.

That it is not a proper function of the Congress of the United States, or of any agency thereof, to try to bring about the discharge of specific individuals from private employment hardly requires argument. And for such a function to be exercised by such a poorly supervised and generally irresponsible body as the Un-American Activities Committee is a shocking thing. It may be, as certain authorities have suggested, that there are times when Congress must serve as "the grand inquest" or "high court" of the nation.[3] In the face of the per-

[2] The ten "unfriendly" Hollywood witnesses were, of course, tried in the federal courts on contempt charges, but they were never tried for the substantive offense with which the committee in effect charged them—membership in the Communist Party and introduction of subversive propaganda into motion pictures. See also Malcolm Hobbs, "The Subversive Drugstore," 169 *The Nation* (Nov. 26, 1949), 417.

[3] See Lindsay Rogers, "The Problem and Its Solution," 18 *Univ. of Chicago Law Review* (Spring, 1951), 464, 465n.

sistent and far-reaching breakdown of law enforcement machinery of government it may be that the legislature must concern itself with the character and extent of criminal wrongdoing in terms of specific individuals and particular offenses. But surely Congress has an obligation to conduct such an inquest with dignity, impartiality, and scrupulous regard for the rights of individuals whose conduct may be brought under scrutiny. Here the American Congress has lagged far behind the practices of legislative bodies in other democratic nations. For example, there is a shocking contrast between the procedure that the British Parliament follows under the Tribunals of Inquiry Act in investigating charges of wrongdoing on the part of government employees and the procedure used by the Un-American Activities Committee in its search for subversives in the federal service.[4]

Another way of putting this same criticism is to say that the committee has sometimes seemed more interested in exposing allegedly subversive *persons* than it has in exposing subversive *activity*. Admittedly, the committee has many times sought and obtained evidence showing that actual misdeeds have been committed. Its hearings on atomic espionage and on espionage in the government service were certainly concerned with such misdeeds. But all too frequently the committee has been content to put the finger on Communists or fellow travelers while making little or no attempt to demonstrate that they have engaged in any acts of a subversive character. Thus its Hollywood hearings revealed the presence of Communists in the motion picture industry but failed to show that these Communists had engaged in subversive activity. Or again in its search for evidence of atomic espionage the committee was at times content to show that some scientists are, or once *were*, Communists, and did not even so much as hint that they had engaged in espionage or any other improper activity.

To be sure, as of 1951, it is possible to take the position that any dyed-in-the-wool Communist is a member of a criminal conspiracy, and a potential if not actual agent of subversive activity, and that accordingly it is enough for the House committee to expose Communists without showing also that they have actually engaged in subversive activity. Perhaps this is true of any continuing member of the Communist Party. But in investigating persons who have broken with the party, such as Frank Oppenheimer and David Hawkins—

[4] See *ibid.*, pp. 472–476, and also Herman Finer, "The British System," *ibid.*, pp. 521, 561–569.

concerning whom there is not a scintilla of evidence to suggest that they ever engaged in subversive activity—the committee has wandered rather far from the task assigned to it by the House of Representatives and has thereby emphasized its seeming desire to attack and even destroy certain individuals whether they have been guilty of misconduct or not.

It is deplorable that a private person who has done no wrong should so find himself under attack by the committee. But even more serious are the consequences of such a policy to the national welfare. What is supposed to happen to a person who is not shown to have engaged in subversive activity but who is publicly exposed by a committee of Congress as a Communist, an ex-Communist, or perhaps just a fellow traveler? He may well find his reputation sullied, his means of livelihood curtailed or entirely cut off—results that the committee can only be supposed to have intended. But then what? Can it be supposed that such a man is thereby won back to "good citizenship," that he thereafter becomes a staunch, loyal American? Clearly the only reasonable supposition is that he will become an embittered, frustrated misfit, an Ishmael, whose "hand will be against every man, and every man's hand against him." Do we wish to force all persons who have ever held status as Communists into this position? Is it not reasonable to suppose that many of these people, if treated with understanding and compassion, can be rehabilitated as loyal Americans, if, indeed, they have not already themselves completed their rehabilitation? Have not the House committee, and the patriots' and professional organizations that have followed its lead and used its findings, instead seemed determined to force the final and complete de-Americanization of these people? Perhaps the evil they might then do would be minimized if they were all locked up, or, like Ishmael, thrown out into the wilderness. But the House committee seems content to see them merely lose jobs and reputations and then left free to wander through the back streets of American life, angry, embittered, and—who knows?—waiting only a good opportunity to strike back against a society which returned a verdict of guilt by association against them.

Secondly, the House committee must be held responsible for having encouraged a widespread witch-hunting spirit both in government and in private life. This spirit has reached its peak in the shameful attacks made by Senator McCarthy upon federal employees and private persons. It may fairly be asserted that McCarthyism would never have been possible had not the Un-American Activities

Committee, and its predecessor, the Dies committee, paved the way from 1938 on. It may be granted that the Un-American Activities Committee, even in its most irresponsible moments during the 80th Congress, never quite descended to the indecent level on which Senator McCarthy has operated. Moreover, Senator McCarthy began his obscene attacks at a moment when the House committee was trying hard to mend its ways. But this perverse turn of affairs may well prove that having earlier indulged in an irresponsible course of action the committee could not suddenly mend its ways without having someone else seize the initiative from it.

The House committee has spawned a number of state committees which have eagerly joined the hunt for disloyal Americans. Many of these state committees have copied the Congressional committee's most disgraceful methods.[5] The House committee has also stimulated private patriots' groups into action. Of every conceivable variety, these groups have acted as self-appointed agencies to threaten and harass those persons who have deviated in the slightest degree from the narrow confines of "Americanism" as defined by the groups.

Thirdly, the committee has played a part in the demoralization of the federal service brought about by the emphasis of recent years upon loyalty testing. There is no doubt that in issuing his executive order in March, 1947, establishing the federal loyalty program, President Truman acted to head off much more extreme demands being made by such Congressional agencies as the House committee. This is not the place to evaluate the President's loyalty program.[6] That few disloyal employees have been found under it is clearly proved by the facts of its operation.[7] That it has excluded any truly dangerous agents of espionage or subversion from the federal service is exceedingly unlikely. But that it has had an unfortunate effect upon the morale and caliber of the federal civil service has been indicated again and again. It is clear that the emphasis that has been placed upon loyalty and orthodoxy among public employees has served to encourage mediocrity in the public service. Federal work-

[5] See Walter Gellhorn, ed., *The States and Subversion* (Ithaca, N.Y.: Cornell University Press, 1952).

[6] See Eleanor Bontecou, *The Federal Loyalty-Security Program*, to be published by Cornell University Press in 1953.

[7] A report of the Loyalty Review Board, April 29, 1951, revealed that only 308 persons had been dismissed from the federal service under the loyalty program since 1947. However, some 3,000 additional persons who were under investigation quit their jobs before their cases could be decided. *N.Y. Times*, April 30, 1951.

ers have learned that it is wise to think no unusual thought, read no unusual books, join no unusual organizations, and have no unusual friends. What this has cost the government in terms of loss of independence, courage, initiative, and imagination on the part of its employees is impossible to say, but it is clear that the cost has been great. For generations it has been traditional to deplore the civil servant as a dull, mediocre nonentity. And yet it would be difficult to imagine any force better calculated to encourage this result than the loyalty program itself. For this result the House committee must assume a large measure of responsibility.

In particular, the activity of the House committee has obstructed the recruitment of scientists into the public service. The members of no profession have been harassed with more regularity or greater injustice by the committee than American scientists. Such things as the Condon report and the perennial search for subversives among atomic scientists have left deep scars. Certainly the members of no profession have been more bitter in their criticism of the committee. The resulting lack of enthusiasm among scientists for service with the federal government has been a fearful price to pay for the committee's bumbling and ineffectual investigations in the field of atomic espionage.[8]

Fourth, by constantly exaggerating the subversive threat the committee has impaired the good judgment of many intelligent citizens. Such people have so often been repelled by the committee's grossly unfair procedures, by the antics of its members, by its highly prejudiced findings, and by its persistent overstatement of the extent of subversive activity in the United States that they have allowed themselves to be persuaded that everything the committee has done is bad, that there is no such thing as subversive activity in this country, and that the Communists offer no threat to the national security. As the *New York Herald Tribune* has put it, the committee "has endlessly confused and diverted attention from a rational approach to the true problems of Communist conspiracy in a democracy."[9] The result has been that our ablest statesmen and scholars have been slow to provide leadership in this area; they have hesitated to undertake the calm, dispassionate analysis of this social problem that has been their historic role in similar situations. In other words, as a nation we have failed to bring our best intelligence to bear upon

[8] See Walter Gellhorn, *Security, Loyalty, and Science* (Ithaca: Cornell University Press, 1950), pp. 55–62, 122–123, 157–174.

[9] March 11, 1948.

a difficult problem of statecraft—the preservation of the democratic way of life in a world threatened by the revolutionary force of communism. By its own incompetent and discredited efforts to cope with this problem the House committee has dulled the sensitivity of many of our wisest citizens and discouraged them from giving their attention to the problem of subversion. Indeed, it has so confused the situation that consideration of the problem has become in large measure the concern of crackpots and fanatics.

Fifth, the committee has succeeded in discrediting the Congress of the United States in the eyes of many Americans. It has done this at a moment in world history when the preservation of healthy, vigorous representative assemblies is an essential condition to the survival of the democratic way of life. The Un-American Activities Committee by providing an opportunity for certain of the most incompetent and thoughtless members of Congress to run hog-wild and to obtain almost unlimited publicity for their irresponsible acts has unquestionably encouraged many people to hold the national legislature in contempt. In particular, it has discredited the investigating power of Congress and thereby weakened what has always been one of the most important and useful Congressional functions. Moreover, it is not enough to say that in the 81st Congress the committee mended its ways and demonstrated that it could conduct an investigation into subversive activity in a calm, fair manner. Taking the long view of the committee's work, this brief period of responsible activity stands out as the exception rather than the rule. There is no guarantee that the committee has permanently mended its ways; its personnel has always been extremely unstable. Moreover, the committee is one to which the least competent and responsible members of the House of Representatives have always gravitated. A change in party control of the House, or even the addition of three or four new members (which has happened every two years since the committee's creation), might well at some early moment turn the committee back to the kind of policies it pursued during the 80th Congress. As long as the committee continues to exist, the most reactionary forces in American life are certain to seek to control it and to use it as an instrument of witch-hunting and suppression. They have succeeded in doing so in the past. Is there any reason to suppose they will never do so again?

Sixth, the committee has adversely affected the moral and intellectual atmosphere of the nation. This it has done by constantly reiterating the idea that our social structure is honeycombed with disloyal persons: that our public officers are spies for the Soviet Union, our teachers are Communists, our scientists are weak links in our security system, our motion pictures are tainted with foreign propaganda, and our labor movement is shot through with subversion. The committee has made us distrustful of each other; it has made us suspicious of organizations which are the very fabric of our democratic order. The committee would have us believe that we are weak and corrupt; it would have us forget the vitality and stability of our nation, the abiding courage and faith of the American people in the democratic way of life. The committee has also adversely affected the thinking of the nation by focusing attention almost exclusively upon the evil of communism and almost totally ignoring the evils that produce communism—such things as economic insecurity, racial discrimination, and social injustice. Communism has come to be viewed by many Americans as a cancer which need only be excised by surgery to restore the body to a state of health and vitality. That communism might better be viewed as a germ-caused infection particularly dangerous to a body weakened by other ills and disabilities seems not to have occurred to the committee or those whom it has influenced. At the moment of this writing, the American Congress has for some three months failed to take positive action concerning such a seemingly obvious method of fighting international communism as sending grain to an India threatened by famine. Yet many members of the same Congress seem perfectly prepared to support policies looking toward direct and total warfare with the Communist world. The Un-American Activities Committee has done much to encourage this delusion that we need only throw American Communists out of their jobs or defeat international communism on the battlefield to safeguard our present way of life.

All things considered, it appears that the record of the Un-American Activities Committee between 1945 and 1950 (and of the predecessor Dies committee) is such that the wisest policy to follow would be the complete abolition of the committee. This would not mean that the threat of subversion would go totally unstudied by Congress. The threat offered by international communism might properly be the concern—as indeed it is—of the foreign relations and armed services committees of the two houses.[10] Because they deal with all

[10] For example, in May, 1947, the House Committee on Foreign Affairs created a Subcommittee on National and International Movements, under the chairmanship of Representative Frances P. Bolton. In 1948 it published a report, *The Strategy and Tactics of World Communism* (80th Cong., 2d Sess.,

aspects of our relations with the rest of the world and with our military preparedness, there is every reason to believe that these committees can bring a greater measure of sophistication to an examination of the international Communist threat and are far better qualified to place this threat in its proper perspective than is the Un-American Activities Committee. Similarly, the judiciary committees of the two houses would seem to be the proper watchdogs with respect to the threat of internal subversion. Actually, the present Senate Judiciary Committee does have jurisdiction over legislation concerning espionage, sedition, sabotage, and similar subversive acts. Moreover, the Legislative Reorganization Act of 1946 gives the House Judiciary Committee jurisdiction over espionage laws.

It may be doubted whether the Senate Judiciary Committee under the chairmanship of Pat McCarran is in any sense to be preferred to the House Un-American Activities Committee as a dispassionate agency for the study of internal subversion in the United States. This doubt has become particularly pertinent now that a standing subcommittee of the McCarran committee has been established in the 82d Congress to deal with matters of internal security. This subcommittee, which is also chairmanned by Senator McCarran, is already being referred to as the Senate "Un-American Activities Committee." Granted that such a committee under the direction of a McCarran may well make a record no better than that of a committee headed by a Wood or even a Thomas, the arrangement is vastly to be preferred to that existing in the House of Representatives. For one thing, as a subcommittee there is at least the possibility that it will be subject in the long run to supervision and checking by the full Judiciary Committee. There is no such possibility in the House as long as the Un-American Activities Committee remains an independent agency. Furthermore, the members of the Senate Judiciary Committee (including the ones appointed to the internal security subcommittee) are concerned with a legislative area far broader than subversive activity, since the entire body of federal criminal law falls within the jurisdiction of this committee (as it does also to the House Judiciary Committee). Accordingly, the two judiciary committees are not likely to develop quite the same obsession for a study of un-American activities as is a committee that has such a study as its sole assignment. And with their broader background of concern for all forms

House Doc. No. 619) which, together with several accompanying supplements, compared very favorably with any of the publications of the Un-American Activities Committee dealing with international communism.

of criminal activity there is a fair chance that the judiciary committees would evaluate their findings respecting subversive activity more calmly and dispassionately than has the House Un-American Activities Committee. Again, the personnel of the foreign relations, armed services, and judiciary committees of Congress is much more stable than that of the Un-American Activities Committee. It is reasonable to suppose that this condition would lead these committees to approach the problems posed by communism with a greater understanding and a deeper sense of responsibility than have marked the work of an Un-American Activities Committee whose membership has undergone great changes every two years.

Unfortunately, the House of Representatives is not apt to abolish the Un-American Activities Committee in the foreseeable future. For that reason, and because other Congressional committees might well make some of the same mistakes even if the authority of the Un-American Activities Committee were transferred to them, it is highly desirable that every effort be made to correct the shortcomings that six years of experience with a standing committee investigating subversion have produced. These shortcomings have been of two types, one substantive and the other procedural in character.

On the substantive side the greatest need is to delimit and define more carefully the subject matter under investigation. It is hard to say which is more unsatisfactory: the name of the committee or the phraseology of the resolution setting forth its authority. The vagueness of any such concept as "un-American activity" has been set forth again and again and hardly calls for further comment. The essential meaninglessness of the concept is perhaps suggested by measuring one's reaction to the suggestion that our neighbor to the north might set up a similar committee "on un-Canadian activities," or that our friends in Europe perhaps have need for committees "on un-English activities," or "un-French activities." Similarly, a search for "subversive and un-American propaganda that is instigated from foreign countries or of a domestic origin and attacks the principle of the form of government as guaranteed by our Constitution" is essentially an undefined undertaking which allows its maker freedom to probe well beyond the limits of truly subversive activity. At no time since this ridiculous language made its appearance in the original Dies committee resolution in 1938 has the House shown any inclination to work out a more carefully worded set of directions for its Un-American Activities Committee to follow. Granted the difficulties to be overcome in devising a satisfactory charter for a committee investigating subversion, "un-American activity" might at least be defined so as to give it specific reference to the use of force and violence to change the American constitutional system or to conduct that reflects a desire to advance the interests of a foreign power at the expense of those of the United States.

Another way in which the substantive shortcomings in the committee's record might be overcome would be by House action directing the committee to concentrate upon a search for information concerning the adequacy of existing federal laws dealing with espionage, sedition, and sabotage, and concerning the enforcement of these laws by the executive agencies responsible for their administration. If the committee's hearings were to be limited more strictly to these issues closely related to the legislative function, it is possible that many of the worst abuses of the past might hereafter be prevented. It is when the committee has wandered far afield and has regarded itself as having a mission to educate the American people concerning the dangers of communism or as being responsible for the exposure of actual Communists that the committee has erred most grievously. In other words, it seems highly desirable that the committee's "informing function" should be minimized, for the record clearly reveals that subversion is not a subject concerning which Congress is well equipped, in terms of either understanding or dispassion, to undertake to influence the minds of the American people. It is also clear that the House should force the committee to cease altogether its efforts to demonstrate the "guilt" of particular individuals. The depersonalization of the work of the Un-American Activities Committee is the single most important change that is necessary if the threat offered by the committee to the American way of life is to be overcome.

It is less easy to say what procedural reforms are essential to improvement in the committee's record. It must be admitted that the record of the committee in the 81st Congress is a vastly better one in this respect than that made by the committee in any earlier Congress. Nevertheless, the need for Congress to prescribe a general code of fair procedures for its investigating committees remains great. Numerous proposals for such a code have been made in recent years.[11] To date neither house of Congress has shown much inclination to act upon them. It is not the purpose of this study to analyze the details of the proposals that have been made or to suggest the specific pro-

[11] For an excellent summary of these proposals see George B. Galloway, "Proposed Reforms," 18 *Univ. of Chicago Law Review* (Spring, 1951), 478–502.

cedural changes that are necessary. It should be pointed out that the problem is admittedly a more complex one than has been generally recognized. Care must be taken not to place unnecessary and unworkable restraints upon the committees of Congress. It is desirable that the great contrast between a court of law and a legislative investigating committee be preserved, for the functions of these two agencies are—or should be—very different. Accordingly, it will not do simply to impose upon the legislative committee the procedural rules common to judicial proceedings. At the same time, of course, legislative committees must be careful not to usurp the judicial function. But in spite of the difficulty of evolving a satisfactory set of workable rules the time has come when Congress must face and meet this responsibility. If it be true that the answer to the mistakes and abuses of the Un-American Activities Committee must and should be found in the national legislature itself, then further delay in the formulation and adoption by Congress of sound, workable rules governing the organization and operation of its committees endangers the continuing usefulness and vitality of the investigating function —surely one of the most important functions of Congress.

Appendix

Table I. List of Publications of the House Committee on Un-American Activities

The dates given in connection with the hearings are the actual days on which committee sessions were conducted; the dates given in connection with the reports refer to the submission of the reports to the House of Representatives and their public release. Hearings and reports are published by the Government Printing Office.

THE COMMITTEE IN THE 79TH CONGRESS

First Session: 1945

Hearings (2 volumes):

Investigation of Un-American Propaganda Activities in the United States (Office of Price Administration), June 20, 21, 27, 1945. Abbrev. to *OPA Hearings*.

Investigation of Un-American Propaganda Activities in the United States (Communist Party), Sept. 26, 27, Oct. 17–19, 1945, Abbrev. to *Communist Party Hearings*.

Second Session: 1946

Hearings (3 volumes):

Investigation of Un-American Propaganda Activities in the United States (Gerald L. K. Smith), Jan. 30, 1946.

Investigation of Un-American Propaganda Activities in the United States: Executive Board: Joint Anti-Fascist Refugee Committee, April 4, 1946. Abbrev. to *Joint Anti-Fascist Refugee Committee Hearing*.

Investigaion of Un-American Propaganda Activities in the United States: Louis F. Budenz, Nov. 22, 1946. A "revised" version of this hearing was issued in 1947.

Reports (3 volumes):

Sources of Financial Aid for Subversive and Un-American Propaganda, House Rept. No. 1996, May 10, 1946.

Report of the Committee on Un-American Activities, House Rept. No. 2233, June 7, 1946. Abbrev. to *Annual Rept.,* June 7, 1946.

Report of the Committee on Un-American Activities, House Rept. No. 2742, Jan. 2, 1947. Abbrev. to *Annual Rept.,* Jan. 2, 1947.

THE COMMITTEE IN THE 80TH CONGRESS

First Session: 1947

Hearings (11 volumes):

Hearings on Gerhart Eisler, Feb. 6, 1947.

Hearings regarding Communism in Labor Unions in the United States, Feb. 27, July 23–25, 1947. Abbrev. to *1947 Hearings regarding Communism in Labor Unions.*

Investigation of Un-American Propaganda Activities in the United States (regarding Leon Josephson and Samuel Liptzen), March 5, 21, 1947.

Investigation of Un-American Propaganda Activities in the United States: Hearings on H.R. 1884 and H.R. 2122: Bills to Curb or Outlaw the Communist Party of the United States. Abbrev. to *Hearings on H.R. 1884 and H.R. 2122.*

General, March 24–28, 1947.

Part 1: Testimony of Hon. William C. Bullitt, March 24, 1947.

Part 2: Testimony of J. Edgar Hoover, March 26, 1947.

Testimony of Walter S. Steele regarding Communist Activities in the United States, July 21, 1947.

Testimony of Victor A. Kravchenko, July 22, 1947.

Investigation of Un-American Propaganda Activities in the United States (regarding Eugene Dennis), April 9, 1947.

Hearings regarding Hanns Eisler, Sept. 24–26, 1947.

Hearings regarding the Communist Infiltration of the Motion Picture Industry, Oct. 20–24, 27–30, 1947. Abbrev. to *Mot. Pict. Ind. Hearings.*

Reports (4 volumes):

The Communist Party of the United States as an Agent of a Foreign Power, House Rept. No. 209, April 1, 1947. Abbrev. to *1947 Communist Party Rept.*

Report on American Youth for Democracy, House Rept. No. 271, April 17, 1947. Abbrev. to *AYD Rept.*

Report on Southern Conference for Human Welfare, House Rept. No. 592, June 16, 1947. Abbrev. to *Southern Conference Rept.*

Report on Civil Rights Congress as a Communist Front Organization, House Rept. No. 1115, Sept. 2, 1947.

Second Session: 1948

Hearings (4 volumes):

Hearings on Proposed Legislation to Curb or Control the Communist Party of the United States, Feb. 5, 6, 9–11, 19, 20, 1948.

Hearings regarding Communist Espionage in the United States Government, July 31, Aug. 3–5, 7, 9–13, 16–18, 20, 24–27, 30, Sept. 8, 9, 1948. [This is actually Part One of the hearings listed fourth in this section, and the pagination of *Part Two* is continuous.] Abbrev. to *Communist Espionage Hearings.*

Excerpts from Hearings regarding Investigation of Communist Activities in Connection with the Atom Bomb, Sept. 9, 14, 16, 1948. Abbrev. to *1948 Atom Bomb Hearings.*

Hearings regarding Communist Espionage in the United States Government—Part Two, Dec. 7–10, 14, 1948. Abbrev. to *Communist Espionage Hearings, Part Two.*

Reports (8 volumes):

Report to the Full Committee of the Special Subcommittee on National Security of the Committee on Un-American Activities, March 1, 1948. Abbrev. to *Rept. to the Full Committee.*

Report of the Subcommittee on Legislation of the Committee on Un-American Activities on Proposed Legislation to Control Subversive Communist Activities in the United States, April 10, 1948. Abbrev. to *Rept. of the Subcommittee on Legislation.*

Protecting the United States against Un-American and Subversive Activities, House Rept. No. 1844, April 30, 1948.

Report on the Communist Party of the United States as an Advocate of Overthrow of Government by Force and Violence, House Rept. No. 1920, May 11, 1948. Abbrev. to *1948 Communist Party Report.*

Interim Report on Hearings regarding Communist Espionage in the United States Government, Aug. 28, 1948. Abbrev. to *Interim Rept.*

Report on Soviet Espionage Activities in Connection with the Atom Bomb, Sept. 28, 1948. Abbrev. to *1948 Atom Bomb Rept.*

Soviet Espionage within the United States Government: Second Report, Dec. 31, 1948. Abbrev. to *Soviet Espionage, Second Rept.*

Report of the Committee on Un-American Activities to the United States House of Representatives, Eightieth Congress, Dec. 31, 1948. Abbrev. to *Annual Rept.,* Dec. 31, 1948.

Other publications:

Index II to Publications of Special Committee on Un-American Activities (Dies Committee) and the Committee on Un-American Activities (1942–1947 Inclusive.) Supplement to 1942 Index, Oct. 21, 1948.

Citations by Official Government Agencies of Organizations and Publications Found to Be Communist or Communist Fronts, Dec. 18, 1948.

The "100 Things You Should Know about Communism" series. Published originally as five separate pamphlets dealing with: *Communism in the U.S.A.; Communism and Religion; Communism and Education; Communism and Labor; Communism and Government.* These five pamphlets were repaged and bound with *Spotlight on Spies* into one pamphlet (with minor changes) as House Doc. No. 136, 82d Cong., 1st Sess., May 14, 1951.

THE COMMITTEE IN THE 81ST CONGRESS

First Session: 1949

Hearings (35 volumes):

For this Congress, the hearings are numbered consecutively from p. 1 to p. 3626. Pages 775–796 seem to be unaccounted for. For convenience of reference, hearings are listed here in chronological order, according to the date of the first hearing.

Documentary Testimony of Gen. Izyador Modelski, March 31, April 1, 1949.

Hearings regarding Communist Infiltration at Radiation Laboratory and Atomic Bomb Project at the University of California, Berkeley, Calif.—Vol. I, April 22, 26, May 25, June 10, 14, 1949. Abbrev. to *1949 Radiation Lab. Hearings, Vol. I.*

Testimony of Paul Crouch, May 6, 1949.

Hearings regarding Clarence Hiskey including Testimony of Paul Crouch, May 24, 1949.

Testimony of Philip O. Keeney and Mary Jane Keeney and Statement reparding Their Background, May 24, 25, June 9, 1949.

Hearings regarding Toma Babin, May 27, July 6, 1949.

Soviet Espionage Activities in Connection with Jet Propulsion and Aircraft, June 6, 1949.

Hearings regarding Steve Nelson, June 8, 1949.

Hearings regarding Communism in the District of Columbia—Part I, June 28, 29, July 6, 12, 28, 1949.

Hearings regarding Communist Infiltration of Minority Groups—Part I, July 13, 14, 18, 1949.

Hearings regarding Communist Infiltration of Minority Groups—Part II, (*Testimony of Manning Johnson*), July 14, 1949.

Hearings regarding Communist Infiltration of Labor Unions—Part I, Aug. 9–11, 1949.

Testimony of James Sterling Murray and Edward Tiers Manning (regarding Clarence Hiskey and Arthur Adams), Aug. 14, Oct. 5, 1949.

Hearings regarding Communist Infiltration of Radiation Laboratory and Atomic Bomb Project at the University of California, Berkeley, Calif.—Vol. II, Aug. 26, 1949; July 1, Sept. 10, 1948; Aug. 14, Sept. 14, 27, 1949. Abbrev. to *1949 Radiation Lab. Hearings, Vol. II.*

Hearings regarding Communist Espionage, Nov. 8, Dec. 2, 1949 (continued in Second Session).

Hearings regarding Communist Infiltration of Labor Unions—Part II, Dec. 5, 6, 1949.

Hearings regarding Shipment of Atomic Material to the Soviet Union during World War II, Dec. 5, 7, 1949 (continued in Second Session). Abbrev. to *Hearings regarding Shipment.*

Reports (4 volumes):

Review of the Scientific and Cultural Conference for World Peace, April 19, 1949.

Report on the American Slav Congress, June 26, 1949.

Report on Atomic Espionage, Sept. 29, 1949. Abbrev. to *1949 Atomic Espionage Rept.*

Report on the Congress of American Women, Oct. 23, 1949, Abbrev. to *CAW Rept.*

Second Session: 1950

Hearings (20 volumes):

Hearings regarding Shipment of Atomic Material to the Soviet Union during World War II (continued), Jan. 23–26, March 2, 3, 7, 1950. Abbrev. to *Hearings regarding Shipment.*

Hearings regarding Communist Espionage (continued), Feb. 27, March 1, 1950.

Exposé of the Communist Party of Western Pennsylvania (Based upon Testimony of Matthew Cvetic), Feb. 21–23, March 13, 14, 24, 1950.

Exposé of the Communist Party of Western Pennsylvania—Part II, March 24, 25, 1950.

Hearings on Legislation to Outlaw Certain Un-American and Subversive Activities, March 21–24, 28–30, April 4, May 2–4, 1950.

Hearings regarding Communist Activities in the Territory of Hawaii— Part I, April 10–12, 1950. Three hearings abbrev. to *Communism in Hawaii Hearings.*

Hearings regarding Communist Activities in the Territory of Hawaii— Part II, April 13–15, 1950.

Hearings regarding Communist Activities in the Territory of Hawaii— Part III, April 17–19, 1950.

Hearings regarding Communism in the United States Government— Part I, April 20, 21, 25, 29, May 4–6, 1950; July 30, Aug. 7, 1948; June 8, 1950.

Testimony of Philip A. Bart (General Manager of Freedom of the Press, Publishers of the Daily Worker, Official Organ of the Communist Party) and Marcel Scherer (Coordinator, New York Labor Conference for Peace, and Formerly District Representative of District 4, United Electrical, Radio, and Machine Workers of America, CIO), June 21, 1950.

Exposé of the Communist Party of Western Pennsylvania—Part III, June 22, Sept. 28, Oct. 13, 21, 1950.

Hearings regarding Communist Activities in the Cincinnati, Ohio, Area —Part I, July 12–15, Aug. 8, 1950.

American Aspects of Assassination of Leon Trotsky, July 26, Aug. 30, Oct. 18, 19, Dec. 4, 1950.

Hearings regarding Communism in the United States Government— Part II, Aug. 28, 31, Sept. 1, 15, 1950.

Hearings regarding Communist Infiltration of Labor Unions—Part III, Aug. 29, 30, 1950.

Hearings regarding Communist Infiltration of Minority Groups—Part III (Testimony of "Josh White"), Sept. 1, 1950.

Testimony of Hazel Scott Powell, Sept. 22, 1950.

Testimony of Edward G. Robinson, Oct. 27, Dec. 21, 1950.

Hearings regarding Communism in the District of Columbia—Part II, Dec. 6, 11–13, 1950.

Hearings regarding Communist infiltration of Radiation Laboratory and Atomic Bomb Project at the University of California, Berkeley, Calif., Vol. III, Dec. 20–22, 1950. Abbrev. to *Radiation Lab. Hearings, Vol. III,* Dec., 1950.

Reports (7 volumes):

Annual Report of the Committee on Un-American Activities for the Year 1949, March 15, 1950. Abbrev. to *Annual Rept.,* March 15, 1950.

Report on Hawaii Civil Liberties Committee—A Communist Front, June 23, 1950.

The Communist "Peace Petition" Campaign, July 13, 1950.

Protection of the United States against Un-American and Subversive Activities, House Rept. No. 2980 (to accompany H.R. 9490), Aug. 22, 1950.

Report on the National Lawyers Guild—Legal Bulwark of the Communist Party, Sept. 17, 1950. Abbrev. to *NLG Rept.*

Report on the National Committee to Defeat the Mundt Bill, Dec. 7, 1950.

Annual Report of the Committee on Un-American Activities for the Year 1950, Jan. 2, 1951. Abbrev. to *Annual Rept.,* Jan. 2, 1951.

Other Publications:

Index III to Publications of the Committee on Un-American Activities, June 28, 1950.

Table II. Membership of the House Committee on Un-American Activities (1938–1950)

Democrats	*Republicans*
1938	
Martin Dies, Tex. (Ch.)	Noah M. Mason, Ill.
Arthur D. Healey, Mass.	J. Parnell Thomas, N.J.
John J. Dempsey, N.M.	
Joe Starnes, Ala.	
Harold G. Mosier, Ohio [1]	
1939–1940	
Martin Dies, Tex. (Ch.)	Noah M. Mason, Ill.
Arthur Healey, Mass.[2]	J. Parnell Thomas, N.J.
John J. Dempsey, N.M.[3]	
Joe Starnes, Ala.	
Jerry Voorhis, Calif.[4]	
Joseph E. Casey, Mass.[5]	
1941–1942	
Martin Dies, Tex. (Ch.)	Noah M. Mason, Ill.
Joe Starnes, Ala.	J. Parnell Thomas, N.J.
Jerry Voorhis, Calif.	
Joseph E. Casey, Mass.	
Harry P. Beam, Ill.[6]	
1943–1944	
Martin Dies, Tex. (Ch.)[7]	Noah M. Mason, Ill.[11]
Joe Starnes, Ala.[8]	J. Parnell Thomas, N.J.
Jerry Voorhis, Calif.[9]	Karl E. Mundt, S.D.
Wirt Courtney, Tenn.[10]	Fred E. Busbey, Ill.[12]
John M. Costello, Calif.[8]	
Herman P. Eberharter, Pa.[10]	
1945–1946	
Edward J. Hart, N.J. (Ch.)[13]	J. Parnell Thomas, N.J.
John S. Wood, Ga. (Ch.)[14]	Karl E. Mundt, S.D.
John E. Rankin, Miss.	Gerald W. Landis, Ind.[15]
J. Hardin Peterson, Fla.	
J. W. Robinson, Utah	
John R. Murdock, Ariz.[15]	
Herbert C. Bonner, N.C.	

1947–1948

John S. Wood, Ga.

John E. Rankin, Miss.[16]

J. Hardin Peterson, Fla.[17]

Herbert C. Bonner, N.C.[18]

F. Edward Hébert, La.[19]

J. Parnell Thomas, N.J. (Ch.)

Karl E. Mundt, S.D.[20]

John McDowell, Pa.[21]

Richard M. Nixon, Calif.

Richard B. Vail, Ill.[21]

1949–1950

John S. Wood, Ga.

Francis E. Walter, Pa.

Burr P. Harrison, Va.

John McSweeney, Ohio

Morgan M. Moulder, Mo.

J. Parnell Thomas, N.J.[22]

Richard M. Nixon, Calif. [23]

Francis Case, S.D.

Harold H. Velde, Ill.

Bernard W. Kearney, N.Y.[24]

Donald L. Jackson, Calif.[25]

---

[1] Defeated for renomination, May, 1938.   [2] Resigned August 5, 1939.

[3] Did not seek re-election to House in 1940.

[4] Appointed Feb. 8, 1939, to take place of Mosier.

[5] Appointed Sept. 2, 1939, to take place of Healey.

[6] Appointed Feb. 11, 1941, to take place of Dempsey; resigned from House on Dec. 6, 1942.   [7] Did not seek re-election to House in 1944.

[8] Defeated for renomination in 1944.

[9] Defeated for re-election by Richard M. Nixon in 1946.

[10] Re-elected to House Nov., 1944, but declined to continue service on committee in 1945.   [11] Resigned from committee Dec. 17, 1943.

[12] Appointed Dec. 17, 1943, to take place of Mason; defeated for re-election, Nov., 1944.

[13] Appointed member and chairman, Jan. 16, 1945; resigned from committee June 29, 1945.

[14] Appointed member and chairman, July 12, 1945.

[15] Re-elected to House Nov., 1946, but declined to serve on committee in 1947.

[16] Forced to give up membership on committee in 1949 on the ground that committee chairmen should serve on only one committee. (Rankin was chairman of the House Committee on Veterans' Affairs.)

[17] Re-elected to House Nov., 1948, but declined to serve on committee in 1949.

[18] Resigned from committee Nov. 17, 1947.

[19] Appointed Dec. 9, 1947, to take place of Bonner; dropped from committee in 1949, because he was not a lawyer.

[20] Resigned from House, Dec. 31, 1948, after his election to the U.S. Senate.

[21] Defeated for re-election, Nov., 1948.

[22] Resigned from House Jan. 2, 1950, after conviction in a federal court.

[23] Resigned from House of Representatives, Nov. 30, 1950, and took his seat in the Senate Dec. 4.   [24] Appointed Jan. 9, 1950, to take Thomas' place.

[25] Appointed Dec. 14, 1950, to take Nixon's place.

SOURCES: *Cong. Rec., Cong. Directory, N.Y. Times,* and August R. Ogden, *The Dies Committee* (2d rev. ed.; Catholic University Press, 1945).

Table III. Staff and Payrolls of the House Un-American Activities Committee (1947–1950) as Reported by the Committee

Staff Personnel	Position	Total Gross Salary			
		1947	1948	1949	1950
Robert E. Stripling [1]	Chief Investigator	$9,416.62	$10,164.96	$7,136.64	$10,846.02
Frank S. Tavenner, Jr. [2]	Counsel				10,846.02
Louis J. Russell	Senior Investigator	7,356.63	8,717.97	9,954.80	10,846.02
Benjamin Mandel	Director of Research	6,969.20	8,942.92	9,405.08	9,805.29
Donald T. Appell	Investigator	6,071.40	7,693.48	8,510.79	9,067.92
William A. Wheeler [3]	Investigator		7,450.68	7,927.36	8,514.53
Courtney Owens [3]	Investigator		1,903.92	7,615.68	8,134.71
William J. Jones [3]	Investigator			6,801.01	8,030.91
Alvin W. Stokes [3]	Investigator		7,187.40	7,352.42	7,996.44
Chas. E. McKillips [3]	Investigator		3,152.03	7,615.68	3,101.45
James A. Andrews	Investigator				
Robert B. Gaston [3, 4]	Investigator		7,450.68		
Walter Wieczerzak [3]	Investigator		5,120.40		
James H. Walter [3, 5]	Investigator		782.41		
Total number on professional staff		4	10	9	10

John W. Carrington	Clerk	$6,364.72	$7,681.26	$8,691.78	$10,024.16
Anne D. Turner	File Clerk	6,316.19	7,187.40	7,878.76	8,134.74
Rosella A. Purdy	Secretary to Counsel	4,038.50	5,177.82	6,013.57	6,635.92
Thelma A. Scearce [6]	Secretary to Sr. Investigator			5,308.33	6,056.56
Juliette P. Joray	Secretary to Clerk	4,038.50	4,453.78	4,657.16	5,187.52
Caroline Roberts	Asst. File Chief	714.78	4,867.55	5,213.52	5,622.08
Margaret S. Kerwan [7]	Clerk-Steno.	4,038.50	4,628.56	3,538.88	

[1] Resigned at close of 1948.   [2] Appointed early in 1949.   [3] Not carried on permanent House payroll.
[4] Services terminated Feb. 15, 1949.   [5] Services terminated July 1, 1948.
[6] Carried on voucher payroll until June 30, 1949.   [7] Services terminated August 31, 1949.

Table IV. Committee Attendance during Hearings regarding Communist Espionage in the United States Government

Date	Public or Executive	Committee or Sub-committee	No. Present	Names of Members Present	Subject
July 31	Public	Com.	7	Thomas (Ch.), Hébert, McDowell, Mundt, Nixon, Peterson, Rankin	1st Bentley
Aug. 3	Public	Com.	6	Mundt (Act. Ch.), Hébert, McDowell, Nixon, Peterson, Rankin	1st Chambers
4	Public	Com.	6	Mundt (Act. Ch.), Hébert, McDowell, Nixon, Peterson, Rankin	2d Bentley
5	Public	Com.	5	Mundt (Act. Ch.), Hébert, McDowell, Nixon, Rankin	1st Hiss
7	Exec.	Subc.	3	Nixon (Presiding), Hébert, McDowell	2d Chambers
9	Public	Subc.	5	Nixon (Presiding), McDowell, Hébert, Thomas, Mundt	Koral
9	Public	Com.	6	Thomas (Ch.), Hébert, McDowell, Mundt, Nixon, Peterson	3d Bentley
10	Public	Subc.	4	Thomas (Ch.), Hébert, McDowell, Mundt	4th Bentley
10	Public	Com.	5	Thomas (Ch.), Hébert, McDowell, Mundt, Nixon	Lee, Ullmann, Miller
11	Public	Subc.	5	Thomas (Ch.), Hébert, McDowell, Mundt, Nixon	5th Bentley
12	Public	Subc.	5	Thomas (Ch.), Hébert, McDowell, Mundt, Nixon	Kramer, Silverman
13	Public	Com.	5	Thomas (Ch.), Hébert, McDowell, Mundt, Nixon	Currie, White, D. Hiss
16	Exec.	Subc.	4	Thomas (Ch.), Hébert, McDowell, Nixon	2d Hiss

Date				Members Present	Witnesses
17	Exec.	Subc.	3	McDowell (Presiding), Thomas, Nixon	1st Hiss–Chambers Confrontation
18	Exec.	Subc.	1	Nixon	I. D. Levine, Mrs. A. Hiss
20	Exec.	Subc.	1	Nixon	Abt, Pressman, Witt
24	Exec.	Subc.	1	Nixon	Budenz, et al.
25	Public	Com.	6	Thomas (Ch.), Hébert, McDowell, Mundt, Nixon, Vail	2d Hiss–Chambers Confrontation
26	Exec.	Subc.	3	McDowell (Presiding), Nixon, Vail	Rosen
27	Exec.	Subc.	3	McDowell (Presiding), Nixon, Vail	Cherner, Bialek
27	Exec.	Subc.	2	Mundt (Presiding), Nixon	Chambers
30	Public	Subc.	2	McDowell (Presiding), Nixon	J. Peters, Chambers
30	Exec.	Subc.	2	McDowell (Presiding), Nixon	Berle
Sept.					
8	Exec.	Subc.	3	Thomas (Ch.), McDowell, Vail	Rosen, Cherner
9	Exec.	Subc.	3	Thomas (Ch.), McDowell, Vail	Rosen, Braverman
Dec.					
7	Public	Subc.	6	Mundt (Act. Ch.), Hébert, McDowell, Nixon, Rankin, Vail	S. Welles, J. Peurifoy
8	Public	Subc.	6	Mundt (Act. Ch.), Hébert, McDowell, Nixon, Rankin, Vail	I. D. Levine
9	Public	Subc.	6	Mundt (Act. Ch.), Hébert, McDowell, Nixon, Rankin, Vail	Wadleigh, Owens
10	Public	Subc.	6	Mundt (Act. Ch.), Hébert, McDowell, Nixon, Rankin, Vail	Nathan L. Levine
14	Public	Subc.	5	Mundt (Act. Ch.), Hébert, McDowell, Nixon, Rankin	Marion Bachrach

Index